Memory
From A to Z

Keywords, Concepts, and Beyond

Yadin Dudai

The Weizmann Institute of Science, Rehovot, Israel

OXFORD
UNIVERSITY PRESS

OXFORD
UNIVERSITY PRESS

Great Clarendon Street, Oxford OX2 6DP

Oxford University Press is a department of the University of Oxford.
It furthers the University's objective of excellence in research, scholarship,
and education by publishing worldwide in

Oxford New York

Auckland Bangkok Buenos Aires Cape Town Chennai
Dar es Salaam Delhi Hong Kong Istanbul Karachi Kolkata
Kuala Lumpur Madrid Melbourne Mexico City Mumbai Nairobi
São Paulo Shanghai Taipei Tokyo Toronto

and an associated company in
Berlin

Published in the United States
by Oxford University Press Inc., New York

First published 2002

British Library Cataloguing in Publication Data

Data available

Library of Congress Cataloging in Publication Data

ISBN 0 19 850267 2

10 9 8 7 6 5 4 3 2 1

Typeset by Cepha Imaging Pvt. Ltd., Bangalore, India

Printed in Great Britain

on acid-free paper by T.J. International, Padstow, Cornwall, UK

Preface

This book contains terms that I wish my students to know. I hope that the book will also be of interest to additional audiences. Over the years, the members of my research group have joined in from a variety of backgrounds, ranging from psychology via biology to computer science. The common denominator was always keen interest in the marvels of *memory.[1] To facilitate the translation of this interest into science, the members of the team must master a language. This is an attempt to present and explain selected elements in this language. The fact that the science of memory is but one branch of science, combined with the unavoidable idiosyncrasy in the selection, resulted in the inclusion in the book of some terms that are shared by other sectors of the scientific *culture as well.

The entries can be read as is. They may also be used as a versatile tool kit: a source for definitions, information, and further reading; a trigger for contemplation and discussion; and an aid to study, teaching, and debates in classes and seminars. The entries are not a replacement for comprehensive professional reviews; they could, however, incite interest in further delving into the literature. In writing the entries, I tried to follow the advice of Poe (1846) that the optimal length of an item should fit to be read in a single sitting. I do realize that cutural respect for the exploitation of human *attention span has probably declined over the past 150 years, but still, I hope that I did not deviate much from Poe's *criterion.

The definition(s) at the beginning of each entry, and the ones scattered throughout the text introduce into this book elements of a lexicon. The humble fate of lexicographers did not escape my notice: '…these unhappy mortals… can only hope to escape reproach, and even this negative recompense has been granted to very few' (Johnson 1755). A number of colleagues have read versions of selected entries and provided the right combination of encouragement and reproach. Among them were Ehud Ahissar, Amos Arieli, Diego Berman, Aline Desmedt, Haim Garty, Patricia Goldman-Rakic,

Howard Eichenbaum, Mark Konishi, Serge Laroche, Joseph LeDoux, Rafi Malach, Henry Markram, Randolf Menzel, Richard Morris, Karim Nader, Lars Nyberg, Noa Ofen-Noy, Robert Rescorla, Nava Rubin, Dov Sagi, Menahem Segal, Roni Seger, Alcino Silva, Burton Slotnick, Wendy Suzuki, and Misha Tsodyks. I am grateful to them all for their wise advice, although, of course, they should be blamed for nothing.

I am particularly grateful to my wife, Rina, for her loving support, keen interest, and shrewd comments.

I also appreciate the reactions of many students who attended my lectures at the Weizmann Institute of Science, the University of Edinburgh, New York University, and the Gulbenkian Institute of Science, Oeiras, Portugal. Major parts of this book were written at the Weizmann Institute, and others at the Center for Neuroscience, University of Edinburgh, and at the Center for Neural Science, New York University. I am grateful to Joe LeDoux and Richard Morris for their friendship and for being such patient and kind hosts. Thanks go also to Tom Boyd from the Royal Society, London, for the reference on the first use of the *mouse in scientific experiments; to Francis Colpaert for advice on the *state-dependent learning literature and for Collin's The moonstone (1868/1992); to Liba Cehrnobrov and Anna Llionsky from the Wix Central Library services at the Weizmann Institute, to Shoshi Hazvi from the Department of Neurobiology at the Weizmann Institute, and to librarians at the University of Edinburgh and New York University, for assisting me in obtaining hard-to-get copies of enjoyable books and articles. Reading these sources reinforced my conviction that some important questions, ideas, and even answers are much older than we tend to pretend, a fact of life that should be occasionally *recalled and re*consolidated in our *collective memory.

---

[1] Throughout the text, terms preceded by an asterisk refer to entries in the book.

Acknowledgements

Permission granted by authors and publishers to adapt material for the preparation of figures is gratefully acknowledged; the particular sources are accredited in the appropriate figure legends. Material copyrighted by the following publishers was used with permission in preparation of the following figures: *Fig. 1*, Oxford University Press; *Fig. 2*, Society for Neuroscience, Washington, DC; *Fig. 3*, Oxford University Press; *Fig. 6*, Wiley-Liss, a subsidiary of John Wiley & Sons, Inc.; *Fig. 7*, Springer-Verlag; Fig. 8, Pearson Education, UK; *Fig. 9*, National Academy of Science, Washington, DC; *Fig. 10*, Kluwer Academic/Plenum Publishers and MIT Press; *Fig. 11*, Oxford University Press and The American Physiological Society; *Fig. 18*, Nature Publishing Group, London; *Fig. 20*, British Psychological Society and Cambridge University Press; *Fig. 22*, Elsevier Science; *Fig. 23*, Nature Publishing Group, London; *Fig. 24*, Carl Donner, Scientific American Inc., NY and Oxford University Press; *Fig. 26*, Cambridge University Press; *Fig. 27*, Nature Publishing Group, London; *Fig. 31*, Elsevier Science; *Fig. 32*, American Psychological Association; *Fig. 33*, Academic Press; *Fig. 34*, Cambridge University Press; *Fig. 35*, Oxford University Press; *Fig. 36*, Cambridge University Press; *Fig. 38*, Yale University Library; *Fig. 40*, Elsevier Science; *Fig. 44*, Elsevier Science; *Fig. 45*, Elsevier Science; *Fig. 47*, Nature Publishing Group, London; *Fig. 50*, Oxford University Press; *Fig. 51*, University of Nebraska Press; *Fig. 54*, American Psychological Association; *Fig. 56*, Elsevier Science; *Fig. 60*, Taylor & Francis, UK and The Psychonomic Society, Austin, TX; *Fig. 61*, The Guildford Press, NY; *Fig. 64*, Clarendon Press, Oxford; *Fig. 65*, The Psychonomic Society, Austin, TX.

Cover: Insets (from left to right): Augustine, as depicted by Botticeli (Uffizi Gallery, Florence; *classic); Learning-dependent changes in the activity of human cortex, as detected by fMRI (*functional neuroimaging, *skill; courtesy of Avi Karni); Neurons in the *cerebral cortex (courtesy of Henry Markram).

Contents

Contents

The conceptual framework

The premises that underlie the selection of entries, the adaptation and formulation of definitions, and the views expressed in this book.

I am a functionalist[1] with a biologist's *bias and with *conscious awareness of other disciplines. My approach to memory research is guided by the following tenets: (a) the function of the brain is to create and retain *internal representations of the world that could guide behaviour; (b) the function of *learning is to permit the adaptation of internal representations to a changing world (*memory is the retention of these adaptations over time); (c) learning and memory require neural *plasticity for their actualization; and (d) learning and memory are *system properties, made possible by the concerted operation of multiple *levels of the system.

The aforementioned tenets yield two important consequences for memory research. First, the comprehensive investigation of the processes and mechanisms of biological learning and memory requires a multilevel approach. Second, in the analysis of learning and memory, two levels of functional organization are particularly critical. One is the behavioural level. It does not make sense to address the function of the system without addressing its input–output relationships. The other is the level in which the specific content (semantics) of internal representations emerges in the brain. Identification of the behavioural level is self-evident. Identification of the level that encodes internal representations is not. It is currently believed that the level critical for encoding the semantics of internal representations in the brain is the circuit level, or the cellular-and-circuit level. More reduced levels implement plasticity, but in the absence of the circuit *context, do not suffice to endow the representation with its semantics. It is essential, therefore, that research programmes on memory never lose sight of the circuit and the behavioural levels. This is not easy. The circuit level is often excessively complex, the behavioural level amazingly tricky. Furthermore, the remarkable success of molecular neurobiology is enticing. I thus believe in a focused, restrained *reductionistic approach to memory research (Dudai 1992). I hope that this is aptly reflected in the entries throughout this book.

Each entry opens with a definition, or a set of definitions. What a definition is, is extremely difficult to define. A liberal list contains no less than 18 different species of definitions, and multiple candidate definitions of the definitions in each species (Robinson 1954). Whenever possible, I tried to adhere to one of the following meanings of definition: (a) the minimal set of attributes that uniquely describes an item or a concept; and (b) the formulation of a thing in terms of a more elementary level of organization or theory. These meanings are not mutually exclusive, and reflect, respectively, an attempt to adhere to *Ockham's razor, and the basic reductionistic approach, which has been restrained above. It is evident, however, at the outset, that each of these types of definitions requires quite a lot of *a priori knowledge about the item to be defined.[2] In the case of many items and concepts in the field of memory research, the relevant knowledge is yet unavailable. I had, therefore, to use an additional type of definition: explanation of the meaning of the term as it is to be used (*stipulated definition*). And as terms in memory research are occasionally used in more than one way, I provided multiple definitions when appropriate. The difficulties and uncertainties involved in definitions bring to mind the view that attempts to define entities at the cutting edge of knowledge could cause more harm than good: 'For when we define, we seem in danger of circumscribing nature within the bounds of our own notions' (Burke 1757). There is, however, the opposite view, that the risk is well worth taking. Socrates leads Meno to admit that definitions are always a must for a fertile, constructive dialogue (Plato, *Meno* 79d; *culture). In this debate, while being aware of Burke's caveat, I am much in favour of Meno's conviction.

Each entry ends with a short string of *associations. Bodies of knowledge in general are associative systems. I tried to *reinforce this notion by proposing selected associations. The reader is invited to form additional ones. Associations are not only aids to understanding, they are also proven *mnemonic devices: the richer the associative network, the higher the probability that the item will be stored (*metaphor) and *retrieved.

The conceptual framework

[1]Functionalism in its broadest sense is any view that analyses something in terms of how it functions (Lacey 1996). There are several versions of functionalism, one of which is 'functional analysis' (Cummins 1975). This is the research strategy that relies on the decomposition of a *system into its component parts while attempting to explain the working of the system in terms of the capacities of the parts and the way they are integrated with each other (Block 1980). Still, the structure of the parts and of the integrative system matters solely as much as it implements or shapes the function. Functional analysis is the sense of functionalism implied here.

[2]On this difficulty, which is also called 'the problem of the criterion', see *criterion.

A Priori

1. Independent of experience.
2. Beforehand.

A priori it could be assumed that students and aficionados of memory will benefit from contemplating the concept of 'a priori'. Before defending the aforesaid statement, however, a brief clarification of the different meanings and uses of 'a priori' is appropriate.

Prior to the eighteenth century, the pair of terms 'a priori'/'a posteriori' (Latin for 'from what is earlier'/'for what comes after') was used to distinguish between modes of reasoning: 'The mind can discover and understand the truth … by demonstration. When the mind reasons from causes to effects, the demonstration is called a priori; when from effects to causes, the demonstration is called a posteriori' (Arnauld 1662). Only later were these nonidentical terminological-twins used to refer to types of knowledge: knowledge independent of experience is 'a priori', that which is grounded in experience is 'a posteriori' (Kant 1781). Traditionally since then, the pair 'a priori'/'a posteriori' is associated in the philosophical discourse with two other pairs of opposites: 'analytic' vs. 'synthetic', and 'necessary' vs. 'contingent' (Moser 1987; Grayling 1997). A statement is 'analytic' if its truth value can be determined by understanding the concepts or terms contained in it, whereas it is 'synthetic' if in order to determine its truth value we must know how the concepts or terms involved relate to other constituents of the world. Hence, adapting a commonly used illustration, 'singles are unmarried' is analytic, because 'single' is 'unmarried', whereas 'singles are happy' is synthetic, because it is not evident from 'singles' how their mood should be (the latter statement also demonstrates that some kinds of truth are *context specific or in the eye of the beholder, but this is another story). In formal terms, an analytic statement is thus a tautology, and its truth value follows necessarily. The latter property leads us to the third related pair of opposites: 'necessary' vs. 'contingent'. 'Necessary' refers to statements that must be either true or false due to what they state, whereas in 'contingent' statements the truth value is contingent upon other occurrences or relationships in the world. Discussion of the 'necessary'/'contingent' pair is within the realm of metaphysics, the 'analytic'/'synthetic' pair deprives logicians of sound sleep, whereas 'a priori'/'a posteriori' is within the domain of epistemology (the science of knowledge) (Moser 1987; Grayling 1997; Bealer 1999).

It is the epistemological connotation of 'a priori' that interests us here. Furthermore, we focus on only a limited portion of the universe: the *individual* organism, its brain, behaviour, and memory. Construing 'experience' in definition 1 as any behavioural or physiological experience of the individual, leaves only one source of a priori knowledge in the individual brain: the genetic material. Genes carry information about a variety of behavioural capabilities and capacities (*neurogenetics). This information is hence 'innate'.[1] As far as the individual is concerned, this is *bona fide* a-priori knowledge. For the species it is not, because the knowledge is supposed to have been acquired over time, a posteriori, by natural selection in evolution. However, it is also useful to consider as 'a priori' that knowledge that cannot be explained *solely* by the individual's experience. Such knowledge is generated by *developmental processes, via the interaction of genes and environment in prenatal and early postnatal periods. It is also produced throughout life by the endogenous activity of the brain, which depends on the processing of both innate and acquired knowledge. Definition 2 is colloquial: according to it, 'experience' is 'experience at the present time', e.g. while on a learning task. Hence according to this liberal interpretation any experience provides a priori knowledge for future experiences. This connotation of a priori gravitates toward the trivial, and will not be further discussed here.

A priori knowledge of both innate and postnatal origin fulfils multiple roles in behaviour and behavioural *plasticity:

1. Innate knowledge underlies reflexes and predetermined behavioural routines such as used in feeding, mating, fighting, and fleeing (Lorenz 1981; Dudai 1989). These behaviours vary in their dependency on postnatal experience. Some are essentially independent of experience, although they still may be perfected or modified by it, e.g. α-type *classical conditioning. Other behaviours require experience for maturation, fine tuning, and optimal *performance. This experience may have to be provided during a restricted 'sensitive period' in life, as in *imprinting (Lorenz 1981) and *birdsong (Nelson and Marler 1994). Another, more general type of 'prepared' or 'constrained learning', in which the type of associations, but not their actual content, is constrained a priori, is *conditioned taste aversion: we are inclined a priori to associate the taste of foodstuff with subsequent visceral malaise but not with a painful blow to the skin (Garcia et al. 1968). Admittedly, most philosophers would not like the use of the term 'knowledge' in the context of such 'simple' behaviours: 'No philosopher will be disturbed if Lorenz

tells him that young geese follow the farmer around without previous conditioning or training. If Lorenz were to add that the young goose knows that it should follow the farmer, or that the farmer is a friend, philosophical ears would be pricked' (Cooper 1972). However, first of all, 'knowledge' is here used in its most *reductive connotation, not necessarily involving *conscious awareness (*internal representation); second, irrespective of the status of philosophical ears, the question whether animals are 'consciously aware' or not is not yet settled (*declarative memory).

2. Innate knowledge underlies capacities and operational rules of higher brain faculties such as language and mathematical abstraction in humans ('the speaker of a language knows a great deal that he has not learned', Chomsky (1966); compare Socrates on geometry: 'Try to discover by recollection what you do not know, or rather what you do not remember', Plato, *Meno* 86b).

3. Perhaps most intriguing is the notion that a priori knowledge that draws from a combination of innate and acquired resources permits our brain to anticipate the world on a momentary basis (e.g. Anokhin 1974). This issue relates to one of the most profound problems in the neurosciences and the philosophy of mind: the relationships of internal representations to the outside world. Let us consider two basic possibilities. One is that input from the world somehow *instructs* the brain to generate specific internal representations of reality. This type of process does not necessitate a priori knowledge, although it may still benefit from it. The other possibility is that the world somehow *selects* representations among 'pre-representations', which are generated endogenously in the brain (Young 1979; Heidmann *et al.* 1984; Dudai 1989; Edelman 1993; *stimulus). The 'selectionist' view has a Darwinian flavour, and likens the ontogenesis of our mind to the phylogenesis of our species. According to this view, the mammalian brain is not a passive observer but rather an active agent that anticipates the immediate future (*planning), and toward that end keeps itself busy by generating internal *models of reality. The postulated rules that guide 'the survival of the fittest internal models' may take into account predictions based on both innate knowledge and accumulated experience, and congruency with the on-line demands of the real world as conveyed by the senses. Such capacity is hence expected to be subserved in every individual of the species by two tiers of a priori knowledge. First there are the species-specific innate components responsible for much of the rules and the hardware, namely the computations, *algorithms and neuronal devices that enable the brain to generate and stabilize the aforementioned pre-representations

(*level). Then there is the ongoing flux of the short-lived pre-representations themselves, which are unique to each individual of the species, and could be regarded as flashes of subjective knowledge preceding *perception and the *acquisition of memories. In this case, the past literally chases the present, and 'a priori' may refer to a time-scale of seconds only. Still, this is 'a priori', because at least part of the information is not derived from actual experience in the outside world.

The 'selectionist' hypothesis hence implies that we continuously anticipate the world and generate approximate models of it, and that both endogenous and exogenous information combine to represent reality (e.g. Arieli *et al.* 1996). This raises the question how faithful to reality are our internal representations (*false memory, *real-life memory). We may assume that in the course of evolution, our ability to model the world, learn about it, and interact with it has been shaped to reach a reasonable correspondence of the internal models to reality. The fact that organisms succeed in negotiating with an ever changing milieu attests to that. But not all our memory *systems (*taxonomy) have been subjected to the same selective pressures, such as the pressure for improved precision and detail. Hence, whether a specific type of memory, such as *declarative, is inherently faithful to reality or not, is itself a priori influenced by evolutionary forces.

Last, we should not *forget that in daily life we are all constrained by a priori assumptions that could *bias our personal (or *cultural) attitude toward events, facts, and disciplines. The attitude toward 'memory' is not expected to be an exception.

Selected associations: Acquisition, Bias, Development, Palimpsest

---

[1] For *classic philosophical attitudes to innate knowledge in general, see Locke (1690) and Leibniz (1704).

Acetylcholine

A *neurotransmitter at central *synapses and at the vertebrate neuromuscular junction.

Acetylcholine (ACh; the acetic acid ester of choline) was among the first chemicals to be proposed as a neurotransmitter, and the first neurotransmitter to be identified in and isolated from neural tissue (Dale 1914; Loewi 1921). It was also the first for which the existence of a proteineous membrane *receptor had been suggested (Nachmansohn 1959).[1] *In vivo* ACh is synthesized from the amino alcohol choline and acetyl coenzyme A. The job is done by the enzyme choline acetyltransferase (Kitamoto *et al.* 1992). ACh is hydrolysed by another enzyme, acetylcholinesterase, one of the fastest enzymes ever (Taylor and Radic 1994). Receptors for ACh are of two major types:

1. 'Nicotinic', so-called because they bind nicotine (the tobacco poison). Nicotinic receptors are *ion-channel receptors, i.e. they contain a pore that mediates the flux of ions across the membrane and is gated by the neurotransmitter (Karlin and Akabas 1996).
2. 'Muscarinic', so-called because they bind muscarine (a mushroom poison that kills flies, *Musca*). Muscarinic receptors are 'metabotropic', i.e. they do not include a channel but rather exert their effect by modulation of *intracellular signal transduction cascades (Wess 1993).

Each of these receptor types can be further classified into subtypes. The subtypes are commonly characterized by their affinity and specificity for activators (agonists) and inhibitors (antagonists); the identity of the intracellular signal transduction cascades coupled to the receptor; and the cellular localization (presynaptic or postsynaptic).

A neuronal *system in which ACh is a neurotransmitter or neuromodulator is termed 'cholinergic'. Cholinergic innervation of various brain areas such as the *cerebral cortex could be described as either extrinsic, e.g. stemming from central cholinergic nuclei in the brain, or intrinsic (Johnston *et al.* 1981; Mesulam *et al.* 1983). The central cholinergic nuclei in the mammalian brain are located in the basal forebrain and the brainstem (Figure 1). The major ones are in the basal forebrain and they innervate the neocortex, *hippocampus, and parts of the *amygdaloid complex. Those in the brainstem innervate among other the thalamus. The innervation by the central cholinergic nuclei is an example of a 'diffused neuromodulatory system' i.e. a neuromodulatory system that does not target specific synapses or neurons but rather a whole region or multiple regions (see also *dopamine, *noradrenaline).

The cholinergic basal forebrain system, itself a collection of nuclei, has been repeatedly implicated in cognition, including *attention, learning, and memory. A correlation was found in a number of studies between degeneration of basal forebrain nuclei, cholinergic dysfunction and cognitive deterioration in Alzheimer's disease (*dementia) and in aged humans and rodents. This has led to the 'cholinergic hypothesis of memory dysfunction' (Bartus *et al.* 1982). This hypothesis proposes that cholinergic dysfunction is not only a correlate, but also a cause of cognitive and behavioural deficits in dementia. The 'cholinergic hypothesis' was highly successful at least on one front: it generated a surge of research on the potential role of cholinergic modulation in learning and memory, and served as an incentive for the development of cholinergic drugs to treat dementia (see below).

Multiple processes and mechanisms have been suggested to underlie the postulated roles of ACh in

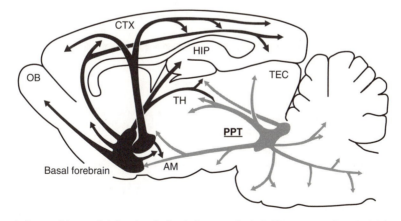

Fig. 1 A schematic diagram of the central cholinergic projections in the mammalian brain. There are two major projectional networks: from the basal forebrain, innervating among others the *cerebral cortex (CTX), *hippocampus (HIP) and *amygdala (AM); and from the penducolopontine and laterodorsal tegmental nuclei (marked in the figure as PPT), innervating among others the thalamus (TH) and tectum (TEC). OB, olfactory bulb. Local cholinergic circuits are not shown. (Adapted from Cooper *et al.* 1996.)

learning and memory. As is the case with other neuro-transmitters and neuromodulators, the physiological roles of ACh in brain should be judged not only by its independent activation of specific cellular receptors and their downstream intracellular signal transduction cas-cades, but also by its contribution to the activation and cross-talk of webs of signalling cascades induced by coactive sets of neurotransmitters and neuromodulators (*coincidence detector, *context). Similarly, at the cir-cuit *level, the function of the cholinergic system must be assessed in the context of the concerted activity of multiple neurotransmission and neuromodulatory path-ways on the target circuit (Decker and McGaugh 1991). ACh was portrayed as a cellular code for saliency (*sur-prise), *attention, *state dependency, and even as a direct 'storage signal' that instructs the appropriate circuits to encode novel information as lasting *internal representa-tions (Mishkin and Murray 1994; Naor and Dudai 1996; Everitt and Robbins 1997; Wenk 1997; Shulz et al. 2000). All the above functions could actually be different mani-festations of similar cellular and circuit mechanisms, with the specific role of the cholinergic function in a given cognitive and behavioural situation being dependent upon the task, the context, and the identity of the brain areas involved. At the *algorithmic level, brain ACh, similarly to other neuromodulators such as *noradrena-line, was proposed to enhance the signal-to-noise ratio in the target circuit (Barkai and Hasselmo 1997).

In recent years, the function of ACh in the mam-malian brain has been scrutinized by a variety of novel *methodologies, techniques, and preparations. Not all the data so obtained fit smoothly into the hypothesis that ACh is indeed obligatory for learning, certainly not in all types of learning, but the overall picture favours the idea that it does play an important part in many learning situations. A somewhat surprising finding was reported by several laboratories following the introduction of a powerful experimental tool, the chimera-immunotoxin 192IgG-saporin. This toxin is a synthetic chimera between the toxin saporin, that kills cells, and an antibody to a subtype of a receptor for nerve growth factor that resides on most types of cholinergic neurons in the basal forebrain. The compound guides itself to these cholinergic neurons and destroys them selectively, while leaving other neu-rons, the majority of which are noncholinergic, intact. In disparity with the effect of less selective lesions of basal forebrain cholinergic nuclei, in several prepara-tions, the guided toxin had only a small effect if at all on memory (e.g. Baxter et al. 1995; but see, for example, Power et al. 2002). In contrast, a variety of other new experimental manipulations did support a correlative

and in certain cases an obligatory role of ACh, acting either via muscarinic or via nicotinic receptors, in a variety of learning situations and of neuronal *plastic-ity mechanisms that *model attention and learning (Auerbach and Segal 1996; Gray et al. 1996; Picciotto et al. 1998; Berman et al. 2000; Mansvelder and McGehee 2000; Nail-Boucherie et al. 2000; Rasmusson 2000; Shulz et al. 2000). For example, in many preparations, ACh enhances transmitter release, and in some it sup-ports *long-term potentiation. Stimulation of the basal forebrain cholinergic input was shown to enable the reorganization (*plasticity) of cortical sensory *maps, and hence possibly *internal representations, in response to modality-specific input (Bjordahl et al. 1998; Kilgard and Merzenich 1998); a caveat is, how-ever, appropriate regarding such an approach, because, as noted above, the basal forebrain is also a source of noncholinergic innervation to the cortex. Another report that made it to the headlines was that transplan-tation into the brain of cells engineered to release ACh alleviates cognitive deficits in rats with a cholinergically denervated cortex (Winkler et al. 1995).

A good deal of support for the role of the cholinergic system in cognition stems from human pharmacology. Drugs that increase the availability of ACh, mostly inhibitors of acetylcholinesterase, have beneficial effects on cognitive function at the early stages of dementia. Furthermore, to the understandable dismay of non-smokers, nicotine appears to be moderately beneficial to attention and memory (Di Carlo et al. 2000). It thus appears that cholinergic drugs establish themselves as cog-nitive boosters (*nootropics) before the exact and task-specific roles of ACh in cognition and memory are fully understood. This, of course, is not unique to the choliner-gic drugs; if understanding the mechanism of action was a *criterion for the introduction of a drug, many of our most efficient medications would not be in use.

Selected associations: Attention, Dementia, Neurotrans-mitter, Receptor, Synapse

---

[1]For an early suggestion that there should be a receptor, long before ACh itself was discovered, see Langley (1878).

Acquisition

1. The initial *phase in the formation of a *memory trace.

2. The process by which new information is converted into a memory trace.

3. The change in *performance during training that is taken to represent the progression of *learning.

Memories are like people—they are born, live, and die. Acquisition is their moment of birth. The other major phases in the life history of a memory are *consolidation (if it is ever to become a long-term memory), storage, *retrieval, and extinction (*experimental extinction, *forgetting). Depending on the context of discussion, 'acquisition' implies a temporal phase (definition 1, e.g. Stillings *et al.* 1987); or a process that takes place during this phase (definition 2, e.g. Tulving 1983); or a change in *performance that reflects this process (definition 3, e.g. *behaviourism). This change in performance is quantified by an 'acquisition curve' or 'learning curve', in which performance is plotted against the amount of practice (e.g. Skinner 1938; e.g. Figure 41, p. 144). Commonly, the *subject is said to have completed the acquisition of the task if its performance has reached a preset *criterion, such as time to reach the goal in a *maze or a certain probability of success on a discrimination problem (e.g. *delay task). The process of acquisition was termed 'engraphy' by Semon (1904), meaning the engraving of an *engram, but 'engraphy' has never caught on. 'Acquisition' is sometimes used as a synonym for '*learning', but the latter term has a broader meaning and usage.

Acquisition is composed of subprocesses. The first is 'encoding', which in general refers the conversion of a message from one language, or code, to another. 'Encoding' is frequently used in the learning literature as a synonym for 'acquisition', but this is unsatisfactory, because there is more to 'acquisition' than 'encoding'. In neuronal encoding, information is transformed into the neuronal codes used in computation and representation (Churchland and Sejnowski 1992). This information arrives from either the external or the internal world. In the first case, the electromagnetic, mechanical, or chemical information is converted via the sense organs into neuronal activity. In the second case, information from the body itself is conveyed by specialized neuronal circuits, or via body fluids in the form of chemical messages (hormones) that evoke neuronal activity. No information can be handled by the central nervous system without first being encoded into the appropriate neuronal code. Encoding is thus involved in brain activities that do not necessarily culminate in the acquisition of a memory, such as on-line processing of information (*attention, *percept), or control of ongoing physiological routines. For a memory to be born, an additional process, of initial 'registration' ('recording'), is also needed. This permits the *internal representations of transient *stimuli, once formed, to become or induce an engram. From what we know from physiology and psychophysics, the decay time of transient representations is in the subsecond range (Dudai 1997b, see also 'encoding time' in Ganz 1975; *cell assembly, *percept, *phase). The registration mechanisms hence differentiate transitory from lasting internal representations, where 'lasting' is anything that is significantly longer than the aforementioned decay time.

How much time does acquisition require? This depends on the learning *paradigm and protocol. It is convenient to distinguish 'instant' from incremental ('repetitive', 'rote') acquisition. Instant acquisition refers to single-trial learning. This takes place in certain situations of intense aversive conditioning (*conditioned taste aversion, *fear conditioning); in some types of *imprinting; in the formation of *flashbulb memories; and probably in some other situations, in which acquisition curves have a step-function shape (e.g. *insight). In contrast, incremental acquisition refers to situations in which information accumulates over multiple experiences to construct the memory (Pavlov 1927; Skinner 1938; Hebb 1949; Dudai 1989). Gradual acquisition of *habits and *skills is such a case. The repetitive practice is expected to involve gradual modification of internal representations over hours, days, even months. But does incremental acquisition involve accumulative modifications that are restricted to the original representation formed at the beginning of training? This assumption might be naive. Internal representations are expected to form dynamic distributed networks (*cell assembly). Therefore, a more realistic view is that recurrent discrete events of acquisition and consolidation, that stem from each accumulative experience, alter existing internal representations that encode the information in question, but at the same time generate new representations and link them to the old ones (*palimpsest).

Ample data, supported by learning theory, indicate that whatever happens in acquisition, in terms of perceptual *cues and cognitive processes, determines not only the lifespan of the resulting memory, whether short or long (Craik and Lockhart 1972; Baddeley 1997), but also how efficiently will this memory be *retrieved in due time. Two influential concepts that reflect this notion will be mentioned here. One is the 'encoding-specificity principle' (Tulving 1983). It states that memory performance is best when the *cues* present at retrieval match those present in acquisition. The other is termed '*transfer-appropriate processing*' (Morris *et al*. 1977). It states that memory performance is best when the cognitive *processes* invoked at retrieval (say, semantic as opposed to phonetic processing in verbal tasks) match those used in acquisition.

Multiple approaches are used to investigate the neurobiology of acquisition. Cellular physiology, neuropharmacology, neurochemistry, and molecular biology are all applied to dissect the molecular and cellular mechanisms involved. Candidate 'cellular acquisition devices' are *ion channels and membrane *receptors on synaptic terminals that receive the teaching input, itself encoded in ion currents and *neurotransmitters (*Aplysia*, *long-term potentiation). A substantial amount of information is also available on the processes downstream from the synaptic membrane, that involve activation of *intracellular signal transduction cascades, and couple acquisition to consolidation. We even seem to start to understand in molecular terms why is it that in many learning situations, distributed training with intercalated intervals between repetitive acquisition trials, is more efficient than massed, continuous training, in which acquisition mechanisms are expected to function nonstop (*spaced training).

Brain areas and neuronal circuits that subserve acquisition have been identified in *habituation, *sensitization, *classical, and *instrumental conditioning in a variety of *simple or less-simple *systems (e.g. *Aplysia*, *classical conditioning, *conditioned taste aversion, *Drosophila*, *fear conditioning, *honeybee). In recent years, *functional neuroimaging has made a remarkable contribution to the identification of brain systems that subserve acquisition in the human brain (e.g. Nyberg *et al*. 1996; Fletcher *et al*. 1997; Tulving and Markowitsch 1997; Buckner and Koutstaal 1998; Epstein *et al*. 1999; Fernández *et al*. 1999). The circuits that acquire information about a memory vary with the type of memory, but a few general conclusions emerge from the studies so far: (a) acquisition of *declarative memories engages widely distributed areas, which include modality specific *cortex, and in addition supramodal areas, particularly in the mediotemporal lobe (*hippocampus, *limbic system); (b) these areas partially overlap brain areas that later retrieve the learned information; and (c) in some studies it was possible to show a correlation between the activation of an identified brain region during the training experience and the subsequent ability to remember this experience. For example, the ability to remember verbal information could be predicted by the magnitude of activation in the left prefrontal and temporal cortex

during the training (Wagner *et al*. 1998b). It is not yet known, however, which of the activated areas is indispensable for acquisition (*criterion), which area is causally related to the strength of the engram, and what are the specific roles of each of the areas in the encoding and registration of information in the first milliseconds and seconds after engraphy has been triggered.

Selected associations: Consolidation, Experimental extinction, Retrieval, Transfer

---

Algorithm

A procedure for solving a problem or achieving a goal in a finite number of steps.

'Begin at the beginning', said the King of Hearts, 'and go on till you come to the end: then stop'. He thus provided White Rabbit with an algorithm (Carroll 1865). The term 'algorithm' is derived from Latinization of the name of one of the most creative mathematician in medieval Islam, Al-Kwarizmi (780–*c*. 850; Boyer 1989; Colish 1997). In modern times algorithmics is a field fundamental to the science of computing (Harel 1987). In the neurosciences algorithms are encountered in multiple contexts (Marr 1982; Hinton 1989; Churchland and Sejnowski 1992). One of these is in *models of biological learning. It is noteworthy that in discussion of such models the terms 'law', 'rule', and 'algorithm' are sometimes intermixed. It is therefore useful to distinguish among them. A 'law' is a scientifically proven formal statement with theoretical underpinning that describes a quantitative relationship between entities. Strictly speaking, there aren't yet *bona fide* 'laws' specific to the discipline of biological memory. It is sensible, therefore, not to misuse the term. 'Rule' describes a standard procedure for solving a class of problems. It is hence close to 'algorithm'. However, they are not equivalent. 'Algorithm' is a formal term referring to a detailed recipe, whereas 'rule' may be vaguer. Furthermore, a 'rule' may connote knowledge by the executing agent of the input–output relationship, 'algorithm' does not. A *system can execute algorithms perfectly without having the faintest idea what it is doing, why it is all done, and what the outcome is likely to be. As there is no *a priori reason to assume that biological learning at the *synaptic or circuit *level is governed by a knowledgeable supervisor (*homunculus), it does not make a lot of sense to claim that synapses or circuits follow 'rules'; rather, they execute algorithms. Finally, an assumption (usually tacit) of the neuroscience of learning, and an incentive for the analysis of *simple systems, is that a great variety of biological learning systems, in different species, share general laws/rules/algorithms. This posit makes sense if evolution is considered, but is definitely not itself a law, and its generality must be scrutinized in every experimental system anew (e.g. Seligman 1970).

The most popular algorithms in the neuroscience are synaptic ones, and are associated with a postulate of synaptic *plasticity dubbed 'Hebb's postulate'. In its original version it states the following: 'When an axon of cell A is near enough to excite a cell B and repeatedly or persistently takes part in firing it, some growth process or metabolic change takes place in one or both cells such that A's efficiency, as one of the cells firing B, is increased' (Hebb 1949; for rudimentary precedents see James 1890; Kappers 1917). In a Hebbian synapse, the increase in synaptic weight is thus a function of the correlation of pre- and postsynaptic activity. Hebb postulated the process to account for experience-dependent modification of local nodes in *cell assemblies. In formal notation, Hebb's postulate is of the type $w_{i,j}(t+1) = w_{i,j}(t) + \Delta w_{i,j}(t)$, where $\Delta w_{i,j}(t) = f[a_i(t), a_j(t)]$; $w_{i,j}$ is the strength ('weight') of connection from presynaptic unit u_j to postsynaptic unit u_i, $\Delta w_{i,j}(t)$ is the change in synaptic strength, $a_j(t)$ and $a_i(t)$ are measures of pre- and postsynaptic activity (Brown *et al.* 1990). Each step in the algorithm is thus a computation of the aforementioned type, and the algorithm consists of proceeding step-by-step over time (at a more *reduced level, the Hebbian computation itself is based on multiple subordinate algorithms, such as summation and multiplication, but this should not concern us here). The original 'Hebbian' became a generic term as well as a reference for many variants of synaptic modification algorithms. Terms composed of 'Hebb-plus-a-modifier' to mark their relationship to the Hebbian are common, and sometimes a bit confusing. For example, 'anti-Hebb' is used to describe rather different types of algorithms that culminate in decrement of synaptic efficacy (e.g. Lisman 1989; Bell *et al.* 1993; *long-term potentiation, *metaplasticity). Over the years multiple attempts have been made to demonstrate how Hebbian algorithms might be implemented in synapses in *development and learning (e.g. Lisman 1989; Fregnac and Shulz 1994; Buonomano and Merzenich 1998; Lechner and Byrne 1998; but see a critical review in Cruikshank and Weinberger 1996).

A discipline in which synaptic learning algorithms became particularly popular and useful is that of artificial neural networks (ANN; Fausett 1994). These are artificial systems (i.e. either abstract *models or the physical implementation of such models) composed of a large number of interconnected computational units ('neurons'). Signals are passed between neurons over connections, which manipulate the signal in a typical way. Each neuron applies an activation function to its net input to determine its output signal. Specific networks are characterized by the pattern of their connectivity ('architecture'), the algorithm that determines the weight on the connections, and the activation function of the neurons. The collective behaviours of such networks could mimic various dynamic properties of neuronal circuits, such as *perception and learning. Certain subclasses of ANN use Hebbian algorithms to achieve 'unsupervised' learning (see above) in local nodes. Other algorithms refer to 'supervised' learning, in which some type of global information or 'instructor' informs the node what the desired end-point is. An algorithm of the latter type that has gained considerable popularity is 'back-propagation' (or 'back-propagation of errors'). Here the error for each unit (the desired minus the actual output) is calculated at the output of the network, and recursively propagated backward into the network, so that ultimately, the weights of connections are adjusted to approach the desired output vector of the network (Rumelhart *et al.* 1986a).

A number of algorithms have been proposed to underlie learning at the more global levels of brain and behaviour (Thorndike 1911; Dickinson 1980; Wasserman and Miller 1997). An influential one is associated with the Rescorla and Wagner model of learning (1972; for precursors, see Hull 1943; Bush and Mosteller 1951). Basically, Rescorla and Wagner posited that in *associative learning, changing the associative strength of a stimulus with a *reinforcer, depends upon the concurrent associative strength of all present stimuli with that reinforcer; if in a given training trial the composite associative strength is already high, learning will be less effective. In formal notation, Rescorla–Wagner propose that $\Delta V_X = \alpha_X \beta_R (\lambda_R - V_\Sigma)$, where ΔV_X is the change produced by a given training trial in the strength of the association (V_X) between stimulus X, and reinforcer R; α_X and β_R are learning rate parameters (associability parameters) representing properties such as the intensity and saliency of X and R; λ_R is the maximal conditioning supportable by R; and V_Σ is the total associative strength with respect to R of all the stimuli present on the aforementioned trial. The expression $\lambda_R - V_\Sigma$ can be said to represent the disparity between expectation and reality on a given trial; the smaller it is, the weaker is the learning. In other words, as many a reader might have concluded from their own experience, the amount of learning is proportional to the amount of *surprise (see also *attention). Here again, each step in the algorithm is a computation of the aforementioned type, and the algorithm consists of proceeding step-by-step over time. The Rescorla–Wagner model can explain multiple behavioural phenomena in conditioning, including cases of *cue revaluation (Dickinson 1980; Wasserman and Miller 1997; *classical conditioning).

Over the years multiple attempts have been made to account for the operation of selected brain regions by proposing identified synaptic and circuit algorithms (For notable examples, see Marr 1969; Albus 1971; Zipser and Andersen 1988). At the current state of the art in brain research, synapses and model circuits still provide a more suitable arena than whole real-life circuits to identify and test learning algorithms, because the input–output relationship of real-life brain circuits is seldom understood in reasonable detail, if at all. Still, advances are being made at more global levels of brain function as well; for example, Schultz *et al.* (1997) report that in the course of multitrial instrumental training, *dopaminergic activity in the primate brain encodes expectations and prediction errors for reward. The dopaminergic neuro-modulatory system may thus be part of a circuit that performs computations of the type $\lambda_R - V_\Sigma$ in the Rescorla–Wagner model.

New classes of algorithms are expected to emerge at the cellular, circuit, and system levels with the intensification of the mechanistic revolution in biology. One of these days, much of descriptive neurobiology is bound to give way to a science of biological engineering, in which algorithms and quantitative relations will become the rule rather than the exception. This has profound implications concerning the proper education of future neurobiologists (e.g. Alberts 1998).

Selected associations: Learning, Models, Level, Plasticity, Synapse

Amnesia

1. **The loss or absence of memory.**

2. **The *amnestic syndrome*: A marked, chronic impairment in memory in the absence of other major cognitive deficits.**

Amnesia is 'forgetfulness' in Greek (*mnemonics). The adverse effect of certain types of brain injury and mental trauma on memory was recognized long ago. But the systematic analysis of amnesia started only in the nineteenth century, with Ribot (1882) and Korsakoff (1887). Till the introduction of *functional neuroimaging, the study of amnesia has been the only practical approach to the investigation of brain substrates of memory in humans. Some information could be also obtained from electrical stimulation of patients undergoing brain surgery, but this was very limited in scope and controversial in interpretation (*engram). The investigation of amnesia is still a very powerful, unique approach to the analysis of human memory: whereas the application of functional neuroimaging could identify *correlations* between the activity of distinct brain regions and the *performance on memory tasks, the study of amnesiacs could potentially identify those brain structures that are *obligatory* for normal memory (*criterion, *method).[1]

Amnesia is not a unitary syndrome (Whitty and Zangwill 1966; Parkin 1987; Mayes 1995). A *taxonomy based on etiology distinguishes among 'organic amnesia', 'substance-induced amnesia', and 'functional amnesia'. These subtypes of amnesia are also known by other names, as explained below.

1. *Organic amnesia* is a consequence of damage to the brain inflicted by injury, disease (e.g. tumour, stroke, viral infection), or surgical intervention (DSM-IV 1994).

2. *Substance-induced amnesia* results from the intake of poisons, drugs of abuse, or medications with amnestic side-effects (for example, certain anxiolytics, *lotus). Chronic excessive consumption of alcohol could result in vitamin deficiency and encephalopathy (brain inflammation), which is manifested in Korsakoff's amnesia, at which stage it is also categorized as organic amnesia (Shimamura *et al.* 1988).

3. *Functional amnesia* develops after severe mental stress or trauma, or as a result of certain affective disorders. This type of amnesia is also termed 'psychogenic', or 'dissociative' ('dissociative disorders' in general are disruptions in the integrated functions of *consciousness, perception, personal identity, or memory).

The amnestic syndrome impairs learning and memory while leaving other cognitive faculties relatively intact. It is hence distinguished from *dementia, which involves multiple cognitive deficits, and from delirium, which impairs consciousness. Whereas some amnesia are modality specific (e.g. Rubin and Greenberg 1998), the 'amnestic syndrome' is 'global' and independent of sensory modality. Global organic amnesia is *chronic*; some improvement may be observed over time, but the patient does not regain normal memory. There is also a separate syndrome termed 'transient global amnesia'. This is a benign neurological syndrome in which the onset of amnesia is sudden and the recovery fast (usually < 1 day). Transient amnesia could also follow head trauma or electroconvulsive therapy.

An additional *criterion used to classify amnesia is the temporal window to which the memory loss refers. Here a distinction is made between '*retrograde*' and '*anterograde*' amnesia. Retrograde (premorbid) amnesia affects memory from the onset of the pathology backward. Anterograde (postmorbid) amnesia affects memory from the onset of the pathology forward. For example, in a typical case of the amnestic syndrome, there is dense anterograde amnesia and usually only a partial, graded retrograde amnesia. Memory of the recent past is commonly affected more than memory of the distant past; this observation is termed 'the law of regression', or 'Ribot's law' (it is noteworthy that Ribot regarded the phenomenon as the manifestation of a Darwinian principle, in which 'progressive destruction advances progressively from the unstable to the stable'; Ribot 1882).

The *classical, most widely cited case of a global amnesia is that of H.M. He became amnestic in 1953 at the age of 23, following 'a frankly experimental operation' (Scoville and Milner 1957) to alleviate uncontrollable epilepsy. The operation removed bilaterally the medial temporal polar *cortex, most of the *amygdaloid complex, the entorhinal cortex, and approximately half of the rostrocaudal extent of the intraventricular portion of the *hippocampal formation (Corkin *et al.* 1997). The operation reduced the frequency of seizures, but produced a severe, permanent anterograde amnesia, with only a limited effect on memory of events prior to the operation (and no effect on more remote events). Postoperationally, H.M. scored above average on a general intelligence test, showed no decline on immediate memory (*capacity), but was unable to store any new *declarative information. He was, however, capable of learning new *skills. Thus even in this severe case, the amnesia was not really 'global'.

The study of H.M., as well as of many other amnesics since then, gave rise to major insights concerning human memory (Squire and Zola 1997; Milner *et al.* 1998). These studies have demonstrated that the brain

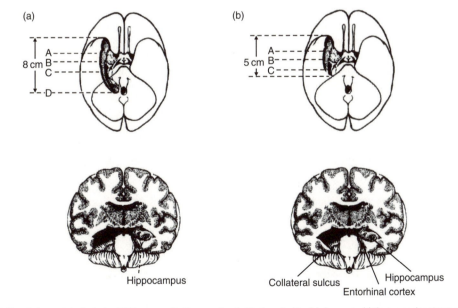

Fig. 2 The missing parts in the brain of H.M., removed in the operation that had resulted in global amnesia. (a) The surgeon's estimate after the surgery (Scoville and Milner 1957). (b) The outcome of the surgical resection as unveiled by magnetic resonance imaging (MRI) 40 years later (Corkin *et al.* 1997). The upper diagrams depict ventral views of the brain, the lower ones depict coronal sections. A through D in the ventral views mark the planes of coronal sections in the original drawings, but only plane B is shown here. The operation was bilateral but in the drawing one hemisphere is shown intact for comparison. Adapted from Corkin *et al.* (1997). The case of H.M. drew much attention to the role of the medial temporal lobe in general, and the hippocampus in particular, in long-term memory.

contains distinct declarative (explicit) and nondeclarative (implicit) memory systems; and that long-term declarative memory is dependent on medial temporal lobe structures. Additional research has shown that nondeclarative amnesia could result from damage to a different, corticostriatal system (Mishkin *et al.* 1984; Knowlton *et al.* 1996; *skill). Support for the above conclusions has also emerged from studies of circumscribed brain lesions in *monkey *models of human amnesia (e.g. Mishkin *et al.* 1984; Ridley and Baker 1991; Meunier *et al.* 1993; Zola-Morgan *et al.* 1993; Gaffan 1994; Leonard *et al.* 1995). Indeed, the neuroscience of amnesia is characterized by a remarkable degree of integration of human and animal research.

Despite the impressive advances in our understanding of amnesia, many outstanding questions still await resolution (Warrington and Weiskrantz 1982; Mishkin *et al.* 1997; Nadel and Moscovitch 1997; Squire and Zola 1997; Weiskrantz 1997; Milner *et al.* 1998; Aggleton and Brown 1999). Among these: Is amnesia due to impairment in the *acquisition, *consolidation, storage, or *retrieval of memory? Although most authorities consider acquisition of information to remain intact in global amnesics, because of the good performance on the immediate memory tasks (see H.M. above), still, even subtle deficits in the way information is encoded and registered could markedly affect later retrieval. Another question is what is the specific contribution of medial temporal lobe structures (such as the hippocampal formation and adjacent cortici), and medial diencephalic structures (such as the medial thalamus and the mammillary bodies), to different manifestations of the amnestic syndrome, such as anterograde vs. retrograde amnesia, or *recall vs. *recognition deficits? And what is the contribution to amnesia of other brain areas, such as the basal forebrain (*acetylcholine, *dementia), or the frontal cortex and its interconnections with the diencephalon?

Each amnestic *subject is a unique individual, and probably in none are the lesions confined to a single well-circumscribed functional location in the brain. This makes the research inherently difficult. Animal models do help a lot, but still, it must be proven that what is considered amnesia in a monkey, even more so in a rodent, is sufficiently similar to the human amnesia to warrant adaptation of the conclusions from the animal to the human. Solutions are expected to emerge from the systematic analysis of additional cases of amnesia (e.g. Reed and Squire 1998), using universally accepted batteries of memory tests; from a greater sophistication of such tests in humans, primates, and rodents; and possibly also from a more extensive

integration of novel functional neuroimaging methods in the study of amnestic brains.

Selected associaions: Conscious awareness, Declarative memory, Episodic memory, Dementia, Infantile amnesia

---

[1] Reversible disruption of activity by transcranial magnetic stimulation (TMS) might also be used to identify brain areas obligatory for learning and memory (e.g. Grafman *et al.* 1999; Rossi *et al.* 2001), but it has not yet been widely employed.

Amygdala

A heterogeneous collection of nuclei and cortical areas in the temporal lobe, considered to subserve emotional and social behaviour, learning, and memory.

The amygdala (alias the amygdaloid or amygdalar complex), first described and named by the German anatomist Burdach in the early nineteenth century (Meyer 1971), is so called because in the primate brain its shape resembles an almond (*amugdalē* in Greek). About a dozen different nuclei and specialized cortical areas are currently discerned in the amygdala, and many intra- and extra-amygdalar connections have been identified (Amaral *et al.* 1992; Pitkanen *et al.* 1997; Swanson and Petrovich 1998; Aggleton 2000). Indeed, the heterogeneity of the nuclei, areas, and pathways raised some doubts whether 'amygdala' as a whole is a discrete anatomical entity *in situ*, or only an artificial construct of the human mind (e.g. Kirkpatrick 1996; Swanson and Petrovich 1998; de Olmos and Heimer 1999). Whether a well-defined natural kind or merely a convenient concept, judging by its connectivity, the amygdaloid complex fits well to serve as a central processor for some facets of sensory and supramodal *representations. This is because sets of amygdaloid nuclei interconnect heavily with the unimodal and polymodal *cortex, as well as with subcortical structures. Some of these pathways are asymmetrical (more extensive in one direction, e.g. from amygdala to hippocampus), and the information flows into one amygdaloid nucleus but comes out at another.

The peculiar behavioural effects of bilateral lesions of the temporal lobe, including the amygdala, were noted over a century ago in *monkeys (Brown and Schafer 1888), and later further characterized (Kluver and Bucy 1938) and termed the 'Kluver–Bucy syndrome'. The overall impression was that the lesion produced 'a condition resembling idiocy' (Brown and Schafer 1888). A more detailed look described the lesioned animals as tamed, over-attentive but fearless, devoid of the ability to assess the significance of inanimate and animate objects, and indiscriminately phagic and sexual. A similar syndrome was shown to result from ablations confined to the amygdaloid complex and the medial temporal polar cortex (Weiskrantz 1956). It is indeed likely that many functions used to be attributed to the so-called *'limbic system', including control of phylogenetically primitive drives, emotions, and elementary social interactions, are carried out by the amygdala (LeDoux 1991).

Over the years, circumscribed lesions in monkeys and rodents, cases of diseased and injured amygdala in humans, and recently *functional neuroimaging, have all been employed to investigate the role of the amygdala in learning and behaviour. The effect of amygdala dysfunction on a number of *recognition tasks, including *delay tasks and visual and cross-modal associations, was first taken to imply that the amygdala plays a major part in these tasks; however, later studies indicated that the impairment was due to damage to the adjacent rhinal cortex, which was injured together with the amygdala in the original lesion experiments (Zola-Morgan et al. 1989a,b; Murray et al. 1993). In contrast, conclusive evidence for the involvement of amygdala in learning and memory was found in other types of tasks, which engage fear and emotional memory (Adolphs et al. 1995; Maren and Fanslow 1996; Rogan and LeDoux 1996; Scott et al. 1997; Walker and Davis 1997; Cahill and McGaugh 1998; Lamprecht and Dudai 2000; Parkinson et al. 2000). A most popular paradigm in this context is Pavlovian *fear conditioning, a ubiquitous form of *classical conditioning. In Pavlovian fear conditioning, a conditioned stimulus (e.g. tone) is associated with an aversive unconditioned stimulus (e.g. electric shock), to yield fear (e.g. freezing, increased blood pressure and heart rate) as the conditioned response. Amygdalar nuclei, including a subset dubbed the 'amygdalar basolateral complex', were specifically implicated in this simple type of conditioning (the identity of nuclei recruited in fear conditioning is probably also a function of the task complexity; Killcross et al. 1997; Nader and LeDoux 1997).

The meticulous analysis of fear conditioning in the amygdala had clearly paid off: it has yielded the first demonstration of *long-term potentiation induced by training in an identified pathway that subserves learning in the behaving rat (Rogan et al. 1997). The cellular analysis of fear conditioning also strengthened the assumption that the amygdala itself is a structure that stores information (see also Lamprecht et al. 1997). A different view is that the amygdala, occupying a strategic position in the network of widespread neuromodulatory systems in the brain, does not itself store memory, but rather modulates other circuits that store it (Cahill and McGaugh 1998). The clash between these opposing views has raised central issues concerning memory traces: is the evidence for the requirement for *protein synthesis and gene expression in training sufficient to prove that a certain brain area *consolidates a given memory? And if it is, will the memory be stored in that area forever after? And which parts of a circuit that subserves a memory should be considered as an integral part of the postulated *engram? On top of it all, there is actually no reason to assume that the 'storage' and the 'modulation' views are mutually exclusive. Moreover, even a close look at the Kluver–Bucy syndrome indicates that there is more to the amygdala than storage, and that it regulates *attention and additional facets of cognition (Gallagher and Holland 1994).

The study of the role of amygdala in fear conditioning is a beautiful example of a cross-*level analysis that has led from the behaving organism to circuits, *synapses, and molecules, and vice versa. An issue that deserves further emphasis is the ethological context of the findings. The amygdala fulfils an important role in navigating the individual in its species-specific milieu, enabling it to construe sign-*stimuli correctly, and react

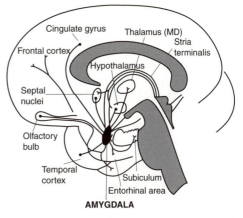

AMYGDALA

Fig. 3 The amygdaloid complex maintains extensive interconnections with multiple brain areas, including the hypothalamus, thalamus (MD, mediodorsal), *hippocampal formation, and temporal and frontal *cortex. This schematic diagram depicts the amygdala as a single area for simplicity, but in reality it is a collection of about a dozen main nuclei and cortical areas that interconnect differentially with targets over widely distributed brain areas, and subserve diverse functions, among them emotional behaviour and learning. (Adapted from Brodal 1998.)

to them appropriately (e.g. see the role of amygdala in perception, memory, and judgement of facial as well as verbal expression in humans, Adolphs *et al.* 1998; Morris *et al.* 1998; Isenberg *et al.* 1999). This is definitely a place to look for brain defects that underlie some neurotic and affective disorders and asocial behaviours.

Selected associations: Fear conditioning, Functional neuroimaging, Limbic system, Long-term potentiation

Anthropomorphism

The attribution of human attributes to mythical creatures, inanimate objects, or nonhuman organisms.

The term is derived from Greek: *ánthropōs*—human being, *morphé*—form. Anthropomorphism owes much to anthropocentricity, i.e. our *a priori inclination to regard ourselves as the centre of the universe and see the world through our *biased eyes. By doing so we probably hope to gain some illusory control over reality. Anthropomorphism is intensively and recurrently exemplified in ancient myths, literature, and art (e.g. Burkert 1985). Occasionally, it had also infiltrated other social activities: throughout Europe in the Middle Ages, horses and pigs were dragged to public trial because it was believed that they are *consciously aware of their own acts and hence are liable for them (Evans 1906). In the early days of experimental psychology, anthropomorphism was popular (Boakes 1984), being influenced by the Darwinian theory of evolution that suggested a mental continuum along with the physical one. The *classics of the anthropomorphic tradition in animal psychology are books by Darwin (1872) and Romanes (1882). The transformation of psychology into a more objective and quantitative scientific enterprise was accompanied by attempts to abandon anthropomorphic anecdotes that portrayed pets as geniuses, and to adhere to parsimonious explanations of animal behaviour, such as advocated by Loyd Morgan's canon (*Ockham's razor). However, anthropomorphism still pops out between, and occasionally in, the lines of current research articles in biology and psychology (e.g. see discussions in Kennedy 1992; Sullivan 1995).

Anthropomorphic accounts could be classified into two kinds: *metaphorical and explanatory. The metaphorical are the more innocent ones. They may add colour to an otherwise rather dry scientific account. To describe the behaviour of protozoa as '… if they did not enjoy being alone and had passed the word along to gather and hold a mass meeting' (Jennings 1899) is a matter of style only, as far as the description does not lead the reader (and even more so the writer) to assign to the unicellular organism *declarative human-like social drives. Explanatory anthropomorphism, however, may result in embarrassing errors. A trivial example is the exposure of teeth in monkeys; what could be construed by the approaching novice as a friendly smile might actually be an expression of threat.

Possibly most relevant to current neurobiological research is our innate tendency for implicit anthropomorphism, i.e. tacitly construing the behaviour of animals in terms of problem solving *algorithms that could have been used by the human observer. This should especially be taken into account in cases in which sophisticated cognitive faculties are suggested, for example the formation of cognitive *maps in insects (Wehner and Menzel 1990), of *learning sets in rodents (Reid and Morris 1993), or of *observational learning in invertebrates (Fiorito and Scotto 1992). Implicit anthropomorphism may result not only in superfluously complex explanations but also in excessively austere ones. As these lines are being written, hundreds of diligent postdocs are running rats or mice in water *mazes, assuming that from the outset, all that the wet animal has in mind from the outset of the experiment is the urge to learn the shortest way to the platform and take a break, because this is what the experimenter would have done. While still wishing to escape the water, in reality, some of the drives and strategies pursued by the swimming rodent are species specific (e.g. Wolfer *et al.* 1998).

There is, however, a twist to the story. In spite of the aforementioned caveats and reservations, the mere fact that an explanation has an anthropomorphic connotation is not sufficient to demote it. In other words, 'anthropomorphism' *per se* cannot be used as a *criterion in refuting or accepting explanations and *models. The truth is that we do not really know the borders between the mental faculties of other mammals and those that are sometimes considered as exclusive privileges of *Homo sapiens*. For example, when rodents associate events, are they *consciously aware of it (Clark and Squire 1998; *declarative memory)? And if they are, what is the depth and quality of their conscious awareness? In recent years, the more we learn about the physiology and psychophysics of animals, the more we become astonished to discover that even species far remote from us on the phylogenetic scale seem to perceive some aspects of the world not so differently from us (e.g. Nieder and Wagner 1999). This raises the possibility that underestimating the capabilities of their brain is as misleading as overestimating it. There is no reason why we should not expect to find in evolution a gradient of antropolikeness on a great variety of faculties, such as *planning, *prospective memory, complex problem solving, or *insight. It is even still debated whether symbolic language had really emerged in humans only (Walker 1983; Griffin 1984; Cheney and Seyfarth 1990).

But, whereas some anthropolike mental faculties, such as numerical competence, are amenable to objective measurement (Davis and Perusse 1988; Brannon and Terrace 1998; Kawai and Matsuzawa 2000), others, e.g. subtle emotions, are not. We may therefore never be able to really know what it is like to be a bat (Nagel 1974). We are hence left with the humble conclusion that the interplay between prudent adherence to Ockham's razor on the one hand, and proper appreciation of the phylogenetic and ecological specialization of other species' brains on the other, is delicate indeed.

Selected associations: Artefact, Bias, Clever Hans, Declarative memory, Subject

Fig. 4 It works both ways: an apeomorphized version of Charles Darwin in a contemporary caricature. Faithful to the *zeitgeist that his theory of evolution reinforced, Darwin himself anthropomorphized animal behaviour in *The expression of the emotions in man and animals* (1872).

Aplysia

The sea-hare, a marine snail.

Aplysia, a hind-gilled (opistobranch) marine snail (Kandel 1979), is one of the heroes of the cellular revolution in the neurosciences. Its external resemblance to the rabbit earned it the name sea-hare. Yet it is the insides of *Aplysia* that has turned it into such a highly successful *system in the cellular analysis of simple memory. Quinn (pers. comm.) had defined an ideal *subject for the neurobiological analysis of learning as a creature with 10 large neurons, 10 genes, a generation time of 1 week, and the ability to play the cello and recite Shakespeare. Indeed this is not a faithful description of *Aplysia*, but in the real world, the sea-hare became a useful compromise. Its main assets are a relatively simple nervous system that is readily accessible to experimentation, a simple behavioural repertoire, and a group of capable investigators that have become fascinated by the virtues of the slug.[1]

The central nervous system of *Aplysia* is composed of about 20 000 nerve cells arranged in widely spaced ganglia (masses of nerve cells). Some secretory neurons are as big as the entire brain of *Drosophila*. Some neurons can be identified from one individual to another by their location, shape, and firing pattern. The system had attracted cellular physiologists (Arvanitaki and Chalazonitis 1958; Tauc and Gershenfeld 1961; Kandel and Tauc 1965). It was, however, the research on *plasticity and learning that has endowed *Aplysia*, especially *Aplysia californica*, with its fame (Kandel and Schwartz 1982; Byrne and Kandel 1996). Following a series of reductive and simplifying steps (*reduction), the cellular and molecular mechanisms of learning in *Aplysia* have been pursued from the behaving animal, via preparations of isolated ganglia, to identified nerve cells and *synapses in culture (Carew *et al.* 1971; Rayport and Schacher 1986; Bartsch *et al.* 1995; Frost *et al.* 1997; Hawkins *et al.* 1998). This system is the epitome of the reductionist approach to memory, and as such demonstrates both the advantages and the shortcomings of the approach.

Like all organisms with a nervous system, *Aplysia* display a repertoire of defensive (e.g. withdrawal) and appetitive (e.g. feeding) reflexes. The analysis of learning in *Aplysia* has focused mainly on the defensive reflexes (Kandel 1976; Byrne 1985). These can be illustrated by the gill-and-siphon withdrawal reflex (GSWR). The gill is the external respiratory organ of *Aplysia*. It is housed in the mantle cavity on the dorsal side of the animal. The cavity is a respiratory chamber covered by the mantle shelf. At its posterior end, the shelf forms a fleshy spout, called the siphon. The siphon protrudes out of the mantle cavity between wing-like extensions of the body wall, called parapodia. If a tactile *stimulus is applied to the siphon or mantle shelf, a two-component reflex is elicited. One component is contraction of the siphon and its withdrawal behind the parapodia. The other is contraction of the gill and its withdrawal into the mantle cavity. The GSWR can be *habituated by repetitive monotonous tactile stimuli to the skin; *sensitized by noxious stimuli to the tail or head; and undergo *classical conditioning. This is achieved by pairing a gentle stimulus to the siphon or gill (the conditioned stimulus) with a noxious stimulus to the tail or head (the unconditioned stimulus), so that the conditioned stimulus comes to evoke intense withdrawal (the conditioned response).

In intact *Aplysia* the GSWR is controlled by both the central and the peripheral nervous systems. Most of the cellular analysis of learning has been performed in the central nervous system, particularly in the abdominal ganglion. This ganglion was found to subserve a substantial portion of the habituation, sensitization, and classical conditioning of the GSWR. Multiple sites of plasticity have been identified in the abdominal ganglion, but the attention has been focused primarily on one site: the synapse between the sensory neurons and the gill or siphon motor neurons (Kandel and Schwartz 1982; Byrne and Kandel 1996; Figure 5). It has been proposed that part of the behavioural plasticity of the GSWR could be accounted for by use-dependent modifications in this synapse. In brief, the cellular analogue of habituation was portrayed as presynaptic depression, induced by repetitive monotonous firing. As this depression involves only the modified synapse, it is said to be 'homosynaptic'. Sensitization was portrayed as synaptic facilitation, induced in the presynaptic terminal of the aforementioned sensory-to-motor

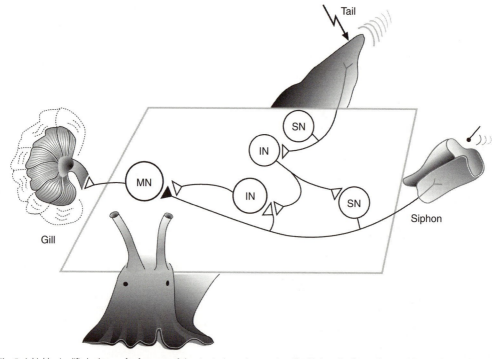

Fig. 5 A highly simplified scheme of a fragment of the circuit that subserves the gill-withdrawal reflex and its modification by experience in *Aplysia*. The reflex could be elicited by a tactile stimulus applied to the siphon skin. Repetitive, monotonous tactile stimuli result in habituation of the reflex. A shock to the tail results in sensitization of the reflex. Classical conditioning is obtained by pairing the shock to the tail with a light tactile stimulus to the siphon, so that this tactile stimulus comes to evoke intense withdrawal on subsequent applications in the absence of the shock. Probably hundreds of nerve cells and thousands of synapses subserve the reflex in the intact animal; only a selection of types of cells and synapses are depicted in the scheme. IN, interneuron; MN, motor neuron; SN, sensory neuron. The presynaptic terminal of the sensory-to-motor synapse, denoted by a black triangle (left-hand side), was so far the focus of much of the cellular and molecular analysis of the reflex. *Plasticity of this synapse contributes both to the short- and to the long-term *phases of memory in the reflex. For further details see text.

synapse by *neurotransmitters that are released from interneurons and encode the sensitizing stimulus (Figure 5). As this facilitation involves multiple types of synapses, it is 'heterosynaptic'. Classical conditioning of the GSWR was portrayed as sharing cellular mechanisms with sensitization. It is also activity-dependent presynaptic facilitation; however, in contrast with sensitization, which enhances the responsiveness to subsequent stimulation of the skin at any location, the facilitation in classical conditioning is specific to the pathway that has mediated the conditioned input (*coincidence detection). This is hence a pathway-specific, activity-dependent presynaptic facilitation. Multiple molecular mechanisms have been suggested to account for the *acquisition and short-term retention of the synaptic facilitation. They include activation of *intracellular signal transduction cascades by the facilitatory neurotransmitter(s), phosphorylation (by *protein kinases) of synaptic proteins (e.g. *ion channels), and modulation of transmitter release (Kandel and Schwartz 1982). These simplified cellular *models were later extended, enriched, and modified to include additional synaptic sites and mechanisms (e.g. Byrne and Kandel 1996).

Because of lack of space, we will not concern ourselves here with the fine details of the *Aplysia* story, but rather with a few generalizations only. The cellular analysis of *Aplysia* reflexes has shown that a significant component of the circuit that subserves simple learning could be pinned down to the *level of identified neurons and synapses. This analysis was the first to demonstrate the central role of cyclic adenosine monophosphate in memory (Cedar *et al.* 1972; *CREB), and the multiplicity of time- and *context-dependent mechanisms of plasticity in a single cell. It has also demonstrated that at least part of the loci that subserve short-term memory also subserve long-term memory. Further, analysis of plasticity in the GSWR has provided much support for the *zeitgeist proposal that long-term memory storage relies on modulation of gene expression (Goelet *et al.* 1986; Martin *et al.* 1997a,b; *consolidation, *immediate early genes, *protein synthesis). It is noteworthy that in recent years, much of the analysis of learning in *Aplysia* has practically merged with the cellular biology of *development. This may reflect a genuine homology between learning and development. Yet the focus on molecular and cellular mechanisms, which are shared with other disciplines in the life sciences, may also attest to the current difficulty in switching, even in a *simple system, to the more global level of analysis, which is critical for understanding memory, i.e. that of concerted circuit activity that ultimately encodes *internal representations in the behaving organism.

Over the years, the appreciation of the complexity of the *Aplysia* system has increased, and the highly simplified models gradually matured into more realistic ones (Glanzman 1995; Byrne and Kandel 1996; Fischer *et al.* 1997; Bao *et al.* 1998; Lechner and Byrne 1998; Royer *et al.* 2000). Attempts are also being made to elucidate the cellular bases of apetitive reflexes (Lechner *et al.* 2000), as well as of a more complex form of learning, *instrumental conditioning (Nargeot *et al.* 1999). *Aplysia* is still our main source of information about the molecular changes that take place in neurons up to a few days after training (*long-term potentiation addresses a shorter time window). This is evident among others from the references made to it in many entries in this book. Admittedly, the memory feats of *Aplysia* are modest (even the classical conditioning of the GSWR is only of the α type, namely, modification of a pre-existing behaviour and not acquisition of a novel one). But no doubt, without the remarkable work on *Aplysia*, the molecular and cellular biology of neuronal plasticity, learning, and memory would have been much, much duller. There is still one take home message that is worth mentioning here. The analysis of neuronal plasticity in *Aplysia* has unveiled an impressive inter- and intra-cellular molecular complexity that keeps growing. This should be noted by orthodox reductionists, who erroneously think that reducing a system implies simplifying it. The opposite might be the case.

Selected associations: CREB, Reduction, Simple system, Synapse

---

[1]The major driving force behind the *Aplysia* project, Eric Kandel, shared the 2000 Nobel prize for Medicine.

Artefact

1. **Man-made object.**

2. **A phenomenon, process, or mechanism that does not normally exist in nature but is introduced by experimental manipulation of the *system.**

3. **A phenomenon, process, or mechanism that does not exist in nature but is believed to exist, due to erroneous interpretation of data or theories.**

Artefact stems from the Latin 'something made with skill', but occasionally, in science, the major skill at stake is how to distinguish an artefact from a natural phenomenon. Artefacts have haunted the experimental sciences since the emergence of the latter, much before the term was introduced into English at the beginning of the nineteenth century. In biology, 'artefact' was first used to denote aberrations produced in histological specimens by the fixation methods used to prepare the tissue for microscopic examination. However, with time, it came to embrace many types and tokens of artificial constructs,[1] either concrete or conceptual, which are confused with the real thing.

It is useful to distinguish two major classes of artefacts: technical (definitions 1,2) and conceptual, or interpretational (definitions 1,3). A harsh fixative or an unreliable stain leading to the appearance of an imaginary brain structure could be the cause of technical artefacts. Similar illusions may result from non-specific antibodies in an immunoblot, sloppy development of an autoradiogram, or tricky electrophysiological set-ups with a will of their own. Expert scientists come to master and prune the potential sources of artefacts in their trade, but new *methods and techniques generate new artefacts. For example, with more and more data analysis being relegated to fancy computer systems, the computers themselves become a source of technical artefacts before the data even reach the scientist. It takes a careful team leader to identify the problem (e.g. Katz *et al.* 1998).

A common potential source of interpretational artefacts is the so-called *post hoc* argumentation (*post hoc ergo propter hoc*, Latin for 'after this hence because of this'). *Post hoc* means arguing that because one event was correlated later in time with another, the second happened because of the first. This could sometimes be straightened out by performing *control experiments in which the order of events is altered or the suspected cause omitted from the protocol. For example, suppose we are tempted to conclude that a *receptor for the *neurotransmitter *glutamate in the *rat *hippocampus is phosphorylated (*protein kinase) as a consequence of learning to navigate in a *maze, because the receptor molecule appears phosphorylated after the experience; this might be a *post-hoc* artefact rather than a real consequence of the learning experience (e.g. see *criterion).

Interpretational artefacts could also result from lack of expertise in, or awareness of, a domain of knowledge that is relevant to the finding. This is a risk encountered especially, but definitely not solely, by investigators who shift from one field to another. A study of conditioning illustrates the case. In the first half of the last century, many operant conditioning paradigms ignored the species-specific behavioural repertoires of the experimental animals. This led to questionable conclusions.

Probably hundreds of Ph.D. theses interpreted the pecking of pigeons in a Skinner box as an *instrumentally conditioned response; however, pecking is an innate response, the pigeons emit it anyway, and the situation might not have been instrumental but rather *classical conditioning (Jenkins and Moore 1973). Similarly, over the years, cats were reported to be meticulously conditioned to emit stereotypic behaviours in order to escape from puzzle boxes; but some of the typical behaviours, such as rubbing the flank or head against a pole, were later pointed out as species-specific feline greeting reactions, emitted in response to the observer rather than conditioned by the escape (Moore and Stuttard 1979). Note that here the artefact is both technical (due to the improper design of the experiment, allowing the observer to affect the behavioural response of the *subject), and interpretational. The role of the observer is probably continued to be ignored to this day in many labs; it would be of interest to enquire how often an unexpected behaviour of a rat in a *maze reflects an artefact due to the introduction into the room of a new perfume or after-shave or an admiring visitor. *Anthropomorphism is another potential source of interpretational artefacts, confusing innate (*a priori) species-specific behaviours with higher-order cognitive faculties (*clever Hans, *Ockham's razor).

Interpretational artefacts could also be due to variables unknown in the discipline at the time that the interpretation is being attempted. An example is provided by a study of the effect of exploratory behaviour on hippocampal neurons. When rats are transferred to an unfamiliar environment they explore and learn it. It has been reported that such exploration is accompanied by hippocampal *plasticity, including persistent facilitation of evoked neuronal responses (Green *et al.* 1990). Although the basic finding was confirmed (Moser *et al.* 1994), it later became clear that the effect is much smaller than first reported. The reason: fluctuations of up to 2–3°C in brain temperature, occurring during the exploratory activity, modify neuronal properties *in vivo* and account for a substantial part of the observed 'plasticity' (Andersen and Moser 1995). The aforementioned temperature effect and the resulting potential artefacts were not recognized at the time. In this case, the artefact was not a waste of intellect; its exploration led to new insights on the tricks of brain physiology. In other words, it is absolutely possible to learn even from artefacts.

Whether the suspected artefact is of the technical or the interpretational type, the first-law-of-the-artefact frequently holds: the more important is the message, the faster is the artefact exposed. Artefacts that lead to boring conclusions gain immortality in obscure journals. But if the news is smashing, for example, that specific memories can be transferred from one individual to another in brain extracts (Babich *et al.* 1965; Ungar and Oceguera-Navarro 1965), the scientific community does its best to sort the facts out, even if the causes of the artefact, or at least what appears to be an artefact to the contemporary eye, do not always become clear in the process (Byrne *et al.* 1966; Nicholls *et al.* 1967; Smalheiser *et al.* 2001).

Selected associations: Anthropomorphism, Control, Red herring, Scoopophobia

---

[1]On 'types' and 'tokens', see *system.

Assay

A procedure or technique for the analysis of a phenomenon, process, or mechanism; a test.

Assays (from *exagiere*, Latin for 'to weigh out') are not merely research tools. They play a decisive part in the development and workings of scientific disciplines. They are also important in shaping the feasibility, progression, and outcome of particular research programmes. Sometimes they even play a decisive part in moulding the fate of individual academic careers.

Scientific assays are the nuts and bolts of scientific *methods and *paradigms. In experimental science, they are the end instrument used to embody the objectives of a 'method' and test the concepts of a 'paradigm'. They are thus more specific than 'methods'. The same method may be implemented by using a variety of assays. For example, one could employ a correlative *method* to probe the role of an *immediate early gene in memory in a given brain region, but use different *assays* to determine whether the expression of that gene is correlated with the behavioural change. A useful assay yields results that are then subjected to analysis and construed according to selected *criteria.

The spectrum of assays used in the neurosciences is rich and heterogeneous. Practically all these assays could also be incorporated into research programmes that target learning and memory. One useful classification of assays (*taxonomy) is by the *level of analysis involved. Other classifications are of course possible; for example, by the method that guides and utilizes the assay (i.e. correlation, intervention, etc.). Straightforward classification by level is into molecular, cellular, neuroanatomical, *system, and behavioural. In considering levels of analysis, one should note differences in the dialects of the scientific *culture. The term 'assay' is mostly popular in molecular and cellular studies. Neuroanatomists prefer to use 'technique' or 'method' (which, as noted above, is better reserved for a more comprehensive activity). Psychologists cling to 'test'. The latter term commonly carries the connotation of 'success' or 'failure' in *performance; 'assay' does not. 'Test' can also be used to denote particular instantiation of a type of assay in an experimental protocol.

Molecular assays, such as binding of drugs to *receptors or measuring enzyme activity, are shared by many branches of molecular and cellular biology (R. Martin 1997; e.g. *development). Cellular, neuroanatomical, and system procedures are shared by many subdisciplines of the neurosciences and are not unique to the study of plasticity and memory. One notable exception that comes to mind is *long-term potentiation, which under certain circumstances may be regarded as an assay to determine induction and maintenance of cellular *plasticity, although it is also a method, and moreover, a *paradigm. In contrast to molecular, cellular, and system assays, behavioural assays used in the field of learning and memory are unique to this field: they are specific 'memory assays' or 'tests'.

Some memory tests were groundbreaking at the time of their introduction. For a field of knowledge to become a scientific discipline, research techniques and assays are required that permit quantification of phenomena addressed in that field: '…the forces and actions of bodies are circumscribed and measured either by spatial intervals, or by moments of time, or by concentration of quantity, or by predominance of power; and unless these four are accurately and carefully weighed, the sciences concerned will be elegant speculations perhaps but of no practical use' (Bacon 1620). A handful of tests, by the mere fact that they had enabled for the first time the quantification of memory, had transformed the study of memory into a science. A prominent example is provided by tests involving *recall of series of so-called 'nonsense' syllables, introduced by Ebbinghaus to measure *forgetting (1885; see also Jacobs 1887). This type of experiment is considered to have opened the scientific era in research of human memory. Similarly, introduction of *classical and *instrumental conditioning has permitted the systematic experimental investigation of animal learning (Thorndike 1911; Pavlov 1927; for more on the history, see Boakes 1984).

Still another class of assays includes those that alter and reroute the course of a discipline. Here are some examples: Introduction of the *maze (Small 1901;

*classic) has paved the way to research on spatial learning, cognitive *maps, and other facets of memory. A popular descendent of those original mazes is the extensively used water maze (Morris 1981). Introduction of the *delay task (Hunter 1913) has permitted analysis of *recognition and *working memory, and development of *monkey models of *amnesia. Very useful versions are the trial-unique delay tasks, such as trial-unique delayed non-matching-to-sample (Gaffan 1974; Mishkin and Delacour 1975; *delay task). In some cases, adaptation of a well-known type of memory assay to a new organism could open a whole new field. An example is provided by olfactory conditioning in the fruit fly, *Drosophila. Sophisticated *neurogenetic analysis of memory became feasible only after classical conditioning had been adapted to the special needs of the fly (Quinn et al. 1974). And, of course, there are those many assays that are variations on a theme, introducing important improvements and modifications to already existing methods.

Lack of an appropriate assay may hinder the development of a field or the resolution of a major research problem. For example, some types of behavioural assays engage the *hippocampus and are sensitive to hippocampal damage. However, at the time of writing there is still no satisfying behavioural assay to tap exclusively into hippocampal function in primates. Such a task will be very useful in clarifying the role of the hippocampus in memory. The hippocampus can also be invoked to illustrate a potential problem in the use of assays. This is the problem of 'circular argumentation'. Thus, given that a hippocampal lesion impairs performance on task X under condition A, some investigators are quick to use task X under conditions other than A to determine whether the hippocampus is involved, as if task X is an established probe for hippocampal involvement. Failure or success on task X, however, may result from parameters specific to condition A that do not *generalize to other conditions of the *subject or the experiment. The problematics are further augmented when inference is made from one species to another. Here is an example that relates not only to the hippocampus but also to a profound issue in the evolution of mind: 'trace conditioning' of the eyelid reflex (*classical conditioning) is sensitive to hippocampal damage and involves *conscious awareness in normal human individuals (Clark and Squire 1998). However, this by itself is insufficient to propose trace conditioning as a cross-species assay for awareness, because other potential explanations (*Ockham's razor) must first be scrutinized, such as a failure to hold information off-line irrespective of awareness.

Another caveat that should be considered is that occasionally, an assay becomes a prison to imagination. This problem runs in two versions: individual and generic. Some individuals flirt with a single method, even a single assay, throughout their career, from their Ph.D. thesis on. Being inflicted with some unique version of separation anxiety, they refuse to give up a procedure that has worked for them, and entrust their future in the hands of the past. A more serious problem arises when an entire subdiscipline falls into the procedural drain. For example, in its first few years, the newly emerging discipline of mammalian neurogenetics has followed as a routine a very limited number of standard versions of the otherwise very useful water maze assay. This was also occasionally accompanied by the simplistic interpretation of performance in the maze, probably resulting in neglect of some intriguing effects of mutations on behaviour (on some of the complexities involved, see Bannerman et al. 1995; Wolfer et al. 1998).

It is likely that in due time, memory research will generate memory-specific assays based on direct observation of experience-dependent alterations in *internal representations of the nervous system (*map, *functional neuroimaging; example in *honeybee).

Selected associations: Delay task, Maze, Method, Paradigm

Associative learning

1. **The formation of new mental links among events.**[1]
2. **Learning that depends on the parameters of more than a single *stimulus.**

The notion of 'association' is central to both the philosophical and the experimental study of the mind. In philosophy it can be traced back to Aristotle, who proposed that similarity, contrast, and contiguity of images subserve recollection (On memory; Sorabji 1972). 'Associationism', the philosophical doctrine that the mind learns and construes the world bottom-up by associating elementary events, has emerged with British empiricism in the seventeenth century (Warren 1921). Hobbes (1651) talks about 'the train of thoughts' and of 'compounded imagination … as when from the sight of a man at one time, and of a horse at another, we conceive in our mind a Centaure'. It was, however, Locke (1690) who first used the phrase 'association of ideas', as the title of a chapter in *Essay concerning human understanding*.

When psychology became an independent empirical discipline towards the end of the nineteenth century, associationism was part of its conceptual heritage. Ebbingahus (1885) was influenced by it when he designed the first quantitative *recall experiments, involving perceptual 'atoms' and their associations. Similarly, Wundt (1896), the founder of the first laboratory of experimental psychology, advocated the study of elementary mental elements and their association in learning, recollection, and thought (Boring 1950a). Over the years the integration of associationism into psychology has also been accompanied by the development of theories[2] that kept the centrality of associations yet disposed of the assumption that the mind works solely bottom-up from simple ideas and 'psychic atoms' (e.g. James 1890; Freud 1901; Hebb 1949; Tversky 1977).

Associations play a part in all the faculties of the mind: learning (the formation of new associations, definition 1); recollection (the use of associations as *cues, *priming, *retrieval); and thought (which involves both the generation of new *internal representations, definition 1, and recollection of old ones).[3] Here we refer to one aspect only, that of *learning. A popular *taxonomy of learning is based on a dichotomy between 'associative' and 'nonassociative' learning. In contrast with associative learning (definition 2), in nonassociative learning, i.e. *habituation and *sensitization, learning is assumed to depend solely on the parameters of the unconditioned stimulus. Whether in *real-life this is indeed the case, is questionable. Even habituation and sensitization involve associations not only with the history of the subject and its interaction with the stimulus, but also with the *context (Hall and Honey 1989; Rankin 2000). Incidental learning and *insight are occasionally depicted as nonassociative as well, but again, this is a great simplification, as in both cases associations are formed in the mind. Incidental learning involves associations between an input and saliency or motivation. Insight is expected to involve sequential implicit associations of internal representations and their *binding. All in all, therefore, it is possible to conclude that associations of some kind or another are universal, and instrumental in learning in even the simplest organisms and tasks.

The study of associative learning has gained tremendously from the use of animal behaviour *paradigms. At the beginning of the twentieth century two major types of paradigms emerged, which permitted for the first time the investigation of elementary forms of associative learning in laboratory animals, and hence a more *reductive and mechanistic analysis of associations at multiple *levels of analysis. One paradigm was *classical conditioning, associated mainly with Pavlov (1927) and his school. The other was *instrumental conditioning or operant conditioning, associated mainly with Thorndike (1911) and later Skinner (1938) and their schools (*behaviourism). In both types of paradigms, the *subject learns relations among events (definition 1). In classical conditioning these relations are among stimuli, whereas in instrumental conditioning, these relations are among actions and their consequences.

The availability of *controllable protocols of associative learning in animals has provided a fertile ground for the development and test of multiple types of laws and theories of associative learning. These theories differ in the identification of the associated variable and of the principles of association. Main types of associated variables considered in these theories are stimulus–stimulus (S–S), stimulus–response (S–R), response–response (R–R), and response–*reinforcer (e.g. see *instrumental conditioning). Stimulus in these theories is commonly an external, sensory stimulus. Note, however, that in definition 2, 'stimulus' is more general and refers to any event that triggers a response in the brain, whether of an external or an internal source, hence it includes also the feedback of motor response. Further, in reality, those are of course not the stimuli themselves that are associated, but rather their on-line *percepts or off-line stored representations. Principles of associations that are considered in theories of associative learning are the frequency of occurrence of the events, their co-occurrence in time and space (contiguity), the probability of linkage (contingency), and the effect or reinforcement (Dickinson 1980; Bower and Hilgard 1981; Mackintosh 1983).

At least in one basic assumption the original British associationism clearly went wrong. This is the depiction of our mental life as dependent only on postnatal associations. Many associations in our brain have innate predispositions. Some authors would even go further to propose that all the associations in our brain are predisposed, and therefore all learning is 'prepared' to some degree or another. This could be due to the existence of certain neural pathways but not others. The generation over time of endogenous pre-representations, which are partially independent of external-world experience but selected by it (Heidmann *et al.* 1984), could also be constrained by *a priori patterns of connectivity in the brain. An example of a simple type of prepared learning is provided by the form of classical conditioning called α conditioning, in which the modified response is pre-existent. Other examples of prepared associations are *imprinting and *conditioned taste aversion. Whether learning is 'prepared' or not should be taken into account in the search for the cellular and molecular algorithms and mechanisms of learning. For example, presynaptic facilitation of active synapses in the circuit that subserves behaviour (*Aplysia) fits to subserve prepared learning, whereas the activation of silent synapses or the growth of new synapses fit to subserve de novo associations as well.

Selected associations: Classical conditioning, Instrumental conditioning, Priming, Taxonomy

---

[1]This definition also fits certain artificial systems, such as smart robots, if 'mental' is construed *metaphorically.

[2]As noted in *algorithm, these are not genuine theories in the mathematical sense of the term, but rather conceptual generalizations. The same is true for 'laws' below.

[3]For the role of associations in completing memories from partial input in artificial neural networks *models, see Hopfield (1982), Amit (1989), and Mehrota et al. (1997).

Attention

1. **The focusing on part of one's own sensory or cognitive space.**
2. **The selection by the brain of *percepts or longer-lasting *internal representations for *conscious processing and action.**
3. **The selection by the brain of percepts or longer-lasting representations to control ongoing behaviour.**
4. **The alert state required for the above.**

So prominent is the position of attention in the scientific discourse on behaviour, that Titchner (1908) regarded it as 'the nerve of the whole psychological system', and added that 'as men judge of it, so shall they be judged before the general tribunal of psychology'. James (1890) was convinced that 'everybody knows what attention is' and described it as '… the taking possession by the mind in clear and vivid form of one of what seem several simultaneous objects or trains of thought'. James was right in stating that intuitively we know what attention is, but, probably because the concept is so inclusive, a consensus on its definition is not easy to attain.

Not always was attention at the focus of attention of psychology. *Behaviourism intentionally ignored postulated inner faculties of the mind, including attention. The interest was renewed only after the Second World War, with the application of information processing theory, originally developed for warfare purposes, to the cognitive sciences (Broadbent 1958). A large body of work on attention has been accumulated since then, both in psychology and neurobiology. It ranges from investigation of the orienting reflex (*sensitization) to auditory and visual perception. A substantial part of what we currently know on attention stems from the analysis of vision in primates, at *levels ranging from behaviour via *functional neuroimaging and neuroanatomy to single cell activity (Posner and Petersen 1990; Desimone and Duncan 1995; Egeth and Yantis 1997; Kanwisher and Wojciulik 2000).

'Attention' refers to multiple mental states and activities, involving vigilance, orientation, and selection of information. The spectrum of activities thus ranges from the distributed to the selective and to the focused in time and space. These activities engage to various degrees on-line information (percepts of sensory attributes, location and timing) as well as off-line information (i.e. lasting internal representations). Similarly, attention could be *stimulus-driven (a bottom-up process) or task-driven (a top-down process). The latter dichotomy is illustrated in vision. Here selective attention was explained in terms of two consecutive, partially overlapping processes. The first is stimulus-driven, automatic, instantaneous and transient. The second is task-driven, slower, sustained and requires cognitive effort (Sperling and Weichselgratner 1987). Early stimulus-driven processing is frequently referred to as 'preattentive' (Neisser 1967), because it involves parallel processing of primitive features over the sensory space in the apparent absence of mental-resource limitation (Julesz 1981; Treisman 1985). Indeed, central to the notion of attention is resource-limited 'selection' (Norman and Bobrow 1975), which is detected at multiple points between post-receptor input and response (Desimone and Duncan 1995). Hence, lack of resource competition is taken by some authors to indicate lack of 'real' attention. More recent findings suggest, however, that even 'preattentive' vision is constrained by mental resources (Joseph et al. 1997).

A common connotation of attention is *conscious awareness (definition 2). Does this mean that attentive nonhuman species can be consciously aware of their dids, and if so, which species? Definitions 1 and 3 above fit situations in which conscious awareness cannot be proven or even assumed. Another definition, suggested by Hebb, also does not specify consciousness: 'central facilitation of the activation of one assembly by the previous one' (Hebb 1949); this view of attention depends, however, on the validity of the notion of *cell assembly. As far as the relationship of attention to conscious awareness is concerned, it is noteworthy that on the one hand, even humans may not be aware of activity in a cortical area assumed to be involved in some attentional tasks (Crick and Koch 1995); on the other hand, some degree of conscious awareness is expected to exist in other species as well (example in *classical conditioning). It is therefore useful to regard attention as involving a spectrum of awareness. Attention has been proposed to be the *binding agent of consciousness, and it is tempting to speculate that it has been a driving force in the emergence of consciousness. Seen that way, one could not escape the humble conclusion that the most precious niches of our inner world owe their existence to the emergence in evolution of the primitive, elementary orienting reflex.

Developments in two *methodologies have contributed much to the contemporary research on brain mechanisms of attention. One is cellular physiology, used in the *monkey, the other is functional neuroimaging, used in research on human *subjects (Desimone and Duncan 1995; Kawashima et al. 1995; Kastner et al. 1998; Reynolds et al. 1999; Kanwisher and Wojciulik 2000). The combination of both methodologies has led to the identification of brain circuits and cellular processes that are engaged in attention either correlatively or casually (*criterion).

At the system level, research on visual attention shows that areas in the frontoparietal, inferotemporal and occipital *cortex are involved. Among the visual processing areas, high-order cortex is particularly engaged, but there is also evidence for attentional activity already at the primary visual cortex. Attending a stimulus modulates the activity in cortex, even when the subject only expects to attend the stimulus before stimulus onset[1] (Chawla et al. 1999). This is taken to reflect the task-driven, top-down attentional facilitation of the processing in the area that expects the signal. There is also evidence for hemispheric lateralization, with a right hemispheric bias for tasks involving attention to locations in space and left hemispheric bias for tasks involving attention to timing (Coull and Nobre 1998). As to the frontal cortex, it is considered to subserve a 'supervisory attentional system' or 'central executive system', which co-ordinates and prioritizes attention across sensory and internal modalities (Shallice 1988; Baddeley 1993). This is the same cortex involved in *working memory. This should not be surprising, since clearly, attention and working memory are complementary and closely related (James 1890;

Cowan 1988; Baddeley 1993). Attention identifies where the action is (a popular *metaphor likens it to a searchlight, Crick 1984a); working memory then immediately takes note of that action for further use. By so doing, it not only permits an instantaneous *plastic response, but also prevents superfluous exploitation of attentional resources. Whereas some of the automaticity in stimulus-driven attention is innate (*a priori), it is clear that the system has to be capable to quickly compare stimuli with use-dependent internal representations in order to decide whether focused attention and further processing and action are warranted. This interplay of attention and memory takes place within a fraction of a second of perception. Working memory is therefore also 'working attention' (Baddeley 1993).

At the cellular level, attention was found to increase the magnitude of the response of neurons in higher-order visual cortex to the attended stimulus in the receptive field;[2] when multiple stimuli are within the receptive field, the activity is larger when attention is directed at the target stimulus (Moran and Desimone 1985; Reynolds et al. 1999). This gain and gating control could involve multiple circuit and system mechanisms, including the action of diffused neuromodulatory systems (*neurotransmitter). The function of these neuromodulatory systems in learning is assumed to involve regulation of gain and gating control as well; hence at the *synaptic level, certain molecular mechanisms of learning and attention merge.

A variety of pathologies impair attention. Among these are parietal and frontal lesions (Shallice 1993), schizophrenia (Andreasen et al. 1994), and attention-deficit/hyperactivity disorder, one manifestation of which is learning difficulties (Shaywitz et al. 1997). It has been suggested that attention and memory are also co-impaired in chronic fatigue syndrome, and the hypothetical 'central executive' was implicated (Joyce et al. 1996). In *real-life, multiple methods could be used to enhance attention, and, good news, some of these methods are clearly devoid of any side effect: a comparison of memory for humorous and non-humorous versions of sentences shows that the humorous ones are remembered better, probably because they are associated with increased attention (Schmidt 1994).

Selected associations: Binding, Homunculus, Metaphor, Percept, Working memory

---

[1]Expecting to attend is actually an 'attentional set'; for more on what is meant by 'set', see *learning set.

[2]A receptive field is that sector of the sensory space that could be sensed by the neuron.

Behaviourism

1. The conceptual framework and the school of psychology that consider only overt behaviour as the subject matter of scientific psychology.
2. The philosophical stand that considers propositions about mental states identical to propositions about behavioural dispositions.

The tenet of behaviourism is that behaviour rather than mind or brain is the subject matter of psychology, and that only publicly observed behaviour can be used as psychological datum. Although its roots can be traced to earlier materialistic philosophy and physiology, the formal emergence of behaviourism in psychology is associated with a manifesto entitled 'Psychology as the behaviorist views it' (Watson 1913):

> Psychology as the behaviorist views it is a purely objective experimental branch of natural science. Its theoretical goal is the prediction and control of behaviour. Introspection forms no essential part of its methods, nor is the scientific value of its data dependent upon the readiness with which they lend themselves to interpretation in terms of consciousness. The behaviorist, in his efforts to get a unitary scheme of animal response, recognizes no dividing line between man and brute.

Several points deserve special attention in Watson's manifesto. First, the rejection of introspection as a valid scientific method, opposing a major trend in psychology at the turn of the twentieth century (Boring 1950; Boakes 1984). Second, the rejection of *consciousness as the subject matter of psychology, again, in contrast to contemporary trends (*ibid.*). Third, the emphasis on the phylogenetic continuity, drawing from Darwinism and legitimizing animal psychology as an approach to the study of human behaviour (Boakes 1984). And fourth, aiming at control of behaviour. The latter objective is clearly not a necessary element of behaviourism, but did recur in the history of the field, occasionally endowing it with Orwellian connotations. The pragmatic attitude (Watson ended up in commercial advertising) culminated on the one hand in rather outrageous experimentation on *fear conditioning of human babies (Watson and Rayner 1920), and on the other in attempts to convince pigeons to guide missiles across enemy lines (Skinner 1960). In a more practical endeavour, it also set foundations for behavioural psychotherapy (Wolpe 1963).

Despite recurrent premature elegies, behaviourism retained its vigour over many years. Like other influential concepts, the original notions mutated. Several *taxonomies are noteworthy. One of these classifies behaviourism by period or school. 'Classical behaviourism' is Watson's. It is also dubbed 'molecular', because it treats behaviour in terms of individual 'atoms' of *stimuli, responses, and single stage stimulus–response operations. 'Neobehaviourism', itself a mixed bag, is associated mainly with Tolman (1932), Skinner (1938), and Hull (1943). It treats behaviour in molar terms of classes and types, and its variants incorporate not only stimuli, responses, and *reinforcers (i.e. operations performed on the organism), but also mediating variables that are not directly observable but thought to be necessary for explaining behaviour (see *algorithms). The Skinnerian version of behaviourism (Skinner 1938) is called 'radical behaviourism', although the same term was initially used to denote classical behaviourism (Calkins 1921). It intentionally ignores mind and brain processes (in his later writings Skinner said that brain sciences are indeed relevant, but not useful in analysing behaviour; Skinner 1988). Radical behaviourism advocates a world view in which behaviour is explained in terms of responses to stimuli and modification of probability of responses by contingencies with reinforcements. It disposes of mental causes; the unobservable 'mind' is replaced with mechanistic responses of various complexities, selected either in the species' evolution (*a priori), or by the reinforcement history of the individual *subject. The pinnacle of Skinnerian behaviourism was the attempt to explain human language (Skinner 1957), an attempt ardently rebutted by linguists and cognitive psychologists (Chomsky 1959).

Another taxonomy distinguishes 'methodological' from 'philosophical' behaviourism (on either one or both, see Carnap 1933; Ryle 1949; Zuriff 1986; Collins 1987; Todd and Morris 1995). Methodological behaviourism advocates the aforementioned principle that scientific understanding of the mind has to rest entirely on publicly observable facts, yet without necessarily taking a stand on inner mental realities (definition 1 above). In contrast, philosophical behaviourism does make statements about mental realities (definition 2), which comes in at least two versions: 'metaphysical' and 'logical'. Metaphysical behaviourism makes life easy by denying mental phenomena, period. Logical behaviourism considers propositions about mental states identical to propositions about behavioural dispositions. It can therefore be said to *reduce mental into behavioural acts.

Over the years, behaviourism has experienced fierce attacks from biological and cognitive psychology, linguistics, and philosophy (for arguments related to the insufficiency of behaviourism to account for learning, see Dickinson 1980). As noted above, behaviourism excluded itself from the biological arena in which much of the excitement of modern memory research takes place. Nevertheless, even with the recent developments in the neurosciences, behaviourism is still highly relevant to basic concepts addressed in this book. For example, the mere definition of *memory raises the issue of the relevance of observable facts to inferred processes. Behaviouristic definitions of learning and memory cannot guide neurobiological research because they are not expressed in biologish. But similarly, data on *ion channels and *synapses cannot advance memory research unless they are expressed in a behaviourally relevant language. Skinner (1988) pointed out that 'Sherrington never saw the action of the synapse about which he spoke so confidently'.[1] We do see it now. An aim of modern neuroscience is to observe neuronal function in the context of circuits and neuronal populations (*cell assembly) that encode *internal representations and guide behaviour. The *level of internal representations, which the classical and radical behaviourist tabooed, is hence expected to bridge the organismic and the molecular approaches to memory. We distanced ourselves long ago from the hegemony of introspection that the fathers of behaviourism so much distrusted, but we are still striving to reach the stage in which brain activity will provide accountable, reliable, and objective measures of behaviour.

Selected associations: Culture, Instrumental conditioning, Paradigm, Performance

---

[1]On Sherrington, see under *synapse.

Bias

1. **A preference or inclination that impairs impartial judgement.**
2. **The favouring of some outcomes over others as a result of systematic errors in procedures or interpretations.**

Frances Bacon, trusting that 'the subtlety of nature is greater many times over than the subtlety of the senses and understanding' (Bacon 1620), distinguished four classes of 'idols' (illusions) that beset the human mind: Idols of the 'Tribe' (inherent in the *a priori limited capacity of the species' senses and mind), of the 'Cave' (resulting from the individual's education and experience), of the 'Market-Place' (originating in social influence and public opinion), and of the 'Theatre' (stemming from dogmas and illusory knowledge). The analysis of error and bias in science has since became richer and more sophisticated, but the basic illusions still haunt us: those that stem from the senses, faulty logic, acquired prejudices, and suffocating *paradigms. Science has learned to cope with the shortcomings of the senses, yet finds it rather difficult to struggle with other faults of human nature, be them conscious or not.

Bias could be explicit (definition 1) or implicit (definitions 1 and 2). But even if explicit, it should definitely be distinguished from explicit distortion, which falsifies the data. The latter deplorable disease will not be discussed here further. At the other end of the spectrum stand the 'idols of the tribe', the elementary sensory and cognitive illusions that bias reality and usually transcend culture, education, and profession (Gregory 1966; Kahneman and Tversky 1982); they will not be referred to here either.

In the context of the present discussion, it is methodologically useful to distinguish four major domains in which bias could emerge: The behaviour of the experimental *subject, that of the experimenter, the interaction between the subject and the experimenter, and the scientific community that judges the research project. A notable source of potential *perceptual, *attentional, mnemonic, and judgement bias in the subject, is the emotional state (Power and Dalgleish 1997). For example, depression imposes a bias toward recalling unpleasant rather then pleasant memories (Clark and Teasdale 1982; see also 'mood congruency' under *state-dependent learning). In some situations, interactions unknown to the experimenter among individual subjects in a shared experimental situation, could lead to biased response by the subjects and *artefacts on the side of the experimenter (e.g. Heyes *et al.* 1994; *observational learning). In addition, multiple sources of bias stem from implicit interactions of the subject with the *context and the experimenter. In many behavioural experiments, the subject is actively involved more than the experimenter is inclined to admit. The subject pays attention to the experimental demands, could try to extract *cues about the objective of the test, reacts to involuntary signs emitted by the experimenter (*Clever Hans), and sometimes attempts to comply with a perceived goal (Pierce 1908). The cues that convey an experimental 'hypothesis' to the subject and hence influence the subject's behaviour are termed 'demand characteristics' (Orne 1962). Their influence on the behavioural outcome of an experiment were mostly studied in humans, but they clearly exist in experiments involving other species as well. Demand characteristics may lead to biased responses by the subjects and to potential artefacts on the side of the experimenter. And finally, the experimenter is itself a potential source of bias (Rosenthal and Rubin 1978; Martin and Bateson 1993). An almost trivial source is self-deception, motivated by a wish to obtain certain results but not others (a potential negative spin-off of *scoopophobia). In such situations minor acts of sampling bias and even data selection throughout the experiment could accumulate to a significant impairment in the overall outcome.

Proper *controls in the experimental design are a must if one wishes to minimize bias due to the subject, experimenter, or experimenter–subject interactions. For example, the potential for some facets of bias could be reduced by strictly following a 'blind' design, in which the person making the measurements does not know the treatment each subject has received until after the experiment is over. In human experiments (such as those that test the effect of drugs on behaviour), a 'double-blind' design should be followed, in which the subject as well does not know the treatment. Furthermore, experimenters must be well aware of their own behaviour. For example, the location and the bodily gestures of the experimenter could markedly bias the behaviour of a *rat or *mouse in a *maze. The design and execution of reliable learning and memory experiments is a complex mixture of science and art, and at least the science part (Martin and Bateson 1993; Kerlinger and Lee 2000) should be mastered before the first experiment is trusted.

But the ordeal of overcoming bias in the experimental design and in its execution is not over even when the manuscript is finally ready for publication. The idols of the market-place and of the theatre could still pose substantial obstacles. The attitude of referees and editors is sometimes biased by *zeitgeist, by a prevalent conceptual paradigm, or, even worse, by the fame of the senior author or the institution in which the work had been done. The refusal over years to accept papers on *conditioned taste aversion, because it had seemed to defy some ideas about what conditioning should be (Garcia 1981; *classical conditioning), provides but one example of referees and editors being biased by a conceptual paradigm. In other cases, the wish of referees and editors to appear politically correct in their scientific milieu or in society at large may also introduce bias into the scientific literature.

Selected associations: Control, Culture, Paradigm, Subject

Binding

1. **The phenomenon or process in which elements in space and time cohere into a perceived whole.**
2. **The phenomenon or process in which perceptual features integrate into a coherent sensory *precept.**
3. **The phenomenon or process in which representational elements fuse into a coherent *internal representation.**

There are several facets of 'binding' (definition 1) that excite philosophers. A classical aspect has to do with the persistence of the identity of things whose constituents turn-over with time, such as the self (see the 'Ship of Theseus' problem in *persistence). Neuroscience and the philosophy of mind presently focus on a distinct type of the 'binding problem', which refers to the ability of the brain to bind, within a fraction of a second, the features of a complex *stimulus into a coherent, meaningful percept (definition 2). Interest in this type of problem has a long history (e.g. Hume 1739). Neuroscience has dragged it into the laboratory, although for many scientists it still retains an excessively 'soft' connotation (also see below). Consider vision: different types and combinations of visual attributes are processed in the brain in multiple streams (Knierim and Van Essen 1992). How do they recombine to yield a coherent visual percept (Treisman 1993; Singer and Gray 1995; Shadlen and Movshon 1999)? This is the 'Humpty Dumpty' problem: 'Humpty Dumpty sat on a wall/ Humpty Dumpty had a great fall/All the King's horses and all the King's men/ Couldn't put Humpty together again' (Carroll 1872). In the brain Humpty is put together again. Or at least so we sense. How sad is it not to: 'On an incredibly clear day/… I saw …/That Great Mystery the false poets speak of…/That there are hills, valleys and plains/That there are trees, flowers and grass/There are rivers and stones/But there is no whole to which all this belongs/ That a true and real ensemble/ Is a disease of our own ideas.' (Pessoa 1914).[1]

Binding is related to the coherency of all kinds of internal representations (definition 3), not necessarily in the context of sensory perception. Hence it surfaces, either implicitly or explicitly, in discussions of *memory (Squire *et al.* 1984; Teyler and DiScenna 1986; Damasio 1989; Hommel 1998; Dudai and Morris 2000). These discussions usually refer to *declarative memory, but sometimes generalize to simple stimulus–response representations. Clearly, although the mainstream interest in the 'binding problem' is still in the context of perception, whatever will be gained there will contribute to the understanding of memory as well.

The binding problem binds several subproblems. Here is a selection:

1. *Parsing:* How are the relevant elements selected among other elements in the perceptual or mental space (Treisman 1999)? And how much of this selection is constrained by *a priori rules?
2. *Encoding:* How is the binding marked, maintained, and read by other systems in the brain (*ibid.*; *cell assembly)?
3. *Mapping:* How are the elements, once bound, kept in the correct structured relations (*ibid.*; *map)?
4. *Flexibility:* How are the bound elements reused in binding without lingering interference of the previous binding(s)?

Each of these questions could be tackled at multiple *levels, from that of the computational theory, via the *algorithms that implement the computations, down to the biological hardware that implements the algorithms. Discussion of binding in cellular neurobiology is still rather uncommon. The main focus is on the higher levels of neuronal circuits, brain systems, and cognition. At these levels, it is methodologically convenient to distinguish two types of approaches: top-down or cognitive, and bottom-up or neurobiological.[2] The *classic top-down approach is that of the Gestalt School (*Gestalt*, from German for '*shape*'; Koffka 1935; Hochberg 1998; *insight). This school of psychology, founded in Germany in the early twentieth century, has promoted the view that the nature of perceptual parts is determined by the whole, and that enquiry into the mind should consider global organization and proceed top-down. Unfortunately not much top-down analysis of the brain was possible during the formative years of the Gestalt. In more recent cognitive psychology, an influential *model is that of 'feature integration' (Treisman and Gelade 1980; Treisman 1993). This model considers *attention as the binding agent. It proposes that simple perceptual features are registered in parallel across the visual field, in a number of specialized subsystems. Focused attention scans serially, within milliseconds, through a 'master-map' of locations, accessing the features

present there at that point in time. The features are integrated, or 'glued', by the attentional 'beam' (*metaphor; for critical discussions of 'feature integration', see M. Green 1991; Van der Heijden 1995; Treisman 1995).

The neurobiological approach attempts to identify computations and algorithms relevant to binding in the brain and their physiological implementation. It focuses on the *cortex and on thalamocortical interconnections; in discussions of the role of binding in memory, attention is also devoted to the *hippocampal formation and to its role in coherency of internal representations. Two major types of solutions come up in neurobiological models of binding. The first type of solution is that binding is based on a *place code* (*map), and is performed by hierarchical combination of coding units, which converge anatomically on a master location (*homunculus; Barlow 1972; also discussions in Singer and Gray 1995; Grossberg *et al.* 1997; Bartels and Zeki 1998). The second type of solution proposes that binding is based on a *temporal code* (Eckhorn *et al.* 1988; Hardcastle 1994; von der Malsburg 1995; Engel *et al.* 1997). The basic idea in this case is that feature-detecting neurons are bound into coherent representations of objects if they fire in synchrony. Neurons in the cortex have been indeed observed to engage in recurrent bursts at frequencies of 30–70 Hz, and this has specifically been proposed as a candidate mechanism of binding. It also fits psychophysical data, which suggest 20–30 ms as the time scale of a 'cognitive beat' (*capacity, *percept). At this stage, the temporal synchrony hypothesis is still mostly phenomenological. It is not yet clear whether the oscillations represent a causal mechanism, a phenomenon, or an epiphenomenon (*criterion). To understand what's going on, one would wish to identify the semantics of the representational code(s), the source of the oscillations (i.e. intrinsic, emergent ensemble properties, top-down induction or executive control), and the hardware components (e.g. *coincidence detector).

So is 'binding' as defined above a problem, or a pseudoproblem? The same question applies to other *enigmas of the brain. What distinguishes 'binding' from some other unresolved brain processes and mechanisms, and occasionally endows it with a mystic flavour, is probably its association with major philosophical aspects (or some would say 'spin-offs') of the neurosciences. These include the mind–body problem and *consciousness (e.g. Crick and Koch 1990). Many scientists hesitate to touch these issues, others do it rather enthusiastically. Crick (1994) remarks on the 'binding problem' that 'it is not completely certain that this is a real problem or the brain gets around it by some unknown trick'. Sure the brain does its trick, and the problem is hence only ours to solve. 'That wonder is the effect of ignorance has been often observed' (Johnson 1751). It is therefore likely that with time, the 'binding' will stay but the 'problem' dissipate.

Selected associations: Algorithm, Attention, Cell assembly, Coincidence detection, Percept

---

[1]Pessoa's lines seem to echo a neurological disorder, Balint's syndrome, in which the ability to perceive the visual field as a whole is disturbed due to bilateral damage to the occipitoparietal region (Halligan and Marshall 1996).

[2]Bottom-up analysis of perceptual binding commonly attempts to account for cognitive phenomena by circuit and multicircuit properties. In the process, it could still employ top-down analysis of synaptic properties.

Birdsong

Complex, stereotyped vocalizations, accompanied by characteristic body postures, produced predominantly by mature male birds during the breeding season.

Male birds sing to selected audiences. The male is a landlord and potential warrior, notifying other males that it is ready to defend its territory. It is also a charming troubadour attempting to convince females that it is the best in town. The song occupies such a cardinal role in the male's life that it may even dream about it (Dave and Margoliash 2000). Whereas we humans could enjoy the song repertoire regardless of gender, the male and the female of songbirds are probably each tuned to understand only that part of the song that speaks to their heart (Williams and Nottebohm 1985). The *plasticity of birdsong has been well known to bird fanciers in the Orient since ancient times, and expert manipulations of song were exploited for aesthetic and commercial purposes (Konishi 1985). This neuronal and behavioural plasticity has also long attracted scientists' attention (Darwin 1871; Mertfessel 1935; Koehler 1951; Thorpe 1954). In addition to being a beautiful system to investigate ethology and learning, the study of birdsong taps into several central issues in brain research. These include the role of genetic constraints on learning ('prepared learning', see *a priori, *imprinting); the interplay of *development and learning; the contribution of 'instruction' and 'selection'

processes in learning (see *a priori, *stimulus); and the role of neurogenesis in the adult brain.

A song is a series of sounds with silent intervals between them. It is different from a 'call' that is a simple, brief vocalization uttered by both species in all seasons in response to particular stimuli such as a predator. Calls are not unique to birds. Birdsongs are. The most elementary sound in a song is a note, lasting 10–100 ms. Notes form syllables, syllables phrases, and phrases songs. Songs are commonly 1–5 s in duration. Different songs form a repertoire. The size of the repertoire ranges from one to many hundreds songs, depending on the species. Repertoires of geographically distinct populations of the same species often differ, and are termed 'dialects' (Baker and Cunningham 1985). Some species perform all or most of their repertoire in cycles that takes many minutes to complete (Marler 1984). Terms such as 'dialect' should not lure us to regard birdsong as an analogue of human language, as there is much more to language than structured stereotyped vocalization. But still, the song repertoire provides the bird with a complex expressive and communicative system, which may require special strategies to ensure prompt *retrieval and correct response (e.g. Todt and Hultsch 1998).

The ontogenesis of song involves discrete stages. Take the wild chaffinch as an example (Nottebohm 1970). In the spring, immediately after hatching, chaffinches begin to emit various food-begging calls. Within a few weeks, the male starts to emit a loose, rambling aggregation of low volume notes of varying complexity. This vocal pattern is called 'subsong'. The subsong keeps changing, and discrete passages, resembling the adult song, gradually emerge. These passages are called 'plastic song'. During the breeding season the subsong vanishes and the plastic song crystallizes into the full adult song. The singing posture typical of the adult also matures. The final crystallization takes place before the end of the winter.

Although there are remarkable species differences in song development, data from experiments involving sensory and social isolation (e.g. Marler and Tamura 1964; Konishi 1965) generalize to portray the following *model of song ontogeny: the bird is born with a song motor-control system that needs input in order to generate a normal song. This input is provided in two stages, 'sensory' and 'sensorimotor', which may partially overlap, depending on the species. First comes the 'sensory stage', during which the bird listens to a tutor. There is a genetically determined predisposition to prefer a conspecific tutor. Thus, even if we raise a chaffinch in Pavarotti's house, the chances that it will learn to sing *La Bohème* are very slim indeed. In the sensory stage, elements of the tutor's song are confined to memory. In the 'sensorimotor' stage, which corresponds to the subsong, plastic song, and crystallization, the bird must listen to itself to match its vocal output with its innate template as well as with the memorized template of the tutor's song. The entire process combines elements of instruction (by the tutor) and selection (among endogenous innately constrained song templates; see Marler 1997). In the absence of a tutor, only the innate information is used. Some species can generate species-specific song solely on the basis of an innate template, in the absence of tutors and auditory feedback. Species differ also in the stability of song. In some 'age-limited learners', such as the zebrafinch and white-crowned sparrow, learning is limited to the first year of life, and crystallized song is maintained throughout adulthood. In 'open-ended learners', such as the canary, new songs are added in adulthood. But even adult 'age-limited learners' retain a significant amount of plasticity, and use auditory feedback in adulthood to maintain the stability of song structure (Leonardo and Konishi 1999).

One of the advantages of birdsong as an experimental *system is the well defined and quantifiable behavioural output that provides a convenient and faithful *assay to determine whether learning has occurred. Moreover, song is generated by a single organ, the syrinx. This facilitates the tracing of pathways from central motor centres and ultimately identification of brain circuits that subserve *acquisition and execution of the motor programme. Over the years, in series of elegant studies combining anatomical and cellular *methods, a picture has been generated that depicts the major elements of the central song system as composed of two major forebrain pathways (Figure 6). The posteriomedial pathway is traditionally termed 'the motor pathway', and includes, in ascending order, the nucleus Uva, the nucleus NIf, the higher vocal centre (HVc, originally so abbreviated because it was thought to be 'hyperstriatum ventrale'), and finally nucleus RA, that innervates the tracheosyringeal portion of the hypoglossal nerve nucleus (nXIIts), itself innervating the syrinx. This pathway is fed by auditory input, and is obligatory for both song development and production (Nottebohm *et al.* 1976). Lesions in HVc and RA result in 'silent song': upon noticing a female, the lesioned male adopts a singing position but emits no song, becoming a very sad bird indeed. The HVc and RA are organized hierarchically, with HVc neurons representing syllables and RA neurons representing notes. Uva and NIf may help organize syllables into higher units of song. Some of the sites afferent to Uva

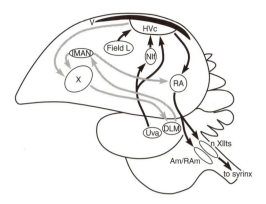

Fig. 6 A schematic representation of the songbird brain, showing the brain centres and pathways that subserve the development, learning, and production of song. The *system is composed of two major forebrain pathways. The posteriomedial ('motor') pathway (*black*) includes the nuclei Uva, NIf, HVc, and RA. The RA innervates the tracheosyringeal portion of the hypoglossal nerve nucleus, which in turn innervates the song organ, the syrinx. The anterior forebrain pathway (*grey*), which is obligatory for song development and learning, connects the HVc to RA via area X, the thalamic nucleus DLM, and nucleus IMAN. Also shown is the auditory area L, which feeds into the HVc. Abbreviations: AM, nucleus ambiguus; DLM, medial portion of the dorsolateral nucleus of the thalamus; HVc, higher vocal centre in the neostriatum; IMAN, lateral portion of the magnocellular nucleus of the anterior neostriatum; Field L, auditory region in the neostriatum; NIf, nucleus interface; RA, robust nucleus of the archistriatum; RAm, nucleus retroambigualis; Uva, nucleus uvaeformis; V, ventricle; X, area X; n XIIts, tracheosyringeal part of the hypoglossal nucleus. (Adapted from Brenowitz et al. 1997.)

may also take part in sensory acquisition during song development (Margoliash 1997).

Another interconnected pathway, the anterior forebrain pathway, is considered essential for song development, learning and recognition. It is not obligatory for the mature song production, but still plays a part in feedback evaluation and adaptivity of singing in the adult bird (*ibid.*; Brainard and Doupe 2000). This pathway indirectly connects HVc to RA via area X, the thalamic nucleus DLM, and the nucleus lMAN. All in all, the song system is distributed over nuclei and circuits, and no single site 'stores' the entire score (*engram, *metaphor). Furthermore, a clear-cut dissociation between central 'sensorimotor' and 'learning centres is probably not honoured by the brain.

An intriguing finding is that many new neurons are born in the brain of the adult bird (Goldman and Nottebohm 1983; Alvarez-Buylla and Kirn 1997). Such neurogenesis is not limited to song nuclei, to males, or to species that sing. However, in songbirds, it is prominent in HVc, and correlates with seasonal variations in song and sex hormone levels. (Sex hormones play a part in moulding song circuits and behaviour; Bottjer and Johnson 1997.) The role of neurogenesis in song memory, if at all, is not yet clear. In recent years neurogenesis has also been noted in the adult mammalian brain, and, furthermore, reported to be enhanced in learning (Gould et al. 1999; *hippocampus; but see concerns in Rakic 2002). Neurogenesis in birds in general and songbirds in particular may therefore reflect a more general process. This is surely a finding that can defeat the popular notion that old brains only fade out.

Selected associations: Development, Engram, Imprinting, Observational learning, Skill

Calcium

A metallic element that comprises about 3% of the earth crust and is essential for many biological processes, including neural *plasticity.

Calcium (*calx*, Latin for lime) fulfils many regulatory, computational, and representational functions in the brain. Furthermore, it is instrumental in translating information across *levels and time domains in the brain (see below). In recent years much has been learned about the ways in which calcium ions (Ca^{2+}) encode and modulate neuronal information, but the picture is far from being comprehensive.

In resting cells, intracellular Ca^{2+} is in the range of 10–100 nanomolar. Upon stimulation it could rise by several orders of magnitude. In many cases the information in the Ca^{2+} signal is encoded as spatiotemporal patterns of change rather than a tonic increase in concentration. Changes in cellular Ca^{2+} are due to influx from the extracellular milieu and release from intracellular stores. Both mechanisms generate elementary all-or-none Ca^{2+} signals, which are brief and localized (Bootman and Berridge 1995). Stimulus-induced combinations of intensity, timing, and location of these primitives of the 'Ca^{2+} language' generate a repertoire of Ca^{2+} codes (Bootman et al. 1997). The latter control cellular metabolism, structural dynamics, signal transduction, hormone release, differentiation, and growth (Berridge 1993; Petersen et al. 1994; Ghosh and Greenberg 1995; Matthews 1996). The introduction of novel technologies of molecular biology, cellular electrophysiology, and imaging has opened new vistas in the analysis of Ca^{2+} in neurons.

Especially noteworthy in the context of plasticity are the studies on the role of Ca^{2+} in mediating and modulating excitability and integrative properties in dendritic compartments (Markram et al. 1995; Magee et al. 1998); control of *neurotransmitter release (Matthews 1996; Goda and Sudhof 1997); modification of membrane *receptors (Barria et al. 1997); and modulation of gene expression (Bito et al. 1996; Dolmetsch et al. 1998).

The ubiquitousness of Ca^{2+} signalling in the nervous system makes it impractical to mention all its major functions in experience-dependent neuronal modification. These functions are performed at locations ranging from neuronal subcompartments to circuits, and on time-scales ranging from milliseconds to days and more. Ca^{2+} is required for elementary short-lived processes of *synaptic plasticity (Thomson 2001), and for the induction of *long-term potentiation, a popular cellular *model of longer-term neuronal plasticity (Nicoll and Malenka 1995). A few examples will serve to illustrate the role of Ca^{2+} in *acquisition, retention, and consolidation of learned behaviours. In the circuits that subserve *classical conditioning of defensive reflexes in *Aplysia, Ca^{2+} encodes information about the conditioned stimulus (CS). Furthermore, convergence of the CS and the unconditioned stimulus (US) takes place on a Ca^{2+}/calmodulin-activated adenylyl cyclase (*coincidence detection; *intracellular signal transduction cascade). The optimal activation of the enzyme requires that Ca^{2+} preceded the transmitter, hence mimicking the order dependency of CS–US presentation in classical conditioning (Yovell and Abrams 1992). Another Ca^{2+}-regulated enzyme, the multifunctional Ca^{2+}/calmodulin activated *protein kinase type II (CaMKII; Braun and Schulman 1995; De Koninck and Schulman 1998), was found to be essential in learning (Bach et al. 1995), *long-term potentiation (Barria et al. 1997), and neuronal development (Wu and Cline 1998). CaMKII is a major component of the postsynaptic density. It phosphorylates and modifies receptors, channels, and cytoskeletal elements. Experience-dependent autophosphorylation of the enzyme complex was proposed as a molecular storage mechanism immune to molecular turnover (Miller and Kennedy 1986). Another family of Ca^{2+} regulated protein kinase, PKC, was also implicated in learning (e.g. Scharenberg et al. 1991.) In addition, Ca^{2+} is involved in cellular consolidation: it regulates the activity of *CREB, and hence of the expression of cyclic adenosine monophosphate-response element (CRE)-regulated genes (Bito et al. 1996; *immediate early genes).

Why is it that Ca^{2+}, rather than any other ion, plays such a key part in cellular activity in general and in plasticity in particular? Though in essence a teleological question with speculative answers, it does warrant consideration, because it could illuminate interesting properties of Ca^{2+} signalling systems. Possibly the physicochemical parameters of Ca^{2+}, when considered in combination with those of critical Ca^{2+}-binding sites in the cell, had from the early days of evolution fitted the demands of cellular function and plasticity better than those of other ions. The problem with this line of reasoning is that it is of the egg-and-the-hen type: was the cause the abundance of Ca^{2+}, or the availability of the biological binding sites? This inherent issue notwithstanding, one appealing argument in favour of Ca^{2+} at the current stage of evolution is that the affinity of Ca^{2+} for important macromolecules in the cell is strong enough to allow rapid binding but not too strong to prevent rapid dissociation. This is important in cellular signalling in general and in fast plasticity in particular. For example, magnesium binds stronger to phospho-groups (Dawson *et al.* 1986); and monovalent ions are in general much worse in getting bound to biological macromolecules. The problem is highly complex, because, as mentioned above, it is not tonic Ca^{2+}, but rather Ca^{2+} transients, which are most important in signalling. The life-span of these transients may not be sufficient for Ca^{2+} to equilibrate with binding sites in the cell (Markram *et al.* 1998b). Analysis of Ca^{2+} signalling, therefore, requires gigantic calculations of nonequilibrium Ca^{2+} dynamics. For our purpose suffice it to remember that the real-life role of Ca^{2+} in neuronal plasticity must be considered in the context of the simultaneous interaction of this ion with the network of the many Ca^{2+} binding molecules in the neuron.

It is also noteworthy that overall, the actions of Ca^{2+} in the neuron span orders of magnitude in time, space, and complexity (Bootman *et al.* 1997). This endows Ca^{2+} with a unique position to bridge molecular, cellular, and system levels of brain action (Dudai 1997b). The spatiotemporal pattern of Ca^{2+} is therefore a candidate parameter for future equations of the not-yet-available interlevel 'correspondence rules' in brain models and theories (*reduction).

Selected associations: Intracellular signal transduction cascade, Ion channel, Plasticity, Reduction, Stimulus

Capacity

1. The ability of a *system to receive, process, store, represent or transmit items.

2. The measure of this ability.

3. The upper limit of this ability.

Pondering the capacity of our memory carries with it the risk of being enslaved to the common *metaphor of memory as a static storehouse (Roediger 1980). This misconception should be avoided at the outset. Furthermore, in the case of the nervous system, even the definition itself evokes cardinal issues: What is the meaning of 'store' (definition 1)? Are *internal representations stored as such, reactivated, or reconstructed anew each time they are *retrieved?[1] If memory is reconstructed, then the capacity of the system should involve the ability to decompress and recreate information; however, something must eventually be stored as, clearly, the brain does not reconstruct memories from void. And as if all this is not enough, it is likely that different memory systems encode information in different ways, possess different capacities, and exploit the capacity to different extents. Having said all this, it is still of interest to wonder whether in terms of capacity (definition 3), our brain is any match to a notebook computer.

The data are still scarce. The Swiss-German physiologist Haller, who in the eighteenth century performed the first documented experiments on the timing of psychic processes, reached the conclusion that a third of a second is sufficient time for the production of one idea. Hence assuming only eight mentally useful hours per day (!), in 50 years a person has a chance to collect up to 1 577 880 000 traces (Burnham 1889). More recent (yet not necessarily less controversial) estimates of how much information we perceive during an average lifetime, yield the very wide range of $\alpha 10^{13}$–$\alpha 10^{17}$ bits (reviewed in Dudai 1997a; 'bit' is the basic unit in information theory; see *system). In considering the information that becomes available to the brain, we must take into account not only the information that is obtained from the external world, but also that information that is generated endogenously by the brain (*a priori, *internal representation, *stimulus). We do not yet have the bases to estimate the magnitude of contribution of this type of information to the potential representational pool of the brain. *Modelling of artificial 'neuronal' networks of the estimated size of the human brain yields an upper representational capacity of $\alpha 10^{13}$ (Palm 1982) to $\alpha 10^{15}$ bits (Amit 1989). There have been also attempts to estimate the representational capacity of parts of the brain, such as *cortex (Gochin et al. 1994; Rolls *et al.* 1997). The conclusion was that the available representational capacity is probably more than required to subserve our actual mental and behavioural repertoire.

But how much of this information could be stored in our memory over time? Some agreement exists only on the maximal capacity of short-term, or better, *working memory (*phase). The discussion digresses here from the bits of the formal models to vague, almost impressionistic units. The most popular estimate is that our working memory can hold only seven-plus-minus-two chunks of information at one time. This estimate stems from experiments in psychology (Jacobs 1887; Miller 1956) and from observations in anthropology (Wallace 1961; Berlin 1992).[2] Despite the catchy title of Miller's classic article, seven-plus-minus-two is not a sacred number. There are lower estimates as well (down to only three separate registers; Broadbent 1975). Miller's idea was not to determine a precise value, but rather to point out that the brain is an information processing system of limited capacity, which had evolved to recode information into chunks in order to be able to deal with it efficiently (Baddeley 1994; Shiffrin and Nosofsky 1994). Attempts have been made to estimate the size of a chunk in terms of digits, syllables, words, and patterns (Simon 1974). Some individuals develop a remarkable *skill for chunking, and by combining it with efficient *retrieval from long-term stores, can handle huge amounts of information simultaneously (e.g. more than a 10-fold increase in the normal digit span; Chase and Ericsson 1982).

It has been estimated by Simon (1974), on the basis of the contemporary psychological literature, that 5–10 s are needed to transfer a chunk from short- into long-term stores. When it comes to both the maximal and the actual capacity of the latter, the issue of magnitude becomes even more evasive. In what units should long-term memory be measured? Which 'chunks' should be used to estimate the size of, say, an *episodic scene or a motor skill? Furthermore, how can one compare the capacity of different long-term memory systems? A variety of experimental methods have been deployed, ranging from introspection (Galton 1879), via controlled recalling of personal experience (Wagenaar 1986), to measurement of *real-life capabilities such as picture *recognition, language, or the feats of *mnemonists (Table 1). There are no definite answers, only estimates expressed in *ad-hoc*, somewhat fuzzy units. A conservative estimate is that a normal human long-term memory retains $\alpha 10^5$–10^6 items, where item means a word, a fact, an autobiographical episode—what might intuitively be

Table 1 Estimates of the actual capacity of selected human long-term memory stores

Store	Size	Reference
Words in language (mother tongue)	25 000–50 000	Nagy and Anderson (1984)
Pictures recognized	> 10 000	Standing (1973)
Game patterns by a chess master	10 000–100 000	Chase and Simon (1973)
Facts by mnemonists	100 000	Yates (1966)
Core personal episodes	Thousands	Dudai (1997a)
Items in expert databases in orally-reliant societies	500–2000	Levi-Strauss (1966); Berlin (1992)

called a unit of memory, but formally is very unsatisfactory indeed (Dudai 1997).

The capacity of brains and memory systems is no doubt of interest, but it would do no harm to scrutinize the assumptions that underlie this interest. One assumption, which is definitely wrong as a *generalization, is that the bigger, the better. The capacity of memory systems is the outcome of the interplay among multiple drives and elements. These include the functions that this memory system is supposed to accomplish; the mechanistic constraints imposed by the biological machinery; the feasibility of *algorithms; the energy resources that are required to *develop and operate the system; and, finally, the current stage in the evolution of the system. Here is but one concrete example: is it phylogenetically advantageous for the system of *declarative, autobiographical memory to have a large capacity? Not necessarily (see in *false memory).

It would be naive to expect real advances in the estimation of memory capacity before two developments materialize. First, we must decipher the codes of internal representations, in order to be better equipped to estimate the requirements for representational and computational space in the brain. Second, we must gain a much better understanding into the processes and mechanisms of *persistence, *forgetting, relearning in *extinction, and particularly, retrieval of memory. Retrieval that tolerates liberal reconstructions of internal representations, and is heavily dependent on on-line information, is expected to place different demands on capacity than retrieval that involves faithful reactivation of fine-grained stored information. The issue of capacity is hence intimately associated with some of the most profound *enigmas of memory research.

Selected associations: Episodic memory, Internal representation, Persistence, Working memory

---

[1]This issue is further discussed in *persistence.

[2]By the way, the working-memory capacity of the chimpanzee is not much less: >5 items, the same as preschool children (Kawai and Matsuzawa 2000).

Cell assembly

A hypothetical concept referring to *phasic sets of coactive neurons that are assumed to encode *internal representations and perform computations over representations.

In 1949, Hebb published *The organization of behavior*, later to become the most influential book in the history of modern neuroscience (*classic). 'In this book', he wrote, 'I have tried … to bridge the gap between neurophysiology and psychology'. In essence, Hebb's monograph was about how the brain *perceives and represents the world. It has yielded important insights into brain function, as well as two major concepts. Typical of Hebb's integrative view of the brain, these concepts related to two *levels: the *synaptic and the *system. At the synaptic level, Hebb coined a postulate of use-dependent synaptic *plasticity (see *algorithm). At the system level, he proposed the existence of neuronal assemblies as vehicles for perception, *attention, *association, memory, and thought. Hebb (1949) envisaged that in the brain

> … stimulation will lead to the slow development of 'cell assembly', a diffuse structure comprising cells in the cortex and diencephalon … capable of acting briefly as a closed system, delivering facilitation to other such systems … A series of such events constitutes a 'phase sequence'—the thought process. Each assembly action may be aroused by a preceding assembly, by a sensory event, or—normally—by both. The central facilitation from one of these activities on the next is the prototype of 'attention'.

Although with time Hebb's synaptic postulate may have gained more popularity (despite being regarded by Hebb himself as less original; Milner 1986), it is the 'cell assembly' that was at the heart of his seminal book. In the past 50 years or so, the concept of 'cell assembly' has remained viable in both experimental and theoretical research on perception, learning, and memory (e.g. Palm 1982; Crick 1984a; Dudai *et al.* 1987; von der Malsburg 1987; Gerstein *et al.* 1989; Singer *et al.* 1990; Nicolelis *et al.* 1997; Sakurai 1998).

The platonic cell assembly has the following attributes: (a) it encodes internal *representations*, in a *spatiotemporal* code; (b) a representation is *distributed* over many units in the set; (c) each unit may be a member of *several* assemblies; (d) the units in the assembly become *coactive*, and hence actualize the assembly and what it represents, in brief time-locked *phases*;[1] and (e) the assembly is *plastic*, meaning that the representations could change over time, either in response to input or by endogenous rearrangements. That the cell assembly uses a distributed, alias ensemble, alias population code means that in big-enough assemblies, no single neuron is essential to any percept or memory; put in other terms, the assembly denies the existence of single-cell *homunculi.

Hebb's assemblies did not emerge out of the blue. As is the case with other great ideas, this one as well stood on the shoulders of giants.[2] The possibility that sensorimotor information is processed by populations of neurons was raised much earlier (Young 1802). Sherrington, the great advocate of the cellular view of brain function, assumed that individual neurons do not have the representational complexity to account for higher properties of the nervous system (Sherrington 1941). Hebb was a student of Lashley, who attempted in vain to localize memory traces to specific brain regions, and reached the conclusion that the *engram is widely distributed (Lashley 1929). At about the same time, de No (1938), himself relying on earlier observations, singled out the role of neuronal loops and recurrent circuits in information processing in the nervous system. This was contrary to contemporary naive switchboard *metaphor, which described the brain in terms of many yet rather simple (sensory) input–(motor) output connectors. Hebb took the aforementioned ideas further. He formulated a comprehensive conceptual framework of brain function in which populations of neurons represent information about the world. As representations (and hence memories) are distributed over many nodes, localized lesions could fail to abolish memory. Furthermore, assemblies according to Hebb are dynamic entities. They form, *develop (first in the immature and later in the mature brain), associate, and disengage. This calls for synaptic plasticity; Hebb's famous synaptic postulate, mentioned above, was his solution to the mechanism of use-dependent modifications in local nodes in the assembly. The first attempts to model neuronal assemblies on a digital computer were carried out a few years after Hebb's book was published (Rochester *et al.* 1956). Since then, various mathematical *models have been suggested for the representation of information in neuronal assemblies, based on the principle of ensemble encoding; some of these models incorporate Hebbian local modification rules.

Do cell assemblies exist in real life? Many attempts have been made to identify them and observe their action. These attempts have involved combinations of cellular physiology, neuroanatomy, *functional neuroimaging, and behaviour. The *zeitgeist is that population coding, which is in line with the assembly notion, plays a part in higher brain function (Jones 1972; Lee *et al.* 1988; Singer *et al.* 1990; Hurlbert and Derrington 1993; Tanaka 1993; Arieli *et al.* 1995; Goldman-Rakic 1996; Nicolelis *et al.* 1997; Sakurai 1998; Stopfer and Laurent 1999; Tsodyks *et al.* 1999). Time-locked phasic activity of large neuronal populations is also detected (e.g. *binding). Yet the inference that these are cell assemblies that encode and control behaviour requires more than that. One must establish a necessary, causal, and sufficient link between the coactive populations and specific instances of perception, memory, and behaviour (*criterion). Taking the devil's advocate stand, one could claim, for example, that what is construed as time-locked phasic population coding is manifestation of a *homeostatic device, or a process permissive for coding but not the code itself, or a step on the road to another type of coding, even on the road to the evasive homunculus.

Suppose cell assemblies do indeed encode internal representations; in that case, how big are the assemblies? The minimal number of neurons that is needed to encode and transmit physiologically meaningful information reliably in the cortex was proposed to be only < 100 (Shadlen and Newsome 1998). Similarly, it has been estimated that the number of neurons required to collectively encode a meaningful aspect of a visual scene is closer to 10^2–10^3 than to 10^4–10^6 (Crick and Koch 1998). The lower limit attest at most to 'mini-assemblies'. But a postulated assembly representing a complex scene could bind together many such mini-assemblies, each encoding an attribute of the representation. In such a case, the overall number of coactive neurons could reach $\gg 10^6$. Each coactivation phase of the hypothetical assembly is expected to be in the millisecond to second range. Limits on the coactivation time can be deduced from the observation that 40–150 ms are sufficient to complete complex perceptual and cognitive tasks (Thorpe *et al.* 1996; Van Turennout *et al.* 1998).

The cell assembly illustrates a fruitful concept in the neurosciences that had preceded by three to four scientific generations the development of experimental tools to prove or refute it. Such tools now become available: sophisticated cellular physiology, functional neuroimaging, behavioural protocols, advanced data analysis, and, preferably, all combined. The hunt for the assembly *reduces the search for the engram from gross neuroanatomical cartography to the analysis of functional circuits and their interconnections. This by itself is instrumental in advancing our understanding of memory.

Selected associations: Cerebral cortex, Engram, Homunculus, Internal representation, Model

---

[1] During this period, the system can be said to become locked in a quasi-stable state of an energy minimum.

[2] For a fascinating history of this aphorism, commonly attributed to Newton, including some lessons on the intricacies of *culture and *collective memory, see Merton (1993).

Cerebellum

A brain organ at the rear of the brain overlying the brainstem, composed of a cortex and a core of white matter, which contains deep nuclei, interconnected with all major subdivisions of the central nervous system, and involved in sensorimotor and cognitive function.

The conspicuous location and distinct shape of the cerebellum (Latin for *little brain*) had attracted the attention of neuroanatomists long ago; at the time it was even considered as the seat of the soul, although this was soon rejected: '... this marvelous instinct, which is developed by education into mind, and which always has its seat in the brain ... and never in the cerebellum; for I have often seen the cerebellum injured ... when the soul has not ceased to fulfill its functions' (La Mettrie 1748). Others thought that the spirits which put the body in motion flow from the cerebrum for voluntary movements, but from the cerebellum for unconscious movements (Hoffman 1695, cited in Brazier 1984). This latter proposal (spirits excluded) was not too far from certain more recent notions of cerebellar function. But the picture is changing. And so is the view of the role of the cerebellum in learning.

The cerebellum in mammals constitutes only about 10% of the total volume of the brain, yet contains more than half of all the neurons (Ghez 1991). It is composed of a thin cortex and a core of white matter containing pairs of deep nuclei (the fastigial, anterior and posterior interposed, and dentate nuclei; Figure 7). The cerebellar input and output pathways course through the cerebellar peduncles that connect the cerebellum to the brainstem. The cerebellar input is carried by two fibre systems, mossy fibres and climbing fibres, which reach the cerebellar cortex and send collaterals to the deep nuclei. The mossy fibres originate in the brainstem. The climbing fibres originate in the inferior olive in the medulla, itself receiving input from the spinal cord and the cerebral cortex. The cerebellar cortex is neatly organized in three layers, containing altogether only a few types of neurons (Figure 8): Purkinje cells (large GABAergic neurons), granule cells (small *glutamatergic neurons), Golgi cells (GABAergic/glycinergic), and stellate/basket cells (GABAergic) (Voogd and Glickstein 1998).[1] Each Purkinje cell

receives converging input from a large number of mossy fibres, via parallel fibres sent by the granule cells. In contrast, each Purkinje cell receives input from only one climbing fibre. The Purkinje cells, the only cerebral cortex efferent system, project inhibitory connections to the deep nuclei, which relay the cerebellar output further.

Over the years, the relative simplicity and quasi-crystalline microstructure of the cerebellar cortex has enticed a wide variety of investigators, ranging from neuroanatomists to cell biologists to theoreticians, to propose *models for cerebellar function (e.g. Braitenberg 1967; Marr 1969; Albus 1971; Ito 1972, 1984; Eccles 1973; Raymond et al. 1996; Braitenberg et al. 1997). Two points concerning these models are particularly noteworthy. First, the models consider the cerebellum to be either an orchestrator of motor function,[2] a motor learning machine, or a clock. It is now evident

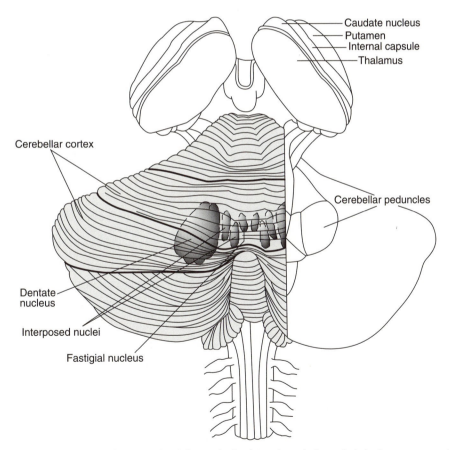

Fig. 7 A simplified macroscopic view of the exposed cerebellum. In this dorsal view, the cerebral cortex is depicted as transparent to show the deep nuclei, and the right hemisphere is cut out to show the underlying cerebellar peduncles. (Adapted from Niewwenhuys et al. 1988.)

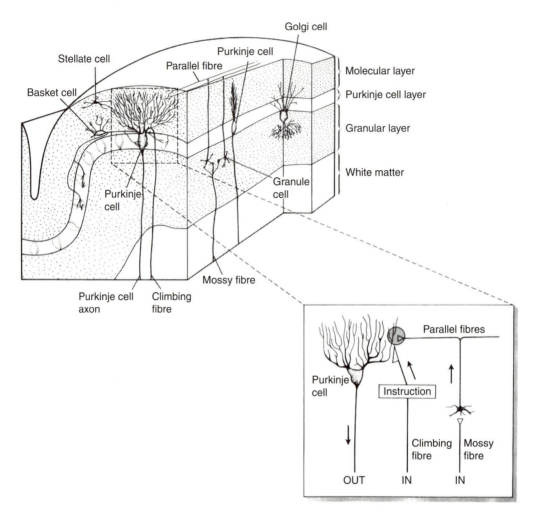

Fig. 8 A simplified microscopic view of the cerebellar cortex. Only five types of neurons (Purkinje, granule, Golgi, stellate, and basket) are organized into the three layers of the cerebellar cortex. The sole output, which is inhibitory, is provided by the Purkinje cells. Input reaches the cerebellum via two excitatory fibre systems, the mossy and the climbing fibres. Each Purkinje cell receives converging input from a large number of mossy fibres via many parallel fibres that are sent by the granule cells. In contrast, each Purkinje cell receives input from only one climbing fibre. *Inset*: A scheme depicting the convergence of the two major cerebellar inputs on the Purkinje cell. The influential Marr–Albus *model (Marr 1969; Albus 1971) proposed that the climbing fibre instructs the Purkinje cell to respond specifically to the concurrent pattern of parallel fibre activity; the modified synapse is encircled. (Adapted from Ghez 1991.)

that these possibilities are not mutually exclusive. Second, a highly influential model has proposed a locus of *plasticity in the cerebellar cortex as the key to cerebellar learning (Marr 1969; Albus 1971). This locus is the *synapse from the parallel fibres to the Purkinje cell (Figure 8). The basic idea is that information arriving via the climbing fibre conditions the Purkinje cell to respond specifically to the concurrent pattern of parallel fibre activity. Certain lines of experimental evidence support this prediction.

Much of the data on the role of cerebellar circuits in plasticity and learning stems from two *systems. One is the adaptation of the vestibulo-ocular reflex (VOR; du Lac *et al.* 1995; Ito 1998); the other is *classical conditioning of the eyeblink reflex (Yeo and Hesslow 1998; Steinmetz 2000; Thompson *et al.* 2000).[3] The basic motor pathways for both reflexes are in the brainstem, but their use-dependent modification relies on other brain structures, particularly the cerebellum. The VOR evokes eye movements in the direction opposite to head movement. It stabilizes vision, by keeping images from slipping across the retina. The reflex is capable of remarkable adaptation, e.g. after wearing reversing prisms, eye movements go with, instead of against, head movement. The visual information and the vestibular information involved in this adaptation converge both in the deep cerebral nuclei and in the cerebellar cortex. Although significant pieces of the puzzle are still missing, it is now believed by most authors that both these sites are involved in the adaptation. Furthermore, it is proposed that the convergence on the Purkinje cell of the visual information, mediated by the climbing fibres, with the vestibular information, mediated by the mossy-fibre—parallel fibre, induces long-term depression (LTD) in the parallel fibre—Purkinje cell synapse (Lisberger 1998; Ito 2001).[4] This LTD is considered to contribute to the behavioural change of the VOR.

The other system that has contributed tremendously to our knowledge about the role of the cerebellum in behavioural plasticity is classical conditioning of the eyeblink reflex, in which the *subject blinks in response to a noxious stimulus applied o the eye area. This is one of the most studied cases of simple learning in mammals. It has been studied in multiple protocols and species. A popular preparation involves the response of the external eyelid or of the nictitating membrane in the rabbit.[5] Commonly in this preparation the conditioned stimulus is a tone, and the unconditioned stimulus is an air puff to the eye (Figure 9). With training, the rabbit learns to blink in response to the tone alone. It can be shown, using ablations, that elemental delay conditioning of eyeblink is dependent on the cerebellum but independent of the *cerebral cortex and *hippocampus.

Studies using cellular physiology, anatomical, pharmacological, and *neurogenetic lesions, and electrical stimulation of discrete brain sites (*criterion, *method), have identified the cerebellar cortex and the interpositus nuclei in the cerebellum as sites of *association and plasticity in this type of learning. Additional learning-related plasticity changes can, however, be detected in other sites in the brain, particularly if the conditioning protocol becomes more complex than elemental conditioning. Furthermore, when a trace conditioning protocol is used instead of delay conditioning (Figure 14, p. 46), the hippocampus becomes obligatory for conditioning (e.g. Moyer et al. 1990). There is also evidence that trace conditioning of the eyeblink reflex, as opposed to delay conditioning, requires *conscious awareness (Clark and Squire 1998), which should be expected to engage cerebral cortex as well.

Though controlling different behaviours, and involving different brainstem nuclei, cerebellar cortex

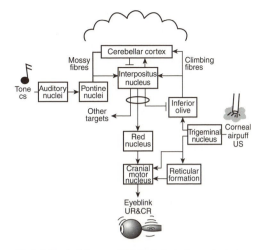

Fig. 9 A flowchart diagram of the circuits that subserve classical conditioning of eyeblink in the rabbit. In a typical protocol, tone is the conditioned stimulus and periorbital air puff the unconditioned stimulus. The unconditioned stimulus elicits closure of the eyelid as well as extension across the cornea of the nictitating membrane (the internal eyelid). The cerebellar cortex and the interpositus nuclei are sites of *association and *plasticity in this type of learning. When trace instead of delay conditioning, or complex protocols of *classical conditioning are used, additional brain organs, such as the *hippocampus, become obligatory as well (*criterion). -> , excitatory *synapse; ⊣, inhibitory synapse. (Adapted from Thompson and Kim 1996.)

areas and deep cerebral nuclei, the use-dependent modification of the VOR and of the eyeblink share a lot in common (e.g. Raymond et al. 1996). In both cases, as noted above, the basic reflex does not require the cerebellum, but modification of the reflex does. We hence encounter tiers of neuronal circuits, the core of which subserves the most elementary form of the behaviour while the others add adaptability. This is particularly evident in eyeblink conditioning, where the more complex forms of conditioning engage additional brain areas. In both cases, the conditioned input—vestibular in the VOR, auditory in the standard protocol of eyeblink conditioning—projects in parallel to the cerebellar cortex and to the deep nuclei. In both cases, the teaching input—visual in the VOR, somatosensory in eyeblink conditioning—has the opportunity to converge with the conditioned input in both the cerebellar cortex and the deep nuclei (*coincidence detector). In both cases, the convergence in the cerebellar cortex could result in modification of the Purkinje response to the conditioned input. The modified Purkinje output, via the cerebellar nuclei, may guide the motor circuits to adjust the reflex to the new conditions. Finally, in both cases, the relative contribution of the cerebellar nuclei and the cerebellar cortex, respectively, to learning, and the site(s) of the lasting memory trace, are still debated.

Recent evidence, including *functional neuroimaging data, unveils cerebellar involvement in *declarative memory, *working memory, and language (Leiner et al. 1993; Desmond and Fiez 1998; Thach 1998; Wiggs et al. 1999). The role of the cerebellum in these higher brain functions is possibly based on the same computational abilities, such as the spatiotemporal orchestration of strings of events, which contribute to the adaptive control of simple motor reflexes. Whatever the computations are, it becomes clear that depiction of the cerebellum merely as a motor centre is outdated.

Selected associations: Acquisition, Classical conditioning, Engram, Performance, Skill

---

[1] GABAergic neurons are so called because they release the inhibiting *neurotransmitter γ-aminobutyric acid (GABA). Glycinergic cells release glycine (see *glutamate).

[2] Proposals that the cerebellum is involved in the control of posture and movement surfaced in the literature already in the seventeenth century (Brazier 1984). These proposals were augmented and substantiated in the nineteenth century, and validated after the First World War by reports on the behavioural consequences of cerebellar injuries (e.g. Holmes 1930). Though most current models consider the cerebellum to control movement, there is also the view that it is the inferior olive in the medulla rather than the intrinsic cerebellar circuits that is the pacemaker and spatial organizer of movement (Welsh and Llinas 1997).

[3] For examples of additional experimental systems that are used to investigate cerebellar function and plasticity, see Kitazawa et al. (1998), Thach (1998).

[4] On LTD, see *long-term potentiation, *metaplasticity.

[5] The nictitating membrane is an internal eyelid, a curved plate of cartilage covered with glandular epithelium, which is drawn from the inner canthus laterally across the cornea when a noxious stimulus is applied to the eye. The movement of both external and internal eyelids is controlled by nuclei in the brainstem.

Cerebral cortex

The outer layer of the cerebral hemispheres of the brain.

The cerebral cortex (Latin for bark, rind, shell) is a multilayered, convoluted sheet of tissue overlaying the cerebral hemispheres. In humans it is 3–4 mm thick, covering ~2600 cm^2. It contains at least 10^{10} neurons and about the same number of glia cells. From a phylogenetic perspective, three types of cortices are discerned: archicortex (*hippocampal formation), paleocortex (olfactory, enthorhinal, and peri*amygdaloid cortex), and neocortex. The neocortex forms the bulk of the mammalian cerebral cortex, and is critical for the most advanced mental abilities of our species.[1]

Multiple macroscopic and microscopic *criteria are used in the cartography of the cortex (Jones and Peters 1984–94; White 1989; Mountcastle 1997). First and foremost, the cortex can be described as composed of lobes, the major ones being the frontal, temporal, parietal, and occipital (Figure 10a). The cortex can also be mapped on the basis of function and functional hierarchy (sensory, motor, and 'association cortex'; or primary and higher-order cortex; or unimodal, polymodal, and supramodal cortex[2]). Finer parcellation into areas is based on cellular architectonics. The most popular map, containing 52 areas, was introduced by Brodmann about 100 years ago. The cytoarchitecture of the cortex is usually described in term of laminar and columnar organization. A six-layer classification, I–VI, first introduced by Brodmann, is conventionally used to describe the laminar structure of the neocortical sheet (Figure 10b). Further subdivision of the major layers is added, e.g. VIa–c. Layer I is the one immediately beneath the pia matter, and layer VI the closest to the white matter. The layers contain pyramidal cells, which are the most abundant neurons in the cortex, and various types of nonpyramidal neurons. The arrangement of afferents and efferents in each layer depends on the area and the species, but in general, thalamocortical afferents end predominantly in the middle layers, whereas corticocortical afferents synapse on to neurons in layers I–IV. Several diffused neuromodulatory systems (e.g. *acetylcholine, *dopamine, *noradrenaline) reach the cortex mostly in layers I and VI. In most cases, cortical neurons in layers II–III project to other cortical areas and those in deeper layers project to subcortical structures. The other organizational principle in the cortex is the division into columns. The column, 0.1–0.5 mm wide, is regarded by many authors as the universal organizational and computational unit of the cortex (Mountcastle 1997).[3] Most of the axonal arbour of cortical neurons lies within the cortical column (Douglas et al. 1995). Even in layers that are major recipients of thalamic input, the great majority of the *synapses still mediate information from within the column (Ahmed et al. 1994). Another interesting observation is that about 85% of the synapses of the excitatory neurons synapse on to other excitatory neurons. The computational theory and algorithms (*level) beyond all this gigantic collection of recurrent mini-circuits is still mostly an enigma.

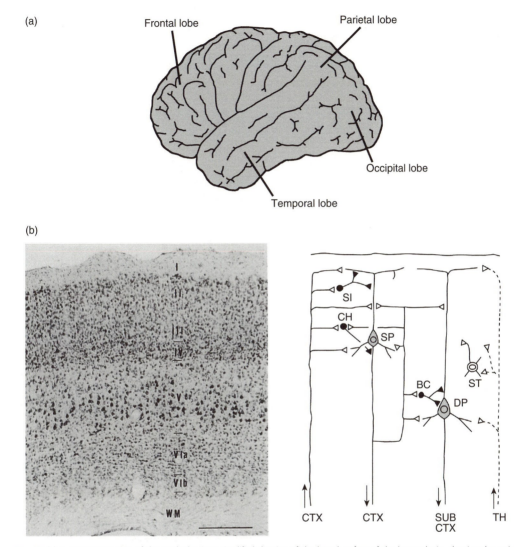

Fig. 10 (a) A macroscopic view of the cerebral cortex: simplified drawing of the lateral surface of the human brain, showing the major cortical lobes. The primary visual cortex is in the occipital lobe, and higher-order visual areas reside in the occipital, temporal, and parietal lobes. The primary and higher-order auditory cortex is in the temporal lobe; primary and higher-order somatosensory areas in the parietal lobe; and primary and higher-order motor cortex in the frontal lobe. The primary taste area is in the insular cortex, which is in the medial wall of the lateral sulcus (groove) that separates the frontal from the temporal lobe, and is invisible on this lateral view, and higher-order taste cortex is in the orbitofrontal cortex. The olfactory (piriform) cortex, on the ventrolateral surface of the brain, which is also invisible in this view, is an ancient part of the cortex (paleocortex). Areas that subserve higher cognitive functions, including *planning, *prospective memory, and *working memory, are in the frontal lobe. (b) A microscopic view of the cortex: *Left*, stained frontal section of the rat primary visual cortex, showing nerve cell bodies in different cortical layers. WM, white matter. (From Peters 1985.) *Right*, simplified diagram of elements of cortical circuits. BC, basket cell; CH, chandelier cell; DP, deep pyramidal neuron; SI, superficial inhibitory neuron; SP, superficial pyramidal neuron; ST, stellate cell. Shown also are major afferent and efferent pathways. CTX, cortex; SUBCTX, subcortical areas; TH, thalamus. Open triangles—excitatory synapses; closed triangles—inhibitory synapses. The great majority of the connections of cortical cells are formed with other cortical cells. (After Shepherd 1988.)

A few *generalizations that emerge from the functional neuroanatomy of the cortex are of potential relevance to memory. First, although different areas of the cortex share the basic design of local circuits, the particular afferent and efferent destinations of discrete cortical areas turn the cortex functionally nonhomogeneous. This differentiation, evident already from the macroscopic functional map of the cortex (Figure 10a), imposes gross limits on the distribution of storage of each item in memory, especially if this item is modality specific, such as a visual scene, tone, or taste. The adult cortex is hence not really equipotential, as was inferred from certain early attempts to search for the *engram. Second, at the same time, long-range connections in the cortex provide it with the potential to subserve rich associativity, potentially permitting the same item in memory to be ultimately accessed and *retrieved via different *cues. And third, the configuration of afferents and efferents of cortical columns fits neatly to subserve processing of target information (thalamic input), *context (diffused systems input, corticocortical connectivity), and *associations (corticocortical connectivity). However, the relevance of this hardware configuration to the computation and encoding of discrete *stimuli, context, and associations, respectively, is yet unclear.

Ample evidence shows that the cortex indeed subserves some types of learning and memory. This evidence is either suggestive, or correlational, or proves necessity, but in no case so far does it prove sufficiency and exclusiveness (*criterion). Sufficiency and exclusiveness, we should remember, are hardly to be expected: the cortex interacts with other brain systems in locating, associating, construing, and assessing information about the world.

1. *The cortex is highly *plastic.* Remarkable morphological and functional plasticity is evident in *development as well as in the adult brain in response to sensory stimuli and injury (e.g. Krech *et al.* 1960; Wiesel 1982; Sadato *et al.* 1996; Buonomano and Merzenich 1998; Crair *et al.* 1998; *map). This plasticity is a candidate vehicle for learning and memory.
2. *The cortex is rich in synaptic components that subserve learning.* These components can be shown to be altered with learning, and further, their disruption in cortex blocks learning, *consolidation, and *experimental extinction of memory (e.g. Berman and Dudai 2001; *coincidence detector; *CREB, *immediate early genes, *glutamate; *long-term potentiation; *protein kinase; *receptor).
3. *Cortical lesions impair learning and memory.* This can be shown by inducing circumscribed lesions in animals or by observing the effect of brain damage in human patients (e.g. Luria 1966; Penfield and Rasmussen 1968; Shallice 1988; Squire and Zola-Morgan 1991; Suzuki *et al.* 1993; Mishkin and Murray 1994; *amnesia, *planning, *working memory).
4. *The activity of specific cortical areas is altered in *acquisition and retrieval of memory.* This can be shown by *functional neuroimaging (e.g. Nyberg *et al.* 1996; Karni *et al.* 1998; Kelley *et al.* 1998; Wagner *et al.* 1998a,b; Wheeler *et al.* 2000).
5. *The activity of cortical neurons correlates with the acquisition and retention of memory.* The activity of nerve cells in unimodal, polymodal, and supramodal cortex in the *monkey and in the *rat was found to be specifically correlated with mnemonic performance in a variety of tasks (e.g. Funahashi *et al.* 1989; Schoenbaum and Eichenbaum 1995; Fuster 1995a,b; Quirk *et al.* 1997; Zhou and Fuster 1997; Erickson and Desimone 1999; Super *et al.* 2001). Two general types of findings are noteworthy (Eichenbaum 1997b): (a) cortical neurons can modulate their response to the target stimulus over the course of learning, and retain the change afterwards, and (b) cortical neurons can sustain or reactivate responses over the task in the absence of the stimulus (Figure 11).

The particular role(s) of the cortex in learning and memory is far from being understood. Such understanding requires, among others, deciphering the neuronal code(s) used by the cortex in registration and reactivation of *internal representations (for a selection of approaches, see Abeles 1991; Gawne and Richmond 1993; Konig *et al.* 1996; Shadlen and Newsome 1994; *cell assembly). In the meantime, it might be useful to think about memory in cortex in the following way: *percepts are formed in modality specific cortex, or in a combination of such cortici, and are registered in collaboration with activity in supramodal cortex and extracortical circuits, such as limbic circuits in the case of *declarative information, striatal circuits in the case of *skill and *habit, and neuromodulatory pathways (*neurotransmitter) in all these cases. Upon consolidation, the representation may become independent of some of the circuits that were obligatory for its encoding and registration (e.g. hippocampus in declarative memory). The representation may also invade new circuits, hence become associated with additional representations. The registered information is ultimately distributed over the relevant unimodal and polymodal cortical areas. Retrieval of the information may require

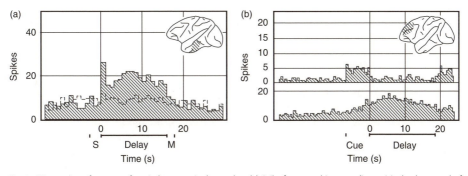

Fig. 11 Mnemonic performance of cortical neurons in the monkey. (a) Spike frequency histogram (i.e. activity level measure) of a unit in the inferotemporal cortex during a delayed matching to sample task (*delay task). The *subject selected one of several colours to match a sample presented before the delay. The unit increased its activity only during the delay if the sample was red (solid line, shaded histogram) but not green (broken line, superimposed on the red response histogram). S, sample, M, match. (After Fuster and Jervey 1982.) (b) Spike frequency histograms of two units in the dorsolateral prefrontal cortex during a visuospatial delayed response task, in which the monkey learned which of two identical wooden blocks covers a baited food well. The upper unit increased firing in the *cue period, during which the monkey observed the baiting and covering of the wells, and in the choice period, following the delay. In contrast, the lower unit increased activity during the delay. (After Fuster 1973.) One interpretation of the data is that the neurons in both cortici (which are depicted in the insets, respectively) retain task-specific information.

activation, co-ordination, and monitoring by the supramodal cortex, particularly the prefrontal cortex. In retrieval, cortical areas that have subserved the acquisition of the information in the first place, may become activated again. This reactivation, however, is unlikely to generate a representation identical to the one at the moment of acquisition. This is because the information has been pruned and associated over time, and, furthermore, is affected by the context of retrieval, which is contributed by exogenous stimuli as well as by the spontaneous, endogenous activity of the cortex at the moment of retrieval. Hence, we may use many *metaphors to describe the cortex, but a hard disk is clearly not a suitable one.

Selected associations: Cell assembly, Conscious awareness, Engram, Functional neuroimaging, Recall

---

[1] For the sake of convenience, 'cortex' will be used throughout this text to refer to the neocortex, or the neocortex and paleocortex (archicortex is discussed separately under *hippocampus). The accurate term is, however, cerebral cortex, as the *cerebellum also has a cortex.

[2] Modal refers to sensory modality. As to the notion of association cortex, it can be traced back to the observation that some cortical areas did not display sensory or motor response in lesion or stimulation experiments. These areas were first called 'silent areas' and later 'association areas' because it was thought that they associate the sensory and motor information. The term association cortex is losing favour, and in any case should not be taken to imply that only these areas perform associations; all cortical areas are probably capable of some or another type of associations.

[3] The concept of cortical column is based on structural and functional observations. Neuroanatomy has shown that columns of nerve cells are discrete structural units. Cellular physiology has shown that vertical aggregates of cortical neurons could be discerned on the basis of their response to a certain *stimulus *dimensions. Columns can also be detected nowadays by *functional neuroimaging (Kim *et al.* 2000). The concept of cortical column appeals to *reductionists because it reinforces the notion that cortical function can be dissected into elementary modules. There are, however, voices who oppose this atomistic approach to cortical function (e.g. Fuster 2000a).

Classic

1. Of acknowledgeable excellence.

2. Serving as a standard or a model.

'Classic' in its classical sense is borrowed from the Romans. '*Classici*' were citizens who possessed a substantial income. The word was used also to refer to the armed forces, and '*classicum*' was the trumpet call signalling the battle. The Latin author Aulus Gellius (second century AD) was probably the first to refer to writers of worth and distinction as classic writers (Saint-Beuve 1850). The French philologist Littre later adapted the term to refer to literary works 'used in the classes of colleges and schools' (Harvey 1937). 'Classical' then became the adjective used when reference was made to the arts and literature of ancient Greece and Rome;

with time it also came to denote formative periods in other segments of *culture, such as Western music in the last half of the eighteenth century, or physics before relativity and quantum mechanics. Strictly speaking, 'classics' are works of letters produced in the 'classical', Greek– Roman period, and 'classic' is a signal work in any discipline and period (Burchfield 1996), but this distinction is not usually honoured in daily language.

What are the *criteria for a 'classic'? High quality is of course a must, but is not enough. The work must also exert a strong impact, either explicit or implicit, on later generations. Hence, it must withstand the test of time. It is therefore good practice to refrain from crowning pieces of work as 'classic', be they as impressive as they are, before they pass the judgement of at least a few scientific generations. A reasonable estimate of a generation time in the neuroscience is 8–10 years; a time window of >30 years seems therefore sufficient to judge the impact of publications on the field. Admittedly, by choosing to label as 'classic' signal works published at least 30 years ago, one surely minimizes the number of enemies among his or her contemporaries. But the latter argument is of course merely a fringe benefit. Not all selections of 'classic' publications in the life sciences follow the test-of-time rule. M.H. Green (1991) compiled 'classic' publications in molecular biology over the period 1958–88, i.e. up to 2–3 years earlier. Peters (1959) covered genetics during the period 1865–1955, i.e. up to 3–4 years earlier. And Shaw et al. (1990), compiled a reprint volume of 82 influential publications in the neurobiology of learning and memory, including papers published only a year or two earlier. The stand taken here is that there is no need to rush.

The method of choosing 'classic' publications in science is another issue. One way is by vox populi, i.e. citations. This is now common in other areas of culture as well, e.g. poetry (Harmon 1998). However, citation indices have their own pitfalls, including the tendency to cite 'trendy spikes' or mundane methods in over-crowded fields. At the end of the day, selection of a short-list of 'classics' in a scientific discipline boils down to a mix of a few unchallenged choices, strong professional *bias, and an unavoidable touch of idiosyncrasy. It does mean, of course, that different people will generate somewhat different lists (e.g. Baddeley 1994). But this only adds to the fun. Having said all that, here is a biased canonic list, limited *a priori to 10 items only, although a few additional ones are actually sneaked-in in the process. This selection unavoidably leaves aside very important publications by very influential authors, including, among others, Pavlov (*classical conditioning), Thorndike (*instrumental conditioning),

Skinner (*behaviourism), and Konorski (*plasticity). Yet the list does not refer to the corpus of authors, but rather to selected, individual papers or books; and in any case, one must make decisions, even if painful. The list is arranged chronologically:

1. St Augustine's philosophy of memory, book 10 in his autobiographical *Confessions* (~ 400). Augustine (354–430), a prominent Christian philosopher (Colish 1997), and a marvellous writer, composed his autobiography in the service of theology. Embedded in it is a gem of introspective psychology. Augustine was not the first in antiquity to write about memory,[1] but his treatise is probably the most readable and surely the most poetic. Those who take the joy of reading Augustine's philosophy of memory, especially chapters 8–19 in book 10, will encounter reference to issues of *taxonomy, *metamemory, *binding, problems of *retrieval and *forgetting, imagery, and more. Augustine is included in this list to remind us that as far as the phenomenology of memory is concerned, although we have perfected it tremendously, we did not invent the wheel.

2. James' *The principles of psychology* (1890). The bible of Western psychology, James' *tour de force* still provides not only an object of intellectual admiration but also a rich source of inspiration. When many later works in psychology are analysed, they appear to contain *palimpsestic fragments that trace back to James. In three studies conducted to establish a consensual list of psychology's great books, polling colleges and professional psychologists, *The principles* received the highest rating (Norcross and Tomcho 1994).

3. *Experimental study of the mental processes of the rat*, by Small (1901). Fans and slaves of *mazes, please note: here it all started, in a small-scale model of the Londonian Hampton Court Labyrinth, copied from the *Encyclopaedia Britannica* (Fig. 46, p.156). This is a perfect example of the importance of matching a *subject with an *assay in the field of memory research. In such matching, ethology could always provide the guide to success: as Small put is, to rodents, maze experiments are 'couched in a familiar language'. Since then, mazes have become the most popular tool to measure the memory of the most popular species of laboratory animals.

4. *Remembering, a study in experimental and social psychology* by Bartlett (1932). This is the epitome of the attempt to understand human memory in real life. Bartlett became disappointed with the investigation of the memory of nonsense material under artificial conditions, a *paradigm introduced by Ebbingahus

(1885) at the birth of quantitative experimental psychology. Instead, he started to use *methods that unveil how the memory of meaningful items works in normal conditions and surroundings. 'Remembering is a function of daily life. So our memories are constantly mingled with our constructions, are perhaps themselves to be treated as constructive in character. It is true that they claim the confirmation of past, perceptual, personal experience; but the claim must not, psychologically speaking, be taken too seriously…' (Bartlett 1932, p. 16). It took almost half a century before this view has started to infiltrate the *zeitgeist of memory research at large (*false memory, *real-life memory, *retrieval). By the way, part I of *Remembering* is a source of inspiration for perceptual and memory experiments to try on family and friends.

5. Hebb's *The organization of behavior* (1949). Another holy scripture of modern neuroscience, and probably the most cited and influential publication on neural *plasticity and memory in the past 50 years. Judging by the trends in the field, it is likely to remain the most cited classic for generations to come. A uniquely coherent conceptual statement, *The organization of behavior* maintains an extensive dialogue with earlier literature (with primary sources as well as the excellent textbook of Hilgard and Marquis, 1940). *The organization of behavior* is mostly cited for two notions: *cell assemblies and their maturation, and, most of all, Hebb's postulate of learning (*algorithm). Hebb was rather astonished to see that this postulate gained so much popularity, as he himself did not consider it as his most original contribution (Milner 1986). Nevertheless, the crispness of the formulation, and its integration in a creative exposition of a theory of brain function, clearly justify the naming of the postulate as 'Hebbian'.

6. *The formation of learning sets*, by Harlow (1949). This is an outstanding example of the ability to extract new *levels of information from a seemingly simple experimental set-up. No big grants were required to make the breakthrough here. Harlow shows how by using discrimination tasks, one could unveil not only the *ad-hoc* *performance of the *subject, but also learn about the ability of that subject to learn how to learn and form rudimentary concepts (*learning set).

7. *The magical number seven, plus or minus two: Some limits on our capacity for processing information*, by Miller (1956). Here is a title that has become a legend. This work is a decedent of earlier attempts to quantify universals of human memory (e.g.

Ebbinghuas 1885; Jacobs 1887). It is anchored in the concepts and measures of information theory, and demonstrates that the brain is an information processing system of limited *capacity. Although Miller's intention was not to determine a precise value, his estimate of short-term memory capacity of seven-plus-or-minus-two chunks became almost a mantra (not without challenges; e.g. Baddeley 1994).

8. *Loss of recent memory after bilateral hippocampal lesions*, by Scoville and Milner (1957). This is the beginning of a major chapter in the research on *amnesia, on the role of medial temporal lobe in *consolidation and memory, and on the *taxonomy of memory. The real hero is the amnesic patient, H.M., unfortunately unaware of his profound continual role in modern neuroscience. The incentive for many studies on human amnesics, primate models of amnesia (*delay task, *monkey), and the role of the *hippocampus in learning, could be traced to Scoville and Milner's report. It is a classic case of a fruitful interaction of the clinic with basic research (Code *et al.* 1996; Corkin *et al.* 1997; Milner *et al.* 1998).

9. *The information available in brief visual presentations*, Sperling (1960). In this condensation of his Ph.D. thesis, a beautiful example of a smart and focused experimental design and execution, Sperling demonstrates the existence of an 'iconic memory' store, or *phase, which lasts for a fraction of a second to a few seconds at most. The giants on the shoulders of which this study is standing are duly accredited in the monograph, something to be longed for in many papers nowadays. Sperling's paper boosted the whole field of 'immediate' or 'sensory' memory (for a perspective 40 years later, see Dosher and Sperling 1998).

10. This place is reserved to three papers, each published by an independent research team. These papers promoted what was later to become a most productive chapter in the molecular biology of learning: investigation of the role of macromolecular synthesis and growth in consolidation and long-term memory. Taken together, the studies of Flexner *et al.* (1963), Agranoff and Klinger (1964), and Barondes and Cohen (1966), have demonstrated that inhibition of protein synthesis during or immediately after training prevents the formation of long-term memory, without affecting short-term memory. These papers complement each other in their experimental details. They have paved the way to decades of research on neuronal proteins, genes, plasticity, and memory. By doing so, they have contributed remarkably to an important ingredient in the current neurobiological

Fig. 12 Authors of some classic classics: Augustine (left, *Confessions*, 400); William James (centre, *The principles of psychology*, 1890); Donald Hebb (right, *The organization of behavior*, 1949; courtesy of Peter Milner).

zeitgeist (*CREB, *development, *immediate-early genes, *late response genes, *protein synthesis). Close contenders for this slot are McGaugh (1966), a well-cited epitome of the view that the *engram is not completed when training is over (*consolidation); and Kandel and Spencer (1968), a manifesto of the *reductionist, cellular approach to learning and a harbinger of the highly successful research program on *Aplysia*.

Naturally, because of the aforementioned self-imposed criterion of a 30-year moratorium on canonization, this list does not refer to many developments that have revolutionized memory research in recent years. It is indeed rather tempting to single out already at this stage some more recent papers, in disciplines ranging from molecular neurobiology to cellular physiology, neuroanatomy, imaging, behaviour, and psychophysics, which are almost certain to withstand the test of time and compete for a respectable seat in the classics pantheon. At the same time, however, it is also tempting to suggest that many of the older papers cited above will retain their status in years to come. In the highly dynamic field of memory research, keeping the classics list short is bound to become only more and more difficult with time.

Selected associations: Bias, Culture, Insight, Paradigm, Persistence

---

[1] Two other notable examples are Aristotle's *On memory*, and Quintillian's *On the education of the orator* (first century AD; *consolidation).

Classical conditioning

1. **Types of *associative learning in which the *subject learns that one *stimulus predicts another.**

2. **Types of training procedures in which two stimuli, the conditioned stimulus (CS) and the unconditioned stimulus (US), are paired with each other, so that the CS comes to evoke a conditioned response (CR), which is similar to the unconditioned response (UR) elicited by the US.**

Pavlov and his dogs are probably the first association that comes to mind in most people when prompted to contemplate experiments on animal learning. Indeed, a century after its formalization (Pavlov 1906), the *paradigm of classical conditioning[1] (alias *Pavlovian conditioning, conditioned reflex type I, respondent conditioning, type S(timulus) conditioning*) is still a cornerstone of learning research. Following the pioneering work of Sechenov (1862), the father figure of Russian physiology, Pavlov (Figure 13) led a systematic attempt to *reduce the study of higher brain function to that of quantifiable atoms of reflexive behaviour. In doing so he relied mainly on gustatory stimuli as the US, gustatory reflexes as the UR, and auditory or visual stimuli as the CS (Pavlov 1927). Since then, Pavlovian conditioning became *classical. In the past three decades, it has accumulated renewed momentum, due to the impressive developments in behavioural, cognitive,

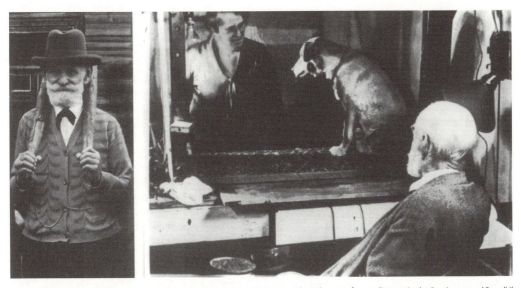

Fig. 13 Pavlov, assistant, dog, and Pavlov. The heavy sticks (left) are thrown at selected targets from a distance in the Russian game 'Gorodki' ('small towns', or 'Russian pyramids'), on which Pavlov was a very proud expert. The dog seems a bit tired of being classically conditioned, but this might merely be an *anthropomorphic interpretation. (Courtesy of K. Anokhin and P. Balaban, Moscow.)

*system, and cellular neuroscience (Holland 1993; Bao *et al.* 1998; Kim *et al.* 1998; Pearce and Bouton 2001).

In classical conditioning, the subject learns relations among stimuli (definition 1). This is different from *instrumental conditioning, in which the subject learns relations among actions and their outcome.[2] The behaviour of the experimenter in classical conditioning (definition 2) is almost as important as the behaviour of the experimental subject: it is the investigator who chooses and manipulates the CS and the US, and selects the CR from the overall behavioural response of the subject.[3] In 'true' classical conditioning, the CR is supposed to be a novel response to the CS, but probably more often than realized, the CR is an intensification of a pre-existing (innate, *a priori) response to the CS. The latter case is termed α-conditioning. If random pairing of the CS and US , or presentation of the CS alone, elicit with time a response similar to the CR, then conditioning is by definition nonassociative. Nonassociative elicitation of a CR to a previously neutral CS is termed *pseudoconditioning*. Nonassociative α-conditioning is *sensitization. In some protocols of classical conditioning, the CS, after coming to elicit a CR, is used as a US in a subsequent phase of conditioning. This is termed *second-order conditioning* (Rescorla 1980); higher-order conditioning can be similarly obtained.

In the first *phases of its investigation, ample attention has been devoted to the role in classical conditioning of the timing and the order of the presentation of the CS and US. This emerged from the observation that, whereas certain conditioning protocols culminate in successful learning, others do not (e.g. Pavlov 1927; Konorski 1948; Mackintosh 1983; Figure 14). An effective protocol is *delay conditioning*, in which the CS is presented first and the US onset precedes the CS offset or coincides with it. *Trace conditioning*, in which the CS starts and ends before the US starts, is also effective, provided that the interstimulus interval is kept sufficiently short (usually in the subsecond to the second range; but see a striking exception in *conditioned taste aversion). *Simultaneous conditioning*, in which the CS and US onset coincide in time, is less effective, unless the CS offset precedes the US offset. *Backward conditioning*, in which the US onset precedes the CS onset, and the US terminates before the CS, is usually ineffective. It can therefore be concluded that order dependency and temporal contiguity are critical factors in ensuring effective conditioning. Contiguity was noted already by Aristotle as important in recollection, and marked as a condition for association in early associative psychology in the seventeenth and eighteenth century (Warren 1921; *associative learning). Classical conditioning permitted, however, for the first time, a systematic, experimental analysis of the temporal parameters involved, in a variety of species. Reductionist analysis has ultimately chased *coincidence

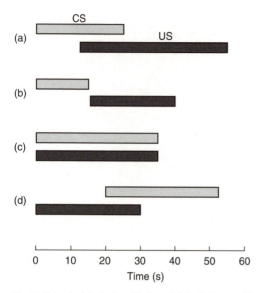

Fig. 14 Protocols of classical conditioning and their effectiveness. (a) Delay conditioning, which is usually successful. (b) Trace conditioning, which is usually successful provided the interval between the offset of the CS and the onset of the US is kept sufficiently short (but see *conditioned taste aversion for a striking exception). (c) Simultaneous conditioning, which is not an effective procedure. (d) Backward conditioning, which is usually unsuccessful.

detectors, that could implement contiguity, down to the molecular *level (Dudai 1985; Abrams and Kandel 1988; Bourne and Nicoll 1993).

As much as order dependency and temporal contiguity are important, more sophisticated conditioning protocols have demonstrated that temporal contiguity *per se* is insufficient, and the emphasis shifted to the role of contingency (Rescorla 1968, 1988; Mackintosh 1983; Wasserman and Miller 1997). Contingency in this context means comparison of the probability of the occurrence of the US in the presence of the CS as contrasted with the probability of the occurrence of the US in the absence of the CS; conditioning is assumed to occur only when the aforesaid probabilities differ (Rescorla 1968, 1988). Still, contingency *per se* may also not suffice to account for all the facets of conditioning (Mackintosh 1983; Rescorla 1988; Papini and Bitterman 1990; Wasserman and Miller 1997). So far, in spite of a number of sophisticated theories of associations, there is no accepted unified theory covering all manifestations and properties of classical conditioning (Pearce and Bouton 2001). There might never be, because classical conditioning encompasses multiple training protocols, behavioural phenomena, neuronal

circuits and possibly mechanisms (*algorithm). Compare, for example, trace conditioning to delay conditioning (Figure 14); whereas in delay conditioning the CS and US overlap on-line part of the time, in trace conditioning, the subject must hold off-line information about the CS before the US onset. Therefore, trace conditioning is expected to engage brain regions that are not required for conditioning that depends on on-line information only. This was indeed found (Moyer *et al.* 1990; Clark and Squire 1998; *conscious awareness, *declarative learning). This also raises the question whether classical conditioning should be considered as a distinct type of memory system, specifically, a nondeclarative memory system, as is advocated by the current *zeitgeist (*taxonomy).

Classical conditioning is considered by the majority of scholars in the field to involve reconstruction of knowledge about stimuli, their relationships, and their predictability (Dickinson 1980; Holland 1993; Wasserman and Miller 1997; Pearce and Bouton 2001). A major impetus to this 'cognitive revolution' in the portrayal of classical conditioning was contributed by the study of a rich set of phenomena, which show that the ability of a stimulus to enter into association and control behaviour is altered markedly by the history of the subject with this or other stimuli either before, during, or after training. Many of these stimulus–revaluation phenomena could be construed as reflecting interaction of the *internal representations of the stimuli involved. Here are selected examples (for additional ones, see *cue):[4]

1. In *sensory pre-conditioning*, two practically 'neutral' sensory stimuli, CS_i and CS_j, are repeatedly presented together, followed by the conditioning of CS_i to a particular response. Sensory pre-conditioning is said to have occurred if CS_j also evokes the response on a test trial (Brogden 1939; Kimmel 1977). Sensory pre-conditioning was demonstrated first in Pavlov's laboratory. It provides a demonstration that associations can take place among stimuli in the absence of an overt response.

2. In *conditioned inhibition*, a CS- that is conditioned to predict the absence of the US, later inhibits the development of the CR to a composed CS-+CS+ stimulus (Pavlov 1927; Zimmer-Hart and Rescorla 1974). This is construed to imply that the subject anticipates no US in the presence of the CS-, and must overcome this anticipation to form the association of the compound stimulus with the US.

3. Uncorrelated presentation of the CS and US is used as a control for classical conditioning (Rescorla

1967). It also retards, however, subsequent associative conditioning of the same CS–US pair (Kremer 1971). This phenomenon came to be known as *learned irrelevance* (Mackintosh 1973; Baker 1976).

4. *Latent inhibition* (Lubow and Moore 1959; Lubow 1989) is attenuation of the associability of the CS as a result of its non*reinforced pre-exposure. For example, in conditioned taste aversion, if instead of pairing an unfamiliar taste with malaise, one pre-exposes the subject briefly to that taste a few days before training, the aversion developed after pairing with the US is significantly weaker (e.g. Rosenblum *et al.* 1997). Several explanations have been proposed to account for latent inhibition. Some of these suggest that pre-exposure reduces subsequent *attention to the CS (Lubow 1989); others propose that the formation of a CS–context association during pre-exposure interferes either with subsequent acquisition of the new CS–US association, or with its expression (e.g. Grahame *et al.* 1994).

5. *Pre-conditioning* exposure *to the US* could also retard the formation of a CR (Randich and LoLordo 1979). The explanations invoke *habituation, or alternatively, again, the formation of stimulus–context associations, which later compete with the formation of new CS–US association (e.g. Cole *et al.* 1996), or with its expression (Miller *et al.* 1993).

6. Responding to a CS is also sensitive to post-training alterations in the ability of the US to control behaviour (Rescorla 1973; Holland and Straub 1979). This is termed *US devaluation*. It is construed to imply that the internal representation of the CS gains access to adjustment in the value of the US at the time of *performance.

7. And, last but not least on our brief tour of the *surprising world of conditioning phenomena: a CS may also come to modulate the response of the conditioned subject even independently of its direct association with the US, in which case this CS is said to 'set the occasion' for responding to another CS. *Occasion setting* was first described by Skinner (1938) in the context of instrumental conditioning. He noted that animals can use a discriminative cue, which has been present upon the occasion of a previous reinforcement, to decide whether to emit the conditioned response or not; the cue itself, however, did not elicit the response. Occasion setting was subsequently investigated mostly in classical conditioning (Holland 1992). It is argued that occasion setting is easier to fit into 'configural theories' of conditioning (Pearce and Bouton 2001; on what configural theories are see footnote 3).

All in all, the picture that emerges is hence of the *performance of classically conditioned behaviour as the surface structure, and the dynamic interaction of internal representations of stimuli and of the probability of their co-occurrence as the deep structure.

Selected associations: Associative learning, Cerebellum, Coincidence detector, Instrumental conditioning, Taxonomy

---

[1]Definition 3 in *paradigm.

[2]The truth is that the subject in instrumental conditioning learns other types of relations as well; see there.

[3]In *real-life, the CS rarely appears in isolation (*context). A single-stimulus CS is called 'elemental', and the conditioning protocol 'elemental conditioning'. Otherwise, the CS is 'composite' or 'compound'. Theories of conditioning debate whether elements of composite stimuli associate with the US independently ('elemental theories') or as a unitary *internal representation ('configural theories'; Pearce and Bouton 2001). But this issue already relates to the knowledge acquired in classical conditioning, which is further referred to in the text.

[4]Most of these revaluation phenomena could be demonstrated, employed as research tools, and used to infer knowledge structures in instrumental conditioning as well.

Clever Hans

A horse in Berlin at the beginning of the twentieth century, claimed to have mastered human language and arithmetic.

Hans was purchased by a retired German schoolteacher, Wilhelm von Osten, in 1900 with the aim of reproducing the remarkable behaviour originally noted by von Osten in an earlier Hans. Soon the feats of Hans II overshadowed those of his predecessor, endowed him with the respectable title 'Clever Hans' (Pfungst 1911), and earned him an honourable position in the history of experimental psychology.

Surely Clever Hans was not the first animal to which human-like mental capabilities have been attributed. Neither was he the first horse to gain eternal fame. Nineteen centuries earlier, the Roman Emperor Caligula invited his beloved Incitatus to banquets and may had even announced his intention to appoint the horse to a Consul, probably in a lurch of doubtful Imperial humour (Barrett 1990). Throughout history individuals of many other species have been regarded as possessing some degree or another of human reason, although they did not attend such a high respect in government. This *anthropomorphism was not always taken in the animals' favour, and in some cases even led them to the gallows (Evans 1906). Clever Hans was, however, different in that he was treated seriously by respected professors, and the investigation of his alleged wit unveiled and singled out some basic issues in behavioural research, which are highly relevant to memory research to date.

Hans was clearly clever, however, in his own equine way. Mr von Osten trained Hans to provide answers to a plethora of questions by either tapping with its front hoof or pointing its snout to symbols on a board. Hans could apparently do arithmetic, including fractions, categorize objects, and even read German (e.g. in response to the question 'What is the woman holding in her hand', he would gallantly reply, letter by letter, 'Schrimm', i.e. parasol). His wisdom was so impressive that a scientific commission was called to exclude any deceit, and indeed, in 1904, the committee declared confidentially that von Osten used no tricks. But the rest remained a puzzle even to the high ranking academics: 'This is a case', they wrote, 'which appears in

principle to differ from any hitherto discovered' (cited in Rosenthal 1965). The *enigma led to a signal research programme, executed by Oskar Pfungst in collaboration with Carl Stumpf (Pfungst 1911), which finally shed light on the Clever Hand phenomenon, although leaving some issues unresolved (Hediger 1981). Briefly, Pfungst showed that Hans learned to respond to subtle human bodily movements, unleashed unintentionally when the horse came to a correct answer. The horse came out rather stupid unless someone he could watch had the answers. Hans clearly knew nothing about math, logic, or the German language, yet knew a great deal about human gestures. Pfungst even stepped further and became himself a 'Clever Hans' in a *control experiment, only to find out that with proper attention, he could come up with correct answers to questions merely by observing the experimenter in front of him.

The Clever Hans phenomenon turned attention to critical issues in experimental psychology. These include: (a) the importance of a systematic research *methodology, including appropriate controls, as well as 'blind tests' in which the experimenter could not know the relevant history of the experimental *subject

Fig. 15 Clever Hans, Clever von Osten, and blackboards in an equine classroom. The horse learned to respond to subtle human gestures.

and the expected outcome; (b) the effect of 'demand characteristics', i.e. unintentionally influencing the performance of an experimental subject by expecting a certain outcome (Orne 1962; *bias); (c) the importance of *Ockham's razor, i.e. preferring a simple explanation to a more complex one; (d) the subtlety of innate and acquired communication abilities of animals (e.g. Sebeok and Rosenthal 1981; *a priori); (e) the need to become well versed in the natural behavioural repertoire of animal subjects; (f) the pitfalls of anthropomorphism; (g) the lack of correlation between one's academic title to success in animal training (Hediger 1981); and finally, last but not least (h) the absence of correlation between the academic statue of members of a site visit team to the robustness of their conclusions.

During the early days of experimental psychology Clever Hans occupied a key position in textbooks (Watson 1914), but then dwindled into footnotes (though see Sebeok and Rosenthal 1981). The lesson should, however, be refreshed, as if forgotten, a mouse in a *maze might be deemed smarter than it is, or at least for the wrong reasons. With time, horses ceased to be favourable subjects for learning research, yet not utterly forgotten (e.g. Heird et al. 1981; Houpt et al. 1990).

Selected associations: Anthropomorphism, Artefact, Control, Subject

Coincidence detector

1. A device that responds only on receiving two signals simultaneously.
2. A device that responds only on receiving a complete set of two or more signals.

Many brain faculties depend on the ability to detect and encode associations and correlations among events. Coincidence detectors are essential for this ability. The most straightforward type of coincidence detector senses the occurrence of two events at the same time (definition 1). However, what is meant by 'at the same time' depends on the scientific discipline and on the *level of analysis. Simultaneity in particle physics has a different meaning than in physiology and psychology. Hence, although an ideal coincidence detector responds only when the time difference between events is $t=0$, in practice, a response is emitted to $t=0\pm\Delta t$. It is safe to say that in the context of neuroscience, two events can be said to occur 'at the same time' if that time is

in the order of magnitude of milliseconds (less then a millisecond to a few milliseconds in synaptic events, e.g. Markram et al. 1997; <100 ms in perception and cognition, e.g. Thorpe et al. 1996; van Turennout et al. 1998; *percept). Note that if $\Delta t>0$, the order of events may also make a difference, i.e. whether i arrives before j or vice versa (see *classical conditioning and below). Another type of coincidence detector generates the desired output only after receiving two or more *stimuli in a number of steps within a defined, commonly short time window ('graded coincidence detector'; definition 2). Still another type of integrating device, which is also sometimes referred to as a 'coincidence detector', is characterized by more relaxed temporal constraints, and in this case 'coincidence' refers to occurrence at the same place rather than at the same time (definition 2). An additional point that requires clarification is what is meant by 'device'. In the context of the present discussion, a device is either a macromolecule, a *synapse, a nerve cell, or a neuronal circuit.

The majority of experimental evidence for the involvement of identified coincidence detectors in learning and memory, relates to the molecular and synaptic level. An example is provided by the enzyme *calcium/calmodulin-sensitive adenylyl cyclase, that generates the second messenger cyclic adenosine monophosphate (cAMP; *intracellular signal transduction cascades, *CREB). In the circuit that subserves the conditioning of defensive reflexes in *Aplysia, a modulatory *neurotransmitter is assumed to encode the unconditioned stimulus (US), and calcium the conditioned stimulus (CS). Both activate adenylyl cyclase, culminating in intracellular cascades that subserve memory of the modified reflex (see also *Drosophila, *immediate early genes). Interestingly, the activation of the cyclase was reported to be larger when the calcium pulse immediately preceded the transmitter (Yovell and Abrams 1992). This led to the proposal that temporal asymmetry in the activation of the cyclase underlies temporal asymmetry of the CS–US pairing in the behaving organism (ibid., also Abrams and Kandel 1988, and *classical conditioning).

Another molecular coincidence detector with a proposed role in *plasticity and learning is the *glutamatergic N-methyl-D-aspartate (NMDA) *receptor (NMDAR; Seeburg et al. 1995). Here, the receptor-*channel complex detects coincidence of presynaptic activity (glutamate, which activates the receptor) and postsynaptic electrical activity (depolarization, which removes a magnesium block from the channel, Figure 16). Convergence in this case is permitted within tens to hundreds of milliseconds. Furthermore, at least

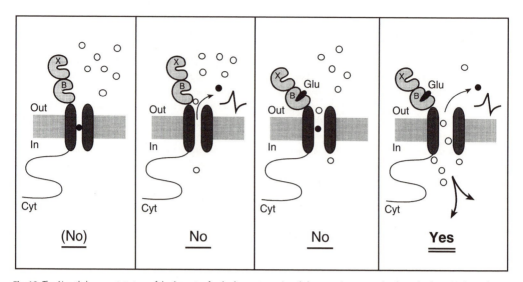

Fig. 16 The *N*-methyl-D-aspartate-type of the *receptor for the *neurotransmitter *glutamate is an example of a molecular coincidence detector that takes part in cellular *plasticity mechanisms, such as *long-term potentiation, which are assumed to subserve learning and memory. In the resting state (left panel in this highly simplified scheme), the extracellular (Out) binding site (B) for glutamate (Glu) is vacant and the *ion channel, which can permit influx of *calcium (o) into the neuron, is blocked by magnesium (●). Electrical activity that results in post*synaptic depolarization can relieve the magnesium block, but this by itself is not sufficient to allow a significant calcium influx. Occupation of the glutamate binding site by the transmitter is also insufficient to open the channel. Only coincident activity of glutamate and depolarization (right panel) leads to calcium influx (heavy arrows, Yes), which may culminate in plastic changes in the neuron. Cyt, cytoskeleton, with which the intracellular (In) portion of the receptor interacts; X, binding sites for other molecular *stimuli.

one additional type of input, glycine, and possibly more, are required for optimal activation. The relevance of the coincidence detection properties of NMDAR to identified behaviours has not yet been determined. Other macromolecules have been shown to function as coincidence detectors (Bourne and Nicoll 1993; Caroll *et al.* 1995). Notable among them are transcriptional regulation elements, including transcription factors and promoters (Impey *et al.* 1994; Janknecht *et al.* 1995; Deisseroth *et al.* 1996; *CREB, *immediate early genes, *protein synthesis). Some cellular scaffold proteins (e.g. such that mediate *protein kinase activation; Whitmarsh *et al.* 1998) can also be considered as signal integrators (definition 2). Two major conclusions can be drawn from the data. First, coincidence detectors exist at multiple tiers of intracellular signal transduction cascades, from the membrane downstream to the cell nucleus, hence yielding many permutations in the interaction of stimuli and as a consequence, high response specificity. Second, 'coincidence' should be considered as an intracellular representational code, which is embodied in intracellular molecular networks (*reduction).

Coincidence detection has been described in several circuits that process and encode sensory information (Sullivan and Konishi 1986; Hopfield 1995; Edwards *et al.* 1998), although the relevance of these findings at the circuit level to learning and memory, if at all, has not yet been determined. One of the best known examples is coincidence detection in the circuit that encodes interaural phase differences in the brainstem of birds and mammals, and permits very precise localization of sounds. In this system, coincidence detection combines with the use of neuronal delay lines, which carry the auditory information from each ear separately, to convert a code that is based on the time of arrival of neuronal firing from the ear ('time code') into a code that is based on the location of the firing neurons in the brain ('place code'; Sullivan and Konishi 1986; also Agmon-Snir *et al.* 1998; *map). In general, discussion of coincidence detection at the circuit level relates to two classes of issues: on the one hand, the spontaneous and the evoked responses of the neurons in the circuit; on the other, the putative *representational codes used by the circuit (de No 1938; Hebb 1949; von der Malsburg 1987; Abeles 1991; Hopfield 1995; Konig *et al.* 1996; Dan *et al.* 1998). The neurons in the circuit integrate incoming synaptic potentials before they fire a 'spike'. The kinetics of this integration is a parameter that determines whether the neuron can serve only as an integrator (definition 2) or also as a *bona fide* temporal coincidence detector (definition 1). Only if the integration time interval is shorter than the inter-spike time interval, can the neuron act as a coincidence detector for the incoming spikes. The synchronized information, which is then relayed to other neurons, might encode the coherency of a sensory *percept or a mental concept (Konig *et al.* 1996).

All in all, it is difficult to envisage how without the evolution of coincidence detectors, be they molecules, neurons, or circuits, our brain would have had the capability to detect correlations and causal relations in the external world, and *bind together meaningful narratives in the internal world.

Selected associations: Algorithm, Cell assembly, Internal representation, Intracellular signal transduction cascade

Collective memory

A set of historical narratives, beliefs, and customs shared by a social group over generations.

When the 'star of England', Henry V, set out to boost the spirit of his few troops before the battle of Agincourt, he recruited future history (Shakespeare 1600):

> Harry the king, Bedford and Exeter,
> Warwick and Talbot, Salisbury and Gloucester,
> Be in their flowing cups freshly remember'd
> This story shall the good man teach his son;
> And Crispin Crispian shall ne'er go by,
> From this day to the ending of the world,
> But we in it shall be remembered;
> We few, we happy few, we band of brothers;

And as the outcome of that battle attests to, the urge to enter the collective memory of a nation is at times stronger than the fear of death.

Discussion of collective memory is at the interface of psychology, sociology, and history (Halbwachs 1925; Pennebaker and Banasik 1997). Collective memory is unique among the types of memory covered in this book because it is not confined to an individual nervous system. Rather, at any given moment in time it is encoded in a distributed *system of individual brains in the relevant social group, as well as in elements of the

contemporary *culture of that group (Bartlett 1932; Wertsch 1985; d'Andrade 1995; *context, *real-life memory). Thus, although portions of the collective memory can be encoded in individual brains, as a whole, both the formation and the retention of this type of memory is an emergent property of the group (*reduction). Collective memory is a primitive of human societies (d'Azevedo 1962).[1] Together with other ingredients of culture, it permits nongenetic information to transcend the limited lifespan of individuals.

The term 'collective memory' actually refers to three entities: a *body of knowledge*, an *attribute*, and a *process*. The *body of knowledge* is a cardinal element of culture. It is characteristic of the given social group, yet changes over time (*plasticity). The *attribute* is the distinctive holistic image of the past in the group, an image which itself may be used as a definer of the group. The *process* is a constant dialogue between individuals and their social group. By selecting ongoing information that is relevant to the group, filtering it, retaining it, and dispersing it in society, each individual could potentially alter the collective memory of the group. This in turn could affect the subsequent acquisition and use of memory in the individual, which could further affect the memory and behaviour of the group, and so forth. In other words, individuals could contribute over time to the collective memory of the group(s) to which they belong, but collective memory at any given point in time could also affect the perception and the memory in the brain of the individual members of the group. By virtue of their social affiliations and beliefs, individuals belong simultaneously to multiple groups centred on family, friends, age group, profession, hobby, politics, religion, and nation. Therefore, individual brains subserve the encoding of multiple systems of collective memory, some of which could be conflicting or even contradictory. The conflict may result in psychological and social tension.

In spite of the fact that collective memory is not a property of the individual, it is tempting to compare it with memory in individual brains. Only a few heuristic analogies will be noted here. Similarly to a popular *taxonomy of human memory, over the years collective memory has been portrayed as being composed of explicit and implicit systems. 'Collective consciousness', a term used by Durkheim (1895) in defining 'social facts' (i.e. the subject matter of sociology), refers to the emergence in a society of collective knowledge, attitudes, values, and behaviour, and is mostly an explicit memory system. Jung (1969) put forward the idea that humans also have a 'collective unconscious', deep strata of the psyche harbouring universal primordial memories or images ('archetypes'; see also Ellenberger 1970). This is an implicit memory system, which, according to Jung, can be studied through myths. In a scientific context, the Jungian account of collective unconscious is vague (and see Bartlett 1932); but one does not have to be a Jungian in order to assume a body of implicit universals of human mental faculties, which has been built into the human brain in the course of its long evolution (*a priori) and mould societal function. Other analogies between individual and collective memory can be proposed. Similarly to other types of memory, *retrieval of collective memory involves reconstruction (Halbwachs 1925), in which the representation of the original event is adapted to the context of recollection (e.g. Schwartz et al. 1986). And similarly to individual real-life memory, one encounters *false collective memory and possibly also *flashbulb collective memory (Schudson 1995; Baumeister and Hastings 1997).

Only little is known on the actual mechanisms of *acquisition, *consolidation, *extinction, and *forgetting of collective memory. Retention is less of a mystery: as noted above, the collective *engram is distributed in the brains of individuals with overlapping lifespan that transmit the information from one generation to another, as well as in artefacts of culture. Adolescence and early adulthood appear to comprise a 'sensitive period' for the acquisition and the consolidation of the collective memory (Schuman and Scott 1989; *development, *imprinting). In a world whose public and government opinion is dominated by massive media coverage of events in real-time, the kinetics of acquisition and extinction of collective memory is probably faster than it has ever been (Lynch 1996; Cox 2000).

The encoding and stability of collective memory are of extreme importance to issues of national and international policy, social policy, economy, war, and peace. Sectarian and national myths are still major powers on the national and international arenas. But not only there. Collective memory has a role in selecting and constructing our attitude toward nature and science as well (Midgley 1992; Eder 1996). One of the toughest challenges facing a scientist is to identify potential *bias in the approach to a problem or in the interpretation of data due to collective predispositions.

Selected associations: Bias, Culture, Observational learning, Paradigm, Zeitgeist

---

[1]An intriguing question is whether nonhuman social species, such as *monkeys, have rudimentary forms of collective memory, as opposed to other manifestations of culture (Bonner 1980).

Conditioned taste aversion

A learned association of taste with visceral distress.

Farmers know, probably from the dawn of farming, that animals tend to avoid poisonous bait if they survive their first encounter with it. The farmers themselves may have probably noticed that foodstuff comes to evoke disgust if consuming it results in nausea and intestinal distress. However, common knowledge does not always penetrate academic barriers: it has taken John Garcia and his colleagues several distressful years to convince the referees of respectable scientific journals that conditioned taste aversion (CTA) does occur (Garcia 1981). This almost became a case of CSA (conditioned submission aversion).

Also dubbed the Garcia Effect, Bait Shyness, or the Béarnaise Sauce Effect (many a reader can probably offer idiosyncratic terms based on unpleasant personal experience), CTA does differ in a critical parameter from other *associative learning *paradigms. This parameter is the interstimulus interval (ISI), i.e. the time interval between the conditioned (CS) and the unconditioned (US) *stimuli. Whereas in *classical and *instrumental conditioning an ISI of more than seconds commonly renders training ineffective, CTA training tolerates an ISI of several hours. It is this deviation from the widely accepted paradigm, namely that two stimuli must come close together in time in order to become associated in mind, that has led respectable psychologists to doubt the early scientific accounts of CTA.

The first systematic studies of CTA were reported by Rzoska (1953) and by Garcia et al. (1955). Both conducted their experiments on the *rat. Rzoska investigated the effect of poisoned bait on the subsequent rejection of the same bait; Garcia noticed that the association of a saccharin solution with exposure to γ-irradiation, which induces malaise, suppresses subsequent consumption of saccharin. He later produced CTA by associating the saccharin with the delayed injection of malaise-inducing compounds (Garcia et al. 1966). Saccharin is used to this day as a standard CS in CTA experiments. Many other tastes can be used as well; they are most effective if unfamiliar to the *subject at the time of conditioning (Revusky and Bedarf 1967). The US could also vary, from rotation and irradiation to drugs and poisons. A standard US is an intraperitoneal (i.p.) injection of a LiCl solution, which produces transient visceral distress within a few minutes of injection. In a commonly used protocol, the rat (or mouse) is made slightly thirsty, and then given to drink the diluted taste solution for 10–20 min. This is followed after 1–3 h by the US. A few days later, the *subject is tested for taste avoidance, either by presenting it with the CS only (single-bottle test), or by permitting it to choose between the CS and another 'innocent' tastant (multiple-bottle test).

On the one hand, the ISI in CTA can extend up to 6–8 h, but, on the other, it cannot be made too short: 10 s only is ineffective (Schafe *et al.* 1995). It seems that the brain has an *a priori tendency to distinguish ingestion-induced malaise, which requires at least several minutes to develop, from other types of negative *reinforcers. Similarly, stimuli that act on non-visceral receptors and have less intimate association with food, such as tones, visual *cues, or cutaneous pain, although very effective in classical and instrumental conditioning, are ineffective in CTA (Garcia *et al.* 1968). Odours can be used as CS in long delay conditioning (Slotnick *et al.* 1997), but are less effective, and work best when associated with taste ('taste potentiated odour aversion', TPOA; Rusiniak *et al.* 1979).

CTA offers significant advantages for the investigation of the phenomena and mechanisms of simple associative learning. The single-trial *acquisition facilitates the correlation of neuronal events with learning, and targeted interventions in the process by drugs or other treatments (*criterion, *method). The CTA protocol is highly reproducible and the resulting memory is long lasting, which permits analysis of multiple memory phases. The extended ISI enables the dissociation of the CS acquisition from the CS–US association. And since rodents are involved, a multi*level analysis of learning and memory, from the behaviour to the molecules and back, is feasible. CTA has therefore become a popular *assay and *paradigm in memory research. Whereas the behavioural parameters of CTA have been described in detail (Bures *et al.* 1988, 1998), less is known about the brain circuits that subserve this behaviour. It is generally accepted that the gustatory area in the insular *cortex plays a part in processing the detection of taste unfamiliarity and in encoding the taste *representation; the parabrachial nucleus is involved in the association of the taste with the malaise; and the *amygdala subserves the hedonic assessment of the taste, as well as the integration and expression of CTA (Figure 17)

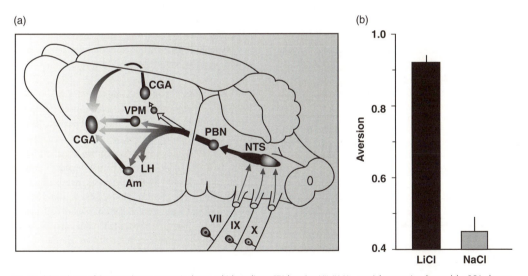

Fig. 17 (a) A scheme of the central taste system in the rat, which mediates CTA learning. VII, IX, X—cranial nerves; Am, *amygdala; CGA, the central gustatory area in the insular *cortex; LH, lateral hypothalamus; NTS, the nucleus of the solitary tract in the brainstem; PBN, the parabrachial nucleus in the pons; VPM, the ventroposteriomedial nucleus of the thalamus, which contains the thalamic taste area(s). The CGA is involved in detection of taste familiarity and in the taste memory; the amygdala in encoding the hedonic valence of the taste and in the acquisition and performance of CTA; and the PBN particularly in the association of the CS with US in CTA. (b) Rats injected i.p. with LiCl an hour after consuming an unfamiliar solution of saccharin display high aversion toward saccharin when tested 3 days later. The test involves a choice between saccharin and water; 0.5 means equal preference, and a low score means preference of saccharin. It can be seen that rats injected in training with NaCl, which does not induce malaise (*control), come to prefer the saccharin to water.

(Yamamoto *et al.* 1994; Bures *et al.* 1998; Lamprecht and Dudai 2000).

It is unlikely that the tolerance of CTA training to long ISI stems from unique types of molecular *coincidence detectors in the central taste circuit. Information gathered so far indicates that the molecular mechanisms that subserve CTA are similar to those that subserve other forms of learning, such as the activation of *glutamate and *acetylcholine receptors and the modulation of *immediate early gene expression (Lamprecht *et al.* 1997; Rosenblum *et al.* 1997; Berman *et al.* 1998, 2000; Gutierrez *et al.* 1999). Probably, the tolerance to long delays results from special circuit properties, shaped in evolution to ensure 'prepared learning' (*a priori) of the avoidance of food toxins (e.g. Shipley and Sanders 1982). An appealing hypothesis is that sampling a taste, especially an unfamiliar one, creates an 'active' (*taxonomy), short-term memory trace in the gustatory cortex, and possibly in some other stations in the central taste pathway (Figure 17). This memory of the CS lasts for only a few hours and is accessed by stations in the central taste circuit that can also detect malaise. Candidate mechanisms that could encode this type of memory are the *persistent phosphorylation of synaptic proteins (Rosenblum *et al.* 1997; *protein kinase), local *protein synthesis, and other types of tagging of the active synapses (Frey and Morris 1997; *consolidation). If malaise is sensed while the short-term taste memory is still active, the CS and the US information converge, probably in the parabrachial nucleus and possibly also in the amygdala. This in turn triggers the cellular mechanisms that register the long-lasting taste-malaise association.

Selected associations: A Priori, Associative learning, Classical conditioning, Paradigm, Surprise

Confabulation

1. The making up of narratives and details, or the filling in of gaps in memory.
2. Falsification of memory in the absence of deceitfulness occurring in clear *consciousness in association with *amnesia.

In Latin *confābulāri* is 'to chat', *fābula*—'a tale', and *fābulae!*—'nonsense'. The confabulator indeed tells a story, but this story is not complete nonsense. In many cases it is more or less coherent and internally consistent, yet false in the *context named (Talland 1965; Moscovitch 1989). Typically, the account concerns the person who tells it, who is unaware of its memory deficit.

Confabulation in its broader meaning (definition 1) refers to a wide spectrum of phenomena. Some of these phenomena are within the normal range of the human behavioural repertoire. Minor, innocent confabulations may pop-up occasionally in some individuals in stressful social situations; they could be considered a sort of defence mechanism.[1] Creative confabulations could contribute to mythology, literature, and the fine arts, as noted, for example, by Hobbes (1651):

> Much memory, or memory of many things, is called *experience*. Againe, Imagination being only of those things which have been formerly perceived by Sense … the imaging of the whole object, as it was presented to the senses is *simple Imagination*; as when one imagineth a man, or horse, which he hath seen before. The other is *compounded*; as when from the sight of a man at one time, and of a horse at another, we conceive in our mind a Centaure. So when a man compoundeth the image of his own person, with the image of the actions of an other man; as when a man imagins himself a Hercules, or an Alexander (which happeneth often to then that are much taken with reading of Romants) it is compound imagination, and properly but a Fiction of the mind.

Only pathological confabulations are of interest to us here. More specifically, only selected aspects of pathological confabulations. Hence antisocial personality disorder, which is expressed among others in deceitfulness (DSM-IV 1994), is not of our concern here; neither is Munchausen's syndrome, a psychiatric disorder in which an otherwise healthy individual seeks invasive medical treatment for feigned or self-induced symptoms (Ahser 1951).[2] Left out is also confabulation in states of delirium and dense *dementia. To the student of memory, the most intriguing is confabulation in clear consciousness, which is adjunct to amnesia (definition 2). It fits the oxymoron 'honest lying'. Two types of confabulations are discerned in this case (Berlyne 1972; Kopelman 1987; Schnider *et al.* 1996a). One is 'momentary' or 'provoked'; the other is 'fantastic' or 'spontaneous'.[3]

Momentary or provoked confabulation is so called because it is fleeting and provoked by questions probing the *subject's memory. It is seen in amnesics, as well as in demented patients in the early stages of their

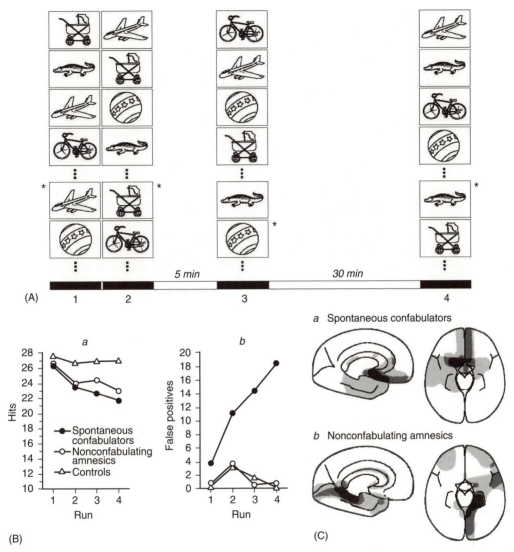

Fig. 18 A laboratory test that confabulators fail. Schnider and Ptak (1999) subjected spontaneous confabulators, nonconfabulating amnesics, and nonamnesic *controls, to a continuous *recognition task. In each run of the task, 80 pictures were presented one after the other on a computer screen for 2 s each (A). Some of the items recurred (targets, marked by asterisk, total 28 in each run), whereas the other items did not recur (distractors, total 52 in each run). The subjects were requested to indicate item recurrence. Immediately after the completion of the first run, a second run was made, with a different selection of targets and distractors. At the beginning of the second run the subjects were asked to ignore the first run and indicate item recurrence only within the second run. Similarly, 5 min after the second run, the third run was made, and 30 min after the third run, the fourth run was made. As expected, spontaneous confabulators and nonconfabulating amnesics did not fare well on target detection (Ba); but most striking was the steep increase of false positive identification by the spontaneous confabulators (Bb). The experiment was replicated with nonsense instead of meaningful pictures (not shown), with similar results. These data were construed to indicate that the confabulators fail to suppress currently irrelevant memory traces. (C). The overlapping lesions in the brain of the spontaneous confabulators (a) and the noncofabulating amnesics (b). The basal forebrain and the medial orbitofrontal cortex were damaged in confabulators but not in nonconfabulating amnesics; in the latter, the lesions covered the posterior mediotemporal lobe and the dorsolateral prefrontal cortex. (Adapted from Schnider and Ptak 1999.)

cognitive deterioration. For example, a subject asked to recognize a picture of the British Royal couple, might reply that they are celebrated movie stars, and go on fabricating details about the last movie in which they allegedly starred. This confabulation is momentary, does not significantly affect the subject's behaviour, and can be understood in terms of compensation for the deficient recollection; some nonamnesics and nondemented occasionally do just this, if weakness of character prevents them from simply admitting that they do not remember. In contrast, fantastic or spontaneous confabulation is unprompted, sustained, refers to wide-ranging narratives, may contain elements of grandiose, and has a persistent effect on the subject's behaviour. Spontaneous confabulation is not always fantastic. It could include sensible reminiscences that are out of their spatiotemporal context. Consider, for example, the patient who suffered from brain haemorrhage, and who for weeks afterwards confabulated about performing stocktaking in a certain store, although the last time he was supposed to do that was years earlier (Burgess and McNeil 1999). At the other side of the spectrum are confabulations whose source is more difficult to identify, as that of the Korsakoff's patient (*amnesia) recovering from a motorcycle accident in Britain, who came to believe she was in Royal Air Force and that her accident occurred while flying over France. Although over time she changed some details in the story, the flying theme remained prominent throughout for several months (Berlyne 1972).

The neuropathology of confabulation commonly involves damage to frontal structures (Figure 18), which could result from a variety of insults (Alexander and Freedman 1984; Stuss and Benson 1984; Shallice 1988; DeLuca and Cicerone 1991). These include rupture of aneurysm of the anterior communicating artery, causing damage the ventromedial frontal lobe;[4] Korsakoff's syndrome (*amnesia); and physical injury. That frontal lobe amnesia is associated with confabulations suggests that some impairment of executive function is involved (*working memory). But this by itself still doesn't explain why confabulators confabulate.

So why do they? In searching for candidate neurological causes, it is first useful to *recall the distinction between spontaneous and provoked confabulation. As noted above, provoked confabulations may basically reflect a normal compensatory strategy (Kopelman 1987; Schnider et al. 1996a). Spontaneous confabulation, on the other hand, is much farther from normal, and therefore more interesting. Poor memory per se is not the reason, or at least is not a sufficient one, because many amnesics do not confabulate. Most investigators now believe that the problem is related to *retrieval.

Either the retrieval set is faulty to begin with, or the proper retrieval *cues become ineffective, or improper cues intrude, or the information gets mixed up in ecphory,[5] or the *metamemory system does not monitor the retrieval process properly and fails to eliminate wrong results. The literature contains arguments for and against any of the above hypotheses.

A particularly fruitful hypothesis is that confabulation is a disorder of mnemonic chronology, and that the confabulated account is composed of bits of experiences taken out of their proper chronological and, hence also, factual context (Van der Horst, cited in Berlyne 1972; Schnider et al. 1996a,b). Even bizarre confabulations might assimilate information that has been encountered earlier, although not necessarily experienced, by the patient. Disorders of mnemonic chronology are probably insufficient to explain confabulation per se—many amnesics err in the chronology of experiences yet do not confabulate—but it might be a necessary condition for confabulation to occur. A variant of the mnemonic chronology deficit was proposed and tested by Schnider and Ptak (1999). They compared the *performance of confabulating and nonconfabulating amnesics on a continuous *recognition task. In this task, the subjects had to identify recurrent pictures within ongoing test sessions (Figure 18). The confabulators made an increasingly growing number of false positive responses to pictures that were presented in the former but not in the ongoing session. It seemed that they recognized information encountered many minutes ago as if it had been presented in the present. This was construed to indicate that the confabulators lose the temporal label of stored information, and fail to suppress activated *internal representations even if these representations are irrelevant to current reality.

An intriguing spin-off of the aforementioned study is the suggestion that failure to recall properly may result from activation or reconstruction of too many memory traces, rather than from the lack of traces to retrieve. This mnemonic failure of certain amnesics reminds one of the severe problems that their antipodes, the hyperamnesics, have in daily life (*mnemonics). In the storage (*metaphor) and recall of memory, as in so many other aspects of life, too much may be too much indeed.

Selected associations: Amnesia, Episodic memory, False memory, Recall, Retrieval

---

[1]On defence mechanisms in general, see *forgetting.

[2]A related syndrome is Munchausen's syndrome by proxy, which is illness fabricated by one person, usually a parent, in another, usually a child (Meadow 1977). These syndromes are called after Baron von Munchausen (1720–90), a retired German officer whose after dinner

confabulations became a literary *classic (Raspe 1785). It is noteworthy that Munchausen's syndromes might be facilitated by the spread of the Internet (Feldman 2000).

[3]The distinction between 'momentary' and 'fantastic' is not based on dissociation along the same *dimension, whereas that between 'provoked' and 'spontaneous' is. Most authors now prefer the latter dichotomy. Both pairs of terms are, however, mentioned here because both are still used, sometimes interchangeably, in the literature.

[4]Aneurysm is a localized pathological dilatation of a blood vessel caused by congenital or acquired structural deficiency or inflammation of the vessel's wall. An aneurysm may rupture and cause haemorrhage, or it can become sufficiently large to displace and damage adjacent tissue.

[5]Ecphory is the actual act of retrieving or reconstructing the information, see *retrieval.

Conscious awareness

The mental state in which one experiences, notices, and is directly apprised of one's own *percepts, *memories, emotions, beliefs, thoughts, and actions.

Books on memory tend to shy away from the discussion of consciousness and related issues. This is surprising on the one hand yet understandable on the other. It is surprising because the relation of consciousness to memory is of great importance in memory research (*amnesia, *declarative memory, *episodic memory), and conscious awareness is a major *criterion in the *zeitgeist *taxonomy of memory *systems. Avoiding the discussion of consciousness is, however, understandable, because despite many centuries of systematic thinking, and the fact that we all know subjectively what it is, consciousness is still an *enigma. All authors point to the great difficulty in even defining it (e.g. Crick and Koch 1992; Searle 1992; Block 1995). Because we know so little about consciousness, many authors also believe that premature definitions are counterproductive.

The purpose of this discussion is to outline briefly only very limited aspects of conscious awareness that are directly relevant to the discussion of memory. To do so, we must, first, and in spite of the aforementioned caveat, attempt to formulate an operational, heuristic definition of the subject of discussion. This definition does not aspire to explain what conscious awareness is in the context of a theory of mind and brain, it merely delineates the subject.[1] Second, as the terms 'consciousness', 'conscious', 'awareness', and 'conscious awareness' are often used interchangeably in the literature, the meaning of these terms as intended in this book should be clarified before further use.

Consciousness is an umbrella term that refers to a particular type of mental faculty, state, and process in living systems, which involves subjective experiencing of ongoing occurrences. *Stimuli are sensed and perceived by their perceiver in a private version, with phenomenological qualities that are transparent to the *subject only.[2] Emotions, beliefs, thoughts, and actions involve private experiences as well, inaccessible to the outside observer. Consciousness could also involve reflexive perception of oneself, or 'self-consciousness'.[3] Consciousness is treated in a variety of contexts in philosophical discourses, whose spectrum of discussion ranges from issues of soul and self, to speculations about emergent properties of highly complex systems (e.g. Kant 1781; James 1890; Freud 1900; Bergson 1908; Ryle 1949; Edelman 1990, 1995; Dennett 1991; Searle 1992; Crick 1994; Damasio 2000; for a tiny glimpse of the sophistication of treatment of consciousness in eastern philosophy, see Harvey 1990; Keown 2000). Consciousness is manifested in multiple varieties, differing along the *dimensions of arousal, *attention, qualia experience, and reflexivity. For example, there are states of altered consciousness on waking up from deep sleep, or in some diseases (e.g. *dementia), or under the influence of drugs, or in meditation. Consciousness is assumed to mean very different things in different species (Ristau 1991; Heyes and Huber 2000). Being *conscious* refers to the exercising of some or another variety of consciousness.

Awareness per se refers here to the ability of the central nervous system to sense and process ongoing stimuli from the outside world, irrespective of the particular state of consciousness. This is a *reductionist use of the term. According to this use, awareness of a target stimulus can be inferred objectively from observing the input–output relationships, provided appropriate *controls for input–output causality are being used. Hence the brain could react to information and use it to act on the world, without the subject, as the active agent, paying attention and becoming directly apprised of this information. Examples in humans are non*declarative memories, such as *habit, *skill, and *priming. Or consider an even simpler case, the stimulus that evokes the gill withdrawal reflex in *Aplysia; it makes sense to talk about *Aplysia* being aware of this stimulus, but it is questionable whether the slug is really conscious of the stimulus; so far we have no *method to determine if it is and if so, to what degree.[4]

Conscious awareness is a higher form of awareness. To say that the subject is consciously aware of something is to say that in addition to the nervous system of the subject being aware of this thing, the subject is also conscious that this thing happens. A subject may, of course, be in a fully conscious state but unaware of the target information. Stating that the subject is specifically conscious of the target information implies that the subject is also aware of this information; however, the use of the solo term conscious (or consciousness) in experimental science might be somewhat problematic from the point of view of pragmatics. This is because these terms, as noted above, are used in a broad spectrum of conceptual frameworks, some of which do not necessarily refer to concrete behaviour. Conscious awareness intends to connote a more tangible cognitive state, of being directly apprised of one's ongoing behavioural acts, and fits better to be used in the context of experimental science. This is, therefore, the term preferred in this book. Note that many authors do equate 'conscious' with 'aware', yet still use the term 'consciously aware', which in this case becomes a redundancy (*Ockham's razor).

A compact matrix of memory systems-by-consciousness, proposed by Tulving (1985b), illustrates the kind of interactions possible among different types of memory and consciousness. Tulving lists three varieties of consciousness, which he terms *anoetic* (not comprehending), *noetic* (comprehending), and *autonoetic* (self-comprehending).[5] Anoetic is similar to awareness as defined above; the subject is capable of registering, representing, and responding to aspects of the present environment, but is not consciously aware of these events. Anoetic consciousness corresponds to procedural, nondeclarative memory systems. Noetic consciousness allows the subject privately to experience and operate cognitively on objects and events and on the relations among them. This corresponds to conscious awareness as used here, and is correlated with semantic memory (*declarative memory). Autonoetic consciousness confers in addition the capability of experiencing the private phenomenological flavour of personal episodes, is correlated with *episodic, autobiographical memory, and corresponds to an advanced, reflexive form of conscious awareness as defined here.

It is hence evident from the discussion so far that consciousness is not an all-or-none state, and therefore we should indeed expect to find various degrees of conscious awareness in different species as well as in different states of the organism. Furthermore, different task conditions may involve different varieties of conscious awareness. Consider, for example, *classical conditioning; whereas simultaneous and delay conditioning require only awareness, i.e. anoetic consciousness, trace conditioning may already require conscious awareness, i.e. noetic consciousness (Clark and Squire

1998). Another noteworthy point is that the role of conscious awareness in *acquisition and in *retrieval of an item could differ. For example, learning to drive a car should better involve conscious awareness, but an expert driver can drive for hours in the absence of conscious awareness of the activation of the driving skill. Thus, conscious awareness is not a cognitive *system* that becomes permanently linked to particular types of memory; rather, it is a brain *state*, which is either obligatory, or permissive, or optional for the acquisition or retrieval of an item.

What are the brain substrates of conscious awareness? This question is the focus of many studies that combine multiple experimental methodologies, occasionally augmented by a provocative hypothesis and by input from professional philosophers (for a selection of approaches and commentaries, see Griffin 1985; Crick and Koch 1992, 1995; Nagel 1993; Bogen 1995; Weiskrantz 1995; Block 1996; Duzel *et al.* 1997; Clark and Squire 1998; McIntosh *et al.* 1999). Two major experimental methods stand out. One is the analysis of conscious awareness in brain damaged patients. These are patients that suffer from amnesia; or agnosia (the loss of ability to *recognize and identify a class of stimuli in the absence of impairment in the ability to sense these stimuli; Shallice 1988); or disconnection syndrome (a set of deficits following interruption of large tracts of nerve fibres in the brain, such as the corpus callosum; Zaidel *et al.* 1996). This type of approach unveils circumscribed disturbances of conscious phenomena, and identifies brain sites that subserve these phenomena. The second approach is combination of *functional neuroimaging with neuropsychology, and its main objective is to identify neural correlates of conscious awareness. It seems that conscious awareness depends on the activity of distributed brain circuits; an *homunculus explanation is currently out of favour. Thalamo*cortical circuits are the prime candidates.[6] The prefrontal cortex probably plays a global, executive role (*working memory), whereas other cortici participate according to the type of information accessed. From studies of amnesics we also learn that the *hippocampal formation and adjacent cortici are particularly important for the access of items in memory to conscious awareness.

Selected associations: Attention, Declarative memory, Enigma, Persistence, Working memory

---

[1]For more on the nature of definitions, see *The conceptual framework*, in the introduction.

[2]These privately experienced qualities are called qualia (singular: quala). Qualia are types of 'sense data', i.e. entities that are assumed to exist only because they are sensed; see *stimulus.

[3]Some authors consider consciousness to always involve self-consciousness (e.g. Kant 1800), others do not (e.g. Searle 1992). Kant's definition draws on this relationship: 'All our cognition has twofold relation, first to the object, second to the subject. In the former respect it is related to presentation, in the latter to consciousness, the general condition of all cognition in general. (Actually consciousness is a presentation that another presentation is in me.)' (Kant 1800).

[4]There is also the view that we will never know what is it like to be an *Aplysia* (Nagel 1974). Some dispute this view (Dennett 1991).

[5]In Aristotelian philosophy, *nous* meant comprehension, or intellectual intuition (Guthrie 1981).

[6]These circuits are necessary but not sufficient. Conscious awareness requires more basic forms of awareness, that depend on arousal, itself controlled by the brainstem (Magoun 1952).

Consolidation

1. **The progressive post-*acquisition stabilization of the *engram.**
2. **The memory *phase(s) during which this stabilization takes place.**

It took the Muses, daughters of Memory, a single encounter with Hesiod on Mount Helicon to breathe into the poet divine voice and knowledge (Hesiod 8thC BC). Yet for most of us, who are not granted the privilege to mingle with the immortals, learning is often a much more lengthy, complicated, and frustrating process. Even if we do devote to training sufficient effort, memory may still betray us (*false memory, *forgetting). And as if the burden of confusion and forgetfulness stemming from the continuing passage of time is not enough, the period immediately after learning also contributes its share to the fragility of our engrams. It has long been recognized that fresh memories need time to stabilize (Quintillian 1stC AD), and are particularly labile and prone to interference by agents ranging from distracting *stimuli to injury and drugs (Muller and Pilzecker 1900; McGaugh 1966, 2000; Dudai and Morris 2000). This brittle phase in the life of a memory is assumed to reflect the process of consolidation (*consolidāre*, Latin for 'to make firm'). Consolidation, however, is not necessarily completed within a short time after learning; in some types of memory it may continue for weeks, months, even longer.

Consolidation is a term used to denote memory stabilization processes at different *levels of brain organization. Molecular and cellular neurobiologists use it to refer to 'local', or *cellular consolidation* (Dudai and Morris 2000). This is the time-dependent stabilization of information storage at local nodes, or *synapses and their cell body, in the neuronal circuit that encodes the memory. Cellular consolidation is accomplished within a few hours after training (e.g. Montarolo *et al.* 1986). In practice, it is commonly defined as that time window during which the formation of the long-term form of the newly acquired memory can be blocked by inhibitors of *protein or RNA synthesis. Certain other drugs, or electric shock, could also be used to block consolidation. The temporal parameters of the consolidation period will, however, depend on which treatment is used. This is because cellular consolidation involves multiple phases, some of which are sensitive to some treatments but not to others (Grecksch and Matthies 1980; Rosenzweig *et al.* 1993; DeZazzo and Tully 1995; Freeman *et al.* 1995; Ghirardi *et al.* 1995). The understanding of cellular consolidation has advanced impressively in recent years, as a consequence of the remarkable achievements in molecular and cellular neurobiology. We now know that in cellular consolidation, post-translational modifications, induced by activation of *intracellular signal transduction cascades, culminate in the modulation of neuronal gene expression and ultimately in the synthesis of new proteins (*CREB, *immediate early genes, *late response genes). These processes involve local synaptic mechanisms, cell-wide mechanisms, and cross-talk between the synapse, cell body, and nucleus (Frey and Morris 1997; Martin *et al.* 1997*a*; Casadio *et al.* 1999; Dudai and Morris 2000). The new proteins are believed to embody and subserve long-term modifications in the functional properties of the synapse. This probably involves morphological *plasticity as well (Bailey and Kandel 1993; *development). It is thought that once the use-dependent modulation of gene expression is triggered, the plasticity change becomes immune to molecular turnover and independent of certain signal transduction cascades, and a consequence, is no more sensitive to the consolidation blockers.

Cellular consolidation has been identified in the brain of every species that learns, and in every type of memory that lasts for more than a few hours or days. *Model neural networks can be shown to be capable of a consolidation-like process solely on the basis of modifications in local nodes (Rumelhart *et al.* 1986*c*); this may also be the case in simple neuronal circuits. However, local, cellular consolidation is not the whole story in some more complex circuits. In the mammalian brain, and possibly in other vertebrates, additional consolidating processes operate at the system level. These processes of *system consolidation* involve gradual recruitment and continuous reorganization of distributed brain circuits long after acquisition has occurred. System consolidation can be detected by noting the time-dependent sensitivity of certain types of memory to circumscribed brain lesions, or the change over time in the activation of specific brain circuits in a memory task, as revealed by *functional neuroimaging.[1] System consolidation in some systems occurs within a few hours (Shadmehr and Holcomb 1997a,b), but in other systems it can take much more time: several days (Winocur 1990), weeks (Cho *et al.* 1993; Bontempi *et al.* 1999), even years (Schmidtke and Vollmer 1997; Reed and Squire 1998; Teng and Squire 1999; Haist *et al.* 2001; but see Nadel and Moscovitch 1997). It is believed to be promoted by endogenous brain activity, sensory input, and their interactions; the triggers and the circuit mechanisms are unknown, but the cellular mechanisms are likely to be similar to those mentioned above for cellular consolidation. The most notable example of system consolidation is provided by *declarative memories. These memories are assumed to be stored in the long run in circuits that involve the *cerebral cortex. But in the first period after learning, they depend on the *hippocampal formation. With time, this dependency disappears (*ibid.*; *amnesia).

An intriguing question, which has received much attention and stirred much debate in recent years, is whether for any memorized item, consolidation starts and ends just once. The data from cognitive psychology indicate that memory traces are reconstructed with use, and that *retrieving a memory item could involve mingling the *internal representations of the past with the *percepts of the present (e.g. Bartlett 1932; Tulving 1983; Schacter *et al.* 1998; *false memory). This mnemonic reconstruction process raises the possibility that engrams may be reconsolidated upon retrieval. There is evidence that a cellular consolidation phase may indeed ensue retrieval (Misanin *et al.* 1968; Spear and Mueller 1984; Nader *et al.* 2000; Sara 2000; but see, for example, Dawson and McGaugh 1969). It is not yet established, however, whether the entire reactivated trace[2] could become sensitive to interference in this assumed reconsolidation, or, alternatively, whether a 'core memory' has privileged stability. What already becomes apparent is that the cellular mechanisms that consolidate novel and reactivated traces, respectively, differ from each other (Berman and Dudai 2001; Taubenfeld *et al.* 2001); and that the stability of the retrieved trace

after post-retrieval interference is task and region dependent (Berman and Dudai 2001).

Why do memories consolidate in the first place? One could envisage a situation in which newly formed memories stabilize instantaneously, evading the risk of erasure by sensory and metabolic interference (*flashbulb memory). An appealing explanation is that instant acquisition of every percepts is bound to waste brain space on useless items (*capacity). Another possibility is that the post-stimulus time window of consolidation, during which the new information is particularly malleable and associates easily with other inputs, could assist the encoding and registration of selected, meaningful mental narratives (Frey and Morris 1997; Dudai and Morris 2000). Similarly, it has been suggested that system consolidation promotes better categorization and hence a more coherent, effective, and parsimonious construe of the world (McClelland *et al.* 1995). All these arguments share a teleological flavour. There is also the other, anti-zeitgeist type of possibility, that cellular consolidation, system consolidation, or both, are

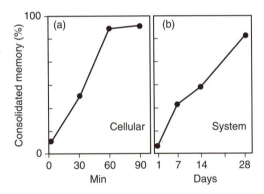

Fig. 19 Two types of consolidation windows in behaving animals. (a) The time course of cellular consolidation, determined by measuring the sensitivity of memory to the inhibition of *protein synthesis. Consolidated memory is defined as treatment-resistant long-term memory. The data are from experiments on shuttle box learning in the goldfish (Agranoff *et al.* 1966; *classic). The protein synthesis inhibitor was administered to the *subject at the indicated time point after training. The sensitivity of memory to protein synthesis inhibition is over by about 1 h. A consolidation process that depends on protein synthesis during and immediately after training is a universal property of the nervous system. (b) The time course of system consolidation, determined by measuring the sensitivity of long-term memory of *contextual *fear conditioning to a lesion in the rat *hippocampus. The lesions were inflicted at the indicated time points after training. The dependence on the hippocampus in this case is over by about 1 month. Data from Kim and Fanselow (1992). A system consolidation process that lasts weeks or even longer, during which the memory becomes independent of the hippocampus, is observed in *declarative memory tasks.

spin-offs of the constraints imposed on biological memory systems by the design and maintenance of the biological hardware, rather than functional properties selected in evolution.[3]

Selected associations: Acquisition, Immediate early genes, Phase, Protein synthesis, Retrieval

---

[1]Long-term memory may be subjected to continuous reorganization throughout life. Reorganization alone is therefore insufficient as a *criterion for consolidation, because otherwise one will reach the conclusion (that some authors indeed reach) that system consolidation proceeds forever, which deprives the notion of consolidation phase of its usefulness. The criteria for system consolidation should therefore ultimately include a limited period of obligatory dependency on the activity of a specific brain region. This could be demonstrated by time-limited sensitivity to lesions or to inactivation of this region.

[2]On the distinction between active and inactive trace, see Lewis (1979); *retrieval, *taxonomy.

[3]This tension between adaptive selection and built-in biological constraints is a recurrent issue in this book; see the Panglossian paradigm, in *paradigm.

Context

The surroundings and circumstances in which an event takes place.

Events always occur in some context (from Latin *contextus*, 'joined together', 'woven together'). The dissociation between a memorized 'target' event and its context is not trivial. This is beautifully illustrated by Locke (1690): '… a young gentleman, who, having learnt to dance, and that to great perfection, there happened to stand an old trunk in the room where he learnt. The idea of this remarkable piece of household stuff had so mixed itself with the turns and steps of all his dances, that though in that chamber he could dance excellently well, yet it was only whilst the trunk was there; nor could he perform well in any other place, unless that or some such other trunk had its due position in the room'. Had the young gentleman been the subject of a controlled experiment on the acquisition of dancing *skill, it would have been fairly easy for the experimenter to discern the target task (dancing) from its context (the trunk). Furthermore, in this case, the context was an innocent part of the environmental surrounds, not expected to influence the target *stimulus in any significant way. This is in contrast to another type of 'context', which always affects the significance or

meaning of the stimulus, such as the context of a figure in a visual scene, a note in a musical score, or a word in a sentence (Wickens 1987). Having made this distinction, it is still useful to remember Locke's gentleman: what is regarded by the experimenter as an irrelevant context may not so be regarded by the brain of the *subject.[1]

In the behavioural literature, 'context' typically refers to environmental stimuli that are kept relatively constant in the course of the experiment, and is hence synonymous with apparatus, environment, and background stimuli (e.g. Lubow and Gewirtz 1995). In *real-life, the background often varies significantly from one moment to another, but still is not usually considered the target of learning or *retrieval. The information about the time and place in which the target was acquired is referred to as 'source information'. The context itself could, however, become the experimental variable. This is illustrated in a study by Godden and Baddeley (1975), in which divers were instructed to learn word lists both on land and underwater, and subsequently *recall the lists either on land or underwater. After learning on land, recall was better on land, and after learning underwater, recall was better underwater (Figure 20). It is likely that in this experiment, the context was not only the underwater milieu, but also the physiological state of the subject, generated

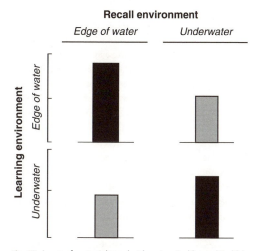

Fig. 20 A case of context-dependent learning. Godden and Baddeley (1975) instructed groups of members of a university diving club to learn lists of words either while seating 20 feet under water or while seating by the edge of the water. The *subjects were then requested to recall the lists either underwater or on land. The lists learned underwater were recalled best underwater, whereas the lists learned on land were recalled best on land. The height of each bar represents the success on performance in the task. (Adapted from Godden and Baddeley 1975.)

by the underwater experience. Learning that is dependent on the endogenous state of the subject is called *state-dependent learning. Distinct endogenous states are usually induced, either in real-life or in the laboratory, by chemical substances, but could also be instated by the external context.[2] In such case, the distinction between context-dependent learning and state-dependent learning becomes a matter of taste or professional *bias.

In their ability to reinstate context, be it internal or external, not all senses are equal. In his famous *Remembrance of things past* (which is probably cited many more times than thoroughly read), Marcel Proust (1913) retrieves his childhood memories to the flavour of madeleine cakes soaked in tea. His literary account of the mnemonic power of the chemical senses appears to have received experimental validation: odours are superior to colours in supplying context for target information (Pointer and Bond 1998). Proust's account also points to the flavour of the madeleines as a retrieval *cue, i.e. a stimulus that elicits retrieval by activating an *engram and interacting with it. Retrieval cues are effective to the extent that they help reinstate or recreate processes involved in the original learning (McGeoch 1932; Tulving 1983). They may hence point either to target information, or to source information, or both. An interesting case in which the target information serves as a retrieval cue to bring to mind source information is *flashbulb memory.

Compelling evidence for the functional dissociation of target and source information in the brain comes from the study of human *amnesia. In some types of amnesia, the patient can recall facts or events, but not when and where this information was acquired. This is therefore termed 'source amnesia' (Schacter *et al.* 1984; Mayes 1988; Lishman 1998). A *classic case of source amnesia was described by Claparede (1911) in a lady with Korsakoff amnesia. Claparede used a trick that probably would not have been accepted nowadays by editors and readers, but still brought him fame. He struck the hand of the patient with a pin hidden between his fingers. Later, when trying again to reach out for the patient's hand, she pulled it back without being able to explain why. In another experiment, Claparede read to her stories, which she was able to recollect while being totally unaware of how these stories were learned. Source amnesia has since been reconfirmed to affect Korsakoff patients, and has also been demonstrated in other amnestic and demented patients (Shimamura and Squire 1987; Brandt *et al.* 1995; Schnider *et al.* 1996*b*). The pathology is considered to result from damage to multiple areas, including the thalamus and frontal *cortex.

In animal studies, the brain organ recurrently implicated in contextual memory is the *hippocampal formation (Penick and Solomon 1991; Holland and Bouton 1999). This is also supported by studies of human subjects (Chun and Phelps 1999). Coming to think about it, this is not surprising. Since context refers to combinations of features contributed by input from multiple modalities, one should expect brain circuits that encode context to process complex polymodal associations, and the hippocampus does just that. Currently, a popular *assay of contextual learning in rodents is a version of *fear conditioning. In the common classical fear conditioning *paradigm, a tone is associated with a shock, and the subject comes to fear the tone. However, as is often the case in seemingly simple *classical conditioning paradigms, there is also learning of the context in which training is performed, e.g. the conditioning chamber. Hippocampal lesions impair the acquired fear of context but not of the tone (Phillips and LeDoux 1992). The effect of hippocampal damage on context learning is, however, detected only when certain protocols or measures of fear conditioning are used, but not others. This implies that some elements of contextual learning can do without a fully functional hippocampus (McNish *et al.* 1997; Frankland *et al.* 1998; Maren *et al.* 1998; Gewirtz *et al.* 2000).

An notable development in the study of context in recent years is the large increase in the reports of cellular correlates and candidate mechanisms of context (e.g. Zipser *et al.* 1996; Christensen *et al.* 2000; Shulz *et al.* 2000). Such studies identify responses of neuronal populations or single neurons to target stimuli, that are affected by the surroundings and the circumstances. Discussion of *plasticity- and learning-related context has even been *reduced to the *synaptic and molecular level. A striking example is provided by the report that the ability of weak synaptic stimuli to establish *long-term potentiation depends on the recent history (<3 h) of the other synapses on the same neuron; this means that stimuli that are ineffective in one context are effective in another (Frey and Morris 1997). But whether this intersynaptic gating of stimuli indeed subserves the effects of context in acquisition or retrieval of memory is still an open question.

Selected associations: Cue, Real-life memory, Retrieval, State-dependent learning

---

[1]This applies even to the simplest of learning in *simple systems: 'non*associative' learning, such as *habituation, could involve an association between the unconditioned stimulus and the context (Marlin and Miller 1981; Rankin 2000).

[2]Indeed, Locke's trunk-dependent dancer, mentioned above, could also be described as trapped in state-dependency, where the retrieval-permissive state is reinstated in the brain by the presence of the trunk. The formation of the state dependency might have been promoted by the emotions involved in acquiring the dancing skill.

Controls

The elements and protocols that are included in the experiment in order to dissociate the contribution of the experimental variable from that of other factors.

In the Middle Ages 'control' meant a 'duplicate register', or 'duplicate roll' (*contra–rotulus* in Latin). Rolls were the standard material for writing administrative and financial records (Clanchy 1993), and the duplicate rolls were used by one officer of the law to check upon the rolls of another officer. The transition from the language of bureaucracy and commerce to that of scientific *culture has its roots in the *Methods of experimental inquiry* proposed by the British philosopher John Stuart Mill. One of these methods was 'The method of difference', whose canon reads as follows: 'If two or more instances in which the phenomenon occurs have only one circumstance in common, while two or more instances in which it does not occur have nothing in common save the absence of that circumstance, the circumstance in which alone the two sets of instances differ is the effect, or the cause, of an indispensable part of the cause, of the phenomenon' (Mill 1884). Hence, to demonstrate that a certain variable (the manipulated, or 'independent' variable) is the cause of an effect (on the 'dependent variable'), one should perform the experiment under two conditions, which should ideally be identical except for the omission of the change in the independent variable. The condition in which the change in the independent variable is omitted came to be known as the 'control' (Coover and Angell 1907). Controlled experiments may involve multiple treatments of the same *subject(s), 'experimental' vs. 'control', or different groups, ideally matched for their composition (e.g. gender, age, history), in which case we have the 'experimental group' vs. the 'control groups'. As it is usually impractical to have truly matched groups, the alternative is to assign subjects in a population to groups at random to smoothen variability (Fisher 1966). Statistics is then used to quantify the effect of the experimental variable, and further, to identify interactions among

seemingly controlled variables, and to unveil potential latent variables (Fisher 1966; Martin and Bateson 1993; Kerlinger and Lee 2000; *dimension).

The use of controls in experimental science has started to gain popularity in early psychophysics (reviewed in Solomon 1949; Boring 1954; Dehue 1997), and later in educational research (Thorndike and Woodworth 1901*b*; Coover and Angell 1907; Winch 1908). But the concept was occasionally appreciated by others as well: a *classic example is the *gedanken* experiment ('thought experiment') that proposed to test the effect of prayer on life in two groups of individuals, matched for everything except for practising 'prudent pious' (i.e. experimental) vs. 'prudent materialistic' (i.e. control) life-styles (Galton 1872).[1] In the discipline of memory research, subjecting the same group alternately to experimental vs. control conditions is inherently problematic, as the mere experience may itself affect the outcome on subsequent tests. It is therefore advisable, whenever feasible, to use separate control groups. This, evidently, is easier said than done. Consider, for example, *functional neuroimaging of complex tasks in humans, or *delay tasks in *monkeys, in which suitable *subjects could be hard to get and train. Under such conditions, an experimental design with control groups often remains an Utopia, and protocols must be devised to reliably dissociate experimental and control responses in the same individual despite the expected order- and temporal experience-dependent effects (e.g. Buckner *et al.* 1996).

The canny use of controls is one of the most important tricks that newcomers to the experimental sciences must learn. On the one hand, the basic desire should be to control for whatever possible in order to make sure that the effect, if any, is indeed due to the independent variable, and to avoid embarrassing remarks of anonymous referees when the paper finally gets reviewed; on the other hand, multiple controls imply excessive expenses and delay in the completion of the work. Controlling the economy of controlled experimental designs is hence an art. In this context, 'internal controls' are a blessing: those are elements embedded in the protocol of the experiment that spare the need for separate controls. For example, suppose that we set out to test the effect of a circumscribed brain lesion on long-term memory. We could include in the protocol a test for short-term memory as well, because if long-term memory is impaired but short-term memory is not, we have an internal control for the lack of the effect of the lesion on the sensory and motor faculties that are required to perform the task. This eliminates the need for a separate control group to test the effect of the lesion on these faculties. A protocol well-designed may include a matrix of 'balanced' or 'reciprocal' controls, i.e. a combination of control groups or treatments that complement each other. A classic example is provided by the 'double-dissociation' lesion protocol (Teuber 1955). In this protocol the effect of two different circumscribed lesions, A and B, is tested on two different phenotypes, X and Y. If lesion A yields a defect in X but not in Y, while lesion B yields a defect in Y but not in X, then the defects in X and Y are not due to general damage but rather to specific dissociable contributions of A and B (see *declarative memory).

Memory research is of course not unique in benefiting from the proper application of controls in experimental design. Some elementary issues that require appropriate controls are shared by many other experimental disciplines. These issues include, for example, the need to distinguish correlation from causality (*criteria, *method). But several potential pitfalls do call for controls that to some degree or another are specific to the discipline of memory research. Here is a short list:

1. Controls for species-specific behaviour vs. learning. Motor patterns that emerge in training and testing may comprise an innate (*a priori) response to specific *stimuli ('sign stimuli') rather than learning (Breland and Breland 1961; Moore and Stuttard 1979; Wolfer et al. 1998). In parentheses, it is worthwhile to repeat here the ever-valid advice to those investigators who mingle with the behaviour of experimental subjects (*Homo included): know your subject!

2. Controls for *development vs. learning. This is especially important in behaviours whose *capacity matures gradually, or materializes in restricted sensitive periods (*birdsong, *imprinting). The rule of thumb, however, is that a definitive dissociation of learning from development could be unrealistic, as both are interwoven in the emergence and refinement of even the most elementary sensory and motor faculties (e.g. Crair et al. 1998).

3. Controls for one type of learning vs. another. For example, is an alteration in behaviour that is obtained in a conditioning protocol due to the *association among stimuli, or to nonassociative processes (*sensitization, 'pseudoconditioning' in *classical conditioning; Rescorla 1967)? Is a particular conditioned response due to stimulus–stimulus (*classical) or stimulus–response (*instrumental) conditioning (Jenkins and Moore 1973)? And when a horse 'reads', is it because it has mastered human language, or because it has realized that responding to the subtle bodily gestures of its master yields a sweet reward (*Clever Hans; Pfungst 1911)?

4. Controls to distinguish learning from alterations in *performance due to changes in the experimental conditions. An often neglected need is to control for *state-dependent memory in studies that investigate the effect of drugs or of modulation of gene expression on memory. In such cases, if the subject flunks on the memory test, it could be a consequence of the change in its endogenous state, due to the presence of the specific drug or gene product in training but not in testing, rather than to memory failure (Overton 1964; also *context).

5. Controls for premature conclusions about the fate of memories. When *forgetting is detected, is it because the *engram has indeed vanished? A control test performed after a while may unveil 'spontaneous recovery'.

6. Other controls to unearth factors that could alter the behaviour but have nothing to do with learning and memory. For example, drug effects that result from the mere expectation by the subject that something will happen (a 'placebo effect', Swartzman and Burkell 1998; Kvavilashvili and Ellis 1999). Or lesion effects that are actually a consequence of the surgical procedures, not of damage to the targeted brain area. This is why lesion experiments always require 'sham' treatments, in which the skull is treated the same way as in the lesioned animal but no brain lesion is induced.

Occasionally what is expected to be a routine, boring control, *surprises and becomes a mind twister. Here is such a case. A subject is conditioned by a certain *reinforcement. A naive expectation is that the more intensive the reinforcement schedule, the stronger the memory. A simple set of controls would include a non-reinforced group, and, possibly, a group reinforced only occasionally. Alas, the group whose behaviour is reinforced only intermittently remembers the best (Humphreys 1939). This is the kind of controls that opens a whole new field of research (see *experimental extinction). Similarly, devising innovative controls has unveiled much about the sophistication of *classical conditioning (e.g. Kremer 1971). The take home message: don't look for excuses, add all the control groups you can think of, they may prove even more interesting than the experimental ones.

Selected associations: Artefact, Bias, Culture, Method

---

[1]This gedanken experiment finally made it, 129 years later, into the *functional neuroimaging lab (Azari et al. 2001).

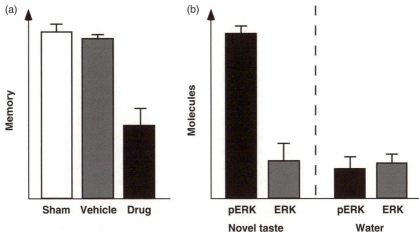

Fig. 21 Controls at two *levels of analysis of *conditioned taste aversion. (a) Microinfusion into the taste *cortex of scopolamine (*Drug*), an inhibitor of the *receptor for *acetylcholine, during training, blocks the formation of long-term memory of conditioned taste aversion in the rat (black bar). A control, in which only a drug-free solution (the vehicle) is microinfused into the taste cortex, has no such effect (grey bar). The 'sham' control (i.e. surgery but no microinfusion into the brain) is also shown for comparison (open bar). Hence the effect on memory is due to the drug and not to the manipulations involved in its administration. Data from Naor and Dudai (1996). (b) Sampling a novel taste, but not a familiar taste (water), causes activation of the enzyme mitogen-activated *protein kinase (ERK) in the taste cortex of the rat. This activation is caused by the phosphorylation of the ERK, and it can detected by the use of specific antibodies, that bind only to the phosphorylated form of the enzyme (pERK, black bar). However, the population of the ERK molecules includes a certain proportion of pERK even in the absence of any taste stimulus. This implies that the increase in the number of molecules detected by the anti-pERK antibodies after the experience of the novel taste, could be due to an increase in the overall number of the ERK molecules (*protein synthesis), without a change in the proportion of the pERK molecules. A control is therefore necessary in which the overall number of ERK molecules is measured in parallel, with antibodies that recognize the ERK molecule regardless of whether it is phosphorylated or not (grey bar). Such a control shows that the total number of ERK molecules does not change, and that the effect of the novel taste experience is activation of the existing ERK molecules. Data from Berman *et al.* (1998).

CREB

A type of protein that regulates the expression of genes, and fulfils a key role in neuronal *plasticity.

In technical terms, which will be explained below, CREB, cAMP-response element-binding protein, is a protein that modulates the transcription of genes with cAMP-response elements in their promoters. CREB is one of the most commonly used acronyms in neurobiology these days, and also one of the few words in the jargon of molecular biology that even experimental psychologists and computational neuroscientists might have encountered. And if they didn't, they should. Because the more we advance our knowledge in molecular neurobiology, the more we realize that CREB plays a pivotal role in the response of neurons to external stimuli. CREB is a transcription factor. This means that it participates in the control of gene expression at the level of transcription, i.e. the production of RNA

complementary to a strand of DNA. Transcription factors bind to specific DNA elements in the promoter (the region that binds or facilitates the binding of RNA polymerase, which is the enzyme that synthesizes RNA), or in other regions that control transcription (e.g. enhancers; Lewin 1994). These elements, because they permit a gene to respond to regulatory factors, are called 'response elements'. Multiple families of response elements are known. Genes are controlled by the conjoint regulation of multiple response elements, belonging to the same or different families.

One type of response elements is the cAMP-response element (abbreviated CRE; Sassone-Corsi 1995). It mediates transcriptional regulation in response to altered levels of the *intracellular signal cAMP (cyclic adenosine monophosphate). CRE is found in the promoter region of many genes. A related element is the activating transcription factor element (ATF). Therefore the terms CRE/ATF, or CRE-like elements, are also in use. CREB binds to CRE, and is a member of the CREB/ATF family of transcription factors. Multiple genes encode these transcription factors, and alternative splicing yields an even larger number of factors.

All the members of the CREB/ATF family have in their carboxy terminus a conserved 'leucine zipper' dimerization domain (i.e. a stretch of amino acids with interspersed residues of the amino acid leucine, which interacts with a 'zipper' in another polypeptide to form a dimer), juxtaposed to a DNA-binding domain rich in basic amino acids (Brindle and Montminy 1992; Sassone-Corsi 1995). Different CREB/ATF transcription factors are able to heterodimerize with each other in certain combinations. Proteins that bind to CRE act as both activators and repressors. For example, CREB, CREMτ (CRE-modulator, alternatively spliced variant τ), and ATF1 are transcriptional activator, whereas CREB-2 and CREMα antagonize cAMP-induced transcription. Unless otherwise specified, the common usage of the term CREB in memory literature refers to the activator form.

At this point molecular biologists may already feel that they have taken enough revenge on psychologists in the contest for the most graceless terminology. Yet what should interest us is not the competition between scientific *cultures, but rather the relevance of all this to learning and memory. There are many members in the CREB/ATF family; unless otherwise indicated, we will limit ourselves here to the discussion of CREB only. CREB is present in cells under nonstimulated conditions, mostly in a nonactivated form (some other members of the CREB/ATF family are expressed only in response to a stimulus, see *immediate early genes). Appropriate extracellular stimuli activate CREB by phosphorylating it. CREB can be phosphorylated on multiple sites by multiple *protein kinases. Phosphorylation on residue Serine-133 is critical for activation, and is mediated via an increase in the level of intracellular cAMP and activation of cAMP-dependent protein kinase (PKA; Brindle and Montminy 1992; Sassone-Corsi 1995), or via an increase in intracellular *calcium and activation of calcium/calmodulin-activated protein kinase (Sheng et al. 1991; Bito et al. 1996; Deisseroth et al. 1998).[1] The phosphorylation and dephosphorylation of CREB by different intracellular signalling pathways provides a mechanism for signal convergence and *coincidence detection (e.g. Perkinton et al. 1999). Phosphorylated CREB binds to the CREB-binding protein, recruits other components of the transcription machinery on the promoter, and initiates transcription, e.g. of other transcription factors (Figure 22).

It is this initiation of transcription in response to cAMP that has placed CREB in the spotlight of memory research (Silva et al. 1998). In recent years, multiple lines of evidence have shown that: (a) the cAMP cascade is stimulated in learning (e.g. *Aplysia, *Drosophila), and (b) *protein synthesis and modulation of gene expression are required for *consolidation. CREB links these two lines of evidence. The first to implicate CREB in neuronal *plasticity were Dash et al. (1990), in Aplysia neurons. Subsequent studies in a variety of species have indicated that the involvement of CREB, and CRE-regulated gene expression in general, in neuronal plasticity and memory formation, is possibly universal, and that CREB activation is correlated with, and necessary for, the formation of *long-term memory (e.g. Bourtchuladze et al. 1994; Bartch et al. 1995; Yin et al. 1995; Bito et al. 1996; Impey et al. 1996, 1998; Guszowski and McGaugh 1997; Lamprecht et al. 1997).[2] The experience-dependent balance between the activator and repressor isoforms of CREB may be critical in determining the fate of a memory. On the one hand, it could switch on very fast acquisition and consolidation of robust long-term memory (Yin et al. 1995; *flashbulb memory). On the other, it could culminate in the suppression of memory storage (Bartsch et al. 1995; Abel and Kandel 1998).

The CREB story leads us to the interface of *developmental and behavioural plasticity. It is now well established that CRE-regulated gene expression plays a key part in developing tissues (e.g. Davis et al. 1996; Liu and Graybiel 1996; Pham et al. 1999). The resemblance of CREB-related mechanisms in developmental and adult plasticity is so striking, that it was used as an argument in favour of the conceptual *paradigm of long-term-memory = f(growth) (Martin and Kandel 1996; *zeitgeist). But at the same time, these shared mechanisms imply that we are looking at a very basic *level of cellular response, which is not unique to learning and memory. CREB is probably essential in retaining cellular *homeostasis and in the protective response to stressful stimuli. It is clearly important in promoting the survival of many types of cells, not only neurons (Finkbeiner 2000; Walton and Dragunow 2000). The question thus remains what is the relevance of CREB to memory: Is the role permissive, supportive, or causal (see *criterion)? CREB could actually fulfil any of these roles, depending on the physiological and molecular *context. Understanding the functional implications of the fine tuning of the CREB machinery, might also cast light on pathological conditions in which neuronal homeostasis and plasticity malfunction. Such conditions could contribute to neurodegenerative disease (*dementia). Future drugs that target CREB might hence find multiple uses, including neuroprotection, the

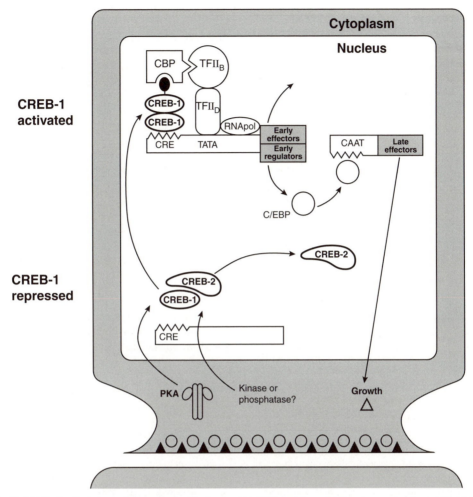

CREB-1 activated

CREB-1 repressed

Fig. 22 A highly simplified scheme of the proposed mechanism by which CREB regulates modulation of gene expression and the subsequent growth processes that accompany long-term use-dependent neuronal *plasticity. The box represents a pre*synaptic terminal; the postsynaptic membrane is across the synaptic cleft at the bottom. CAAT, or 'CAAT box', a conserved nucleotide sequence located upstream of the start point of a gene transcription unit, recognized by a variety of transcription factors; CBP, CREB-binding protein; C/EBP, CAAT/enhancer binding protein; CRE, cAMP response element; CREB-1, CREB-2, activator and repressor isoforms of CREB, respectively. CREB-2 is here depicted as a direct repressor of CREB-1, for simplicity; PKA, *protein kinase A, the cAMP-dependent protein kinase; RNApol, RNA polymerase, an enzyme that synthesizes RNA from a DNA template; TATA, or 'TATA Box', a conserved nucleotide sequence that may be involved in positioning RNApol for correct initiation; TFII$_B$, TFII$_D$, general transcription factors. According to this scheme, the balance between the activator and repressor isoforms of CREB, which is regulated by a variety of intracellular signal transduction cascades (of which only the one involving cAMP is partially depicted in the scheme), determines whether remodelling of the synapse will indeed take place. Hence, certain combinations of inputs could lead to long-term change, whereas others may not, or could even abort memory at its outset. This property may pave the way to novel specific memory-blocking drugs, which target CREB and might be used, for example, in treating some types of trauma (e.g. *fear conditioning). (Adapted from Carew 1996.)

blocking of undesired memories (*lotus), or the enhancement of desired ones (*nootropics).

Selected associations: Consolidation, Immediate early genes, Protein synthesis, Reduction, Spaced training

[1]CREB should therefore better be termed 'cAMP/calcium response element-binding protein'.

[2]For a dissident claim that the role of CREB in neuronal plasticity is, however, dispensable, see Frey *et al.* (2000).

Criterion

1. A standard by which something is judged.
2. A condition considered *a priori to provide reliable evidence for something else.

Meaning 'standard' in Greek, 'criterion' was advanced already by Plato, in a very capitalistic connotation: 'Your success, I admit, is fine evidence of the wisdom of the present generation as compared with their predecessors, and it is a popular sentiment that the wise man must above all be wise for himself; of such wisdom the criterion is in the end the ability to make the most money' (*Hipp. Maj.* 283*b*). Although to the naive mind the mere notion of 'criterion' may look straightforward, to philosophers it poses a real problem. Consider the following statements: in order to reach the conclusion that one knows a thing, one must posses criteria for the instantiation of that thing; but in order to know the criteria, one must already know what the thing is. This Catch-22 situation is termed 'the problem of the criterion'. It has haunted philosophers since ancient times, and even brought the Greek sceptics to conclude that we know nothing for real because the aforementioned statements are both correct (Amico 1993). Not surprisingly, 'the problem of the criterion' was dubbed as 'one of the most important and difficult problems in philosophy' (Chisholm 1982). Modern epistemology and philosophy of language are occupied with various facets of the meaning and use of criteria (e.g. see discussion in Glock 1996). For our purpose, before taking a much more limited yet pragmatic attitude, suffice it to note that a criterion provides indication that something is the case (definition 2), but unless specifically qualified as such, its satisfaction does not entail the occurrence of what it indicates.

Now to the pragmatics. The fact that 'criterion' stirs debates among philosophers should not discourage neuroscientists from using qualified criteria as powerful tools in experiments[1] and *models. Suppose we were to contemplate an elementary and pressing problem in memory research, namely, the relevance of neurobiological observations to learning and memory (Dudai 1994*b*). Attempts to address this issue can benefit from application of a number of criteria, which refer to the following.

1. *Correlation.* Some biological models of learning and memory are proposed, at least at the time of their inception, on the basis of *correlations* in space or time of certain biological observations with the behavioural phenomena of learning and memory. In practice, the correlation may be of the first or higher order. It is of the first order if the molecular, cellular, or *system phenomenon is directly correlated with learning and memory. It is of a higher order if the phenomenon is correlated with another intermediate phenomenon, which itself was earlier correlated with learning and memory. For example, correlation of synaptic facilitation in *Aplysia with behavioural *sensitization (Castellucci and Kandel 1976) was of the first order; but correlation of the molecular changes that take place in cultured *Aplysia neurons with the sensitization is of a higher order, as the events in the culture are correlated with the synaptic facilitation rather than directly with the behaviour (Sun and Schacher 1998). Correlation is a very popular criterion, and at the same time a rather weak one. Phenomenological correlation does not necessarily imply mechanistic correlation. A common correlative fallacy is the *post hoc* argumentation (*post hoc ergo propter hoc*, Latin for 'after this hence because of this'), which argues that because one event was correlated later in time with another, the second happened because of the first. Correlation nevertheless is a useful guideline for the design of further experiments intended to establish more stringent criteria (see below).

2. *Similarity.* Sometimes phenomenological *similarity* is used to conclude that a process or mechanism are related to learning and memory. For example, some authors promote the claim that *long-term potentiation plays a part in memory because it displays properties expected of memory, such as *persistence following a brief stimulus, *associativity, order-dependency in associativity, and localization in brain regions assumed to subserve memory (see in Dudai 1995). Such similarity is appealing, but could be misleading. Furthermore, there is no reason to assume that parts of a whole should display the properties of the whole and vice versa, hence that the molecular and cellular devices should display the properties of the behaving organism (e.g. Bechtel 1982; *reduction).

3. *Usefulness.* Are the mechanisms or processes *useful* for memory? There are two versions to this criterion. The first is 'pragmatical usefulness', i.e. can the process or mechanism be used in an experimental protocol to induce learning-related alterations in a given preparation. For example, serotonin is useful in inducing presynaptic facilitation in *Aplysia (Sun and Schacher 1998), and *acetylcholine in inducing lasting plasticity changes in *hippocampal neurons (Markram and Segal 1990), supporting the notion that these *neurotransmitters play a role in memory. Experiments of this kind occasionally merge with an attempt to demonstrate that the manipulated agent is sufficient to induce the change (see below). A second version of the usefulness criteria

is 'conceptual usefulness', i.e. can the implicated mechanism be productively incorporated into models of learning and memory, leading to a more coherent model and new testable hypotheses. An example is provided by the introduction of the unique kinetic properties of the cyclic adenosine monophosphate-dependent *protein kinase into models that attempt to explain the persistence of use-dependent *plasticity in neurons that encode memory (Buxbaum and Dudai 1989). Usefulness is suggestive, but does not prove that the process or mechanism involved do play a part in learning and memory *in vivo*.

4. *Necessity*. Is the mechanism *necessary* for learning and memory? The *methodology here is to intervene in the physiological process and infer normal function from dysfunction. This is an extremely popular approach. Many types of intervention are possible, involving anatomical lesions (Glassman 1978), mutations (*neurogenetics), or pharmacological agents (e.g. Morris *et al.* 1986; Berman *et al.* 1998). Many examples for each of the above are mentioned throughout this book. The types of caveats that typically arise involve *post hoc* argumentation (see 'correlation' above), doubts about the specificity of the intervention, and the possibility that the effect of the lesion is masked by compensatory mechanisms *in vivo*.

5. *Sufficiency*. Does the mechanism *suffice* for memory formation? In practice, this criterion is more difficult to satisfy than the previous ones. It requires mapping candidate loci of the *engram. The methodology involves mimicry experiments, resembling those mentioned in 3 above. It is common practice to infer that if event A is both necessary and sufficient for event B to take place, B is caused by A.[2] The following examples illustrate the use of this criterion: induction of conditioned phototaxis in the mollusc *Hermissenda* by altering membrane properties of photoreceptors *in vivo* (Farley *et al.* 1983); microinfusion of the neurotransmitter octopamine into the brain to show that octopamine encodes the unconditioned stimulus in *classical conditioning of the *honeybee (Hammer and Menzel 1998); a similar experiment with serotonin and long-term facilitation in *Aplysia* (Sun and Schacher 1998); switching on *gluatamtergic *N*-methyl-D-aspartate *receptors in the *mouse in an attempt to prove that this receptor is crucial in *consolidation (Shimizu *et al.* 2000); induction of long-term memory in *Aplysia*, *Drosophila*, or the *honeybee* by activation of the cyclic adenosine monophosphate *intracellular signal transduction cascade, *CREB, and modulation of gene expression (Yin and Tully 1996; Muller 2000); reversible inactivation of the *cerebellum and brainstem pathways to show that they are necessary

and sufficient for conditioning the nictitating membrane reflex in the rabbit (Thompson *et al.* 2000); and microstimulation of visual cortex in order to alter the behavioural response of the behaving *monkey (Groh *et al.* 1997). Considering the number of variables involved in any brain function, it is rather unlikely that a single molecular or cellular event will suffice to induce memory faithfully. Nevertheless, activation or inhibition of key 'molecular switches', such as CREB, could have substantial behavioural effects.

6. *Exclusiveness*. The most demanding criterion is *exclusiveness*. Such a claim cannot be currently made for any candidate mechanism in learning. Some discussions of CREB do dare to hint that the manipulated cellular process plays an exclusive part in memory consolidation (e.g. Yin and Tully 1996). Again, as in the case of the criterion of sufficiency but even more so, the question is whether exclusiveness can at all be expected, as multiplicity of mechanisms and parallel pathways appear to be the rule in the brain systems that subserve learning.

The above or other criteria (e.g. Rose 1981) are applicable and useful in multiple domains of memory research. Here is another central question that calls for the formulation of criteria: How should one delineate and classify memory systems? (Shettleworth 1993; *taxonomy.) Occasionally the discussion of such issues leads us back to the good old philosophical 'problem of the criterion', even if this problem is not explicitly stated (see Sherry and Schacter 1987).

Selected associations: Method, Reduction, System

---

[1]An example of the use in learning experiments of a generic type of criterion that fits definition 1, is 'learning to criterion' in *acquisition.

[2]This inference is not a given. Some philosophers will raise the possibility that B is merely 'supervenient' upon A. Briefly speaking, a 'supervenient', or 'consequential' attribute comes along in addition to other attributes but is not necessarily entailed by them (Kim 1978; Davidson 1980; Hare 1984; *reduction). This is not an argument commonly employed by brain scientists. It does come up in discussions that concern the mind–body problem.

Cue

1. That aspect of the *stimulus that guides behaviour.

2. That aspect of the stimulus that distinguishes one stimulus from another in a discrimination task.

3. A stimulus that signals the need to respond.
4. A stimulus that triggers *retrieval.

'Cue' originated in the medieval theatre, and is the spelled name of the letter q, the abbreviation of *quandō*, Latin for 'when'. For a while it was also spelled qu or cu. It meant a signal that prompts another event in the performance, such as the entrance of an actor (Harrison 1998). Cues fulfil fundamental roles in all the paradigms and assays of learning and memory. Definition 1 is the generic one. It refers to both learned and innate (*a priori) cues. Definitions 2–4 are also presented because they express particular uses of 'cue' in the learning literature. Definition 2 specifically refers to cues as discriminators, a particularly useful notion in *instrumental learning situations, and also in ethology (Tinbergen 1969). Definition 3 marks cues as the timing signal, again, particularly useful in instrumental tasks (for an example of 'cues' per definitions 2 and 3, see Figure 23). Finally, definition 4 refers to cues as triggers of retrieval. The role of cues in retrieval is more critical than usually meets the inexperienced eye: an influential hypothesis that binds *acquisition, *context, retrieval, and *forgetting, termed 'the encoding specificity principle', proposes that memory is retrieved better when tested in the presence of the same cues that were present in acquisition (Tulving 1983).

Cues could be external or internal. External cues are not only those provided by the experimenter, but also those that the experimenter erroneously ignores. The latter are cues in the seemingly *controlled stimulus and context, including the behaviour of the experimenter (*bias, *Clever Hans). Internal cues are endogenous states of the organism, including circadian rhythms, which, again, are too often neglected in behavioural experiments.

An important thing to remember about cues is that they are seldom invariant over an experiment or across *subjects, even if the particular stimulus is kept constant. The behavioural significance of stimuli, hence their 'cueness', is altered by the experience of the subject with the same or other cues, which is as a matter of fact a trivial statement because this is simply learning, but also by the physiological and external context, including the presence of other cues, which is much less trivial. Multiple processes of cue revaluation are illustrated in *classical conditioning. A special case is when that portion of the stimulus that serves as a cue for a distinctive behaviour shrinks with training; this is called 'cue reduction'. Another important subset of processes is called 'cue competition' (Wasserman and Miller 1997). This refers to inhibition of the behavioural

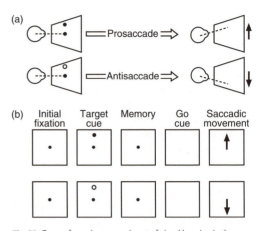

Fig. 23 Types of cues in an experiment of visual learning in the monkey (Zhang and Barash 2000). (a) The monkey was trained to make a brief, rapid eye movement (a saccade) either toward the stimulus (prosaccade) or in the opposite direction (antisaccade). This was done in the course of the analysis of neuronal correlates of visual decision making and performance in the posterioparietal *cortex, but for our purpose, only the behavioural part of the experiment will be mentioned. (b) The monkey was placed in front of a computer screen, and trained in successive stages ('shaped') to fixate on a stimulus at the centre of the visual field. A coloured stimulus, either red (full circle) or green (open circle), was then presented for 250 ms away from the fixating point. The colour was the 'target cue', instructing the monkey which type of saccade should be performed at the later part of the task (definitions 1 and 2). After an additional working memory interval of 1 s, the fixation stimulus disappeared. This signalled to the monkey to make the response (the 'GO' cue, definitions 1 and 3): prosaccade if the target stimulus was red, antisaccade if it was green. A proper response was rewarded (*reinforced) with juice. (Adapted from Zhang and Barash 2000.)

control by a conditioned stimulus (CS) due to the presence in training of another conditioned stimulus, that is more salient or is a better predictor of the unconditioned stimulus (US) or the *reinforcement. Two notable types of 'cue competition' are overshadowing and blocking.

Overshadowing is an increase in the associability of the more salient or more predictive of two or more stimuli present at the same time, at the expense of the other stimuli. Pavlov (1927) noted that when a conditioned salivary reflex was established in a dog to a simultaneous application of two stimuli, the more salient stimulus came to evoke salivation when presented alone, whereas the less salient stimulus was ineffective by itself. His conclusion was that 'When the stimuli making up the compound act upon different analysers, the effect of one of them when tested singly was found very commonly to overshadow the effect of the others' (*ibid.*). An example of overshadowing in instrumental conditioning was provided by Pearce and Hall (1978): two groups of rats were trained to press a lever for food. In one group, the delivery of the food was always preceded by a brief flash of light. In the other group, the light was uncorrelated with the food. In the test, the rats that had experienced the light–food correlated schedule pressed the lever at a slower rate than those trained under the uncorrelated light–food schedule. The authors concluded that pairing the light with food retarded the development of normal instrumental conditioning, because the light was a better predictor of the food, and therefore the stimulus–reinforcer association overshadowed the formation of the response–reinforcer association. The literature contains many other examples of overshadowing in classical and instrumental conditioning.

Blocking is inhibition of the conditioning to a stimulus, CS_1, in a compound $CS_1 + CS_2$ stimulus, by previous pairing of CS_2 with the US (Kamin 1968). In a classical experiment, Kamin (*ibid.*) used a conditional emotional response procedure (*fear conditioning). Rats were trained to press a bar for food, and upon mastering the operant task, were further conditioned to associate a CS with a fear-inducing US (electric shock). The fear response resulted in suppression of bar pressing in response to the CS. This was observed regardless of whether the CS was light, white noise, or a compound stimulus of both. But in the consecutive phases of the experiment, an interesting phenomenon emerged. When the rats were first conditioned to fear the noise, then conditioned to the compound stimulus, and then tested on the light, they showed essentially no fear response to the light. A similar phenomenon was noted when the animals were first conditioned to the light, then to the compound stimulus, and then tested on the noise. Thus prior training to an element of the compound stimulus blocked conditioning to the new, superimposed element. The interpretation is that in order for an association between a CS and a US to be formed, the US must *surprise the animal. If the animal already knows that CS_2 predicts the US, addition of CS_1 does not involve much additional surprise, and therefore association of CS_1 with the US is weak. (On the role of the unexpected in learning, see also *algorithm; on additional aspects of blocking phenomena; see Miller and Matute 1996; Holland 1988.)

The analysis of 'cue competition' has contributed to the compelling evidence that even apparently 'simple' forms of classical conditioning are actually manifestations of rather complex information processing in the brain, which involves interactions among the *internal representations of the associated stimuli. Hence in this respect, the cues have provided a valuable cue to the mechanisms underlying conditioning.

Selected associations: Attention, Clever Hans, Context, Recall, Stimulus

Culture

The collective body of institutions and traditions, material artefacts, regulations and procedures, *habits, rituals, and beliefs, created over time by a society or a group, and usually transmitted, both implicitly and explicitly, from one generation to another.

Cultūra in Latin meant tilling and husbandry, and *cultor* was a planter, inhabitant, and worshipper of gods (Cassell's *Concise Latin dictionary* 1966). In modern society, the agricultural connotations of culture are largely gone, but the sense of belonging to a physical or virtual niche remains; some kind of worshipping, be it religious or secular, is also often retained. So versatile are the uses and implications of 'culture', that dictionaries give up on defining it in a comprehensive manner. 'Culture' is widely discussed from different points of views in anthropology, sociology, archaeology, history, political science, critical theory and aesthetics, philosophy, ethology, and sociobiology (Kroeber and Kluckhohn 1963).

Three aspects of culture should interest us in the context of the present discussion. The first is culture as a process and vehicle for the transfer of information by behavioural means. This involves a number of channels, such as instruction via *observational learning, or cultural artefacts. A common manifestation of culture is *collective memory. The two, although related, should not be confused. Members of a group can share a collective memory but belong to separate cultures. Culture also includes material artefacts as well as contemporary institutions, regulations, and beliefs that do not necessarily make it into the collective memory of the group. Furthermore, certain social species in addition to *Homo sapiens are said to display rudiments of culture (Bonner 1980; Whiten *et al.* 1999; *birdsong, *monkey), but it is doubtful whether the members of any of these species share even a rudimentary collective memory, in terms of sets of historical narratives and beliefs.

The two other aspects of culture that are of interest to us here relate to certain anthropological and sociological aspects of the concept. More specifically, to science, of which brain and memory research are a prominent part, as a culture, and to the interaction of this culture with the rest of culture.

For Geertz (1983), culture was the 'webs of significance (man) himself has spun' and in which human beings are 'suspended'. These webs are composed of multiple types of threads, some material, some mental. In the world of science, 'culture' is hence the physical, procedural, intellectual, and emotional milieu, or 'webs of significance', in which scientists are entangled during most if not all their waking hours, and frequently also during the rest of the day. The notion that there are two intellectual cultures, that of scientists and that of 'literary intellectuals' or 'humanists' (Snow 1963), has turned over the years into a given in popular discourse on modern society. The question can be raised whether the split in the intellectual community is indeed so deep; whether it is inherently so or due mostly to mutual laziness; and, moreover, whether it is static. But clearly, in daily life, scientists do have their typical dialects, *methods (not necessarily generalizable to many facets of life), rituals, and worries, which altogether justifies their classification as members of a separate culture. Furthermore, within science, many separate subcultures could be discerned, according to the discipline and subdiscipline.

As far as the scientific culture in general is concerned, one of the most intriguing issues is indeed its interaction with society at large. This has been the topic of numerous novels and movies, too many of which depict the scientist as a dangerous lunatic or a weirdo at best (Haynes 1994). The interaction of science and society, including its potential futuristic outcome, has occasionally been the topic of works of letters composed by distinguished members of the scientific culture (e.g. Haldane 1923; Skinner 1961). And, of course, it is also the subject matter of serious academic work (for an introductory selection of scholarly themes and stands, see Olby et al. 1990; for a provocative point of view, see Midgley 1992; and for a recent view concerning the unwritten science–society 'contract', see Gibbons 1999).

But there is another aspect to the culture of science, which usually gains less publicity. This is the inner workings of scientific culture itself. Occasionally, a best-seller allows the public to glimpse at the *modus operandi* of the scientific community (e.g. Watson 1968). In recent years, unfortunately, a few fraud scandals and greed-driven rivalries have also attracted much attention. The truth, as every practising scientist knows, is less heroic and more complicated than depicted by egocentric accounts that make it to the

book-of-the-month shelf (for a few refreshing exceptions, see Brenner 1997; Weiner 1999; also some of the chapters in Hodgkin et al. 1977).

The culture of any scientific discipline, memory research no exception, could be depicted as a collection of conceptual, pragmatic, and ritualistic attributes that are partially shared with other scientific disciplines. They range from the philosophical to the mundane. The philosophical include, among others, the elementary, universal sets of the scientific methods and *criteria. These themselves are cognitive + cultural constructs. Being so, and to the justified dismay of scientists, these tenets of the scientific culture are a recurrent target for vicious attacks by the so-called 'postmodernists', who seem to capitalize on the inherent fallibility of the senses and the cognition of the human individual, yet utterly ignore the built-in safeguards that the scientific *system as a whole has painstakingly devised to hold a grip on reality, as well as the great successes of science and technology (for minute glimpses into these issues, see Midgley 1992; Gottfried and Wilson 1997). Other attributes of the scientific culture are on the more mundane side and include laboratory practices and rites (Lynch 1985, 1988; Pickering 1992), extensive overtime, lengthy seminars, international meetings, workshops, lecture and poster habits, manuscript and reviewer routines, worries about priority (*scoopophobia), etc. Whoever wishes to taste these facets of the scientific culture and never did, is cordially invited to mingle with the crowd in the yearly meeting of the American Society for Neuroscience (> 25,000 participants, a sure prescription for agoraphobia). And then there are those more specific elements of the culture of memory research that break down into further subdisciplines or, better, subcultures—those of the physiologists and their electrodes, the molecular biologists and their clones, the geneticists and their mutations, the psychologist and their *subjects, the neurologists and their *amnesics, the computational people and their *models, etc., etc.

In addition to the differences in training and occasionally in the *zeitgeist, and to the idiosyncratic *esprit de corps* and folklore, a major obstacle to intercultural and sometimes even to intracultural communication is the language barrier. Not only is the scientific jargon incomprehensible to the nonscientists, it is also frequently gibberish to scientists from other disciplines (for an informative scale of language obscureness see Hayes 1992). In this respect, there are two steps that scientists could take to facilitate mutual understanding and gain from it. First, it would be nice to stop using all these nonstop awkward acronyms without explaining them; they certainly turn into a mission impossible any attempt to follow seminars or read papers, even in the so-called general interest journals. How many neuroscientists can even dare to understand a sentence such as 'Kir6.2 produces K-ATP in the absence of SUR1'?[1] And is 'CSBs-CSAs-USs ISIs in DMTS' better? Second, it might be useful to recall what Socrates said to Meno (Plato, *Meno, 79c,d*):

'*Socrates:* … Does anyone know what a part of a virtue is, without knowing the whole?

'*Meno:* I suppose not.

'*Socrates:* No, and if you remember, when I replied to you about shape just now, I believe we rejected the type of answer that employs terms which are still in question and not yet agreed upon.

'*Meno:* We did, and rightly.

'*Socrates:* Then please do the same.'

Selected associations: Birdsong, Collective memory, Homo sapiens, Observational learning, Paradigm

---

[1]For another example related to the molecular neurobiology of learning, see ZENK in *immediate early genes.

Declarative memory

1. The *conscious recollection of facts and episodes.
2. The *internal representations of facts and episodes that are accessible to conscious recollection.
3. The memory *system that subserves the above.

The term 'declarative memory', depending on the *context of the discussion, refers to a faculty and experience of memory (definition 1), the material stored and *retrieved (definition 2), and the relevant brain system(s) (definition 3). That part of our memory is directly accessible to conscious recollection but part is not, was first explicitly stated by philosophers (e.g. de Biran 1804; Bergson 1908).[1] Ryle (1949) formulated it as the distinction between 'knowing that' and 'knowing how'. 'Knowing how' refers to *skills and procedures, 'knowing that' to information that can be 'declared', i.e. declarative memory.[2] Declarative memory is conventionally further subdivided into memory

for facts ('semantic'), and memory for episodes ('episodal', 'autobiographical'; Tulving 1983; *episodic memory). Episodic memory, and sometimes semantic memory, single-trial learning, yet could be modified over time, either by additional facts, new experiences, or retrieval in new contexts. Episodic memory includes information about an experience locked to a particular time and place, whereas semantic memory is not locked to specific coordinates in these *dimensions. Some authors classify 'episodic' apart from 'declarative' (Tulving and Markowitsch 1998). Similarly, in epistemology, 'knowledge by acquaintance', i.e. of people, places, and things, is distinguished from propositional or factual knowledge (Bernecker and Dretske 2000). The term 'cognitive memory' is also occasionally used for recollection with conscious awareness (Mishkin *et al*. 1997). 'Explicit' and 'implicit' (Graf and Schacter 1985; Schacter 1987) are sometimes used in the literature instead of 'declarative' and 'nondeclarative', respectively. Others, however, prefer to consider the explicit/ implicit dichotomy to be used in the *taxonomy of learning tasks and memory tests (*assay) rather than for that of memory *systems and mechanisms (e.g. Johnson and Hasher 1987; N.J. Cohen *et al*. 1997).[3]

Support in favour of the declarative/nondeclarative distinction has surfaced over the years not only via introspection but also in *controlled experiments in normal individuals (e.g. McDougall 1923; Eriksen 1960; Richardson-Klavehn and Bjork 1988). Yet the evidence that the brain indeed honours this distinction was ultimately provided by the neuropsychological investigation of *amnesia in humans and its *models in the *monkey (Cohen and Squire 1980; Squire and Zola 1996). It has been noted for years that the memory deficits in 'global' amnesics are not really global (e.g. Corkin 1968; Warrington and Weiskrantz 1968). A *classic study illustrates this point. Cohen and Squire (1980) subjected amnesic patients to a mirror-reading skill test, involving presentation of mirror-reflected words over consecutive sessions. Some words were presented only once and some were repeated. The reading time of the unique words was used to evaluate the ability to *acquire the procedure of mirror-reading, while the reading time of the repeated words reflected, in addition, the ability to remember specific data. Amnesic patients learned the mirror-reading skill, as indicated by the decrease with training of the time required to read the unique words. Their performance, however, did not improve further on tests of repeated words as it did in controls. Furthermore, none of the amnesics reported that the repeated words were indeed encountered beforehand. Hence, the nonamnesics learned both 'how' and 'that'; the amnesics only 'how'. Similar conclusions were obtained in different types of 'global' amnesics, using a variety of tasks that assay 'rule' ('how') vs. 'data' ('that') knowledge (Squire and Zola 1996).

The aforementioned data have been taken to indicate that amnesics can acquire nondeclarative information, and that mediotemporal brain structures damaged in 'global' amnesics (*hippocampus, *limbic system) are necessary for declarative but not for nondeclarative tasks. But is this indeed due to the existence of different brain circuits for declarative and nondeclarative information, respectively? The argument could still be raised that declarative and nondeclarative memory are subserved by the same circuits, but there is a general impairment in the processing of information in the brain, that affects only declarative memory.[4] Compelling evidence against this single-system hypothesis was provided by double-dissociation experiments. 'Double-dissociation' refers to a protocol in which the effect of two different circumscribed lesions, in areas A and B, is tested on two different phenotypes, X and Y (Teuber 1955; *control). If lesion A yields a defect in X but not in Y, while lesion B yields a defect in Y but not in X, then the defects in X and Y are not due to some across-the-board damage but rather to specific damage in the dissociable functions of areas A and B, respectively. The 'global' amnesics mentioned above showed only a 'single dissociation', i.e. lesion A yielded a defect in X but not in Y. For double dissociation, patients were sought that fail on nondeclarative but not on declarative tasks. Such patients were indeed identified (Gabrieli et al. 1995; Knowlton et al. 1996). For example, Parkinson's patients failed on a task that involved the acquisition of a mental *habit, i.e. nondeclarative knowledge, in spite of being able to acquire and *retrieve new declarative knowledge (Knowlton et al. 1996). Furthermore, this identifies the neostriatum, which is damaged in Parkinson disease, as critically involved in nondeclarative, but not declarative, memory.

*Functional neuroimaging *methods have further reinforced the conclusion that in humans the mediotemporal lobe subserves the acquisition and retrieval of declarative memory, in concert with the prefrontal cortex (e.g. Nyberg et al. 1996; Wagner et al. 1998a; Kirchhoff et al. 2000). There is, however, an ongoing debate in the literature whether the hippocampal formation contributes equally to both episodic and semantic memory, or primarily to episodic memory (Mishkin et al. 1997; Squire and Zola 1998; Tulving and Markowitsch 1998).

As a hallmark of the expression of declarativeness in humans is language, the task of identifying declarative

memory in subhuman species could become tricky.[5] There are three basic approaches to the problem.

1. Investigation in animals of the performance and brain mechanisms of *tasks that are declarative in humans*. These could be either tasks that normal *subjects report as involving awareness, or tasks sensitive to human amnesia (e.g. Zola-Morgan and Squire 1985; Clark and Squire 1998; Manns et al. 2000; *monkey). Some pure *recognition tasks (see *delay task) could be useful in this respect. The main problem is that different species, even different individuals and the same individual under different circumstances, can solve the same problem using different strategies.

2. Investigation in animals of the effect on learning and memory of *circumscribed lesions in* mediotemporal and diencephalic *brain regions that are assumed to subserve declarative memory in humans* (e.g. Zola-Morgan and Squire 1985; Squire and Zola 1996; Mishkin et al. 1997; *hippocampus, *monkey). Here the difficulties are, first, it is unlikely that brain circuits that subserve declarative tasks in humans do only that; the hippocampus, for example, is involved in memory with or without conscious awareness (e.g. Chun and Phelps 1999). Second, the same brain regions may fulfil different functions in different species. Further, the rationale risks circularity: a task may be deemed declarative in humans because it depends on a brain region that is postulated to subserve declarativeness, and then is labelled declarative in animals because it depends on this same region.

3. A different approach is to attempt to identify *primitives of declarative memory*, which are shared by prehuman manifestations of declarativity. The assumption is that declarative systems have emerged in evolution prior to the ability of *Homo sapiens* to experience and express declarativity the human way. This assumption is taken by the followers of approaches 1 and 2 above as well, but here it is bolder and more speculative, because it searches for the deep structure of the computational theory (*level) of the memory system. It is further assumed that 'declarativess' is not necessarily the decisive distinctive attribute of declarative memory systems. It has been argued, for example, that the elementary characteristic of declarative memory is the ability to encode internal representations according to relationships among specific items, and flexibly *generalize and integrate this information in novel situations (N.J. Cohen et al. 1997; Eichenbaum 1997a). This, so goes the claim, differs from nondeclarative memory, which is more rigid (for opposition to this view, see Willingham 1998). Guided by this line of argument, 'paired associates tasks' were employed to tap into inferential, flexible memory. In paired associates tasks, the subject learns a list of

discrete pairs of associations, denoted generically A–B, where typically A is to serve as a *cue for the recall of B or for a response that stems from the recall of B. Paired-associate learning involves multiple cognitive processes (e.g. McGuire 1961), including acquisition of associations among discrete *stimuli and of stimulus–response rules. In humans, A–B could be arbitrary verbal stimuli, whereas in laboratory animals, A–B are nonverbal sensory cues. Hippocampally lesioned animals fail on some versions of paired associates tasks that tax flexibility of response, for example, on the ability to associate paired elements presented in the reverse of training order (Eichenbaum 1997*a*). This was taken to support the idea that such tasks can be used to test declarative memory in nonhuman species.

A nice spin-off of the flexibility + generalization = declarativeness hypothesis is that it is in line with the classification of *priming as an intermediate stage between nondeclarative and declarative capabilities, with repetition priming being less flexible and less generalizable, conceptual priming being more flexible and more generalizable, yet both still independent of conscious awareness.[6] But identification of the flexibility of representational reconstruction as the core attribute of declarative memory system is only a working hypothesis. Note that if primitives of declarative memory independent of conscious awareness were to be identified, the definitions of declarative memory above will have to be modified, or become a subtype of a more comprehensive definition.

All this leads us to the question whether the term 'declarative' is appropriate to be used in animal studies. The distinction 'explicit'/'implicit', despite the aforementioned occasional claim that it fits tests better than systems, may be more useful in animal studies, especially because it does not explicitly refer to 'declarativeness' with its linguistic roots and connotations. It also blunts the need for conscious awareness, which is problematic, especially in *simple systems. We do not know at which stage of evolution conscious awareness has entered the scene (Tulving 1983; Moscovitch 1996; Eichenbaum 1999). This is definitely an issue in which the prudent use of *Ockham's razor to eliminate superfluous *anthropomorphism is advisable.

Selected associations: Amnesia, Episodic memory, Hippocampus, Learning, Taxonomy

---

[1]'Recollection' refers here to both *recall and *recognition, see there.

[2]In linguistics, a 'declarative sentence' makes a statement, i.e. informs someone of something (Winograd 1972; Lyons 1977).

[3]See also on tasks of implicit vs. explicit learning, under *learning. In many cases, information learned implicitly can later be used either in a declarative or in a nondeclarative mode, and the same is true for information learned explicitly.

[4]For example, it could be argued that amnesics are incapable of processing information at a *level that permits proper *acquisition and *retrieval of declarative information, but still capable of processing at a 'shallower' level, presumably sufficient for nondeclarative memory. On levels of processing in acquisition and retrieval, see also *dimension.

[5]For the sake of simplicity, no distinction is made here between memory of facts and memory of episodes. It is clearly possible that some nonhuman species have declarative memory of one type but not the other. See also *episodic memory.

[6]On the hypothetical place of priming in the evolution of memory systems, see also Tulving (1983).

Delay task

1. **A task in which a delay is interposed between a *stimulus and the opportunity to respond to it.**

2. **A task in which response is guided by an *internal representation of a stimulus in the absence of that stimulus.**

Delay tasks were introduced into experimental psychology by Hunter (1913), who found that a variety of species can learn to respond to a light stimulus after a delay, which in his hands ranged from a few seconds in rats to about half an hour in children. The procedures were later refined by Yerkes and Yerkes (1928) in their investigation on mnemonic capabilities in the chimpanzee. Since then, a variety of delay tasks have been developed and proven highly useful in the measurement of short-term and *working memory, *recognition, and *recall.

Delay tasks comprise an heterogeneous family whose members are united solely by the fact that a delay is introduced between the stimulus and the opportunity to respond to it (definition 1).[1] Other than that, these tasks could be used to tax different facets of learning and memory, *attention and motivation, innate response predispositions (*a priori), response strategies, and *planning. The delay period may be blank, or, alternatively, the delay is filled with other stimuli, which could serve as distracters. A common assumption is that in all the delay tasks, correct *performance taps into the ability to hold in memory information about the stimulus in the absence of that stimulus (definition 2). In some delay tasks, the validity of this assumption must not be taken for granted. For example, consider the *spatial delayed alternation* task. The subject is first rewarded for selecting one of two positions in a response chamber or a *maze. This is followed by a delay, after which the correct response is choosing the alternate position. Thus the subject must remember over the delay that it had responded to position A, and master the rule that the next response is B, and so on (*learning set). The memory used is a combination of recall (of the last response) and recognition (of the situation after the delay). The problem with this type of spatially guided delay paradigm is that the subject could adopt a strategy of orienting toward the correct position while still in the sample phase, hence eliminating the need to rely on the internal representation of the stimulus over the delay (Hunter 1913; Steckler *et al.* 1998a).

Indeed some authors distinguish 'delayed response' from 'delayed comparison' tasks (Steckler *et al.* 1998a). In delayed response tasks, all the information necessary for the internal representation of the correct response is available before the delay, and the behaviour could represent a *habit response that only awaits the *cue in the test. In delayed comparison, additional information must be supplied during the test, involving the comparison of past and present situations. To emit a correct response, the subject must recombine the information carried over the delay with the on-line test information. Examples for delayed comparison tasks are provided by the *delayed matching to sample* (DMTS) and the *delayed nonmatching to sample* (DNMTS) tasks. Here the sample stimulus, usually a visual one, is presented and then withdrawn. After a delay, the sample stimulus is presented again along with one or more additional stimuli. The subject has to respond by either choosing the previous stimulus (DMTS) or a different stimulus (DNMTS). As it is not a spatially guided response to a recurrent situation (compare with delayed spatial alternation above), the subject cannot 'cheat' by orienting during the training phase and merely release the planned motor response in the test.

A particularly useful DNMTS task is the *trial unique* DNMTS (Gaffan 1974; Mishkin and Delacour 1975).

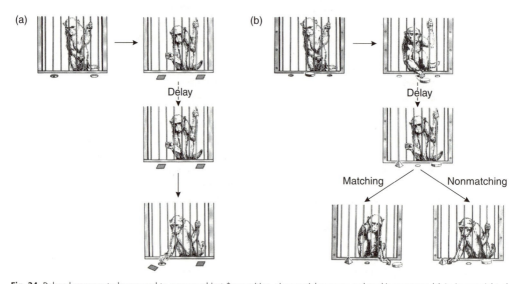

Fig. 24 Delayed response tasks are used to measure object *recognition, visuospatial memory, and working memory. (a) A visuospatial task. The monkey is placed in a Wisconsin General Testing Apparatus (Harlow and Bromer 1938). A food reward is placed in one of two wells in front of the cage. Both wells are then covered. After a delay (usually a few seconds or minutes), the monkey has to uncover the baited well. This task measures the ability to remember visuospatial information over the delay. (b) Delayed matching and nonmatching to sample tasks. A visually conspicuous object is placed over a central reward-baited well. The monkey replaces the object to obtain the food reward. After a delay, the monkey is confronted with the same object paired with a new one. In the delayed matching-to-sample task (left), displacement of the familiar object is rewarded. This test measures visual recognition and the association of an object with reward. In the delayed nonmatching-to-sample task (right), displacement of the nonfamiliar object is rewarded. In the trial-unique version of this task, each object is seen in only one trial during the whole series of tests. The trial-unique nonmatching-to-sample is appropriate for quantifying recognition memory, because reward is only an incentive to perform the task, and the ability to associate a specific object with reward does not contribute to success on the test. The monkey masters the nonmatching tasks faster than the matching tasks, because it has an *a priori tendency to explore novelty. (Modified from Mishkin and Appenzeller 1987; Dudai 1989.)

This paradigm has been extensively used in the analysis of visual recognition in the *monkey. In brief, a monkey is placed in a test enclosure, such as the Wisconsin General Testing Apparatus (WGTA, Figure 24) (Harlow and Bromer 1938), and presented with a visually conspicuous 'junk' object over a central baited food well. The monkey learns to uncover the well and retrieve the food reward. After a delay, in which a screen is lowered to hide the manipulation of stimulus tray from the monkey, the same object is paired with another, novel 'junk' object, each presented over a lateral well. The monkey must now avoid the familiar object and displace the new one. The procedure is repeated, with new 'junk' objects in each trial. As the objects are unique to each trial, no object–reward associations are formed (the reward here is merely an incentive to perform the test). The results could therefore be construed as representing 'pure' visual recognition combined with the innately dispositioned rule of 'go for the new one'. Furthermore, the information from one trial is irrelevant to the next, and therefore this procedure is also useful in tapping *working memory.

Selected delay tasks are key components of test batteries used in the analysis of monkey *models of the human *amnesic syndrome (Zola-Morgan and Squire 1985). This is because performance on such tasks, e.g. DNMTS, maps on to multiple features of the amnesic syndrome, including the dependence on the length of the delay, the sensitivity to interference, and the independence of sensory modality. Attempts have been made to develop reliable DNMTS procedures for rodents as well, to facilitate the molecular and *neurogenetic analysis of amnesia models, but the interpretation of the behavioural data is still unsettled (e.g. Mumby 1995); it is not unlikely that monkeys will run happily in huge *mazes in memory labs around the world before rats will be able to solve the monkey's favourite delay tasks.

Performance on delay tasks is subserved by multiple brain regions, including *cortical and subcortical (Eichenbaum et al. 1994; Mishkin and Murray 1994; Brown and Xiang 1998; Parker and Gaffan 1998; Steckler et al. 1998b; *hippocampus, *limbic system). The involvement of some cortical regions is modality specific, e.g. inferotemporal cortex in vision (Mishkin and Murray 1994) or somatosensory cortex in haptic tasks (Zhou and Fuster 1996), whereas the involvement of other cortical regions, i.e. perirhinal and parahippocampal cortex, is modality independent (Suzuki et al. 1993). Visuospatial delayed response tasks rely heavily on frontal function (Jacobsen and Niseen 1937; Mishkin 1957), and the performance on these tasks is correlated with prefrontal neuronal activity (Fuster 1973; Friedman and Goldman-Rakic 1994; *retrieval, *working memory). Delay tasks are also useful in assessment and research of human neurological and affective disorders. For example, poor performance of chronic schizophrenics on visuospatial delay tasks is cited to support the notion that frontal pathology is involved (Pantelis et al. 1997).

Selected associations: Attention, Instrumental conditioning, Learning set, Monkey, Working memory

---

[1]'Delay task' should not be confused with 'delay conditioning', which is a protocol of *classical conditioning. In delay conditioning, the onset of the unconditioned stimulus occurs after the onset, but prior to the offset, of the conditioned stimulus; hence the response in delay conditioning does not have to be guided by off-line information.

Dementia

A chronic syndrome of heterogeneous aetiology characterized by multiple cognitive deficits that include severe memory impairment.

The common feature of all the dementias is multiple cognitive deficits that include severe memory impairment, and at least one of the following cognitive disturbances: aphasia (deterioration of language function); apraxia (impaired ability to execute motor activities despite intact sensorimotor function); agnosia (failure to identify objects despite intact sensory function); or disturbance in executive function (the ability to reason, *plan and execute complex behaviour) (DSM-IV 1994). Severe memory impairment in the absence of other cognitive disturbances is *amnesia. Hence demented patients suffer from amnesic disturbances, but 'global amnesics' with selective mediotemporal and telencephalic lesions are not demented. Dementia usually displays insidious onset and progressive exacerbation of symptoms. The dementias are differentiated on the basis of their aetiology (Fraser 1987; Edwards 1993; Knopman 1993; DSM-IV 1994; Larson and Imai 1996). The most prevalent (>30%) is Alzheimer's disease (AD) (see below). Other prevalent causes of dementia are: cerebrovascular accidents (vascular or multi-infarct dementia, 15–20% of cases); chronic alcoholism; head trauma; Parkinson's disease; Huntington disease; Pick's disease; Creutzfeldt–Jacob disease; and complications of AIDS. The incidence of dementia increases with age. Estimates for the prevalence of dementia are 2–10% at >65 years of age, increasing to 20–40% at >80 years of age (Jorm *et al.* 1987; DSM-IV 1994; Price and Sisodia 1998). Dementias that become apparent at <65 years of age are termed 'early-onset'; those that become apparent later are 'late-onset' or 'senile'.

In many societies there is a remarkable shift toward extended life expectancy. Therefore, diseases of old age that were rarely encountered only a century ago are now becoming an epidemic. In 1900, less than 1% of the world's population was over 65 years of age, in 2000, it was already about 7%, and the predication for 2050 is 15–20% (Olshansky *et al.* 1993; Heilig 1997). The main concern is AD. Named after the physician who first described it (Alzheimer 1907), it typically starts with significant recurrent lapses of *episodic (*declarative) and *prospective memory. At first impaired encoding is possibly more significant than increased *forgetting (Granholm and Butters 1988), and *metamemory is relatively spared (Moulin *et al.* 2000). The disease progresses to severe global memory deficits accompanied by other cognitive and emotional disturbances, and culminates in dissolution of personality and inability to perform even the simplest of tasks (McKhann *et al.* 1984; DSM-IV 1994). AD destroys the *hippocampal formation, neo*cortex, basal forebrain, and additional brain organs and circuits. The affected brain displays two distinguishing pathologies: extracellular plaques and intracellular tangles. The plaques are extracellular deposits of aggregated insoluble fragments of proteins (peptides), called the β-amyloid peptides (AβP). The AβPs are cleaved by enzymes, secretases, from the extracellular segment of a larger membrane protein, the amyloid precursor protein (APP), which normally plays a role in cell–cell and cell–matrix interactions. Tangles are intracellular deposits of hyperphosphorylated tau proteins, constituents of the cellular skeleton (Kosik 1994; Edelberg and Wei 1996).

We do not yet understand AD, but some candidate cellular clues are already available. One line of incriminating evidence points to the severe loss of cholinergic neurons (i.e. neurons that secret *acetylcholine) that is detected in the basal forebrain of AD patients (Bartus *et al.* 1982; McGeer *et al.* 1984). As acetylcholine is proposed to subserve widespread cognitive functions, the hypothesis was raised that cholinergic dysfunction is the cause of dementia. Furthermore, as there is some decline in cholinergic function even in normal ageing subjects, the suggestion was further made that all dementia, including modest, 'benign' senile dementia,

result from cholinergic deficits; and that in AD, the number of cholinergic neurons is reduced below a threshold (<25%, McGeer *et al.* 1984) that is required for minimal cognitive function. This is 'the cholinergic hypothesis' of dementia. Drugs that increase the availability of acetylcholine in brain were introduced as cognitive boosters in early stages of AD, so far with modest success (Giacobini and McGeer 2000; also *nootropics). Actually, nicotine, an activator of some acetylcholine *receptors, may be the only real reason why smokers could justify their addiction (e.g. Di Carlo *et al.* 2000; but smokers should not feel good about it, because smoking reduces pulmonary function, depriving the brain of oxygen and impairing cognition; Emery *et al.* 1997). The beneficial impact of cholinergic activators on memory is possibly due to their effects on arousal, *attention, and *performance (Everitt and Robbins 1997), rather than memory *per se*.

Another type of potential breakthrough in understanding AD was made possible by *neurogenetics.[1] AD occurs in two main forms. Some variants of the disease, mostly early-onset, propagate in families ('familial AD'). Other, late onset variants, occur sporadically in the general population ('sporadic AD', 'senile dementia of the AD type'). Familial AD provides an opportunity to hunt AD-related mutations. Some were indeed identified (Goate *et al.* 1991; Edelberg and Wei 1996; Levi-Lahad and Bird 1996; Hardy *et al.* 1998; Price and Sisodia 1998). To date, familial AD has been linked to mutations in three genes, that encode APP, presenilin-1 (PS1) and presenilin-2 (PS2). APP is the amyloid precursor protein mentioned above. The presenilins are membrane proteins thought to affect the activity of the secretases that act on APP and lead to accumulation of the insoluble AβPs in plaques. An additional gene, encoding apolipoprotein E (ApoE), is related to the aetiology of AD. Together with other lipoproteins, ApoE plays a part in the metabolism and transport of cholesterol and triglycerides. One of its forms, ApoE4, has been associated with increased susceptibility to sporadic, late-onset AD. ApoE4 interacts with AβPs and tau (Edelberg and Wei 1996). The identification of mutations that comprise a risk factor in AD has led to a number of genetic *models of AD in mice (Price *et al.* 2000). The relevance of these animal models to the human AD pathology must yet be established (e.g. Janus *et al.* 2000).

So what triggers AD? Some authors trust that the amyloid cascade is to be blamed (Hardy *et al.* 1998). Others favour the idea that the pathology is initiated elsewhere, and that the plaques and tangles ensue. It is noteworthy that in the mouse, a genetic trick that reduces nerve growth factor and basal forebrain cholinergic activity, gave rise to age-dependent appearance of amyloid plaques and neurofibrillary tangles in the cortex and hippocampus (Capsoni *et al.* 2000). This raises the possibility that lack of growth factors induces AD-like neurodegeneration. However, again, the relevance to the human disease is unclear. Such research is of great interest not merely because it is expected to explain how AD happens, but also because it could identify drugs to prevent the catastrophe. Interestingly, an almost forgotten hallmark of AD, local inflammatory response to plaques, tangles, and neuronal degeneration (Rogers *et al.* 2000), has recently gained renewed interest: certain nonsteroidal anti-inflammatory drugs retard the symptoms of AD (Giacobini and McGeer 2000). After all this sophisticated molecular biology, we may end up swallowing aspirin to combat senility (the reader is strongly urged not to regard this as a practical advice).

Does AD research contribute to memory research? To answer that, we must separate memory from *plasticity. The contribution to memory research *per se* is there, but limited. AD is not a memory-specific pathology. In this respect, it is different from the *amnesic syndrome, or from circumscribed dementias that result from degeneration to localized brain foci (e.g. Graham 1999). Indeed, the analysis of AD does corroborate the preferential role of the *cerebral cortex, hippocampus and basal forebrain in memory. The observation that in AD, event memory is typically degraded before fact memory, and declarative before procedural memory, provides additional support to the conventional *taxonomy of memory systems. But the major contribution of AD research, and dementia research in general, is expected to be in the field of *plasticity, including the role of inter- and *intracellular signalling cascades in plasticity. This is because the common denominator of all dementias might be a catastrophe of neural plasticity (Mesulam 1999; Bothwell and Giniger 2000). Seen this way, dementia could be the heavy price we risk paying at old age for our ability to learn so efficiently throughout life.

Selected associations: Acetylcholine, Attention, Plasticity, Real-life memory

---

[1]Neurogenetics has contributed in recent years to the identification of risk factors of some other dementias as well (e.g. Garcia and Cleveland 2001).

Development

1. **Progression over time of a *system from one state to another according to a programme.**

2. **Progression over time from nonspecialized to specialized structure and function.**

3. **Progression over time from simpler to more complex structure and function.**

Biological development (*des-* + *voloper*, old French for 'to wrap') is manifested in growth, remodelling, and specialization of cells and tissues. This is accompanied by a change in the functional capabilities of the organism, which, in the case of the nervous system, could include modification of learning capabilities (Marcus *et al.* 1988; Hartshorn *et al.* 1998; Stanton 2000). The relationship of development and growth to learning raises some of the most fundamental issues in the neurosciences, abutting molecular biology on the one hand and philosophy on the other. Among these: how do brain circuits achieve their complexity and specificity? How much of learning is merely unravelling by experience of information that is already encoded in the genes? Are the cellular mechanisms of learning an extension of, or even identical to, the mechanisms that operate in development and growth? 'Growth and learning', wrote Holt (1931), 'are one continuous process, to the earlier phases of which we give the one name, and to the later ... phases we give the other.' He was not the first to suggest that. The notion that when we learn our neural tissue grows was explicit in the scientific and philosophical writings of the late nineteenth century. Furthermore, some of the proposals referred specifically to the primary site where growth should occur—the *synapse, which at that time was not even yet known by that name: 'For every act of memory ... there is a specific grouping or coordination of sensations and movements, by virtue of specific growths in the cell junctions' (Bain 1872, cited in Finger 1994). More elaborate experience-dependent growth theories emerged only later (e.g. Kappers 1917; Hebb 1949), paving the way first to the proposal (Monne 1949), and later to the discovery (Flexner *et al.* 1963; Agranoff and Klinger 1964; Barondes and Cohen 1966), that *de novo* *protein synthesis, hence modulation of gene expression, is required for the encoding of long-term memory (LTM).

The function LTM ~f(Growth), where 'growth' is synaptic remodelling, is hence a *paradigmatic tenet of the current neurobiological *zeitgeist. But it is more than that. It also provides a guideline and framework for experiments on the biological bases of lasting memory. For if growth is concerned, then the study of the cellular mechanisms of LTM can borrow not only concepts but also *methods and data from the study of development. And as developmental processes follow rules shared by different tissues, organisms and phyla (Wolpert *et al.* 1998; Fraser and Harland 2000; Scott 2000), the demarcation line between the mechanisms specific to LTM and those that occur in other developing tissues that are irrelevant to learning, may be blurred. The implications of this will be further noted below. In the meantime, a few generalizations are noteworthy. Similarly to all other tissues (*ibid.*), the development of the nervous system involves cell division, the emergence of pattern, change in form, cell differentiation, and growth. In the process, neurons migrate over distances from their place of birth to their place of work, start to express specific gene products, including enzymes, *receptors, and *ion channels, form connections with their target areas, and then establish specific synaptic contacts. Even a brief account of each of these families of processes and mechanisms far exceeds the scope of this discussion (for guides to neurodevelopment, see Jacobson 1991; Goodman and Shatz 1993; Hatten 1999; for comments on the history of the discipline, Cowan 1998). Suffice it to note that in principle, two types of mechanisms work in concert in the formation of functional circuits in brains: *activity independent*, and *activity dependent*. The former are guided solely or mostly by genetic instructions, and usually occur even before the neurons become functionally active. The latter depend on extracellular signals, such as hormones, growth factors, and ions. The interaction between genetics and experience is especially important during certain 'critical periods' in development (e.g. Katz 1999; *birdsong, *imprinting, *nutrients).

It is useful to consider the relationship between experience-dependent modifications that take place in development and those that occur in learning, in terms of *levels of organization and analysis.

1. *The level of overall computational strategy.* *Stimuli that result in experience-dependent modifications may either 'instruct' a system to change, or 'select' one or a few among multiple endogenous states. The 'selectionist' strategy has 'hardware' and 'software' versions. The 'hardware' version proposes that experience selects and stabilizes certain morphological configurations of the system. The 'software' version only assumes that experience selects and stabilizes certain 'pre-representations', i.e. functional states of the

system, which may or may not be subserved by specific morphological configurations (see *a priori, *internal representations). 'Instructionist' and 'selectionist' strategies, which refer to multiple spatial and temporal *dimensions in the function of the tissue, were proposed for development and for learning alike (Hebb 1949; Pringle 1951; Changeux and Danchin 1976; Young 1979; Lo and Poo 1991; Edelman 1993; Marler 1997; Quartz and Sejnowski 1997).

2. *The level of the *algorithms that implement the strategy.* Similar synaptic algorithms are postulated to operate in experience-dependent modification in development and in adult learning. Foremost in current theories and *modelling are Hebbian algorithms, or their conceptual progenies, including some that restrict plasticity only to 'critical periods' (e.g. Bienenstock *et al.* 1982; *metaplasticity).

3. *The level of the biological mechanisms that implement the algorithms.* Here again, similar molecular and cellular mechanisms are discovered in development and learning. They involve modulation of gene expression by extracellular stimuli, culminating in tissue remodelling (e.g. Corfas and Dudai 1991; Weiler *et al.* 1995; Davis *et al.* 1996; Martin and Kandel 1996; McAllister *et al.* 1999; Pham *et al.* 1999; *CREB, *immediate early genes, *intracellular signal transduction cascade, *late response genes). Whether the mechanisms are only similar or indeed identical is another story, the conclusion of which is not yet known. For example, the similarity between experience-dependent synaptogenesis in the developing brain and *long-term potentiation in the mature brain may be a bit overstated (Constantine-Paton and Cline 1998). Similarly, the role of neurotransmitters in neural development may require a second thought (Verhage *et al.* 2000).

The relationship of development to learning raises a number of real or apparent conceptual problems, which transcend the discussion of the specific neuronal mechanisms.

1. The *specialization paradox.* Definitions 1 and 2 above leave open the possibility that development may restrict the potential and *capacity of a system. (To mention an extreme, apoptosis, programmed cell death, is also a developmental programme; Kuan *et al.* 2000.) For example, the 'hardware' version of 'selectionist' models assume selective elimination of synapses. Yet learning by definition adds *internal representations to our mental repertoire. If learning mimics developmental processes, and developmental processes eliminate degrees of freedoms in the system, is there a paradox here? Only an apparent one. First, elimination of alternatives is itself added information. Second, elimination

of synapses does not necessarily undermine the potential representational complexity and capacity of a circuit, because this is also expected to be determined by functional synaptic capabilities that could be added in development (definition 3). Third, 'hardware' versions of selectionist processes might occur in development but only in some learning systems, e.g. 'prepared learning' (*birdsong, *imprinting), and not in others. And fourth, synaptic remodelling and growth during adult learning may provide the brain with a continuous supply of substrates for further, ongoing development. Moreover, in some brain regions new neurons are added in adulthood (e.g. Gould *et al.* 1999*a,b*; Shors *et al.* 2001; *birdsong, *hippocampus; but see some doubts concerning neurogenesis in the adult mammalian brain, in Rakic 2002). Nobody knows what these new neurons are doing there, but one possibility is that they compensate for reduced capacity induced by specialization.

2. The *relevance issue*. When we do detect growth in circuits that learn, how do we know that this is at all related to memory (*criterion)? Growth and tissue remodelling that are triggered by a training situation may fulfil functions other than learning, such as *homeostasis. At the time of writing, there is not even a single case in which learning-related morphological changes in circuits and synapses have been proven

without doubt to fulfil functional, not to mention causal role in the use-dependent representational change in the circuit. With powerful model systems such as cultured *Aplysia* circuits, that could enable selective lesioning of individual synapses and neurites, the evidence may soon be provided.

3. The *persistence problem*. If indeed LTM ~ f (Growth), and given that circuits undergo substantial changes with time (e.g. Purves *et al.* 1986; Segal *et al.* 2000): How come memory endures in the circuit spite of the turnover of its components? The solution to this problem is discussed under *persistence.

4. What makes memory memory? If cellular mechanisms of development and growth subserve LTM, why not concentrate on development in *simple systems, even in non-neuronal tissues and cell cultures that are much easier to handle than brains, in order to understand the formation of memory? This is what some capable investigators try to do. But a caveat is appropriate. The simple system approach casts some light on *plasticity but not necessarily on *memory. The latter, we should remember, is a functional property of circuits. Therefore, we should not expect to decipher the computations and codes that are used, say, in a cortical circuit, by analysing development in cell culture or a neuromuscular junction. Following the

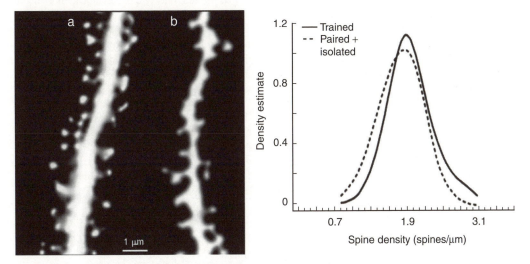

Fig. 25 Ongoing development and growth in the adult brain: The density of dendritic spines in the rat *hippocampus is affected by experience. One group of rats (*trained*) was subjected to a complex, stimulating environment that enhanced their ability to learn their way in a water *maze. Another group was composed of individual rats caged in isolation in a quiet environment (*isolated*), and yet another group of rats caged in pairs in a similar boring environment (*paired*). The picture on the left depicts extremes of variability in the number of dendritic spines in hippocampal area CA1 in *trained* (a) and *isolated* (b) rats. The graph on the right shows the overall increase in spine density in the *trained* vs. *isolated* + *paired* rats. Although the overall difference is small, it is significant and may reflect an important effect of experience on the localized growth of synaptic contacts. Courtesy of Per Andersen; see also Moser *et al.* (1997) and Andersen and Soleng (1998).

same line of argumentation, even if we understand how neuronal circuits develop, we cannot hope to grasp their contribution to memory and behaviour unless we decipher the representations and computations performed by these circuits in the subsecond range. This is clearly a time-scale (*dimension) very different from that addressed in the study of development.

Selected associations: Consolidation, Immediate early genes, Late response genes, Persistence

Dimension

1. **Each of a set of measures of a *system.**
2. **Magnitude.**
3. **Each of a set of independent directions in space.**
4. **The smallest number of coordinates needed to specify uniquely a point in space.**

'Dimension' stems from *dīmētīrī*, Latin for 'to measure out'. Definitions 1 and 2 are the ones most relevant to this discussion, which does not (yet?) involve treatment of spaces with dimensions higher than the familiar four of space–time (definitions 3 and 4).[1]

Brains are considered to have evolved in evolution under pressures that were supposed to lead to the selection of faculties beneficial for survival in a limited niche of the universe.[2] It is therefore likely, in spite of occasional sparks of unjustified hubris that claim otherwise, that the individual human brain perceives only limited dimensions of nature, in terms of both properties and magnitude. That segment of our physical ambience that is directly accessible to our senses and has shaped our intuition[3] can be dubbed, based on its dimensions, as the 'mesoworld'. It refers to properties such as size, number, and location in a four-dimensional space; to scales of millimetres to kilometres, milligrams to kilograms, seconds to years; and to complexities that are subserved by processing a few chunks of information at a time. Whatever transcends the aforementioned properties, scales, or complexities, requires *culturally derived technical and conceptual tools for detection, qualification, quantification, and analysis (e.g. Nicolis and Prigogine 1989; Mainzer 1994; Wilson 1995). Science literates do learn to accommodate in their mind notions of entities such as electrons and atoms, the speed of light, galaxies, and black holes; but whether such dimensions are always assimilated in intuition is open to debate. Similarly, in the analysis of the brain

itself, we should expect to encounter dimensions that are difficult to grasp intuitively. These may involve quantities (e.g. the number of synapses in a human brain), complexities (e.g. the spatiotemporal activity patterns of large *intracellular signalling networks or *cell assemblies), and qualities (e.g. *consciousness).

Contemplating the dimensions of the research object at the outset of the investigation is always useful. It yields a rough estimate of what lies ahead, assists in focusing on the appropriate *levels of analysis and on the right *methodologies, and even provides a safeguard against certain types of *artefacts. The measures (definition 1) that are within the realm of the 'mesoworld' are a straightforward business: we naturally tend to characterize an object in terms of size, location, or time. Other measures are invisible to the naive eye. These are 'latent dimensions', which could be real, or merely useful hypothetical constructs. They may pop out even in the absence of rigorous statistical analysis, although their verification should involve statistics (Martin and Bateson 1993; Kerlinger and Lee 2000). Alternatively, they become apparent only by factor analysis (Spearman 1904; Thurstone 1947; Kerlinger and Lee 2000). In factor analysis the correlations among variables are used to determine which variables vary together and hence could share an underlying factor. Such factors are candidate dimensions. For example, analysis of the results of a battery of common intelligence tests unveils the presence of two major factors, verbal and mathematical ability. We could then pursue the in-depth analysis of the verbal and mathematical dimensions of human cognition. In this case, but not necessarily in others, the unveiled dimensions agree with intuition.

Let's now illustrate some dimensions of memory. The sample below is highly selective. Some important dimensions are omitted, including level, location (*engram), *representational complexity, *development, and emotion. When appropriate, for each dimension (definition 1), the relevant magnitude (definition 2) will be noted.

1. *Time.* This is per definition an essential dimension of memory. In humans, memories can last anywhere between 10^0 and 10^9 s, depending on whether they are sensory, short-term, long-term, or practically permanent (*consolidation, *phase, *taxonomy; *collective memories may extend over 10^{12} s). This immediately implies that it is naive to expect to find a master solution to the mechanisms of memory. A 'cognitive beat' is 10^{-2}–10^{-1} s. Whether a *stimulus triggers the formation of a memory or not is

determined within 10^{-1}–10^{0} s (*attention, *perception, *phase). *Working memory lasts 10^{1}–10^{2} s. Cellular consolidation of long-term memory takes place over 10^{2}–10^{4} s; system consolidation in the mammalian brain requires 10^{3}–10^{6} s and possibly even more (Dudai 1996). All this means that critical events in the biology of *acquisition should be addressed by biophysics (Dudai 1997b). Practically, most of the current research on acquisition actually addresses events that take place long after initial critical decisions have been made, and some even forgotten. This is especially true for molecular studies, which deal with processes and mechanisms in the 10^{2}–10^{5} s range. These are hence expected to tap after-effects of initial encoding and registration, consolidation, and *homeostasis.

2. *Size of the neural machinery.* The number of neurons expected to encode a relatively simple defensive reflex in *Aplysia* is 10^{2}–10^{3}. The minimal number of cortical neurons needed to reliably encode and transmit physiologically meaningful information is estimated to be $<10^{2}$ (e.g. Shadlen and Newsome 1998). However, real-life engrams in the mammalian brain are expected to be distributed over much larger numbers of neurons, reaching even 10^{7}–10^{8}, depending on the complexity of the representation (upper estimates are based on *functional neuroimaging; for some estimates from cellular physiology, see Hurlbert and Derrington 1993).[4]

3. *Capacity.* This is discussed separately (*capacity).

4. *Depth.* Introspection suggests that we devote different amounts of mental resources to the acquisition of different types of information. This intuition is supported by systematic research, which shows that the depth and extent of encoding varies among types of tasks and situations, and further, that this 'level of processing' of the acquired information has much to do with the robustness of retention and subsequent *retrievability (Craik and Lockhart 1972). For example, in verbal tasks, phonetic processing is considered shallower than semantic processing, and semantic encoding commonly results in better retrieval than phonetic encoding. The same applies to depth of processing in sensory *perception and in mastering *skill. 'Depth' is a dimension of memory that has so far been influential in human memory research more than in animal research.

5. *Types.* The *zeitgeist portrays about a dozen types of memory systems in the mammalian brain (e.g. Milner *et al.* 1998; *declarative memory, *taxonomy). All these systems are expected to have evolved in response to specific needs and phylogenetic pressures. Although some basic molecular components are shared by multiple systems (*CREB, *immediate early genes, *ion channels, *receptors), the heterogeneity of types renders it again reasonable to conclude that there is no master solution to the mechanisms of memory.

6. *Subjective dimensions.* The effectiveness of a stimulus is a function of the interaction of the stimulus dimensions (*context included) with the *subject's state. The latter can be measured by subjective dimensions such as arousal, *attention, intention, awareness, familiarity, and expectancy (e.g. Boring 1935; Berman *et al.* 1998; *algorithm, *declarative memory, *learning, *surprise).

*Reductionists are possessed by the search for elementary dimensions. It is useful though to remember that emergent properties are also important dimensions; and, further, that the brain in fact accommodates all the perceived and inferred dimensions within it, and in that respect is omnipotent and dimensionless. This was crisply perceived by Dickinson (1896): 'The Brain—is wider than the Sky/For—put them side by side—/The one the other will contain/With one—and You—beside—/The Brain is deeper than the sea—/For—hold them—Blue to Blue—/The one the other will absorb—/As Sponges—Buckets—do—/The Brain is just the weight of God—/For—Heft them—Pound for Pound—/And they will differ—if they do—/As Syllable from Sound—'.

Selected associations: Cell assembly, Level, Reduction, Stimulus, Synapse

---

[1]Definitions 1 and 3 are different formulations of the same idea, safe that in practice, the 'measures' in definition 1 are not necessarily independent. Broader, more sophisticated definitions of 'dimension' have been developed in the exact sciences, but they far exceed the scope of this discussion (Mandelbrot 1977; Greene 1999).

[2]This argument echoes the Panglossian paradigm, which trusts that natural selection is an optimizing agent (see *paradigm). It is prudent to take into account the possibility that brain and memory systems are what they are not only because of adaptation but also because of accumulative structural and functional constraints. This caveat, however, is unlikely to nullify the subsequent assumption in the text concerning the limitations of our brain.

[3]'Intuition' refers to a fast, mostly innately predisposed system of tacit knowledge about the world.

[4]The potential distinction between the minimal number of neurons obligatory for representing an item and the actual number engaged in representing that item is another issue, the discussion of which exceeds the scope of the present discussion.

Dopamine

A biogenic amine that functions as a *neurotrans-mitter in the brain and as a regulator of physio-logical activity in peripheral tissues.

Dopamine (3,4-dihydroxyphenylethylamine) is the predominant catecholamine neurotransmitter in the mammalian brain. Catecholamines are so called because they are amines (compounds derived by replacing the hydrogen atoms in ammonia with organic groups) that contain the aromatic alcohol catechol. Other catecholamine neurotransmitters and hormones are adrenaline (epinephrine) and *noradrenaline (norepinephrine). The catecholamines in the body are synthesized from the amino acid tyrosine. In fact, till the 1950s, dopamine has been considered merely as an intermediate metabolite in the pathway leading to the synthesis of noradrenaline and adrenaline. Only later was it discovered that dopamine itself is a neuro-transmitter (reviewed in Cooper *et al.* 1996). In periph-eral tissues dopamine regulates renal, cardiovascular, gastrointestinal, and other visceral functions. To the general public dopamine is known mainly because of its role in Parkinson's disease. This disease is caused by the degeneration of dopamine producing nerve cells in the brain. As dopamine does not penetrate the blood–brain barrier, it cannot be administered to the patient to replenish the brain with the missing chemi-cal. Rather, the disease is treated with L-DOPA (L-dihy-droxyphenylalanine), which penetrates the brain and is converted there to dopamine.

A convenient *taxonomy of the dopamine systems in the brain is based on the length of their efferent fibres (*ibid.*). Local, or short projectional systems, exist in the retina and in the olfactory bulb. Intermediate length systems include the tuberohypophysial, incertohypo-thalamic, and medullary periventricular group. Long-range systems originate in dopamine neurons in the ventral tegmentum and substantia nigra and innervate striatal, *limbic, and *cortical areas (Figure 26). They comprise the mid-brain dopaminergic system, which is further differentiated into three pathways. The projec-tion from the substantia nigra to the basal ganglia is termed the 'nigrostriatal pathway'. The projection to the septum, *amygdala, and the piriform cortex, is termed the 'mesolimbic dopaminergic system'. The projection to the prefrontal, cingulate, and entorhinal cortex is termed the 'mesocortical dopaminergic system'. Much has been learned in recent years about the cellular and molecular properties of the dopaminergic systems in the brain, including the metabolism of dopamine, its

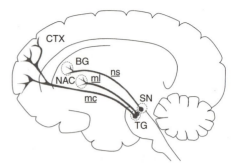

Fig. 26 A schematic diagram of the long-range central dopaminergic systems in the mammalian brain. The nigrostriatal pathway (ns) projects from the substantia nigra (SN) to the basal ganglia (BG). The mesolimbic pathway (ml) projects from the mid-brain ventral tegmen-tal area to some so-called '*limbic structures', e.g. the nucleus accum-bens (NAC). The mesocortical pathway (mc) projects from the ventral tegmental area to the *cerebral cortex, e.g. frontal cortex. (Adapted from Stahl 1996.)

release and re-uptake, and its membrane *receptor families (Cooper *et al.* 1996; Missale *et al.* 1998).

Ample data indicate that dopamine plays a part in several facets of the 'reactivity' of the organism, including arousal, *attention, emotion, motivation, motor control, food intake, and endocrine regulation (Mason 1984; Wise and Rompre 1989; Robbins and Everitt 1996; Spanagel and Weiss 1999). It is also well established that dopamine is important in several types of learning. As the mid-brain dopaminergic systems are anatomically and pharmacologically heterogeneous, they are expected to subserve a number of physiological functions, which could contribute differentially to learning and memory. We will focus only on a few postulated functions.

An hypothesis that has guided the field for many years now is the 'dopamine hypothesis of reward'. It considers the mid-brain dopaminergic system as a common pathway for encoding the *reinforcing attrib-utes of reward (Wise and Rompre 1989; Robbins and Everitt 1996; Nader *et al.* 1997). The dopamine hypoth-esis of reward rests on multiple lines of evidence. Its roots could be traced to a *classic set of experiments, in which Olds and Milner (1954) demonstrated that rats can be made to work hard, even to exhaustion, to self-stimulate certain centres in their brain via implanted electrodes.[1] These 'reward centres' include the mid-brain dopaminergic system. It was later shown that dopaminergic blockers inhibit self-stimulation as well as food-elicited reward (Rolls *et al.* 1974), and addictive drugs, such as morphine, cocaine, amphetamine, and nicotine, increase the activity of mid-brain dopaminer-gic neurons (Pontieri *et al.* 1996; Nestler and Aghajanian

1997; Robbins and Everitt 1999; Berke and Hyman 2000). Furthermore, recording of neuronal activity from the brain of behaving animals has shown that dopaminergic neurons respond preferentially to rewarding stimuli (Schultz 1998).

But do mid-brain dopaminergic neurons actually encode the reward, or do they encode something else, which is required for the actualization of the neuronal and behavioural effect of the *reinforcer? Cellular analysis in the behaving *monkey, engaged in the *acquisition and the performance of a variety of *delay tasks, has shown that dopamine neurons respond to the salient stimuli whose detection is crucial for the learning, but do not themselves encode the reward. During learning, the response of these neurons transfers from the primary reward to the conditioned, reward-predicting stimuli. Moreover, the cellular response to the reward is highly characteristic: activation in response to rewarding events that are better than predicted, no response to events that are as predicted, and depression in response to events that are worse than predicted (Schultz 1998). It seems, hence, that the dopamine neurons encode the prediction error of the reward. Such prediction error drives learning in some formal *models (see the Rescorla–Wagner model in *algorithm; *surprise; Schultz et al. 1997). This is definitely an impressive example of cross-*level *reductive research, which binds learning theory, behavioural phenomena, brain neuroanatomy, and cellular and molecular mechanisms. It provides learning theorists with biological tools to test their predictions, and neurobiologists with conceptual frameworks to accommodate their findings.

Intriguing and influential as it is, the dopamine prediction-error hypothesis is still only one type of interpretation of the data. An alternative interpretation proposes that the fast dopamine response is not a teaching signal but rather an *attentional switch (Redgrave et al. 1999).

Much attention has been focused in recent years on the function of dopamine in the prefrontal cortex, including its role in *working memory (Goldman-Rakic 1995). The attentional-switch hypothesis of dopamine action fits well the proposed dopaminergic role in working memory, in which attention must be shifted quickly on and between the on-line and off-line *internal representations that are required to perform the ongoing memory task. Malfunction of the dopamine system, especially in the prefrontal cortex, is postulated to contribute to cognitive pathologies in which attention is impaired, particularly schizophrenia. This assumption, called the 'dopamine hypothesis of schizophrenia', is guiding the search for

schizophrenia-linked defects in dopaminergic receptors, and for specific dopaminergic drugs to ameliorate the disease (e.g. Okubo et al. 1997; Lidow et al. 1998). The dopaminergic hypothesis, however, is only one of the 'theories' of schizophrenia (Willner 1997; Harrison 1999). By the way, those who find it difficult to think and learn under a distracting loud noise, should note that this could be related as well to dopaminergic prefrontal malfunction: the music in a modest discotheque suffices to push the dopaminergic system in the prefrontal cortex off balance (Arnsten and Goldman-Rakic 1998).

Dopamine could have also played a part in shaping one of the hallmarks of human behaviour, namely, novelty seeking. It has been suggested by some authors (Benjamin et al. 1996; Ebstein et al. 1996), although questioned by others (Gelernter et al 1997), that individuals who persistently seek novelty, owe this personality trait to a certain genetically determined composition of subtypes of dopaminergic receptors. Even if at the end of the day the role of dopamine in novelty seeking will be proven true, we should not expect to become daring adventurers just by swallowing dopaminergic drugs; as any other complex behavioural trait (*neurogenetics), novelty seeking is probably determined by many genes.

Selected associations: Algorithm, Attention, Neurotransmitter, Reduction, Reinforcer

---

[1]The original observation was fortuitous; see *reinforcer. The self-stimulation studies were replicated in many species, ranging from fish and chick, via goats, dogs, *monkeys, and dolphins, to humans (Olds 1969). Luckily, most humans do not normally have the opportunity to self-administer electrical pulses to their own mid-brain dopaminergic centres, but video games, which release striatal dopamine, could provide a safe substitute (Koepp et al. 1998).

Drosophila melanogaster

The common 'fruit fly', which is extensively used in the study of genetics, developmental biology, and neurobiology.

There are over 3000 different species of *Drosophilidae* (Greek for 'dew lovers'), but none is as popular as *Drosophila melanogaster*, which became the pet organism of geneticists already a century ago (*melanogaster* is 'black belly' in Greek, referring to the colour of the male's bottom). The term 'fruit fly' is a misnomer, because *Drosophila* are actually after the yeast that flourishes on rotten fruit rather than after the fruit itself. *D. melanogaster* was one of the first organisms to be adapted and then bred purposely for scientific needs. It was introduced into the laboratory by Castle at Harvard in 1901. This was soon followed by Lutz, Loeb, Morgan, and others (Kohler 1994). The major *D. melanogaster* wild types currently in use date from the 1920s (Ashburner 1989).

What is it that has endowed *Drosophila* with such a successful career in science?[1] Fruit flies are not only cute (at least in the eyes of drosophilists). They are also conveniently small, remarkably inexpensive, clean, harmless (except occasional allergies), and easy to cultivate. Their generation time is only about 10 days at 25°C, and the life cycle includes easily identifiable *phases (Ashburner 1989). Furthermore, *Drosophila* display a rich, hectic behavioural repertoire, including positive phototaxis (movement towards light), negative geotaxis (movement away from the centre of gravity), and gracious courtship. All these attributes sufficed to convince professors at the turn of the twentieth century to use fruit flies in demonstrations of *development and behaviour.

But it is the amenability of *Drosophila* to genetic analysis that has made the real difference. The diploid chromosome number of *D. melanogaster* is only four, including the sex chromosomes X and Y (XX is female, XY male). The giant chromosomes in the larval salivary are real cytological gems. The small number of chromosomes, the convenient chromosomal cytology, the availability of wild types and spontaneous mutants, the short generation time and ease of breeding—all these initiated a meticulous, systematic analysis of *Drosophila* genetics. With time, the accumulation of knowledge, the large number of genetically mapped mutations, and the rich repertoire of experimental *methods, have all reinforced the experimental advantages of *Drosophila*, and made it very popular in the study of genetics in multicellular organisms.[2] Naturally, the genome of *Drosophila* was one of the first to be sequenced in the Genome project (13 600 genes, many more transcription units; Adams *et al.* 2000).

The experimental advantages of *Drosophila* have also attracted animal psychologists and neurobiologists. Initially, polygene analysis was used to assess the contribution of genes to behaviour (e.g. Hirsch 1959). The field has advanced into a new phase with the use of single-gene mutations; the basic idea was to treat the flies as 'atoms' of genetics and behaviour (Benzer 1967). In the pre-genetic engineering era, the mutants were generated at random, usually by feeding the flies with mutagenic chemicals (Ashbruner 1989). Nowadays, mutations are induced by using virus-like transposable genetic elements that mutate the fly by jumping into its

chromosomes, or by other sophisticated methods (e.g. Yin *et al.* 1995; Goodwin *et al.* 1997). The putative mutants are then screened for abnormal performance in discrete behavioural tasks, ranging from phototaxis and geotaxis, via courtship, to sensory discrimination. Even in a species that is readily amenable to genetic analysis, the neurogenetics of memory is clearly useless unless efficient, reproducible memory *assays are available. Luckily enough, when presented with the appropriate problems, fruit flies do prove to be surprisingly intelligent. Paradigms of *habituation, *sensitization, and *classical and *instrumental conditioning are now available, involving use-dependent modification of the response of *Drosophila* to odour, taste, light, touch, potential mates, and *context (Quinn *et al.* 1974; Tully and Quinn 1985; Hall 1986; Dudai 1988; Corfas and Dudai 1989; Rees and Spatz 1989; Liu *et al.* 1999).

A number of single gene mutants in *Drosophila* affect learning and memory rather specifically (Dudai *et al.* 1976; Aceves-Pina *et al.* 1983; Dudai 1988; Boynton and Tully 1992; Folkers *et al.* 1993; Dubnau and Tully 1998; Pinto *et al.* 1999; DeZazzo *et al.* 2000). The modifier 'rather' that precedes 'specifically' in the above sentence is critical; whenever one deals with the effect of mutations (or drugs) on learning and memory, the issue of specificity comes up. Because biological memory systems share molecular and cellular processes with other systems in the organism, no absolute specificity should be expected. Memory mutants in *Drosophila* do display some nonmemory defects (Dudai 1988; Corfas and Dudai 1990; Zhong *et al.* 1992; Préat 1998). The critical question is, however, whether the mutation still provides useful information on the phenomena, processes, and mechanisms of learning and memory. The answer in many cases is yes. Several mutations, including some that impair the function of *intracellular signal transduction cascades, have provided unique insight into the neurobiology of learning and memory (Figure 27). In particular, *Drosophila* neurogenetics has provided independent and remarkable evidence in support of the role of the so-called cyclic adenosine monophosphate (cAMP) signal transduction cascade in learning and memory (see also *Aplysia, *CREB). It has also been useful in dissecting phases of *acquisition and *consolidation of memory (Dudai 1988; DeZazzo and Tully 1995). And on top of it all, studies in *Drosophila* have contributed to the identification of the intimate mechanistic links between developmental and behavioural plasticity (e.g. Corfas and Dudai 1991; Schuster *et al.* 1996).

Attempts have also been made to identify functional centres, neuronal circuits, and the individual neurons that subserve memory in the central nervous system

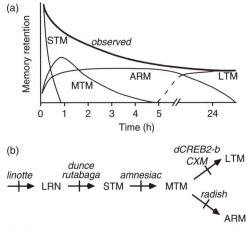

Fig. 27 Genetic dissection has unveiled multiple *phases in the *acquisition and the *consolidation of memory in the fruit fly. (a) Four functionally distinct phases are proposed to underlie the memory curve observed in normal flies trained to avoid a shock-associated odour: STM, short-term memory; MTM, middle-term memory; ARM, memory that is resistant to anaesthesia; LRN, learning; LTM, long-term memory. STM decays the fastest and LTM the slowest. (b) A scheme showing where in the pathway different mutants and pharmacological manipulations exert their primary disruptive effects: *linotte*, a mutant defective in a putative *protein kinase; *dunce*, a mutant defective in a form of the enzyme that degrades cAMP, cAMP-dependent phosphodiesterase; *rutabaga*, a mutant defective in the form of the enzyme that produces cAMP, adenylyl cyclase (this form of the enzyme is sensitive to *calcium and may serve as a *coincidence detector of the *neurotransmitter and calcium signals); *amnesiac*, a mutant defective in the production of a peptide that stimulates cAMP synthesis; *radish*, the product of which is yet unidentified; dCREB2-b, flies engineered to express an antagonist of the transcription factor *CREB; CXM, flies treated with the *protein synthesis inhibitor cycloheximide. The figure is adapted from Dubnau and Tully (1998). For the molecular defects in the indicated mutants, see Dura *et al.* (1995; *linotte*), Byers *et al.* (1981; *dunce*), Dudai *et al.* (1983), Livingstone *et al.* (1984) (*rutabaga*), and Waddell *et al.* (2000; *amnesiac*).

of *Drosophila* (Corfas and Dudai 1990; Davis 1993; Waddell *et al.* 2000; Zars *et al.* 2000; Dubnau *et al.* 2001). This search for the *engram is not too easy, for reasons including the fact that the brain and the thoracic ganglion of the fruit fly are small and compact. *Functional neuroimaging methods, similar to those already in use in the *honeybee, may facilitate the task.

Selected associations: CREB, Intracellular signal transduction cascade, Neurogenetics, Simple system

---

[1]On the virtues of working with flies in general, see Dethier (1962).

[2]The accumulative body of knowledge, procedures, traditions, and rituals of the drosophilists provides an interesting example of scientific sub*culture (Kohler 1994; Weiner 1999).

Engram

The physical record of a *memory; the memory trace.

The notion that *stimuli produce enduring physical changes in the brain, and that these changes are the basis for memory, has been with us since early times (e.g. see Plato's etched wax tablets of memory, *Theaetetus*; *metaphor). About 100 years ago, a German scholar, Richard Semon, termed the material record engraved by a stimulus in living tissue as the 'engram' (Semon 1904). The etymological roots of the term are Greek, and it means 'something converted into writing'. Semon had in mind a rather general theory of experience-dependent records in living organisms, which included not only neural but also *developmental and genetic memory in all types of tissue. In his book, *The mneme*, Semon suggested two mnemic 'laws'. The first is the 'law of engraphy'. It states that 'all simultaneous excitations within an organism form a coherent simultaneous excitation complex which acts engraphically; that is, it leaves behind a connected engram-complex constituting a coherent unity' (*ibid.*, p. 273). The second is the 'law of ecphory'. 'Ecphory' according to Semon is the process that 'awaken(s) the mnemic trace or engram out of its latent state into one of the manifested activity'. The etymological roots of 'ecphory' are also Greek, and it means 'to be made known'. The law of ecphory states that 'the partial recurrence of the excitation complex, which left behind the engram complex, acts ecphorically on this simultaneous engram complex, whether the recurrence be in the form if an original or of a mnemic excitation.' (*ibid.*, p. 274). Elements of Semon's writings are nowadays echoed in the discussions of *cell assemblies, *models of neural networks, and *retrieval. Unfortunately, Semon and his book were almost forgotten (Schacter 1982).

Most of the popularity of 'engram' stems from a noted paper by Lashley (1950), entitled 'In search of the Engram'. Though seemingly an epitome of the crosstalk of scholarly ideas (Semon's chapter V in *The mneme* is entitled 'The Localisation of Engrams'), typically of Semon's fate, Lashley did not cite Semon even once in this paper.[1] Lashley aimed at identifying 'habits of the conditioned reflex type' in the brain. Following the path of Flourens, Franz, and others (Gomulicki 1953; Herrenstein and Boring 1965; Brazier 1988), Lashley used the *methodology of inference of function from dysfunction. He inflicted anatomical lesions on various parts of the *rat or *monkey brain, and tested the effect of the intervention on brightness discrimination and *maze learning (Lashley 1929, 1950). After many years of research, Lashley came to the conclusion that no cortical area, except the relevant primary sensory areas, is obligatory for learning and memory. He summarized his findings in two principles: (a) the *equipotentiality* principle, which states that cortical areas are equipotential for learning, and can generally substitute for each other in learning, and (b) the *mass action* principle, which states that the reduction in learning and memory *performance is roughly proportional to the amount of tissue destroyed, rather to its position. Other conclusions were also drawn from the data, e.g. that the effect of a lesion is proportional in magnitude to the complexity of the task. 'This series of experiments', concluded Lashley, 'has yielded a good bit of information about what and where the memory trace is not … I sometimes feel, in reviewing the evidence on the localization of the memory trace, that the necessary conclusion is that learning just is not possible … Nevertheless, in spite of such evidence against it, learning does sometimes occur' (Lashley 1950).

Lashley's conclusions about the engram were already criticized at the time of their publication (Hunter 1930). The main objections were, first, that the behavioural tasks were not well defined in terms of the sensory inputs and the behavioural strategies required for successful performance, and therefore a *subject with partial brain damage could still succeed in the task by using the undamaged areas; second, the lesions were not delicate enough to differentiate the contribution of distinct functional divisions in the brain. Disappointed with the search for the engram, Lashley came to favour field theories of brain function, which regarded sensations and memories as patterns of excitations being reduplicated throughout the cortical surface like spreading waves in a liquid surface (Lashley 1950). This view was compatible with the Gestalt theories.[2] In the later part of his career, Lashley put this idea to experimental test. He placed pieces of gold on the visual cortex of the monkey. The metal was expected to short-circuit the cortex and therefore disrupt visual perception. This did not happen (Lashley *et al.* 1951). Similar conclusions were reached at about the same time by other investigators. Not surprisingly, Lashley himself remarked that he had destroyed all theories of behaviour, including his own (Hebb 1959). Lashley's seminal contribution to the study of learning was not, however, in his *ad-hoc* experimental conclusions. Rather, it was in the methodology and the concepts. On the methodological side, he was a pioneer in combining careful lesion techniques with behavioural analysis. On the conceptual side, he came to argue that dedicated

effector–affector connections could not be considered as building blocks of high brain function. This notion was influential in shaping later distributed models of brain and memory, for example, those of Lashley's student, Hebb (*algorithm, *cell assembly, *classic).

What is the current status of the search for the engram, a century after Semon and half a century after Lashley? The picture is not simple. At this stage, it could be useful to resort to the basic issues.

1. The *existence* of the engram. Is there an engram? The question where the engram is should not be confounded with the question whether an engram is at all necessary. The answer in a nutshell is definitely yes, there must be some type of engram to ensure *persistence of memory. Whether the term should apply to the entire circuit that encodes the item, or only to those use-dependent changes in the circuit, is already a matter of convention or taste. Even if we consider certain types of memory as selective reactivation (*retrieval) of endogenous spatiotemporal patterns of neuronal activity (*a priori, *cell assembly), use-dependent alterations must leave a material tag at one *level or another of the neural tissue. This tag, however, might be minute, and in some cases even hide as modification in an index of internal representations in a brain area far remote from the area in which the retrieved representation resides.

2. The *locale* of the engram. The question is hence not whether there is an engram to search for, but rather whether the engram is localized to a single location, whether this location is stable over time, and whether the combination of locale and stability permits us to put our hands on it. This becomes a quantitative rather than a qualitative issue, interwoven with methodological and technical difficulties. In a nutshell, it is likely that the engram of modified reflexes in *simple systems will be found in a dedicated pathway, whereas that of complex memories in humans will be highly distributed (*cell assembly). Further, some types of engrams may shift from one locale to another; this, for example, seems to occur routinely in the *consolidation of *declarative memories, in which with time the engram becomes independent of the *hippocampus.

3. The *differentiation* of function in the engram. In spite of the expected multiplicity of locations, and the potential uncertainty in the localization of complex engrams over time, discrete anatomical parts of the brain are clearly implicated by the available data in specific types of memory. For example, it is now evident that the primate mediotemporal lobe subserves *declarative memory, the corticostriatal system *skill memory, and the prefrontal *cortex *working memory.

Candidate engrams have also been identified in classical conditioning in mammals, in lower vertebrates (*birdsong), and in invertebrates (*Aplysia, *Drosophila). In most cases, the question of what are the precise functions of the identified regions in retaining the trace over time remains, however, unresolved. First, the fact that a circumscribed brain region is necessary for a certain type of memory does not entail that this region is sufficient to encode the memory, even more so exclusive in doing so (*criterion). Second, some areas in the candidate engram might be required for only some *phases of memory but not for other phases. And third, the engram may have a 'core', responsible for the persistence over time of the essential attributes of the item, and auxiliary components that either encode additional *dimensions of the item, or are recruited only in the encoding or the expression of the memory. All these issues resurface in the renewed attempts to identify engrams by means of *functional neuroimaging.

4. The *transformation* of the engram. In addition to the differential function of identified brain areas and pathways in a particular experimental protocol, the relative contribution of distinct areas and pathways to the engram could change dramatically when the *acquisition or retrieval parameters of the task are altered. This is the case even in relatively simple forms of learning, for example, in classical conditioning, when a shift is made from delay to trace conditioning, or from elemental to *contextual conditioning (Thompson and Kim 1996; Nader and LeDoux 1997; Desmedt *et al.* 1998). This again calls for the depiction of engrams as multicomponent *systems, the individual components of which are recruited and expressed in a permutable manner depending on the specific task demands.

5. The *level* of the engram. Traditionally, the search for the engram refers to an anatomical expedition. But nowadays it is also cellular and molecular. Problems similar to those concerning the neuroanatomical search haunt the molecular and cellular search. Synapses and neurons modified by experience should carry some type or another of a physical record of the experience (Dudai and Morris 2000). But the change could be minute, distributed, and alternate over time from one site to another. Again, in the molecular like in the circuit level, there might be a core engram and additional tiers of mechanisms that encode additional stimulus dimensions (Berman and Dudai 2001).

In conclusion, whatever the level of analysis, to expect the search for the engram in the mammalian brain to end up in the identification of a single locale is naive. And even if a candidate area is identified as important in maintaining the engram, the problem

becomes that of both resolution and *reduction: Where is it within that area? In a dedicated circuit? In identified neurons? In synapses? To what size of circuit do we hope to nail it down? What answer will finally satisfy our urge to localize things in the world? And if we keep reducing the area, or the number of units in the area— where will the transition be from an engram, to a fragment of that engram, or to a non-engram?[3] These problems could apply to simple brains as well (Glanzman 1995).

And as to term 'engram' *per se*, many experimenters use it, others think that it carries the risk of spilling into purple prose, and prefer the term 'trace'. Most authors, however, simply use 'trace' and 'engram' interchangeably (e.g. Thompson and Kim 1996).

Selected associations: Criterion, Memory, Metaphor, Persistence, Phrenology

---

[1]He was, however, well aware of Semon's writings (Lashley 1933).

[2]For what the Gestalt was, see *insight.

[3]This is another example of the classical sorites paradox, which is explained under *insight; see also *reduction.

Enigma

An open problem, a mystery.

Science is driven by the unknown as much as by the known, and therefore, noting enigmas is often as useful as listing facts (*aînos*, Greek for 'fable', *aínigma*, 'to speak in riddles'). Below is a list of 10 enigmas of memory. Some refer to baffling concepts, others to technological shortcoming, and most to both. Although many investigators may agree with much of the choice, some may not. Scientific enigmas tend to reflect the *bias of their compiler. The reader is fully encouraged to expand or shrink the list unabashedly. But at least, it is a starting point.

1. What are the neuronal codes of *internal representations? This is a central issue not only in memory research, but in neuroscience at large. Without knowing in detail how models of the world are encoded in the brain, there is little hope in providing answers to many of the questions that follow.

2. What are the computational and physical changes that take place in internal representations in *acquisition and *consolidation of memory? Which of

these changes are obligatory for long-term memory? Many alterations are detected in the brain after training, at the molecular, *synaptic, cellular, and *system *levels. Yet some of these alterations may not directly relate to experience-dependent modifications in internal representations (e.g. some could subserve *homeostasis). Are we currently pursuing the processes and mechanisms that are really relevant (*criterion)?

3. How are internal representations retained over time in spite of massive synaptic remodelling in the brain (*persistence)? Furthermore, there is some evidence for turnover of neurons in the mature brain (*birdsong, *hippocampus); if so, how is it that new cells integrate into existing circuits without disrupting old memories? Or do they?

4. How is complex information *retrieved from memory, frequently within a fraction of a second? And how much of retrieval is reconstruction, sometimes with doubtful faithfulness (*false memory)?

5. How much of our knowledge about the external world is due to selection by experience of pre-representations, generated by the endogenous activity of the brain? In other words, how much of our world models is encoded in our brain *a priori, and to what degree can we indeed master truly novel information and concepts?

6. Do all *percepts and thoughts leave a lingering trace in memory? If so, will we be able to tap into the latent information? Similarly, will we be able to restore *engrams once they become unretrievable?

7. Will we be able to increase significantly the physiological *capacity and performance of our memory? Will it be done by pharmacology (*nootropics), by genetic engineering (*neurogenetics), or by bionics, based on the integration of nano-chips with the central nervous system (Moravec 1988; Kuwana et al. 1995; Maher et al. 1999; Weng et al. 2001)?

8. Will we ever be able to download memories directly to and from the Web, in a non-invasive manner, hence linking our brain to a gigantic, global memory 'syncytium'? This will surely provide the term *collective memory with a new meaning. If the possibilities raised here, as well as in 7 above, ever materialize, what will be the biological, emotional, cognitive, and social price for the species and for the individual?

9. Will new types of memory systems evolve in our brain? A great variety of memory systems have already emerge in evolution, each time presumably to comply with the updated needs of the species. These systems include, among others, memory for *skills, for space, for language, for facts, for events, for the self (*taxonomy). Some of these systems may have evolved at first in response to a certain selective pressure but later became adapted to new needs or even paved the way to new faculties and capabilities. Will new memory systems emerge to cope with the new technological environment, what will their capabilities be, and which new opportunities will they open for brain and behaviour?

10. And, finally: What is consciousness (*conscious awareness)? Similarly to enigma 1 above, this issue definitely transcends memory research, yet is intimately related to the function and mechanisms of *declarative, particularly *episodic memory, and to the role of *attention and memory in the *binding of our personality over time. Furthermore, to what degree are other species consciously aware of themselves and the world (*anthropomorphism)? Will we ever be able to really know what is it like to be a bat (Nagel 1974)? And will smart robots (Moravec 1988, Weng et al. 2001) or neuro-silicon hybrids (Kuwana et al. 1995; Maher et al. 1999) become conscious as we are? Will they have episodic, autobiographical memory, and what will it mean to them?

Scientific enigmas are there to be tackled (Duncan and Weston-Smith 1977; Doty 1998). Judging by the remarkable pace of memory research, solutions to some of the aforementioned riddles may become common knowledge sooner than imagined. Other problems, such as the consciousness one, may at the end of the day be resolved formally but resist intuition (*dimension). Note also that what an enigma is, depends on the level and resolution of the analysis. For a molecular neurobiologist, the *developmental regulation of an ion channel is a pressing enigma, as is the physiological relevance of the fMRI (functional magnetic resonance imaging) signal for the *functional neuroimaging expert. Hence, in addition to the aforementioned 'macro-enigmas', many 'micro-enigmas' are hidden in various subdisciplines of memory research. Whether they should be dubbed 'enigma' or simply 'open questions' or 'research objectives', is a matter of taste.

Before concluding, we should also remember that there is an additional type of enigma: that of not yet knowing that we do not yet know. Identifying new dimensions opens new vistas that unveil new enigmas. Even what is now deemed by us as almost trivial and even boring, may with time become a source of wonder and inspiration, if we only come to see it under fresh light. As the English author G.K. Chesterton remarked almost a century ago (cited in Gratzer 1996): 'Is ditch-water dull? Naturalists with microscopes have told me that it teems with quiet fun'.

Selected associations: Classic, Criterion, Culture, Dimension, Homo sapiens

---

Episodic memory

1. The *conscious mental reenactment of personally experienced past events.
2. The *recall or recognition of a unique event and the spatiotemporal *context in which it was experienced.
3. The *internal representations that are accessible to such mental reenactment or recall.
4. The brain *system that endows the *subject with the capacity to perform 1,2 above.

Episodic recollection is conscious time travel into the subjective past[1]. This is considered by many as the most sophisticated faculty of memory, and the one most characteristic of humans. Further, a minority of authors even use the term 'memory' and 'episodic memory' as synonyms. These authors would usually concede that the *declarative memory of impersonal facts is also 'memory', but refuse to consider many other types of use-dependent change in behaviour, such as *classical conditioning, *habit and *skill, as *bona fide* memory. This is evidently not the stand taken in this book (*memory).

The term 'episode' is from the Greek *epi-*, on, at, + *eisodios*, entering; *epeisodion* meant a parenthetic narrative. Indeed an episodic memory item is only one scene in the individual's accumulative personal narrative[2]. That there is memory which is episodic, as opposed to automatic responses, or to the recall of impersonal facts (*taxonomy), was discussed already by Greek philosophers if not earlier. A clear description of this distinct type of memory was given by Agustine (400; *classic): '... I encounter myself and recall myself, and what, and when, and where I did some did, and how I was affected when I did it'. The term 'episodic memory' was, however, introduced into the scientific discourse much later, by Tulving (1972). This was on the background of intensive developments in cognitive research on the different categories of human knowledge. The new computer era opened new vistas for understanding the storage and *retrieval of knowledge, which infiltrated human memory research. In the mid-1960s, Quillian proposed a method by which meaning could be stored optimally in a computer program, and his postulates were adapted by psychologists in their attempt to account for the storage of knowledge in real brains (Collins and Quillian 1969; Tulving and Donaldson 1972). This type of knowledge encoding was termed 'semantic memory' (*declarative memory, *taxonomy). Tulving (1972, 1983) went on to distinguish semantic memory, which he dubbed 'mental thesaurus', from another type of knowledge that humans have about the world, which is about temporally dated events, describable in terms of their perceptible attributes, and the spatiotemporal relations of these events to each other. This memory he termed 'episodic'. The term is now used, depending on the context of discussion, to denote a type of mental act or experience (definitions 1,2), a type of memory items (definition 3), or a type of memory system (definition 4)[3].

Here are a few things to remember about episodic memory:

1. It is not only about *what, how* and *where*, but also about *when*; the ability to place unique experienced events on the temporal axis of personal history, be it distorted and poorly resolved, is characteristic of episodic memory.

2. It refers to unique experiences, hence each episodic item is the outcome of 'single trial' learning (*acquisition). Recalled *real-life episodes, however, refer each to different time windows of experience. Further recollection effort may dissect amalgamated episodes into elementary events.

3. In humans, it involves autonoetic awareness, i.e., the conscious reflexive experience of private phenomena[4]. Whether non-human species are also capable of experiencing such 'mental time travel', and if so, what kind of awareness is involved, is an open question (see below). Definition 2 does not posit awareness and therefore fits particularly to be used in animal research; this definition, however, is considered by many authors to refer to 'episodic-like' rather than to genuine episodic memory.

4. Whereas retrieval of memory is commonly oriented toward the present or the immediate future, i.e. application of knowledge for ongoing needs, retrieval of episodic memory is oriented toward the past, i.e. the past events are recognized as such (Tulving and Markowitsch 1998). The retrieved

information, however, might then be harnessed for identifying and attaining future goals (Conway and Pleydell-Pearce 2000).

5. The retrieval of episodes is expected to involve multiple steps, or components, which ultimately differ in the specificity of the information retrieved, such as the recollection of specific information about the target item ('what') and about its source ('where', 'when', as well as the sequence in which the elements of the episode unrolled), and the recognition of the familiarity of each of these items (e.g., Yonelinas 2001 ; see also 'remembering' vs. 'knowing' in *recognition).

6. Many types of tests could be used to tap into episodic memory, including free recall, cued recall, target and source recognition[5], etc. But not all the tests referred to in the literature as paradigmatic tests of episodic memory, are indicative that such memory has indeed been encoded (*criterion). Paired associates learning is but one example. In this type of learning, the subject is presented in training with a pair of stimuli, and then, in the test, presented with one member of the pair and requested to retrieve the memory of the other. Word pairs are commonly used in humans (e.g. Winocur and Weiskrantz 1976; Shallice et al. 1994), non-verbal stimuli in other species (e.g. Saunders and Weiskrantz 1989; Sakai and Miyashita 1991; see also pp. 74–75). The task is sensitive to mediotemporal damage (*amnesia), substantiating its declarative nature. Paired associates are considered 'episodic' tests because, when the pairs used are unique, their recall unveils the memory formed in a single episode of experience. Yet, depending on the protocol used and particularly when the memory of 'when' is not taxed, success on such tasks might be construed as the outcome of the formation of a semantic association, including sometimes *priming, independent of mental time travel.

Where is it in the brain? Being a declarative type of memory, episodic memory is subserved by *cortical circuits, including dependence on the mediotemporal lobe for acquisition and *consolidation, and on the frontal lobe, among others, for retrieval (e.g., Fletcher et al. 1997; Eldridge et al. 2000; Kirchhoff et al. 2000; Lepage et al. 2000; for more on functional differentiations in these areas by types of tasks and memory *phases, see *acquisition, *declarative memory, *consolidation, *retrieval). A prominent question is whether the brain circuits that subserve episodic memory differ from those that subserve semantic memory[6].

No consensus answer is available to this question. The data that feed the debate stem from the study of brain lesions and from *functional neuroimaging. Whereas functional neuroimaging can unveil correlation of activity in identified brain areas with the performance on episodic tasks, currently, only the study of brain lesions could pinpoint candidate obligatory circuits. In some types of *dementia, the deterioration of semantic and episodic memory is differential, suggesting that the biological substrates of these two types of memory differ (e.g. Hodges et al. 1999; it is noteworthy that normal ageing is often associated as well with preferential impairment of episodic memory, e.g. Nilsson et al. 1997). Studies of amnesic patients provide mixed evidence (reviewed in Mishkin et al. 1997; see Tulving et al. 1988 for a case of 'semantic' amnesia; also Zola-Morgan et al. 1983 for some methodological caveats). A particularly interesting type of information has been provided by the study of patients with amnesia due to hippocampal damage sustained very early in life (Vargha-Khadem et al. 1997). These patients were capable of developing normal language and social competence, and acquire new factual knowledge, in spite of displaying severe loss in episodic memory. Based on these data, a suggestion was made that the *hippocampus and the subhippocampal cortici form a hierarchically organized system for the registration of declarative knowledge. Episodic memory, so goes the idea, which depends on rich associations, is encoded in the hippocampus itself, the top processing level in the hierarchy, whereas semantic memory, less dependent on intricate associations, can be supported by the subhippocampal cortici, lower on the hierarchy (Mishkin et al. 1997, 1998). Alternative interpretations of the data, which do not support such a qualitative distinction between the semantic and the episodic systems, were also raised (Squire and Zola 1998).

Do animals have it? If one posits autonoetic awareness as a critical criterion for episodic memory, the issue of whether animals go on mental time travels becomes complicated indeed and by some accounts insolvable. Investigators who address the problem in non-human species almost always set a more modest, yet still admirable, goal: to prove that the animal has 'episodic-like' memory, which does not presuppose conscious awareness as a defining criterion. An interesting strategy, which is actually recommended as a general strategy in memory research, is to look for the behavioural ecology of the species, and search for natural situations which could benefit from episodic-like memory. Clayton et al. (2001) list a number of potential candidate systems. One is brood parasitism: brood parasitic birds such as the cuckoo deposit eggs in the nests of other species and the young are later cared for by the host species. A successful brood parasite must remember where potential victims have started their nests, and return to that place at the right time to add the egg to those already laid in the nest. This could involve *where*, *what*, and *when* information of a single event. Another potential candidate is a polygynous mating system, such as in the meadow vole, in which a male mates with multiple females that are distributed over a wide area and come into estrus at different times. Successful mating in this case could greatly benefit from remembering who, where, and when. These candidate systems are somewhat difficult to investigate systematically in the laboratory. But another type of suitable behaviour was found amenable to systematic, controlled analysis: food caching in the scrub jay (Clayton and Dickinson 1998; Clayton *et al*. 2001). Scrub jays cache perishable insects and seeds in multiple locations, and it may be adaptive for them to remember what has been cashed where and when. Clayton *et al*. (1998) have trained scrub jays to appreciate that worms, which the birds like a lot, are perishable and therefore degrade over time. They then allowed the birds to recover the perishable worms, or non-perishable peanuts, which the birds had previously cached in distinct sites. The birds searched preferentially for fresh worms, their favorite food, when allowed to recover them shortly after caching, but learned to prefer searching for the less-favorable (but still tasty) peanuts and avoid searching for the worms after longer intervals in which these worms decayed. (Birds that did not have an opportunity to learn that worms degrade over time, continued to search for the cached worms even long after caching; and needless to say, measures were taken in the experiment to prevent odor cues of the degrading food.) This use-dependent modification in the food search strategy was taken to imply that the jays remembered not only what was deposited where, but also when it was deposited there—hence fulfilling the behavioural criteria for episodic-like memory (definition 2).

The story of the scrub jays shows that the demonstration of episodic-like memory in non-human species is possible, given the investigators are smart enough to match the right species with the right *assay (for an example of a different kind of approach, which attempts to identify primitives of episodic memory in the rat, see Fortin *et al*. 2002). But is episodic-like memory a rudimentary form of what we humans experience as episodic memory? And will it ever be

possible for us to identify the conscious awareness of mental time travel, if it ever exists, in other species? Can we ever come to know how is it like to be a bat (Nagel 1974), particularly, a nostalgic bat? Some say that we will never be able to do this. But there might be another, though admittedly remote and less satisfactory solution. Suppose we identify in the human brain a characteristic functional tag of mental travel, e.g. a distinct activity pattern unveiled by functional neuroimaging of the behaving subject. This might be analogous, say, to the identification of candidate dream states by recording brain waves (e.g. Dave and Margoliash 2000). Suppose then that we identify this unique functional tag in the brain of animals when they perform a task that involves episodic retrieval in humans. We may then be able to say that there is a reasonable probability that the non-human subject performs a mental time-travel. Not enough to firmly conclude that this animal feels the same as we do when we recall our private past, but still, a hint that this might indeed be the case.

Selected associations: Amnesia, Conscious awareness, Declarative memory, False memory, Recall

---

[1] This past is assumed by the subject to be veridical, but is not necessarily accurately recalled (see *false memory). *Confabulations and hallucinations are excluded.

[2] How many scenes are there all together is an interesting question; probably less then most of us would predict intuitively (*capacity; Dudai 1997a).

[3] 'Autobiographical memory' is often used interchangeably with 'episodic memory'. It might be preferable to distinguish between the two. Whereas 'episodic' refers to distinct individual episodes, 'autobiographical' connotes the narrative formed from the combination of such episodes (see also Conway 2001).

[4] Autonoetic ('self-comprehending') awareness is regarded in the scientific *culture as the highest form of conscious awareness; certain Eastern philosophies use other *taxonomies, with higher resolutions (e.g., Harvey 1990; Keown 2000).

[5] 'Source information' is a term used in human memory research to refer to the time and place in which the target item was acquired; see also *context.

[6] The question can be posed at various *levels of analysis: is the functional system monolithic? Are the *algorithms the same? And is the hardware implementation identical? The question as posed here refers to the hardware implementation at the circuit level but clearly reflects on the algorithmic and computational levels as well.

Experimental extinction

1. A decline in the frequency or intensity of a conditioned behaviour following the withdrawal of *reinforcement.

2. The experimental protocol used to obtain the aforementioned phenomenon.

3. A modification in the *internal representation of a conditioned association that leads to suppression of the conditioned response, due to behaviourally meaningful rearrangements in the relationship among previously associated *stimuli or stimuli and *reinforcers.

Pavlov noted that once one of his famous dogs (and there were many) had been conditioned to salivate to the sound of a metronome by associating the sound with food, the sound alone came to elicit salivation, as expected (*classical conditioning). However, when the metronome continued to be played without subsequent reward, with time salivation diminished. Pavlov termed this phenomenon 'experimental extinction' (Pavlov 1927). Ever since, experimental extinction (which can easily be demonstrated in *instrumental conditioning as well) became one of the most fundamental problems in learning theory. A naive, *Ockham's razor type of explanation, might construe the situation as rather simple: the dog in the above example forms an association between sound and food, but when the sound is sounded without reinforcement, the association weakens and the dog ultimately *forgets. A simple explanation? Probably, but absolutely wrong. A selection of four types of observations will suffice to illustrate the case.

1. *Spontaneous recovery.* After extinction has occurred, the conditioned response may recover with time without any additional training (Pavlov 1927). This immediately suggests that the original information was preserved. Pavlov himself proposed that in extinction, the conditioned reflex undergoes a process of 'internal inhibition'. To put his proposal in a broader context, we should note that he distinguished central excitatory processes, commanding reflexes, from central inhibitory processes, that act to negate the excitatory processes. Furthermore, he distinguished two types of inhibitory processes, one 'direct' or 'internal', the other 'indirect' or 'external'. 'External' inhibition arises when there is a clash with another excitatory processes in the brain, whereas in 'internal inhibition' the excitatory conditioned reflex itself becomes progressively inhibitory for the behaviour in question.

2. *Reacquisition and saving.* Generally speaking, 'saving' is facilitation of relearning in retraining (in the 'saving method', retention is quantified by comparing learning and relearning scores; Ebbinghaus 1885). In many cases reacquisition of an extinguished behaviour takes fewer trials than the original training (although see Bouton 1993). Such cases imply that the brain saves more information about the original learning than it volunteers to give up at first.

3. *Reinstatement.* After experimental extinction of conditioning, exposure to the unconditioned stimulus alone can partially restore the response to the conditioned stimulus (see *fear conditioning in Rescorla and Heth 1975). This again indicates that the conditioned association was not abolished.

4. *Renewal.* Switching out of the extinction *context could result in re-emergence of the seemingly extinguished response (Bouton and Swartzentruber 1991).

Over the years, the phenomenology of experimental extinction has provided lots of excitement on the one hand, and insights on the other, to experimental psychologists and learning theorists. An additional notable example is the so-called 'partial reinforcement extinction effect' (PREE): behaviour that has been reinforced only intermittently extinguishes more slowly than behaviour that has been reinforced consistently (Humphreys 1939; Weinstock 1954; Amsel 1958; Wagner *et al.* 1964; Rescorla 1999; Figure 28). This seems rather paradoxical, for why should less reinforcement lead to more memory? Several theories have been proposed to account for PREE. Among the most influential ones are the 'Frustration Hypothesis' (Amsel 1958) and the 'Sequential Hypothesis' (Capaldi 1966). The 'Frustration Hypothesis' argues that PREE works because lack of reward creates 'frustration' (note the *anthropomorphism), and as animals trained under a partial reinforcement schedule got accustomed to frustration, they become more stubborn in extinction training. The 'Sequential Hypothesis' proposes that during partial reinforcement regimes, persisting stimulus traces from the nonreinforced trials become conditioned to the next reinforced response provided there is an appropriate nonreinforced–reinforced alternation schedule, and the memory of these associations maintains responding during extinction. It is thus seen that explanations offered for the phenomena of PREE reflect on fundamental issues in learning theory, such as how associations are reinforced and *acquired, retained, and *retrieved.

Indeed, there is no shortage of hypotheses of why brains behave the way they do in experimental extinction. Many of these hypotheses refer to learning and memory processes that transcend issues of extinction (e.g. Bower and Hilgard 1981; Mackintosh 1983; Flaherty 1985; Bouton 1991). In the frame of the present discussion, suffice it to note that experimental extinction can be viewed as a dynamic learning process, in which *internal representations of target and *context stimuli are rearranged (definition 3). Experimental extinction is hence different from forgetting; it involves a *phase of memory *consolidation for the new extinction experience (Braud and Broussard 1973; Berman and Dudai 2001), and could itself be forgotten (Bouton 1994). Seen this way, experimental extinction provides additional support to the *zeitgeist that classical and instrumental conditioning are not at all solely about the contiguity or contingency of pairs of isolated stimuli; rather these types of learning reflect intricate processes

of information processing, only limited facets of which are unveiled under a given experimental situation in the laboratory (for examples see *classical conditioning and *cue). Furthermore, 'experimental extinction' tells us that when we relearn, we preserve the information about previous associations (e.g. Rescorla 1996); hence we constantly create mental *palimpsests.

'Experimental extinction' offers additional take-home messages. Being so widespread, it epitomizes the fact that some general principles and *algorithms are shared by many forms of learning. These learning 'universals' are expected to have selective advantages. Consider, for example, PREE; nothing in life is sure, therefore robust *performance under conditions of uncertainty makes sense. Experimental extinction also illustrates how a phenomenon that at first might appear merely of theoretical interest to a small group of scientists, ultimately becomes important in *real-life. For many years now there is much interest in experimental extinction in psychotherapy, in the treatment of post-traumatic stress syndrome and prevention of its relapse (Bouton and Swartzentruber 1991; Charney et al. 1998).[1] The interest in brain mechanisms of extinction is on the rise as well (Falls et al. 1992; LaBar et al. 1998; Berman et al. 2000). One of the goals is to understand the neuronal mechanisms that differentiate learning the new (i.e. in acquisition of the *engram) from learning anew (i.e. in experimental extinction). This could tell us in due time how to prevent corruption of important learned information by subsequent experience (*false memory).

Selected associations: Associative learning, Consolidation, Forgetting, Persistence

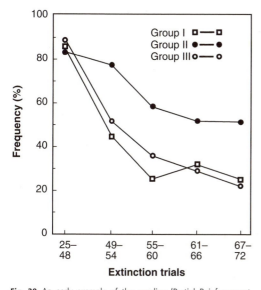

Fig. 28 An early example of the puzzling 'Partial Reinforcement Extinction Effect' (PREE): college students were divided into three groups and trained to blink their eyelid to a light because this light was followed by air puff to the cornea. Group I received in training 96 reinforced trails, group II 96 trials (only half of which were reinforced), and group III only 48 reinforced trials. All groups were then subjected to an experimental extinction protocol. The graph depicts the frequency of conditioned response vs. the extinction trial. The naive prediction is that group I will show the strongest acquisition and extinguish most slowly, whereas group II will show weaker acquisition. In reality, all groups showed similar acquisition, while group II was definitely the most resistant to extinction. For hypothetical explanations, see text. (From Humphreys 1939.)

[1]As the clinic is mentioned, it would be only fair to note that the term 'extinction' carries also a different meaning in neuropsychology. It refers to the situation in which the simultaneous application of two identical tactile stimuli results in the report of only one of the stimuli, although each would have been reported if they were to be presented independently. This type of 'extinction' may indicate a lesion in somatosensory cortex. It is not 'experimental' and has nothing to do with memory.

False memory

1. A retrieved *memory item that does not correspond to veridical experience but believed to be so by the *subject.

2. The phenomena that refer to the report of such items by the subject.

'Footfalls echo in the memory/Down the passage which we did not take/Towards the door we never opened' (Eliot 1963): more often than we tend to concede, memory leads us to passages we never took in reality. Fantasy and facts mix well in poetry, but the charm could become nightmare if they do so in reality. Why does it happen, when and how, are major questions in memory research. These questions have been approached in experimental psychology long ago (Bartlett 1932; Carmichael *et al.* 1932), almost forgotten (*zeitgeist), but regained much interest in recent years. Their renewed discussion has already transcended the domain of science, invading courtrooms and newsrooms alike.

There is a great variety of phenomena that could be regarded as false memory. They range from delusions and *confabulations in diseased states to memory illusions in normal individuals (Kopelman 1999; Koriat *et al.* 2000). In the contemporary literature, however, the term is commonly reserved to refer to the erroneous memory, particularly *episodic memory, in normal subjects. In the past decade, particular attention has been directed at the potential role of false memory in recollection in adulthood of sexual abuse in childhood (Penfold 1996; Pope 1996; Winbolt 1996). It all started with a wave of reports on the recovery of such repressed memories in subjects undergoing psychotherapy. The apparent revival of trauma has culminated in litigations against parents and caretakers. Soon after, however, it became apparent that in some cases (not all!), the memories of abuse could have been acquired by the patient in the course of overenthusiastic therapy. In fact, a new diagnostic criterion has been suggested, termed 'false memory syndrome', which refers to the situation in which an individual uncritically accepts suggestions of the therapist and comes to believe illusory memories of abuse. At this stage, therapists in lieu of parents became fashionable targets for legal suits. This has led to heated debates and emotional flares in the psychotherapeutic community (*ibid.*), and, as expected, to juicy headlines in tabloids.

Yet false memory in *real-life covers many phenomena that have nothing to do with claims of abuse. A pressing and more prevalent problem refers to the questionable validity of courtroom testimony (Wells and Loftus 1984). Ordinary subjects are capable of adopting and assimilating a fabricated autobiography, in the absence of any malicious intention (Loftus 1996). Last but not least, false memories are not confined to individuals; when societies and nations adopt false *collective memories, the resulting fantasies and emotions could lead to global disasters.

Situations that resemble real-life false memory can be simulated in *controlled laboratory settings. The procedures typically involve the *recall or *recognition, often *cued, of stories, other verbal material, or visual scenes (e.g., Bartlett 1932; Carmichael *et al.* 1932; Miller and Gazzaniga 1998; Tversky and Marsh 2000). A *classic study is that of Deese (1959b).[1] The test material in this study was 36 lists of 12 words each. Each list was composed of the 12 primary associations of a target word, which itself was excluded from the list. For example, for the target word 'sleep', the list was 'bed, rest, awake, tired, dream, wake, snooze, blanket, doze, slumber, snore, nap'. The subjects were instructed to listen carefully to each list and then, at the conclusion of each list, recall orally the items from the list. Deese's intention was to identify the occurrence of extralist intrusions of words in the immediate recall. He found that many of the lists induced the subjects to produce the nonpresented target word as an intrusion on the test. 'Sleep', mentioned above, had in his hands the largest probability of intruding into the relevant list; words like 'rough', 'soft', 'chair', 'foot', 'cold', and others also starred as intruders in the recall of their associative list. This is hence a clear-cut case of false memory: the subjects claimed to have heard the target word, which they did not. The method was later improved and expanded to include a recognition test by Roediger and McDermott (1995). Word-intrusion tests are highly recommended for convincing demonstration of false memory in the classroom as well as in public lectures.

Why are some memories false? The question could be posed in two versions: first, what are the brain mechanisms that generate false memories, and second, why haven't some of our memory *systems been perfected in evolution to yield a higher fidelity of output. At the mechanistic *level, multiple possibilities could be entertained, which relate to distinct memory *phases: perception, *acquisition, *consolidation, *persistence, and *retrieval. False memories might stem from perceptual illusions (Roediger 1996), even from dreams (Loftus 1996) and fantasies (Freud 1899). It is, however, questionable whether these should be considered as a source of *bona fide* false memory, because from the point of view of the brain, the raw material for memory was real. Distortions in the processing of *percepts might be due to the amalgamation of the on-line experience with off-line experiences from different times and *contexts, and to reconstruction as well as repression of narratives by fitting them to emotive and cognitive schemata (Freud 1899; Bartlett 1932; Carmichael *et al.* 1932; Neisser 1967; Loftus *et al.* 1995; Koriat *et al.* 2000; Anderson and Green 2001). Consolidation, processes that might take place after a memory item is retrieved in a new context, 'implicit' could particularly provide an opportunity for new information to modify the initial trace (Nader *et al.* 2000; Sara 2000; Berman and Dudai 2001). The cues available in retrieval could also cause subjects to select, rearrange and distort the retrieved information (Tulving 1983; Loftus 1996). The introduction of improved neuropsychological assays of false memory, especially when combined with *functional neuroimaging, will surely cast additional light on the mechanisms involved. It has already led to the identification of frontal areas that are recruited differentially in false vs. veridical recall (Schacter *et al.* 1996c).

As to the phylogenetic considerations, several types of possibilities should be kept in mind. One, that faulty reproduction of information is an inherent constraint of the biological hardware that embodies memory. In other words, the system is imperfect because it could not be otherwise, unless we replace the hardware.[2] Second, the system still undergoes evolution, we are in the process, just give us time and we will fare much better. Only that time here could mean zillions of years, unless, again, we call bionics to the flag (*enigma). And third, which is related to the second, who says that accuracy is always a positive selective pressure in evolution? It could be so for some types of memory systems, such as *skill, but not for others, such as episodic memory. There are no doubt situations in which accurate recollection of episodes is but a burden; Plutarch (1–2C AD/1914a) was among those who recognized that: 'I dislike', he said, 'a drinking-companion with a good memory'. The possibility was raised that autobiographical memory had evolved to bind our personality and allow us to function better as distinct individuals in society; for this, autobiographical memory need not be neither large (Dudai 1997a) nor accurate (Conway 1996). Yet another possibility is that in moulding declarative memory systems, evolution actually selects against accuracy of details, because excessive accuracy may hamper *generalization and categorization (*mnemonics). The Rashomon phenomenon[3] may hence be a price we pay for the cognitive success of our species.

There is much more to the discipline of false memory than the phenomenon itself. The rediscovery and enthusiastic analysis of false memory phenomena in the past few decades has catalysed a conceptual revolution in the field of memory research (Koriat *et al.* 2000). This revolution is concerned with the shattering of the concept of the brain as a faithful mirror of reality, and replacing it with the idea that *internal representations mix the filtered percepts of the world with percepts acquired at other times, as well as with innate

(*a priori) and endogenously generated representations. In addition, the static 'storehouse' *metaphors are passé; many biological memories are *biased, dynamic reconstructions of past occurrences.[4] What comes out of the 'storehouse' is not what was deposited there.

Selected associaitons: Bias, Cue, Real-life memory, Retrieval, Zeitgeist

---

[1] The fate of this signal paper in the years following its publication is discussed in *zeitgeist.

[2] See in this context the 'Panglosian paradigm', in *paradigm.

[3] Termed after the *classic film *Rashomon*, by Akira Kurosawa, in which four conflicting versions of the same traumatic event are offered by four narrators (Kurosawa 1950; Cook 1981).

[4] A caveat is appropriate here. This statement merely claims that the individual human being is an untrustable witness. It does not claim that there are no facts outside there that could be identified and quantified by methods that control for bias in individual memory. This is what science attempts to do. For relevant debates, see Appleby *et al.* (1996); for the occasional misuse of science to support irrelevant claims such as the one this caveat tries to prevent, see Sokal and Bricmont (1998).

Fear conditioning

A type of learning in which a *stimulus or action become associated with fear.

'Show me a man who is not a slave; one is a slave to lust, another to greed, another to ambition, and all men are slaves to fear' (Seneca 63–65). Fear drives fundamental responses to the world in individuals and societies alike (Durkheim 1895; Freud 1908). James (1890), influenced by Darwin (1872), considered fear merely as an instinct. He even thought that the need to exercise this instinct had diminished in evolution, and in a somewhat naive burst of trust in the virtues of human kind, remarked: '…the progress from brute to man is characterized by nothing so much as by the decrease in frequency of proper occasions for fear' (James 1890). Yet already in its early days, experimental psychology became interested in the ways in which fear is acquired and augmented by experience. Pavlov (1928) termed fear as a 'passive defensive reflex', and noted that memory of a traumatic situation lingers for long and can block the expression of other acquired behaviours. Whereas Pavlov experimented on dogs, Watson, in a chilling expression of pragmatic *behaviourism, did it on human infants (Watson and Rayner 1920).

Fear conditioning

He frightened them with unexpected noises or sudden removal of physical support. One of his subjects, Albert B., 9 months old, initially 'stolid and unfearful', came to fear a laboratory rat upon association with a sharp noise that caused the infant to jump violently, fall, and cry. The ordeal led Albert, involuntarily, into the scientific literature (*ibid.*; also Harris 1979) (Figure 29); nowadays, it would have probably led the author into disgrace.

Fear is an emotion. Over the years, 'emotions' were frequently considered as intimate feelings unfit for mechanistic analysis. Most discussions of brain systems of emotion were rather vague and converged on the idea that emotions are subserved by the so-called *limbic system. As in many other chapters in science, a major breakthrough in understanding the neural substrates of emotion was provided by a *reductionist analysis of a *simple system. In this case, the *system was *classical (alias Pavlovian) fear conditioning, and specifically its auditory version. A rat hears a tone (the conditioned stimulus, CS) in conjunction with electric shock to the foot (the unconditioned stimulus, US). The shock elicits a fear response (unconditioned response). The tone then comes to elicit a fear response in the absence of shock (conditioned response, CR). The CR is manifested in multiple physiological responses, including increased blood pressure, secretion of stress hormones, startle, and freezing. The latter is an especially rapid and robust measure of fear (Blanchard and Blanchard 1969), although not necessarily the easiest to quantify. Pavlovian fear conditioning has proven to be a fruitful experimental system (Davis 1992;

Fig. 29 Little Albert undergoes fear conditioning to a rat, as detailed in Watson and Rayner (1920; courtesy of Ben Harris, see also Harris 1979). Conditioning paradigms did change dramatically over the past 80 years: nowadays, the rat is the one that is conditioned, whereas the human *subject only observes.

LeDoux 1996; Maren *et al.* 1996; Rogan and LeDoux 1996; Amorapanth *et al.* 2000). It has already contributed much to our understanding of circuits that subserve classical conditioning in general and emotion in particular in the mammalian brain. It has also cast light the role of *amygdala in learning, memory, modulation, and expression of emotional behaviour. And almost as a fringe benefit, fear conditioning became the first system in which a *long-term potentiation-like mechanism was shown to occur in learning in the behaving organism (Rogan *et al.* 1997).

A combination of studies using lesions, cellular physiology, and pharmacology led to a model of Pavlovian fear conditioning. According to this model, the CS and the US information reach the amygdala and associate in the lateral and basolateral nuclei. Amygdalar output, funnelled via the central nucleus, controls multiple effector systems involved in the expression of fear. After training, the CS alone, upon reaching the amygdala, elicits these responses. Although the circuit seems rather simple, several caveats are in place. First, although many laboratories agree that *acquisition and memory of fear conditioning occur in the amygdala, there are some who propose that the amygdala only modulates fear learning, while fear memory forms somewhere else (Cahill and McGaugh 1998). Second, when fear learning becomes more complex, the neuroanatomical map of this type of learning becomes more complex as well (Killcross *et al.* 1997; Nader and LeDoux 1997). In *real-life, the *context of the fearful situation is also of great importance, in which case the hippocampus becomes involved (Maren *et al.* 1998; but see McNish *et al.* 1997). The *cerebral neocortex is also expected to play a part. Yet, in approaching a complex system, one may be better off in adhering first to *Ockham's razor, and elemental Pavlovian fear conditioning offers an opportunity to do just that.

Fear conditioning unveils how the brain deals with the tension between speed and accuracy of response to danger. Analysis of even simple fear learning shows that the information about the CS reaches the amygdala via two different pathways (LeDoux 1996). A short one travels directly from the sensory thalamus to the amygdala and supplies information on general features of the stimulus but not on its detailed attributes. This short channel makes it possible for the organism to respond immediately. For a wandering rabbit, it is surely advisable to react as fast as possible to a fox-like-shadow and risk a false positive, rather than contemplate the fine *perceptual details of the predators' mouth from within. The other pathway runs from the thalamus to the cortex and from there to the amygdala. This some-what slower route provides information about detailed sensory attributes of the CS and can modulate the initial response. *Functional neuroimaging studies of human volunteers subjected to fear learning show that what is true for the rat is true for *Homo sapiens. The amygdala is active when we acquire and express fear (Adolphs et al. 1995; LaBar et al. 1998),[1] and subcortical, thalamo-amygdalar connections enable us to react to a fearful stimulus before we even get a chance to think about it (Morris et al. 1999).

Under certain circumstances fear conditioning situations could culminate in anxiety, neurosis and phobia. 'Fear' and 'anxiety' share many features (Davis 1992), to the point where some authors used them interchangeably (e.g. Mowrer 1938). However, 'fear' and 'anxiety' are not the same. The first is a response to a specific, identified event or situation; the second is abnormally heightened vigilance in anticipation of an event or situation that are construed, either consciously or subconsciously, as threatening (Rachman 1998). In a neurotic state, the mere fact that the threat can be logically deemed unreal doesn't alleviate the suffering. Our prefrontal cortex is normally capable of monitoring and assessing ongoing fearful and emotional situations (*'working memory' of fear and emotion; Davidson and Irwin 1999). This exerts some control over the response, and anticipates its consequences. However, when danger is subjectively appreciated as immediate and intense, *noradrenergic and *dopaminergic neuromodulation disrupts prefrontal cognitive functions (Arnsten 1998). Hence, when life is in peril, evolution clearly relies more on instinct than on reason, but unfortunately, this is also the case when the danger is only in the mental eyes of the beholder.

Selected associations: Amygdala, A Priori, Classical conditioning, Consolidation, Limbic system

---

[1] In a gender-dependent manner: in emotional situations, the right amygdala is preferentially activated in the male, the left amygdala in the female (Cahill et al. 2001).

Flashbulb memory

Memory for the circumstances in which one first learned of a *surprising, consequential, or emotionally arousing event.

In their now *classic paper, Brown and Kulik (1977) reported that 79 of 80 US citizens remembered vividly the circumstances in which they had first heard about the assassination of President John F. Kennedy, 14 years earlier. The fact that this type of *recall involves mental illumination of a specific scene explains the flashbulb *metaphor. Since then, recollections of additional salient events, such as the Challenger disaster (McCloskey et al. 1988; Neisser and Harsch 1992), have been used to analyse further the flashbulb memory phenomenon. The basic observation that unexpected momentous events, public or personal, do tend to generate an apparently exceptional memory of the circumstances in which they were encountered, is clearly supported by both experimental research and common experience. Some important issues, however, remain unsettled. Among them: Are flashbulb memories faithful? And are the biological mechanisms that subserve such memories unique?

Accounts of flashbulb memory are characterized by lucid, vivid, and detailed recollections. But already at the outset of the investigation of flashbulb memory it became evident that these memories do not preserve all the details of the original scene (Brown and Kulik 1977). In addition, several studies have indicated that the reported details are not necessarily accurate to begin with, and furthermore, could change with time (McCloskey et al. 1988; Neisser and Harsch 1992). A methodological problem, invoked in response to claims that flashbulb memories are unreliable, is that personal consequentiality and emotional significance are not easy to quantify and compare. Even though some signal public events are expected to generate flashbulb memories, in reality they do so in some *subjects but not in others (Conway 1995). The test protocol that is used to identify flashbulb memory could also itself influence the outcome, i.e., whether the recollection will be accurate or not (Koriat and Goldsmith 1996); *collective memory *cues and demand characteristic effects (*bias) may certainly colour the response. Such complications notwithstanding, it does appear that the fidelity of flashbulb memory, similarly to the fidelity of other *episodic recollections, must be treated with caution (*false memory).

Are flashbulb memories unique in their robustness and vividness? Some authors propose that this type of memory is not qualitatively different from other types of emotional memory (Christianson 1992; *fear conditioning). Others claim that flashbulb memories do comprise a distinct class of traces (Conway 1995). One type of suggestions is that the encoding of information during the *acquisition of the flashbulb memory is unique (Brown and Kulik 1977), in that it involves a particularly intense activation of specific brain circuits (e.g. *limbic system; Livingston 1967). This leads to the 'printing' of a highly detailed and robust *internal representation of the association of the salient event with the *context. Other types of explanations propose that there is nothing special about the encoding of flashbulb memory, but that this type of memory is special only because the intense emotional valence of the original event causes the information to be assigned extra importance over time, or be *retrieved extensively, resulting in a more robust, although not necessarily more faithful, memory (Neisser and Harsch 1992).

In recent years, brain research has unveiled clues to the biological mechanisms that encode the memory of intensely emotional and consequential events. These candidate mechanisms deal with two *levels of brain organization: the circuit level and the cellular level. The circuit mechanisms are assumed to involve subcortical modulation of the *cerebral cortex, which causes certain sensory events to be *perceived as highly salient because of the concomitant activation (*coincidence detection) of neuromodulatory systems such as the *acetylcholine and the *noradrenaline systems (Naor and Dudai 1996; McGaugh and Cahill 1997; Tang et al. 1997). This hypothesis is a neurobiological version of the 'unique acquisition' accounts mentioned above (Brown and Kulik 1977). The cellular explanations are based on the assumption that the consolidation of long-term memory is triggered by a certain configuration of transcription factors (*CREB, *immediate early genes, *spaced training). This configuration acts as a molecular switch that induces a wave of activation or de-repression of gene expression at the modulated *synapses, culminating in the remodelling of the network connections and in the stabilization of the memory (Bartsch et al. 1995). The idea is that those momentary events that give rise to a flashbulb memory, induce the right configuration of the transcription factors very rapidly—in a few seconds or a few minutes instead of several hours. If this is true, it implies that the kinetics of memory *consolidation is not fixed, but rather depends on the conditions of training (Frey and Morris 1997; Dudai and Morris 2000). It also suggests that a robust long-term memory trace can be induced by 'instant consolidation', without necessarily going through a labile short-term *phase. By the way, the notion that long-term memory can be established in the absence of short-term memory is in line with evidence from other *systems (e.g. Emptage and Carew 1993).

Whatever the mechanisms of flashbulb memory are, they should also explain why is it that intense emotional experiences lead to remarkable memories in some cases, but to obliteration of memory or repression of its retrieval in others (Loftus and Kaufman 1992).

Selected associations: Attention, Collective memory, Consolidation, Context, Surprise

---

Forgetting

1. **The loss of learned information.**
2. **The inability to *retrieve learned information.**
3. **The deterioration of correspondence between the memory retrieved and the memory *acquired.**

Herman Ebbinghaus, the progenitor of quantitative experimental psychology (Gorfein and Hoffman 1987), remarked that 'all sorts of ideas, if left to themselves, are gradually forgotten' (Ebbinghaus 1885). Whether this statement is acceptable by laypersons and scientists alike, depends on what is meant by 'forgotten'. If 'forgotten' means 'erased from memory', then many, including professional psychologists, tend to believe that everything we learn is never erased (Loftus and Loftus 1980). In contrast, others, starting with Plato (*Theaetetus* 191), trust that memory traces can indeed be obliterated ('drowned in the waters of Lethe', Galton 1879).[1] As it is much more difficult, and frequently impossible, to distinguish an obliterated memory from a nonretrievable one, the use of 'retrieval' in the definition of 'forgetting' (definition 2 above) is therefore a safer bet.

Forgetting occurs in all species (elephants included) and *memory *systems (*taxonomy), but its magnitude and kinetics depend on the type of memory, on its use, and on the conditions under which it is tapped (Baddeley 1997). The variables involved are not straightforward. People display surprising forgetfulness even for personal events that could be expected to rank as important indeed to the *subject, ranging from salient changes in personal status (Jenkins et al. 1979) to routine dietary behaviour (Smith 1991). And when a frequently retrieved memory does seem 'unforgetful'— is it the original *engram that is reinforced with repeated use, or, alternatively, a changing engram that is reconstructed and then *consolidated each time anew (*flashbulb memory, *real-life memory)? In most memory *paradigms one is able to come up with 'forgetting curves' (Ebbinghaus 1885), which show deterioration in *performance over time for almost every material learned, except that in some cases the time-scale is minutes or hours (e.g. nonsense syllables, *ibid*), whereas in others it is years to decades (e.g. a foreign language or autobiographical episodes; Linton 1978; Bahrick 1984). A useful method to quantify forgetting, or actually [1-forgetting], in the laboratory is to measure 'saving'. This is the decrease in the amount of training needed on retraining on the original task (hence measuring 'the saving of work in the case of relearning'; Ebbinghaus 1885). *Real-life approaches to forgetting focus on the determination of the loss in details and veridicality of the memory (definition 3; Koriat *et al.* 2000; *false memory).

One could come up with multiple types of potential explanations for the various manifestations of forgetting. Four types of hypotheses concerning either true or apparent forgetting have specifically attracted the attention of experimentalists and theoreticians (Freud 1901, 1915; Pavlov 1927; McGeoch 1932; Underwood and Extrand 1966; Shiffrin and Atkinson 1969; Tulving 1983; Capaldi and Neath 1995).

1. Forgetting occurs because the biological substrate that encodes the engram disintegrates or decays with time. This decay may involve the entire representation or, more likely, fragments of it, up to a point where degradation ceases to be 'graceful' (*persistence) and becomes catastrophic.

2. Forgetting occurs because the learned information is processed in a way that erases part(s) of the engram. This could be the consequence of either passive or active processes. 'Passive' means that with mere usage, the fidelity of the information deteriorates, and the representation gets noisy and ultimately meaningless. 'Active' means that information is actively being pruned over time, or 'unlearned', to optimize storage *capacity, retrieval, or performance (Hopfield *et al.* 1983; McClelland *et al.* 1995; *consolidation).[2]

3. A related possibility is that forgetting, or at least apparent forgetting (see below), occurs because other information alters the engram or interferes with its expression. The interference may be 'proactive' (of earlier learning on later learning), or 'retroactive' (of later learning on the recall of previously learned information; see examples in *classical conditioning). A notable case is *experimental extinction, in which an acquired *association is inhibited by repetitive post-training presentation of the unrewarded stimulus. The original information could still exist, and in experimental extinction of associative conditioning indeed it does, but it becomes ineffective in controlling behaviour. As noted above, the interaction may also occur in

're*consolidation' of the memory immediately after its retrieval. A special type of interference is promoted in psychoanalytic theory. This is 'repression', a defence mechanism[3] that attempts to turn anxiety-provoking memories non-retrievable (Freud 1915; Laplanche and Pontalis 1973; *infantile amnesia, *palimpsest).[4] Some authors will argue that interference mechanisms are not *bona fide* forgetting, because the original trace is not really obliterated; yet, as already noted, unless one deals with a straightforward case of experimental extinction, practically, it is usually difficult to determine whether a forgotten memory is abolished or only repressed.

4. Forgetting is due to the lack of appropriate retrieval *cues or to the use of an inappropriate processing mode in retrieval (*transfer). This again is apparent forgetting; given the appropriate cues and processing, the memory will be actualized.

Although forgetting is frequently regarded as a nuisance, for example, when it involves tasks to be performed in daily life (*prospective memory), the real nuisance might be not to forget at all. 'Thus even a happy life is possible without remembrance, as the beast shows; but life in any true sense is absolutely impossible without forgetfulness' (Nitzsche, cited in Roth 1989). People who suffer from 'hyperamnesia', the antipode of *amnesia, are miserable and would rather forget [two *classic cases are Monsieur X of Guillons, cited in Roth (1989), and the mnemonist S of Luria (1969)]. Forgetting could permit us to increase the signal-to-noise ratio of our cognitive narratives, and *generalize about the world. Occasionally it could also facilitate the acquisition of new *skills, by weakening distractive, older ones. And, last but not least, forgetting bad memories could smoothen the roughness of life. We should not forget that.

Selected associations: Amnesia, Cue, Experimental extinction, Infantile amnesia, Retrieval

---

[1]Lethe was the mythological river in Hades, the Land of the Dead, whose water induced forgetfulness in those who drank it, *Republic* 621; see *lotus.

[2]An intriguing hypothesis is that 'unlearning', pruning, and reorganization of information occurs in dream sleep (Crick and Mitchison 1983; Sejnowski 1995). If this is the case, then we do not only forget dreams, we also dream to forget.

[3]In psychoanalysis, defence mechanisms are postulated unconscious mental operations that are aimed at the reduction of painful emotions, ideas, and drives (Vaillant 1992).

[4]For candidate repression processes in brain, see Anderson and Green (2001).

Functional neuroimaging

The visualization of the functional organization of the brain by electromagnetic or optical methods.

The search for the *engram is a mapping expedition. It requires *maps that chart both anatomy and function. Anatomy *per se* only rarely tells us what specific brain structures do. This is evident, by the way, from some neuroanatomical terms that mean only a fruit or a sea monster (e.g. *amygdala, *hippocampus). Surely if early anatomists would have known something about what these structures do, they would have called them by other names. Indeed, some idea on function could occasionally be obtained from tracing the connections between various sites, e.g. a pathway from the olfactory bulb to the piriform cortex does suggest that the latter deals with olfaction, not vision. But the insight into function obtained this way is still limited. Anatomical brain mapping was born in antiquity (Galen 2nd century AD; Thorndike 1923). It underwent a revolution in the nineteenth century with the development of microscopy and histology (Brazier 1988; history fans might also wish to see DeFelipe and Jones 1988). The anatomical cartography of the brain has reached new heights in the second half of the twentieth century. This was made possible by the introduction of sophisticated tracing methods, based on specific molecular probes such as lectins (proteins that bind sugars characteristic of specific cells and cellular compartments), radioactive tracers, and enzymatic reactions (Brodal 1998; Cowan 1998).

Functional brain mapping has a long history as well: the same Galen mentioned above was said to have already noted the effect of brain lesions on behaviour (Thorndike 1923). This approach had gained popularity among brain scientists in the nineteenth century; so was the study of the behavioural consequence of stimulation of loci in the brain by electric currents (Brazier 1988; Finger 2000). Almost a century later, the introduction of the microelectrode has already permitted the analysis of the response of single nerve cells in the brain to specific sensory *stimuli. This has yielded the first detailed functional brain maps (for a *classic example, see Hubel and Wiesel 1977). However, the term 'functional neuroimaging' nowadays does not commonly connote the construction of functional brain maps by meticulous analysis of the response of single neurons, nor the inference of function from anatomical or metabolic lesions, but rather the visualization of the function of large terrains of the brain by electromagnetic or optical methods.

Functional neuroimaging is based on electrophysiological methods; or tomographic methods (*tómos*, a 'cut' in Greek, so called because these methods involve construction of three-dimensional images from planar images, or 'cuts'); or optical methods. The various methods will be explained below. Three points should be noted at the outset, which reflect on the contribution of the functional neuroimaging methods to the analysis of learning and memory in brain. First, these methods differ in their spatial and temporal resolution (Figure 30). Second, they differ in the nature of the signal that they measure; some detect electrical activity directly, others only haemodynamic and metabolic changes secondary to electrical activity. And third, these methods differ in the degree of invasiveness, which means that some could be safely applied to behaving volunteers, others to more daring volunteers, yet others to immobilized laboratory animals only.

1. *Electrophysiological imaging.* The earliest functional neuroimaging method was electroencephalography (EEG), which measures electrical potential differences among locations on or in the brain as a function of time and place. (The abbreviation 'EEG' is used both for the method and for the records that it generates, 'electroencephalograms'.) The first to report that spontaneous electrical activity can be recorded from the scalp of animals was Caton (1875). The effect of physiological conditions on these patterns of activity was further investigated by his contemporaries (e.g. Danielvsky, see Brazier 1988). But it took several decades before EEG had captivated the world's attention. Berger (1929) pioneered EEG in humans, including on his own son, and discovered a rhythmic oscillation of electric potential with a frequency of about 8–12 Hz, associated with relaxed wakefulness. Adrian and Matthews (1934) replicated Berger's findings and localized the source of the 'Berger rhythm' to the occipital lobe. This was the first use of EEG in functional brain mapping.

Scalp EEG is assumed to reflect mainly the summation of graded post*synaptic potentials originating in the *cerebral cortex. Detection of EEG sources deep in the brain requires insertion of invasive electrodes. The contribution of cortical neurons to the EEG is itself a function of the endogenous states of the neuron and the activity of its input circuits (Lopes da Silva 1991). To make the story even more complex, the electrical signal of scalp EEG is distorted by the intervening tissue and is highly sensitive to the location of the recording electrode. Not surprisingly, the task of the investigator trying to identify and understand the source and physiological function of scalp EEG has been likened to

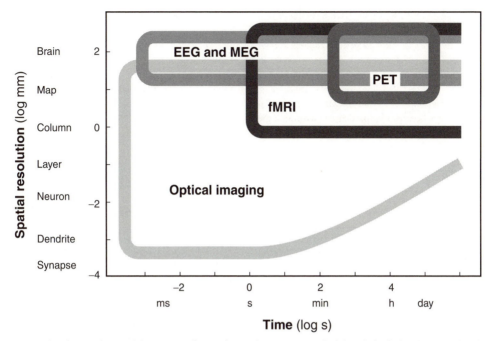

Fig. 30 Spatial resolution and temporal characteristics of various functional neuroimaging methods. 'Time' refers both to the *temporal resolution* (which limit for each method corresponds to the most left-handed point on the time-scale) and to the *duration* of the time window during which experiments could be conducted. *Optical imaging* is the imaging of intrinsic signals, or voltage-sensitive dyes, calcium-sensitive dyes, and other optical probes; these methods differ in their spatial and temporal resolution but are combined in the diagram for the sake of simplicity. EEG, electroencephalography; MEG, magnetoencephalography; fMRI, functional magnetic resonance imaging; PET, positron emission tomography. PET time window is closed because it involves radionucleides that cannot be administered repeatedly over a long time period. Currently, optical imaging is the most invasive of these methods yet provides the highest temporal and spatial resolution. EEG is the least invasive. So far, because of reasons indicated in the text, PET and fMRI have contributed most to the search for the *engram, and fMRI is considered of the highest potential in the field of human memory research.

that of an expert attempting to diagnose the problems of a computer by holding a voltmeter up to it (Bodis-Wollner 1987). Keeping this in mind, still, a lot can be done. The ongoing activity recorded from the scalp of a healthy *subject is at a frequency range of 1–30 Hz, with a few dominant state-dependent frequencies: α (the above 'Berger rhythm'); β (12–30 Hz); δ (0.5–4 Hz); and θ (4–7 Hz). EEG can also be used to detect 'evoked potentials' (EP) or 'event-related potentials' (ERPs, e.g. Picton *et al.* 1995; the term ERP should be preferred to EP, as the latter is also used in cellular electrophysiology to denote the stimulus response of single neurons and *receptor cells). ERPs are time-locked to a sensory stimulus or a cognitive event. For example, *cued expectancy of an imperative stimulus is preceded by a low frequency negative wave ('contingent negative variation', CNV, Walter *et al.* 1964); a rare stimulus in a sequence of frequent stimuli evokes a characteristic positive component after >300 ms ('P300', Sutton *et al.* 1965, *surprise).

EEG is characterized by an excellent temporal resolution, in the millisecond range. Scalp EEG is completely noninvasive, relatively inexpensive, and can be used on freely moving subjects, including in *real-life situations. These are some of the pros. But there are, as usual, cons. The spatial resolution is poor, in the centimetre range, and the correlation of the signals with an identified source, as noted above, is problematic. A sister method, magnetoencephalography (MEG), offers some advantages, including a smaller sensitivity of the magnetic signal to distortion by the skull and simpler localization of the source signal (Wikswo *et al.* 1993). At the time of writing, MEG requires a cumbersome and expensive set-up, and the subject must remain immobilized throughout the measurement. In recent years the use of many electrodes (>100), the improvement in computational power, and the accumulating supporting data from other disciplines such as cellular physiology, has boosted EEG as a functional mapping method (Gevins *et al.* 1999). Still, so far the major proven strength of EEG in research is in detecting and separating, by time and type, broad electrophysiological phenomenological correlates of fast cognitive processes in humans, e.g. in *attention, *acquisition, and *retrieval of memory (e.g. Kutas 1988; Johnson 1995; Paller *et al.* 1995; Friedman *et al.* 1996; Miltner *et al.* 1999). Areas in which EEG has been proven particularly useful are the analysis of *working memory, and the acquisition, retrieval, and the dependence of long-term retrieval on acquisition in *declarative tasks in humans; in all these cases the task typically involves verbal material.

2. *Positron emission tomography* (PET). This method can be used to measure certain aspects of cerebral metabolism, such as local blood flow, glucose utilization (*nutrient), or *receptor occupancy. PET is based on the use of isotopes that decay by the emission of positrons (positive electrons). The emitted positron collides with an electron to produce two γ-rays, which travel 180° apart. Coincident detection of the two γ-rays permits the position of their source to be determined. In practice, a biologically relevant compound, labelled with the appropriate isotope, is injected intravenously or inhaled. The emitted radioactivity is monitored by an external ring scanner and used to compute a map of the distribution of the compound in the tissue. The isotopes used have a short half-life, in the range of minutes, so that large doses of radioactivity can be administered within acceptable safety limits. The short half-life necessitates access to an accelerator to produce the tracers on site. For example, compounds containing ^{15}O, typically $H_2^{15}O$, are used to measure task-related differences in regional cerebral blood flow. The underlying assumption is that such haemodynamic changes reflect alteration in neural activity; this notion can be traced back at least to James (1890) and Roy and Sherrington (1890; for a related pre-scientific idea, see Descartes 1649). Amino acids labelled with ^{11}C are used to measure protein synthesis, ^{18}F-labelled drugs to map receptor occupancy, and 2-deoxy-2-^{18}F-D-glucose (^{18}F-2DG) to map glucose metabolism. The 2DG method was originally used for post-mortem imaging (Sokoloff *et al.* 1977). 2DG is an analogue of glucose that is taken up by the cells, but cannot be metabolized like glucose, and is therefore trapped in an amount proportional to the level of glucose consumption. The assumption is that a high metabolic rate is indicative of increased neuronal activity. In the original method, ^{14}C-2DG was administered before the task, the animal killed afterwards, and the active regions detected by quantitative autoradiography of brain slices. In PET, of course, the subject can live happily afterwards.

PET was developed in the mid-1970s, and since then has contributed tremendously to neurocognitive mapping (Raichle 1983; Cherry and Phelps 1996). Selected examples of the localization of memory systems in the mammalian brain by PET are provided in Buckner and Tulving 1995; Buckner *et al.* 1995; Fletcher *et al.* 1997; Maguire *et al.* 1997, 1998; Smith and Jonides 1997. For example, PET has enabled remarkable insight into the brain systems that subserve spatial memory and its use in navigation in humans, in situations that simulate *real-life (Maguire *et al.* 1997, 1998; *hippocampus). It has also provided a tremendous boost to the analysis of brain substrates of *retrieval (e.g. Buckner *et al.* 1995). PET has a respectable spatial resolution (millimetres), but a poor temporal one (minutes). It is moderately invasive because of the use of radionucleides.

3. *Functional magnetic resonance imaging (fMRI).* MRI detects and measures the characteristic interaction of certain atomic nuclei with radiofrequency waves in a strong magnetic field. (It is also known as 'nuclear magnetic resonance', NMR, only that the use of 'nuclear' was assumed to frighten the public, and dropped except in chemistry.) MRI can detect hydrogen in water, and as the large water content of organisms differs from one tissue to another, the method can be used to map internal organs. It can also detect and delineate lesions, for example, in the brain of *amnesics (e.g. Corkin *et al.* 1997). Early attempts to extend the use of MRI to map functional changes in blood flow (and hence develop fMRI) were based on the introduction into the blood an exogenous contrast agent (Rosen *et al.* 1989). But then a better method has been devised. It was based on the observation that the magnetic properties of oxyhaemoglobin and deoxyhaemoglobin differ (Pauling and Coryell 1936), and that paramagnetic deoxyhaemoglobin in venous blood can serve as a contrast agent for MRI. MRI methodology was thus adapted to obtain *in vivo* images of brain microvasculature with image contrast that reflects blood oxygen level (blood oxygenation level-dependent contrast, abbreviated 'BOLD contrast' or 'BOLD signal'; Ogawa *et al.* 1990, 1998). The underlying tenet, as in some usages of PET, is that the haemodynamic changes reflect regional brain activity.

The temporal resolution of fMRI detectors is in the subsecond range, but the kinetics of the haemodynamic signal is slower, and therefore, practically, the temporal resolution is in the range of a few seconds. The spatial resolution at the time of writing is in the millimetre range (e.g. Logothetis *et al.* 1999; Ugrubil *et al.* 1999). Advanced, high field fMRI methods, based on the detection of early local changes in oxygen consumption rather than the delayed, more diffused alterations in blood flow, could potentially improve the resolution (Kim *et al.* 2000; on this issue see also Vanzetta and Grinvald 1999; Logothetis 2000). In behavioural experiments, to increase the signal-to-noise ratio, paradigms that use fMRI (or PET) commonly collect multiple images over extended time periods that contain successive trials of the same task ('block task paradigms'). Such protocols do not supply information about responses that are time-locked to single trials and about trial-to-trial change—as opposed, for example, to EEG studies of ERPs (see above). In recent years, protocols have been developed that allow analysis of trial-to-trial responses in fMRI as well (Buckner *et al.* 1996). This 'event-related fMRI' is particularly useful in investigating brain response in situations in which different stimuli are mixed over time, and where the response is expected to vary from one stimulus to another.

fMRI is considered noninvasive, although the long-term safety for humans of the high magnetic fields that are already used on the *monkey must still be determined. The advantages of the high resolution and the assumed noninvasiveness clearly outweigh the fact that fMRI does not measure neuronal activity directly. At the same time, this situation emphasizes the need to understand in fine details the source, specificity, and physiological significance of the biological signal (Vanzetta and Grinvald 1999; Kim *et al.* 2000; Logothetis *et al.* 2001). The contribution of fMRI to the field of memory research is clearly on the ascending limb, and the pace of publication is admittedly almost alarming (the question how can a single human being read all this literature certainly deserves a special functional neuroimaging study). Results cited in many entries in this book are either based on or supported by fMRI (e.g. *acquisition, *cerebral cortex, *hippocampus, *retrieval, *skill; for selected examples see Buchel *et al.* 1998; Fernandez *et al.* 1998; Kelley *et al.* 1998; LaBar *et al.* 1998; Poldrack *et al.* 1998; Dolan and Fletcher 1999; Wagner *et al.* 1999; Cabeza *et al.* 2001; Figure 31).

4. *Optical imaging.* Optical functional neuroimaging methods rely on the detection of intrinsic activity-dependent optical changes in neural tissue, or on the use of voltage-sensitive dyes, ion sensitive dyes and other extrinsic optical probes and tracers. Alterations in the intrinsic optical properties of nerve fibres were first reported in the late 1940s (Hill and Keynes 1949). Staining with voltage-sensitive dyes to measure neuronal activity was described by Tasaki *et al.* (1968). The voltage-sensitive-dye imaging methodology was subsequently improved and put to use by a number of groups (e.g. Cohen *et al.* 1974, Grinvald *et al.* 1981).

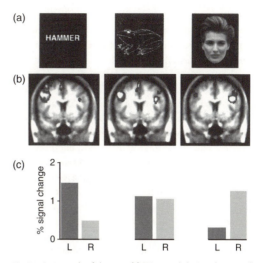

Fig. 31 An example of the use of fMRI to study brain substrates of learning. Human subjects were subjected to fMRI scans while being presented with three types of visual stimuli (a: from left to right): word, nameable object, and face. The instructions were to remember each item for a later memory test. The word-encoding task was expected to depend on verbal processing, the object on both verbal and nonverbal processing, and the face on nonverbal processing. Coronal sections (b) show dorsal frontal cortex activation. Peak activation was observed in the left frontal cortex for word encoding, the left and right dorsal frontal for object encoding, and the right dorsal frontal cortex for face encoding. (c) The per cent signal change in the left (L) and right (R) hemispheres. There is a clear hemispheric asymmetry in the verbal and nonverbal encoding situations. Adapted from Kelley *et al.* (1998; in the original publication, the fMRI images are presented in pseudocolours).

Optical imaging of intrinsic signals relies on activity-dependent changes in light reflected from the imaged tissue. The intrinsic signals stem from activity dependent alterations in local blood volume, oxygenation of haemoglobin, and light scattering caused by the local movement of water, ions, and released *neurotransmitter(s) (Grinvald *et al.* 1986; Malonek *et al.* 1997; Vanzetta and Grinvald 1999). Optical imaging of intrinsic signals in its current state of the art is invasive, as it requires opening the skull. The optical changes can be visualized through intact dura or thinned bone, hence its invasiveness in experimental animals can be minimized. For the imaged tissue itself the process is nondestructive. The spatial resolution is high (µm range), whereas the temporal resolution depends on the rise time of the haemodynamic and metabolic changes. Intrinsic imaging has been extensively employed to analyse the functional architecture of the mammalian brain, especially the visual system. The measurements can be repeatedly performed on the same subject over long periods (in fact, many weeks). The latter property is particularly advantageous in the study of the use and reuse of memory (*phase).

The use of voltage sensitive days involves application of dyes to the brain surface. This is invasive, and restricts the approach to animal studies. The advantage is a high temporal and spatial resolution (Shoham *et al.* 1999). Among the optical imaging methods, this is the one that follows neuronal activity most faithfully, as it monitors real-time alterations in membrane potential. An example of another optical imaging method that relies on extrinsic chromophores is *calcium imaging, i.e. using compounds that change their optical properties as a function of calcium concentration (e.g. Faber *et al.* 1999).

The contribution of optical imaging methods to the neurobiology of memory has so far been limited. These methods, none the less, have a remarkable potential to contribute to the analysis of brain mechanisms of learning and memory in experimental animals. The use of optical imaging in the analysis of the olfactory perception and olfactory memory is only one example. Calcium imaging has been used to detect experience-dependent alterations in odour *maps in the olfactory brain of the *classically conditioned *honeybee (Faber *et al.* 1999). Intrinsic imaging has been used to map the topography of odorant representation in the rat olfactory bulb as well (Rubin and Katz 1999).

All in all, functional neuroimaging is exciting, useful, and popular. Its potential for being even more so in the future is substantial. It has already provided us with remarkable data on the involvement of distinct brain areas and circuits in various phases and types of memory. But it is definitely not a magic bullet. The proper exploitation of its potential depends on proper adaptation of the specific technique to the right question and system, and in combining multiple synergistic methodologies in the experimental protocol. Selected examples include the use of molecular biology to image the dynamics of gene expression in the brain of small laboratory animals (Service 1999), hence creating the opportunity to monitor correlates of *consolidation in real time; the use of behavioural *assays to image brain substrates of memory illusions (Schacter 1996*c*, Cabeza *et al.* 2001, *false memory); and the differential contribution of brain circuits to mathematical thinking (Dehaene *et al.* 1999). Functional neuroimaging will be judged in the history of memory research not by the dazzling feats of the technology or by the impressive aesthetics of pseudocoloured images, but rather by the ability to solve questions (e.g. Kosslyn 1999, *enigma)

that cannot be unravelled without it. Judged by these *criteria, some authors think that so far, the contribution of functional neuroimaging to memory research is a bit overrated, whereas others think that this set of methodologies has already passed the test of memory research in flying colours.

Selected associations: Dimension, Engram, Homo sapiens, Phrenology

Generalization

1. Partial equivalence in the behavioural effect of different *stimuli or responses.

2. The acquired response to a class of stimuli on the basis of experience with exemplars of the class.

3. The occurrence of a learned response in circumstances that differ from those prevailing during *acquisition.

The functional counterpart of 'generalization' is 'discrimination', which is the ability to distinguish one stimulus or response from another. This is why it is convenient to treat these faculties together. Discrimination increases the repertoire of fine-tuned *perception and response, but places a burden on *capacity; generalization diminishes the sensitivity to input noise, but limits the degrees of freedom of the behavioural repertoire and could increase the proportion of false-positive responses. A *subject could be well capable of discriminating among two events, but still generalize its response to them if this pays off behaviourally. The optimal balance between discrimination and generalization is a function of the task and the situation. This balance in nature is nicely illustrated in the primitive *fear conditioning reflex (LeDoux 1996). Suppose we unexpectedly detect a snake-like shadow. The visual information travels to the *amygdala, a brain centre involved in the emotional response, either directly via the thalamus or indirectly via the *cerebral cortex. The thalamo-amygdalar pathway transmits only some general features of the stimulus (that it is a long undulating object), but not detailed sensory attributes (revealing that it is only a loose black water pipe). This channel makes it possible for the organism to respond faster to the generalized gestalt of a snake, risking a false-positive but at the same time minimizing the probability of a fatal false-negative response. The slightly slower thalamocortico-amygdaloid route provides information about the detailed, discriminative sensory attributes of the stimulus (*cue), and prevents further costly physiological and behavioural reactions.

Generalization, discrimination, and their modulation by experience became fashionable research topics early in the history of psychology (Boring 1950*a*; Keller and Schoenfeld 1950). Since then, it is common practice to distinguish 'stimulus generalization' from 'response generalization'. Stimulus generalization refers to situations in which a subject that had learned to respond to a particular stimulus comes to elicit the same response to other, similar stimuli. Response generalization refers to situations in which a subject that had learned to respond to a given stimulus comes to elicit other, similar responses to the same stimulus. A useful measure of stimulus generalization is the 'generalization gradient', which depicts the range of response to a conditioned stimulus (Figure 32). In some paradigms, the more difficult the task, the less the generalization, hence the steeper the generalization gradient (Ahissar and Hochstein 1997). A corresponding measure in discrimination is the 'just-noticeable-difference' ('jnd'). This is the smallest change along a stimulus *dimension that can still be discriminated. The relationship between the change in stimulus intensity that can just be discriminated ($\Delta\phi$) and the intensity of the stimulus (ϕ) is approximated by 'Weber's law': $\Delta\phi/\phi = $ constant. The relation between the stimulus magnitude (ϕ) and the subjective sensation magnitude (ψ) is given by 'Fechner's law': $\psi = k \log \phi$ (where k is a constant; Gescheider 1997). Note that both are not really 'laws' but merely generalizations, which only approximate reality under limited conditions (*algorithm).

Discrimination is invaluable in the study of conditioning paradigms, in which the subject's ability to acquire and store new information is quantified by its ability to distinguish among stimuli and associate the appropriate stimulus with the unconditioned stimulus or *reinforcer (*classical conditioning, *instrumental conditioning). The use of discrimination protocols in probing the functional neuroanatomy of visual cortex and its role in learning in the *monkey is but one example (e.g. Mishkin 1982). A similar use in dissecting the brain systems that process and learn chemical information in the *rat is yet another example (e.g. Schul *et al.* 1996). An important variable in such experiments is the sensory attributes of the objects to be discriminated. Those attributes that support sensory differentiation are traditionally termed 'discriminanda' (Tolman 1932). Appropriate discriminanda, e.g. of food items as

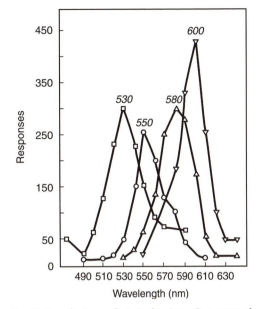

Fig. 32 Generalization gradients in the pigeon. Four groups of pigeons were trained to peck at an illuminated key to get food *reinforcement. One group was trained to respond to illumination at 530 nm, another at 550 nm, still another at 580 nm, and the fourth at 600 nm. Generalization testing was carried out by presenting the pigeons with random series of lights at different wavelengths and measuring their key pecking as a function of the wavelength. The curves depict the range of response for each group. The same graphs can, of course, be treated as discrimination curves. (Adapted from Guttman and Kalish 1956.)

opposed to nonsense objects, can markedly facilitate discrimination learning (Jarvik 1953). Discrimination analysis is routinely used in psychophysics to study perceptual competence and use-dependent modification in perceptual *skill (Green and Swets 1988; Gescheider 1997). Generalization is also used to infer the ability of animals to extract rules and in assessing the phylogeny of cognitive abilities (Harlow 1949; Wright *et al.* 1988; Slotnick 1994; *learning set; for *classics on human ability to generalize and categorize, see Rosch *et al.* 1976; Tversky 1977). Indeed, simple generalization is considered as a rudimentary form of categorization, induction and concept formation. Deficits in generalization could result in marked behavioural disadvantage, and in humans impair *performance on even mildly demanding jobs (*capacity, *mnemonics). Overgeneralization is also no good, as it could lead to inaccuracy of response, and, under certain conditions, even worse, to generalized anxiety and phobias.[1]

*Models of stimulus generalization can be classified according to their *level of analysis. Among the models that address computational and algorithmic levels, two prominent types are 'feature-based' and 'rule-based' (Shanks and Darby 1998). Roughly speaking, feature-based models treat generalization as a bottom-up function of similarity in a feature-representation space, whereas rule-based models envisage generalization as a top-down process, based on abstract rules or categories that are either innate (*a priori) or acquired. Models that address the level of neuronal, 'hardware' implementation of generalization, date back to the early part of the twentieth century. Pavlov proposed that the neuronal basis of generalization is a spread of excitation from one specific brain region to another (Pavlov 1928). The idea was hence that the original stimulus was highly differentiated but the specificity lost due to the rich interconnectivity of the brain. The same type of concept could be applied to response generalization. This contrasts with a later hypothesis, that generalization is the original state and differentiation develops with experience (Lashley and Wade 1946). It is likely that in the brain both processes occur.

The circuit mechanisms of generalization are expected to depend on the type of task. Whenever cognitive generalization is concerned, the *hippocampal–cortical axis immediately comes to mind (McClelland and Goddard 1996). Which cellular and *synaptic mechanisms subserve generalization in these circuits? Is it at all subserved by distinct synaptic properties? Recent observations on *long-term potentiation (LTP) and synaptic specificity suggest candidate processes and mechanisms. LTP is considered as an input-specific mechanism that modifies only use-activated synapses. Engert and Bonhoeffer (1997) reported, however, that this specificity is rather limited: in their preparation, synapses at a distance of up to 70 μm from the focus of potentiation were also potentiated, regardless of their activation history. This is a distance that can accommodate many synapses. Although the contribution of such neighbouring synapses to the relevant *representation is not yet known, this observation hints at a type of local process that might contribute to generalization. In another type of experiment, Frey and Morris (1997) found that the persistence of potentiation over time depends not only on local events at the activated synapse but also on prior activity of other synapses on the same neuron. Weak tetanic stimulation, which ordinarily leads to short-lived LTP only, resulted in long-term LTP, provided repeated tetanization had already been applied as long as 2–3 hours earlier at another input to the same population of neurons. This may be construed as yet another mechanism in which a specific synaptic input expands its sphere of effectiveness to nonactivated synapses (*context; for related findings in *Aplysia, see Martin et al. 1997a). Nevertheless, at present, the possibility that the aforementioned observations at the synaptic level contribute to generalization at the behavioural level should be treated only as provocative speculation.

Selected associations: Cue, Skill, Stimulus, Taxonomy, Transfer

---

[1]A refreshing example of overgeneralization is cited by Bandura and Walters (1963). This is a letter from the advice column of a leading metropolitan newspaper. And so it goes:

Dear Abby:
My girl friend fixed me up with a blind date and I should have known the minute he showed up in a bow tie that he couldn't be trusted. I fell for him like a rock. He got me to love him on purpose and then lied to me and cheated on me. Every time I go with a man who wears a bow tie, the same thing happens. I think girls should be warned about men who wear them.
Against Bow Ties.

Dear Against:
Don't condemn all men who wear bow ties because of your experience. I know many a man behind a bow tie who can be trusted.

Glutamate

An amino acid that functions as the primary excitatory *neurotransmitter in the vertebrate central nervous system.

L-glutamate is present in the mammalian brain at remarkably high concentrations. For a while this observation, coupled with the ability of glutamate to excite neurons all over the brain, cast doubt on its role in neurotransmission; for how can such a 'non-specific' agent mediate specific information? The case for glutamate as a neurotransmitter in the invertebrate neuromuscular junction was easier to establish (Usherwood 1994; *criterion). But with time it became clear that not only is glutamate a transmitter in mammalian brain—it is the major excitatory transmitter, and as such is critical for ongoing activity in the central nervous system. Furthermore, it is now known to play a key part in neuronal *plasticity and learning.

Glutamate belongs to the family of amino acid neurotransmitters. The closely related amino acids L-aspartate and L-homocysteine possibly play a part in excitatory neurotransmission as well. Other amino acids that serve as neurotransmitters are the inhibitory neurotransmitter γ-aminobutyric acid (GABA), and glycine, which serves as an inhibitory neurotransmitter and also as a modulator of glutamatergic transmission (Cooper *et al.* 1996). In neurons, L-glutamate is synthesized from glucose via the Krebs' cycle and transamination of α-oxoglutarate, and from glutamine (imported from glia cells[1]), by glutaminase. Glutamate released from pre*synaptic vesicles interacts with several types and subtypes of glutamate *receptors, depending on the neuronal circuit, synaptic target, and physiological context. Two major types of glutamate receptors are known: ionotropic and metabotropic. The ionotropic receptors are ligand-gated *ionic channels, permeable to cations. There are at least three subtypes of ionotropic receptors, which differ in their ligand binding as well as in channel properties. These receptor subtypes are each named after the glutamate analogue that activates the receptor preferentially: α-amino-3-hydroxy-5-methyl-4-isoxazole propionic acid (AMPA) receptors, N-methyl-D-aspartate (NMDA) receptors, and kainate receptors (Seeburg 1993; Hollman and Heinemann 1994). The metabotropic receptors (mGlu) are coupled to *intracellular signal-transduction cascades, which, again, exist in multiple subtypes (Hollman and Heinemann 1994; Riedel 1996). Additional proteins interact with glutamate in the brain, among them high-affinity glutamate transporters that swiftly terminate the glutamatergic synaptic signal (Auger and Attwell 2000). The glutamate transporters fulfil another function as well. Excess extracellular glutamate is neurotoxic and responsible for neurodegeneration under certain pathological conditions (Meldrum and Garthwaite 1990; Michaelis 1998). The transporters maintain extracellular glutamate levels below those that cause excitotoxic damage. In doing so they contribute to the compartmentalization of glutamate in the brain, without which our brain cells get excessively excited and die.

Glutamate, and multiple types of its neuronal receptors, have been implicated in multiple facets of cellular, *developmental and behavioural plasticity in many species, *paradigms and brain regions (e.g. Morris *et al.* 1986; Bannerman *et al.* 1995; Aamodt *et al.* 1996; Riedel 1996; Riedel *et al.* 1999; Catalano *et al.* 1997; Rosenblum *et al.* 1997; Bortolotto *et al.* 1999; Hayashi *et al.* 2000). Glutamate is also critical for *long-term potentiation, the *zeitgeist cellular *model of learning in the mammalian brain. Three points concerning the role of glutamate in plasticity are noteworthy.

1. Glutamate is a prime candidate for a synaptic *stimulus that triggers *acquisition and *retrieval.

It possibly subserves cellular and circuit operations in other *phases of learning and memory as well.

2. Glutamate plays a part in *coincidence detection in *synapses that detect and encode *associations. A prominent coincidence detector is the NMDA receptor, which associates glutamate, depolarization, and probably additional molecular stimuli, such as glycine. The NMDA receptor is assumed to be instrumental in implementing elementary types of synaptic *algorithms of associative learning.

3. The plasticity at glutamatergic synapses could be expressed not only in use-dependent alterations in the availability of glutamate in the synapse, but also in use-dependent availability of the glutamatergic receptors (Shi *et al.* 1999). Further, these receptors interact with other proteins in the membrane, the cytoplasm and the nucleus. This is achieved via soluble second messengers, and also via mechanical links in a protein–protein network that extends from the membrane deep into the cytoplasm (Ottersen and Landsend 1997; Wyszynski *et al.* 1997). The role of glutamate in plasticity must therefore be considered in the context the spatiotemporal state of the multi*dimensional *system of the transmitter molecules, their receptor sites, and the intracellular macromolecular web that is regulated by the interaction of the transmitter with the receptor. The same argument for complexity holds for other transmitters as well (e.g. Shoop *et al.* 2000), only that at this stage we know more about the complexity of the glutamatergic signalling network because of its universal role in transmission and plasticity. This complexity turns the life of the investigator more interesting (or miserable, depending on the personalities involved), but clearly adds *dimensions* to the processes and mechanisms that implement neuronal plasticity.

Being such a ubiquitous molecular mediator of behaviourally meaningful stimuli, glutamate is an appealing candidate for perturbation experiments, in which learning and memory are blocked by applying receptor antagonists to the postulated site(s) of the *engram (e.g. Morris *et al.* 1986; Bannerman *et al.* 1995; Reidel 1996; Rosenblum *et al.* 1997). The glutamatergic synapse could also become the focus of mimicry experiments, in which the behavioural stimulus is simulated by molecular or cellular manipulations (*method). This type of approach is illustrated by studies of 'pregnancy blocking' in the *mouse (Kaba *et al.* 1994). In the female mouse, post-mating exposure to pheromones of a strange male, but not to those of the mate, blocks pregnancy. The mate is recognized because the female forms olfactory memory of his pheromones during mating (*flashbulb memory?). This memory is subserved by the accessory olfactory system, and involves reduction of GABAergic inhibition by *noradrenaline released in mating. Infusion of agonists of one of the mGlu receptors, which in this system reduce GABAergic inhibition, into the female's accessory olfactory bulb during an exposure to a male pheromone, mimics the effect of mating by establishing a memory for that pheromone without mating.

The strong evidence that glutamate is involved in plasticity and learning marks the components of the glutamate system as targets for candidate mnemonic drugs. Indeed, compounds that bind to the AMPA receptor-channel complex are already under clinical trial as memory boosters (*nootropics).

Selected associations: Acquisition, Long-term potentiation, Neurotransmitter, Receptor, Synapse

---

[1]Glia cells do much more than supplying nerve cells with glutamine and other *nutrients; see *synapse.

Habit

1. A behavioural routine capable of being formed and *performed in the absence of *conscious awareness.

2. A behavioural routine as in 1, *acquired gradually via repetitive experience.

Definition 1 refers to 'habit' irrespective of whether it is innate (*a priori), acquired, or induced by disease or drugs. Definition 2 restricts 'habit' to a type of *learned behaviour; it is a special case of definition 1, but is stated separately because this is what 'habit' commonly means in the contemporary learning literature. In the early learning literature, 'habit' was also occasionally used to denote a learned act in general, but this is now unacceptable. Habits comprise a substantial chunk of our behavioural repertoire, often to a larger degree than we tend to concede. Driving a car becomes a habit, but so is also eating junk food, or delivering the same seminar for the ninth time. Nowhere is the dominance of habit in our lives better epitomized than in James' *classic *Principles of psychology* (1890). Dubbing organisms as 'bundles of habits' (referring to the generic definition 1), James considered habits not only as an inescapable

manifestation of the *plasticity of organic material, but also as driving force of the daily operation of individuals and *cultures: '… Habit a second nature! Habit is ten times nature… Habit is … the enormous fly-wheel of society … it keeps the fisherman and the deck-hand at sea through the winter; it holds the miner in its darkness, and nails the countryman to his log-cabin …'[1] Many a reader nowadays will clearly disagree with James' social conservatism, but not with his appreciation of the role in our life of automatic or semiautomatic procedures, many of which are acquired via repetitive *stimulus–response conditioning (Thorndike 1911; *instrumental conditioning). Habits could be sensorimotor, emotional, or cognitive, or all of the above elements combined in a single assembled routine. They could be highly useful and beneficial, as in vocational training, because they spare *attentional and cognitive resources, perfect performance, and prevent superfluous response; but the same brain circuits that bring all these benefits could also go astray and generate viciously disturbing habits (Long and Miltenberger 1998; Robbins and Everitt 1999; Leckman and Riddle 2000).

Being independent of conscious awareness, habit is by definition a non*declarative (implicit) type of memory (Hirsh 1974; Mishkin *et al.* 1984; Squire and Zola 1996; *skill, *taxonomy). As opposed to *declarative memory, which is subserved by *cortico*limbic circuits, habits are subserved by corticostriatal circuits, i.e. reciprocal connections between the *cerebral cortex and the basal ganglia (Mishkin *et al.* 1984; Salmon and Butters 1995; Knowlton *et al.* 1996; Jog *et al.* 1999). Two selected studies, one in the *rat, the other in *Homo sapiens*, will serve to illustrate the conserved role of the corticostriatal circuits in the formation and expression of habit in mammals.

Let's start with the rat first. McDonald and White (1993) subjected rats to three types of tasks in an eight-arm radial *maze: a *win-shift* task (Olton and Schlosberg 1978), a conditioned *cue preference* task, and a *win-stay* task (*ibid.*). In the *win-shift* task, all the eight arms of the maze are baited with food. The rat is placed on the central platform of the maze, and allowed on each trial to choose an arm. The performance is scored as the number of revisits (i.e. errors) to arms from which the rat has already obtained food within the first eight choices. Success in this type of task demands the rat to identify, classify, and remember multiple spatial locations, i.e. use explicit memory.[2] In the *conditioned cue preference* task, two arms are used and the rest blocked. One arm is cued with light at the entrance to the arm. In the training trials, the rat is conditioned by confining it with food to either the 'light' or the 'dark' arm. In the test, both arms are left unbaited, and the amount of time spent in each arm is recorded. This type of task taps into the ability of the rat to associate a stimulus (light) with a food reward. In the *win-stay* task, four randomly selected arms are baited with food and lit. The rat is placed on to the centre platform of the maze. Immediately after the rat leaves a lit arm having eaten the bait, the arm is rebaited. When the rat retrieves the second pellet for any arm, the light is turned off and no further food is placed there. Overall, the rat is required to visit each of the four lit arms twice, earning eight pellets within a trial. The trial is terminated after a fixed time or after the eight food pellets have been retrieved. Entries into unlit arms are scored as errors. This task involves learning an approach response to a specific sensory cue (light), irrespective of other environmental cues,[3] and repeat the choices to each lit arm within a trial. This is construed to involve the formation of a stimulus–response habit (Packard *et al.* 1989; McDonald and White 1993).

By using groups of rats with circumscribed brain lesions, McDonald and White (1993) found that damage to the *hippocampal formation impaired acquisition of the *win-shift* task but not of the *conditioned cue preference* or the *win-stay* task; damage to the lateral *amygdala impaired acquisition of the *conditioned cue preference* task but not of the *win-shift* or *win-stay* tasks; and damage to the dorsal striatum impaired acquisition of the *win-stay task* but not of the *win-shift* or the *conditioned cue preference* task. Hence, these authors showed, by inferring function from dysfunction (*method), that the formation of a stimulus–response habit depends on the striatum, and that the neural system that subserves habit could be dissociated from the neural systems that subserve explicit and affective memory. Additional evidence for the involvement of the striatum in the formation of the *internal representations of habits was found in correlative studies, in which neuronal activity was recorded from the striatum of the behaving rat while engaged in maze routines (Jog *et al.* 1999).

Whereas McDonald and White (1993) used a 'triple dissociation' approach (three tasks, three lesions), Knowlton *et al.* (1996) used 'double dissociation' to identify the brain substrates of habit and dissociate it from the brain substrates of declarative memory in humans.[4] The two tasks used in this study were a *probabilistic classification* task and a *multiple-choice questionnaire* task. In the *probabilistic classification* task, the *subject is requested to forecast the weather, whether sunny or rainy, on the basis of four visual patterns, each linked to the weather conditions with a prefixed probability, unknown to the subject in advance. On each trial, one, two, or three of these cues are presented side by side on the computer screen, and the response on each trial is *reinforced by visual and auditory feedback. This task involves gradual learning shaped by repetitive stimulus–response–reinforcement loops over multiple trials, and does not require conscious awareness of the information accumulated over trials; these task attributes are characteristic of habit learning. The *probabilistic classification* task can hence be used to tap into the ability to form a habit.[5] The *multiple-choice questionnaire* referred to declarative information about the procedures and episodes of the habit task.

Knowlton *et al.* (1996) used the two tasks to test three groups of subjects: *amnesic patients with bilateral hippocampal or diencephalic damage; non*demented patients with Parkinson's disease, which involves striatal damage; and healthy matched *controls. The amnesic patients learned the habit as well as the controls, but failed on the declarative task. The parkinsonian patients, in contrast, performed well on the declarative task, but could not learn the habit. The conclusion: formation of habit depends on intact striatal circuits, but not on intact mediotemporal circuits, whereas the opposite is true for the declarative task.

To the causal observer, the maze habit and the probabilistic classification habit may look very different. But they do share a lot in common. This is evident first, from the analysis of the behavioural task, which in both cases depends on the formation, via repetitive stimulus–response–reinforcement cycles, of a stimulus–response routine; and second, from the identity of the brain circuits that are essential for the behaviour in both cases. As the striatum subserves different types of habits, which involve different types of information, it is likely to execute generic computations, which are required for the 'syntactic' assembly of pieces of action repertoires into routines (Graybiel 1998). The circuits that encode the internal representations specific to the habit are hence expected to involve additional brain areas, including modality-specific and association cortex. If this is the case, then use-dependent changes in striatal circuits will show larger *transfer than those in other brain areas that encode information about a specific habit. This is why damage to the striatum leads to a 'global' deterioration of habits. This relates to the differentiation between use-dependent changes in particular internal representations, and those that occur in generic computations made over these representations. But this is already a global issue, which exceeds the discussion of habit.

Selected associations: Instrumental conditioning, Learning set, Maze, Skill, Taxonomy

---

[1]Not surprisingly, many authors considered the formation as well as the reversal of habits a key to the success of education at large, e.g. Rousseau (1762), Radstock (1886), and Rowe (1909).

[2]This task also exploits the innate tendency of the rat to shift its search for new locations. When given equal opportunity, the rat will prefer the *win-shift* over the *win-stay* strategy (Olton and Schlosberg 1978). This is hence an example of the interaction of an innate predisposition (*a priori) with learning (for another example, see the delayed nonmatching to sample task in the *monkey; *delay task).

[3]Actually, because the rat is requested to enter the lit arm regardless of the identity and location of the arm, the use of cues other than the light, and of the relationship among cues, becomes counterproductive (McDonald and White 1993). This illustrates that the formation of habit involves not only augmentation of a response, but also what Glaser (1910) calls the '…often painful suppression of irrelevant actions, and the survival of only those that count'.

[4]For the logic and *algorithms of 'multiple dissociations' experiments, see *control.

[5]The habit in this laboratory task forms much faster than must habits in *real-life.

Habituation

The gradual diminution of the response to a *stimulus following the repeated presentation of the same, or a similar, stimulus.

Habituation is commonly classified as a type of non*associative learning (*taxonomy). This is because it is assumed to be governed solely by the parameters of the habituated, unconditioned stimulus, in the absence of associations with other stimuli. This assumption may be wrong. It is questionable whether any type of learning is indeed purely nonassociative. In habituation, associations are formed with the *context (Wagner 1979; Marlin and Miller 1981; Rankin 2000), and possibly also with *palimpsests of the *internal representation, accumulated over the individual's history. Another common myth concerning habituation is that because it involves a diminution of response, no new information is acquired. On the contrary: that a certain stimulus can be safely ignored is

in itself new valuable information, which promotes adaptation to the milieu and prevents superfluous defensive reflexes. Kandel (1976) cites a fable by Aesop, which epitomizes this point: 'A fox, who had never yet seen a turtle, when he fell in with him for the first time in the forest was so frightened that he was near dying with fear. On his meeting with him for the second time, he was still much alarmed but not to the same extent as the first. On seeing him for the third time, he was so increased in boldness that he went up to him and commenced a familiar conversation with him.' Be it a fox or a turtle, a spider (in which it was first described in the scientific literature; Peckham and Peckham 1887), a scientist or a mollusc—habituation is part of the behavioural repertoire of all the cellular organisms analysed so far (Christoffersen 1997), including unicellular organisms and even cells in culture (McFadden and Koshland 1990). From the point of view of the neurosciences, however, there is some advantage in focusing on habituation in organisms that do contain a nervous system.

'Habituation' is a central nervous system process. Use-dependent response decrements that occur because of sensory and peripheral processes, are termed 'adaptation'. Although clearly not a unitary process, several attributes *generalize over many instances of habituation (Thompson and Spencer 1966; Staddon and Higa 1996). These include, among others:

1. *Stimulus specificity.* Habituation to one stimulus does not usually generalize to other stimuli. This distinguishes habituation from response decrements due to adaptation, fatigue, or disease.

2. *Intensity sensitivity.* Commonly, the weaker the habituating stimulus, the more rapid or pronounced is habituation.

3. *Rate sensitivity.* The rate of formation, robustness and *persistence of habituation is a function of the time between the presentations of the stimulus (interstimulus interval, ISI). Habituation is faster when the ISI is short, and more persistent, once achieved, when the ISI is long; the dependence on ISI could, however, be rather tricky (e.g. Davis 1970).

4. *Spontaneous recovery.* Withholding the habituating stimulus commonly results in time-dependent recovery of the response. Recovery is faster if the ISI in habituation training is kept short (see 3 above). Repeated cycles of habituation and spontaneous recovery result in progressively greater habituation.

5. *Undershooting.* Habituation may proceed below the naive response level.

6. *Dishabituation.* The presentation of another (usually noxious) stimulus results in the recovery of the habituated response.

Not all the above parameters are satisfied in every *system that habituates. Dishabituation is considered the most critical *criterion, and is commonly employed to establish that habituation has indeed occurred. Dishabituation resembles *sensitization, which is the facilitation of a nonhabituated response; cellular, circuit, behavioural, and developmental studies have, however, indicated that habituation and sensitization differ in multiple parameters (Rankin and Carew 1988; Byrne and Kandel 1996; Hawkins *et al.* 1998). Is dishabituation only a disruption or removal of habituation (Dodge 1923), or is it an independent process superimposed on habituation (Grether 1938)? Habituation and dishabituation could be shown to have different intrinsic time courses. This supports the idea that they are independent processes that interact to yield the final behavioural outcome ('the dual-trace hypothesis'; Groves and Thompson 1970). Multiple interpretations and functional *models of habituation have been proposed over the years (Coombs 1938; Sharpless and Jasper 1956; Sokolov 1963*a,b*; Glaser 1966; Konorski 1967; Wagner 1979; Staddon and Higa 1996). A useful classification distinguishes 'feedback' from 'feed-forward' models (Staddon and Higa 1996). In 'feedback' models the response is inhibited by the *percept or the immediate memory of the current stimulus. In 'feed-forward' models the integrated longer-term memory of past stimuli is fed forward to dampen the immediate effect of the current stimulus. It is unlikely that any single type of model will generalize to all habituating systems, from the simplest to the complex.

The cellular bases of habituation have been pursued in a number of experimental preparations. Noteworthy among these are the cat spinal reflexes (Spencer *et al.* 1966); the rat acoustic startle reflex (Davis 1970; Jordan and Leaton 1983; *fear conditioning); and the *Aplysia* defensive reflexes (Kandel 1976; Frost *et al.* 1997; Hawkins *et al.* 1998). The studies of short- and long-term forms of habituation in *Aplysia* epitomize a comprehensive reductionist research programme, in which the combination of reductive and simplifying steps (Dudai 1989; *reduction) resulted in the identification of circuit, *synaptic, and molecular correlates of habituation. Interestingly, although considered the simplest of all types of learning, the cellular and molecular analysis of habituation in *Aplysia* has so far yielded less elaborate mechanistic models than the analysis of sensitization or *classical conditioning in the same

organism. The major conclusion was that habituation is due to homosynaptic[1] depression of the monosynaptic sensory–motoneuron connection that mediates the reflex (Fig. 5, page 16). The process involves *inactivation of *calcium channels and depletion of releasable *neurotransmitter molecules (Frost *et al.* 1997). In the long term, morphology is altered as well, and there is a reduction in the frequency and size of the active zones in the synapse (Bailey and Chen 1983). All this portrays habituation as use-dependent modification confined to the elementary, minimal reflex pathway. In real life, the habituated response is more likely to be subserved by heterosynaptic processes in polysynaptic pathways as well (Hawkins *et al.* 1998). Habituation has been reported to involve modulation of pathways that are extrinsic to the minimal reflex pathways in another *simple system, the escape response of the crayfish (Krasne and Teshiba 1995). As expected, multiple pathways are also involved in the habituation of more complex behaviours, such as the orienting reflex in mammals (Kwon *et al.* 1990).

The cellular analysis of habituation could serve to illustrate the problematics of *level shifts in a reductive research programme. Suppose you are interested in the neuronal mechanisms of habituation, have just decided to go cellular, and started to record the response of neurons in the visual cortex of the *monkey. You find a response decrement with repetitive presentation of the same or similar stimuli ('repetition suppression', Desimone 1996). Furthermore, if you present a novel, *surprising stimulus, the response will recover. Is this the cellular analogue of behavioural habituation? Well, probably not. It may actually subserve *priming, which is facilitation of the behavioural response. Or it might also be the cellular correlate of *recognition, resulting in an enhanced rather than a diminished behavioural

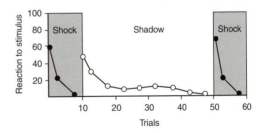

Fig. 33 Simple habituation: the worm *Nereis* contracts in response to a mechanical shock (*full circles*) or a moving shadow (*open circles*). The response habituates readily. Habituation to one type of stimulus is independent of habituation to the other type. This is different from the response decrement due to fatigue, which *generalizes over types of stimuli. Interstimulus interval = 1 min. (Adapted from Clark 1960.)

response. Hence habituation of cellular response may subserve a facilitatory behavioural response, and similarly, facilitation of the cellular response may end up in a decremental behavioural response.[2] The take-home message: the contribution of neuronal *plasticity to behavioural plasticity does not necessarily honour *Ockham's razor.

Selected associations: Context, Cue, Plasticity, Recognition, Sensitization

---

[1]A process is called 'homosynaptic' if it involves only the modulated synapse, and 'heterosynaptic' if it involves modulatory interneurons. A pathway is 'monosynaptic' if it involves only a single synaptic connection, and 'polysynaptic' if it involves multiple synaptic connections.

[2]The relationship of habituation to some other types of use-dependent modification in response is intricate. Priming is an example. Habituation could be regarded as a type of gradual negative priming. Indeed in an influential model of habituation, the decremental behavioural response is formulated in terms of variations in stimulus processing that depend on whether or not the representation of the stimulus, or its associations, has been primed (Wagner 1979). Recognition is another example. Suppose in a recognition paradigm the subject stops responding because the stimulus is recognized as familiar—Is this habituation to the stimulus? Yet for habituation to occur, recognition of the stimulus is a must. In this example the 'recognition' terminology will always be preferred in mammals when the mediotemporal lobe is involved.

Hippocampus

A bilateral archi*cortical structure that extends as a ridge into the lateral ventricle, interconnects with multiple subcortical and cortical areas, and considered to play a critical part in certain types and *phases of memory.

In 1587 the Italian anatomist Arantius introduced the term 'hippocampus' (seahorse) to describe 'an elevation of white substance' that rises at the base of the lateral ventricles (Lewis 1923). He wondered, however, whether 'a white silk-worm' (*Bombyx*) might provide a better description. Two centuries later, a spark of dubious imagination led to a new suggestion, 'hippopotamus'. At about the same time, a structure in that same brain region also came to be called 'ram's horn', or, 'calculated to impress whoever hears it for the first time' (*ibid.*), the 'horns of Ammon' (after the Egyptian deity Ammon, which was represented as a ram or a human form with a ram's head). The road of 'hippocampus' to

glory was hence rather shaky, and the fact that we do not talk nowadays about 'bombycal *long-term potentiation' (LTP) or 'hippopotamal place cells' (see below) is due either to mere chance, or to the convoluted undercurrents of scientific etymology, or both. The seahorse won, and established itself quite firmly as a recurrent protagonist in the dreams or nightmares of brain scientists world-wide. Egyptian theology did leave a mark, nevertheless, in contemporary scientific literature: the hippocampus proper is still frequently referred to in neuroanatomy books and papers as 'Ammon's horn', and *Cornua Ammonis* is the source of the acronym 'CA' used to denote hippocampal subfields (Figure 34) (de No 1934; for additional historical notes, Meyer 1971).

Multiple terms are used in the hippocampal literature to refer to structures in the hippocampal region. The 'hippocampal formation' consists of the hippocampus proper, the dentate gyrus, and the subiculum. Occasionally, authors use the term 'hippocampus' to refer to the hippocampus proper+the dentate gyrus. The 'hippocampal system' includes in addition to the hippocampal formation the parahippocampal region, which contains the entorhinal, perirhinal, and parahippocampal cortices (Witter *et al.* 1989). The issue is not merely nomenclature. When authors report that they have performed an 'hippocampal lesion', it is crucial to note what is it exactly that they lesioned. The hippocampal formation interconnects either directly or indirectly with multiple subcortical and cortical areas. Without delving too much into neuroanatomy, it is useful to remember that the major cortical input to the hippocampus flows from the entorhinal cortex via the perforant path (abbreviated PP), and that major output to the cortex leaves via the subiculum. The intrinsic circuitry consisting of the successive projections from the entorhinal cortex to the dentate gyrus (via the PP), from the dentate gyrus to CA3 (via the mossy fibre pathway, MF), and from CA3 to CA1 (via the Schaffer collateral pathway, SC), is traditionally termed the 'trisynaptic pathway'. Major interconnections of the hippocampus with subcortical regions are mediated via the fornix.

The hippocampus is very popular in the neurosciences in general and in memory research in particular. In 2000, no less than 5640 papers included 'hippocampus' or 'hippocampal' in their title, abstract or keywords. This means on the average more than 15 papers per day, about 0.6% of the total papers published in science throughout that period, double the popularity of the cerebellum and the *amygdala combined, and an almost a fivefold increase over 1989

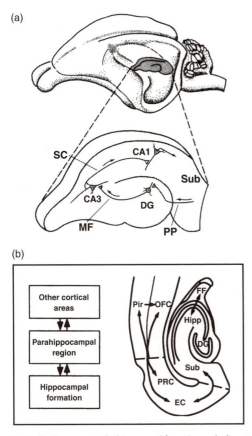

(a)

SC
CA1
Sub
CA3
DG
MF
PP

(b)

| Other cortical areas |
| Parahippocampal region |
| Hippocampal formation |

Pir → OFC
FF
Hipp
DG
Sub
PRC
EC

Fig. 34 The hippocampus, the hippocampal formation, and adjacent cortical areas. (a) A drawing of the rabbit hippocampus *in situ*, as well as of an hippocampal slice. Only part of the pathways are indicated. CA1, CA3, pyramidal cell fields of the hippocampus; DG, dentate gyrus; MF, mossy fibre pathway; PP, perforant path; SC, Schaffer collateral pathway; Sub, subiculum. (Modified from Andersen *et al.* 1971.) (b) Outline of a horizontal rat brain section (right) illustrating the flow of information (schematically depicted on the left) between the hippocampal formation, the parahippocampal region, and some adjacent cortical areas. EC, entorhinal cortex; FF, fimbria-fornix (mediating information to subcortical areas); Hipp, hippocampus; OFC, orbito-frontal cortex; Pir, piriform cortex; PRC, preirhinal cortex; DG, dentate gyrus. Discussion of the role of the hippocampus in learning and memory must take into account not only the hippocampus or the hippocampal formation, but also the interconnections with the adjacent cortex. The computations performed by the hippocampal system are not yet known. (Adapted from Eichenbaum *et al.* 1996.)

(Science Citation Index 2001). Furthermore, about 25% of these 'hippocampal' papers explicitly mentioned learning or memory or LTP in their title or abstract or keywords. The majority of these papers, as did many thousands before them, reach the conclusion

that the hippocampus is involved in learning and memory. But many of them fail to agree on what it does, and how and when it does it. The experimental evidence stems from multiple *methods and experimental *systems. Some data demonstrate correlation of hippocampal function with learning, others indicate an obligatory role (*criteria). Here is a brief illustration of the evidence.

1. *Evidence from lesions.* In *human pathology* it was noted already 100 years ago that damage to the medial temporal lobe, including the hippocampus, impairs memory (reviewed in Zola-Morgan *et al.* 1986). This was substantiated in patient H.M., who underwent bilateral removal of pieces of the medial temporal polar cortex, most of the amygdaloid complex, the entorhinal cortex, and a substantial part of the hippocampal formation, and as a result became densely *amnestic (Fig. 2, p.11; Scoville and Milner 1957; Corkin *et al.* 1997). But rather amazingly, confirmation of whether hippocampal damage is indeed sufficient to induce amnesia proved difficult (e.g. Aggleton and Shaw 1996; Aggleton and Brown 1999). Human amnesia is a consequence of an unfortunate pathology that is seldom restricted to a single region. Accumulative evidence from a number of cases in which hippocampal damage was a major feature was therefore needed to reach the conclusion that *recognition memory is subserved by the hippocampal formation (e.g. Zola-Morgan *et al.* 1986; Kartsounis *et al.* 1995; Reed and Squire 1997, 1998); however, lesions in additional temporal cortex must be present to produce a severe memory loss (Reed and Squire 1998). A few points deserve special notice. First, the deficits are not confined to *declarative information (Chun and Phelps 1999). Second, the role of the hippocampus is important in long-term memory, but very remote memories, acquired before the damage had occurred, are spared (e.g. Teng and Squire 1999). This finding has led to the proposal that the hippocampus is required for a prolonged process of memory *consolidation, which in humans may require months or even years; once consolidated, memories become independent of hippocampal function (McClelland *et al.* 1995; Knowlton and Fanselow 1998; see also Haist *et al.* 2001). This view, supported by animal studies (e.g. Winocur 1990), does have opponents, who propose that the role of the hippocampus in some types of memory is not time limited (Moscovitch and Nadel 1998). And third, the hippocampus may be specifically important in event rather than fact memory (Vargha-Khadem *et al.* 1997); again, this is still debated (Mishkin *et al.* 1998; Squire and Zola 1998; Tulving and Markowitsch 1998; *taxonomy).

The major incentive for studying hippocampal *lesions in the *monkey* was to develop an animal *model for amnesia (reviewed in Squire and Zola-Morgan 1991; Eichenbaum *et al.* 1994; Murray and Mishkin 1998). Many of the studies have focused on *delay tasks, mainly delayed-nonmatching-to-sample (DNMTS), which were considered sensitive to human amnesia. Whereas early results have suggested that hippocampal lesions cause severe memory impairments, later studies unveiled complications. This was because the early lesions were not in fact confined to the hippocampus and included adjacent cortical areas. It was later found that lesions of the perirhinal and parahippocampal cortex that spared the hippocampus produced severe memory impairment on recognition tasks, whereas lesions restricted to the hippocampus yielded only minor deficits if at all (e.g. Zola-Morgan *et al.* 1989b; Murray and Mishkin 1998; *amygdala). To complicate life even further, it was also noted that versions of DNMTS as administered to monkeys may not be sensitive to recognition memory impairment in humans after all, because the extensive training of the monkey on that task involves acquisition of hippocampal-independent rules that facilitate *performance (Aggleton and Shaw 1996; Reed and Squire 1997). But all in all, the data from the monkey lesion studies do suggest that the hippocampus contributes to some aspects of recognition and inter*stimulus-association memory. It also plays a part in encoding spatial information (e.g. Gaffan 1998).

Hippocampal *lesions in other mammals*, such as in rodents and in the rabbit, impair performance on tasks involving spatial memory, *contextual memory, *working memory, and a variety of stimulus–stimulus and stimulus–action associations (e.g. Olton and Feustle 1981; Winocur 1990; Bunsey and Eichenbaum 1996; Clark and Squire 1998; Maren *et al.* 1998; Moser and Moser 1998*a,b*; Steckler *et al.* 1998b; Corbit and Balleine 2000). On some tasks, lesions of dorsal hippocampus were found to be more damaging than those in the ventral hippocampus (Hock and Bunsey 1998; Moser and Moser 1998*a,b*). In recent years, in addition to the *classical anatomical lesions, several other types of lesions have been used. These include transient pharmacological lesions, i.e. inhibition of targeted enzymes and receptors in the hippocampus (e.g. Riedel *et al.* 1999); *neurogenetic lesions, i.e. mutations in identified genes (e.g. Tsien *et al.* 1996*a,b*); and artificial saturation of hippocampal cellular *plasticity mechanisms (LTP; Moser *et al.* 1998).

2. *Evidence from neurogenesis.* There is evidence that neurons continue to be produced in the hippocampus throughout adult life (but see Rakic 2002). Training on learning tasks that depend on the hippocampus, but not on those that do not, was reported to enhance adult neurogenesis (Gould *et al.* 1999*a*).

3. *Evidence from *functional neuroimaging.* Despite some early failures to identify activation of the human hippocampus in *acquisition and *retrieval, many later functional neuroimaging studies of human subjects have delivered the goods (e.g. Lepage *et al.* 1998; Schacter and Wagner 1999; Haist *et al.* 2001). An imaginative example is provided by studies of navigation in virtual reality, in which successful performance was associated with activation of the right hippocampus in volunteers ranging from London taxi drivers (Maguire *et al.* 1997) to their clients (Maguire *et al.* 1998). In these studies, the left hippocampus was found active in nonspatial aspects of the task. Other functional neuroimaging studies of human subjects have used a variety of sensory and verbal tasks, and have identified hippocampal involvement in a number of declarative functions (e.g. Lepage *et al.* 1998; Dolan and Fletcher 1999; Schacter and Wagner 1999; Eldridge *et al.* 2000). Still, in some reports, the focus of activity in learning and memory tasks was identified in parahippocampal regions rather than the hippocampus proper (e.g. Brewer *et al.* 1998). Some neuroimaging studies also suggested differential involvement of anterior vs. posterior hippocampus (as well as other mediotemporal lobe structures) in acquisition (encoding) vs. retrieval, although the nature of the postulated functional segregation remains unclear (e.g. Dolan and Fletcher 1999).

4. *Evidence from cellular physiology.*

a. '*Place cells*'. A breakthrough in understanding the relevance of hippocampal activity to behaviour was attained by O'Keefe and his coworkers (O'Keefe and Dostrovsky 1971; O'Keefe and Conway 1978). They have reported that the firing rate of certain hippocampal neurons is correlated with the animal's location in space. These cells were aptly termed 'place units', or 'place cells'. Their identification was used to support the hypothesis that the hippocampus forms and maintains spatial *maps, or, more generally, 'cognitive maps' of the world (on the concept of 'cognitive map', see Tolman 1948; on its history, see Best and White 1999). Over the years, place cells and their role in encoding experience-dependent spatial maps have become a central topic in hippocampal physiology, modelling, neurogenetics, and molecular neurobiology (e.g. Mehta *et al.* 1997; Wilson and Tonegawa 1997; Kentros *et al.* 1998; O'Keefe 1999). Electrodes mounted into rats hippocampal place cells even made it into outer space (Knierim *et al.* 2000). For our purpose, suffice it to say that in both laboratory and *real-life situations, location in allocentric space[1] could be a major *dimension in world models encoded in the hippocampus (O'Keefe 1999). Physical space is not, however, the sole representational parameter of hippocampal units. Although place cells became quite popular from the outset of their identification, they were never claimed to exploit the response repertoire of hippocampal neurons (e.g. Ranck 1973). More recent studies have demonstrated that the activity of many hippocampal neurons is related to perceptual and behavioural events as well as their interactions, regardless of the location of where these events occurred (Wood et al. 1999).

b. *LTP. All the pathways in the trisynaptic circuit, the PP, MF, and SC (Figure 34), sustain LTP (Bliss and Collingridge 1993), a *synaptic plasticity mechanism that is assumed to subserve learning. If we indeed assume that LTP contributes to learning, then the hippocampus is surely equipped with the right cellular machinery.

5. Evidence from biochemistry and molecular biology. A number of studies have reported changes in hippocampal enzymes, growth factors, *neurotransmitters, and gene expression, that were correlated with learning and memory (e.g. Sunayashiki-Kusuzaki et al. 1993; Meyer et al. 1996; Cavallaro et al. 1997; Atkins et al. 1998; Hall et al. 2000).

So what is the role of hippocampus in learning and memory? Despite thousands of man-years, smart paradigms, fascinating data, stimulating models (e.g. Treves and Rolls 1994), and the apparent neuroanatomical simplicity that has always attracted anatomists and physiologists, the truth is that we do not yet know for sure what the hippocampus does. One way of looking at the issue is within the framework of the expectation that there should be differentiation in *engrams along the following lines: some parts of the trace should reside in brain regions that deal with modality-, task- or content-specific information (e.g. spatial maps in the hippocampus—Gaffan 1998; see also *cerebral cortex). Other parts could depend on regions that subserve many types of engrams by performing 'global' operations (Hirsh 1974, 1980; Teyler and DiScenna 1986; Wallenstein et al. 1998; Holland and Bouton 1999). Judged by its connectivity to other brain areas, the hippocampus does fit to execute global operations. These could be of two types, which possibly overlap. First, computations necessary for the generation and processing of internal representations that are stored elsewhere. Examples are temporary *binding of multiple representations to promote the formation of new ones, or ad-hoc evaluation of the *contextual importance of on-line input or of retrieved information.

Second, operations that involve activation of high-order representations that are themselves stored, at least partially, in the hippocampus; these could involve representations of specific times and settings of episodes (*episodic memory), or of sets of other representations catalogued by yet unknown attributes. This latter view considers the hippocampus as some sort of a mental index that is used in the storage and retrieval of other representations.

With all this wealth of data, interpretations, and hypotheses, an attempt to encapsulate the proposed functions of the hippocampus in a catchy phrase, even if speculative, partial, and *metaphoric, is worth a try. So let's try this one. In that same moment in a mental time travel in which we *recall the specific contents, time, and setting of an episode all together, and suddenly experience that familiar sense of 'I remember' (Buckner 2000; Eldridge et al. 2000), it is the hippocampal system that is ticking in the background.

Selected associations: Amnesia, Consolidation, Declarative memory, Maze, Recognition

---

[1] 'Allocentric' means independent of the location of the observer, as opposed to 'egocentric', in which spatial position is determined relative to the observer. An example of 'egocentric' units is provided by 'head-direction cells' in the *limbic cortex and subiculum, which fire as a function of the animal's head direction in the horizontal plane (Taube et al. 1990).

Homeostasis

The maintenance of steady state(s) by a *system in the face of change.

'Homeostasis' stems from Greek, meaning same stand or same state. The term was coined by Cannon: '…The coordinated physiological processes which maintain most of the steady states in the organism are so complex and so peculiar to living beings … that I have suggested a special designation for these states, homeostasis. The word does not imply something set and immobile, a stagnation. It means a condition—a condition which may vary, but which is relatively constant' (Cannon 1932). Antecedents of the concept of 'homeostasis' can be traced back to ancient Greece (Adolph 1961). In the nineteenth century, the identification of a variety of physiological regulatory mechanisms has led to the notion that the body maintains a stable internal environment, for example stable temperature, blood pressure, or sugar level, in spite of changing conditions (Cannon 1932; Adolph 1961; Brazier 1988). Most notable was Claude Bernard's conclusion: '... all the vital mechanisms ... have only one object, that of preserving constant the conditions of life in the internal environment' (1878, translated and cited in Cannon 1929; Olmsted 1938). This idea that a stable internal milieu is characteristic of, and essential for, life became a tenet of biology (Jones 1973; Houk 1980*a*,*b*). It is also central to discussions of adaptive control in artificial systems (Wiener 1961). Unfortunately, that biological systems are inherently homeostatic is not always properly remembered by students of the nervous system; too frequently authors disregard the possibility that the goal of a neuronal change might not be to bring about a long-lasting alteration in the system, but rather, on the contrary, to prevent it.

Brain scientists are bound to encounter homeostasis, and face the delicate interplay between stability and change, in many branches of the neuroscience, ranging from the study of membrane properties, via neuro*development, up to widespread autonomic regulation, drives, motivation, emotion, cognition, and behaviour (for selected discussions, see Blessing 1997; McEwen 1997; Risold *et al.* 1997; Zhou *et al.* 1997; Davis and Goodman 1998; Fanselow 1998; Mattson 1998; Damasio 1999). All the aforementioned manifestations of homeostasis are relevant to learning. Here we will focus briefly on one aspect of homeostasis only, which is not yet sufficiently elaborated in the current literature. This is the potential relevance of homeostasis to candidate cellular mechanisms of learning and memory, and to the interpretation of data and *models.

For our purpose, suffice it to reiterate that in order to fulfil their basic roles in *perceiving the world and reacting to it, nervous systems must maintain relative stability that ensures sustainment of input–output relationships ('gain control') within a desired limit. This is done under conditions in which the system is 'open', i.e. exchanges materials and energy with the world, and the world itself is in an ever-lasting flux. Homeostatic mechanisms that secure emission of a given range of behavioural response to a given range of stimuli include various types of feedback and forward regulation (Jones 1973; Houk 1980). Such mechanisms usually involve comparison of output with a 'reference' signal, or 'set point', which represents the desired value of the output. In some 'innate' or reflexive behaviours, which had been moulded in evolution to allow fast reaction and survival (*a priori), the 'set point' by which the system judges the aptness

of its *performance is rather rigid. In such cases, use-dependent modifications in the operation of local nodes in the system, e.g. *synapses, may represent the operation of the regulatory mechanisms that restore proper operational conditions, keep the system stable, and at most perform some fine tuning. Thus, although a local change is observed, its role might be to *prevent* a lasting overall alteration in the performance of the system rather than promote it.

One way of construing neuronal *plasticity in learning and development is to regard it as a process that involves a lasting modification in the set point of the homeostatic system (definition 2 in *plasticity; also Bienenstock *et al.* 1982; Bear 1995; *metaplasticity). In such case, the use-dependent neuronal modifications detected by the experimenter might indeed constitute lasting changes in *internal representations, hence be causally related to learning and memory.[1] Alternatively, however, the observed modification might still reflect only a homeostatic, restorative process in the circuit, which does not culminate in a lasting representational change. The distinction between these two types of change is important but not easy. For it to be made, one should be able to identify the representation encoded in the circuit, and prove that the observed molecular, cellular, or morphological modification indeed subserves a lasting change in the internal representation. What makes life even more complicated, is that in complex systems, modification of individual components is not necessarily informative as far as alteration in the properties of the system as a whole is concerned. This means that, although some local changes in synapses and neurons, such as use-dependent change in *receptor availability or *neurotransmitter release, are plausible candidates for subserving representational change in the circuit—they may not do so, after all.

The distinction between the role of candidate synaptic plasticity mechanisms, such as unveiled in *LTP, in homeostatic control as opposed to lasting representational change, is thus one of the current challenges of the cellular biology of learning.

Selected associations: Persistence, Plasticity, System

---

[1]One could come up with the remark that even if the circuit is altered to encode a new lasting representation, hence a new memory is formed, the ultimate goal of this memory is to retain the steady state of the organism as such in its milieu. In other words, the goal of learning is to maintain homeostasis. This reflects the importance of defining the *level of discussion.

Homo sapiens sapiens

Human, the only extant species of the primate family Hominidae.

Humans are a very popular species in memory research. Over the years, far more memory experiments have been published on humans than on *monkeys, or on all invertebrate species combined. Only rodents still keep an edge in popularity in labs that specialize in the neurobiology of memory, but this could change, with the widespread availability of *functional neuroimaging. And yet, human beings almost always identify themselves with the side of the experimenter, even in situations in which they themselves suffer the fate of the experimental *subject, be it involuntarily in evolution or disease, or voluntarily in the lab. This raises some additional doubts on whether *Homo* (from 'earth' in Latin, a reminder of old myths) is indeed always *sapiens* (from 'to be wise = to taste' in Latin, another reminder of a biblical story).

There used to be additional *Homo* (Wood and Collard 1999). At least with one of these, *neanderthalensis*, we shared this planet for a while. It is questionable whether we remember the experience, a sort of *infantile *sapiens* amnesia, although it is still possible that some reminiscences do linger in the obscure legends of our *collective memory. It is generally assumed that *sapiens* emerged $1-2 \times 10^5$ years ago, probably in Africa, and made the first massive out-of-Africa exodus $0.6-1 \times 10^5$ years ago (Quintana-Murci *et al.* 1999).[1] Assuming 20 years per generation, it means that the distance between us and the first true human may be only 5000 generations, not an astronomic number (try to imagine several thousand individuals holding hands; this is it). What was the brain power of the lost hominids species? And which cognitive capabilities, memory included, enabled us to win over the Neanderthal, or at least to linger longer? Attempts to unearth the answers combine prehistoric archaeology with anatomy, molecular biology, and common sense (Wilkins and Wakefield 1995; Wood 1996; Wood and Collard 1999; Yamei *et al.* 2000). Our current ideas on the memory *capacity of our ancestors are mostly speculations. The scientific community will no doubt be delighted if one day a method is devised to determine the problem-solving ability or *working memory *capacity in early hominids (cloning from hominid DNA could yield big surprises, but is unlikely to occur). However, at this point in time, the only clues to human memory emerge from what we get from experiments on living humans.

The study of memory in general had probably started with human subjects. First it involved sporadic observations intermingled with philosophical speculations and pedagogical generalizations (e.g. Sorabji 1972). These were followed by systematic introspection, in both its pre-scientific (Quintillian 1C AD; Augustine 400) and scientific versions (e.g. Wundt in Germany, Titchener in the USA, Boring 1950*a*). Objective *methods for quantifying memory were first documented only a bit more than a century ago (Ebbinghaus 1885). Darwinism, combined with practical considerations and the need to use methods that would not have been tolerated on humans, have provided the background and incentive for the study of memory in experimental animals (e.g. Boakes 1984). But even when animals became preferred subjects in the study of learning, a prevalent notion was that they are primarily convenient *models for understanding humans and the general 'laws' of mind: 'Most of the formal underlying laws of intelligence ... can still be studied in rats ... more easily than in men ... (rats) do not go on binges the night before one has planned the experiment ... they avoid politics, economics and papers on psychology' (Tolman 1945; *rat, *simple system).

Let us list briefly the pros and cons of conducting memory research on human subjects. First, here is a short list of selected pros:

1. Only humans have a human brain. Whatever we find about the *engram in experimental animals, even in tasks in which these animals excel (e.g. *maze), or in animal models of human pathology (e.g. *amnesia), must still be adapted to and verified in the human brain.

2. The highest forms of learning, involving language, reasoning, and imagery, as well as intricate emotional experiences and the memory of the self (Conway and Pleydell-Pearce 2000), can only be studied in humans. Attempts to identify rudiments of these capabilities in non-human species are far from yielding satisfactory alternatives to human subjects (*anthropomorphism, *declarative memory, *episodic memory, *monkey, *Ockham's razor).

3. Humans (usually, admittedly not always) can follow instructions quickly and efficiently (the reader is cordially invited to take a breath and imagine, eyes closed, what is it like to be a lonely, frightened, perplexed *mouse in its first encounter with a bizarre problem box).

4. Only humans can report their experience verbally, in detail and in response to specific questions.

5. Human volunteers take care of themselves. No need for animal rooms, costly maintenance, even not quality-time according to NIH guidance. Unless they are a real nuisance, human subjects come and go as requested, and the experimenter can simply forget about them in between experiments.

And now here is a selection of cons, for a balance:

1. Invasive methods are out of question. This is probably the critical disadvantage of working with humans. We clearly cannot test a hypothesis, or replicate an amnestic pathology (e.g. Scoville and Milner 1957), by inducing brain lesion in a human subject[2]. Only observations in the course of mandatory medical treatment, e.g. surgery, are allowed. New functional neuroimaging methods provide alternatives for certain invasive experimental designs (such as the recording of neuronal activity from the insides of the brain) but not for others (lesions). Gone are even the days when psychologists were allowed to frighten babies to advance their own career (Watson and Rayner 1920; Jones 1930). Intentional *neurogenetic manipulations are also a no-go.

2. In some protocols, overenthusiastic human subjects are particularly prone to 'demand characteristics' and other sorts of *biases that could undermine the validity of the results. This, however, may not be unique to humans (*Clever Hans).

3. You do not have to be a scientist to discover that humans are not easy to work with. In most places it is difficult to get a sufficient number of human subjects for lengthy experimentations, unless, probably, you are the dean or run a prison. And in most of the cases the subjects available are heterogeneous in their biology and personal history. Further, most human subjects tend to shy away from though, or boring, tasks. They may start the experiment and then disappear. Animals have no choice, although even monkeys revolt from time to time. Animals also do not request payment for their participation in an experiment and surely will not request a raise. Also, animals are not required to sign a letter of consent, and will not sue the experimenter even if they become confident that their neurosis is due to their experience as subjects in a demanding experiment. It is not surprising, therefore, to discover occasionally that the acronyms of subjects in human psychophysics or neuroimaging papers are those of the names of the authors themselves.

Over the years, a large variety of similar tasks have been used in the investigation of both human and animal memory. On the one hand, sheep were trained to recognize faces (Kendrick and Baldwin 1987), horses convinced to read prose (Pfungst 1911, they cheated), and monkeys to master math (Kawai and Matsuzawa 2000). On the other, human subjects were expected to salivate like Pavlovian dogs (Lashley 1916), run in mazes like rats (Woodsworth and Schlosenberg 1954), and fear unexpected noises like rabbits (Watson and Rayner 1920). In general, in memory research it is best to choose a task that fits the species and permits it to disclose its full potential. As is the case with other species, humans are better in some tasks than in others, for example, in problem solving in a variety of environments, or in *planning. But we are not the ultimate memory machine. Rodents are superior in labyrinths, dogs in olfactory discriminations, bats in spatial localizations, and chicks in telling one individual hen from another (*imprinting). Even in some human-specific memory tasks we perform rather miserably, e.g. assigning names to faces (McWeeny *et al.* 1987); this is probably due to the fairly recent appearance of human names in evolution. To our favour it should be added that we are unique in trying to overcome by technology the limitations of our innate, *a priori capabilities, and improve our memory (*mnemonics, *nootropics). We also create new artificial worlds to which our memory systems must rapidly adapt. Virtual reality (e.g. Maguire *et al.* 1998) is but an example. The Web is another. Such new environments impose great demands on *working memory, the ability to categorize, and the *plasticity of cognitive *skills. They also open the possibility of intimate interfacing between human brains and electronic systems. In the future, some engrams may actually be engraved (*metaphor) in neurosilicon hybrids.

Selected associations: Amnesia, Anthropomorphism, Enigma, Monkey, Real-life memory

---

[1]Estimates of the structure and timetable of hominid lineages are characterized by substantial uncertainties and large standard deviations. The discovery of even a single new type of skeleton, or of a new site with hominid artefacts, could shift these estimates remarkably. See, for example, Leakey *et al.* (2001); also Humans on the move, *Science*, **291**: 1721–1753 (2001).

[2]Transient functional lesious using transcranial magnetic stimulation (TMS, see *amnesia) are explored but their future as acceptable routine experimental procedure is doubtful.

Homunculus

1. **A diminutive human being.**
2. **In the theory of mind, an intelligent supervisor in the brain that reads information and commands action.**

Homunculi (Latin, diminutive of *homo*, man) have a rich history in science and philosophy, but not all homunculi were created equal. As a term in biology, 'homunculus' is a close relative of 'animalculus' ('little animal'). The latter was a generic term used by the early microscopists of the seventeenth century to refer to the microorganisms discovered under the magnifying lens (Wilson 1995). Guided by a combination of naive observations and wishful thinking, animalculi were occasionally depicted as miniature editions of full-sized animals. Probably the most famous one was invented by the Dutch microscopist Nicolaas Hartsoeker. While investigating sperm, he portrayed the first 'homunculus': a curled-up tiny human being enclosed inside a spermatozoon like a passenger on an aeroplane diving for a crash. Hartsoeker actually wrote that what he drew was not what he saw but what one might hope to see, yet this remark was rapidly forgotten, whereas the homunculus was not (*ibid.*). The mythical homunculi in sperms are currently of interest primarily to historians of biology. In this discussion we will deal with another species of homunculus, created in philosophy to account for the operation of the mind. Basically, so goes this version of the homunculus story, there is a little man inside our head, that sees, hears, smells and tastes, feels, contemplates and plans, pulls pulleys, presses levers, and makes us think what we think and do what we do. Admittedly, such an homunculus does have an intuitive appeal. How nice would it be to be able to explain the *enigmas of the brain by *reducing them to a search for a little fellow that hides somewhere there and is responsible for it all. The problem is that the solution simply postpones the difficulty, is clearly too *anthropomorphic, and any smart homunculus would have rejected it.

Rephrasing Eliot on cats (Eliot 1939), the naming of homunculi is a difficult matter. In psychology they become variants of 'central executives' (see *working memory). In physiology they resurface disguised as 'grandmother cells', 'command neurons', and more (see below). In philosophy, homunculi have been discussed many years before they were so named. Descartes' proposal that the pineal gland is the site of the soul (Descartes 1649) is a version of the homunculus with assigned neuroanatomical coordinates. Other thinkers were much less enthusiastic; Leibniz, for example, opposed those searching for explanations in 'little demons or imps which can without ado perform whatever is wanted' (Leibniz 1704). More than two centuries later, Homunculi found their way into the debates on *behaviourism in psychology. Homunculi-based explanations of behaviour were inherently problematic for behaviourism. On the one hand, homunculi could relieve psychology from the need to explain inner mental processes; on the other, themselves they were postulated inner mental structures. 'The function of the inner man is to provide an explanation which will not be explained in turn', so Skinner (1971), '… Explanation stops with him'. But he also added: 'Science does not dehumanize man; it de-homunculizes him' (*ibid.*).

Another window through which the homunculus stares at us is artificial intelligence. In this discipline, the assumption that intelligent systems must ultimately harbour an intelligent executive agent, that is more-or-less in the image of its host, is dubbed 'the homunculus fallacy' (Kenny 1971). Some authors argue that depiction of 'homunculi' does not necessarily implies adapting this fallacy, because homunculi can be discharged with a hierarchy of progressively sillier homunculi: 'Homunculi are bogeymen only if they duplicate entire the talents they are rung to explain… If one can get a team or committee of relatively ignorant, narrow-minded, blind homunculi to produce the intelligent behavior of the whole, this is progress' (Dennett 1978; see also Minsky 1985). Note, however, that if the homunculus is multiplied extensively and made really stupid, one disposes of the homunculus rather than of the fallacy.

Most neuroscientists are familiar with another, more tangible use of the term 'homunculus', in neuroanatomy and neurology. Resting on the shoulders of the great European neuroanatomists of the nineteenth century, several teams of investigators have mapped the representation of body surface in the brain (Marshall *et al.* 1941; Penfield and Rasmussen 1950). They came up with the finding that somatic sensations arising from the body surface map on to specific areas of the primary somatosensory cortex, although the *map is distorted: different surfaces of the body occupy areas that are disproportional to their actual physical size. This cortical topographical map is termed 'sensory homunculus'. An analogous 'motor homunculus' exists in the primary motor cortex. Despite the graphic representation of bodily figures on cortical areas in neurology books, the use of the term 'homunculus' in this context does not imply that a supervisor resides in those

121

areas, even if some newcomers to brain research might erroneously suppose that it does.

From the point of view of memory research, the concept of 'homunculus' is pertinent to two critical albeit related issues: the encoding of *internal representations, and the localization of the *engram. For if there were homunculi, one possibility would have been that learning involves changes in the way they read and govern. There are two extreme views on the nature of representational codes in the brain. One is that complex representations are realized in single neurons ('unitary code', e.g. Barlow 1972). Such units are dubbed 'grandmother', 'gnostic', or 'pontifical' cells or units (Konorski 1967; Baum *et al.* 1988).[1] A related concept exists for motor programmes: the 'command neuron', a neuron responsible for a certain behaviour and critical in generating it (Wiersma and Ikeda 1964; Kupfermann and Weiss 1978; Edwards *et al.* 1999). Now, single units that encode complex representations do carry a connotation of 'homunculi': if there are cells that encode the grandmother, why not cells that encode complete autobiographical narratives, and yet others that read the whole brain, encode, and navigate our consciousness? The opposing view considers internal representations as distributed over many neurons, while none of the individual units encodes a significant part of the representation ('population code', *cell assembly). In between these views one may envisage neuronal populations of various sizes, the members of which respond to complex stimuli and possibly even represent meaningful chunks of complex representations, e.g. cells that respond to hands or faces (Gross *et al.* 1972; Desimone 1991). Such cells are detected in circuits in multiple locations in the brain (Desimone 1991; Ó *Scalaidhe *et al.* 1997). Similarly, even 'command neurons' in simple systems are commonly described as groups of cells (Kupfermann and Weiss 1978). Internal representations seem thus distributed, even though the critical number of units that encode a meaningful chunk of the representation might be small (e.g. Young and Yamane 1992; Shadlen *et al.* 1996; *cell assembly). At least in the mammalian brain, the search for the engram should therefore focus on distributed neuronal populations, not on a single cell in a fixed address or on an elusive *plastic homunculus.

The main virtue of the 'homunculus' is that as a concept it forces us to think about how the brain understands and controls itself. All this notwithstanding, it is tempting to assume that the homunculus *per se* is still popular, more than we tend to concede, even in the mind of serious neuroscientists. We must

overcome some very basic intuitions in order to drive him, or her, out.

Selected associations: Anthropomorphism, Reduction, Subject

---

[1] The important element in the concept is the convergence on a single processor. Gnostic units, for example, were not depicted necessarily as single cells, but were always contrasted with a representation that is distributed over many cells (Konorski 1967).

Honeybee

A winged social insect of the family *Apidea*, sub-family *Apinae*, genus *Apis*, characterized by special organs of pollen and nectar collection and of honey production.

Humankind has displayed keen interest in bees since the dawn of history. There is no evidence that the opposite was ever true. Cave paintings dating 10 000 years ago already depict bold honey harvesters driving away the stinging bees with smoke (Menzel and Mercer 1987). A few millennia later, when the Almighty led the Israelites from slavery to freedom, he promised 'a good and large land, a land flowing with milk and honey' (*Exodus* 3:8). To this day, cultivation of the common honeybee, *Apis mellifera* L. (Rutner 1988), is a significant source of income to some, and a hobby to others; a cult encyclopaedia detailing whatever-you-ever-wanted-to-know-about-bees-and-never-dared-to-ask-them is claimed to have sold over the years more than half a million copies (Root 1972).

Bees are endowed with a remarkable behavioural repertoire that is manifested in both solitary adventures and social life. It is subserved by acute visual, odour, taste and tactile perceptions and discriminations, a magnetic sense, expert long-range navigation, skilful flight, dance 'language', and more (e.g. von Frisch 1967; Menzel and Mercer 1987; Getz and Page 1991; Seeley 1995; Menzel *et al.* 1996; Giurfa and Menzel 1997; Sirinivasan *et al.* 2000; Esch *et al.* 2001). There is a long and occasionally heated debate in the bee literature on how much of bee behaviour is innate and how much acquired throughout life (e.g. Lindauer 1967; Gould 1984), but clearly, under certain circumstances, bees are proficient learners (Bitterman *et al.* 1983; Lehrer 1993; Hammer and Menzel 1995; Brown *et al.* 1998; Erber *et al.* 1998). They manage to do all their tricks with a tiny brain (1 mm³, not strikingly larger than a single giant neuron in *Aplysia*), that contains less than a million nerve cells. Despite the brain's compactness, compartmentalized sensory and associative centres, connecting pathways and certain individual neurons can be identified and manipulated. Bees are hence amenable not only to ethological and behavioural analysis, but also to neuroanatomical, neuropharmacological, and cellular investigation.

Yet those are not the cognitive or neuronal virtues of the bee that have carried it to these pages. Clearly, many species do outperform the bee in behavioural complexity and brain power. The bee is of interest here because it is the subject of a systematic, multi*level, top-down research programme, that has successfully managed to link the phenomenology of ecological behaviour to the mechanistics of circuits and molecules. Furthermore, this programme attempts to explain concretely *real-life learning in terms of alterations in identifiable *internal representations. This critical step in bridging behaviour and brain is still a rather uncommon enterprise in the neurobiology of learning and memory.

Bees can be tested for memory as freely-behaving populations, freely-flying individuals, or restrained individuals. The latter situation offers advantages for mechanistic studies. The most popular paradigm is olfactory *classical conditioning (Bitterman *et al.* 1983; Hammer and Menzel 1995). A bee extends its proboscis (the insect's version of a tongue) when chemoreceptors on the proboscis or antennae are stimulated by food, e.g. a sucrose solution. This is called the 'proboscis extension reflex' (PER). In the context of classical conditioning, the sucrose is the unconditioned stimulus (US) and the PER the unconditioned response (UR). The response can be conditioned by pairing an odour, which initially is practically neutral with respect to the PER, with sucrose. Pursuing the terminology of classical conditioning, the odour is the conditioned stimulus (CS), and with conditioning comes to evoke the PER (the conditioned response, CR). Such learning is used in foraging, hence is couched in a language familiar to the bee. This is probably the reason why this learning is fast and robust.

Both the CS and the US pathways of the modifiable reflex have been mapped in the bee's brain. The CS pathway starts with the olfactory chemoreceptors, which project to the antennal lobes, the functional analogue of the mammalian olfactory bulb. In the lobes, the information is processed by approximately 5000 interneurons and 1000 projection neurons. The projection neurons reach other parts of the brain, including the 'mushroom bodies', a central processing area shown to play a part in learning in other insects as well (*Drosophila*). The US pathway begins with the chemoreceptors that sense the sucrose. They send information to central motor neurons that control the proboscis, and to interneurons that innervate a number of brain areas and subserve the modulatory function of the US. Activity of one of these modulatory neurons, named VUMmx1, was shown to correlate with the US and, furthermore, to be capable of substituting for it (Hammer 1993; see 'mimicry' under *criterion, *method). The reward function of food can be substituted by microinjection of the *neurotransmitter octopamine into the mushroom bodies or the antennal lobes (Hammer and Menzel 1998). Specific temporal patterns of activation of cAMP-dependent *protein kinase sustain the associative long-term PER memory in the lobes (Muller 2000). The presence of extensive projections of US-related interneurons in the brain indicates that there are multiple sites of convergence of the CS and US in this system (*coincidence detection). The multiplicity of association loci is in accord with data from cellular and circuit analysis of classical conditioning in other organisms (e.g. *Aplysia). It is plausible to assume that the multiple sites of association in PER conditioning in the bee's brain are not functionally equivalent.

The analysis of conditioning in the honeybee has recently proceeded to target experience-dependent changes in the coherent activity of neuronal populations that are expected to encode internal representations of odours and their hedonic valence. *Functional neuroimaging of neuronal *calcium currents unveiled specific odour-induced spatiotemporal activity *maps in the antennal lobes (Joerges *et al.* 1997), that were specifically modified in associative learning (Faber *et al.* 1999). Further research is needed to determine the causal relevance of these alterations in circuit activity to representational change (this caveat applies as well to the use-dependent morphological alterations that were detected in the olfactory glomeruli; Sigg *et al.* 1997). But already at this stage, the tiny brain of the bee is one of the first places in which the discussion of learning mechanisms addresses not only anatomical pathways, *synapses, and molecules, but also putative population-encoded internal representations—a real must for understanding the neurobiology of memory. The bee thus appears to navigate us in the right direction.

Selected associations: Associative learning, Classical conditioning, Simple system

Immediate early genes

Genes whose products are induced rapidly and transiently in response to extracellular *stimulation.

The term immediate early gene (IEG) was borrowed from virology. During the infectious cycle, the viral proteins are expressed in an orderly programme, which involves immediate early, delayed early, and late proteins (Honess and Roizman 1974; Weinheimer and McKnight 1987). For example, in the virus *Herpes simplex*, products of IEGs are detectable at 1 h of infection, of delayed early genes at 3 h, and of *late response genes at 6–7 h (Weinheimer and McKnight 1987). Each *phase in the cascade is required for the initiation of the next phase. An analogous picture was later unveiled in the response of mammalian cells to extracellular stimuli (Nathans *et al.* 1988; Lanahan *et al.* 1992). The modified expression of cellular IEGs is detected within minutes of the extracellular stimulation, and commonly lasts only for a short time (e.g. tens of minutes; Sheng and Greenberg 1990).

Some IEGs encode transcription factors (TFs). These are intracellular proteins that control the expression of genes and hence the differentiation, *development, function, and *plasticity of the cell.[1] Many TFs are known. A few common encounters in the neurobiological literature are c-Fos, c-Jun, Zif/268, and members of the *CREB/ATF family (Sheng and Greenberg 1990; Hill and Treisman 1995; Herdegen and Leah 1998).[2]

The genes for certain TFs, such as CREB, are always expressed in the cell to some degree or another. Their products, termed 'constitutive transcription factors' or CTFs, are activated or inhibited by stimulus-triggered post-translational modifications. Other TFs, such as c-Jun, are transiently expressed only upon the proper stimulation. They are termed 'inducible transcription factors', or ITFs. They also undergo post-translational modifications. The post-translational modification of TFs commonly involves phosphorylation by *protein kinases, such as the cyclic adenosine monophosphate-dependent kinases, or the mitogen-activated protein kinase (Hunter and Karin 1992; Xia *et al.* 1996). TFs are hence components as well as targets of *intracellular signalling pathways. They are capable of coupling short-term events, encoded in the state of the intracellular signal transduction pathways, to long-term alterations in the structure and function of the cell. These long-term effects could be mediated by the modulation of the expression of late response genes (Hill and Treisman 1995).

Not all IEGs, however, encode TFs. Many encode membrane and cytoskeletal elements, regulatory proteins, enzymes, and secreted proteins. For example, the extracellular protease (an enzyme that degrades proteins), tissue plasminogen activator, is induced by experience as an IEG in the *hippocampus (Qian *et al.* 1993). Its role in this case is probably to 'clean' the extracellular space in order to permit tissue remodelling. Another example: a growth factor, brain derived neurotrophic factor, known to be involved in synaptic plasticity in brain, is expressed in the hippocampus as an IEG during *contextual learning (Hall *et al.* 2000).

Ample data show that the induction of IEGs is correlated with, and sometimes obligatory for, long-term (but not short-term) plasticity and memory (e.g. Impey *et al.* 1996; Yin and Tully 1996). This is construed within the prevailing conceptual framework (*zeitgeist), which describes the *consolidation of long-term memory as a growth process that endows the memory with immunity to molecular turnover (Goelet *et al.* 1986; Dudai 1989; Milner *et al.* 1998; *development, *protein synthesis). The idea is that, whereas weak training results in only transient post-translational modifications in the neurons, training that involves repetitive or *coincident stimuli induces IEGs, culminating in long-term circuit alterations and therefore long-term memory. The products of the IEGs, or at least of those IEGs that encode TFs, are hence regarded as intracellular switches that transform short-term into long-term plasticity. IEGs have also become a major focus of research in developmental neurobiology (Curran and Morgan 1994; Davis *et al.* 1996). Indeed, the analysis of the role of gene expression in plasticity is currently an industrious interface between developmental neurobiology on the one hand and the molecular analysis of learning on the other; the two subdisciplines of the neuroscience use the same methodology and terminology (Martin and Kandel 1996; but to put the similarity in proportion, see Constantine-Paton and Kline 1998).

The sensitivity to behavioural and physiological manipulations render the induction of IEGs as well as the activation of TFs useful metabolic markers of neuronal activity, which could identify functional circuits in the brain. This is the molecular equivalent of *functional neuroimaging. For example, by monitoring the behaviourally driven expression of the IEG *ZENK*, Jarvis *et al.* (2000) have been able to identify a set of forebrain nuclei that subserve the production of *birdsong in the hummingbird. Similarly, *c-Fos* and other

IEGs have been used to map the circuits of *conditioned taste aversion in the rat (Swank and Bernstein 1994; Lamprecht and Dudai 1995). Given the appropriate IEGs, the *method could also be adapted to supply information on the dynamics of circuit recruitment in a task. This was done using *Arc*, an IEG that encodes a cytoskeletal-associated protein. The mRNA of *Arc* is delivered within minutes of its production from the nucleus into the cytoplasm and ultimately into the dendrites. Guzowski *et al.* (1999) have exploited this property to infer the history of activity of individual neurons in the rat hippocampus at two close time points, as a function of exposure to a novel or familiar environment. As predicted by physiological evidence and by *models of spatial *maps in the hippocampus, *Arc* was induced in a single subset of hippocampal neurons upon sequential visits of the rat to the same environment, but in two overlapping neuronal subsets upon sequential visits to two different environments.

In spite of the impressive evidence on the involvement of IEGs in learning and memory, the question is yet unsettled whether their role is permissive, or causal, or both. The waves of gene expression that are observed after training could induce alterations in the *internal representations in the circuit, yet could also fulfil *homeostatic functions unrelated to the representational change. Further, IEGs are universal devices; they are induced in all tissues in response to a great variety of stimuli. In neurons, they are also induced in response to stimuli that do not result in a memory. We must therefore identify those contributions of IEGs that are specific to learning and memory, and elucidate their particular contribution in each case. Whether specific, permissive, or obligatory—IEGs are definitely useful (*criterion) in providing cellular explanations for some intriguing behavioural phenomena of learning and memory. For noteworthy examples, see *flashbulb memory and *spaced training.

Selected associations: Consolidation, CREB, Late response genes, Protein synthesis

---

[1]For more on transcription factors, see *CREB.

[2]The names of transcription factors, and hence many IEGs, are usually acronyms that reflect the activity of the molecule, its structure, or the idiosyncratic preferences of the person who first described it. Here is the meaning of names that are mentioned in the text. *c-fos* stands for 'Finkel–Biskis–Jinkins murine osteogenic sarcoma virus', with the 'c' standing for 'cellular', to distinguish it from the viral gene, which is preceded by 'v'. *jun* is 'ju-nana', Japanese for 'number 17', because *v-jun* was isolated from the avian sarcoma virus 17. *zif/268* stands for 'zinc finger binding protein clone number 268'; zinc finger denotes a

protein DNA-binding domain that centres on a zinc ion. *CREB* and *ATF* are explained in *CREB. *Arc* is 'activity regulated cytoskeletal-associated protein'. Guessing the origin of the name of a transcription factor could be rather frustrating. For example, *ZENK* is an acronym of the second order, standing for *Zif/268, Egr-1, NGFI-A,* and *Krox-24.* *Egr* is 'early growth response gene', *NGFI* 'nerve growth factor inducible gene', and *Krox* is Kruppel-box, where *Kruppel* is the German-originating name for a mutation that causes bodily deformation in *Drosophila,* and 'box' is a generic term for a DNA motif. *zif/268, Egr-1, NGFI-A,* and *Krox-24* all refer to the same of molecular species. Conventionally names of genes are in italics, and of their protein products in regular font. It is not such a bad idea to organize trivia contests on the etymology of the names of transcription factors.

Imprinting

The process in which an individual learns, during a sensitive period usually early in life, to restrict its social preferences to an object or to a class of objects.

When we select a partner, we often proudly consider it to be an epitome of free choice of a mature human being. Well, we may be wrong. Members of many species learn very early in life to restrict their social preferences to a specific class of objects. This acquired *bias comes to restrict the choice of the mate much later on. It is called 'sexual imprinting'. In other words, there are always traces of one's parents in one's spouse. The basic phylogenetic function of sexual imprinting is considered to ensure that in due time, individuals do not waste their energy in courting the wrong species. Most readers of both the scientific and the general literature are much more aware of another type of imprinting, filial imprinting, in which a juvenile of the species forms attachment to the mother immediately after hatching. Here the idea is to provide the newborn with much needed food and care.[1]

Different types of imprinting, even in the same species, are established in different time windows and last for different times (Hess 1959; Bateson 1966; Immelmann 1972; Vidal 1980; Leon 1992; Hudson 1993; ten Cate and Vos 1999). Multiple sensory modalities are involved, depending on the species, the object to be imprinted, and the occasion. Indeed, the world of imprinting is astonishingly rich: imprinting navigates Salmons across oceans and rivers to their natal habitat (Dittman and Quinn 1996), socializes dogs with humans (Pfaffenberger and Scott 1959), and can turn a laboratory mouse into a Mozart fan (doesn't work with

Schoenberg; Cross *et al.* 1967). Although usually characteristic of the young, learning to restrict social preferences during a sensitive time window could occur in the adult (Hudson 1993). For example, reciprocal ewe–lamb bonding is established by olfactory imprinting in parturition. Imprinting also plays a part in the mother–infant bonding in humans (Kennell *et al.* 1979), and here, again, olfactory cues are important (Leon 1992). As even days-old babies readily recognize their mother's perfume (Schleidt and Genzel 1990), we might expect to find out that a nursing mother who switches too many fragrances cultivates a potential neurotic.

Filial imprinting is especially striking in precocial birds and was the subject of systematic observations already during the early days of experimental psychology (Spalding 1873). A few hours after hatching, the chick approaches and follows a conspicuous moving object, which may or may not be the mother. In nature it usually is; in the laboratory it may actually be an earnest scientist (Lorenz 1937). 'After hatching and becoming able to look around, a greyleg gosling utters its lost piping, to which... its mother answers with a rhythmic cackle. To this the gosling responds by greeting. The mutually releasing sequence of piping-cackle-greeting is predictable with a high degree of probability... The program timing the period of sensibility of that irreversible learning process for this particular moment is obviously adaptive. The built-in mechanism conveys to the gosling information which, if verbalized, would say: 'When you first feel lonely, utter your lost piping, then look for somebody who moves and says 'gang, gang, gang' and never, never forget who that is, because it is your mother" (Lorenz 1981). This imprinting process involves at least two distinct, interactive components. One is the innate (*a priori) predisposition to approach *stimuli that have the characteristics of the natural mother. The other is the learning to approach a stimulus to which the chick is exposed during the sensitive period—which may be the natural mother, Lorenz, or an artificial stimulus in the lab.

The approach behaviour of the domestic chick, although not as long-lasting as the one in Lorenz's narration, became a useful *system for investigating the behavioural, neuroanatomical, cellular, and molecular substrates of filial imprinting (Horn 1985; Rogers 1994; Bolhuis 1999). The chick is imprinted on a combination of visual and auditory *cues, which are *bound synergistically (Smith and Bird 1963; Bolhuis 1999). Candidate forebrain substrates of both visual and acoustic imprinting have been identified (Maier and Scheich 1983; Horn 1985; Bolhuis 1999; Bock and Braun 1999a) (Figure 35). Noteworthy among those regions that subserve visual imprinting is the intermediate and medial part of the hyperstriatum ventrale (IMHV), lesions in which impair the learning process but not the innate predisposition (Johnson and Horn 1987; Bolhuis 1999). The IMHV may hence be a critical station in the circuit that enables the chick to *recognize *individual* birds.

The molecular and cellular mechanisms unveiled in the brain regions that subserve imprinting in the chick are similar to those identified in other types of *acquisition and *consolidation. They involve, among

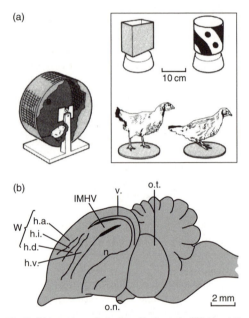

Fig. 35 (a) Apparatus and stimuli used in the study of filial imprinting in the domestic chick. Imprinting is quantified by measuring the approach toward the imprinted object. The chick is placed in a training wheel, which is here drawn with one of its opaque sides exposed. The *subject runs on the mesh towards a visually conspicuous object, such as those depicted in the inset. As the wheel rotates on its axle, the distance to the object remains constant. The rate of rotation is an index of the approach *performance. Acoustic *stimuli could be combined with the visual ones. (b) A diagrammatic longitudinal section in the brain of a 2-day-old chick, cut laterally to the mid-line; h.a., hyperstriatum accessorium; h.d., hyperstriatum dorsale; h.i., hyperstriatum intercalatus; h.v., hyperstriatum ventrale; IMHV, intermediate and medial part of the hyperstriatum ventrale, delineated ventrally and dorsally by heavy lines; n., neostriatum; o.n., optic nerve; o.t., optic tectum; W, visual Wulst. The IMHV has been particularly implicated in the process of learning to *recognize individual members of the species in imprinting. (Adapted from Bateson and Wainwright 1972; Horn 1985.)

others, *glutamatergic *N*-methyl-D-aspartate *receptors, other *neurotransmitter systems, *protein kinases, *immediate early genes, cell adhesion molecules, and morphological synaptic *plasticity (Horn and McCabe 1990; Sheu *et al.* 1993; Solomonia *et al.* 1998; Ambalavanar *et al.* 1999; Bock and Braun 1999*a,b*).

Imprinting could be considered a subclass of 'prepared learning' processes, in which brain maturation (*development) is modified by sensory experience during a sensitive period. This sensitive period is constrained, among others, by the growth potential of the neuronal circuits and by hormonal states. Other examples are visual (Wiesel 1982; Crair *et al.* 1998) and auditory (Knudsen 1998) sensory learning early in life, and the learning of *birdsong. Such learning could leave in the young brain dormant *engrams, which, given the appropriate conditions and cues, are capable of being reactivated after many years in the adult (Knudsen 1998).

Selected associations: A Priori, Acquisition, Birdsong, Development

---

[1]In biology, the term 'imprinting' is also used in an utterly different *context. 'Gametic' or 'genomic imprinting' is the process whereby the expression of certain genes in the embryo is restricted to either the maternal or paternal allele, although both are present.

Infantile amnesia

The lack of *recall of autobiographical memories dating to infancy.

The observation that infancy is not remembered was noted with interest by students of the mind, and probably by others as well, throughout the ages (Augustine 400; Rousseau 1798; Freud 1901). The experimental data confirm folk psychology: adults do not remember autobiographical episodes that had occurred prior to the age of about 3 or 4 years, and report that their inner personal narratives begin to make sense (if they ever do) only about the age of 6 or 7 years (Dudycha and Dudycha 1941; Wetzler and Sweeney 1986; Nelson 1992; Eacott and Crawley 1998). Claims for the 'rediscovery' in adulthood of the memories of early infancy should be treated with great caution, as they could reflect *false memory.

Why do individual life histories begin with a period of oblivion? Over the years, several types of explanations for infantile amnesia have been proposed. They involve different conceptual frameworks (biological, cognitive, psychosocial), and some of them refer to different *phases of memory (*acquisition, *consolidation, retention, *retrieval).

One class of explanations suggests that the problem lies already at the acquisition phase: early personal memories are not retained to begin with, because the brain systems that are required for autobiographical, *episodic memory simply do not mature before the age of 3–4 years (Nadel and Zola-Morgan 1984; Nelson 1998; *declarative memory). A related suggestion implicates both acquisition and retention and rests on cognitive rather than neurological arguments. It claims that the infant's mind cannot form the appropriate mental structures that serve as inner frameworks for organizing new information in a sensible manner. The generic term for such abstract mental structures is 'schemata' (Bartlett 1932; Piaget 1969; Cohen 1996). In the absence of mature schemata, so goes the argument, autobiographical experiences cannot be stored in an effective, retrievable form. A version of this argument considers the intense episodes of infantile memory inconsistent with the categories of the adult schemata, hence incapable of being assimilated into the adult memory (Schachtel 1947; see also Freud's suppression hypothesis below). Similar suggestions invoke the lack in infancy of linguistic competence, which is assumed to be required in encoding autobiographical episodes (Nelson 1992); immaturity of a 'me' system, postulated to be necessary for integration of episodic information into the internal personal nar-rative (Howe and Courage 1997); or, similarly, immaturity of a 'self-memory system', postulated to hold the autobiographical memory base together with the current goals of the self (Conway and Pleydell-Pearce 2000).

Deficiencies in retrieval comprise another class of explanations for infantile amnesia. Here the most famous argument is that early memories are formed but later suppressed to become non-retrievable, because of their damaging emotional load; furthermore, those early memories that are recalled are actually 'screens', which hide the real, difficult experience (Freud 1901). No experimental evidence has been reported so far to support this psychoanalytical account.[1] Similarly, there is no firm experimental evidence to support the popular view that special methods, such as hypnosis, can retrieve repressed or forgotten infantile memories.

And there are also psychosocial explanations, which search for the roots of infantile amnesia within the framework of the interaction of the individual with society. Autobiographical episodes, so it is suggested, become encoded properly only after the infant becomes aware of the social function of autobiographical memory, which is postulated to be, according to this view, the development of a life history that can be shared with others (Nelson 1993).

Many of the aforementioned explanations are not mutually exclusive. Immature brain circuits in infancy, such as frontal *cortex and cortico*limbic circuits, may be yet unable to subserve the cognitive and the psychosocial faculties of categorization, 'inner language', self-comprehension, or social understanding. All this does not imply that very young infants do not have the ability to acquire *ad-hoc* declarative knowledge (they

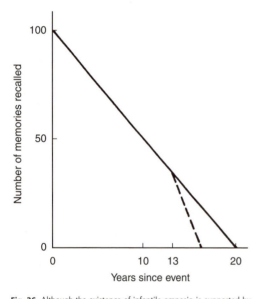

Fig. 36 Although the existence of infantile amnesia is supported by introspection, personal accounts, and anecdotal evidence, its objective verification under *controlled conditions is not trivial. Three major types of variables are involved in such experiments: the age at learning, the age at retrieval, and the length of the retention interval. The ideal experiment should control the age at retrieval, vary the age of learning, and, most importantly, define the expected normal forgetting over the retention interval. Infantile amnesia will then become apparent as accelerated forgetting below a certain early age at learning. The graph depicts the hypothetical distribution of memories across the lifetime of a 20-year-old human *subject. The solid line represents an ideal function of normal forgetting, while the inflected broken line represents the accelerated forgetting that one should observe in infantile amnesia. Based on the analysis of the data in the scientific literature, Wetzler and Sweeney (1986) confirmed that indeed, phenomena that approximate the hypothetical curve are observed in reality, and that there is accelerated forgetting for memories acquired below the age of 5. (Adopted from Wetzler and Sweeney 1986.)

do; Rovee-Collier 1997), or that their brain is incapable of amazing feats of learning and memory (it does; Saffran *et al.* 1996; Jusczyk and Aohne 1997). Even fetuses may have learning and memory capabilities that parents-to-be commonly disregard (Hepper 1996). In estimating the mental capacity of infants, it took a lot of grant money to reach the conclusion reached by every normal parent: these babies outperform us in many ways.

So, regardless of the exact mechanism, what could be the phylogenetic and ontogenetic rationales for preventing adults from remembering their adventures in the crib? It might be related to a mix of biological constraints and selective pressures. First, evolution did not come up (yet?) with the ability to construct instantly a perfect brain; it takes years to *develop. Second, slow brain maturation may have an advantage in coping with a changing environment, as it reduces the chance of fast and robust encoding of erroneous outcomes of certain types of learning in early infancy. Third, autobiographical memory could lack significant phylogenetic advantage early in life (and see *capacity). All the above combined, it probably pays better to dedicate first the brain power of the newborn to the acquisition of critical, basic *skills, rather than to the long-term declarative memory of the pains and the joys of the first months of life.

Selected associations: Amnesia, Development, Episodic memory, Persistence, Real-life memory

---

[1]The frontal cortex can suppress unwanted memories (Anderson and Green 2001), but there is no evidence that this is involved in infantile amnesia.

Insight

1. **The sudden realization of a solution to a problem.**

2. **Abrupt improvement in the *performance on a task.**

Some types of learning, such as the acquisition of *skill, progress gradually, through numerous repetitions. This is termed 'incremental learning', or 'rote learning' (Hebb 1949). In contrast, other types of learning, both in *real-life and in laboratory setting, occur abruptly, following a step function. Two examples are *flashbulb memory and *conditioned taste aversion. There is, however, a type of abrupt learning that differs from these examples. It cannot be described as fast acquisition of information about an on-line event. Rather, the *subject is presented with a problem, which it finds difficult to solve. After a typical period of either fruitless overt attempts or behavioural silence, suddenly, a solution comes to mind. We all are familiar with these situations. There is even a special term that conveys the subjective flavour: the 'AHA! experience' (Kaplan and Simon 1990; Sternberg and Davidson 1995). When we watch animals under situations that seem to involve sudden realization of a solution to a problem, we tend to *anthropomorphize and conclude that they also have their 'insight', uttering 'AHA!' in doglish or chimpanzeesh.

Some cases of alleged insight are anecdotal. It is told that the chemist Kekule suddenly saw in reverie the structure of the benzene ring, although doubts were raised whether the story is true (Gruber 1995). The most famous of all 'AHA!' experiences is that of Archimedes, who allegedly jumped naked from his bath shouting 'Eureka' (Greek for '*I have found it*'), after suddenly realizing a *method to determine the amount of alloy mixed with the gold in the crown of the king of Syracuse. Again, the story is surely refreshing, but already Galileo considered it implausible (*ibid.*). As science cannot rely on anecdotes, various protocols were developed to demonstrate insight under controlled conditions. The following are two *classic examples. Kohler (1917, 1925) reported a number of 'insightful' or 'intelligent' experience-dependent behaviours in the chimpanzee. In a typical experiment, he placed a chimpanzee behind an array of vertical bars, and a heavy stone with a cord tied around it on the other side (Figure 37). Food was attached to the cord halfway between the anchoring stone and the bars. The cord was inserted through the bars in an angle that prevented the chimp from reaching the food. The only way to get the reward was to shift the cord between the bars until it formed a straight angle with the array of bars. The chimp tried at first to pull the cord, but in vein. Suddenly she somehow realized that she can take the cord in one hand, pass it around the bar to the other hand, and hence move it from one inter-bar spacing to another, step by step, till it formed the required angle, culminating in happy end. Individual chimps differed in the kinetics of their response, but most reached the right solution.

Other classic 'insight' experiments were carried out by Maier (1931) on humans. A typical one is 'the pendulum experiment'. Subjects were introduced into a room that had two strings hanging from the ceiling, and a number of other objects, including poles, pliers, and

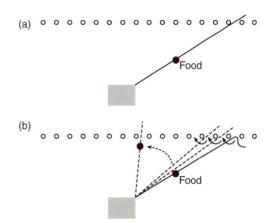

Fig. 37 A *classic insight experiment. Kohler (1917) placed a chimpanzee behind an array of vertical bars, and a heavy stone with a cord tied around it on the other side. Fruit was attached to the cord halfway between the stone and the bars, and the cord was inserted through the bars in an angle that prevented the *subject from reaching the reward (a). The only way to get it was to shift the cord between the bars until it formed a straight angle with the array of bars. Just pulling the cord was of no avail. Suddenly the chimp realized that she can take the cord in one hand, pass it around the bar to the other hand, and hence move it, step by step, from one inter-bar spacing to the other, till it formed the required angle (b). (Adapted from Kohler 1917.)

cords. The subjects were asked to tie together the two hanging strings. However, the distance between the strings was too large. After a while, the subjects suddenly realized that they can tie the pliers to one of the strings, swing it like a pendulum, and catch it in its up-swing while holding the other string. Reports of 'insight' are not confined to anthropoids. Over the years, cases of apparent 'insight' were described, although some also disputed, in cats in problem boxes and rodents in *mazes (e.g. Walker 1983). An interesting example of 'insight' in lower vertebrates involves pigeons who pushed a box in order to be able to climb and peck a hanging banana (Epstein *et al.* 1984). In all these experiments, it is important to discern between chance successes occurring via repetitive attempts of *instrumental learning, and a sudden solution to a problem after behavioural silence.

Reports of 'insight' made *behaviourists sad and Gestaltists happy.[1] The mere idea that learning involves internal reorganization in the brain in the absence of explicit *stimulus–response coupling contradicted the orthodox behaviouristic tenet that only public behaviour is the subject matter of psychology and that internal processes should be ignored. Attempts have been made either to play reports of 'insight' down, or to explain 'insight' by rather complex chaining of stimulus–response contingencies (Keller and Schoenfeld 1950; Bower and Hilgard 1981). In contrast, the Gestalt trusted that the nature of *perceptual and mental parts is determined by the whole, and that enquiry into the mind should consider global organization and proceed top-down (Kohler 1925; Koffka 1935; Hochberg 1998). The idea that mental structures are restructured to achieve a new meaning in the *context of previous knowledge was exactly in line with what they were preaching for. With time, 'insight' became a focus of interest in cognitive psychology in relation to information processing and problem solving (e.g. Weisberg and Alba 1981; Kaplan and Simon 1990; Ohlsson 1994a,b; Sternberg and Davidson 1995). Several *models have been proposed for insightful behaviours. They involve elements such as reshuffling and recategorization of building blocks of prior problem-related knowledge, the sudden identification of *cues, the use of multiple heuristic solutions and the identification of invariants in such solutions. Among these elements, the need for prior problem-related knowledge stands out in species far away on the phylogenetic scale (e.g. Epstein et al. 1984); again, it appears that in order to learn something, we must already know a lot (*a priori). However, as noted by Kaplan and Simon (1990), knowledge is a two-edged sword, as inflexible knowledge may guide the search for the solution astray.

A major question concerning insight is whether it a special type of learning, differing in its computational strategy, the *algorithms and their biological implementation from rote learning. For example, is insight restricted to higher processing *levels because it seems to affect 'global' cognitive structures? And are there any specific circuit properties that play a part in insight only? Hebb (1949), for example, who considered insight as the most advanced form of adult learning, did not think that its basic mechanisms differ from those of rote learning. So far, one of the difficulties in comparing insight to incremental learning was the traditional use of different types of behavioural paradigms—problem solving in the study of insight, skill acquisition in the study of incremental learning. The use of certain *perceptual learning tasks, involving visual detection and discrimination, could provide a solution, because these tasks tap into elements of both skill learning and insight (Ahissar and Hochstein 1997; Rubin et al. 1997). In these tasks, if the task is made easy, learning *generalizes over *dimensions of the stimuli, matching the properties of high-level visual areas, whereas when the task is made difficult, learning shows little *transfer if at all, typical of low-level perceptual skill. Under certain

conditions, performance on these skill-like tasks shows sudden improvement, resembling insight, either on the particular task, or on the ability to solve the type of tasks (*learning set). It was suggested that this abrupt improvement on 'low-level' learning depends on increments in 'high-level' knowledge (Rubin et al. 1997). Although this conclusion could prove to be *paradigm-specific, it does cast doubts on the generality of type-distinction between rote learning and insight.

The attempt to separate abrupt from gradual learning brings to mind the so-called 'Sorites paradox' (soros, Greek for 'heap'; Williamson 1994). It is attributed to Eubulides of Miletus, a contemporary of Aristotle, and it goes like this: does one grain of wheat make a heap? Do two grains? Three? Ten thousands? Where is the transition point? For those remote from agriculture, the 'bald man' version may evoke more empathy: Is a man with one hair on his head bald? With two? Three? If the addition of any single hair is not critical, one is led to admit that a man with 10 000 hairs is bald. The boundaries of the terms 'heap', 'bald', 'incremental', or 'abrupt learning' are therefore vague. Attempts to distinguish insight from incremental learning resemble attempts to consider '*flashbulb memory' as inherently different from other episodic memories. Naturally, we are impressed by the extreme cases. But in real life, a spectrum should be expected of time-scales, interactive levels of processing, and complexity of *internal representations. Insight may involve latent increments in knowledge, and rote learning may involve 'microinsights'. Sharp *taxonomies may exist only in the eye of our cognition.

Selected associations: Acquisition, Binding, Delay task, Learning

---

[1] For more on the Gestalt school of psychology see *binding.

Instrumental conditioning

1. Types of *associative learning in which the probability or intensity of behaviour changes as a result of its consequences.[1]

2. Types of training protocols in which *reinforcement is made contingent upon *performance of the proper behaviour.

In *classical conditioning the subject learns relations among *stimuli; in instrumental conditioning (also 'instrumental learning') it learns the impact of its actions on the world. The scientific interest in this type of learning can be traced to Bain (1859), who, impressed by his experience in the Scottish Highlands, noted 'association of movement with the effects produced on outward things' in animals trying to leap over obstacles: '… spontaneous impulses of locomotion lead them to make attempts … any attempt causing a hurt is desisted from; after a number of trials and failures, the proper adjustment is come to, and finally cemented'. Morgan (1894; see *Ockham's Razor) reported experiments on trial-and-error learning in birds and in Tony, his fox terrier. But it is to Thorndike (1911) that we owe the introduction of the systematic study of instrumental conditioning into the laboratory.

In a typical experiment, Thorndike placed a hungry cat into a puzzle box, a small crate hammered together from wooden slats (no fat grants those days) (Figure 38). A piece of fish was placed visibly outside. The box had systems of pulleys, strings, and catches so arranged that pulling a loop, or pressing a lever, allowed a door to fall open, and the cat to jump out and devour

Fig. 38 Two of the puzzle boxes used by Thorndike in his studies of instrumental conditioning. For more on Thorndike's puzzle boxes, see Thorndike (1911); Chance (1999). (Courtesy of Yale University Library.)

the fish. The cat, restlessly exploring the box, would operate the mechanism by chance. As the door fell open immediately, the cat would apparently learn to associate its deeds with the outcome, resulting in a striking improvement in performance over time. The behaviour was not necessarily related to the mechanism of door opening; in some experiments Thorndike manipulated his cats to lick themselves in order to get out. Note, however, that, whereas in classical conditioning the experimenter controls (ideally) all the experimental parameters, in instrumental conditioning there is a more democratic division of labour: the subject decides which response to emit, and the experimenter decides how and when to reinforce it.

Instrumental conditioning is so termed because the individual's behaviour is instrumental in the materialization of the reinforcement. This family of conditioning *paradigms is also known by other names: conditioned reflex type II (Miller and Konorski 1928; they modified Pavlov's paradigm and trained a dog to flex a leg in response to a buzzer in order to get food); Thorndikian conditioning; type R conditioning (R for response, Skinner 1938); trial-and-error conditioning; operant conditioning (operant because the spontaneous behavioural response operates on the environment, and is in turn affected by the environmental effects; ibid.);[2] and Skinnerian conditioning, after Skinner, whose problem boxes, descendants of Thorndike's puzzle boxes, came to epitomize the social and educational philosophy that all behaviour is malleable by operant conditioning ('operant *behaviourism'; Skinner 1984).[3] A *taxonomy of instrumental conditioning lists no less than 16 different subtypes, differing in the relationship of the behaviour (or its omission) to the outcome (or its prevention), and in the presence or absence of an antecedent signalling stimulus (Woods 1974). Among the most popular subtypes: signalled reward conditioning, in which a signal signifies that the reward will follow if the behaviour is executed (a 'go' situation); signalled omission reward conditioning, which is similar to the above only that the behaviour has to be withheld (a 'no-go' situation); active avoidance conditioning, in which following a signal, punishment is avoided provided the response is made; and passive avoidance conditioning, in which punishment is avoided if the response is withheld.

What is it that gets associated in instrumental conditioning? The theory of instrumental conditioning, similar to that of classical conditioning, has developed remarkably since the introduction of the paradigm. Thorndike himself extracted from his experimental findings a 'law' (*algorithm) that he called 'the law of effect'. This influential 'law' appears in several forms in Thorndike's writings. Here is the formulation at the behavioural and *system *levels: 'Of several responses made to the same situation, those which are accompanied or closely followed by satisfaction to the animal will, other things being equal, be more firmly connected with the situation, so that, when it recurs, they will be more likely to recur; those which are accompanied or closely followed by discomfort to the animal will, other things being equal, have their connections with that situation weakened, so that, when it recurs, will be less likely to recur. The greater the satisfaction or discomfort, the greater the strengthening or weakening of the bond' (Thorndike 1911). And here is the formulation at the circuit, cellular or *synaptic levels: '*Connections between neurones are strengthened every time they are used with indifferent or pleasurable results and weakened every time they are used with resulting discomfort.* This law includes the action of two factors, frequency and pleasurable result. It might be stated in a compound form as follows: *(1) The line of least resistance is, other things being equal, that resulting in the greatest satisfaction to the animal, and (2) the line of least resistance is, other things being equal, that oftenest traversed by the nerve impulse.* We may call (1) the *Law of Effect*, and (2) the *Law of Habit*' (Thorndike 1907; italics in the original).[4] Two points deserve particular attention. One, the law of effect is an adaptation of Darwinian selectionism (*a priori, *stimulus). Second, Thorndike's attitude was rather modern: he explicitly treated learning as multilevel phenomena and processes, and well appreciated that whatever is observed at the behavioural level, is manifested at the neuronal level as well, and vice versa.

The law of effect continues to drive research to this day in both the behavioural and the brain sciences (e.g. Ahissar *et al.* 1992). It does not, however, have the power to explain all the processes that occur in instrumental conditioning. Any attempt to understand these processes and their interaction must take into account three types of elements that play a part in every instrumental conditioning situation: the *response* whose probability or intensity is modified, the *reinforcer* that is contingent upon this response, and the *stimulus* in the presence of which this contingency takes place. Three types of associative configurations have dominated the theoretical discussion of the interaction of response, reinforcer, and stimulus in instrumental conditioning (Colwill and Rescorla 1986): (a) stimulus–response association ('S–R theories'; e.g. Guthrie 1952; *associative learning). (b) Pavlovian S–reinforcer association, occurring in parallel with the S–R association

('two-process theories'; Rescorla and Solomon 1967); (c) response–reinforcer, or action–outcome association ('A–O theories'; Colwill and Rescorla 1986; Dickinson and Balleine 1994).

Experimental evidence could be provided for the involvement of each of the above associative structures in instrumental conditioning, but, at the same time, none of these postulated associations could serve as a sufficient, much less so exclusive explanation (*criterion) for the behaviour. It is likely, therefore, that in instrumental conditioning, *internal representations could be formed that link the three elements, S, R, and O, with associative weights that depend on the task, *context, and a priori knowledge of the subject. Just as an example to illustrate that instrumental conditioning involves more knowledge than detected by the naive eye, consider the following experiment (Colwill and Rescorla 1985): rats were trained on two different instrumental responses, lever pressing and chain pulling, each associated with a different reinforcer, sucrose solution or food pellets. Then each rat received pairing of one of the reinforcers with a malaise-inducing injection of LiCl (*conditioned taste aversion, CTA), to decrease the hedonic value of that reinforcer (this is called 'stimulus devaluation', see *classical conditioning, *cue). When the rats were again given access to the instrumental response in the absence of the reinforcers, each rat preferred to make the specific instrumental response that had not been devalued by CTA. This suggests that the rats encoded the reinforcer identity and A–O contingency as part of the knowledge about the instrumental learning situation, and that this knowledge was susceptible to post-training experience. The picture that emerges is hence of instrumental conditioning leading to the *acquisition of specific knowledge bases, rather different from the picture depicted by the early minimalist S–R theories. This is similar to the current *zeitgeist in the study of classical conditioning. Further, from the aforementioned discussion it becomes evident that in spite of the difference in the training protocols and the particular types of knowledge, the processes that occur in instrumental conditioning overlap some that occur in classical conditioning (on this issue, see also Dickinson 1980; Mackintosh 1983).[5]

The incentive to understand the computational theories, algorithms, and biological hardware (*level) of instrumental conditioning is high. Much of what we learn in our lifetime is by trial and error. Furthermore, together with *observational learning, instrumental conditioning is contemplated as the method of choice to train the smart robots that will share this planet with us in the future (e.g. Saksida *et al.* 1997), and we had better find the way to teach them efficiently and, what's even more important, the right things only. The neurobiology of instrumental conditioning is, however, still fragmentary. At the system level, brain circuits have been identified that perform selected types of computations in instrumental conditioning. Special interest is dedicated in recent years to those circuits that encode the reinforcement and the A–O associations. These include *cortico*limbic–striatal–pallidal circuits (Robbins and Everitt 1997), with specific structures assumed to play distinct roles such as anticipation of reward, computing the deviation of the actual from the expected outcome, control of response and its adaptive correction, and possibly also representation of A–O causality (Schultz *et al.* 1997; Trembley and Schultz 1999; Balleine and Dickinson 2000; Baxter *et al.* 2000; Corbit and Balleine 2000; Corbit *et al.* 2001; see also *dopamine, *habit, *reinforcer). As to the cellular, synaptic, and molecular mechanisms of instrumental conditioning—their study could benefit from the use of *simple systems and, although the analysis of trial-and-error learning in simple systems is so far less developed than that of classical conditioning, some promising preparations are already available (Cook and Carew 1989; Chen and Wolpaw 1995; Nargeot *et al.* 1997). We might expect the molecular mechanisms of instrumental conditioning to be similar to those of classical conditioning and many other forms of learning; the characteristic instrumental contingencies are probably encoded at the circuit level.

Selected associations: Associative learning, Classical conditioning, Maze, Reinforcer, Skill

---

[1]Excluding, of course, consequences that eliminate the opportunity to perform this behaviour again.

[2]Operant conditioning is sometimes distinguished from instrumental conditioning in that the latter involves distinct responses within a structured task, whereas the former refers in addition to repeated emission of spontaneous behaviour that results in obtaining the goal. This distinction, however, is not systematically honoured in the literature and will not be further elaborated here.

[3]Operant behaviourism aspired to explain all types of behaviour, including human language (Skinner 1957). This was belligerently confuted by linguists and cognitive psychologists alike (Chomsky 1959). By the way, Skinner's methods found their way even into top-secret war projects: during the Second World War he was engaged in an attempt to train pigeons to guide missiles by operating problem boxes in the warhead (Skinner 1960).

[4]On precedents of Thorndikes' law, and on its place in the history of the behavioural sciences, see Cason (1932) and Wilcoxon (1969); see also *reinforcer. The empirical *generalization that the

consequences of the response is an important determiner of whether this response will be learned, is called 'the empirical law of effect', and can be used independently of Thorndike's theoretical assumptions (*reinforcer).

[5]The relevance of classical- to instrumental conditioning has multiple facets and all should be taken into account in the interpretation of the data. One is the postulated processes shared by these two types of learning. A very different facet is the possibility that conditioning that is considered instrumental is actually Pavlovian. Consider, for example, a pigeon trained to peck an illuminated disk in a Skinner box to obtain food. The classical interpretation is that food delivery is contingent upon pecking, i.e. an operant conditioning situation. However, if the experimenter simply illuminated the disk before each food delivery, irrespective of the pigeons' behaviour, the pigeons still pecked at the light as if there were an instrumental contingency (Jenkins and Moore 1973). Pecking is a component of the pigeon's consummatory response, and the contingency was probably between a conditioned stimulus (illuminated disk) and an unconditioned one (food). Hence, in this case, Skinner's famous pigeons were disguised Pavlovian dogs.

Internal representation

1. A *map of event space in neuronal coding space.

2. A neuronally encoded structured version of the world which could potentially guide behaviour.

'Representation' and 'internal representation' are used in multiple senses in philosophy, linguistics, and the cognitive sciences. The meaning of 'internal representation' as used here deserves, therefore, careful clarification, especially as it is ardently *reductionistic. Generally speaking, 'representation' is the expression of things in one language transformed into another. 'Language' is any set of symbols with rules for putting them together (Marr 1982). We are not engaged here, however, in the formal treatment of representations at large, but rather in the application of the concept to memory research. In the context of brain sciences, 'representation' means encoding of things in the world, such as objects, events, and processes, in neuronal language(s). This encoding is done in a way that enables the nervous system to manipulate the representations, modify and transform them, while maintaining: (a) *parsing*, which is the distinctiveness of things represented, and (b) *structural relationships* between the things represented. Both are needed for useful interaction with the world.

'Representations' have a long and rich history in the philosophy of mind, referring to some kind or another of 'mental images', or elements of an inner 'private language' or a 'language of the mind'. Some aspects of this usage can be traced back to 'phantasia', which meant 'appearance' or 'perception' in Greek philosophies (Irwin 1991; Long 1991; Annas 1992). A limited yet highly varied selection of notable examples includes treatments by British *associationism (Hobbes 1651; Warren 1921), Kant (Kant 1781; Caygill 1995), Bergson (1908), Wittgenstein (McGinn 1997), and more recent philosophers and cognitive theorists (Stich and Warfield 1994; Markman and Dietrich 2000). In modern discourse, it is useful to distinguish between two *levels of treatment of 'representation'. One is cognitive, mental, 'semantic', or 'symbolic'. 'Mental representations' in this sense are theoretical postulates invoked to account for 'propositional attitudes'. The latter are regarded as 'mental sentences' characterized by a specific content, being about something in the world ('intentional'), and conditions that can satisfy the proposition. For example, believing that x, being angry at y, or desiring z are all 'propositional attitudes'. The other level of analysis in which 'representations' are currently used is the computational or implementational level, which some philosophers of the mind refer to as 'subsymbolic'; here representations are activated vectors in neuronal coding space (e.g. Cooper 1973; Churchland and Sejnowski 1992; definition 1). The relevance of 'symbolic' representations to 'subsymbolic' ones is a matter of heated debates (e.g. Fodor and Pylyshyn 1988). Phylogenetic considerations as well as *Ockham's razor lead to the assumption that 'subsymbolic' and 'symbolic' representations are the micro- and the macrolevels of the same brain and mental faculty. This is clearly a case in which interlevel translation via 'correspondence rules' is badly needed (*reduction). For our purpose, we should also note that often, even computational neuroscientists who manipulate 'subsymbolic' representations do hope to explain complex mental states at the end of the day.

The stand taken here is strictly reductive. The tenet is that nervous systems, even the most primitive of them all, had evolved to encode knowledge about the world. 'Knowledge' is used in the most elementary sense and is devoid of *anthropomorphic connotations of awareness and *consciousness. It refers to structured bodies of information possessed by the organism about the world, and capable of setting the organism's reaction to the world. 'World' means both the external milieu and the external states of the organism, and the organism means, specifically, the nervous system. These neuronally encoded structured versions of the world that could potentially guide behaviour are the 'internal

representations' (definition 2). Representation is hence an inherent and fundamental function of *all* nervous systems. Therefore, internal representations are expected to vary tremendously in their complexity. Some are very simple, for example, a neuronal circuit subserving withdrawal in response to pain (e.g. *Aplysia*), encodes a representation of 'no pain' or various intensities of pain, and the appropriate motor response programme.[1] Other internal representations are far more complex, and many, for example representations of propositional attitudes, are highly complex. However, regardless of their complexity, all internal representations as considered here: (a) are encoded in some way or another in neuronal systems; (b) determine the behavioural output to an input; and (c) when altered, may modify the potential to react rather than immediate action or reaction to an input (Dudai 1989, 1992; *learning, *memory).

In computational neurosciences, a further distinction is sometimes being made, between 'representations' and 'internal representations'. This stems from *models of associative networks. The simplest associative network is composed of two layers, input and output. A set of input patterns arriving at the input layer is mapped directly into a set of output patters at an output layer. Under these conditions, the *system is said to lack 'internal representations', because the coding provided by the external world suffices to generate the output. In contrast, when the number of layers increase and intermediate, 'hidden' layers are added, the representation is said to be 'internal' (Rumelhart *et al.* 1986c). However, this distinction does not hold water when real nervous systems are considered. In even the simplest nervous systems, sensory information is recoded and manipulated in neuronal language, be it at the level of cells or circuits (*percept). Therefore, any representation of information by the nervous system should be considered 'internal'.

'Internal representation' is thus a generic term, referring to the most fundamental functional property of nervous systems. Indeed, with evolution, it became manifested in many forms and realized in a variety of codes. But as an umbrella term, it is highly valuable. At the conceptual level, it focuses our attention on the essence of brain function. At the practical level, it guides us to search for representational codes and look for the most important changes, i.e. the representational ones, in systems that learn. Admittedly, we are still short of even a mini-dictionary that translates neuronal activity from representational code into behavioural change.[2] But that day will soon come. And from that day on, the philosopher shall dwell with the neurobiologist, and the mutual interest in 'representations' will no doubt lead them once-in-a-while to dare and attend each other's seminars.

Selected associations: Attention, Binding, Learning, Map, Memory

---

[1] In the intact organism, even in this simple case, the representation encoded in the reflex circuit is in fact but one element in a structured body of information encoded by the nervous system *in toto*.

[2] For a limited selection of expeditions for the neuronal Rosetta stones that might yield this interlevel translation: see Lee *et al.* (1988), Shadlen *et al.* (1996), Dan *et al.* (1998), Kitazawa *et al.* (1998), Stanley *et al.* (1999), Miyashita and Hayashi (2000), and Zhang and Barash (2000); see also **Aplysia, *hippocampus,* and **honeybee*.

Intracellular signal transduction cascade

Any of the specialized molecular pathways in the cell that decode extracellular signals and convert the information into cellular response.

Intracellular signal transduction cascades (*Trānsdūcere*, Latin for 'to transfer'), also termed 'signalling pathways', are intracellular molecular pathways that decode and distribute within the cell specific information conveyed by distinct extracellular *stimuli, such as hormones, growth factors, and *neurotransmitters. (Special types of signal transduction cascades are activated by sensory stimuli in specialized sensory receptor cells, but they will not be further discussed here.) Intracellular signal transduction cascades span multiple cellular compartments, from the cell membrane via the cytoplasm to the nucleus. They are ubiquitous in all species and tissues, and involved in all aspects of cellular life, from differentiation and proliferation, via *homeostasis and *plasticity, to death.

The information in intracellular signal transduction cascades flows from transmembrane *receptor(s) to *systems of interacting enzymes and regulatory proteins, which are linked to each other by adaptor and scaffold proteins to provide the right signal channelling (Koch *et al.* 1991; Niethammer *et al.* 1996; Whitmarsh *et al.* 1998). Specific nodes in these cascades are linked via smaller diffusable substances such as cyclic adenosine-3′,5′-monophosphate (cAMP), *calcium, inositol triphosphate, or eicosanoids (a family of lipid molecules), whose level is modulated following the stimulus–receptor interaction. These substances

distribute and markedly amplify the message. They are termed 'second messengers', as opposed to the 'first messengers' which are the extracellular stimuli (Sutherland *et al.* 1965). About 20 families of intracellular signal transduction cascades have been identified so far. For a tiny selection, to be used merely as an appetizer or an entry point to the intricate world of intracellular signalling cascades, see Cantley *et al.* (1991), Berridge (1993), Hunter (1995), and Seger and Krebs (1995). Furthermore, in real life signalling pathways are intimately interwoven into complex networks (Figure 39) (Weng *et al.* 1999), to the point were their *taxonomy looks like a heroic feat.

The first intracellular signal transduction cascade to be identified was the 'cAMP cascade'. This was during the biochemical revolution that has swept biology in the mid-twentieth century (Sutherland and Rall 1960). It so happened that the same cascade was also later identified as critical for neuronal plasticity mechanisms that are engaged in *development and memory. A few words about the cAMP cascade can therefore illustrate not only the operation of signalling pathways in general, but also their role in neuronal plasticity in particular. Hormones or neurotransmitters that regulate the cAMP cascade, such as catecholamines (e.g. *noradrenaline), do so by binding to specific transmembrane receptors coupled, via a detachable transducer called G-protein (Knall and Johnson 1998), to the enzyme adenylyl cyclase. This enzyme produces cAMP (Sunahara *et al.* 1996; Tesmer *et al.* 1999). Depending on the specific type of G-protein, the level of cAMP in the cell increases or decreases in response to the stimulus. Before it is degraded by the enzyme cAMP-phosphodiesterase, cAMP activates the cAMP-dependent *protein kinase (PKA). It does so by dissociating the inhibitory regulatory subunits from the catalytic subunits of the enzyme. The latter alter target proteins in the cytoplasm and in the nucleus, by phosphorylation, which is the addition of a phosphoryl moiety to proteins (phosphorylation is a ubiquitous 'modifying tool' of intracellular signal transduction cascades). Some of the modified proteins are other enzymes, others are signalling and regulatory molecules, still others are transcription factors,[1] which modulate gene expression.

There are at least two identified mechanisms by which the cAMP cascade can itself sustain information over time, hence serving as a cellular 'information storage' device and potentially contributing to the *persistence of experience-dependent modifications in neuronal circuits. One involves the experience-dependent degradation of the regulatory subunit of

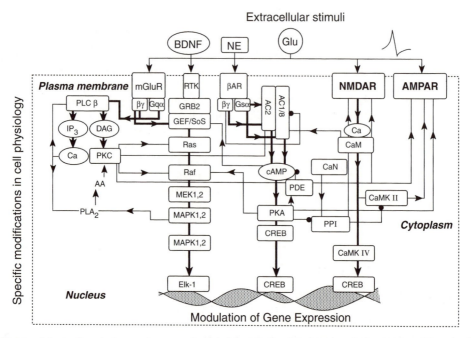

Fig. 39 Intracellular signal transduction cascades convey extracellular information from the cell membrane to the cytoplasm and the nucleus. They interact to form complex signalling networks, whose spatiotemporal pattern of activity at any given points in time controls cellular function. Intracellular signalling cascades in neurons subserve the *acquisition, *consolidation, *persistence (at least in the short-term), and *retrieval of memory. This highly simplified scheme depicts the information flow and the interactions of only a few cascades. Selected acronyms: AC, adenylate cyclase, the enzyme that produces cAMP; AMPAR, NMDAR, mGluR, types of *glutamateric *receptors; βAR, β-adrenergic receptor; βγ, Gqα, Gsα, subunits of G-proteins; BDNF, brain-derived neurotrophic factor, which is a growth factor; CaM, calmodulin, a *calcium-binding protein; CaMK, calcium/calmodulin *protein kinase; *CREB, Elk-1 — transcription factors; Glu, *glutamate; GRB, growth factor-binding protein; MAPK, mitogen-activated protein kinase; NA, noradrenaline; PLC, the enzyme phospholipase C; PKA, protein kinase A; PKC, protein kinase C; Ras, a small G protein; RTK, receptor tyrosine protein kinase. The spike pattern above the membrane on the upper right-hand side represents electrical activity. (Adapted from Weng *et al.* 1999.)

PKA, which results in an increase in the availability of the free, active catalytic subunits. This mechanism has been specifically implicated in memory in conditioning of defensive reflexes in *Aplysia* (Chain *et al.* 1999). The other mechanism involves modulation of gene expression (*immediate early genes). A most prominent substrate of PKA in this case is *CREB, which in many systems is instrumental in switching on the long-term *phase of neuronal plasticity (*Aplysia*, *long-term potentiation). CREB itself is a substrate for multiple signalling pathways. cAMP also regulates certain proteins in a PKA-independent manner (Kawasaki *et al.* 1998). All in all, stimulus-induced modulation of the cAMP cascade results in multiple molecular modifications, some of which involve existing proteins, others the synthesis of new ones.

Research on the role of intracellular signal transduction cascades in plasticity, learning, and memory is overwhelmingly rich (for only a few selected examples, see Thomas *et al.* 1994; Byrne and Kandel 1996; Deisseroth *et al.* 1996; Kornhauser and Greenberg 1997; Berman *et al.* 1998). It is useful, though, to focus on a few generalizations:

1. Intracellular signal transduction cascades encode at the cellular *level facets of the internal *representations* of neurons and neuronal circuits. In the not-yet-available *reductive theories of memory, values representing spatiotemporal patterns of activity of signalling pathways will probably be terms in the 'laws' that *bind representational events at the different levels of operation of the brain (see also 3 below). We do not yet know, however, which parameters of signalling pathways are critical for computations and representations by neurons and neuronal circuits. Such parameters may not necessarily be the

mere level of a second messenger, or the activity of a key enzyme in the cascade (e.g. Barkai and Leibler 1997).

2. The spatial and temporal *complexity* of intracellular signal transduction cascades contributes to the representational and computational repertoire of neurons and hence probably also of neuronal circuits. The combinatorial interaction between cascades increases the intracellular complexity while providing additional options for signalling specificity (e.g. Madhani and Fink 1998; Crabtree 1999; Weng *et al.* 1999). All this also implies that the idea that reduction culminates in simplification is a myth. As every cellular biologist knows, the more we understand the inner working of a cell, the more we complicate life.

3. Intracellular signal transduction cascades *couple* multiple *temporal domains* in the nervous system: they respond to transient biophysical events, occurring at the millisecond range, by inducing biochemical change that last much longer (Dudai 1997*b*; *calcium). They are therefore expected to be instrumental in subserving the transformation of *percepts into *engrams.

4. Intracellular signal transduction cascades provide multiple loci of *integration* for information stemming from different extracellular stimuli. They are therefore candidate 'associative devices' in biological learning machines (Dudai 1994*a*; *coincidence detector).

5. Intracellular signal transduction cascades implement *transitions* from short- to long-term plasticity in the process of memory *consolidation. They are therefore candidate 'consolidation devices' in biological learning machines (*ibid.*).

6. Intracellular signal transduction cascades *retain* information over time by becoming *persistently active long after the activating stimulus had dissipated. They are therefore candidate 'information storage devices' in biological learning machines, at least in the context of short-term memory (*ibid.*).

Bearing all the above in mind, we should still note that, although every neurotransmitter or hormone is expected to modulate the activity of some intracellular signal transduction cascades in its neuronal target, it does not follow that the ensuing cellular alterations are necessarily relevant to learning. Whether they do or not depends on whether the neuronal modifications culminate in a representational change in the neuron and in the neuronal circuit. Lasting modulation of signal transduction cascades is hence always relevant to neuronal maintenance and plasticity, but only sometimes to memory.

Selected associations: Acquisition, Consolidation, Coincidence detector, Receptor, Reduction

---

[1]For what transcription factors are, see *CREB, *immediate early genes.

Ion channel

A protein containing a regulated, selective pore, which mediates the flow of particular ions down their electrochemical gradient from one side of a biological membrane to the other.

Ion channels belong to families of proteins that translocate substances across biological membranes. These families include channels, pumps, and transporters (Aidley 1998). Channels open to permit the flow of ions down their electrochemical gradient. They are fundamental to all types of excitable cells. Pumps drive ions against their electrochemical gradient. Transporters bind specific ligands and undergo a conformational change that releases the ligand on the other side of the membrane (Reith 1997; Amara 1998). In some cases the distinction between a channel and a transporter is blurred (Valverde *et al.* 1992).

Ion channels are classified on the basis of their ion selectivity and the cellular signal that opens or closes ('gates') them (Hille 1992; Rudy and Iverson 1992; Johnston and Wu 1995; Aidley 1998; Conn 1998). *Taxonomy on the basis of the preferred translocated ion distinguishes among sodium (Na^+), potassium (K^+), *calcium (Ca^{2+}), and chloride (Cl^-) channels. Each of these types is further classified on the basis of some phenotypic or functional characteristic, such as kinetics of activation and inactivation, modulation by ligands, or assumed physiological role. Taxonomy on the basis of gating distinguishes between 'voltage'-, 'second messenger'-, and 'agonist'-gated channels. 'Voltage-gated' channels are regulated by membrane potential, 'second messenger-gated' channels by second messengers such as cyclic nucleotides or Ca^{2+} (*intracellular signal transduction cascade), and 'agonist-' or 'ligand-gated' channels by *neurotransmitters (see *receptor). Voltage-gated and second messenger-gated channels are considered as members of the same superfamily. With the advances in molecular biology and the identification of hundreds of genes that encode channel proteins, additional taxonomies are now possible, which take into account previously unknown 'evolutionary kinship' (e.g. Jan and Jan 1992).

Ion channel

The history of research on ion channels is an intriguing chapter in biophysics and neurobiology, now spanning over a century (reviewed in Hille 1992; Armstrong and Hille 1998; Colquhoun and Sakmann 1998). It began with pioneering observations on the phenomenology of excitable membranes (Bernstein 1902, cited in Hille 1992). It then evolved through a set of methodological and conceptual breakthroughs to yield robust, quantitative *models of excitability (e.g. Hodgkin and Huxley 1952). In recent years, a combination of cellular physiology and molecular biology started to unveil the detailed structure–function relationship of individual channels and their interaction with other cellular components. One of the hallmarks of the field is an attempt to comprehend the computations, temporal dynamics, and use-dependent modification of multiple types of channels in neuronal compartments (e.g. Koester and Sakmann 1998). The molecular and cellular biology of ion channels is no doubt one of the most booming subdisciplines of neuroscience. At the time of writing, 5000 papers a year are published on voltage-gated channels alone. Our interest here lies in the role of channels in learning and memory, which narrows the field a bit, but still not enough to do minimal justice to its rich spectrum of themes in a few sentences. Hence, only a few prominent examples will be noted.

It is useful to consider the role of channels in learning and memory in the context of the operation of hypothetical cellular 'learning machines'. Such 'biological machines' are expected to include several types of molecular devices that embody *acquisition, association, storage, and readout of information (Dudai 1993). Cellular acquisition devices are receptors capable of responding to incoming stimuli. Cellular conjuncture devices are *coincidence detectors, associating multiple stimuli. Cellular storage devices are capable of retaining a change in cellular function over time. Readout devices are macromolecules whose activity in *retrieval expresses the experience-dependent alteration in cellular activity. Several of the above roles can be realized in a single molecule.

Ligand-gated channels fit to serve as cellular acquisition devices, although they can also subserve association, retention, and retrieval of information. The

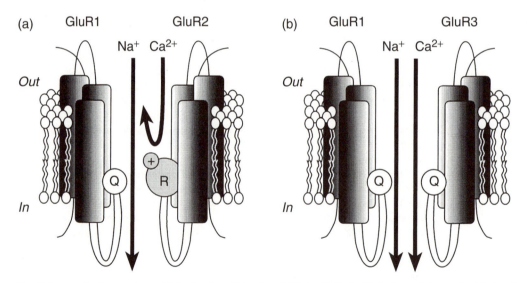

Fig. 40 An example of an agonist-gated (alias ligand-gated) ion channel. This is a highly simplified scheme of the α-amino-3-hydroxy-5-methyl-4-isoxazole propionic acid (AMPA)-type *glutamate receptor, which mediates fast excitatory transmission in the vertebrate brain, and is considered to subserve neuronal plasticity, e.g. *LTP, and possibly memory. For example, it is proposed that AMPA receptor channel availability increases upon use-dependent facilitation of central *synapses (e.g. Nayak *et al.* 1998). It is also a target for experimental memory-enhancing drugs (*nootropics). Glutamate binds to a site on the extracellular domain (not indicated in the drawing), and activates the channel. The channel itself is a central aqueous pore engulfed by multiple types of subunits (GluR) that transverse the neuronal membrane. The pore mediates primarily sodium (Na^+) influx, potassium efflux (not shown), and, depending on the composition of the subunits that form the channel 'wall', *calcium (Ca^{2+}) influx. (a) The activated channel allows only Na^+ in. (b) The activated channel allows calcium influx as well. Q is the amino acid glutamine, R is arginine, which is positively charged and can block calcium entry. Some naturally occurring poisons, e.g. certain spider toxins, can also block calcium permeability. *Out, In*—outer and inner faces of the neuronal membrane, respectively. (Adapted from Pellegrini-Giampietro *et al.* 1997.)

N-methyl-D-aspartate receptor channel (NMDAR) is but one example. This macromolecular complex is composed of two types of subunits, NR1 and NR2. The NR2 subunit contains the recognition site for the *neurotransmitter *glutamate, and NR1, for glycine (Anson *et al.* 1998).[1] The channel is basically the inner pore formed by the aggregation of four subunits (e.g. Rosenmund *et al.* 1998), always containing NR1 and at least one of multiple NR2 subtypes. It is a Ca^{2+} channel that is blocked by magnesium ions under resting conditions. Binding of glutamate activates the receptor but does not remove the magnesium block. To release the latter, the membrane must become depolarized. The NMDA receptor channel is hence a coincident detector, gated by both agonist and voltage (e.g. Seeburg *et al.* 1995). It is assumed to play a decisive part in acquisition of certain forms of *long-term potentiation and learning. The NMDA receptor channel is probably more than a cellular acquisition device; it is known to undergo lasting changes in response to neuronal activation (Rosenblum *et al.* 1996). Some of these changes may not relate to the properties of the current but rather to the interfacing of the complex with intracellular cascades. These post-translational modifications may turn the complex into a device that stores information (i.e. functional change in the nerve cell) over the first few hours after training.

Another example for the role of channels in learning relates to *synaptic facilitation in the circuit that subserves *sensitization of defensive reflexes in *Aplysia (Byrne and Kandel 1996). In this system a major contribution to synaptic facilitation, a cellular analogue of *sensitization, is made by use-dependent enhancement of excitability and neurotransmitter release in the sensory-to-motor synapses in the circuit. It involves state- and time-dependent modulation of voltage-dependent as well as voltage-independent potassium (K^+) conductances. For our purpose, suffice it to note that: (a) K^+ channels are critical for the synaptic change that contributes to the behavioural change in the reflex; (b) these channels play a part in storage (part of the memory at the cellular *level is the lasting modification in K^+ conductances, although the memory-keeping step may not be in the channel itself, but rather in a *protein kinase that keeps modifying the re-modified as well as the newly synthesized copies of channel molecules); and (c) K^+ channels are also readout devices, at least in the short-term (in retrieval, the action potential, which encodes the test stimulus in the sensory neuron, encounters a presynaptic membrane with modified channel(s), and therefore triggers a modified sensory-to-motor signal). Whether the same or similar channels

also play a part in storage and retrieval of long-term memory is still unclear (*late response genes).

The roles of NMDAR in NMDA-dependent LTP and of K^+ channels in learning in *Aplysia* are only selected examples (for additional proven or postulated roles of channels in neuronal and behavioural *plasticity, see Changeux *et al.* 1998; Blackwell and Alkon 1999; MacDermott *et al.* 1999). Computations performed by batteries of channels will surely occupy prominent positions in future *algorithms of biological learning, and in *models that interrelate events at the molecular, cellular, circuit, and behaviour levels (Dudai 1997b; *reduction). And, finally, on the more pragmatic side: ion channels also provide promising targets for cognitive enhancers (Eid and Rose 1999, *nootropics).

Selected associations: Coincidence detector, Neurotransmitter, Receptor, Reduction

---

[1] The reader may wonder why, if this is the case, the receptor channel is named after glutamate rather than glycine. Well, this has partially to do with the history of the field, but is utterly justified: under physiological conditions the concentration of glycine is usually sufficient to occupy the glycine site, whereas the concentration of glutamate is a sensitive function of incoming stimuli and hence critical in determining the activity state of the complex.

Late response genes

Genes whose products are induced in response to extracellular stimulation with a delay of a few hours.

Similarly to *immediate early genes, late response genes (or simply 'late genes') is a term born in virology (Honess and Roizman 1974; Weinheimer and McKnight 1987). In mammalian cells, the expression of immediate early genes is detectable within minutes of stimulation, followed by the expression of delayed early genes, and finally, starting a few hours after stimulation, late response genes (Nathans *et al.* 1988; Lanahan *et al.* 1992). The latter encode a variety of proteins, including transcription factors,[1] enzymes that produce other cellular products (biosynthetic enzymes), enzymes that degrade other proteins (proteases), and cytoskeletal elements.

The role of the late response genes in learning and memory is commonly construed within the prevailing conceptual framework, which describes *consolidation of long-term memory as involving *synaptic remodelling and growth (Goelet *et al.* 1986; Dudai 1989; Milner *et al.*

1998; *development). Only little, however, is currently known about the identity of the late genes that are supposed to subserve these postulated remodelling and growth processes. The problem is that, whereas the careful analysis of the pattern of gene expression during the first hours and days after a training experience is likely to reveal many changes, determining the relevance of these changes to learning and memory is a tricky business.

Here are a few examples of genes whose modulated expression following training lags after that of the immediate early genes. In *Aplysia*, BiP/GRP78, an endoplasmic-reticulum resident protein involved in folding and assembly of newly synthesized proteins (a type of protein termed 'chaperon'), was found to be synthesized in neurons 3 hours after the onset of long-term facilitation, which is considered the cellular analogue of long-term *sensitization (Kuhl et al. 1992). This fits the time course expected of a delayed early gene product. In the same *system, calreticulin, a major *calcium-binding protein in the endoplasmic reticulum, also displayed a delayed time course of post-training expression (Kennedy et al. 1992). In the mammalian brain, 24 hours after the induction of *LTP in the rat *hippocampus, a transient increase was observed in the expression of the messenger RNA (mRNA) of ERK-2 and raf-B, two components of a major *intracellular signal transduction cascade (Thomas et al. 1994). Two gene products with the kinetics of late genes were also reported to increase transiently in the rat hippocampus after water *maze training (Cavallaro et al. 1997). One of these genes encodes the enzyme glutamate dehydrogenase (mRNA peaking at 6 h post-training), the other a ryanodine *receptor (an intracellular *ion channel involved in *homeostasis of cellular calcium; its mRNA peaked at 6–12 hours post-training).

Although it is rather straightforward to try and incorporate the aforementioned findings and the like into *models of synaptic *plasticity and neuronal remodelling, the truth is that the real function of the identified late genes in consolidation and memory is yet unclear. Do their products fulfil a causal role in altering the *internal representations in the neuronal circuits that encode memory? Are they ultimately stabilizing or augmenting the molecular machinery that is altered in the short term, e.g. post-translationally modified ion channels, enzymes (e.g. *protein kinase), or receptors? Are they required for growth processes to supply active neurons with sufficient synaptic space for future computations? Or, alternatively, are they only manifestations of homeostatic processes that provide *nutrients and restore function to the exhausted, stressed cells?

In some potential scenarios, the expression of the late genes could be transient, whereas in others, the cell could commit itself to expressing these genes differently from the time of consolidation on. The distinction between transient and lasting modulation reflects on the candidate role(s) of the late gene products in the cellular machinery of learning. If the modulation of the expression of the late response genes is only transient, the products of these genes could function as cellular switches that trigger the shift of the cell from one stable state to another, but not as storage or *retrieval devices. In contrast, if the expression of these genes itself switches into a different lasting state, this implies that the products of the late genes could be storage or read-out components in the neuronal machinery of memory.

The investigation of identified neurons in identified circuits that subserve identified behaviours, e.g. in *Aplysia*, offers significant advantages in the search for the concrete role of late response genes in the formation of persistent memories. The fast developments in molecular neurobiology ensures that pretty soon, relevant information will become available from *in situ* analysis of identified circuits in the brain of behaving mammals, which learn, for example, to avoid a taste (*conditioned taste aversion), fear a tone (*fear conditioning), or navigate in space (*hippocampus).

Selected associations: Consolidation, Development, Immediate early genes, Phase, Protein synthesis

---

[1]For what transcription factors are, see *CREB and *immediate early genes.

Learning

1. The act or process of induction of a lasting alteration in behaviour or in the behavioural potential, due to the individual's behavioural experience.

2. The *acquisition of information, or the reorganization of information that results in new knowledge.

3. Experience-dependent generation of enduring *internal representations, or lasting modifications in such representations.

The above definitions apply to smart inanimate *systems as well (Moravec 1988; Weng et al. 2001). We limit our discussion, however, to learning in biological organisms with nervous systems. Definition 1 is of the *classical, 'behavioural' type (e.g. Bower and Hilgard 1981). The term 'behavioural experience' in it refers to the wide gamut of sensory, motor, emotional, and cognitive events that take place in a lifetime; the modifier 'behavioural' is introduced to eliminate the need to exclude specifically the experience of disease, injury, and poisoning, which is not traditionally considered to result in learning. Definitions 2 and 3 are variants of the 'informational' type, which refers to the behavioural *performance and behavioural capacity of the organism in terms of 'knowledge' (Plato; James 1890; Squire 1987). Definition 3 (Dudai 1989, 1992) expresses information in terms of internal representations, which are neuronally encoded structured *models of the world that could potentially guide behaviour. This is the preferred definition of learning in this book. This definition implies that *all* learning, be it in *Aplysia* or human, is alteration in an internal representation of some type or another.

The pursuit of internal representations and their modification by experience is thus identified as the crux of learning research, at all the *levels of analysis of learning. In the *reductive analysis of learning, the focus on representational properties is meant to guide the investigator to identify those changes in one level, e.g. the cellular, that cause or reflect the representational alterations in another level, e.g. the circuit. Changes that do not contribute to the representational alteration are irrelevant to learning *per se*, although, of course, they may still be critical for other functions of the nervous system, such as *homeostasis. Further, the assumption in this book is that internal representations are encoded in the spatiotemporal activity of neuronal circuits. Hence, molecules, isolated *synapses, and in many cases even individual nerve cells, are not expected to encode independently appreciable chunks of behaviourally meaningful models of the world. In order to gain behavioural meaning, the contribution of the molecular and cellular change must be construed within the *context of the circuit (Dudai 1989, 1994b).[1]

A caveat is appropriate here. Molecular states within an individual nerve cell clearly have a meaning as well. But this meaning is at a level of organization that does not *suffice* to guide directly behaviour and cognition. 'Meaning' is level-dependent, and levels transmit only limited information to other levels (Simon and Ando 1961).[2] Therefore, although states at level L_i could embody unique meaning at level L_i, these states only provide elementary building blocks, or terms, that are used to construct a variety of meanings at a higher level

L_j. For example, suppose a *neurotransmitter activates its *receptor in a synapse. The downstream cascade culminates in modification of an *ion channel. The identity of the modified channel, determined by the *stimulus and its context, conveys a specific meaning to the synaptic state, e.g. modified channel $X = +\Delta y$ synaptic excitability. But this altered synaptic state could be employed in different ways to construct meaning at the circuit level; for example, it means something very different if the synapse is inhibitory or excitatory, or, at a higher level, if the circuit enhances or suppresses the behaviour. The contribution of the molecular change to the representational meanings ('semantics') hence depends on the synaptic context, and that of the synapse, on the circuit context.

Learning has multiple *dimensions. Here are a selected few:

1. *Innateness.* Some types of learning involve information that is constrained *a priori by innate predispositions. These types of learning are termed 'prepared learning'. They could be ubiquitous in the animal kingdom, for example, *conditioned taste aversion, or species-specific, for example, filial *imprinting, *bird song. Imprinting and bird-song are good examples for the role of *development in learning. Some behavioural definitions of learning explicitly exclude the role of rigid, autonomous developmental programmes, which do not require interaction with the environment, in the modification of behaviour. But it is doubtful whether genuine use-independent programs exist in real-life. The demarcation line between 'development' and 'learning' is inherently blurred. The two types of processes share molecular and cellular hardware (e.g. *immediate early genes), and it is possible to consider learning as an extension of brain development. Still, the position of different types of learning on the 'deterministic', 'preparedness' or 'developmental' axes vary. An example is provided by *classical conditioning. Some instances of classical conditioning involve only augmentation by experience of the response to the conditioned stimulus. This is called α-conditioning (*Aplysia*). In other instances there is no significant pre-conditioning response to the conditioned stimulus. This is *bona fide* classical conditioning. These two types of classical conditioning are hence separable on the axis of 'preparedness'.

2. *Strategy.* There are two major strategies by which a 'teacher' stimulus could modify internal representations (Young 1979; Changeux 1985; Edelman 1987; Dudai 1989). First, the teacher could impose new

order in the system by directly *instructing* it to modify in a certain way. Secondly, it could induce the new structure by *selecting* an internal representation among multiple endogenous variations, i.e. existing 'pre-representations'. The instructive and the selective mechanisms of learning could coexist.

3. *Domain.* Learning may involve the acquisition of motor, sensory, emotional, or cognitive information, or to all of the above.

4. *Associativity.* Certain types of learning are governed solely by the parameters of the unconditioned stimulus. These types of learning therefore do not result in the association of the unconditioned stimulus with other stimuli. Examples are provided by *habituation and *sensitization.[3] Most types of learning involve the formation of association among stimuli or among stimuli and actions. Examples are provided by classical and *instrumental conditioning.

5. *Specificity.* Types and instances of learning differ in the specificity of the acquired information (*generalization, *transfer).

6. *Intention.* We learn about the world either incidentally or intentionally. The term 'incidental learning' has come with time to acquire multiple meanings (Hilgard and Marquis 1940; Spence *et al.* 1950; Morton 1967; Hyde and Jenkins 1973; Craik and Tulving 1975; Glass and Holyoak 1986; Rugg *et al.* 1997; Berman *et al.* 1998). These are: (a) learning that occurs unintentionally as a by-product of a sensory, motor, or cognitive process; (b) learning in the absence of *attention; (c) learning in the absence of an identified *reinforcer; and (d) an experimental situation in which the *subject is not told that memory would be tested later. Note that in (c) the lack of an identified *reinforcer is used as a *criterion; however, in real life, the reinforcer is always there, only hidden, either in the context or in the endogenous activity of brain circuits.

7. *Awareness.* The presence or absence of *conscious awareness is a major criterion in the *zeitgeist *taxonomy of learning and memory. Suffice it to note in the present context that conscious awareness in learning does not entail conscious awareness in retention and *retrieval, and vice versa (*declarative memory). When information is acquired in an incidental manner, without awareness of what has been learned, the process is termed 'implicit learning', as opposed to 'explicit learning' (Seger 1994; Whittlesea and Wright 1997). The distinction between 'implicit' and 'explicit' learning has been used extensively in tasks involving rule learning in

humans, e.g. grammar learning. In these experiments 'explicit' came to mean that deliberate instructions are given to search for rules that underlie the presented material, whereas 'implicit' is when the subject learns without such instructions but acquires information about the underlying rules nevertheless (Reber 1967; Berry and Broadbent 1988). The term 'latent learning' is occasionally applied to either incidental or implicit learning (Stevenson 1954), but this is not recommended, because 'latency' does not necessarily imply neither incidentality nor implicitness of learning (Dudai 1989; *insight).

8. *Novelty.* Certain types or tokens of information are unexpected, others are. A useful rule of thumb is that the more *surprising the information, the better it is learned (*algorithm). The novelty dimension of the stimulus to be learned should not, however, be confused with naiveté of the subject. Even when the role of innateness is recognized (1 above), many investigators still err to think that the subject's brain enters the new experimental situation as a blank surface (*tabula rasa*, Locke 1690). This rarely is the case; almost always the subject brings to the task knowledge and expectations (*a priori). This is now evident even at the cellular level. For example, whether a modest input induces a long-term change in the target neuron (*long-term potentiation) depends on what the same cell has experienced 2–3 h before (Frey and Morris 1998). It is hence appropriate to consider even new learning experiments as manipulations of an already opinionated brain (*palimpsest).

9. *Rate.* Certain types or instances of learning occur in a single trial, as a step function (*flashbulb memory). Others are incremental and require repetitive training. An example for the latter is rote learning (Hebb 1949; Irion 1959), manifested in the acquisition of *skill. The kinetics of learning is commonly depicted as a learning curve. This is the representation of performance, which itself is taken to represent learning, as a function of the amount of experience (e.g. Figure 41, p. 144).

10. *Fate.* Depending on its type and on the parameters of acquisition, learning could result in *engrams that last from seconds up to engrams that last for a lifetime (*percept, *consolidation, *taxonomy). Furthermore, in some types of learning the information is a priori intended to subserve only the transient task and then be *forgotten (*working memory).

The multiplicity of dimensions clearly hints at the richness of the computational theories, neuronal algorithms and their cellular and molecular implementation, which one should expect to identify in neuronal circuits that learn. It also implies that a master solution to the mechanisms of learning is unlikely to exist.

Selected associations: Acquisition, Engram, Development, Internal representation, Memory

---

[1]Although there is no doubt that the contribution of individual neurons to a representation must be evaluated in the context of the entire circuit, the role of single neurons in encoding representations is still unsettled. In any case, this role is circuit and task dependent. Single neurons may execute meaningful computations, but it is unlikely that they encode meaningful parts of complex representations. For further discussion, including estimates of the number of neurons that encode a representation, see *cell assembly.

[2]Theoretically, one might envisage a computational system with practically unlimited *capacity that could read simultaneously all the information in all the levels of a biological system. Such a system is however impractical, and, most importantly, disposes of the advantage of being able to save computational resources by using only the important information extracted at each level.

[3]It is doubtful, however, whether pure nonassociativity exists in nature; see discussion in *habituation.

Learning set

1. **A learned tendency to follow a particular cognitive strategy in response to a particular type of *stimulus.**

2. **Learning to learn.**

3. **Progressive improvement in the rate of learning of successive object discrimination problems of a given type, culminating in single-trial learning of novel problems of that type.**

The roots of 'learning set' can be traced back to the beginning of the twentieth century, to a group of psychologists at Würzburg University, Germany, known collectively as 'The Würzburg School'. They pioneered experimental approaches to thought processes (Boring 1950). In the course of their investigation they noted that with proper preparation of a *subject for a mental task, upon the presentation of the stimulus the thoughts of the subject would run off automatically to perform the task. This was taken to indicate that the particular task and the instructions that have preceded

it ('*Aufgabe*' in German) imposed certain constraints on *attention and thought, yielding a tendency to use a particular mental strategy. This learned tendency to respond in a particular manner to a type of stimulus was termed '*Einstellung*' (German for 'set', 'attitude').

For a while, the concept of a cognitive or mental 'set' had been used rather liberally by multiple schools in psychology, dealing with topics as diverse as perception, conditioning, volition, or neurosis. This cast some doubts on the usefulness of 'set', leading Gibson (1941) to comment that 'The concept of set or attitude is a nearly universal one in psychological thinking despite the fact that the underlying meaning is indefinite, the terminology chaotic, and the usage by psychologists highly individualistic'. It was Harlow (1949) who reinvigorated the concept by focusing on one aspect of it, which he termed 'learning set', and devising *assays to quantify it. Harlow felt uneasy with the fact that many in the contemporary field of animal learning study their subjects in short, isolated learning episodes only. He called this approach the '*Blitzkrieg*' technique. Animals, so ran his argument, do not learn about the world merely by taking isolated snapshots of it; they are expected to benefit from *transfer from one situation to another and ultimately form some *generalizations and predictive 'hypotheses' that facilitate the proper response to familiar types of situations. This, at least, is the way we humans behave, and there is no reason to assume *a priori that other species are radically different.

What Harlow did was to place *monkeys in a special test enclosure ('Wisconsin general test apparatus', *delay task), and present them with a series of visual discrimination food–reward problems. In each problem, the monkey was required to choose on a front tray the rewarded one of two different objects. Different pairs of objects were used for each individual problem, and the left–right position of the rewarded object was varied in an overall balanced manner. Each of the problems was run for multiple trials. At the beginning, it took the monkeys many trials to respond correctly. But then, a remarkable increase was noted in *performance, reaching after a while > 95% successful discrimination on the second trial of each new problem (Harlow 1949). Harlow suggested that the remarkable level of performance was achieved because the monkey 'learned to learn'. He defined this 'metalearning' as the formation of a 'learning set'. Harlow further found that the monkey could acquire a set that allowed for swift alternation of the response tendency. This was done by using 'discrimination reversal' problems. In this type of problem, the subject was first run on a discrimination problem for a number of trials, but then the reward value of the stimuli was reversed for another series of trials, i.e. the stimulus previously correct was made incorrect and vice versa. After experiencing a number of problems of this type, the monkey learned to respond correctly already in the second trial on the discrimination reversal type of problem. It is noteworthy that in spite of the fact that the discrimination reversal task might have been expected to be at least as difficult, the learning set was actually formed more rapidly (Figure 41); this was attributed to interproblem *transfer from the earlier discrimination training.

The experimental procedure developed by Harlow, namely measuring the improvement in performance on successive discrimination problems, gave rise to a restricted operational definition of 'learning set', which is frequently used in the literature (definition 3, 'discrimination learning set'). However, definitions 1 and 2 are more comprehensive and capture the essence of the concept better. For the change in behaviour noted by Harlow and by many investigators after him (Hodos 1970) could be safely construed as manifestation of the ability of the organism to acquire a response strategy, and not only the particular stimulus–*reinforcer association in an isolated task (*instrumental conditioning). It is important to appreciate that the acquisition of a learning set is conventionally measured in terms of the number of *problems* solved before the subject has acquired the postulated response strategy, just as the formation of *habit is measured in terms of the number

of *trials* required to acquire the specific habit. Hence the former yields an *interproblem* 'learning curve' (*learning), whereas the latter an *intraproblem* learning curve. It is also noteworthy that the formation of a learning set involves gradual improvement in performance, and this is different from *insight, in which an hypothesis or concept form abruptly after a period of latency. It is not a grave sin, though, to refer to the acquisition of a learning set as sluggish insight.

What is it that is actually acquired in a learning set? Harlow himself entertained the idea that the subject acquires the *skill of eliminating inappropriate response tendencies ('error factors', Harlow 1959). Others have emphasized that in forming a learning set, the subject acquires a conceptual understanding of the type of problem (Restle 1958; Levine 1959; Schusterman 1962; Warren 1966). In the case of the types of discrimination problems described above (but not necessarily in other types of problems), the evidence points to the acquisition of an hypothesis, or abstract *algorithm, of the type 'win-stay, lose-shift': the subject remembers the outcome of the preceding trial as being either rewarded ('win') or unrewarded ('lose'), and selects on the next trial the same *cue if previously rewarded ('win-stay') or the alternative cue if unrewarded ('lose-shift').[1] Note that this requires the use of *working memory, and is expected to be sensitive to intertrial interval in each problem (e.g. Kamil and Mauldin 1975).

As the acquisition of a learning set implies mastering some type or another of abstract rules, it was soon adapted as an intelligence test in comparative animal psychology. For the purpose of comparison, a useful convention is to measure the mean per cent correct on trial 2 of a given problem as a function of the number of problems experienced of the same type (Figure 41; success on trial 2 reflects single trial learning because trial 1 is the instruction trial). The idea is that the more problems required to form a set, the duller is the brain. This type of *assay has been applied to estimate the difference in intelligence in phylogeny, ontogeny, and among individual members of a species, even in *Homo sapiens* (Hayes *et al.* 1953; Harlow 1959; Warren 1966; Doty *et al.* 1967; Hodos 1970). Learning sets have also been used as *model behaviours to explore the role of identified brain organs, such as *cortex, *hippocampus, thalamus and striatum, in advanced learning capabilities in various species (Riopelle *et al.* 1953; Chow 1954; Staubli *et al.* 1984; Eichenbaum *et al.* 1986; Lu and Slotnick 1990; Tremblay *et al.* 1998). However, several caveats are appropriate. First, it is advisable to keep *Ockham's razor in mind, and scrutinize the data even if they do suggest a learning set. Over the years, some

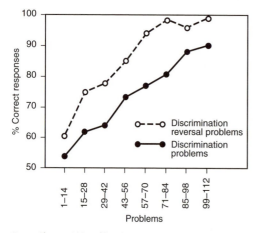

Fig. 41 The acquisition of learning sets. Learning curves of discrimination (closed circles) and discrimination reversal problems (open circles) in the monkey are plotted as responses on trial 2 in each problem as a function of successive groups of problems. The discrimination reversal learning set was formed more rapidly, probably due to interproblem training *transfer (reproduced from Harlow 1949).

interesting debates have taken place in the scientific literature concerning the question whether a marked improvement in performance by a given species on successive presentation of a given type of problem indeed proves the formation of a *bona fide* learning set (Menzel and Juno 1982; Schrier and Thompson 1984; Reid and Morris 1992; Slotnick 1994). Second, the above notwithstanding, it is important to remember that species differ in the way they sense the world and in the importance they assign to different kinds of problems. It is therefore unlikely that a single type of discrimination problem will do justice to the intelligence of different species. For example, primates are visual animals, whereas for the rat the world is mostly smell and taste and touch. It is hence not surprising to discover that if learning sets are at all formed in the rat, *performance on series of odour discriminations rather than visual discriminations is the place to look for them (Slotnick and Katz 1974).

Selected associations: A Priori, Classic, Habit, Subject, Transfer

---

[1]For more on this and similar types of response strategies, see *habit.

Level

1. A stratum in a hierarchy.

2. A bounded interval on a scale of structural, functional, or conceptual complexity.

'Level' originated in *lībella*, diminutive of 'balance' in Latin. It was adapted to denote gadgets used to establish flat surfaces. That led to the use of 'level' to denote a stratum in a hierarchy, because components at the same level are considered, mostly *metaphorically, to be at the same height or rank. The question whether the *taxonomy of levels in a *system follows natural divisions or is merely a convenient *artefact of human cognition, is an issue that needs to be addressed separately in each case. Whatever the particular answer is, in real-life levels in any system are dependent on each other. But in practice, in the analysis and *modelling of systems, the borders between the levels are delineated in an attempt to optimize their apparent segregation and permit their separate treatment. This ordinarily involves the assumption that variables at other levels are for all practical means either constant or irrelevant. This is referred to as the *ceteris paribus* assumption (Latin for

'*other things being equal*'). It is a risky heuristic that must be retested from time to time by using the appropriate *control procedures.[1]

When neuroscientists say 'level' they refer to one of three things: level of *organization*, level of *processing*, and level of description and *analysis* (Dudai 1989; Churchland and Sejnowski 1992). 'Level of organization' refers to the structural hierarchy in the nervous system. It is the most common usage of 'level' in the popularization of science. A conventional top-down organizational hierarchy depicts the nervous system as composed of behavioural, brain, organ, circuit, cellular, and molecular levels. These levels differ in their physical scale, ranging from metres (behaviour) to angstroms (molecules). It is useful to note that on the one hand, a higher level of organization means a higher complexity of the system as a whole, but on the other, the complexity within each of the levels is still immense. For example, it is evident that the biophysical properties of single neurons, and the molecular networks within a single cell, are amazingly intricate (Alberts *et al.* 1994; Aidley 1998). Therefore, transition from the brain or the circuit to the cellular or the molecular level *per se* does not really imply simplification; hence one should not confuse 'reductive steps' with 'simplifying steps' (Dudai 1989; *reduction).

'Levels of processing' refer to the neuroanatomical and physiological hierarchy of information processing in the nervous system. A bottom-up view depicts them from the lower to the higher. 'Higher' means a larger distance from sensory receptors, or a more global representation of an item. Brain systems that process sensory information used to be portrayed as strictly hierarchical, whereby information from 'low level' centres converges on 'high level' centres (*homunculus). This picture is currently replaced with the one that portrays central sensory systems as concurrent streams of processing, with 'low level' *cortical areas already dealing with rather complex attributes (e.g. DeYoe *et al.* 1994). Picturing *perceptual systems in the brain as neuroanatomical 'pyramids', each composed of low strata supporting higher ones, is thus considered today as a somewhat naive simplification. Still, at a certain stage the processing is expected to culminate in a more global *internal representation (*binding). 'Levels of processing' is also a concept used, initially without explicit neuroanatomical or physiological connotations, in the theory of memory (Craik and Lockhart 1972).[2] The proposal is that processing of sensory information in the brain begins with 'shallow' levels and proceeds to 'deeper', cognitive ones, and that the deeper the processing, the more robust is the resulting *engram.

For example, phonological processing of a word could be regarded as 'shallow' and semantic as 'deep', and the latter is bound to generate stronger memories than the former. A major conclusion from such a model is hence that the levels of processing engaged in the first second in the life of a memory determine much about the whole future of that memory (*acquisition, *retrieval).

'Levels of description' or 'analysis' are concepts that refer to the operation of the brain as an information-processing, problem-solving machine. An influential account of such levels is that of Marr (1982). He distinguished three levels in the operation of any machine carrying out information-processing tasks: (a) the level of the *computational theory*, involving the goals of computations and the logic of the strategy to carry them out; (b) the level of *representations and *algorithms*, i.e. how can the computations be implemented in terms of 'input' and 'output' representations and of the algorithms for the transformation of 'input' to 'output'; and (c) the level of *hardware implementation*, i.e. the way the representations and algorithms are implemented in the 'nuts and bolts', or 'silicon and wires', or 'neurons and *channels' of the machine. For example, consider the implementation in a brain circuit of a Hebbian algorithm by an *long-term potentiation-like *synaptic mechanism that involves *calcium currents and subtypes of *glutamate receptors.

Three comments are appropriate here: first, the same computation can be performed in different species, or in different circuits in the same species, by different algorithms. Similarly, the same algorithm may be implemented by different molecular, cellular, and circuit devices. For example, an algorithm of multiplication may be implemented in an AND gate in two different systems, but the AND gates may be realized by different *coincidence detectors in each of the systems. Second, the complexity of algorithm should not be expected to be a function of the complexity of the brain or the behaviour. This means that a certain task may be implemented by a cumbersome algorithm in a simple brain but by a simple algorithm in a complex brain. In other words, *simple systems are not guaranteed to yield simple solutions. And third, the different conceptual levels of analysis, i.e. the computational, algorithmic, and implementational levels, could be identified at any level of processing or organization in the nervous system. This means that even cellular and molecular neurobiologists will soon have to learn to struggle with information-processing theories, representations, and algorithms, if they ever wish to understand what neurons do (e.g. Bray 1995).

Note that the term 'levels of analysis' is also used in the literature in a more colloquial manner, to simply indicate the level in which the research is performed by an experimenter. In this context, reference to the afore-mentioned 'organizational levels' is the most common. The choice of the level of experimental analysis depends on a personal *bias, anchored in philosophical attitudes, training, expertise, *paradigms, zeitgeist, opportunities, and chance—not necessarily in that order. The choice of the level of experimental analysis places constraints on the expected outcome of research programmes and academic careers. For example, in the field of memory research, adherence to a molecular level of analysis means that the research will yield, if successful, insight on general building blocks of *plasticity and on synaptic information-storage mechanisms, but probably not on the specific mechanisms that embody a specific internal representation. For the latter, circuit analysis is required (Dudai 1989, 1992). And *vice versa*, a choice of a brain and organ level is not expected to illuminate the physiological implementation of synaptic algorithms. A research programme that aims at elucidating learning and memory as they really are, i.e. multilevel phenomena, must therefore combine the expertise of multiple subdisciplines, ranging from molecular biology to experimental psychology to modelling. How to integrate all these disciplines in a coherent project, and especially how to make their practitioners talk the same language and comprehend each other, is itself not an easy problem. It surely cannot be solved at the administrative level.

Selected associations: Binding, Homunculus, Reduction, System, Taxonomy

---

[1]The *ceteris paribus* assumption is further encountered in *system. For selected approaches to levels, their taxonomy, decomposability, and other assumptions required in dealing with them in a variety of system types, see Bunge (1960), Simon and Ando (1961), Simon (1962), Fisher and Ando (1963), Whyte *et al.* (1969), Mesarovic *et al.* (1970), and Yagil (1999).

[2]For the application of this concept in *functional neuroimaging studies, see Kapur *et al.* (1994).

Limbic system

A disputed concept, referring to an interconnected collection of cortical and subcortical structures in the medial parts of the mammalian brain that are implicated in autonomic, emotional, and cognitive functions.

Limbus is *rim* or *border* in Latin. Already in 1664, Willis described the brain area that surrounds the brainstem as 'the limbus' (cited in Witter *et al.* 1989). He was followed by Broca, who termed more or less the same part of the brain as the 'great limbic lobe' (Broca 1878; see also Schiller 1992). Later, MacLean (1952) referred to the limbic lobe together with subcortical structures interconnected to it as 'the limbic system', or 'visceral brain'. MacLean further suggested that this visceral brain processes emotions and guides some 'primitive' types of behaviour essential for the preservation of the individual and the species (MacLean 1970). With time, multiple lines of evidence have led to the notion that the limbic system plays a central part in learning and memory. Interestingly, the idea that 'limbic' is associated with memory echoes Dante; *Limbo* was the first circle in Inferno, and according to an hermeneutic analogy made between the circles and the human body, Limbo was the site of memory (Dante 1314/1996).

The definition of the limbic system given above is rather vague. This is intentionally so. Almost from the outset, no two authorities agreed on the precise anatomy and function of the limbic system (Swanson 1987; LeDoux 1991; Kotter and Meyer 1992). A popular, *classical morphological description of the limbic system portrayed it as being composed of two interconnected circuits (Livingston and Escobar 1971). One circuit is centred on the *hippocampal formation, and is called the medial or 'Papez circuit' (Papez 1937). In this circuit, information flows from the entorhinal cortex to the hippocampal formation, from there through the fornix to the anterior thalamus (directly or via the mammillary bodies), from the anterior thalamus to the cingulate gyrus, and from there back to the entorhinal *cortex via the cingulum bundle. The other major limbic circuit, called the basolateral or 'Yakovlev circuit' (Yakovlev 1948), is centred on the *amygdala. It includes the orbitofrontal, insular, and anterior temporal cortical areas, together with their interconnections to the amygdala and the dorsomedial nucleus of the thalamus.

Over the years, two major trends have characterized the research on the limbic system. The first involved the attribution of a growing number of physiological and behavioural deficits to limbic dysfunction. This was done on the basis of the effect of circumscribed brain damage resulting from disease, injuries, and lesions. The identified deficits were related to a large spectrum of normal functions. At first the emphasis was on emotion and sociopathology (Papez 1937; Kluver and Bucy 1938). These limbic functions are now attributed mostly to the *amygdala (LeDoux 1991). Later the

discussion came to stress also visceral functions and sensory integration (MacLean 1952, 1970), as well as learning and memory (Scoville and Milner 1957). In the context of learning and memory, certain limbic lesions were specifically related to *amnesia, and limbic functions to both non*declarative (Pavlovian *fear conditioning) and declarative memory (e.g. see Fernandez *et al.* 1999 for a recent study of real-time tracking of declarative memory formation in limbic circuits). One possibility raised was that limbic circuits contribute to the evaluation of saliency and importance of neocortical input, and instruct neocortical circuits whether to form lasting *internal representations of that input (Dudai 1989).

A second trend, a natural outcome of the first, involved the expansion of the limbic system concept to include more and more brain regions interconnected with the 'original' limbic components, up to a stage in which very substantial portions of the brain were included (LeDoux 1991; Kotter and Meyer 1992). This growing scope of the limbic system concept, combined with the generality and fuzziness of the functions attributed to the system, have contributed to a growing concern whether the limbic system represents a natural structure or rather is an artificial concept (*taxonomy). Furthermore, the mere usefulness of the concept was questioned (e.g. Brodal 1981; LeDoux 1991, 1996; Kotter and Meyer 1992; Blessing 1997). Judging by our current knowledge of the functional anatomy of the widespread so-called 'limbic' structures and circuits, and of their multifaceted role in physiology and behaviour, the conclusion might indeed be reached that the 'limbic system' does not exist in reality as such. As Kotter and Meyer (1992) put it, '(it) is a non-empirical explanatory concept for poorly understood brain functions'. This is, however, a case in which a concept, in spite of being at some odds with reality, succeeded in stimulating tremendously influential research. The use of the modifier 'limbic' in the scientific literature is still prominent (*ibid.*). It even found its way long ago into the popular press.

So what is it that still keeps the limbic system concept going? Some suggest that whatever the real limbic system is, it is useful to think in terms of 'limbic-ness' (Isaacson 1992), which refers to basic and 'primitive' brain functions in the domain of emotions, *homeostatic behaviour, and phylogenetically ancient drives such as hunger and sex (e.g. MacLean 1970). This 'limbic-ness' is different from 'neocortical-ness', which involves high-order processing and retention of sensory and cognitive representations. Others may claim that such a division is artificial, simplistic, and misleading.

For example, the *hippocampus is a classical limbic structure, but is involved in functions that are characterized by more 'neocortical-ness' than 'limbic-ness'; so are 'limbic' cortici (e.g. Suzuki *et al.* 1993).

After so many viable years it is unlikely that the limbic system notion will suddenly disappear. It will probably give way to more sophisticated classifications of brain structure and function. But in that respect it does not differ from some other concepts of brain organization and function, that may reflect an artificial entity rather than a natural one (e.g. Kirkpatrick 1996).

Selected associations: Amygdala, Amnesia, Fear conditioning, Hippocampus

Long-term potentiation

An increase in *synaptic efficacy that persists for hours to more than days after the delivery of a brief induction *stimulus.

In the field of memory research, interest in activity dependent lasting synaptic *plasticity is a natural sequel to the tenet that learning involves synaptic modifications. Over the years, cellular physiologists have identified a number of stimulation protocols that unveil synaptic plasticity (Johnston and Wu 1995). For example, in many types of synapses, when a pair of stimuli are delivered sequentially within a fraction of a second, the response to the second stimulus is larger than that to the first (del Castillo and Katz 1954). This is 'paired-pulse facilitation' (PPF). Stimulation by a train of stimuli ('tetanic stimulation') could result in augmentation of synaptic response that lasts seconds to minutes (Larrabee and Bronk 1947; Lloyd 1949). This is 'post-tetanic potentiation' (PTP). The short life of PPF and PTP, and the fact that they were initially investigated in synapses that do not connote learning such as the neuromuscular junction, did not stir much excitation in the memory community. This situation changed when investigators in the laboratory of Per Andersen in Oslo noted that in the *hippocampus, certain tetanic stimulation protocols resulted in enhanced synaptic efficacy (Lomo 1966; Andersen and Lomo 1967), which could *persist for hours to days (Bliss and Lomo 1973; Bliss and Gardner-Medwin 1973).[1] Enter long-term potentiation (LTP).

LTP is a generic term. It is now used to refer to a heterogeneous form of neuronal plasticity observed in many types of synapses. Many neuroscientists consider LTP a mechanism that implements learning, short-term and intermediate-term memory at the cellular *level. But by no means is this accepted by all. To gain insight into the phenomenon and the controversy that encircles it, it helps to recall the original observation. Bliss and Lomo (1973) stimulated the perforant path leading from the entorhinal *cortex to the dentate gyrus in the hippocampal formation of the anaesthetized rabbit, and found that after a conditioning train at 100 Hz for 3–4 s or 10–20 Hz for 10–15, the dentate response to a single afferent volley was potentiated for hours, and in the unanaesthetized rabbit, even for weeks (Bliss and Gardner-Medwin 1973). This change was noted in the amplitude of the excitatory postsynaptic potential (EPSP) and in the amplitude and latency of the population spike (EPSP-to-spike potentiation, abbreviated E–S potentiation). This implied that both the synaptic strength and postsynaptic excitability have changed. LTP was hence discovered by applying non-physiological stimuli in a paradigm that did not involve learning. Bliss and Lomo (1973) were well aware of that, but also realized the potential of their finding: 'Our experiments show that there exists at least one group of synapses in the hippocampus whose efficiency is influenced by activity that may have occurred several hours previously—a time-scale long enough to be potentially useful for information storage. Whether or not the intact animal makes use in real life of a property which has been revealed by synchronous, repetitive volleys to a population of fibers … is another matter'. With time, variants of LTP have been demonstrated in other hippocampal synapses, the Schaffer collateral/commissural synapses in area CA1 and the mossy fibres synapses in area CA3. It was also demonstrated in other brain regions, including the cerebral cortex, but hippocampal LTP remained the dominant *model of activity dependent synaptic plasticity in the mammalian brain (Bliss and Collingridge 1993; Nicoll and Malenka 1995). The Yin of the LTP-Yang is long-term depression (LTD), elicited after specific stimulation protocols in synapses that can or cannot sustain LTP (Bear and Malenka 1994; Lisberger 1998). A dominant model system for investigating LTD and its potential role in learning is the *cerebellum.

Breakthroughs in understanding LTP started to emerge when the analysis shifted from the macroscopic to the microscopic level. This benefited from the use of brain slices, and from a variety of new techniques in cellular physiology, neuropharmacology, molecular biology, and *neurogenetics. In the hippocampus, LTP appears in two major forms, one in which induction is dependent on *N*-methyl-D-aspartate (NMDA) *receptors (NMDAR, *glutamate), the other on which it does not. The original dentate LTP as well as CA1 LTP are NMDAR dependent, whereas CA3 LTP is NMDAR independent. Here is a partial sketch of the current picture of NMDAR-dependent LTP, with a few comparisons with NMDAR-independent LTP.

1. *Induction*. LTP is induced by glutamate activation of NMDAR under conditions that remove the magnesium block from the NMDAR-*ion channel (*coincidence detector). This leads to calcium (Ca^{2+}) influx, resulting in activation of Ca^{2+}-/calmodulin-activated *protein kinase (CaMKII) and other kinase systems, and in the modulation of activity of a variety of *intracellular signal transduction cascades. Other types of glutamate receptors, such as the metabotropic receptors, might also be required in the induction *phase. The site of induction is postsynaptic. In contrast, NMDAR-independent LTP is probably induced by presynaptic Ca^{2+} influx.

2. *Maintenance and expression*. Short-term changes ('early LTP', less than an hour) involve modification in existing proteins. Longer-lasting LTP ('late LTP') involves modulation in gene expression (Frey *et al.* 1988; Nguyen *et al.* 1994; *immediate early genes, *late response genes, *protein synthesis). In both phases, a major part is played by glutamatergic receptors of the α-amino-3-hydroxy-5-methyl-4-isoxazole propionic acid (AMPA) type (APMAR). They are phosphorylated (Barria *et al.* 1997), and their synthesis (Nayak *et al.* 1998) and density in the synapse (Hayashi *et al.* 2000) increase. This results in enhanced AMPAR-mediated transmission. In addition, growth processes possibly contribute to enhanced synaptic efficacy (e.g. Andersen and Soleng 1998). All in all, the long-term processes involve an intricate step-wise dialogue among synaptic and cell-wide mechanisms (Frey and Morris 1997; Dudai and Morris 2000). Although the focus of change in NMDAR-dependent LTP is postsynaptic, presynaptic mechanisms, possibly regulated by a message that travels from the postsynaptic to the presynaptic terminal ('retrograde message', e.g. nitric oxide), also contribute to potentiation. In contrast, in NMDAR-independent LTP, the major site of expression is assumed to be presynaptic, involving enhanced transmitter release, which is induced by activation of intracellular signal transduction cascades such as the cAMP cascade (Nicoll and Malenka 1995).

The aforementioned sketch does no justice to the potential complexity of LTP (to tell the truth, discovering that a molecule is involved in LTP is now the rule rather than the exception; Sanes and Lichtman 1999).

Still, it conveys the flavour of the core mechanisms involved. The $64000 question (inflation notwithstanding, Stevens 1998) is whether LTP implements memory. The phenomenology of LTP does look attractive. In addition to the initiation by a brief stimulus and to poststimulus persistence, other properties of LTP are frequently taken as evidence that it is indeed related to learning. These properties include: (a) *input specificity* (LTP is restricted to the conditioning path; Andersen *et al.* 1977; Lynch *et al.* 1977); (b) *cooperativity* (LTP has a stimulus intensity threshold, below which only PTP may develop, and above which LTP is a function of the number of activated fibres; McNaughton *et al.* 1978); and (c) *associativity* (activation of adjacent, convergent afferents can yield greater LTP in one of these afferents, and, furthermore, a weak input, incapable of sustaining LTP, can sustain it if activated concurrently with a strong stimulus to another, convergent path; Levy and Steward 1979; Gustafsson and Wigstrom 1986). Note, however, that the similarity argument suffers from the *homunculus fallacy: it assumes that within the brain resides a miniature creature, the long-term potentiated synapse, which displays the properties of the behaving organism, whereas *reduction does not entail that the part displays the properties of the whole. We must look for better arguments. Those were supplied by a combination of *methods. Here is a sample:

1. *Correlation*. Auditory *fear conditioning, which is subserved by the *amygdala, alters the auditory evoked responses in the amygdala in the same way as LTP induction. The change parallels the acquisition of the fear behaviour, and does not occur if the tone and the shock remain unpaired (Rogan *et al.* 1997).

2. *Perturbation*. This is a popular approach. Drugs that block NMDAR also block certain types of learning, including *maze tasks that depend on hippocampal function (Morris *et al.* 1986). Some versions of these tasks are, however, unaffected (Bannerman *et al.* 1995). A few mutations that impair LTP impair learning (Silva *et al.* 1992), others do not (Zamanillo *et al.* 1999). The pharmacological and genetic data can be used to show that certain cellular components and mechanisms are shared by LTP and learning, but not that both are the same. A different type of interventional approach is based on the prediction that if learning is subserved by LTP, driving all the synapses to their maximal LTP might saturate the *capacity of the system and block the ability to acquire new information. Saturation of hippocampal LTP in the rat was indeed found to impair maze learning (E.I. Moser *et al.* 1998). The inverse is

also true: training rats on a reach-and-grasp motor task results in reduced ability of the neurons in the motor cortex to sustain LTP, as if learning has exploited a part of the LTP capacity in that region (Rioult-Pedotti *et al.* 2000).

3. *Modelling.* The concept of LTP is useful in some models that mimic the performance of brain circuits (e.g. Mehta *et al.* 2000).

So what are the conclusions? It is heated debate. The participants are divided into three congregations: those that adhere to St Anselm's motto, *credo ut intelligam* (Anselm ~ 1100), 'unless I believe I shall not understand'; the opposing atheists, admittedly a minority; and in between, those that do not feel that questioning the role of LTP in learning is blasphemy. All in all, the

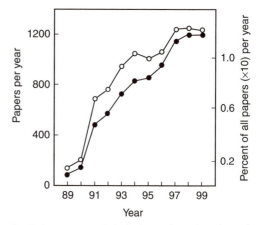

Fig. 43 Long-term potentiation in the popularity of LTP. The graph depicts the number of papers that mentioned either 'long-term-potentiation' or 'LTP' in their title, abstract or keywords, per year, in the period 1989–99 (Full circles). The percentage of these papers of all the papers listed in the Science Citation Index throughout this period is also presented (open circles). Both plots show a more than an order of magnitude increase in the popularity of LTP over that decade, with an almost step function increase in popularity between 1990 and 1991. Note, however, the plateau in the last years in the graph, which appears also to be retained in the year 2000 (data not shown). This indicates that the interest in LTP, or the capacity of the neuroscience community to deal with it, may have reached at least a temporary saturation. About a third of all the papers that have mentioned LTP throughout the above decade also referred specifically to learning and memory. See also *zeitgeist. (Compiled from the Science Citation Index Expanded, Web of Science V. 4.1, ©ISI, Institute for Scientific Information.)

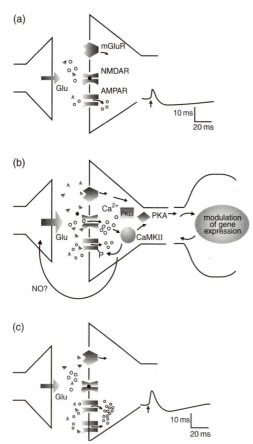

Fig. 42 A highly simplified scheme of the cellular mechanisms of LTP in *hippocampal area CA1. In the absence of an LTP induction stimulus (a), excitatory *neurotransmission is mediated via two major types of *glutamate *receptors: AMPA (AMPAR) and metabotropic (mGluR) receptors. The first is an *ion channel preferentially permeable to sodium (small open circles), the latter is linked to *intracellular

signal transduction cascades. A third type of glutamatergic receptor, the NMDA receptor channel (NMDAR), is a *calcium (Ca^{2+}) channel, blocked under resting conditions by magnesium (closed circle). Induction of LTP (b) involves removal of the magnesium block, resulting in an NMDAR-mediated Ca^{2+} influx (large open circles). Ca^{2+} activates, either directly or indirectly, a number of signal transduction cascades, involving a number of *protein kinases. A key role is played by the Ca^{2+}-dependent kinase CaMKII. This leads to phosphorylation and activation of AMPAR, and, furthermore, to translocation of new functional AMPAR molecules into the synapse. A retrograde message (nitric oxide, NO?) could modify presynaptic activity. The potentiation involves additional processes, including, in the case of long-lasting ('late') LTP, modulation of gene expression (see *immediate early genes, *late response genes, *protein synthesis). Proliferation of synaptic contacts may also ensue (*development, not shown for simplicity). A stimulus arriving at the presynaptic terminal of the potentiated synapse (c), releases glutamate again, but now the transmitter (whose release may be augmented because of the aforementioned presynaptic modifications) encounters additional AMPAR, resulting in marked synaptic facilitation (compare the synaptic response, inset in a and c, respectively). (Based on Nicoll and Malenka 1995; Hayashi *et al.* 2000.)

jury is yet out (e.g. Shors and Matzel 1997). As it is an umbrella term, the simplistic question 'is LTP = memory' is meaningless; one must specify exactly which LTP. In each system, the relevance of the phenomenon to learning should be assessed on the basis of physiological and behavioural data that are relevant to this same system. Next, one should consider the possible role of LTP in learning at the computational, algorithmic, and implementational levels. The computational level is a tricky issue, because in spite of the intuitive idea that a stronger synapse means stronger memory, the ultimate contribution of enhanced synaptic efficacy to the representational properties of circuits is far from simple (e.g. Markram and Tsodyks 1996). An example of a role at the algorithmic level is the AND gate function provided by NMDAR-dependent LTP. And as to implementation, similar algorithms may be implemented in different neurons by different receptors and signalling cascades. In most cases we are still ignorant as to what the crucial parameters of intracellular molecular networks are, and what they actually represent (e.g. Barkai and Leibler 1997). Nevertheless, it is safe to conclude that multiple receptors and signalling cascades are shared by LTP and other processes of use-dependent synaptic plasticity that are not LTP (e.g. *Aplysia, *development; Constantine-Paton and Cline 1998). In other words, LTP itself may not be learning, but it surely unveils cellular mechanisms that are used in learning.

Selected associations: Associative learning, Model, Plasticity, Synapse

---

[1]At the time of LTP discovery, the probable role of the hippocampus in learning was not on the mind of most cellular physiologists. The hippocampus was initially chosen because it is a convenient preparation for investigating cellular physiology (Andersen, personal communication).

Lotus

An imaginary fruit that makes its eaters forget their way home.

The Lotophagi (lotus eaters in Greek) were encountered by Odysseus and his sailors on an island in the troubled sea, shortly before facing the Cyclope (Homer, Odyssey IX 83–104). Whoever tasted the honey-sweet fruit of the flowering lotus, forgot the way home and desired to stay in lotus land. The fabulous lotus, never identified, is hence the ancient counterpart of modern *amnestic drugs. Actually, lotus was not the only potion renown in ancient times for its alleged amnestic powers. Drinking the water of the River Lethe (forgetfulness) in the Plain of Oblivion in Hades (the underworld, to which the souls travel) was supposed to erase all memory of earthly life (Plato, Republic 621).

A variety of real agents interfere with memory. Some are physical treatments, such as electric shock (Duncan 1948), including electroconvulsive therapy (ECT, Daniel and Crovitz 1983). In laboratory animals, a brief electric shock produces amnesia for a recently acquired task, provided that the treatment is administered during the first few hours after training. In humans, ECT induces a gradient of retrograde amnesia that may cover memories acquired up to 3 years before treatment (Squire et al. 1975). The effect of electric shock is construed as interference with *consolidation (Duncan 1948; McGaugh 1966; Squire et al. 1975).

Certain types of drugs produce amnestic effects as well. This could be due to their effect on arousal, on *attention, or on *acquisition, consolidation, or *retrieval of information. Drugs that impair recent memory when administered immediately after training, e.g. inhibitors of macromolecular synthesis or of *protein kinases, are highly useful in dissecting memory into *phases and in identifying the molecular and cellular mechanisms of short- and long-term *plasticity (Davis and Squire 1984; Montarolo et al. 1986; Rosenzweig et al. 1993). In general, if a drug enhances attention or *learning (Hock 1995; *nootropics), the antagonist has the opposite effect. Furthermore, the effects are dose dependent; some compounds that have beneficial effects on learning and memory have an opposite effect at higher concentrations. For example, caffeine at moderate doses is used to increase alertness and attention and hence creates favourable conditions for learning (Weiss and Laties 1962); but at high doses it impairs learning (Lashley 1917). The same is seen with other stimulants (e.g. Wetzel et al. 1981).

Perhaps most interesting for the general public is the amnestic effect of drugs widely prescribed in medical practice. 'Sedatives or hypnotics… taken in large doses retard the circulation. A clergyman was obliged to discontinue its use; he had very nearly lost his memory, which returned when the medicine was suspended' (Ribot 1882). Nowadays, anxiolytics of the benzodiazepine family (e.g. Valium) stand out as the most striking example. Benzodiazepines augment the efficacy of inhibitory neurotransmission by interacting with the

GABA$_A$ receptor complex in brain (Cooper *et al.* 1996). They are widely used as anxiolytics, hypnotics, muscle relaxants, and anticonvulsants. They also impair some cognitive abilities (Ghoneim and Mewaldt 1990; Izquierdo and Medina 1991; Danion *et al.* 1993; Gorenstein *et al.* 1995). Benzodiazepines are capable of interfering with long-term encoding of new episodic information without significantly affecting previously stored memory. They have little effect if at all on semantic memory or on non*declarative memory (*taxonomy). The amnestic effect is not correlated with the sedative and hypnotic effects of the drugs. Repeated administration results in some tolerance to the amnestic effect but does not abolish it (Ghoneim and Mewaldt 1990). Members of the benzodiazepine family have qualitatively similar effects on cognition, but in practice, some have more severe effects than others (*ibid.*). The most renown in terms of its amnestic effect is Flunitrazepam (Rohypnol). This drug has acquired the unflattering nickname of 'the rape drug' or 'date rape drug', because cases have been reported in which it was used as a prelude to sexual assault (Anglin *et al.* 1997). Flunitrazepam induces drowsiness and sleep, impairs motor function, and, most importantly, is remarkably amnestic. As the compound is water soluble, colourless, tasteless, and odourless, it can be slipped into a drink and afterwards, the victim may be unable to recall details of the assault. Owing to its abuse potential, flunitrazepam is now illegal in some countries.

With proper use, amnestic drugs do have a beneficial potential. They could be considered in severe shock and trauma. It is likely that in the years to come medicine will be equipped with an arsenal of specific memory erasers side by side with memory enhancers. In both cases, identification of specific steps in the encoding and the consolidation of new information (e.g. see *CREB, *immediate early genes) is expected to permit development of better memory targeted agents. Again, as is the case of other types of sophisticated technology, decisive regulations should be ensured to prevent abuse. In the meantime, benzodiazepines are already employed in anaesthesia and to calm unanaesthetized patients undergoing invasive and painful medical procedures. Forgetfulness of the unpleasant experience is in this case not an undesired side-effect but rather a blessing.

Selected associations: Amnesia, Attention, Fear conditioning, Nootropics

Map

1. A function that associates each member of a set *A* with a member of a set *B*.
2. Representation of space.
3. Representation of attributes of space *A* in space *B*, that keeps a systematic variation in the value of at least one salient attribute of *A* across a *dimension of *B*.
4. *Central sensory* or *central motor map*: A map (as in definition 3) of attributes of sensory or motor space, respectively, in a brain area.
5. *Cognitive map*: Mental *model of physical or imaginary space.

Mappa is a cloth or napkin in Latin; yet the first maps were probably drawn not on cloth but rather on clay, by the Babylonians. In the neurosciences, the term is occasionally used in its everyday connotation (definition 2), to denote functional architecture and spatiotemporal activity patterns in discrete brain areas (e.g. in *functional neuroimaging), without necessarily making assumptions about the code and the fine properties of the map. This usage needs no further elaboration. But 'map' is also used more specifically in two different contexts or *levels of analysis. One refers to the mode of representation of sensorimotor space in neuronal space (definitions 3 and 4), the other to cognitive representation of the world (definition 5). The first requires *reductive analysis of brains, the latter may even satisfy psychologists and philosophers who prefer not to map the world in terms of circuits and spikes.

Let us navigate our way in the neuroscience map-world top-down, from behaviour to neurons. Cognitive maps are mental models of the world. In its most common usage, a 'cognitive map' is meant to be a mental analogue of a topographic map. The idea dates back much before scientific psychology was born, and is reflected, for example, in ancient methods of *mnemonics. It was Tolman's neo*behaviourism that has endowed the concept with a stronger scientific flavour. Tolman trusted that mental maps are instrumental in enabling the organism to locate goals and get from one place to another (Tolman 1948). The spatial map concept was later supported and much expanded in a series of elegant experiments on the role of *hippocampus in guiding *rats in *mazes (O'Keefe and Nadel 1978). One can entertain multiple versions of such maps, differing, for example, in their resolution and behavioural control—from detailed plans that exploit salient landmarks to permit navigational plasticity, to less-detailed global representations of space (*ibid*; Gallistel 1989). Analysis of experience-dependent modifications in so-called hippocampal 'place maps' and their candidate components, 'place cells', is a fruitful branch of the molecular neurobiology and *neurogenetics of learning and memory (e.g. Wilson and Tonegawa 1997). Whether the major role of the hippocampus is to encode topography is still debated. Some authors propose that the mapping functions of the hippocampus much exceed the spatial domain (e.g. Wood *et al.* 1999). Few, though, will dispute that spatial coordinates do fulfil a major role in our cognition. The need to map space in order to navigate to food and away from predators may have provided many species, including invertebrates, with the capacity for cognitive maps. However, the risk of *anthropomorphizing in construing animal behaviour should always be considered; complex navigational abilities in *'simple' species may

not necessarily require off-line 'cognitive maps' (e.g. Wehner and Menzel 1990; Bennett 1996). Note that the concept of 'cognitive map' is not limited to representation of physical space, and *generalizes to faculties that do not rely directly on sensory attributes, such as mental depiction of *taxonomies, or of social status (Aronson 1995; Laszlo *et al.* 1996). Such nonspatial mapping may still involve imagery of imaginary or *metaphorical spatial coordinates. There was even a proposal that spatial mapping has provided a phylogenetic platform for the emergence of human language (O'Keefe 1996).

Another context in which mapping is employed in the neurosciences is sensory or motor encoding in brain circuits. When the neurons in such circuits are arranged so that their spatial relationship conserve those in the peripheral sensory epithelium, the map so formed is termed 'projectional', or 'topographical' (Konishi 1986; Kaas 1997) (Figure 44). A *classic example is the

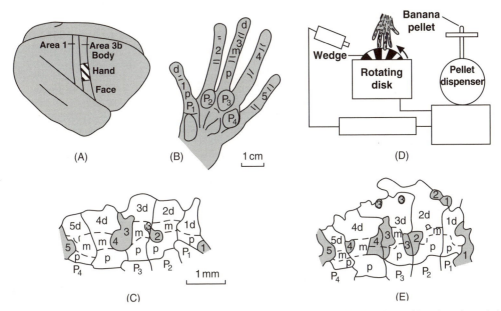

(A)   (B)   1 cm   (D)

(C)   1 mm   (E)

Fig. 44 A central topographical map of sensory space and its modification by experience. (A) A simplified lateral view of the right neo*cortex in the owl monkey. Areas 1–3b in the primary somatosensory cortex contain a somatotopic representation of the body surfaces (*homunculus). The location of the hand representation is marked by hatching. (B) The hand surface of an adult monkey. Numbers 1–5 denote the digits (1 is the thumb); distal (d), middle (m), and proximal (p) phalanges; P_{1-4}, the palmar pads at the base of the digits. (C) A map of the representation of hand surfaces indicated in B, in area 3b of the somatosensory cortex. The map is rotated 90° counterclockwise with respect to A. Grey areas, dorsal (hairy) skin on each digit. (D) The behavioural apparatus used for studying the effect of differential stimulation of restricted skin surfaces of the hand on the representation of these surfaces in area 3b. The monkey was trained to maintain contact with a rotating disk in order to get banana pellets. Only the distal aspect of the distal segment of digits 2, 3, and occasionally 4, contacted the disk. (E) The cortical hand representation of the same monkey as in C, after about 20 weeks of daily training (1.5 h/day) in the apparatus depicted in D. Note the remodelling of the map and the marked expansion of the representations of the distal aspects of digits 2, 3, and, to a lesser degree, 4. (Adapted from Jenkins and Merzenich 1987.)

somatotopic *homunculus in the primary sensorimotor *cortex (Penfield and Rasmussen 1968). When the map does not conserve the topography of the corresponding sensory epithelium, it is 'centrally synthesized' or 'computational' (Knudsen *et al.* 1987). The distinction is methodologically convenient but should be taken with a pinch of salt; 'projectional' mapping involves central computations as well. Examples for 'computational maps' are many (e.g. Knudsen *et al.* 1987; Knierim and Van Essen 1992; Schreiner 1995), although in most cases the contribution to the overall *internal representation is still not fully appreciated. A *classic example in which the contribution of a centrally synthesized map to an internal representation is evident, is that of the map that encodes interaural time differences of the barn owl: here spike time-code is transformed into place code by a brain-stem circuit that uses delay lines and *coincidence detectors (Konishi 1986) (Figure 45).

Some general issues concerning sensory maps are noteworthy:

1. Traditionally, 'central maps' are expected to display systematic variation in the value of at least one sensory attribute across at least one dimension of neural structure. The lack of apparent systematicity was actually taken to indicate that mapping is not indispensable for neural computation (Knudsen *et al.* 1987). However, in some brain circuits we cannot yet conclude whether there is an orderly, systematic variation in the encoding of an important attribute across a dimension of neural structure. In other cases, miniature ordered maps are discovered dispersed in a seemingly irregular mosaic (e.g. pinwheel-like patterns of orientation selectivity in the mammalian visual cortex; Bonhoeffer and Grinvald 1993). Declaring a representation 'non-map' by the criteria of definition 3 may therefore prove premature. It might be useful to relax the constraints and extend the concept of 'brain map' to all cases in which world attributes are represented in a confined, dedicated brain area (definitions 1 and 2). In that case, 'map' becomes more of a generic term for localized candidate internal representations (that can of course map into each other)—but see 6 below.

2. Mapping involves transformation of codes, for example from time code (see above, Figure 45) or chemical code (e.g. Rubin and Katz 1999) into place code.

3. Maps recombine to produce higher-order maps. In the process, topographical and computational maps of different modalities interact and align,

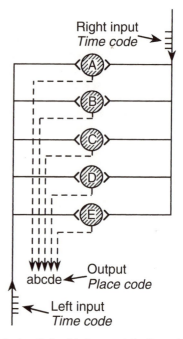

Fig. 45 A schematic *model of a computational map of acoustic representation in the brainstem of the barn owl. The map converts spike time code into place code. The circuit uses delay lines and *coincidence detection for measuring and encoding interaural time differences. Neurons A–E are arranged in an array and fire maximally only when signals from the left and from the right arrive simultaneously. Temporal information about the acoustic signal is encoded by spike timing. The axonal path increases in opposite directions for the two sources, thus creating a left–right asymmetry in transmission delays. When binaural disparities in the acoustic signals exactly compensate for this asymmetry, the neurons fire maximally. The output of the neurons does not use spike timing to encode time, but rather the position of the neuron in the array signals the interaural time differences for which the neuron responds maximally. (Adapted from Konishi 1986.)

presumably to permit coherent *perception and action (e.g. Wallace *et al.* 1996; Feldman and Knudsen 1997). This indicates that the brain uses general strategies to process codes regardless of the original modality or of whether the map was topographical or computational to begin with.

4. The shape of maps may reflect developmental constraints, or phylogenetic pressures to optimize wiring or facilitate computations (Konishi 1986; Schreiner 1995; Kaas 1997; Van Essen 1997). The possibility should, however, be considered that in some maps topography has little to do with the ultimate representational meaning (see 6 below).

5. Suppose the spatiotemporal states of brain maps could be recorded in physiologically meaningful time windows—will we be able to read in individual maps only *types* of computations, or also *tokens*, namely statements with a specific representational 'semantics' which encode a unique physiological and behavioural situation?[1]

6. Ample evidence now indicates that central maps can be altered by experience (e.g. Weinberger 1995; Kilgard and Merzenich 1998; Faber *et al.* 1999). What is the relevance of such changes to learning and memory? Does the observed experience-dependent modifications in the map reflect lasting representational alterations, or solely changes auxiliary to the representational change, for example, expansion of computational space (Dudai 1999)? With the impressive advances in *methods such as functional neuroimaging and molecular neurobiology, more and more experience-dependent alterations are bound to be detected in brain maps. The temptation to declare each of these a manifestation of learning should be better quenched until we understand what the map really charts.

Selected associations: Internal representation, Model, Plasticity, System

---

[1]For more on type vs. token, see *system.

Maze

1. **An intricate, usually confusing network of interconnecting pathways.**

2. **Physical space containing multiple potential routes to a goal, at least one of which is productive or optimal.**

Mazes (*amasian*, 'to confound' in old English) are for some current students of learning what the pen is for a literary critic: indispensable but occasionally abused. Although employed mainly to probe the memory of rodents (Olton 1979), over the years, mazes have been applied to the analysis of other species as well, ranging from flies (Dudai 1988) to monkeys (Murray *et al.* 1988) and humans (Woodworth and Schlosberg 1954). The systematic use of mazes in the psychological laboratory was initiated by Kline in Clark University in 1898. He was searching for an appropriate *system to experiment on 'the migratory impulse vs. the love of home' (the title of his PhD thesis, admittedly rather poetic). The idea to use the laboratory *rat and the maze for 'home finding' experiments was suggested to him by Sanford (Miles 1930). Furthermore, Sanford suggested specifically to model the Hampton Court Garden labyrinth in London for these experiments. Up to that stage all this had nothing to do with learning research. But soon after, Small (1901), in the same department, started to use the Hampton Court maze for learning experiments. With time, rats in mazes became highly popular in studies of behaviour and learning. By the 1930s–1950s, they almost monopolized experimental psychology. The contemporary *zeitgeist culminated in *paradigmatic statements such as 'everything important in psychology (except such matters as building of a super-ego ...) can be investigated in essence through ... determinants of rat behavior at a choice point in the maze' (Tolman 1938).

There was reason behind the mazomania. Against a background of some rather artificial and sometimes bizarre paradigms of *instrumental learning, mazes have provided a reproducible experimental environment adapted to the rodent sensory-motor ecological disposition: '(for the rat)', said Small (1901), '... the experiments were couched in a familiar language'. Inter alia, mazes became a major test ground for two rivalling types of theories in the psychology of learning. One, the stimulus–response (S–R) type, trusted that whatever an animal learns is due to *reinforcement by trial and error of atomistic sensory stimulus–motor response connections. The other type of theory was cognitive, claiming that with experience, animals accumulate structured bodies of knowledge that they use to construe, react to, and even anticipate the world. Hence, whereas the first type of theories denied the existence of inferred mental processes that bridge S to R (*behaviourism), the second type deemed such internal intervening processes as obligatory; and whereas S–R theories portrayed laboratory animals as having a somewhat impoverished picture of their milieu, the cognitive theories were ready to endow them with a much more intricate psyche (Boakes 1984).

Proponents of the cognitive view have tried to convince themselves and their opponents that when a rat runs a maze, its behaviour reflects a molar cognitive purpose (as opposed to reacting to local cues like a kinesthetic automaton). The innate predisposition of the rat to navigate in space (*a priori), combined with the varied complexity of the task and the substantial number of response strategies permitted in certain mazes, rendered maze paradigms especially fit to be used in the attempts to resolve the aforementioned debate (e.g. Tolman 1938; Olton 1979). The maze studies matured into a dynamic, multifaceted research field, addressing cognitive *maps and brain regions that retain *engrams of such maps. Sophisticated cellular physiology, molecular biology, and computational science now permit, for the first time, attempts to close the gap between the observed behaviour, the postulated cognitive maps, the circuits that are assumed to encode the maps, and the cellular and molecular mechanisms that embody the *internal representation in these circuits (e.g. Burgess and O'Keefe 1996; Wilson and Tonegawa 1997; *reduction).

Mazes come in many variants. A convenient distinction is between 'defined paths' and 'open-field' mazes. The former (definition 1) have bordered passages and cul-de-sacs as intuitively expected of labyrinths. The passages could be delineated by walls (in which case it is an 'alley maze') or by elevated paths ('elevated maze', with the dead ends being the termination of the elevated alley into open space rather than a wall; Olton 1979). Alternatively, mazes may have no defined

physical paths within the maze enclosure (conforming to the more inclusive definition 2 above). Such mazes are thus of an 'open-field' type.[1] The term 'enclosed' or 'closed' field is sometimes used to denote defined paths mazes within a closed environment (Hebb and Williams 1946), but this is questionable because unless virtual (Maguire *et al.* 1998), all mazes are enclosed in physical space in one way or another. In their shape, defined path mazes range from a straightforward I, T, or Y, useful for example in simple discrimination or avoidance tasks, to more complex multiple-arm radial mazes, permitting sophisticated spatial and *working memory tests (Olton and Samuelson 1976; see also example in *habit). An 'open-field' type of maze that has gained impressive usefulness and popularity in recent years is the water maze (also known as the 'Morris maze'; Morris 1981). In this type of maze rodents are trained to escape from water on to a hidden platform located within a large unobstructed pool (for earlier variants of water mazes, although with defined paths, see Glaser 1910; Rosvold and Mirsky 1954). The 'Morris

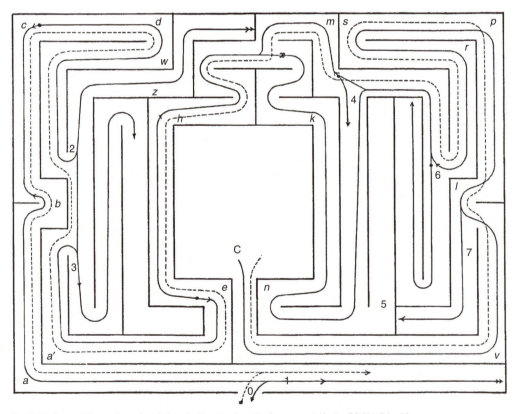

Fig. 46 The first maze in experimental psychology: the Hampton Court Garden maze, used by Small (1901; *classic).

maze' has been seminal in reinforcing the notion that rodents can form stable overall spatial maps of their milieu, independent of local cues (Morris 1981). It has also been instrumental in analysing the function of the *hippocampus in learning and memory, as well as the relevance of *long-term potentiation to behavioural plasticity (e.g. Bannerman *et al.* 1995; Wilson and Tonegawa 1997). Many other types of maze are, however, highly useful as well in such studies (e.g. O'Keefe and Speakman 1987; Markus *et al.* 1995).

The rapid and impressive advances in molecular neurobiology in general, and in mice *neurogenetics in particular, have promoted the popularity of mazes among neurobiologists at large, because mazes could provide a seemingly simple learning *assay. Thus, it has become almost routine for new transgenic and knockout mice to be declared either smart or stupid on the basis of passing or flunking the test in the water maze. However, the simplicity of the procedures facing the experimenter may mask the complexities facing the mouse (e.g. Bannerman *et al.* 1995; Day *et al.* 1999). It may also blur the finesse of species-specific innate behaviours (Wolfer *et al.* 1998). A maze is clearly not an instant assay kit, and the experimenter should devote ample attention to the *performance of the *subject and to what this performance really means.

Selected associations: Assay, Hippocampus, Map, Mouse, Rat, Paradigm

---

[1]For a beautiful distinction between alley and open field mazes in fiction, see Borges (1949).

Memory

1. **An enduring change in behaviour, or in the behavioural potential, that results from the individual's behavioural experience.**

2. **The retention over time of *learned information.**

3. **The retention over time of experience-dependent *internal representations, or of the capacity to reactivate or reconstruct such representations.**

Memory, the mother of all the muses (Hesiod 8C BC, *mnemonics), resides in many types of *systems, including inanimates (Moravec 1988; Weng *et al.* 2001). We will refer here solely to memory in biological organisms with a nervous system. As in the case of *learning, the term 'behavioural experience' in definition 1 refers to the wide gamut of sensory, motor, emotional, and cognitive events that take place throughout a lifetime. Other types of experience, such as the unfolding of a rigid *developmental programme independent of the environment, or disease, injury and poisoning, are excluded. The term 'enduring' means longer than the perceptual or the cognitive present, which is a fraction of a second to a few seconds at most (*phase). Another type of definition refers to memory in terms of 'information' (definition 2). It is noteworthy that brains and nervous systems are not at all mentioned in the behavioural or informational types of definitions. This lack of reference to the biological substrate of behaviour is the combined heritage of multiple schools in psychology, information, and system theory (reviewed in Bower and Hilgard 1981; Baddeley 1997). Over the years, only rarely were complaints expressed in the literature that 'few dictionaries contain any reference to memory as a feature of a physical system' (Young 1987). Definition 3 refers to memory as retention over time of experience-dependent modifications in *internal representations, where internal representations are neuronally encoded models of the world that could guide behaviour (Dudai 1989). The focus on the representational properties of neural systems is meant to guide the identification of the relevance to memory of findings at multiple *levels of analysis (*reduction). This attitude fits the multilevel nature of research in the neurosciences better than the attitude reflected in the behavioural and/or the informational definitions (Dudai 1989, 1992; Crick 1994).

The view taken here is that *all* memories, regardless of the species and the task, are biological *internal representations. Similarly to 'learning', the difference among types of memory is in the ecological function, computational theory, *algorithms, and neural implementation of the internal representation. The pursuit of internal representations and their modification by experience is thus tagged as the gist of memory research. Internal representations are assumed to be encoded in the spatiotemporal states of neural circuits (*cell assembly, *homunculus). In contemporary neurobiology, quite a few research programmes that claim to target memory concentrate solely on the molecular and the isolated single-cell level. Such programmes address cellular information storage, or neuronal *plasticity, not 'memory'. This of course should not all belittle the huge excitement, signal importance, and immense usefulness of the molecular and cellular approach; it only means that molecular and cellular neurobiologists shall aim at integrating their programs with higher level approaches if they wish to focus on memory. And vice versa: system neurobiologists should tune to molecular and cellular biology, and exploit its tools, if they wish to understand the nuts and bolts of biological information-storage machinery in the brain.

'Memory' could be subjected to multiple *taxonomies, based on different *dimensions, such as duration, associativity, *conscious awareness, and behavioural function (e.g. Augustine 400; de Biran 1804; James 1890; Bergson 1908; Hebb 1949; Ryle 1949; Tolman 1949; Milner *et al.* 1998). Such taxonomies are exemplified under *learning above. The rationale and evidence for selected classifications of memory are detailed in the relevant entries in this book. At this point, it is useful to consider briefly only a few general properties of memory.

1. By definition, not all internal representations that guide behaviour are memories. Internal representations could also be *a priori, innate constructs, encoded by the genes and established by developmental programmes even in the absence of learning. *Percepts are also internal representations but not memory. Memories are only those species of internal representations that result from learning. At the same time, it is important to note that the concept of 'learning' used in this book is comprehensive, and includes not only physiological or behavioural experience but also rearrangements of internal representations that yield new knowledge. Therefore, in brains, probably also in very simple brains and ganglia, even the innate internal representations are expected to undergo a process of change with experience and become *bona fide* memory.

2. In contrast with what is connoted by popular *metaphors, memories, being spatiotemporal activity states of the nervous system, are unlikely to be stored over time as such. Rather, they are probably reactivated or reconstructed each time anew, to regain their meaning, content-wise, only in *retrieval (Tulving 1991). Retrieval is any *stimulus-induced or spontaneous activation of the representation, whether accompanied by behavioural *performance or not. So what is it that is stored over time? This profound issue is discussed under *persistence; suffice it to note here only two basic types of scenarios. One, that *recognition or *recall is the activation of a dedicated circuit, probably identical to the one activated in training. One could expect to encounter this scenario in simple circuits that subserve simple behaviours, such a reflexes (*Aplysia). Another possibility is that what is stored is only a compressed 'core memory', or index, that permits the reactivation or reconstruction of a full-blown representation. The activated circuit could be different from that employed in

learning or previous retrieval. Further, retrieval itself could induce use-dependent alterations in the circuit, including re-*consolidation of the modified-anew trace. Add to this the *association of the *context at the time of retrieval with the retrieved *engram, and the result is the potential *falsification of memory.

3. A balance is expected in the evolution of biological memory between universal processes and components, that subserve many types of memory systems, and particular processes and components, that subserve only a particular type of memory system. Whereas economy in evolution could favour universals, the need to endow the system with new capabilities, as well as opportunism in evolution, could favour the addition of particular molecular, cellular, or system *algorithms and devices. The point to note is that even if two learned behaviours seem to share the phenomenology, or two memory circuits seem to share algorithms, such as the Hebbian, and hardware devices, such as the *glutamate N-methyl-D-aspartate receptor, a closer look may unveil many particulars among the apparent universals. In any case, as memory refers to so many different types of internal representations, neuronal systems, functions, and behaviours, as in the case of learning, it is unlikely to expect a master solution to the mechanisms of memory.

Selected associations: Engram, Internal representation, Learning, Palimpsest, Plasticity

---

Metamemory

Self-appreciation, monitoring, and control of one's own memory.

Although some authors consider the study of metamemory a newcomer to the field of memory research, its roots are rather ancient. Already St Augustine (400) referred to 'Memory of memories... I have remembered that I have remembered'. Interest in the self-appreciation of one's own knowledge and performance was shared by introspectionists during the early days of experimental psychology, especially the so-called 'Würzburg school' of 'systematic experimental introspection' (Boring 1950a).[1] However, systematic reports on *subjects' ability to predict their own learning ability had to await the development of more rigorous research *methods (e.g. Underwood 1966). Soon after, Tulving and Madigan (1970) noted that 'one of the truly unique characteristics of human memory (is) its own knowledge', and added that '... if there is ever going to be a genuine breakthrough in the psychological study of memory ... it will ... relate the knowledge stored in the individual's memory to his knowledge of that knowledge'. Finally, the term 'metamemory' itself (*meta*- Greek for 'beyond', 'after') was coined by Flavell (1971). This was in the context of research on the development of learning and memory in children in general, and children's knowledge about their own memory in particular. Flavell and his coworkers became interested in questions such as whether kids appreciate that some types of material are harder to remember than others, and whether they have any idea of how to improve their learning *performance. For example, do kindergarten kids realize that it is easier to remember the gist of a short story rather than its exact wording? In suggesting 'metamemory', Flavell had in mind the analogy with 'metalanguage' (a language used to describe a language under study) (Flavell and Wellman 1977). 'Metamemory' is hence a 'higher-order' memory, and as such is 'metacognitive' faculty ('metacognition', the ability to reflect on one own's cognitive processes and performance, e.g. Yzerbyt *et al.* 1998). Viewed this way, metamemory is part of a belief system that comprises a 'private theory of mind'.[2]

The research on metamemory still occupies a central position in developmental psychology (reviewed in Schneider 1999), but has long transcended into other subdisciplines of memory research. There are multiple facets to metamemory, some implicit, others accessible to *conscious recollection (*declarative), some involved in self-appreciation and self-monitoring of performance, others in controlling it. Here are some measures; all have been used to infer that metamemory does exist, and to then analyse it:

1. *Ease of learning*, refers to the subject's judgement of how easy is the task to be learned (Underwood 1966).
2. *Judgement of learning*, refers to the subject's prediction of whether the information was indeed *acquired and whether it will be successfully *retrieved (Arbuckle and Cuddy 1969).
3. *Feeling of knowing (FOK)*, refers to the subject's judgement of whether an item is in memory despite a failure to retrieve it at present time (Hart 1965). A related term is the *metaphor depicting verbal information in an incomplete *retrieval situation as residing on the 'tip of the tongue' (Brown and McNeill 1966).
4. *Control of learning strategy*, refers to the subject's self-appreciation of the effectiveness of learning strategies, their applicability to the target in

question, and their recruitment, for example, whether to use *spaced, rather than massed, training.
5. *Control of retrieval strategy*, refers to the subject's self-appreciation of retrieval strategies and effectiveness. Consider, for example, the decision whether to terminate a retrieval attempt or to pursue it (as appreciated intuitively, this could be related to FOK, see above). Control of retrieval and learning strategies, as well as other facets of metamemory, were considered as a potential leverages to memory improvement (Hertzog 1992; *mnemonics).

The self-belief and predictions about one's own memory could sometimes be deceiving (e.g. Herrmann 1982; Benjamin *et al.* 1998), but still, in many situations they are well above chance level, and sometimes are dependable indeed (e.g. Kelemen and Weaver 1997). Thus, while keeping in mind occasional criticism concerning the research methodology and the conclusions (e.g. Cavanaugh and Perlmutter 1982), metamemory is now regarded not only as a theoretical concept but also as a concrete cognitive faculty that we routinely use in *real-life. It improves throughout childhood and probably remains fairly stable in normal ageing, in spite of some decline in self-confidence (Cohen 1996). How is it at all possible for us to know whether we know or do not know an item in memory without specifically retrieving that item, is mostly still a mystery. Understanding the processes and mechanisms involved is bound to tell us a lot about how acquisition, storage, and retrieval really work in a complex brain. For example, are FOK and control of retrieval due to some 'internal monitor', a type of *homunculus, that gauges the inventory of our *engrams from an outside-of-store position? Alternatively, metamemory may reflect the monitoring of the system by itself, an outcome of computations performed within the memory system in the course of an attempt to retrieve. The latter possibility (e.g. Koriat 1993) is more in line with what we currently feel that we know about how the brain operates. It is, however, prudent to note that at least in some situations, the 'K' in FOK could be misleading, as the 'F' may be based on familiarity of the problem rather than judgement of the availability of information (e.g. Reder and Ritter 1992; Klin *et al.* 1997). In that case, it is even questionable what is 'meta' in the 'metamemory'.

What brain circuits subserve metamemory? There are two ways of approaching the problem. One is to assess the effect of brain lesions and pathology, such as *dementia and *amnesia, on the performance in metamemory tasks (Kaszniak and Zak 1996). Some aspects of memory monitoring remain intact even in dementia of the Alzheimer type (Moulin *et al.* 2000). Impairment in FOK is evident in Korsakoff's patients, but is not an obligatory feature of amnesia (Shimamura and Squire 1986). One of the characteristics of Korsakoff's patients is frontal *cortex dysfunction. Frontal patients that are not amnesics also show impairment on FOK. All this has led to the proposal that the frontal lobe is critical for self-monitoring of memory (Shimamura 1995; but see doubts in O'Shea *et al.* 1994). Another potential approach is to use *functional neuroimaging to observe brain areas in metamemory tasks, although the differentiation between engagement of 'metamemory' and 'memory' circuits may not be easy.

As noted above, Tulving and Madigan (1970) deemed metamemory unique to human memory. Is it true? Over the years attempts have been made to prove that other species also know what they know and what they don't. Verbal tests are unfortunately out of question in nonhuman subjects. The anecdotal testimony of pet owners is also useless as a respectable research methodology. All this makes it necessary to devise some sophisticated tricks to overcome the communication barrier (e.g. Smith *et al.* 1998; Inman and Shettleworth 1999; Hampton 2001). Some will claim that this need for the indirect approach is actually an advantage, because not having to rely on questionnaires, opinion polls, and subjective verbal accounts, does only good to the field. Without going too much into details, here is an illustrative approach: suppose we train a pigeon on a delayed matching-to-sample task (*delay task), and occasionally allow it to choose between a test of memory for the sample with a hefty *reinforcement, or pecking a safe key for a meagre reinforcement. Will the pigeon prefer the safe key when it senses that its own memory is feeble, say, after a long delay? As Inman and Shettleworth (1999) show, even when such a behaviour is observed, interpretations other than the use of metamemory are still possible. Nevertheless, this kind of experimental design might in principle be further explored and *controlled to identify metamemory. Among the nonhuman contenders for a personal theory of memory, *monkeys and anthropoid apes are probably a better bet than pigeons. In any case, this is definitely an area of research where smart application of *Ockham's razor is an effective antidote for *anthropomorphism and *red herrings.

Selected associations: Cerebral cortex, Mnemonics, Real-life memory, Retrieval

---

[1]On the Würzburg School see also *learning set.

[2]A subject is said to have a 'theory of mind' if it can impute mental states to itself and others (*observational learning).

Metaphor

A figure of speech in which one entity is described in terms of another.

Metaphora is 'a transfer' in Greek, the transference consisting 'in giving the thing a name that belongs to something else' (Aristotle, *Poetics* 1457b7–8). In a more formal notation, metaphors can be described as statements in figurative language, composed of two juxtaposed elements, the 'tenor' and the 'vehicle', which are presented as sharing common attributes or 'ground' (Richards 1936). The tenor is the subject of the metaphor, while the vehicle is the means by which the subject is referred to. (More recent discourse refers to the subject as the 'target domain' and to the vehicle as 'source domain'; Gibbs 1994.) For example, in 'memory is a storehouse' (after Locke 1690, and see below), 'memory' is the tenor (the target domain), 'storehouse' the vehicle (the source domain), and 'space' the ground. The interaction of the tenor with the vehicle, or the target with the source domain, produces an emergent meaning for the entire statement.

Classically, metaphors were regarded as artful, poetic decorations: 'Metaphor gives style clearness, charm, and distinction as nothing else can' (Aristotle, *Rhetoric* 1405a8–9). But in modern psychology and linguistics, metaphors are also considered essential in ordinary language, language development and change, and thought and conceptualization (Lakoff and Johnson 1980). Three major motives were proposed for using metaphors (Gibbs 1994). The first is similar to the classical poetic view, namely, metaphors capture effectively the vividness of experience. The second is to provide compactness in verbal communication. The third, to express what is otherwise inexpressible in literal language. It is this latter property that endows metaphors a central position in musing, hypothesizing and writing about learning and memory.

Ordinarily, there are two main reasons for inexpressibility in a normal person. The first is related to evolution of human brain and cognition. It is tempting to presume that *Homo sapiens has so far evolved to deal intuitively[1] with only selected manifestations of the universe, characterized by circumscribed physical *dimensions (millimetres to kilometres, seconds to years), limited complexity (e.g. *attention, *capacity), and restricted access to inner mental processes. These segments of the universe comprise the 'mesoworld', to be contrasted with the 'micro' and 'macro' world, which are not accessible to the bare senses. It is also tempting to assume that ordinary language lags beyond the potential of the human brain to transcend the mesoworld into the micro, the macro, as well as the inner universe. Ultimately, the accumulated *insight of our *culture is formalized in formal, scientific terminology, some of which gravitates with time toward intuitiveness. But often, an interim stage is needed in which comprehension of the unfamiliar is mediated via the familiar. Here metaphors are useful. For a layperson, it is tough to comprehend intuitively what an electron is; depicting it by a process of analogical *transfer as a small planet encircling the nucleus-sun, makes life easier. A second reason for inexpressibility is simply the lack of appropriate knowledge.

Brain research uses metaphors for both aforementioned reasons. To describe the mind and memory, multiple classes of metaphors have been generated, most of them antedating the scientific era (Abrams 1953; Roediger 1980). The vehicle and ground in these metaphors involve either space, written records, vision, or technology. Especially common are spatial metaphors, depicting memory as a physical repository, and *retrieval as a search for the location of an item filed in storage (for classical examples see Plato, *Theaetetus* 197c–e; Augustine 400; Locke 1690; *engram, *mnemonics). Written record metaphors (which could be regarded as a subset of the spatial ones) advanced from etched wax tablets (Plato, *Theaetetus* 193a–a95a) to more fancy writing pads (Freud 1925). In an influential *model of *working memory, we encounter a subsystem termed the 'visuospatial scratch pad' or 'sketchpad' (Baddley 1986).[2] Working memory as such was also referred to as 'the blackboard of the mind' (Goldman-Rakic 1996).

Visual metaphors of brain and memory often intermingle with spatial or written record metaphors. They refer to *perception and *acquisition in terms of passively perceiving the world or actively throwing light on it (Abrams 1953), and to *retrieval as illumination of items in mind (e.g. by an internal searchlight, Baars 1998). Visual metaphors are common when the discussion involves *attention and *conscious awareness (*ibid.*). Whereas the images in some of the above metaphors, e.g. the storehouse, remain rather similar over the ages, technological metaphors reflect the machines and gadgets of their period. They tend to be more dynamic than spatial metaphors and describe multiple phases in learning and memory. Examples of technological metaphors include hydraulic networks in the Renaissance (Descartes 1633), and electronics and computers nowadays (Churchland and Sejnowski 1992). Operational and system research by the Allies in the Second World War was influential in shaping metaphors of attention and working memory. In current discussions, working memory is occasionally referred to as the brain's 'desktop'; this is an interesting example of a second-order, or *palimpsestic metaphor: 'desktop' is borrowed from the computer world, which was imported from the pre-computer office environment.

Although metaphors of memory may help us in organizing our thoughts and even in proposing creative research ideas, their value is limited. A few caveats are appropriate here. First, metaphors are potential source for misunderstanding: 'Metaphor is the dreamwork of language and, like all dreamwork, its interpretation reflects as much on the interpreter as on the originator' (Davidson 1979). Second, in the absence of new data and theory, merely adding or exchanging metaphors could simply augment confusion. This is not unique to the scientific language: it was noted that 'mixed metaphors' (i.e. the application of two or more inconsistent metaphors to a given situation) 'always arouses derision' (Fowler and Burchfield 1996). Third, dominant metaphors (*zeitgeist) could hinder progress by fixating conceptual *paradigms (Watkins 1990; Koriat and Goldsmith 1996). For example, storage metaphors may lure us to think about memory as static, which is wrong. Only time will tell whether recent metaphors that drew from computer science and modern physics are distractive or not. In conclusion, in memory research, as in science in general, metaphors should better be regarded only as vehicles on the winding and bumpy road to formal understanding. But this is already another metaphor.

Selected associations: Engram, Flashbulb memory, Model, Palimpsest, Transfer

---

[1] For what is meant by 'intuition', see *dimension.

[2] The 'central executive', used to describe the postulated supervisory controlling system in working memory, could also be considered a metaphor, but of a different ground. It belongs to the family of the *homunculus metaphors.

Metaplasticity

The *plasticity of neural plasticity.

Metaplasticity is the modulation by experience of neuronal plasticity. It is a family of adaptive processes that have probably evolved to form a dynamic balance among the need for change (*plasticity), the need to resist too much change (*homeostasis, *memory, *persistence), and the metabolic price of both, at various periods in the life of the organism (*development). Metaplasticity is commonly referred to as the plasticity of *synaptic plasticity (Abraham and Bear 1996; Abraham and Tate, 1997), but there is good reason to believe that the underlying mechanisms involve the neuronal cell body as well. The concept of metaplasticity fits to be used in the discussion of higher *levels of organization as well. For example, it is legitimate to say that the language areas of the brain undergo metaplastic changes with age. It is, however, assumed that metaplastic changes that are manifested at the circuit or *system level, are the consequence of metaplasticity at the synaptic level.

Most research on metaplasticity concerns activity that primes the expression of subsequently induced *long-term potentiation (LTP) or of long-term depression (LTD). Part of this work is conducted on *hippocampal preparations (e.g. Huang *et al.* 1992; Christie and Abraham 1992), and part on *cortical preparations with special emphasis on developmental plasticity in the visual cortex (Kirkwood *et al.* 1996). In these systems, under appropriate conditions, prior activity can be shown to regulate the capacity to undergo LTP and LTD (Abraham and Tate 1997).

An influential theoretical framework for metaplasticity in the mammalian brain was proposed by Bienenstock, Cooper, and Monro (known in the field as the BCM *model; Bienenstock *et al.* 1982). This model was developed to account for the developmental plasticity of *stimulus selectivity in the mammalian sensory cortex. The model makes two basic assumptions. One, that synaptic modification varies as a nonlinear function of postsynaptic activity, such that low levels of afferent activity result in LTD whereas high levels in LTP. The crossover from LTD to LTP occurs at the modification threshold θ_m. The second assumption of the model is that θ_m slides as a function of synaptic history, hence endowing the system with metaplasticity. This sliding threshold keeps the active synapse within a dynamic range, preventing saturation of LTP on the one hand and complete depression by LTD on the other (*ibid.*). Some experimental data echo the assumptions of the BCM model. For example, Kirkwood *et al.* (1996) found that in the developing cortex, θ_m indeed depends on sensory experience (Figure 47): in the visual cortex of light-deprived rats, LTP is enhanced and LTD diminished over a range of stimulation frequencies, but the effect is reversed by brief light exposure. This shift may contribute to the experience-dependent modifications of visual receptive fields in

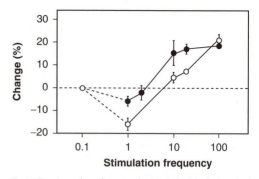

Fig. 47 Experience-dependent metaplasticity in the *developing visual system. Kirkwood et al. (1996) have measured the change in synaptic responses in slices prepared from the visual *cortex of light-deprived (closed circles) and *control (open circles) 4–6-week-old rats. The measurement was done at 20–30 min after the stimulation. The per cent change in synaptic response is depicted as a function of the stimulation frequency. It can be seen that visual experience shifts the long-term depression (LTD, negative change)—long-term potentiation (*LTP, positive change) cross-over point (termed θ_m in the BCM *model, see text). (Adapted from Kirkwood et al. 1996.)

the cortex following manipulation of visual experience (*development).

Multiple molecular and cellular mechanisms may account for metaplasticity over a spectrum of developmental stages, brain regions, synaptic specificities, and time courses. The experience-dependent release of growth factors and neuromodulators probably primes circuits to respond differentially to subsequent plasticity-inducing stimuli (e.g. Markram and Segal 1990; Kaneko *et al.* 1997; Abraham and Tate 1997). At their cellular targets, these stimuli modulate receptors, *intracellular signalling cascades, and their downstream substrates. It has been particularly proposed that variations in the *calcium-independent activity of the enzyme calcium-calmodulin dependent *protein kinase type II (CaMKII), shifts θ_m in the hippocampus (Mayford *et al.* 1995; see also commentary in Deisseroth *et al.* 1995). Another type of candidate mechanism for metaplasticity is local tagging and local *protein synthesis in synapses; during the synaptic *consolidation time window, the recent history of the neuron could determine whether a stimulus will be encoded in long-term memory or, alternatively, forgotten (Frey and Morris 1997).

Metaplasticity was also explored in an invertebrate, *Aplysia*. The advantage of studying this system lies in the ability to relate events at the cellular, circuit, and behavioural level, respectively. The circuits that encode the defensive withdrawal reflexes in *Aplysia* are composed of a number of cell types, including sensory neurons that receive the tactile information from the skin, motor neurons that execute the withdrawal reflex, and interneurons that feed into the sensory and motor neurons information from various parts of the organism (Figure 5, p. 16). In the circuit that mediates the siphon withdrawal reflex, the L29 excitatory interneurons synapse on to the motor neurons, whereas the L30 inhibitory interneurons synapse on to L29. By inhibiting L29, activation of L30 suppresses the ability of siphon stimulation to elicit the reflex. L30 receives input from the excitatory interneurons that relay tactile information from the siphon skin; this forms a negative feedback loop, which limits the activation of the reflex. Activation of L30 can induce multiple types of plasticity. One type, frequency facilitation (FF), involves a steady increase in the strength of the synaptic connection during the burst of nerve impulses. Another type of plasticity, short-term enhancement (STE), involves augmentation of response that outlasts the stimulus by about 1 min. The most important findings in the context of this discussion is that L30 is also influenced by tactile information from the tail. If a weak tactile stimulus is applied to the tail shortly before a tactile stimulus is applied to the siphon, the inhibition of L30 by siphon stimulation is enhanced. If instead the tail is shocked (or the *neurotransmitter serotonin is applied in an imitation experiment, *method), the capacity for STE in the L30–L29 inhibitory synapse is suppressed, while leaving the capacity for FF intact (Fischer *et al.* 1997). In other words, the tail shock selectively modulates the ability of the synapse to undergo short-term use-dependent plasticity, i.e. it induces metaplasticity. Similarly, in the behaving animal, tail shock suppresses the inhibitory modulation of the siphon withdrawal reflex after tactile stimulation of the tail. This phenomenon was termed 'modulatory metaplasticity', because its induction does not require activity of the synapse whose plasticity is being regulated, as tail shock itself does not activate L30 (*ibid.*).

A valuable take-home message from the metaplasticity studies relates to the importance of the history of the experimental *subject or preparation and to the influence of this history on the outcome of the experiment. The investigation of metaplasticity reminds us that individual subjects or preparations, even if *controlled for age, gender, *nutrition, or *context at the time of experiment, etc., could still differ not only in terms of their particular past experience on a specific activity or item of information, but also in their activity dependent *capacity to undergo plastic changes at any particular moment in time.

Selected associations: Development, Homeostasis, Long-term potentiation, Plasticity

Method

1. **A systematic procedure to attain a goal.**

2. **The set of procedures and techniques that guide the *planning, execution, and analysis of a type of tasks.**

Selecting a method and following it is like choosing a road and embarking on a journey (this indeed is the origin of the word: *meta-*, which is Greek for beyond, after, along with, and *hodos*, which is way, journey). The road may guide to the goal but at the same time impose *a priori limits on the terrain travelled and on the expected outcome. 'Methods' are fundamental to human cognition and action (definition 1; e.g. Newell and Simon 1972). Here we shall confine ourselves to scientific methods (included in definition 2, which is an elaboration of definition 1), and particularly, to methods used in the experimental sciences. Discussion of the methodology of science at large far exceeds the scope of this treatment (Nagel 1979; Bechtel 1988). Therefore, we shall identify only a few basic notions that are helpful in the discussion, classification, and evaluation of research.

Despite the fact that experimental science is wonderfully rich and heterogeneous, the number of elementary types of methods, or better 'metamethods', is modest indeed (Dudai 1993). The mythological muses of art and intellectual pursuit, daughters of Zeus and Mnemosyne (*mnemonics), were nine in number (Hesiod 8C BC); the practical muses of experimental science, daughters of logic, are fewer, but still as inspiring as the mythological ones. The core experimental methods are *observation, intervention,* and *simulation.* To these one should add complementary analytical methods, mostly *comparison* and *correlation.* The data that all these methods generate are further analysed and manipulated in various ways to yield heuristic *hypotheses,* conceptual frameworks, attitudes, and *paradigms, which temporarily govern mainstream knowledge in a given domain of science. If influential, these hypotheses, concepts, and paradigms come to sustain and cultivate recurrent rounds of observations, interventions, modelling, etc. A scientific career, a smashing discovery or an entire scientific discipline may start at any point along this never-ending methodological ritual. The aforementioned description is surely simplistic from the point of view of the history and the philosophy of science, but it does encapsulate the essence of the reality of scientific practice and *culture. The 'metamethods' are shared by different scientific disciplines. In addition, distinct disciplines have their own sets of domain-specific methods, which transform the general methods into specific procedures and techniques.

So let's encounter the metamethods, one by one. First come the core experimental methods.

1. *Observation.* This is the most fundamental of all the experimental methods, clearly preceding modern science. 'Observation' sometimes connotes non-*controlled as opposed to controlled experimental situations (e.g. Freedman *et al.* 1998). This is not the intention here. Careful observation in the course of controlled experiments could yield highly valuable and sometimes ground-breaking discoveries. Unfortunately, the good old practice of observation, which requires ample patience, openness, and experience, tends nowadays to be neglected by too many hyper-active investigators in their rush for tenure (*scoopophobia). Heuristic classifications, longer-lived *taxonomies, and signal hypotheses may emanate from smart observations (Hodgkin *et al.* 1977; for a notable example, see Darwin 1871). However, to contribute usefully to a scientific discipline, observations must usually be followed by the additional methods of intervention and simulation, to test hypotheses and generate *models. (On a special type of 'observation', 'introspection', which occupied a prominent position in the methodology of the early days of memory research, see *behaviourism.)

2. *Intervention.* This is a very popular type of research method. It is adored in *reductive research programmes. The aim of interventional methods is to infer function from dysfunction or hyperfunction. It is hence the *classical generic type of scientific experiment that involves active interference with nature to see what will happen. In the brain sciences, the agents used include interference in perception or in behavioural *performance; perturbation of metabolic cascades (e.g. *intracellular signal transduction cascades), using drugs or mutations; perturbation of the electrical activity of neurons and neuronal circuits: and anatomical lesions. Concrete examples are to be found in many entries in this book; e.g. *amnesia, *consolidation, *neurogenetics, to cite merely a few. For selected methodological issues related to the use and misuse of interventional studies, see Bechtel 1982, Glassman 1978.

3. *Simulation.* This type of methods attempts to imitate or simulate natural phenomena, processes, or candidate mechanisms. This is done in order to verify assumptions concerning structure and function, test models, predict performance, and generate new hypotheses. Simulation experiments come in two flavours, experimental and theoretical. In the experimental approach, phenomena, processes, or mechanisms are imitated or simulated by discrete experimental manipulations *in situ*. Examples include substitution of a *percept by electrical activity in the brain (Loucas 1936; Romo *et al.* 2000); of a conditioned stimulus (*classical conditioning) by *long-term potentiation (LTP; Skelton *et al.* 1985); of other types of learned input by identified molecular agents (Acosta-Urquidi *et al.* 1984; Kaba *et al.* 1994); and of *consolidation by the activation of *CREB (Yin *et al.* 1995). Some of these manipulations could also be considered 'interventions' (see 2 above), but their aim is specifically to imitate or simulate candidate biological processes and mechanisms of learning in order to prove their postulated physiological role. The theoretical use of this approach includes various types of simulations that are aimed at imitating as well as testing the natural phenomenon or parts of it (*algorithm, *model). In the near future we should expect to see more and more attempts to mimic or simulate living organisms, including their learning and memory capabilities, by electronic devices, creating '*in silico*' in addition to '*in vivo*' *systems (Normile 1999; *enigma). Simulation experiments could also involve 'thought experiments' ('*Gedanken experiments*'); these are controlled speculations, in which the entire 'experimental' manipulation is carried out in the imagination of the experimenter rather than on the bench or in the field (Sorensen 1992). However, fruitful thought experiments may require a more robust theoretical infrastructure than currently available in the neuroscience of memory.

All the above experimental methods are complemented and augmented by several analytical methods (for a *classic treatment, see Mill 1884). Two types are *comparison* and *correlation* (additional ones, related to *hypothesizing*, exceed the scope of this brief pragmatic discussion).

4. *Comparison* of sets of observations of the same variable under different conditions (e.g. memory as a function of *synaptic activity, drug treatment, age, *context), could illuminate the workings of processes and mechanisms in the system. This requires selection of appropriate variables, units of quantification, experimental design (including controls), and statistics (e.g. Martin and Bateson 1993; Freedman *et al.* 1998; Kerlinger and Lee 2000). Quantification, which is essential for scientific comparisons but also for other methods, deserves a special comment. The introduction of quantifiable variables is usually taken to mark the transformation of a field of interest into a scientific discipline. Sometimes the ingenuity of the forefathers of a scientific discipline is not in identifying the important

questions, but rather in identifying or devising the variables that could be quantified and used in order to address these questions. For example, Ebbinghaus (1885) made it possible to first quantify reproducibly the *capacity and the stability of human memory by introducing retention of nonsense syllables as a measured quantity (see also Jacobs 1887; for the first quantitative measures of animal memory, see in Boakes 1984; Gorfein and Hoffman 1987).[1]

5. *Correlation*. Here a natural or manipulated phenomenon is correlated, in time or space, with other phenomena in the same or another *level of analysis, in order to identify links among phenomena. In an important subtype of correlative experiments, and as part of reductive memory research programmes, behavioural phenomena are correlated with neuronal *plasticity. Selected examples are correlation of *fear conditioning with *amygdalar *LTP (Rogan *et al*. 1997), or correlation of learning with neurogenesis in the *hippocampus (Gould *et al*. 1999a). In such cases, the aim is to pinpoint cross-level mechanistic inter dependency. On the general problematics of the attempt to conclude causality from correlations, see Irzik (1996; also the pitfalls of *post-hoc* argumentation in *criteria).

It is easy to notice the affinity of the above 'metamethods' to the *criteria used to assess the contribution of experimental data to the resolution of a given research problem. Observations correlate phenomena, identify similarity, and hint at necessity; interventions identify necessity; and simulations yield information on similarity, usefulness, sufficiency, and even exclusiveness. In general, whereas the methods provide us with the knowledge, the criteria tell us about the relevance of this knowledge to the question posed.

The field of memory research is equipped with its own special repertoire of methods. These are exemplified in *classical conditioning, *cue revaluation, *delay task, *fear conditioning, *habituation, *instrumental conditioning, *LTP, *maze, *priming, *real-life memory, *sensitization, *transfer, and *working memory. But brain research in general is in a special situation. It is a truly multidisciplinary enterprise. The more it advances, the more it is quick to incorporate knowledge and methods from a great variety of other disciplines. These range from molecular, cellular, and *developmental biology, via physiology and anatomy, clinical neurology and *neuroimaging, psychology, and ethology, to computational science and information theory (Dudai 1989; Martin and Bateson 1993; Baddeley 1997; Manning and Dawkins 1998; Zigmond *et al*. 1999; Kandel *et al*. 2000). Not surprisingly, a recent textbook in the neurosciences is authored by no less than 150

experts in different fields and subfields, methods, and techniques, while still leaving some important topics and issues untouched (Zigmond *et al*. 1999).

Selected associations: Control, Criterion, Reduction, Simple system

---

[1]Ebbinghaus' method was very efficient and influential, but not without opponents. For a revolt against the use of nonsense material to test the faculties of human learning and memory, see Bartlett (1932; *classic), and *real-life memory.

Mnemonics

The use of mental techniques for assisting, improving and expanding memory.

Mr Memory, Hitchcock's master of facts, earned his living by performing feats of trivia pursuit in night clubs, while in parallel trusting to memory information for the sake of the notorious spy organization '39 Steps' (Hitchcock 1935). Most mnemonists, both in fiction and in real life, are engaged in much more innocent activities. In modern times mnemonists are either regarded as curiosities or at most as interesting *subjects for research. But only a few centuries ago, mnemonists were still masters of an important and respectable art.

Mneme is 'memory' in Greek (Mnemosyne was the mother of the muses; Hesiod 8C BC). Before writing became widespread (and surely before recording devices became inexpensive), the ability to trust data to memory was highly valuable, and mnemotechniques were extensively developed. From its early days, writing could have turned these mental techniques obsolete for most practical purposes. This was clearly appreciated by philosophers and teachers. Socrates tells us that when the God Theuth praised the newly invented art of writing, claiming that it will make people wiser, the Egyptian King Thamus responded: 'O man full of arts, to one it is given to create the things of art, and to another to judge what measure of harm and of profit they have for those that shall employ them... If men learn this, it will implant forgetfulness in their souls; they will cease to exercise memory because they rely on that which is written' (Plato, *Phaedrus* 274–275). Well, King Thamus panicked prematurely. In practice, for a very long period after its introduction, writing was used mostly for administrative purposes, and most of the population, being illiterate, could not make use of it anyway. Thousands of years after Socrates, in medieval

Europe, it was still common practice to regard written documents with suspicion because texts could not be challenged to defend their statements whereas people could (*false memory was clearly not on the mind of people as it is now). In societies all around the globe, epics and ballads continued to rely for many generations on oral traditions. Even after the invention of printing, printed bibles and books of prayers were considered primarily as aids to memorization by heart (Clanchy 1979; Ong 1982; Rubin 1995). Mnemonics, therefore, was not abandoned for a long while. On the contrary, great intellects devoted their energy to the development and improvement of 'artificial memory systems' composed of mnemonic techniques and procedures (Yates 1966; Carruthers 1990).

In a popular type of artificial memory systems, images of physical items or loci (e.g. rooms in palaces, 'memory theaters'; Figure 48), were associated in memory with specific items or meanings, and later used as a code to *retrieve them. Some expert mnemonists became legends in exploiting these techniques. For example, Peter of Ravena (fifteenth century) was said to

have memorized no less than 100 000 loci, and that '… on his travels, he does not cease to make new places in some monastery or church, remembering through them histories, or fables, or Lenten sermons. … He can repeat from memory the whole of the canon law, text and gloss … two hundred speeches or sayings of Cicero; three hundred sayings of the philosophers; twenty thousands legal points …' (Yates 1966). Superb memory and mnemotechniques were considered highly useful in church and government, and therefore, in *classic education, *Memoria* (trained memory) was part of the curriculum of language arts, side by side with grammar, logic, and rhetoric. It was told of Thomas Aquinas, the scholastic philosopher and theologian of the thirteenth century, that he was able to dictate simultaneously to four secretaries on four different subjects, and even go on dictating while asleep; in that he excelled Julius Caesar, who, fourteen centuries earlier, was said to be capable of dictating to four people while writing a fifth letter in his own hand, but no mention was made of his ability to keep on dictating from memory after falling asleep (Carruthers 1990).

Fig. 48 A popular type of mental 'artificial memory systems' was based on the allocation of items in memory to spatial maps of familiar locations. In this one, items are associated with buildings, rooms, and items in an abbey. (Johannes Rombrach, *Congestium artificiose memorie*, Venice 1533; reprinted in Yates 1966.)

Whether Aquinas was indeed capable of dictating something legible from sleep is questionable; he could have appeared as if in sleep at a state of extreme concentration. This is at least an explanation that would be favoured nowadays by those scientists who doze off in research seminars and then wake up to the applause to ask a question. Naturally, information about past memory feats and mnemonists is mostly anecdotal. However, we do have data on more recent cases (Stratton 1917; Luria 1969; Hunter 1977, 1978; Thompson *et al.* 1993; Brown and Deffenbacher 1995). From this information, based on only a small number of mnemonists, one could draw a conclusion that there are different mnemonic strategies. Compare, for example, the patient Shereshevskii of Luria (1969), and Professor Aitken, a mathematician, mental calculator, and mnemonist (Hunter 1977). Whereas Shereshevskii's mnemonics was of the classical type (see above), using imagery and forming a rich perceptual chain to link and retrieve information, Aitken formed a rich conceptual map to encode and retain his memory (*ibid.*).[1] Another conclusion is that some exceptional mnemonists display pathological traits, even to the degree of becoming 'idiot savants',[2] whereas others are apparently normal. For example, Shereshevskii led a rather miserable life and couldn't adjust to any profession (Luria 1969). Aitken was a professor of mathematics and it is left for the reader to judge whether this is entirely normal. And Rajan Srinivasan Mahadevan, who in 1981 recited from memory the first 31 811 digits of π and entered the Guinness Book of World Records, was described as a 'decently normal', 'average to above-average student' of cognitive psychology (Thompson *et al.* 1993). It would be of great interest to find out which brain systems subserve the performance of mnemonic feats like these of Shereshevskii, Aitken or Mahadevan. Do they use the same brain systems as do individuals with an average memory on the same task? *Functional neuroimaging of mnemonists could provide the answer (Pesenti *et al.* 2001).

Can ordinary individuals with an average memory become memory experts? It is useful to remember that practice and the perfection of *skill are bound to improve the skill-related aspects of memory. Experts do usually have a markedly larger task-related memory than novices in their field of expertise. Take chess as an extreme example. Master chess players clearly outperform novices or middle-range players, and some chess experts can remember as many chess positions as the above mentioned number of loci in the memory of the legendary Peter of Ravena (Chase and Simon 1973). What is it that turns the expert's memory, or the use of memory, so good? The elementary *capacity of memory probably remains the same, but the use of *metamemory, the chunking of information, the retrieval from long-term stores, and the switching from short-term to long-term stores and back, could improve tremendously (Chase and Simon 1973; Hirst 1988; Pesenti *et al.* 2001; *working memory). An improvement in chunking and retrieval rather than in capacity was also detected in controlled laboratory experiments, in which subjects succeeded in improving 10-fold their performance on digit span tests (Chase and Ericsson 1982).

All this suggests that practice, combined with personal mnemonic strategies for chunking, tagging, and association, could improve an average memory (Loisette 1899; Rawles 1978; Hirst 1988; Hertzog 1992). Here are some hints. *Spaced training could be useful. Test-type rehearsals instead of straightforward repetitions could be useful as well, for example, in assigning names to faces and thus preventing social embarrassment in parties (Landauer 1988). In the future, memory enhancing chemicals (*nootropics) and bionic gadgets might become available as well, but this is not really *bona fide* mnemonics any more.

Do we really wish to expand our memory, and if so, to what extent? A modest memory improvement is likely to be beneficial. But remembering too much could mean a decline in the ability to *generalize and to focus on important data. This is another manifestation of the general maxim of *performance, which states that moderation is the key to success. The sad life of Shereshevskii, who was overwhelmed by details and could not generalize, hints at the potential disadvantage of remembering much too much (Luria 1969; Dudai 1997*a*).

Selected associations: Capacity, Metamemory, Nootropics, Performance, Real-life memory

---

[1] Borges, in the marvellous story about Ireneo Funes who lost the ability to forget after being thrown off a horse (1944), endowed the fictitious hero with a mnemonic system in between that of Aitken and that of Shereshevskii: a mental idiosyncratic vocabulary of all the mental images ever encoded in the brain.

[2] Idiot savant (French for 'learned idiot') is a mentally impaired individual who exhibits genius in a highly specialized area, such as calculation or painting (Treffert 2000).

Model

1. **An abstract or concrete *system that represents another, usually more complex or less
familiar system.**
2. **A schematic representation that accounts for
properties of a system, often used to infer
additional properties and to predict the outcome of manipulations.**

All models (*modus*, Latin for 'a measure', 'standard of
measurement') are analogies (things similar but not
identical, Greek for 'proportionate'). Some are only
*metaphors, others sets of quantitative relations among
components of the modelled system, and yet others
somewhere in between. In the context of the present
discussion, it is useful to distinguish among (a) mathematical models, (b) diagrammatic models, and (c) the
use of the term 'model' to describe a *simple system that
could potentially illuminate phenomena of interest in
what is considered a more complex system. Although
different in type and complexity, all models share some
elementary methodological aims, pros and cons.

Basically, models are heuristics devised to explain
and predict (Lakatos 1978; *paradigm). A profound
question is whether we can do without them, i.e. are
they only mental aids, or an inherent necessity for
human understanding of nature (Duhem 1914; Hesse
1963). Some will argue that even what seems to us the
most accurate depiction of a natural phenomenon is
still a schematic model distilled through human cognition (*internal representation). Another issue is when
does a detailed representation loses its modelness,
hence usefulness as a simplifying and explanatory
agent. Borges (1964) has something to say about it:

> … In that Empire, the Art of Cartography reached
> such Perfection that the map of one Province
> alone took up the whole of a city, and the map
> of the empire, the whole of a Province. In time,
> those Unconscionable Maps did not satisfy and
> the Colleges of Cartographers set up a Map of the
> Empire which had the size of the Empire itself and
> coincided with it point by point. Less Addicted
> to the Study of Cartography, Succeeding Genera-
> tions understood that this Widespread Map was
> Useless and not without Impiety they abandoned
> it to the Inclemencies of the Sun and the Winters.
> In the Deserts of the West some mangled Ruins of
> the Map lasted on, inhabited by Animals and
> Beggars; in the whole Country there are no other
> relics of the Disciplines of Geography.

It is not uncommon to find great minds captivated
by their pet model to such an extent that they lose sight
of the initial question and reach a stage where the
model must be modelled to simplify it. This, of course,
is still an utterly legitimate and potentially rewarding
intellectual pursuit, only that its relevance to the original research objective deserves scrutiny.

1. *Mathematical models.* These usually combine an
attempt to *reduce biology into the exact sciences with
the quest for a powerful descriptive and predictive
language. In disciplines such as physics, models could
refer to a theory (Nagel 1979). As there aren't yet real
comprehensive formal theories with theory-derived
laws in the neurosciences, even the most 'formal' models of learning and memory are not formal in the full
sense of the term, but rather an hypothesis or experimental *generalization expressed in mathematical
notations. In the field of memory research, there are
influential formal models at different *levels of analysis.
An example at the level of *synaptic *plasticity is
provided by models that employ the Hebb type of
*algorithm (Hebb 1949), which assumes that the alter-
ation in synaptic weight is a function of the correlation
of pre- and postsynaptic activity. An example at the
level of behavioural learning is provided by models that
employ the Recorla–Wagner algorithm (Rescorla and
Wagner 1972), which proposes that in associative learning, the change in the associative strength of a stimulus
with a *reinforcer, depends upon the concurrent
associative strength of all present stimuli with that
reinforcer. Many other examples exist of semiquantita-
tive models at the system and behavioural level
(e.g. Raaijmakers and Shiffrin 1992).

A particularly important class of mathematical
models is that of artificial neural networks (ANN;
McCulloch and Pitts 1943; Amit 1989; Fausett 1994;
Mehrota *et al.* 1997). These models deal with the collective behaviour of systems that consist of a large number
of interconnected computational units ('neurons').
Signals are passed between units over connections,
which manipulate the signal in a typical way. Each unit
applies an activation function to its net input to determine the output signal. Networks are characterized by
the architecture of connectivity, the algorithm that
determines the weight on the connections, and the activation function of the units. The collective behaviours
of such networks appears to mimic various dynamic
properties of neuronal circuits, such as representation
of *percepts, learning and *retrieval. Certain types of
ANN are implemented in technological systems that
need to perceive, recognize, and learn from experience.

2. *Diagrammatic models.* These are rather common,
often intended as a didactic tool or as a rudimentary

functional explanation in familiar terms. Such models run the danger of being perceived as the real world rather than an analytic tool. Textbooks and papers provide many examples of such models: block and flowchart diagrams of *intracellular signal transduction cascades (Figure 39, p. 136), graphs of *phases in *acquisition, *consolidation, and *retrieval of learned information, or *maps of interconnecting brain circuits (e.g. *limbic system). Models of this kind commonly echo the contemporary technological *zeitgeist, borrowing, for example, from electrical engineering and computer science (*metaphor).

3. *Simple systems* as models. Here 'model' is usually a figure of speech more than a real model. The justification of the usage of the term is sometimes questionable and the outcome of this usage potentially problematic. There are two major types of so-called 'simple models'. One is organisms or naturally occurring biological phenomena that are used to cast light on properties of other organisms or phenomena. Examples include the use of animal systems in studying human cognition and disease (e.g. *dementia), the use of one species as a 'model' for learning and memory in remote species, or of a simple type of learning as a 'model' for other, more complex types of learning (for selected examples, see Thompson and Spencer 1966; Clause 1993; Suppes *et al.* 1994; D'Mello and Steckler 1996; Eichenbaum 1997a; Eisenstein 1997; Gallagher and Rapp 1997; Milner *et al.* 1998; Robbins 1998; also *Aplysia, *Drosophila, *monkey, *mouse, *rat). It should not be forgotten that 'simple organisms' did not evolve to serve as models for other organisms. Although one does expect some similarity to increase in an inverse proportion to the phylogenetic distance, rats and mice are not models for humans; they are rats and mice. If forgotten, this trivial truth may lead to erroneous conclusions on the properties of human brain, behaviour, and pathology, and promote fishing expeditions for *red herrings.

Another caveat concerning the use of simple organisms as models involves the distinction between homology and analogy. Homology (Greek for 'same reason', 'in agreement') refers to having the same phylogenetic or ontogenetic origin but not necessarily the same form or function.[1] Analogy refers to having the same form or function but not the same phylogenetic or ontogenetic origin. Whether one should expect to unveil homologies or analogies depends on the species used as a model, the physiology and behaviour modelled, and the level of analysis. For example, using invertebrate learning to model mammalian learning may unveil homology at the molecular and cellular level but only analogy at best at the circuit and behavioural level.

The other type of simple systems commonly referred to as models involves artificial manipulation of biological systems. A most popular example is *long-term potentiation (Bliss and Collingridge 1993). Such model systems unravel processes and mechanisms that might serve as candidate components of the real thing, e.g. of synaptic plasticity in the behaving brain under physiological conditions. A common problem in this type of models is that their practitioners may become trapped in the *homunculus fallacy: trusting that the *reduced model system should display properties of the complex system that it is supposed to model. Parts of a whole are not expected to display the properties of the whole, and if they do, one should suspect the simplification has gone too far.

Despite all the caveats, models of all the three aforementioned types are indispensable both as conceptual and as practical tools. They unveil phenomena, processes, and mechanisms that could later be pursued in the more complex and less tangible system. The trick is probably in always remembering to distinguish between the role of a system as a model and what it really is, and in having the courage to abandon the model, in spite of the great investment and affection, when its use invokes too many discrepancies with the original research goal.

Selected associations: Metaphor, Map, Paradigm, Simple system, System

---

[1]For the history and usage of this term, see Donoghue (1992).

Monkey

Any of various members of the order Primates, excluding the anthropoid apes and humans.

'This is what I see in my dreams about final exams: /Two monkeys, chained to the floor, sit on the windowsill/ The sky behind them flutters,/The sea is taking its bath./The exam is History of Mankind./I stammer and hedge./One monkey stares and listens with mocking disdain,/the other seems to be dreaming away—/But when it's clear I don't know what to say/He prompts me with a gentle/Clinking of his chain' (Szymborska 1995). It is the appreciation that monkeys are our closest phylogenetic relatives and share some of our intimate biological secrets, that fuels Szymborska's irony. Among all the species around us, the monkey's brain resembles ours the most. It is there that we often go in search for the rudiments of our higher cognitive faculties (*a priori, *declarative memory). 'Plato', remarked Darwin (1838a), "… says in 'Phaedo' that our 'necessary ideas' arise from the preexistence of the soul, are not derivable from experience—read monkeys for preexistence". And he also noted, musing relativity in the universe: 'If all men were dead then monkeys make men.—Men makes angles' (Darwin 1838b).

Monkeys belong to the order Primates, which has two major suborders (Bennett et al. 1995): The Prosimii ('pre' or 'early' monkeys) and the Anthropoidea ('human-like'). In general, prosimians have a long, wet nose, slightly sideways eyes, prominent muzzle and brow whiskers, and large mobile ears. Many of them are nocturnal species that rely on smell and hearing. Anthropoids have flatter faces, a dry short nose, no prominent whiskers, forward-facing eyes, and they rely mostly on vision. The prosimians and the anthropoids each are further classified into suborders: The prosimians into the Lemuriforms and the Lorisiformes, and the anthropoids into the Platyrrhini ('broad nose', New World Monkeys) and the Catarrhini ('hooked nose', Old World monkeys, apes and humans). The term 'monkey' is conventionally reserved to denote only the long-tailed, medium-sized primates, always excluding the anthropoids apes and humans, and frequently excluding also the prosimians. This classification also fits the term 'nonhominoid primates'. The monkey species most commonly used in medical and biological research are the macaques, which are Old World monkeys. They include the rhesus, Macaca mulatta (Bourne 1975), the Japanese macaque, Macaca fuscata, and the cynomolgus monkey, Macaca fascicularis. But other species are used as well.

Monkeys became occasional pets since times unknown. Their resemblance to humans also led to their use in early anatomical investigations (Morris and Morris 1966). They were among the first species to be systematically used in the early days of brain research and experimental psychology. Generally speaking, monkeys are employed in neurobiology for four main purposes:

1. As *models for human brain pathology. The contribution of the monkey to our understanding of the consequences of brain damage cannot be underestimated. The effect of circumscribed brain lesions on monkey's physiology and behaviour was systematically studied already more than a century ago (Brown and Schafer 1888). These studies have led to the discovery that the temporal lobe (Kluver and Bucy 1938) and frontal lobe (Jacobsen and Nissen 1937; Pribram et al. 1952; Fuster 2000b) play a key part in higher brain function, learning, memory, and cognition (*cortex, *limbic system, *working memory). In recent decades, extensive efforts have been devoted to the development of monkey models of human *amnesia. This has led to remarkable sophistication in lesion techniques on the one hand and behavioural testing on the other (e.g. Mishkin 1982; Zola-Morgan and Squire 1985; *delay tasks). Attempts to resolve the debate over the obligatory role (*criterion) of *hippocampus, *amygdala, and various adjacent cortical areas in memory are still largely based on lesions in monkeys (e.g. Suzuki et al. 1993). Even the fast developments in the *functional neuroimaging of human brain do not yet provide a satisfactory alternative.

2. As *systems for the investigation of the role of discrete brain areas and circuits in normal physiology and behaviour, of the alteration of these roles with development and experience, and, ultimately, of the nature of neural codes and *internal representations. Such research programmes rely on a variety of neuronal activity recording methods, including the use of single and multiple invasive electrodes as well as invasive or noninvasive functional neuroimaging, combined with behavioural protocols on the one hand and with modelling on the other (e.g. Miller and Desimone 1994; Vaadia et al. 1995; Britten et al. 1996; Goldman-Rakic 1996; Georgopoulos 1996; Malonek and Grinvald 1996; Nudo et al. 1996; Tanaka 1997; Logothetis et al. 1999).

3. As systems for exploring the capability and applicability of top-notch research and clinical methods, before they can be safely applied to humans (e.g. Logothetis et al. 1999).

4. Monkeys as well as hominoid primates are used to unveil the evolution of human cognitive abilities, including social interactions, self-recognition, tool usage, communication and language, and even rudimentary math (Anderson 1990; Greenfield and Savage-Rumbaugh 1993; Swartz 1997; Brannon and Terrace 1998; Kawai and Matsuzawa 2000; Ramus et al. 2000; on the criticism of the studies of human language in the apes, see Pinker 1994; *anthropomorphism).

Although monkeys are indispensable for multiple facets of brain research, they are not the easiest species to use in the laboratory. They require special handling, infrastructure, attitude, and quality time. They learn at a very slow rate some tasks that look so simple to humans; it may take many months to a year to teach a monkey to master certain *instrumental tasks. This may attest to the remoteness of the experimental protocols from *real life. The frustrated investigator should also ask himself or herself how long would it take for a naive, perplexed human *subject to acquire such tasks in the complete absence of verbal instructions. On top of it all, monkeys are prone to evoke human-like emotions, which may give rise under certain conditions to hesitations and scruples on the side of some human experimenters. Monkeys are also quick to draw the aggression of the so-called 'animal-rights' group. Whoever subjects animals to invasive manipulations should always keep in mind ample respect for the well-being of the other species; in the case of the monkey, this is even more so warranted.

Selected associations: Amnesia, Anthropomorphism, Declarative memory, Model, Subject

Mouse

A small mammal of the genus *Mus*, family *Muridea*, order *Rodentia* (rodents).

The common mouse (*Mus musculus* L.) is a pest for householders, a pet for animal lovers, a blessing for molecular biologists, and a hero for some psychologists. It even shared an Oscar: Cliff Robertson won his 1968 Best-Actor award for beating Algernon, a cute albino mouse, in racing in a *maze (Nelson *et al.* 1968). It is not clear, though, whether Algernon made it to the ceremony. Mice have accompanied human populations since prehistoric times. Similar to rats, they originated in Asia, and from there spread to the rest of the world. They were occasionally used for amusement in both East and West, and a mutant, the 'waltzing' mouse (see below), had been bred in China and Japan specifically for this purpose. Throughout the Middle Ages, mice were used in magic and folk medicine (Thorndike 1923). The first documented use in scientific investigation was by Robert Hook, who in 1663/64 experimented on the survival of the mouse in compressed air, hoping to gain some insight about the ability of man to breathe under water (Nichols 1994). But mice only found their way into the routines of laboratory life during the nineteenth century, when they were started to be employed in large numbers in the study of genetics. Many laboratory strains used today can be traced almost a century back to a few commercial colonies in the USA (Green *et al.* 1966; Hogan *et al.* 1994). DNA analysis shows that several of these strains originated

from a single female of the subspecies *Mus musculus domesticus*, the common house mouse. But as genetic material from other subspecies has been introduced over time into the genetic pool of the laboratory mouse, standard inbred strains are referred to as *M. musculus* only. The genetic making of the mouse can now be easily manipulated (see below), and new strains are produced on demand (mice were also already cloned from somatic cells; Wakayama *et al.* 1998).

The mouse has a lot to offer to biologists and psychologists alike. It is a small mammal (20–35 g), but not small enough to make the life of anatomists and physiologists miserable. The size of the brain is manageable. The generation time is 3–4 months, and the litter size six to eight in inbred lines. Handling is easy and the food inexpensive. Only the smell of the mouse colony is a potential obstacle. The mouse is an agile, social animal (Williams and Scott 1953). It has a rich behavioural repertoire, and is quick to learn, especially in natural situations that involve the chemical senses, spatial information, and social interactions. Perhaps the *classic example of mouse behavioural analysis is that of the dancing (waltzing) mouse by Yerkes (1907). Even Pavlov, whose favourite experimental *subject was the dog (*classical conditioning), switched to the mouse to study the inheritance of conditioned reflexes (Razran 1958). Since those early days, mice have been used extensively in the study of learning and memory (for a useful selection of paradigms, see Crawley and Paylor 1997). During a certain period, though, they seemed to have lost their priority in animal psychology laboratories to the *rat, which is larger and under certain situations less erratic in its behaviour. The undeclared battle was re-won only recently, with the resurrection of the mouse as the king of the *maze, due to the developments in molecular genetics.

Mice clearly beat rats in the field of genetics. For a mammal, the mouse is an impressive genetic machine. Sophisticated *methods have been developed in recent years for the application of reverse genetics to the mouse, i.e. targeting mutations to identified genes or altering gene dosage (*neurogenetics). These techniques are advancing at a very rapid pace, and the literature is almost overwhelmed with the description and analysis of mutant mice and their *development, physiology, pathology, and behaviour (Blake *et al.* 1997; Keverne 1997; Silva *et al.* 1997a; Nelson and Young 1998; Tang *et al.* 1999; Price *et al.* 2000; also the Mouse Genome sites on the Web). Furthermore, novel techniques now permit the generation of tissue-, cell type- and temporally restricted gene knockouts (for the particular application to memory research, see Tsien *et al.* 1996a,b;

Wilson and Tonegawa 1997; Shimizu *et al.* 2000; also *dementia, *hippocampus, *LTP). These techniques offer considerable advantages to the study of learning and memory, because they could be used to dissociate the effect of a mutation on development from those on behavioural plasticity, and, furthermore, localize the defect to specific brain regions and circuits.

The impressive pace of mouse neurogenetics, and the unavoidable (yet frequently justified) hype, turn it pertinent to pin-point several caveats. First, the novelty and smartness of a research method should not be confused with its usefulness. For example, in certain experiments that aim at establishing the specific role of an identified brain region in a narrow temporal *phase of memory *acquisition, *consolidation, or *retrieval, targeted microinfusion of a selective short-lived drug could be as useful as a knockout. It is also cheaper. Second, almost trivial but sometimes forgotten, careful attention must be devoted to the genetic background of mutant mice, because only if the same background is used, can the difference between the phenotype of the wild type and that of the mutant be ascribed to the mutation rather than the background (Silva *et al.* 1997*b*). This is particularly important in the study of behaviour, which, as a rule, is a polygenic trait, hence highly sensitive to modifier genes. Third, those who switch from rats to mice because of the genetic advantages of the latter, should be reminded that mice are not tiny rats. They have their own species-specific physiology and behaviour, and the interpretation of their *performance in learning and memory tasks depends on understanding what is it that the mouse really *perceives and does (e.g. Wolfer *et al.* 1998). And fourth, behavioural paradigms are not a pH indicator paper. You don't insert a mouse and get a reading. Before deciding on the basis of behavioural tests that a mutant, lesion, or drug has a specific effect on memory, one must carefully evaluate and exclude multiple genetic, developmental, environmental, as well as physiological and behavioural parameters that are not directly relevant to memory. This is not easy (e.g. Deutsch 1993; Gingrich and Hen 2000).

Selected associations: Dementia, Maze, Model, Neurogenetics, Subject

Neurogenetics

The use of genetics in the investigation of the structure and function of the nervous system.

Already in its infancy, psychobiology became fascinated by the role of heredity in behaviour. Foci of interest ranged from the inheritance of blushing (Darwin 1872) to that of exceptional talent (Galton 1869).[1] At first the approach was only observational (*method), and mostly anecdotal. But hardly half a century later, leading investigators were already engaged in the systematic selection of 'bright' vs. 'dull' strains in the rodent-in-a-*maze *paradigm (Tolman 1924). This approach was usually 'top-down', from the population and the behaviour to the individual and its genetics; the study of specific mutants, and the analysis of the effect of the mutation on the physical structure of the nervous system was still a rarity (Yerkes 1907). The newly formed discipline of behavioural genetics combined methods from ethology, experimental psychology, and quantitative genetics (Falconer 1960; Hirsch 1963). Only little was known at that time about the physical nature and structure of the genetic material and about the mechanisms by which the genetic information is transformed into physiological processes.

The revolution that has converted neurogenetics into the success story it is today, took place only after the overall strategy has been changed to 'bottom-up', i.e. searching for the role of identified single genes in physiology and behaviour (Benzer 1967). Single-gene analysis of learning and memory started in the fruit fly, *Drosophila* (Dudai *et al.* 1976; Dudai 1988; Tully 1996; Dubnau and Tully 1998). Over the years, learning mutants of *Drosophila* have contributed significantly to our current knowledge about the molecular mechanisms of *acquisition and *consolidation of simple memory (*CREB, *intracellular signal transduction cascade). Yet *Drosophila*, in spite of offering unique advantages to the geneticist, is not the dream machine of the neurophysiologist. With time it became indeed possible to identify the effect of specific mutations in identified brain regions and even single neurons that subserve learning (Corfas and Dudai 1990; Waddell *et al.* 2000; Zars *et al.* 2000; Dubnau *et al.* 2001), but central neurons in the fruit fly do not yet succumb to the electrode in the same way that central mammalian neurons do. Furthermore, being an invertebrate, *Drosophila* is incapable of providing clues to the operation of the mammalian brain at the circuit and *system *level. Neither does it disclose anything about issues such as emotional memory (*amygdala, *fear conditioning) or *declarative memory.

Enters the *mouse. In the past decade or so several spectacular developments have taken place in the field of mouse genetics, which now make it possible to add engineered genes to the mouse genome or remove other genes at will, and generate mouse lines that will express the mutation and propagate it in their progeny. Genes can be added or lesioned in other organisms as well, e.g. *Drosophila* or zebrafish, using a variety of methods. The point is, however, that the ability to engineer the mouse genome in an efficient, flexible, and reproducible manner has swept the mammalian brain for the first time to the forefront of neurogenetic analysis. Among mammals, the mouse is still unique in this respect; appropriate neurogenetic techniques are not yet available, for example, in the rat.

In the present context we need to become familiar with two specific terms only, 'transgenic' (TG) and 'knockout' (KO) mice. Without going into the methods in which TGs and KOs are actually generated (Jaenisch 1988; Joyner 1993; Wassarman and DePamphilis 1993; Nagy 1996; Torres and Kuhn 1997), suffice it to say that TG is the generic term for an organism with foreign pieces of DNA incorporated into its genome, and KO for an organism in which a gene is ablated *in situ*. TGs are used to test the effect on physiology and behaviour of extra genes, normal or mutated. KOs are used for the analysis of the loss of normal gene function. 'First generation KOs' affect the expression of the gene throughout the body, during *development and in adulthood. The absence of regional and temporal specificity makes it impossible to conclude that the effect of

the KO on learning and memory is independent of developmental or general anatomical and physiological impairments. In 'second generation KOs', the KO is targeted to a specific region or cell type (Tsien *et al.* 1996*a*; Wilson and Tonegawa 1997). In 'third generation KOs', the expression of the mutation is also regulated in time in a reversible manner (Mayford *et al.* 1996; Shimizu *et al.* 2000). This permits exploration of the role of the gene in discrete *phases of learning and memory. At the time of writing, the onset or offset time of gene expression in third generation KOs is measured in hours, which is not terrific for the analysis of acquisition, consolidation, or *retrieval of memory, but this is likely to improve.[2]

The use of transgenic mice has already contributed markedly to our knowledge on the role of identified molecular processes in *plasticity, learning, and memory. To name just a few selected examples, KOs have been used to identify the role of types of a variety of *protein kinases, of subtypes *glutamatergic receptors, and of *CREB and other transcription factors in *long-term potentiation and in a variety of *classical and *instrumental learning situations. They have also proved useful in probing the relations between *long-term potentiation and learning, and the role of *hippocampus in learning and memory (Grant *et al.* 1992; Silva *et al.* 1992; Abeliovich *et al.* 1993;

Fig. 49 A suspected case of reverse genetics. The group that has isolated *dunce*, the first memory mutant in the fruit fly, **Drosophila*, headed by Seymour Benzer, shortly after making their discovery at the California Institute of Technology (Dudai *et al.* 1976). This discovery started the now flourishing discipline of the molecular–genetic analysis of learning and memory.

Bourtchuladze *et al.* 1994; Mayford *et al.* 1996; Rotenberg *et al.* 1996; Tsien *et al.* 1996*b*; Wilson and Tonegawa 1997; Shimizu *et al.* 2000). Interestingly, the overexpression of the glutamatergic *N*-methyl-D-aspartate receptor in the forebrain of a transgenic mouse was shown to enhance the performance of some learning tasks (Tang *et al.* 1999), indicating that genetic engineering could potentially be used not only to investigate memory, but also to improve it. In addition to their use in research of neuronal plasticity and elementary learning mechanisms, transgenic mice are employed to *model the aetiology and mechanisms of Alzheimer's disease (Price *et al.* 2000; *dementia).

There is no doubt that state-of-the-art neurogenetics is extremely useful in elucidating the molecular and cellular machinery of developmental and behavioural plasticity. The sophistication of the current molecular neurogenetic methodologies is really impressive. However, from the point of view of learning research, similarly to other cutting-edge techniques such as *functional neuroimaging, it is only a tool, not the goal. To become really useful, it must be teamed with additional methodologies and levels of analysis, such as cellular and circuit physiology, neuroimaging, and, clearly, fine behavioural analysis.

Another point to remember is the distinction between neurogenetics as a research tool and neurogenetics as a philosophy. There is a big gap between the demonstration that a gene product influences learning, memory, or any other cognitive faculty, and the conclusion that the gene product is deterministic for the behaviour in question (Rose 1995*a*). The more we learn about the role of development in moulding physiology and behaviour, the more we understand the complexity of the genome, the more we realize how complicated is the behaviour~*f*(genes) equation. The impressive success of the Human Genome project (International Human Genome Sequencing Consortium 2001; Venter *et al.* 2001), provides us with new powerful experimental tools, and with a marvellous potential for further understanding of the brain. But they also call for proper humbleness: we still have to travel a long way to unravel the real contribution of identified genes to learning, memory, and other aspects of cognition in humans (e.g. Flint 1999; Plomin 1999).

Selected associations: Development, Drosophila, Immediate early genes, Intracellular signal transduction cascade, Mouse

---

[1]Scientists were not, of course, the first to pay attention to the genetics of behaviour. They were preceded by countless animal breeders, pet lovers, circus owners, and other entrepreneurs, who were collecting and breeding useful mutations and strains for commercial purposes or just for fun.

[2]For comparison, the onset and offset time of conditional, temperature-sensitive mutations in *Drosophila* is only a few minutes (Kitamoto 2001).

Neurotransmitter

1. **A chemical substance that is secreted from the pre*synaptic nerve terminal into the synaptic cleft and acts as a *stimulus on the post-synaptic terminal.**

2. **A chemical substance that is released by a neuron and acts as a stimulus on a cellular target.**

'Neurotransmitter' is a term nowadays in use not only by neuroscientists but also by the lay person citing from the popular science columns. Yet both the concept and the term were nonexistent only a century ago. At that time it was thought that nerve–nerve and nerve–muscle communication is always electrical (*synapse). The first to propose explicitly that a chemical substance, adrenaline, is liberated from the sympathetic nerve terminal to act upon its muscle target, was Elliott (1904). But the story actually starts earlier. The mere idea that a nerve may release a chemical substance for communicating with other cells was proposed by Du Bois-Reymond in 1877 (cited in Dale 1938). The first hints of evidence were provided by an English physician, George Oliver, who spent his leisure time inventing clinical instruments and testing them on his own family members (Dale 1948). One of these instruments was designed to measure the thickness of an artery under the skin. Oliver (how horrible) injected extracts of various animal glands into his young son. Using his new instrument, he observed that an extract of the adrenal gland altered the diameter of the artery. He rushed to tell the story to Professor Schafer in London, who was experimenting on blood pressure in dogs. Together they replicated the experiment, this time without Oliver's son, whose name somehow did not enter the scientific literature (Oliver and Schafer 1894). This has led to the identification of some physiological effects of the extract, which was later to become known as 'adrenaline'. Lewandowsky, Langley, and others subsequently described additional physiological properties of adrenaline (e.g. Langley 1905). This was the background for Elliot's suggestion that adrenaline relays information from the nerve to the muscle.

Adrenaline was indeed the first substance to be proposed as a transmitter, but the first transmitter substance to be isolated as such from living tissue was *acetylcholine (Loewi 1936; Dale 1954). Synthesized by chemists and extracted from the rye fungus (ergot), acetylcholine was found to be a potent cardiac blocker. The trail of experiments that had culminated in its identification in the nervous system started with an instance of *state-dependent memory. The person beyond the critical experiment, Otto Loewi, was a restless sleeper. One night he awoke suddenly with the idea that if the vagus nerve inhibits the heart by liberating a chemical substance, this substance might diffuse out into a solution left in contact with the heart, and then transferred to inhibit another heart. He scrabbled the plan of the experiment on a scrap of paper and went to sleep again. Alas, the next morning he could not decipher his scribbles. He spent the whole day trying to understand what he wrote, but in vain. The next night he awoke again, with vivid recall of the experimental plan. There are two versions on what actually happened later (Cannon 1934; Finger 2000). In the more romantic version, which clearly fits a movie script, Loewi dashed off to his lab in the middle of the night to perform the experiment. In the second, more mundane version, he wrote a detailed account of what he had in mind and went to sleep again. In any case, by the subsequent day the experiment was done. Loewi took two frogs, removed their heart, and placed each in a salt solution. He left the terminal of the vagus nerve on one heart but removed it from the other. He then stimulated the vagus nerve on the first heart, collected aliquots of the bath solution, and transferred it to the chamber containing the second heart. The denervated heart slowed down. This meant that the stimulation of the vagus secreted into the solution a compound that was capable of controlling the heart in the absence of the nerve. After much additional work, the compound, first dubbed *Vagusstoff* ('vagus substance'), was identified as acetylcholine. It is told that since that discovery, Loewi became ardently interested in dreams (Finger 2000). But this is another story.

The *classic view of a neurotransmitter is provided in definition 1 above: a substance released from the presynaptic on to the postsynaptic terminal, triggering there a cascade of events that result in excitation (excitatory neurotransmitter) or inhibition (inhibitory neurotransmitter). This is a point-to-point, or one-to-one, unidirectional communication. With time, the concept of 'neurotransmission' was expanded. First, it was found that neurotransmitter molecules could act on the same neuron that releases them, usually to modulate transmitter release (reviewed in Powis and Bunn 1995). This is still a one-to-one communication, but the cellular target is also the source of the signal, i.e. the presynaptic rather than the postsynaptic terminal. Second, it was found that neurotransmitters could act by diffusion on distant targets in the absence of direct synaptic contacts. This one-to-many communication is termed 'volume transmission' (Zoli *et al.* 1999). It is especially relevant to the concept of 'neuromodulation' (see below). Third, it was discovered that some compounds that transmit information between neurons, such as the gas nitric oxide (NO, Zhang and Snyder 1995), are not released via specific synaptic sites to bind to membrane receptors, but instead diffuse out of the membrane to adjacent cells to interact with intracellular receptors. This is either one-to-one or one-to-few communication. Further, these compounds convey information from the postsynaptic into the presynaptic terminal, contrary to the conventional wisdom of neurotransmission; they are therefore termed 'retrograde messengers' (e.g. Figure 42b, p. 150). Finally, neurotransmitters act on and released by glia cells as well, although only little is so far known on this topic (Araque *et al.* 1999).[1] All these modes of transmission are accommodated by the more comprehensive definition 2 above.

We are currently familiar with scores of transmitter substances, and even the simplest nervous system contains a surprising number of them (Brownlee and Fairweather 1999). The classical transmitters are small molecules, such as acetylcholine or *glutamate. About 10 are identified, most of which are amino acids (the building blocks of proteins) or their derivatives (acetylcholine is an exception). To these we should add the neuroactive peptides, which are much more numerous (Cooper *et al.* 1996) Endogenous opioids are only one example. And to these we should add the 'nonconventional' transmitters such as gases and small lipid molecules (Medina and Izquierdo 1995; Zhang and Snyder 1995). At this point in our discussion, two additional points deserve attention. First, how do we decide whether a compound is a neurotransmitter? Several attempts have been made to identify the relevant *criteria (e.g. Werman 1966). These criteria must fit not only the classical view of chemical transmission (definition 1) but also the more modern views (definition 2). The only universal criteria are probably the release from a neuron and the action as a stimulus on a target cell. Of course, the transmitter must be synthesized, and later degraded or removed from its site of action, but these functions must not necessarily be carried out by the source and the target cell, respectively.

Another point is the distinction between a 'neurotransmitter' and a 'neuromodulator' (Kaczmarek and Levitan 1987; Harris-Warrick and Marder 1991; Lopez and Brown 1992; Katz and Frost 1996). Conventionally, when this distinction is used, the term 'neurotransmitter' is reserved to those stimuli that transmit fast information between one neuron and another in a one-to-one mode (definition 1 above). They exert their effect by directly gating *ion channels ('ionotropic *receptors') in the target neuron. In contrast, 'neuromodulators' modify the ability of neurons to respond to neurotransmitters and by other stimuli, commonly by indirectly modulating ionic channel complexes, for example, via 'metabotropic *receptors', their downstream *intracellular signal transduction cascades and *protein kinases. Neuromodulators alter the intrinsic properties of neurons, affect their excitability and ability to extract signal from noise, and hence gate, rescale, and bias incoming information. This enriches the computational and representational *capacity of the circuit and, furthermore, encodes at the cellular *level parameters such as *attention, *context, and internal states (e.g. Hasselmo 1995; Shulz et al. 2000). However, in the literature, and apparently also in real life, the distinction between neurotransmitters and neuromodulators is not rigorous. For example, is glycine acting on the regulatory site of the *glutamatergic N-methyl-D-aspartate receptor, a modulator or transmitter? Or, most authors would consider NO as a transmitter, but it is not limited to a one-to-one communication mode, and does not directly gate channels. It is therefore useful to consider types of transmitter substances as components of a whole spectrum, ranging from fast-acting, bona fide transmitters, to slow-acting, diffusing, bona-fide modulators.

In the context of memory research, we should note that neurotransmitters and neuromodulators are molecular stimuli that in their concerted activity convey to the target neurons and circuit information about *percepts, activated *internal representations, and endogenous brain states (e.g. Hasselmo 1995; McGaugh and Cahill 1997; Arnsten 1998; Fellous 1999). Therefore they are particularly relevant to the *acquisition and *retrieval phases in the operation of those circuits that encode the relevant representations. The specific combination of neurotransmitters and neuromodulators arriving at the synapse at any given point in time is critical in determining whether the synapse will change as a consequence of the experience,

and if so, for how long (e.g. *coincidence detection, *long-term potentiation). But the role of the transmitters themselves is transient. Even in those cases in which the retention of learned information in a circuit is believed to be based on the modulation of transmitter release (e.g. *Aplysia), the transmitter molecules do not store information over a prolonged time; the persistent alteration in their availability is a consequence of a lasting changes in other cellular components, such as channels, receptors, or cytoskeletal elements and transmitter-release mechanisms.

Selected associations: Acetylcholine, Acquisition, Glutamate, Receptor, Synapse

---

[1]Glia (Greek for 'glue'), or neuroglia, is a generic term that refers to multiple types of non-neuronal cells in the nervous system, which fulfil multiple roles in providing a proper microenvironment, and metabolic and functional support for neuronal function. The possibility that glia cells have a computational role in the brain should not be excluded. See also *synapse.

Nootropics

Compounds that enhance cognitive function.

The term 'nootropics' (from Greek, noos—mind, tropos—turn) was originally coined to denote chemical compounds that were reported to enhance cognitive function, including learning and memory, without possessing other significant effects (Giurgea 1973). The best known are piracetam and structurally related compounds (Giurgea 1973; Gouliaev and Senning 1994). Over the years, however, the term has acquired a peculiar flavour. Many authors reserve it for compounds that are reputed to boost cognition, but were not rigorously proven to do so. Others use it to refer to compounds that have proven beneficial effects on cognition but whose mechanism of action is yet unknown. There is actually no reason why 'nootropics' shouldn't be used as a generic term to denote compounds that enhance cognition, whether their mechanism of action is known or not. But this is a matter of taste.

The search for a memory potion clearly antedated the introduction of the term 'nootropics'. It was mostly disappointing. Even the literary imagination did not come up with a simple solution. To learn the fine details of the collective past, the poet in the Divine Comedy, much like Odyssey before him, had to go through Hell

(Dante 1314; *limbic system); and in modern times, Borges' Funes, the ultimate memorizer, was endowed with limitless memory only after knocking his head in an almost fatal horse accident (Borges 1944; *mnemonics). A more realistic and systematic approach to memory enhancement began by the same Lashley who was searching for the *engram. He found that strychnine (a poison that interacts with the *receptor for the *neurotransmitter glycine) accelerates the learning *performance of rats in a maze, albeit only in concentrations that produce tremor and motor incoordination (Lashley 1917). More recent research has provided evidence that other stimulants as well could enhance memory if administered around the time of training (McGaugh 1966; McGaugh et al. 1993), but toxicity prevents these drugs from being used as cognitive enhancers.

In the late 1960s, a new compound with a structural resemblance to the inhibitory neurotransmitter γ-aminobutyric acid (GABA), piracetam (2-pyrrollidoneacetamide), was tested for its effects on motion sickness, and subsequently reported to enhance learning and protect against *amnesic treatments in rats (Giurgea 1973; Gouliaev and Senning 1994). Soon afterwards, additional pyrrollidone derivatives were synthesized and tested, and some reported to improve learning and memory in both rats and humans (Mondadori 1993; Deberdt 1994; Gouliaev and Senning 1994). In parallel, compounds unrelated to the piracetam family were also added to the nootropic list, among them newly synthesized chemicals (e.g. Mondadori et al. 1991), and natural preparations with a respectable history in traditional medicines (e.g. ginkgo biloba extracts; Deberdt 1994). The nootropic efficacy of most of these compounds was, however, debated from the outset. Furthermore, no agreement has been reached on their mechanism of action in the brain. Interactions with neurotransmitter and neuromodulatory systems (and see below), *ion channels, membrane fluidity, steroid hormones, and neuronal energy supply, have all been suggested (Olpe and Lynch 1982; Mondadori 1993; Gouliaev and Senning 1994).

Meanwhile, rational design has led to the development and identification of new classes of cognitive boosters (Staubli et al. 1994; Ingram et al. 1996; Giacobini and McGeer 2000). The first drugs to be approved for alleviating some early symptoms of *dementia act by enhancing transmission via *acetylcholine (Crimson 1994; Giacobini and McGeer 2000). The identification of the role of the α-amino-3-hydroxy-5-methyl-4-isoxazole propionic acid (AMPA) type of *glutamatergic receptors in *plasticity resulted in the synthesis of ampakines, AMPA agonists that cross the blood–brain barrier, enhance excitatory synaptic response and *LTP, and improve memory in rats (Staubli et al. 1994) and humans (Ingvar et al. 1997). In the latter, an ampakine was reported to improve performance on several sensory and spatial learning tasks, but not on cued *recall of verbal information and on tasks that measure arousal and *attention only. Interestingly, facilitation of AMPA receptors is one of the effects seen with piracetams (Gouliaev and Senning 1994). In vivo this glutamatergic effect is probably limited because of the rapid metabolism of piracetam in peripheral tissues (Staubli et al. 1994). Research on agonists of the benzodiazepine binding sites on GABAergic receptors was also considered (Raffalli-Sebille et al. 1990; Izquierdo and Medina 1991; *lotus). The anxiogenic effects of these compounds could pose, however, a severe problem.

Drugs that interact with the cholinergic, glutamatergic, and additional neurotransmitter systems are expected to enhance *acquisition and possibly *retrieval of learned information. Other compounds might boost *consolidation. An appealing target for consolidation boosters is the *CREB system. Other transcription factors and *immediate early genes could be targeted as well. At the time of writing, nootropics that act on these targets are still unavailable. To develop them is not an easy task, because one must identify those elements of the transcriptional and translational regulatory systems in neurons that are critical for learning and memory, but not for other essential cellular processes (e.g. *homeostasis).

Whichever their mechanism of action, either on acquisition, on consolidation or on retrieval, it is likely that safe and effective nootropics will ultimately become available, even as over-the-counter medications. Their effect on the *capacity of *real-life memory, on cognitive functions such as categorization and decision making, and on emotion, should make an interesting topic for countless PhD theses.

Selected associations: CREB, Glutamate, Lotus, Mnemonics, Nutrient

Noradrenaline

A biogenic amine that functions as a *neurotransmitter and a hormone.

Noradrenaline (NA, alias norepinephrine, 2-amino-1-(3,4-dihydroxyphenyl)ethanol) belongs to a family of compounds called catecholamines (see also *dopamine). It is synthesized from dopamine in the brain, sympathetic nerve, adrenal medulla, and heart by the enzyme dopamine-β-hydroxylase (DBH; Cooper et al. 1996). Noradrenaline fulfils multiple roles in *development, physiology, and behaviour (Mason 1984; Thomas et al. 1995; Thomas and Palmiter 1997*a*). A related catecholamine, adrenaline (AD, alias epinephrine) is synthesized from NA by the enzyme phenylethanolamine N-methyltransferase. Adrenaline was the first substance to be proposed as a neurotransmitter (Elliott 1904). In the periphery both NA and AD act as transmitters and hormones. In the brain, NA is much more abundant than AD, and less is known about the function of the latter.

The noradrenergic innervation in the brain is diffused and reaches a large variety of targets. The majority of the noradrenergic innervation originates in the locus ceruleus, in the pontine central grey (Figure 50). This cluster contains about 3000 neurons in the rat and 25,000 in human. Several major noradrenergic tracts travel from the locus ceruleus and innervate targets in most of the brain. Noradrenergic neurons also reside outside the locus ceruleus, in the lateroventral tegmentum. Much of their output intermingles with that of the locus ceruleus but the targets are not identical.

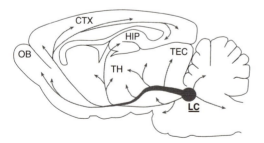

Fig. 50 A schematic diagram of the central noradrenergic projections from the locus ceruleus (LC) in the mammalian brain. Only selected targets are marked. CTX, cerebral cortex; HIP, hippocampus; OB, olfactory bulb; TEC, tectum; TH, thalamus. (Adapted from Cooper et al. 1996.)

NA released from nerve terminals interacts with adrenergic *receptors (adrenoreceptors). These exist in multiple types, which differ in their localization, ligand binding properties, and downstream *intracellular signal-transduction cascades. A major classification of noradrenergic receptors is on the basis of rank affinity for NA, AD, and the synthetic agonist isopernaline (ISO); α-adrenoreceptors are defined as NA > AD ≫ ISO, and β-adrenoreceptors as ISO > AD = NA. All the adrenoreceptors are targets for potent drugs (Milligan et al. 1994). As is the case with many other neurotransmitters and neuromodulators, additional NA binding-proteins exist in brain, including cross-membrane transporters, active in reuptake (Blakely and Bauman 2000). The transporters are also targets for efficient neuroactive drugs.

The fact that noradrenergic drugs affect performance on memory tasks, and that the turnover of NA in the nervous system correlates with certain behavioural states, has led already more than 30 years ago to the suggestion that NA plays a part in learning and memory (Kety 1970). It is now agreed that in a variety behavioural paradigms, memory is enhanced by treatments that induce NA release or activate NA receptors, and impaired by treatments that reduce NA release or block NA receptors (Mason 1984; McGaugh and Cahill 1997; Roullet and Sara 1998). There is especially strong evidence for the involvement of adrenoreceptors in the *amygdala in the storage of information for inhibitory avoidance (McGaugh and Cahill 1997; Ferry et al. 1999). Adrenoreceptors are also obligatory in the *cortex for the formation of memory in another avoidance paradigm, *conditioned taste aversion (Berman et al. 2000). In some other learning situations NA ligands were reported to have no effect (Pontecorvo et al. 1988). Similarly, mice lacking NA because of a knockout (*neurogenetics) in the DBH gene, display only mild defects in some learning and memory tasks and perform normally in others (Thomas and Palmiter 1997*b,c*). All in all, the pharmacological, neuroanatomical and genetic interventions suggest that NA affects functions that are obligatory for memory formation only in certain situations.

What could these functions be? There is evidence that the noradrenergic system contributes to the encoding of selective *attention, vigilance and novelty detection, stress, emotion, and motivation (Steketee et al. 1989; Decker and McGaugh 1991; Aston-Jones et al. 1994; Smith and Nutt 1996). NA does this in concert with other neuromodulatory systems, such as *acetylcholine and dopamine (Hasselmo 1995; McGaugh and Cahill 1997). At the system level, the aforementioned functions could be achieved via noradrenergic activation of the amygdala (McGaugh and Cahill 1997), of the cortex, and of the reciprocal thalamocortical processing (McCormick 1989; the modulation of thalamocortical information could specifically subserve novelty detection, Ahissar *et al.* 1997; *surprise). At the cellular level, it is noteworthy that NA was found to modulate *glutamatergic *N*-methyl-D-aspartate receptors in *hippocampus, via the cyclic adenosine monophosphate cascade (Gereau and Conn 1994; Raman *et al.* 1996). This fits with the idea that NA contributes to the encoding of *context, which modulates glutamatergic input, affects cellular signal-to-noise ratio (Segal and Bloom 1976; Hasselmo 1995; Jiang *et al.* 1996), and contributes to the overall decision made by the neuron and the circuit, whether or not to retain the incoming information.

The possibility could be raised that the activity of the noradrenergic system, similarly to that of the cholinergic and the dopaminergic systems, is not essential for the operation of the 'core' molecular machinery that embodies lasting *synaptic changes in some systems of the mammalian brain. The distinction between a 'core' and an 'accessory' synaptic storage system is not self-evident. Generally speaking, it implies that there are molecular cascades that are essential for synaptic storage and there are others that are indispensable for encoding distinct cellular and circuit states but dispensable for the storage process *per se*. For example, certain subtypes of the intracellular signalling cascades that lead to the modulation of gene expression and to *protein synthesis in *consolidation of long-term memory, could be regarded as components of the core machinery of synaptic storage. It is likely that in a variety of areas of the mammalian brain, glutamatergic transmission is essential for the *in vivo* triggering of this core machinery. In contrast, certain neuromodulatory systems may trigger state-dependent activation of the core machinery or set the threshold of its activation, but storage could take place in their absence, provided the core machinery was set into action by other means. The identity of the core machinery itself, however, may still depend on the task.

Selected associations: Context, Dopamine, Neurotransmitter, Receptor, Synapse

Nutrients

Substances and compounds required by living tissues for metabolism and energy production, growth, maintenance and reproduction, remodelling, and communication.

'Food for thought' is not merely a cliché. The discussion of the association of satisfactory nutrition with efficient cognition has transcended long ago the domains of folk psychology. Ribot, one of the forefathers of modern neurology (see *amnesia), postulated that '... the basis of memory is ... nutrition; that is to say, the vital process per excellence' (Ribot 1882). It is now established that even without too much mental effort, our brain consumes an impressive amount of energy. The adult human brain, while weighing only 2% of the total body weight, consumes 15–20% of the total resting oxygen consumption (Guyton 1991; Ganong 1993); in a 6-year-old child the value is about 50% (Kennedy and Sokoloff 1957). In the resting brain, energy is generated almost exclusively by the oxidation of glucose (Siesjo 1978). A substantial proportion of this energy is used up by molecular pumps that maintain proper concentration gradient of ions, such as *calcium, across the neuronal membrane, thus ensuring neuronal excitability and responsiveness (Guyton 1991; *ion channel). Glucose is derived continuously from the capillary blood, as only a tiny supply of glucose is normally stored as glycogen in the neurons at any given time (*ibid.*). In periods of activity, local metabolic rate and blood flow increase dramatically in the activated area (Roy and Sherrington 1890; Fox *et al.* 1988; Sokoloff 1989; Malonek and Grinvald 1996). These fast activity dependent processes provide the biological basis for a variety of *functional neuroimaging techniques (Raichle 1994). They are also reflected in the intense molecular turnover that is detected in neurons immediately after a physiological or behavioural experience (*consolidation, *homeostasis, *immediate early genes, *protein synthesis). Which metabolic pathways supply the instantaneous surge of energy in activated neural circuits, is still a subject of controversy. Whereas some investigators favour the view that hard-pressed neurons resort to anaerobic metabolism, similarly to exercising muscles (Fox *et al.* 1988), others report that active neurons, similar to resting ones, stick to oxidative metabolism (Malonek and Grinvald 1996).

The fact that a working mind consumes much energy, has led to the idea that the lack of proper foodstuff might impair intelligence. Many types of nutrients in addition to energy sources are also very important for brain and cognition. Vitamins or minerals are examples. Deficiency in these may cause severe neurological and cognitive disorders. For example, thiamine deficiency in chronic alcoholism results in *dementia (Korsakoff's syndrome, Butters 1985). Many other vitamins as well as minerals (e.g. iodine, iron) are also essential for a healthy brain (Ganong 1993; Scrimshaw 1998). Improper intake of vitamins, minerals, and essential amino acids is a pressing problem in undernourished societies, where it may adversely affect child *development and cognitive achievements (Scrimshaw 1998). Lipids, which are required among others in intercellular and *intracellular signal transduction and in regulation of membrane fluidity and excitability, are also important for proper cognitive function. Some lipid preparations were claimed to act as cognitive boosters (*nootropics) and memory enhancers (Yehuda and Carasso 1993, Yehuda *et al.* 1996).

The composition of the diet should also not be ignored by investigators who experiment on laboratory animals. A change of a diet may affect *performance on learning tasks, and under certain conditions, an imbalanced or poor diet may ultimately result in amnesia (e.g. Guo *et al.* 1996).

Even in healthy individuals on a balanced diet, what is placed into the mouth, and especially when it is placed there, may make a lot of difference as far as cognition is considered. This, at least, is the conclusion that emerges from a number of reports in recent years. For example, drinking a glucose-rich beverage was found to improve learning and recall in healthy adults (Manning *et al.* 1998). Similarly, in healthy students, failure to eat breakfast impaired learning and memory throughout the day; the problem was easily amended by drinking a glucose-supplemented drink (Benton and Parker 1998). The improvement in memory performance correlated with blood glucose. It has yet to be determined whether the beneficial effect of sugar on cognition is a consequence of a boost to the energy of the brain, or of augmentation of neurotransmitter synthesis (e.g. *acetylcholine), or other metabolic processes. Nevertheless, all in all, the data imply that children should not be sent to school without breakfast; that politicians should not decide on state matters without ensuring that their blood glucose has reached a sufficiently high level; and that elderly people should pay proper attention to what they eat and when they do that. It also argues against diets that reduce calorie intake to absurdity—unless definitely deemed a must by an expert physician.

Selected associations: Dementia, Development, Homeostasis, Nootropics

Observational learning

1. The *acquisition of novel behaviour by observing its *performance by a model.

2. The generation or modification of lasting *internal representations of actions, or actions and their consequences, by observing the behaviour of a model.

'Whatever you see me do, do like-wise', said Gid'on to his selected three hundred men, blew the shofar, waved the torch, and surprised the Midyanites in their camp (*Judges* 7: 17–22). He was a master demonstrator in an observational learning class. A lot of what we learn in our lifetime, from others we learn, frequently by observing a model and adapting its actions. In *real-life, the model is a conspecific; in the lab it could be an individual of another species or a behaving inanimate.[1] This capability, to gain from the experience of others, clearly expands the behavioural repertoire of individuals much beyond the limits of their own innate (*a priori) responses and solo experience combined.

Behaviours emitted or acquired via social interaction are termed 'socially dependent'. They are widespread and observational learning is but one type. Socially dependent behaviours include: (a) *socially released* behaviour; (b) *socially facilitated* behaviour; (c) *social learning*, which includes imitation and observational learning, instructed learning, and collaborative learning.[2] In socially released behaviour an innately predisposed response pattern, such as courtship or attack, is triggered by the *perception of a specific *stimulus (Lorenz 1981). In socially facilitated behaviour, there is an increase in the frequency or intensity of response that is already in the individual's active repertoire, e.g. eating or locomotion, when in the presence of others that are engaged in the same behaviour (Clayton 1978). In contrast, in social learning, the interaction results in new behaviour. This interaction could be between a model and a learner (imitation and observational learning), an intentional teacher and a learner (instructed learning), or two or more learners (collaborative learning; Tomasello *et al.* 1993). The differentiation among observational, collaborative, and instructed learning is appropriate in the discussion of social learning in humans, but not necessarily in other species, in which the parties in the learning process might be unaware of their 'formal' role in it. Collaborative and instructive learning will not be further discussed here.

Many authors use the terms 'imitation' (or 'imitative learning') and 'observational learning' interchangeably. This should not, however, blur the wide spectrum of complexity of the behaviours involved. Others prefer to reserve 'imitation' to describe a subtype of observational learning, in which the learner faithfully duplicates the behavioural performance of the model. In the more flexible forms of observational learning, the learner emulates the behavioural strategy involved, not only the overt motor acts, and is clearly capable of adapting and improving the learned behaviour to attain the goal. Another point to note is that 'observational learning' connotes visual learning, whereas 'imitation' covers all the sensory modalities. In the rest of this discussion, for the sake of convenience, the term used will be 'imitation and observational learning' (abbreviated IOL).

Our knowledge of IOL draws from research in multiple disciplines: behavioural psychology and ethology; education, developmental and social psychology; and cognitive psychology and the philosophy of mind. The systematic discussion of IOL in behavioural psychology and ethology was initiated already in the nineteenth century; examples from this period are provided in Darwin (1871, 1872), Romanes (1882), and Morgan (1896). Most contemporary reports on species other than humans were mostly anecdotal (*anthropomorphism). The interpretation of the factual or the alleged data was at first rather shaky. In this context, even Darwin erred: he suggested that in evolution, the dog has started to bark in an attempt to imitate its talkative human master (Darwin 1872). Since then, IOL has been documented in a great variety of species, ranging from guppies and octopi, via birds and cats, to *monkeys and apes (John *et al.* 1968; Griffin 1984; Anderson 1990; Cheney and Seyfarth 1990; Fiorito and Scotto 1992; Barresi and Moore 1996; Whiten *et al.* 1996; Marler 1997; Laland and Williams 1997; Templeton 1998). And, reassuringly enough, not only humans find it more rewarding to learn from other's mistakes than from their successes (Templeton 1998).

Research in education and social psychology has contributed tremendously to our understanding of the role of IOL in human *culture (Deahl 1900; Miller and Dollard 1941; Bandura 1962; Bandura and Walters 1963; Bandura 1986). A major question is how much of children's behaviour is moulded by observing their parents, their siblings, their classmates, or TV? The answer is simple: a lot. IOL starts already in the neonate (Meltzoff and Moore 1977), and plays a central part in

shaping behaviour throughout the critical periods of emotional and cognitive *development (Piaget 1962). For example, in a *classic, influential set of studies, it was found that children who observe a model rewarded for aggressive behaviour tend to exhibit more aggressive responses than children who see the model punished (Bandura *et al.* 1963) (Figure 51). This is a case of 'vicarious learning', so called because the *subject sympathizes with the reward or punishment of the model without experiencing it itself (Bandura and Walters 1963). It is difficult to overemphasize the importance of the findings on the role of IOL in children, especially in a TV-dominated society. Some kids may be misled to think that jumping in front of a car is safe and kicking another guy is good, because on TV stuntmen/women are never hurt and villains live happily forever (Potts *et al.* 1996). IOL keeps working throughout life, even in situations in which we are utterly unaware of it; for example, in a restaurant, what we order is influenced by incidental observation of the reaction of others to the food (Bayenes *et al.* 1996).

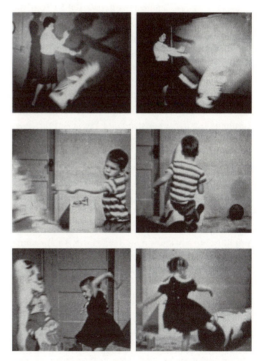

Fig. 51 A *classic study of observational learning: children imitate the aggressive behaviour of an adult model they had observed torturing an inflated doll on film. In this study, on the average, gender had a clear effect: boys displayed more acute aggression toward the doll, whereas girls were more inclined to sit on the doll rather than punch it. (From Bandura *et al.* 1963.)

There used to be in the literature a temptation to use complex forms of IOL as evidence that subhuman species have, similarly to *Homo sapiens*, a 'theory of mind', i.e. that the individual of the species can impute mental states to itself and to others.[3] This is because in some situations it seems as if the observer really 'reads the mind' of the model. This is why cognitive psychologists and philosophers of the mind discuss IOL (e.g. Gallese and Goldman 1998). A caveat is, however, appropriate: even a remarkable capability to learn from the other is not sufficient to prove a 'theory of mind', as the behaviour might still be explained by *associative conditioning, rendering the theory of mind explanation superfluous (*criterion, *Ockham's razor). The acid test for a 'theory of mind' is the ability to compute what the other subject will do on the basis of *false belief*, not *physical reality*, because *cues in physical reality could govern the behaviour of the observer without the need to access the mental state of the other individual. Possibly, in addition to humans, only great apes have a (rudimentary) 'theory of mind' (Barresi and Moore 1996; Frith and Frith 1999).

What brain mechanisms subserve IOL? Given the rich repertoire of IOL performances in various species, no single solution should be expected, at neither the computational, nor the neuronal hardware *level. The problem is easier to approach in the laboratory in tasks that involve elementary motor acts, such as imitation of reaching or grasping in humans and monkeys. The *methods used to analyse the imitating brain are cellular physiology in the behaving monkey, and *functional neuroimaging in humans. A useful conceptual starting point is that IOL of simple motor movements exploits elementary motor subroutines of the learner. The learning therefore does not involve *de novo* generation of the entire movement on the basis of the information received by observation of the model. In other words, here is another example of the rule 'to learn something, you must already know a lot' (*a priori). An appealing hypothesis is that the learner matches the *percept with its own motor representations of motor action, in order to understand (Jeannerod 1994) and learn (Rizzolatti *et al.* 1996; all this is done implicitly; no *declarativity required).

Evidence from both humans and the monkey concur with this 'matching' or 'resonance' hypothesis. In the monkey, neurons were detected in the pre-motor area in the frontal cortex, which fire both when the monkey performs an action and when it observes a similar action made by another monkey or by the experimenter (di Pellegrino *et al.* 1992; Rizzolatti *et al.* 1996). These neurons are termed 'mirror neurons'. Similarly, in humans, areas were identified in the frontal and parietal lobe that are activated both when a movement is performed by instruction or by imitation (Iacoboni *et al.* 1999). In another study, brain regions involved in *planning and generation of action, including frontal cortex, were activated in humans that observed an action with the intention to imitate it, as opposed to observation only (Decety *et al.* 1997). These data indicate that the neuronal circuits that subserve the perception and learning of the action-to-be-imitated overlap with circuits that subserve the preparation and the execution of the same action. If we *generalize a bit, and look at the other facet of the coin, this conclusion echoes the so-called 'motor theories' of speech perception (*birdsong, *performance): in order to understand an action, we must be able to perform it.[4]

Selected associations: Acquisition, Birdsong, Cerebral Cortex, Internal representation, Planning

---

[1]Using inanimate models could be tricky, as animals often distinguish between animates and their inanimate replicas, and might fail to imitate in the absence of the live model; e.g. see discussion in Rizzolatti *et al.* (1996).

[2]Some socially dependent behaviours do not fit easily into this *taxonomy. For example, the transfer of food information from one rat to another via odours (Galef *et al.* 1984) is social learning, but could hardly be considered observational, or *bona fide* collaborative, or instructive. Also, relevant to socially dependent behaviours is biological communication, which includes many types of vocal, visual, olfactory, and somatosensory species-specific communication systems, and, of course, human language.

[3]The 'theory of mind' is termed 'theory' because the mental states are not directly observable but inferred, and this inference is used to make predictions. The term in this meaning was introduced by Premack and Woodruff (1978), in the context of their studies of the chimpanzee. Similar notions are 'mentalizing', and an 'intentional stance'; having an 'intentional stance' means treating the other subject as an agent with intentionality (Dennett 1987; on intentionality as a *criterion for mental systems, see *system).

[4]This also echoes a maxim of scholastic philosophy, resurging in Vico (1710): only the one who makes something can fully uderstand it. Alas, the generalization of this wisdom to most human behaviours is clearly questionable.

Ockham's razor

The maxim that entities are not to be multiplied beyond necessity.

The Franciscan theologian William of Ockham (also spelled Occam; 1285–1347), later of Oxford, was a most influential medieval scholastic (Adams McCord 1987; Colish 1997). In his analysis of the Universe and human ability to perceive it, Ockham proposed that phenomena should be better explained in terms of the simplest causes rather than the more complex ones. Admittedly, he was not the first to suggest such a principle of parsimony. Even more so, his principle was rather qualified: 'No plurality should be assumed', said Ockham, 'unless it can be proved (a) by reason, or (b) by experience, or (c) by some infallible authority' (Adams McCord 1987), meaning that the Bible, the Saints, and the Church can make exceptions, and, furthermore, God is not in the game: 'There are many things that God does with more that he could do with fewer' (*ibid.*). In spite of his hesitation to regard the principle as a sweeping universal, Ockham's name became associated with it forever. Almost half a millennium later, the French philosopher de Condillac referred to Ockham's principle *metaphorically as 'the razor of the Nominalists',[1] paving the way to the current idiom 'Ockham's razor' (Safire 1999). It became and remained 'a most fruitful principle in logical analysis' (Russell 1945).

Ockham's razor has a derivative in the behavioural sciences, termed Lloyd Morgan's Canon: 'In no case may we interpret an action as the outcome of the exercise of a higher psychical faculty, if it can be interpreted as the outcome of the exercise of one which stands lower in the psychological scale ' (Morgan 1894). Lord Morgan's canon was a cautionary reaction to overenthusiastic accounts of animal intelligence, that have dominated late nineteenth century psychology as a consequence of Darwin's theory of evolution. 'There is no fundamental difference between man and the higher mammals in their mental faculties. With respect to animals very low on the scale … their mental powers are much higher than might have been expected' (Darwin 1971). *Anthropomorphism became a trend in leading circles of the discipline of animal behaviour. It attained its pinnacle in the *classic book on animal intelligence by Romanes (1882), in which the author based generous interpretations of animal cognition on anecdotes obtained from secondary sources. Against that background, a canon of parsimony was utterly justified.

To the neuroscientist at the turn of the twenty-first century, Ockham's canon is still a useful guideline, but in practice is easier to quote than to use, and in any case, must not be followed blindly. The major initial successes in modern biology relied on an Ockham's razor-guided world view; modern *neurogenetics drew from the same conceptual source (Benzer 1967). *Models of artificial neuron-like networks focused in their early days on minimalistic neuronal units, but soon afterwards appreciated the need for at least a partial mimicking of

real-life complexity (Segev 1992). The problem is that in general, when scratched beyond the surface, biological *systems display much more complexity than first expected. For example, a brief period of naive hopes that the map of *intracellular signal transduction cascades is around the corner, gave way to the realization that the intricacy and complexity of these signalling networks and their interactions is overwhelming, and that their analysis requires radical rethinking not only of the methodologies but also of the education of biologists (Alberts 1998). Enzymes and *receptors are amazingly intricate machines with multiple regulatory sites and permutational states. The same holds for the regulatory apparatuses of gene expression (Lewin 1994; *immediate early genes). The living cell is hence packed with highly elaborate miniature machines and their understanding in great detail is the subject matter of gargantuan efforts (Alberts and Miake-Lye 1992; Bray 1995). And on top of it all, organisms and neural preparations initially regarded as *'simple systems' soon ceased to be simple anymore (Byrne and Kandel 1996; Wolpaw 1997; see also on the demise of simple explanations of *classical conditioning; Wasserman and Miller 1997). Even the rejection of anthropomorphism is not so trivial nowadays; for example, is the suggestion that in certain conditioning protocols the rabbit becomes *consciously aware of the associated events, in conflict with Ockham's razor (Clark and Squire 1998; *declarative memory)?

The difficulty beyond all this is that we simply do not know whether the complexity that we detect is real and non-parsimonious. In Ockham's own words, we cannot determine whether 'God (did) with more that he could do with fewer' (see above). We also cannot simply conclude that a biological system, assumed to be moulded by aeons of opportunistic evolution, had evolved to take the simplest route to its goal. The remedy to this dilemma is to identify what information a system encodes at each *level of its organization, be it a molecular ensemble within the neuron or a neuronal ensemble within the brain, and then find out whether the so-called 'complexity' is indeed essential for the representation of the relevant information. If it turns out that many detected variations in individual elements, say enzymes in signalling networks, are irrelevant to the encoding of critical information (e.g. Barkai and Liebler 1997), then there is a better hope for a simple explanation of the operation of the seemingly complex system. Admittedly, it is hard to believe that nature has taken all these pains to ensure highly intricate regulation of proteins and cells in order to end up in systems in which this complexity is not important. We are thus back to square one.

Fig. 52 Proponents of parsimony: William of Ockham (*left*) and Lloyd Morgan. Seven hundred years after the introduction of Ockham's maxim, the student of memory struggles to navigate properly between the lure of simple explanations and the complex reality of biological *systems.

So may be the solution to the dilemma presented by Ockham's razor is on the pragmatic level: we should adhere to the maxim of parsimony merely as a reminder that we had better focus first on the simplest facets of our experimental systems, because in real life biology is too complex for us to approach otherwise. And the overall take-home message is that it is not easy to handle biological systems with tools borrowed from logic unless we understand what the logic of the system is.[2]

Selected associations: Anthropomorphism, Clever Hans, Declarative memory, Observational learning, Reduction

---

[1]Nominalists deny the existence of universals. Universals are *generalizations of knowledge, abstract properties and relationships, that contrast with particulars, which are instantiated objects. Generally speaking, nominalists believe only in the existence of particulars, whereas their opponents, the realists, do believe in addition in universals (Armstrong 1989). Compare also 'token' vs. 'type' in *system. Nominalists and realists come in multiple versions, but a discussion of these variants in the present context would certainly defy Ockham's razor.

[2]Which brings us back to the question whether to fully understand we must be able to fully produce the *system; see *criterion, *observational learning.

Palimpsest

1. **A surface, such as vellum or parchment, that has been written on more than once, with the previous writing incompletely erased.**

2. **A text that reflects its history.**

3. A memory system in which new patterns are stored on top of previous ones.

The term had originated from Greek *palimpsestos*, 'scraped again' (*palin*, again, + *psestos*, scraped). It seems to have occurred first in the writings of the Roman poet Catullus (Hammond and Scullard 1970). When vellum was scarce, especially in the early middle ages, early manuscripts were erased and the writing material used again. As the removal of the original writing was seldom complete, valuable religious and classical texts have been recovered from such palimpsests (Lewis and Gibson 1900; Cuddon 1979; Shailor 1988). For example, the important mathematical text called *The method*, by Archimedes, was discovered in Constantinople as a tenth century manuscript on leaves of parchment over which Eastern Orthodox prayers had been added in the thirteenth century (Boyer 1989).

'Palimpsest' has been used as a *metaphor for brain and mind by Romantic writers. 'What else than a natural and mighty palimpsest is the human brain? ... Everlasting layers of ideas, images, feelings, have fallen upon your brain softly as light. Each succession has seemed to bury all that went before. And yet ... not one has been extinguished ... Yes, reader, countless are the mysterious hand-writing of grief or joy which have inscribed themselves successively upon the palimpsest of your brain' (De Quincey 1866). Postulated palimpsestic properties of biological memory systems were also contemplated by Freud (1925). Similarly, Gestalt psychologists have proposed that new memory records are inscribed on top of old ones (Koffka 1935).[1] 'Palimpsest' resurfaced in modern neurosciences with the introduction of *models of artificial neural networks (Nadal *et al.* 1986; Amit 1989; Amit and Fusi 1994). In subclasses of such model networks, which keep a permanent *capacity for learning, new patterns are stored on top of old ones that get progressively erased (*ibid.*).[2]

Palimpsestic memory systems may be classified into two major conceptual classes. In the first, the new memory is an autonomous representation that displaces and nullifies the old one(s). This is a 'winner-takes-all' situation. In the second, the new pattern is superimposed on the old one(s) to yield a representation that is different from both old and new (here too, with repeated learning memories may ultimately be diluted to practical extinction, but they always leave a mark on younger representations). This latter version of the concept retains more faithfully the original connotation of a palimpsest.

Ample theoretical and experimental data support the second aforementioned process in brain, i.e. new experience interacts with previous ones to generate new *internal representations. For example, *percepts interact with endogenous brain activity at any given moment ('pre-representations'; Young 1979; Heidmann *et al.* 1984), activity that itself is expected to be at least partially experience dependent, to yield new patterns of brain activity (e.g. Arieli *et al.* 1996). If this indeed is the case, substantial implications emerge for both philosophical and practical issues such as the degree of objectivity of percepts and knowledge, the role of *a priori knowledge in learning, and the fidelity of memories (*false memories, *real-life memory). It also reflects on the question whether memories could indeed be utterly *forgotten.

Selected associations: A Priori, Cell assembly, Experimental extinction, False memory, Retrieval

---

[1]For more on the Gestalt, see *binding, *insight.

[2]It is noteworthy that 'Palimpsest' found another modern use, in the critical theory of literature and culture, to denote the thesis that literary texts are rewritten versions of earlier texts, and hence writing is rewriting, e.g. Genette (1997).

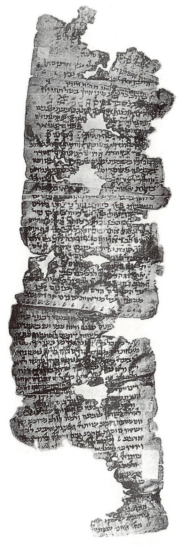

Fig. 53 A palimpsest fragment. A Hebrew script from the tenth/eleventh century, part of a Liturgical poem (*Piyut*), runs on a piece of coarse vellum across an older syriac text, a chapter of Deuteronomy from the tenth century (Lewis and Gibson 1900). The Hebrew letters faded until they have become of essentially the same hue as the older Syriac ones. In palimpsests like this one the different strata of the text are easily discerned. However, in some palimpsests the new text merges with the old one and occasionally a newer text emerges. This is the idea beyond 'palimpsest' in *models of memory.

Paradigm

1. **An ideal instance of a concept.**
2. **An example that serves as a model.**
3. **A standard concept, method, or procedure used in a discipline.**
4. **A set of concepts, practices, findings, and beliefs that dominates a discipline and affects its activity, structure, and progress.**

Paradeigma (Greek for *pattern*) was used by Plato in various meanings of 'example', including an ideal instance of a concept, a model and a standard (e.g. *Statesman* 278b*sq.*; Guthrie 1975). In the scientific literature, 'paradigm' is occasionally used to denote a standard concept, method, or procedure (definition 3, e.g. 'the *classical conditioning paradigm', 'the *conditioned taste aversion paradigm', etc.). It was, however, Kuhn (1962) who endowed 'paradigm' with its broader meaning and central position in the philosophy, sociology, and history of science (definition 4).

Kuhn treated the culture of science from a historical perspective. He differentiated five stages in the ontogeny of a scientific discipline: immaturity, normal science, crisis, revolution, and resolution. 'Immaturity' is characterized by fact gathering in the absence of an accepted conceptual and practical framework. 'Normal science' is 'research firmly based upon one or more past scientific achievements ... that some particular scientific community acknowledges for a time as supplying the foundation for its further practice' (Kuhn 1962).

These achievements form 'paradigms' (definition 4). Paradigms are constructs of thought (shared concepts and beliefs), methodology (standard methods and practices), and sociology (they underlie the behavioural code and *esprit des corpes* of the discipline, as reflected in professional societies, journals, and meetings; *culture). Achievements that give rise to paradigms delineate the workings of the discipline, yet are sufficiently open ended to leave problems for resolution in the future. Crisis arises when anomalies pop-out in the worldview that is advocated by the paradigm, and success in solving problems and advancing the field slows down. The crisis ultimately leads to a revolution, in which a new paradigm starts to emerge. The new and old paradigms, according to Kuhn, are incommensurable, and the revolution is characterized by a struggle between the disciples of each. Finally, the struggle is resolved with the new paradigm prevailing—till the next cycle.

Kuhn's analysis was very influential, itself approaching the status of a paradigm in the philosophy and history of science. Typical of Kuhnian paradigms, it encountered crisis and gave way to new accounts of scientific practice (Hacking 1981; Bechtel 1988), in which 'paradigms' were replaced by other concepts, such as 'research programmes' (Lakatos 1978) or 'traditions' (Laudan 1977). For the purpose of the present discussion, 'programmes' and 'traditions' could be described as families of theories with some shared characteristics, which, in contrast to Kuhnian paradigms, coexist to various extent throughout the ontogenesis of the discipline. Hence, in the philosophy of science, Kuhnian paradigms and revolutions are not so trendy anymore, but still, they retain some usefulness in contemplating the state of the art and the progress of a given discipline.

It is only fair to note that even if Kuhn's account of the ontogeny of scientific disciplines were valid, the question would still remain whether the science of learning and memory has attained the status of 'normal science'. The answer is not simple. Kuhn, similarly to many philosophers and historians of science, drew mostly from the analysis of physics, in which theories and paradigms are easier to delineate. Research on learning and memory combines multiple disciplines, ranging from psychology via neurobiology to computational science. In each of these disciplines, the level of 'normality' (in the Kuhnian sense) is different. Nevertheless, for the sake of argument, analysis of the field of learning and memory with Kuhnian tools is of substantial interest. It sharpens attitudes, illuminates the source of current trends, and provides perspectives on popular scientific as well as social practices.

So which are the paradigms of memory research? The discipline at large draws on some paradigms that are shared by other disciplines in the natural sciences. Because these paradigms are at a higher levels of *generalization, we can consider them as 'metaparadigms'. Here are examples:

1. *Reductionism. Well, this is surely a successful paradigm. The secret of using it smartly is to focus on those *levels of analysis that fit the discipline. This is not at all trivial in memory research (*internal representation, *learning; Dudai 1992).

2. *Modularity.* This paradigm considers biological systems as composed of modules, or elementary systems, either cross or within levels. Modularity serves reductionism. At the same time, it could lure us away from considering the system as an integrated whole. For the fingerprints of the modularity paradigm in the cognitive and the brain sciences, see *engram, *functional neuroimaging, *phrenology; also the critique in Fuster (2000a).

3. *The Panglossian paradigm.*[1] This paradigm posits that natural selection is an optimising agent, and therefore biological systems are neatly adapted to perform particular tasks (Gould and Lewontin 1979; Dennett 1983). The Panglossian paradigm guides us to search for an adaptationist explanation whenever we encounter an incomprehensible system. The truth might be that the system is as is because of built-in, accumulating internal constraints, irrespective of the assumed adaptation; or that the ongoing evolution of the system is still far from the optimum.

In addition to the above 'metaparadigms', other paradigms are more specific to memory research. In the history of psychology, several schools have approached the status of the dominant paradigm at their time (e.g. Weimer and Palermo 1973; Gholson and Barker 1985). Most notable were *introspective psychology*, that has characterized the emergence of the 'new psychology' in Germany a century ago (Boring 1950a), and the subsequent reaction to it, *behaviourism. In current neuroscience, a few paradigms fuel the *zeitgeist. A major example is provided by the prevailing concept that *long-term memory is* embodied in *synaptic remodelling and growth*. This conceptual framework has definitely reached the status of a Kuhnian paradigm, influencing so much of the current research in molecular and cellular neurobiology (see *consolidation, *CREB, *development, *immediate early genes, *late response genes, *protein synthesis). The *classification of memory systems* into *declarative and nondeclarative (*taxonomy) is another contemporary paradigm. And the assumption that *long-term potentiation (LTP) is memory* is yet another example, still a mini-paradigm, but ambitiously aiming higher.

Given the current paradigms of memory research, and adhering for the sake of argument to the Kuhnian terminology—will revolutions ensue? As noted above, when facts are difficult to explain in terms of the existing conceptual framework, be it a paradigm or a research programme or a tradition, they herald new concepts and ultimately change worldviews (e.g. Lightman and Gingerich 1991). It would be naive to assume that statements such as memory=growth, or LTP=memory, will not succumb to anomalies. Behaviourism did, to the complexity of language (Chomsky 1959) and of learning (Dickinson 1980). The exclusiveness of instantaneous associations in *associative learning, if it was ever substantiated in the data, was diminished by the documentation of effective long-delay associations in nature (Garcia 1981). Even the hegemony of laboratory experiments, whose practitioners came to worship reaction times, avoidance boxes, and *mazes, was shattered by the complexity of *real-life memory (Neisser 1978). Interestingly, in all the above cases, the prevailing paradigm did not disappear, but rather lost some of its inflated status, while retaining its usefulness side by side with newer paradigms. The piecemeal evolutionary accounts of Lakatos (1978) and Laudan (1977) seem thus to be more realistic than the Kuhnian sharp survival of the fittest. This means that on the one hand, even paradigms that currently seem amazingly robust are not immortal, but on the other, their spirit will survive in their progeny.

Selected associations: Development, Bias, Culture, Reduction, Zeitgeist

---

[1]Dr Pangloss ('entirely-language'), the teacher of Candide (Voltaire 1759), was the ultimate incurable optimist. He justified every disaster in the world by the *a priori assumption that everything under the sun is for good cause. Pangloss was hanged, which, judged by his own philosophy, couldn't be but good.

Percept

1. A short-lasting *internal representation of an on-line sensory *stimulus.

2. An internal representation of a sensory stimulus.

3. The *conscious experience of sensed energy.

'Percepts' are glimpses of the sensory world captured by the brain in real-time (definition 1; from per- + capere, 'to seize' in Latin). These short-lived representations serve as raw material for more advanced analysis of the sensory world. The brain then decides, within a few milliseconds, whether to pay *attention and use the information for further processing, or simply forget about it. Research on perception is an extremely rich and dynamic discipline at the core of the neural and cognitive sciences (Hochberg 1998). It addresses the whole gamut of processes and mechanisms by which the nervous system extracts information from sensory input. In the context of this type of research, 'percept' is also referred to not as the initial internal representation of the stimulus, but as the intermediate or end-product of central analysis (definitions 2 and 3). Construed this way, 'percept' denotes a *memory, as it outlives the stimulus. As noted below, the distinction between 'percept' and 'memory', specifically 'immediate' memory (*phase), is not trivial. In discussions of learning and memory, however, there are merits to such a distinction. Furthermore, for the purpose of the present discussion, considering percept as dependent on awareness (definition 3), which is central to cognitive treatments of percept, is not obligatory. Hence the more restricted, *reductive definition 1 is here preferred.

Information about the world arrives at our brain via sensory channels. The interaction of sensory energy with peripheral receptors at the front end of these specialized channels is termed 'sensation'. 'Perception' involves processes downstream of the peripheral receptors. Both the peripheral receptors and the central sensory units could be characterized using multiple *criteria; two common ones are modality, i.e. the type of energy detected, and the 'receptive field', i.e. that portion of the world from which that energy can affect the detector. Over the years, philosophers and psychologists have been debating and re-debating the relative role of the external and internal (brain) world in perception. What the frog's eye tells the frog's brain (Lettvin et al. 1959) may depend not only on what is in front of the eye, but also on what is at its back. The debate can be illustrated by contrasting theories of 'direct' vs. 'indirect' perception. Both types of theories agree on the basic good old philosophical tenet that 'perceiving is knowing' (Price 1950; Hall 1964; Burnyeat 1990). They disagree, however, on critical elements of this tenet. Adherents of 'direct' theories (alias 'ecological', 'stimulus-centred') suggest that the focus of perceiving is in the animal–environment interaction rather than in the animal, and perception is merely the selection and capture of information that is awaiting us outside there (Gibson 1979;

Michaels and Carello 1981). In contrast, proponents of the 'indirect' theories (alias 'information-processing', 'constructivist') propose that in perception, sensory data interact with endogenous information and are subjected to neuronal computations before becoming meaningful and useful (Ullman 1980; Rollins 1998). The view taken in this book is the latter. Ample data indicate that sensory areas in the brain function as filters tuned to specific sets of features (Dosher and Sperling 1998; Nakayama 1998). The information flows in both bottom-up and top-down streams (Knierim and Van Essen 1992; Ullman 1996; Jones et al. 1997; Nakayama 1998), with the latter possibly involving interactions with endogenously generated pre-representations (*a priori) as well as with previously acquired representations. The process probably becomes accessible to consciousness only at brain stations far from the sensory periphery (e.g. Crick and Koch 1995). Ultimately it *binds into a coherent percept. Thus, sense data do not represent the whole physical object but only selected aspects of it, biased by the species' and the individual's experience.

The fine tuning of central sensory systems and, as a consequence, the perception of attributes of sensory stimuli, is altered during brain *development in the young and by experience in the adult. This experience-dependent modification in the ability to extract information from sensory stimuli is termed 'perceptual learning' (Hebb 1949; Sagi and Tanne 1994; Goldstone 1998). Perceptual learning is manifested in multiple alterations in perceptual competence, including discrimination, categorization, and the attentional valence attributed to sensory features. It could involve the formation of perceptual 'sets',[1] and is implicated in a wide range of behaviours. In addition to the overall maturation of sensory abilities, these behaviours include, among others, filial and sexual *imprinting during sensitive periods early in life; re-adjustment of sensory capabilities in response to insult (*map, *plasticity); and the acquisition of sensory *skill. Fine discrimination of odours in wine tasters is but one refreshing example for the latter (Bende and Nordin 1997). Whereas the normal brain is destined to benefit from improved perception over time, certain pathologies do the opposite. 'Agnosias' lead to failure in perceptual processing and recognition in the absence of disorders of sensation or language (Peach 1986). Their investigation assists in identifying brain regions that are involved in specific aspects of normal perception.

'Percept' by definition 1 above is a transient internal representation. It refers to the cognitive present. What is 'transient' and 'present' in this context? And can one at all distinguish a percept from very short-term memory?

A reasonable *criterion is to rely on the estimate of the minimal time that is required by the brain to extract information from sensory input. The exact value is expected to vary according to the complexity of input, but still, converging evidence from both cellular and psychophysical investigations points to 20–30 ms as the elementary cognitive stroke (e.g. Rolls and Tovee 1994; Horowitz and Wolfe 1998; *binding, *cell assembly). Even the complete processing of a complex visual scene, including the immediate response to it, requires < 150 ms (Thorpe et al. 1996). This is shorter than the commonly accepted life span of 'sensory memory' (0.25–2 s; Dosher and Sperling 1998). So do 'percepts', as defined above, live 20–200 ms before they either become memories or die out? Possibly, but not necessarily. Circuits encoding percepts may sustain the primordial representation longer than that. First, because of their inherent biophysical properties. Second, because the brain may had evolved to always allow some more time for decision to be taken before sensory data are discarded. For example, is the endurance of evoked activity detected in cortical 'face' cells (200–300 ms after the offset of a stimulus; Rolls and Tovee 1994) evidence for the representation of a percept, or of an immediate memory trace? In real-life, the transition from percept to very short-term memory is probably gradual. Attempts to dissociate the two by behavioural *assays were unsuccessful (Haber 1966; but see Neisser 1967). Advanced psychophysical and cellular methodologies (e.g. Horowitz and Wolfe 1998; Parker and Newsome 1998) may clarify the issue, set new criteria, or declare the problem solely semantic and therefore practically irrelevant.

Yet even if at the end of the day 'percept' as a phase that precedes memory remains hypothetical and elusive, it is still a notion worthwhile to retain. This is because it sharpens the conceptual differentiation among memory phases and subphases. 'Percept' as considered here refers to the 'encoding' but not the 'registration' function in *acquisition (see there). It is also the concrete agent of 'stimulus-driven' attention, capable of pushing the input into the road to the *engram; for the brain, a stimulus has no meaning unless it results in a percept. A percept could also serve as a 'sign stimulus', which activates an innate response programme (Lorenz 1981), in which case the registration of the input is not a must. And, finally, percepts could provide *cues for *retrieval. Percepts thus induce major 'rites of passage' in the life of a memory.

Selected associations: Binding, Cue, Internal representation, Phase, Stimulus

---

[1]On what a 'set' is, see *learning set.

Performance

1. The generation of output by a *system.
2. The execution of a mental or motor act.
3. The execution of overt behaviour.
4. Achievement on a specific task.

In behaving animals, the process or the outcome of learning are measured by monitoring changes in performance. But learning and performance are not equivalent. Learned information may remain latent until the appropriate conditions emerge for its expression as a change in performance ('latent learning'; Tolman 1932). Earlier in the twentieth century, orthodox *behaviourists attempted to shy away from this common knowledge. They claimed that only overt behavioural acts (definition 3) are legitimate psychological data, whereas inferred implicit changes in the potential to behave are not. The distinction between performance and competence, however, is now taken for granted in memory research. It does complicate the life of the experimenter who studies learning and memory in the behaving organism. For how could one be sure whether an apparent failure on a memory test is due to faulty learning, feeble memory, or impaired performance under the test conditions? The impaired performance could be due to trivial causes, such as defective sensorimotor capabilities, but also to more elusive causes, such as lack of *retrieval cues, inappropriate *context, diverted *attention, subthreshold motivation, too little or too much arousal,[1] latent alterations in the ability of *stimuli to control behaviour, and more. The distinction among these types of causes requires smart test designs, which take into account factors that could hinder the expression of behaviour (for selected examples of pitfalls and how to circumvent them, see *experimental extinction, *state dependent learning, *transfer). In other cases, the brain itself may simply need more time to surrender its new knowledge (*insight).

The distinction between performance and competence should be a source of concern in dealing with *reduced preparations as well (definition 1). These preparations range from isolated ganglia (*Aplysia) to brain slices and neuronal cultures (*long-term potentiation). Cellular analogues of learning, such as a lasting *synaptic facilitation, may remain dormant under certain conditions yet become apparent under others. This may due to inappropriate test conditions such as nonpermissive *ionic composition of the solution in which the brain slice is immersed, unfavourable neuromodulatory state (*neurotransmitter), or impaired cellular metabolism (*nutrients). Similarly, even if we knew the representational code in a given neuronal circuit, and were in principle able to infer learning by noting the alteration in the *internal representation in that circuit, we might still fail to identify the change because of certain nonpermissive states of the system or the context. The differentiation between competence and performance may hence pop up at various *levels of analysis, from the behaving organism to its individual synapses.

In some cases competence is not aptly transformed into performance simply because the system can do well without exploiting its full *capacity. This is nicely demonstrated in language. We know many more words than we use in daily life. This is why educated adults tend to estimate their vocabulary at a figure that is only 1–10% of the actual value (Seashore and Eckerson 1940). Whereas the vocabulary used in routine daily activities ranges from a few hundreds to a few thousands words, depending on education and profession, and goes up to 8000–20 000 in literary works,[2] the number of distinct words in printed school English (excluding derivatives and compounds) is about 89 000, of which an average 6-year-old child commands already no less than 13 000 (Pinker 1994), and a high school graduate 27 000–53 000 (Nagy and Anderson 1984). This implies that tests to quantify skill should not only be permissive for the expression of this skill, but also properly designed to allow the expression of its capacity. Training and testing conditions that allow for the expression of maximal performance may, however, yield 'ceiling effects'. Testing under ceiling conditions is not appropriate for measuring delicate alterations in performance, such as caused by learning or *development, because it could mask the effect of the experimental treatment.

Performance has multiple roles in the different *phases in the life history of a memory. It is a key element in *instrumental conditioning, acquired via stimulus–response (S–R) contingencies.[3] Repetitive performance is essential for training on *habits and skills; this, among others, underlies the use of simulators in training (Hammerton 1967; *transfer). And in solving complex problems, performance itself may actually be an essential step in the *algorithm: the subject (an organism or a computer) tries the problem, attempts a solution, which produces a new problem-solving strategy, which is then used to tackle the problem again, and so on. The overall approach involves a sequence of transformations from one attempted strategy to another, each emerging from the one that just preceded it. This is called 'learning by doing' (Anazi and

Simon 1979), a sort of on-the-job training. Performance is also, of course, the embodiment of retrieval. The distinction from competence notwithstanding, performance is the ultimate measure of learning both in the field and in the laboratory (Richardson-Klavehn and Bjork 1988; Martin and Bateson 1993). However, as performance involves activation of neural circuits and therefore *plasticity on the one hand, and adaptive interaction with a dynamic outside world on the other, performance in retrieval may also induce modification of the trace upon its use (re-*consolidation). Thus usually, performance P_i of a task is not an exact replica of performance P_{i-1}, because the performance itself actuates learning. Virtuoso musicians should surely attest to that.

Much has been learned in recent years about *internal representations that underlie motor performance and learning, and about distinct brain regions that monitor the behavioural performance and its deviation from the desired output (Carter *et al.* 1998; Kawato 1999; *dopamine, *planning). Prevalent theories of motor control and motor learning propose that the brain generates, stores, refines with experience, and executes internal models of the world, that mimic the input/output characteristics of the specific motor act, and uses them on-line to calculate the desired motor commands (Jeannerod 1994; Kawato 1999). Imagery may engage such internal models without culminating in overt performance (Jeannerod and Decety 1995). Furthermore, there are reports that imagery can substitute for real action in motor training; under such conditions of 'learning by imaging', the distinction between overt and covert performance becomes even fainter (e.g. Yáguez *et al.* 1998).

At least in certain types of mental operations, performance is also believed to be instrumental in *understanding* the world. There is evidence that in some *perceptual and *recognition tasks, the brain construes the perceived behavioural act by activating internal representations that are capable of performing that same act. This possibility has been suggested specifically by the so-called 'motor theories' of vocal recognition. These theories, which apply to human speech, mammalian calls, and *birdsong, propose that speech sounds are perceived and distinguished by tacit knowledge of the vocal gestures used in their production (Liberman *et al.* 1967; Peterson and Jusczyk 1984; Williams and Nottebohm 1985). If this is the case, then the take-home message is that those who cannot perform cannot understand (for a similar conclusion see also *observational learning). This conclusion, however, should not be taken too orthodoxly and seriously; we can surely enjoy a melody even if we sing notoriously out of tune.

Selected associations: Habit, Insight, Mnemonics, Observational learning, Skill

---

[1]The observation that appropriate performance requires an optimal level of arousal is called 'the Yerkes–Dodson Law' (Yerkes and Dodson 1908). As all the other 'laws' of behaviour, this is not a law but rather a pragmatic *generalization. The Yerkes–Dodson law should be kept in mind when an attempt is made to improve memory, either by behavioural methods (*mnemonics) or by drugs (*nootropics). Hence excessive training could result in a weaker memory (*spaced training), and taking stimulants before an exam may damage attention and performance. This was clearly realized by Maimonides (1180): 'the righteous way is the median measure'. The Yerkes–Dodson law is hence a special case of the 'Maimonides Law', itself a reformulation of the old wisdom that preaches for taking the golden path in life (*aurea mediocritas* in Latin).

[2]Shakespeare used 15 000 words, Milton 8000, but Italian Grand Opera enchanted audiences with 800 words only (Seashore and Eckerson 1940).

[3]But see Deese (1951) and Solomon and Turner (1962) for selected cases in which overt performance is not essential to obtain an instrumental response.

Persistence

1. **Continual existence.**

2. *The metaphysical 'persistence problem'*: Does the whole retain its original identity if all its parts are replaced over time?

3. *The memory 'persistence problems'*: (a) How does biological memory persist over time in spite of cellular and molecular turnover? (b) How do items in memory persist in the brain over time in the absence of continual actualization?

If we only abandon highly simplistic *metaphors of memory storage, such as 'cabinet files' or 'computer disks', 'persistence' (*per-* + *sistere*, Latin for 'to stand') becomes a prominent *enigma of memory research. As memory is the retention of acquired information over time, persistence is clearly its central attribute. Generally speaking, there is a family of 'persistence problems'. The *classic philosophical problem (definition 2 above) is also known in metaphysics as 'The Ship of Theseus': the ship of the mythical Greek hero was placed on display in Athens, and with time, parts of it were replaced, one by one, till none of the original remained. Is this still the same ship? (Plutarch, *Theseus* 1–2C AD/1914b; Kim and Sosa 1999). Metaphysics notwithstanding, this discussion will focus primarily on the more pragmatic 'persistence problems', which relate directly to memory (definition 3a,b). First, how come that in spite of the notorious frailness of the individual components of the biological material in which the trace is registered, the *engram endures, sometimes for a lifetime? This is 'the endurance issue'. Second, how do items in memory persist over those periods in which they are not expressed? This is 'the dormancy issue'. Both issues seem to call for some engineering solutions. They also invoke, however, interesting conceptual and methodological issues. For example, although the 'dormancy issue' can be satisfied rather easily, its probable solution leads to the paradoxical conclusion that specific items in memory are not at all 'stored' in the common sense of the term.

Let's turn to the 'endurance issue' first. Organisms are epitomes of the pre-Socratic saying 'everything flows' ('*Panta Rei*', Guthrie 1962). Their constituents never experience a dull moment. Metabolic instability contributes to *plasticity and adaptation, hence to survival. Stability and completion, probably contrary to intuition, could promote atrophy: 'How long/Do works endure? As long/As they are not completed./Since as long as they demand effort/They do not decay' (Brecht 1929–33). In the mature organism, cells are constantly born and die (Alberts *et al.* 1994). Proteins within cells turnover within minutes to weeks, their actual life expectancy being determined by their type, location and history (Varshavsky 1992; Shi *et al.* 1996; Krupnick and Benovic 1998; Huh and Wentold 1999; Xu and Salpeter 1999). Furthermore, it is now evident that cells are born even in tissues that were traditionally considered to be stable throughout adult life; the brain is no exception (e.g. Kirn *et al.* 1994; Eriksson *et al.* 1998; Gould *et al.* 1999*b*). This situation raises the following questions.

1. *The molecular *level.* If an experience-dependent change is embodied in modified *synaptic components (e.g. **Aplysia*, *long-term potentiation), such as enzymes, *ion channels, and *receptors, which have a limited life span—how does the change outlast the limited life span of the proteins, and becomes immune to the consequences of molecular turnover? Without such resistance to the effect of turnover, no long-term memory would be possible. We should also worry about the persistence of post-translational modifications in protein molecules (*protein synthesis), because these modifications are unlikely to survive immediate re-modification by enzymes *in vivo* (e.g. Shuster *et al.* 1985). Multiple mechanistic solutions have been proposed to account for the immunity of use-dependent

neuronal changes to molecular turnover (Crick 1984*b*; Lisman 1985; Goelet *et al.* 1986; Buxbaum and Dudai 1989; Dudai 1989; Chain *et al.* 1999; Lisman and Fallon 1999). These proposals include molecular positive feedback loops, that, once activated, are shifted into a new stable state, and regenerate the molecular change again and again (*protein kinase); modulation of gene expression, that results in a new, stable expression pattern (*CREB, *immediate early genes, *protein synthesis); or a combination of the above.

2. *The synaptic to circuit levels.* If traces are subserved by synaptic connections, but these connections are continuously remodelled *in vivo*, how is the trace preserved (e.g. Bailey and Kandel 1993; Kleim *et al.* 1997)? At least in complex circuits, the problem is solvable by assuming distributed codes, in which no single node in the net is exclusive in representing a significant chunk of the message (*cell assembly, *homunculus, *model). The idea is thus that at any given moment, the trace is retained by a sufficiently large chunk of the circuit, so that it can tolerate elimination of part of the nodes. This property is termed 'graceful degradation'.

Similarly, if newly-born neurons are incorporated into functional circuits in the adult brain (Kirn *et al.* 1994; Eriksson *et al.* 1998; Gould *et al.* 1999*b*; though see Rakic 2002), how does the perturbed circuitry sustain the old memory? Again, the conceptual difficulty is ameliorated by assuming a distributed code as above. Note that by explaining how hardware turnover does not undermine the persistence of the trace, we do not solve the metaphysical 'Ship of Theseus' identity problem. But at least we can explain how copies of the ship become available. That this is a partial answer is perfectly OK, because neuroscientists should definitely relegate some problems exclusively to philosophers.

And what about the 'dormancy issue'? We have defined '*memory' as the retention over time of experience-dependent *internal representations, and noted that representations are expected to be encoded in the spatiotemporal activity patterns of neuronal circuits. If this is the case, how is the memory retained in our brain when the representation is not actualized? Note that for the sake of argument, it does not really matter whether the representation is activated only in explicit *retrieval of the item in memory, which may occur very rarely, or also, probably more frequently, in the course of hypothetical, implicit 'house-keeping' routines in the brain.

The 'dormancy issue' can be rather easily resolved if we only switch the level of analysis and recall the difference between '*memory' and neuronal and synaptic 'storage'. What is retained over time is not the actual internal representation, but rather the capacity to generate it. The information is stored as 'hardware' alterations in the circuit that is capable of expressing that specific representation. For a memory to be retrieved, certain *cues are required to engage the circuit and generate the relevant activity pattern anew. In other words, memories are not retained 'as is', but reconstructed; what persists after learning is the change in the system that leads to their reconstruction in a certain way but not another; retrieval is not merely an expression of memory, but rather a condition for its mere existence. We can also conclude that the study of synapses and individual nerve cells is expected to generate information on the generic mechanisms of storage, whereas the study of active circuits suits better the search for the fingerprints of specific instances of memory.

Selected associations: Consolidation, Engram, False memory, Metaphor, Plasticity

Phase

1. **Each of the distinct states in a *system or process.**
2. **Stage of *development.**
3. **Each of the distinct stages in a periodic process.**
4. **Period.**

Phases (*phasis*, Greek for 'appearance') are distinct states in time and space. *Acquisition, *consolidation, retention, *retrieval, and *forgetting are all phases of memory. Some authors use the term 'stage' instead of phase to refer to these different periods of memory. 'Phase', however, is more suitable, because in addition to denoting a distinct state (definition 1), including in development (definition 2), it also connotes the recurrence of states (definition 3). This is important, because memory phases could recur. For example, items in memory shift back and forth between active (retrieved) and nonactive (stored) states (Lewis 1979; *persistence), and, upon retrieval, might even be reacquired and reconsolidated (Sara 2000; Nader *et al.* 2000). The expression (*performance), endurance, and susceptibility of the *engram to interference are common *criteria in the *taxonomy of memory phases. Our knowledge, however, about the number, nature, and transition of memory phases is a function not only of the particular memory system and memory task, but

also of the sophistication of the research *methods employed.

A particularly popular distinction of phases in a memory trace, once formed, is between 'short-term' memory (STM) and 'long-term' memory (LTM). That memory can be short or long lived, was probably noted by the first human who forgot the items on his daily hunting list but still remembered the way back to the cave. More formal distinctions emerged in experimental psychology. The results of both contemplation and experimentation gravitated toward *models of two to three memory phases. Here are a few examples. The German physiologist Exner concluded that 'states of mind' vanish, if not caught by *attention, within a few seconds, and dubbed these first few seconds in the life of a memory 'elementary memory' (cited in James 1890). James preferred the term 'primary memory', as opposed to 'secondary memory', or 'memory proper', which is '… the knowledge of a former state of mind after it has already dropped from consciousness' (*ibid.*). Meumann (1913) advocated a three-phase distinction: immediate, temporary, and permanent. Hebb (1949), drawing from earlier data and concepts (Lorente de No 1938; Hilgard and Marquis 1940), returned to the basic two-phase type of models, and proposed a 'dual trace' hypothesis as well as mechanism: a reverberating, transient, unstable trace, that 'carries the memory until the growth change is made' and memory is stabilized in the long term. The introduction of the specific 'short-term' vs. 'long-term' terminology is accredited to Broadbent (1958; *attention), who spoke about 'short-term' and 'long-term' storage systems (see also Peterson and Peterson 1959).

The current terminology of elementary temporal memory phases refers to 'sensory', STM and LTM. Sensory memory of visual and auditory information is termed 'iconic memory' and 'echoic memory', respectively (Sperling 1960; Efron 1970). Sensory memory lasts for less then a second (Figure 54) to a few seconds at most. The duration of STM and LTM depends on whom you talk to. STM lasts for a few minutes for neurologists (Sacktor and Mayeux 1995), up to a few hours for cellular neurobiologists (Goelet *et al.* 1986; Dudai 1989, 1997*b*). LTM, according to this coarse classification, is for neurologists memory that lasts for more than a few minutes, and for neurobiologists, by convention, memory that lasts for more than 24 h. In what is regarded as a cellular analogue of learning, *long-term potentiation in a brain slice, the limits of 'long term' are pushed backwards to 1–3 h only. Similarly, consolidation of LTM could last anything from a few hours ('cellular consolidation', which requires *protein

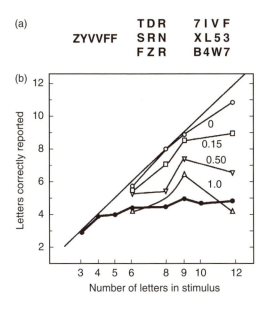

(a)

	TDR	7IVF
ZYVVFF	SRN	XL53
	FZR	B4W7

(b) Letters correctly reported vs Number of letters in stimulus

Curves labeled: 0, 0.15, 0.50, 1.0

Fig. 54 The shortest memory phase. In a *classic experiment, Sperling (1960) presented a group of *subjects with nonsense *stimuli composed of letters (or letters and numbers) in various *arrangements (a). The stimuli were each presented for 50 ms only. The subjects were requested to report all the items in each stimulus immediately afterwards. When the number of items was higher than four, the subjects never reported all the items correctly (heavy curve in b). The subjects were then presented again with stimuli consisting of letters in three symmetric rows (a, middle and left). They were told that a tone would come immediately after the stimulus, and that this tone would be either high, middle, or low. If high, only the upper row should be reported; if middle, only the middle row; if low, only the bottom row. Under this *cued, partial report mode, the amount of information reported was two to three times larger than in the whole report mode. The availability of this information declined within less then a second (b; the straight diagonal is the theoretical curve; the numbers on the other curves are the onset of the tone in seconds after the visual stimulus). This short-lived memory is called 'iconic'.

synthesis) to weeks or longer ('system consolidation', Dudai 1996; *hippocampus). Behavioural, *neurogenetic, pharmacological, and cellular analysis unveils additional, 'intermediate' memory phases, between 'short' and 'long' (Rosenzweig et al. 1993; Tully et al. 1994; Winder et al. 1998; Wüstenberg et al. 1998; Sutton et al. 2001). In *real-life, 'long' itself is evidently not an homogeneous phase, as some LTMs are irretrievable already within a few days, whereas others linger for many years, up to a lifetime (e.g. EBT 1923).

Different memory systems (*taxonomy) may have different types of temporal phases, probably moulded in evolution to comply with the specific functional demands imposed on the particular system. For example, in mammals, *declarative memory is characterized by multiple LTM phases, ranging from weeks (hippocampal-dependent) to years (hippocampal independent), whereas nondeclarative memory appears to be consolidated faster (McClelland et al. 1995; Shadmehr and Brashers-Krug 1997a). Such heterogeneity probably stems from the different properties of the particular circuits that subserve the different memory systems, but not from different building blocks at the molecular *level.

Why are there short- and long-term phases of memory? And are these phases serial or parallel? The favoured answers to the first question are three: (a) transient STM phase(s) provide the organism with the ability to hold information indispensable for *ad hoc* tasks but superfluous in the long run (in this respect, 'short-term' fulfils the role of '*working memory'); (b) transient STM phase(s) provide the organism with a better opportunity to evaluate, prune, classify, and rearrange information before the decision is taken to store it 'permanently' (McClelland et al. 1995); (c) there are phases because biological memory is incapable of operating otherwise, due to the structural and functional constraints of the machinery.[1] As to the second question, namely are the short- and the long-term phases of memory serial or parallel, information from both cellular and system studies suggest that short- and longer-term memory could unfold in parallel; further, there are situations in which LTM is intact but STM is faulty (Shallice and Warrington 1970; McCarthy and Warrington 1990; Emptage and Carew 1993).

Finally, all learning and memory processes could themselves be regarded as a phases in the overall continuous process of the development of the organism. Recent findings in cellular and molecular biology support such view, which has been promoted well before promoters, *immediate early genes and transcription factors were even dreamt of: 'Growth and learning are one continuous process, to the earlier phases of which we give the one name, and to the later … we give the other' (Holt 1931).

Selected associations: Acquisition, Consolidation, Retrieval, System, Taxonomy

---

[1]The reader who is already familiar with *paradigms will recognize in possibilities *a* and *b* the Panglossian paradigm, and in *c* an alternative.

Phrenology

A school in psychology that held the following set of premises:

(a) the mind is composed of distinct mental faculties;

(b) each faculty resides in a specific brain organ;

(c) individuals are innately predisposed to different proficiencies in different mental faculties;

(d) the more developed the mental faculty, the larger the size of the brain organ;

(e) the size of brain organs is manifested in the external configuration of the skull.

Phrenology (*phren*, Greek for 'mind', -*logos*, 'reasoning') was born toward the end of the eighteenth century. It is considered pseudoscience because of postulate *e* above. This postulate is 'craniometry'—the belief that one can determine a mental profile from the shape of the skull. The point is that while craniometry is indeed a preposterous claim, the rest of phrenology's assumptions do deserve proper attention. These are the modularity of mind (*a* above), the localization of function in the brain (*b*), the individual variability in innately predisposed potential (*c*), and the dependence of function on neural space (*d*). All these postulates are echoed in contemporary neuroscience. Assumption *a*, with or without the rest but in the absence of *e*, is 'neophrenology'. Many neuroscientists speak 'neophrenologish' without even being aware of it.

The founder of phrenology was the prominent neuroanatomist Gall (Germany 1758–France 1828; Temkin 1947). Gall himself was not happy with the term 'phrenology', which was introduced by his co-worker, Spurzheim. But Gall never came up with a catchy term as an alternative. He developed his views of brain and mental function against the background of a variety of earlier theories. Quite a number of these theories considered mental function to be subserved by fluids (humours), in amazing disrespect to the tissue of the brain itself. Many also regarded the mind a unitary whole, unresponsive to physical dissection. Gall considered the available data, added his own observations, and spiced it all with the influence of the contemporary practice of 'physiognomy', the art of judging character and disposition from the features of face and body. Phrenology was the outcome. Gall's ideas arouse opposition among some and enthusiasm among others.

An example of the first was the decisive response by Emperor Francis I, who banished Gall from Vienna: 'This doctrine concerning the head, which is taken about with enthusiasm will perhaps cause a few to lose their heads and it leads also to materialism, therefore is opposed to the first principles of morals and religion' (cited in Greenblatt 1995). An epitome of the more enthusiastic reaction was provided, years later, by the poet Walt Whitman, who, swept by admiration for the new science, subjected his own 'splendid head' (*sic.*) to the test of phrenology (Davies 1971).

Phrenology as it became known in the nineteenth century was mostly Spurzheim's modification of Gall's conceptual framework. Gall originally distinguished 27 faculties. These included, among others, multiple memory systems (*taxonomy): memory for facts, memory for persons, and memory for words (Temkin 1947). Some of Galls' proposed faculties pointed to unflattering facets of human nature: the instinct of killing, the desire to possess, pride, and vanity. Spurzheim, while expanding the list of faculties, got rid of the more annoying traits. He also emphasized the ability to improve 'deficient' faculties by training.

We will get a better appreciation of phrenology if we evaluate its premises in the context of present knowledge:

1. *The modularity of mind.* The basic assumption here is that the mind is a collection of different kinds of mental faculties. This view is also known as 'faculty psychology' (Fodor 1983). In principle, a 'module' may refer to a general type of mental function such as *attention, *perception, or memory, irrespective of the specific mental content or behavioural task. It could alternatively refer to a specific behavioural programme, e.g. *imprinting, or a specific mental *skill, e.g. language, musicality, or sociability, each of which requires attention, perception, memory, etc. The original phrenological maps listed mostly specific aptitudes rather than general mental processes that cut across skills (Temkin 1947). This view is shared by modern versions of the modularity of mind (Rozin 1976; Fodor 1983; Gardner 1993). The mere existence of mental modules could make sense from the point of view of the evolution, as different phylogenetic pressures might had advanced distinct mental capacities, to offer specific solutions to specific survival needs. It has furthermore been suggested that the progress in evolution toward more intelligent organisms involves enhanced interaction among different modules (Rozin 1976; see also 'central systems' in Fodor 1983). Neuropsychological analysis of brain-damaged patients with highly circumscribed behavioural deficits has been used as

evidence for the existence of highly specific cognitive modules (Damasio 1990; Baynes *et al.* 1998). However, the relevance of the breakdown unveiled by pathology to the normal divisions of the mind, as well as its relevance to the modules/central processors distinction, awaits clarification. Another central question is to what degree are different modules innate (Karmiloff-Smith 1994; Spelke 1994; Markson and Bloom 1997; Paterson *et al.* 1999).

2. *The localization of function.* Whereas the modularity of mind supposes *mental organs*, the localization of function in brain assumes *neural organs*. The latter assumption is 'organology'. Note that modularity of mind does not entail organology. It is legitimate to assume mental modules while displaying complete indifference to their physical substrates. It is also possible to envisage a model in which the whole brain is induced, either spontaneously or by external *stimuli, to produce distinct mental modules at need. However, given the modularity of mind, some organology becomes a logical possibility. Phrenology prompted systematic attempts to localize brain function, including *engrams, by relying on the effect of disease and injury (Brazier 1988; Finger 1994; *method). We are now experiencing a new wave of this search, this time using *functional neuroimaging. The pitfall that the 'new organologists' (Marshall 1980) must avoid is the tendency to adhere to the descriptive levels,

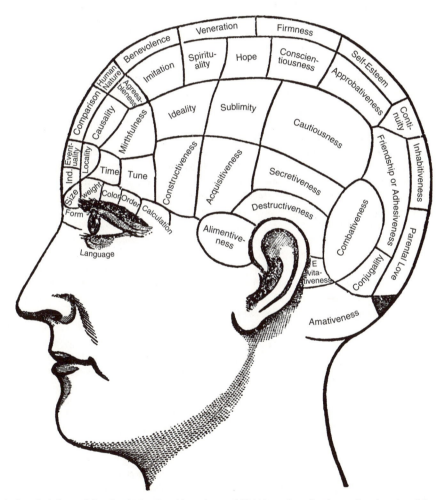

Fig. 55 A phrenological map, delineating the location of 'mental organs'. Multiple versions of such maps have been issued throughout the nineteenth century. They usually depicted memory not as a unitary faculty but as multiple *systems (e.g. memory for words, memory for facts, memory for persons), or as an implied component of other faculties (e.g. language). (Reproduced from Davies 1971.)

rather than create a *model that will account for what the different organs and circuits compute and represent. Also, much as the localization of function is an attempt to dissect the brain into parts, it should not be forgotten that *in situ* these parts function together. The brain is not an homogeneous porridge, but also not a random collection of individual organs.

3. *Individual variability in the innate potential.* Genes influence human behaviour (e.g. McClearn *et al.* 1997; *a priori, *neurogenetics). But each distinct behavioural trait depends on many genes, most of which are pleiotropic (i.e. contribute to more than one phenotype). We also know that the structure and function of cognitive modules depend much on how the brain interacts with the environment (Sadato *et al.* 1996; Paterson *et al.* 1999; *development). Our current view on how much is nature and how much nurture depends on which trait is analysed and how one construes the data (Rose 1995*a*; Gelernter *et al.* 1997; Leboyer *et al.* 1998; Noble *et al.* 1998; Flint 1999).

4. *The dependence of function on neural space.* The idea that brain space is correlated with *performance is not considered far-fetched any more (e.g. *birdsong). Consider, for example, the recent report that professional taxi drivers, who earn their living from navigation in urban streets, have a larger *hippocampus, a brain area critical for spatial memory (Maguire *et al.* 2000). But of course, nobody claims that such an alteration creates bumps on the skull.

5. *Craniometry.* Neither the shape of the skull, nor the overall size of the healthy brain, are indicative of mental power (Gould 1981). Gall himself objected to being called a craniologist, claiming that the focus of his research is the brain, not the skull. Therefore, despite the failure of his mental diagnostic methods, he would have probably been proud of neophrenology.

Selected associations: Engram, Homo sapiens, Red herring, Zeitgeist

---

Planning

1. **The design of a *method or programme for achieving a goal.**
2. **The volitional organization ahead of time of goal-oriented behaviour.**

3. The generation, modification, or selection by the brain of *internal representations of future actions and their anticipated consequences.

'It is a poor sort of memory that only works backwards', said the White Queen to Alice (Carroll 1865). But mocking at the memory of the visitor to Wonderland was rather unjustified. For even without pushing modern physics to its limits, we do have a kind of 'memory of the future' (Fuster 1992). This is planning.[1] This capability should not be belittled: in spite of its alleged reputation, even Destiny, speaking through the Delphic oracle, only rarely dared to give clear predictions of the future (Fontenrose 1978).

'Planning' originally referred to the design of ground plans for the purpose of planting, itself a word derived from *planta*, Latin for 'sole of the foot'. Definition 1 is the generic one; Definition 2 assumes volition.[2] This is what people commonly have in mind in considering planning. The distinction between definitions 1 and 2 touches philosophical issues that exceed the scope of this brief discussion; suffice it to note that definition 2 applies to living organisms (myths and deities notwithstanding), yet in the future will fit smart robots as well. Definition 3 rephrases definition 1 while focusing on the *reduced concept of internal representations, which is central to discussion of *learning and *memory in this book.

Planning could be manifested in a gamut of markedly different behaviours, ranging from fast motor actions to long-term strategic plots. It is therefore methodologically useful to classify it (*taxonomy), using *criteria such as the behavioural domain, complexity, timetable of the anticipated action, flexibility, and the trigger for the plan.

1. *Behavioural domain.* An elementary dichotomy distinguishes motor planning, referring to motor acts and their anticipated consequences, from cognitive planning, referring to cognitive narratives and their mental, behavioural, and social consequences. Multiple taxonomies are possible within the behavioural domain *dimension. Related dimensions are the complexity of the planned goal, and the explicitness of planning (*declarative memory).

2. *Time to attain the goal.* From what has been said above it becomes apparent that different planning acts could refer to very different temporal spans, ranging from seconds on the one hand to years on the other. Compare, for example, a tennis player planning a tricky serve vs. a college student planning a career. In considering the shortest time spans, two issues are noteworthy. One is the automaticity of the plan. This will be further discussed in 3 below. The other is the transformation from the present to the future. As the

cognitive present in not infinitesimally small, plans of brief motor acts raise the question what is 'present' and what is 'future'. Based on psychophysical and physiological data, 'present time' appears be in the order of ~100 ms (this estimate is task dependent; e.g. Thorpe *et al.* 1996; Helenius *et al.* 1998; *percept). In motor tasks such as orienting and reaching, neuronal activity is detected in the brain several hundreds of milliseconds prior to the actual execution of the act (Georgopoulos *et al.* 1989). This could therefore be construed as a candidate neuronal correlate of *bona fide* elementary planning (Georgopoulos 1994; Andersen *et al.* 1997; Flanagan and Wing 1997). Within this narrow temporal window, there is ample time to modify the plan by intervening with the activity of the circuit during the planning phase (Groh *et al.* 1997; *method).

3. *Innateness and flexibility.* But how much of a short-lived motor plan is really a plan, rather than the deterministic unfolding of an automatic response? Even the most sophisticated, imaginative cognitive plans are expected to depend to some degree on *a priori constraints on our perceptual and cognitive faculties, which lead to automaticity of certain elements in the behaviour. Yet clearly, some plans are more constrained by innate predispositions than others. It is phylogenetically advantageous to limit the anticipated alternative outcomes of fast motor plans that are essential for survival, by relying on innately encoded internal representations that can be selected within fraction of a second. The most elementary brief motor plans could be said to differ from elementary reflexive responses in that the former include a component of active selection and decision making by the *system (definition 2), whereas the latter are solely deterministic reaction. The reflexive response could still be fine-tuned by experience, but the action pattern is a given once triggered. This distinction between 'reflexive' and 'nonreflexive' is convenient yet shaky; what appears as a 'voluntary' planned act might still be an intricate reflex shaped by complex input (Luria 1962).

4. *Trigger.* Plans ranging from very simple to rather complex ones (e.g. ambushing a prey) could be triggered by a single 'release *stimulus' (Lorenz 1981). In contrast, complex cognitive plans may be initiated by *retrieved or endogenously generated representations.

In spite of their immense heterogeneity, in all mental plans the internal representations are expected to include a representation of a hierarchical set of sequential actions and of the anticipated outcome (Miller *et al.* 1960). These organized sets of actions, termed 'schemata' (Bartlett 1932), draw from past experience—be it encoded in innate or learned responses or both. In other

words, although plans refer to the future, they always draw from either the species' or the individual's past.

Naturally, the investigation of planning in laboratory setting is limited to tasks that are completed within a few minutes or a few hours at most. Systems that are particularly useful for the cellular and system analysis of elementary planning in the *monkey brain involve limb, head, or eye movement (e.g. Georgopoulos 1994; Thach 1996; Andersen *et al.* 1997; Flanagan and Wing 1997; Zhang and Barash 2000). These studies focus, depending on the specific task, on the role of motor and posterior parietal *cerebral cortex, as well as the *cerebellum. Relevant to this area of research is also the investigation of the role of neuromodulatory systems (*neurotransmitter, *dopamine) in the selection among alternative response patterns.

In the study of planning in humans, the tests commonly involve puzzles that could be solved by mentally testing sequences of moves ahead of time, such as the Tower of London task (Shallice 1982; Figure 56). In this task, three beads, one red, one green, and one blue, have to be moved in a minimal number of steps from the initial configuration on three sticks of unequal length to the designated goal position. The problems vary in complexity, from two to five moves. More recent versions of the task involve the manipulation of coloured shapes on a computer screen (e.g. Dagher *et al.* 1999). Other types of tasks that tap into human planning involve simulation of *real-life situations, such as financial planning (Goel *et al.* 1997). All in all, the combined data from neuropsychological and *functional neuroimaging studies in patients with circumscribed brain lesions and in normal volunteers, implicate frontal cortical areas in the multiple aspects of cognitive planning (Luria 1962; Shallice 1982, 1988; Fuster 1995a; Goel *et al.* 1997; Owen 1997; Bechara *et al.* 1998; Dagher *et al.* 1999; Figure 56; for an example of *modelling of planning in cortex, see Dehaene and Changeux 1997). This cortex is 'where the past and future meet' (Fuster 1995) to integrate past experiences, both declarative and nondeclarative (Bechara *et al.* 1997), in planning ahead.

Selected associations: A Priori, Algorithm, Dimension, Prospective memory, Working memory

---

[1]A related type of memory of the future is *prospective memory, which is discussed separately.

[2]Volition refers in this context to autonomous decision making by a *system regardless of its state of *conscious awareness. Hence 'planning' according to definition 2 could either be *declarative or nondeclarative.

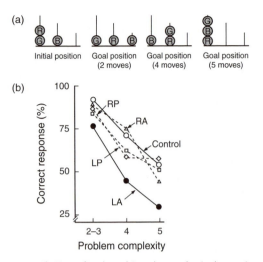

(a) Initial position — Goal position (2 moves) — Goal position (4 moves) — Goal position (5 moves)

(b) Correct response (%) / Problem complexity

RP, RA, Control, LP, LA

Fig. 56 The Tower of London task is used to test planning because it is possible to solve it by mentally testing sequences of moves ahead of time, before actually executing them. (a) In the original version (Shallice 1982), three beads, one red, one green, and one blue, have to be moved from the initial configuration on three sticks of unequal length to the designated goal position in a minimal number of steps. The problems vary in their complexity, from two moves to five moves. More recent versions of the task involve the manipulation of coloured shapes on the computer screen rather than beads and sticks (e.g. Dagher *et al.* 1999). (b) The *performance on the task of *control, healthy volunteers and of brain lesioned patients, plotted as the percentage correct on the first attempt to solve the problem vs. the complexity of the problem. LA, left anterior brain lesion; LP, left posterior lesion; RA, right anterior lesion; RP, right posterior lesion. The patients with left anterior brain lesions, involving the left frontal lobe, were dramatically impaired. (Adapted from Shallice 1982).

Plasticity

1. The ability to undergo modification without immediate relaxation or disintegration.

2. A lasting shift in the set point of a *homeostatic *system.

Plasticity is probably the most widely used term in modern neurobiology, clearly not to be recommended as an effective keyword in literature searches in this field. In its rudimentary form, the notion of plasticity as a vehicle for memory appears already in pre-scientific times: Socrates depicted memory as an impression on wax tablet, too hard in slow learners and oversoft in the forgetful ones (Plato, *Theaetetus*). It is likely that this and similar *metaphors were used much earlier. In the scientific discipline of memory research, 'plasticity' was

formally born at least twice. James (1890) brought it up in his *classic chapter on *habit: 'Plasticity... means the possession of a structure weak enough to yield to an influence, but strong enough not to yield all at once ... Organic matter, especially nervous tissue, seems endowed with a very extraordinary degree of plasticity of this sort ... the phenomena of habit in living beings are due to the plasticity of the organic materials of which their bodies are composed'. Half a century later, Konorski (1948) listed plasticity as one of the two metaprinciples that underlie the operation of the central nervous system. These principles are excitability (later renamed 'reactivity', Konorski 1967), which is the capacity to be activated by stimulation of receptive organs, and plasticity, the capacity to change reactive properties as a result of successive activation.

At about the same time, Hebb (1949) proposed how use-dependent *synaptic growth can subserve learning (*algorithm, *cell assembly), and Monne (1949) suggested that *protein synthesis allows for lasting neural remodelling in the formation of the *engram.[1] These proposals are tenets of neurobiology to date. The current zeitgeist is that *stimulus-induced regulation of *intracellular signal transduction cascades, which culminates in the modulation of gene expression (*immediate early genes) and hence in *de novo* protein synthesis, embodies use-dependent neuronal plasticity; and that much of this action takes place in the synapse. The relation of all this to memory is encapsulated in the *synaptic plasticity and memory hypothesis*: 'Activity-dependent synaptic plasticity is induced at appropriate synapses during memory formation, and is both necessary and sufficient for the information storage underlying the type of memory mediated by the brain area in which that plasticity is observed' (Martin *et al.* 2000).

This zeitgeist deserves a caveat or two. But they will follow later. First, it is useful to consider briefly neural plasticity at multiple *levels of function and analysis. These are the theory level, the algorithmic level, and the implementational, or hardware level.

1. *The theory level.* In the theoretical world of all-possible organisms, it is not a given that adult individuals will show neural plasticity.[2] That in real-life plasticity is the rule rather than the exception, is commonly attributed to the selective pressures of biological evolution. This means that the gain of adult plasticity outweighs the loss. The gain is clear: the ability to fine-tune the *a priori genetic adaptations, and hence survive in an even larger spectrum of mutable habitats. To this one could add the capacity to utilize only part of the potential gene products at one time, and also to amend injured cells and tissues. The loss is the metabolic

price paid for the production of the plasticity machinery, and the risk that plasticity will go astray, resulting in malignancy or degeneration (indeed some authors consider *dementia to be a catastrophe of plasticity, e.g. Mesulam 1999). Another type of explanation, though, is that adult organisms are plastic because of built-in properties of biological material, and not because plasticity was selected for *per se*.[3] This could be due to the ephemeral nature of the stuff of cells, plasticity being the by-product of the ability to replace continuously cellular components and correct mistakes in their production; or to opportunistic capitalization by evolution on processes that permit multicellular organisms to grow postnatally.

The above considerations refer to the overall principle of 'adapt your behaviour to the world'. How is this achieved? The system follows a few computational rules, which refer to the probability of co-occurrence of events. It is methodologically legitimate to describe these rules as though they have a teleological rationale: if events tend to *coincide in time or place, then they are related, one can predict the other, and their *internal representations deserve to be *associated. If an event follows action, then this event has a significant probability to be caused by the action, and again, this apparent causality deserves to be encoded.[4] These rules guide *classical conditioning and *instrumental conditioning, respectively, yet are relevant to other learning situations as well.

2. *The algorithmic level.* The synaptic postulate of Hebb (1949), noted above, which proposes that synaptic connections are *reinforced by coincident activity of pre- and postsynaptic terminals, is the one most discussed in the literature on neural and behavioural plasticity [*algorithm, *long-term potentiation (LTP)]. Additional algorithms at the circuit and system levels are illustrated in *algorithm, *dopamine, *instrumental learning.

3. *The hardware level.* How are the neural algorithms implemented? This is done by multiple types of cellular devices, which include *receptors, *ion channels, *neurotransmitter release machinery, *intracellular signal transduction cascades, *protein kinases, cytoskeletal elements, *immediate and *late response gene products.[5] Among these are *coincidence detectors that operate on a variety of time-scales, and growth regulators. Each of these molecules is itself plastic. Pioneering work in identifying molecules of neural plasticity and their relevance to simple memory has been done on *Aplysia (Kandel 1976; Kandel and Schwartz 1982). Other systems, capable of *LTP, *habituation, *sensitization, and *classical conditioning, are also used extensively.

A recurrent issue in the field of neural plasticity is whether the same cellular machinery that subserves development also subserves learning and memory. Some authors emphasize the similarity (e.g. Martin and Kandel 1996), others the differences (e.g. Constantine-Paton and Cline 1998). It is noteworthy that developmental plasticity, in contradiction to long-held dogma, continues to function in the nervous system throughout life (*birdsong, *hippocampus; interestingly, simple physical activity could activate it; van Praag *et al.* 1999). Even if it does stop, it manages to affect markedly the *capacity of later use-dependent plasticity in the adult (e.g. Martin *et al.* 1991; Carvell and Simons 1996; Rosenzweig and Bennett 1996; Sylva 1997; Crair *et al.* 1998). Another point to remember is that components of the plasticity machinery in neurons are shared by non-neuronal tissues throughout development and in adulthood. This reinforces the notion, mentioned above, that plasticity is a universal biological property; it also supports, by the way, the conviction that cellular plasticity alone will not explain *memory.

The fact that the molecular biology of learning has become predominantly the molecular biology of synaptic plasticity, is an inevitable consequence of the *reductive approach to learning. The remarkable success in deciphering the mechanisms of synaptic plasticity should not, however, distract us from noting some caveats. First, it now becomes evident that the focus on the synapse has led to unjustified neglect of cell-wide processes and mechanisms (Frey and Morris 1997; Casadio *et al.* 1999; Dudai and Morris 2000). Second, the role of glia cells is still an *enigma, and breakthroughs should be expected on this frontier (Araque *et al.* 1999; Ullian *et al.* 2001). And third, most importantly, the crucial issue is whether neural plasticity, be it synaptic or cell-wide or both, is both *necessary* and *sufficient* (*criterion) for learning and memory. Ample evidence, much of which is cited in this book, indicates that neural plasticity is necessary for learning and memory; but a careful survey of the literature shows that few data currently support the notion that synaptic plasticity is sufficient for learning and memory to take place (Martin *et al.* 2000). To prove sufficiency, one should be able to induce artificially controlled plasticity in identified synapses that implement the specific, targeted internal representations. This is not easy, as it requires identification of circuits that encode specific internal representations, and of synapses that are critically important in these circuits. Examples of attempts to follow this line of research are mentioned in *method. Note that even if at the end of the day experiments of this type will indeed show that use-dependent synaptic plasticity is sufficient to register a specific memory, it will still remain to be determined how learning and memory processes are initiated *in vivo*; is it a bottom-up process, from the synaptic to higher levels, or is it a top-down process, in which higher-level activity initiates the plastic change in the appropriate synapses.

Selected associations: Development, Metaplasticity, Persistence, Reduction, Synapse

---

[1] Both Hebb (1949) and Monne (1949) drew, naturally, upon the work of others. The role of synaptic growth in learning has been discussed earlier (e.g. Cason 1925; *development). The precedents of Hebb's synaptic postulate are discussed in *algorithm. The proposal in Monne's paper was based on the pioneering work of contemporary research groups in cellular and chemical biology (e.g. Hamberger and Hyden 1945).

[2] In this discussion, plasticity (definitions 1 and 2), unless otherwise indicated, refers to neural plasticity. But most early authors, such as James (1890) and Semon (1904), aptly emphasized that plasticity, whether called by that name or not, is a universal property of the biological material.

[3] This argument fits the anti-Panglossian paradigm, see *paradigm.

[4] No assumptions are being made here concerning *conscious awareness of this potential causality, or the validity of the assumed causality. See also Macphail (1996) and Heyes and Huber (2000).

[5] This is an appropriate point to note that many authors distinguish functional from structural plasticity. The truth is that 'functional' plasticity also involves modification in some hardware component(s) of the system, hence is structural. It is all a matter of the level of *reduction. What those who speak about structural plasticity mean, is morphological plasticity: those structural changes in the tissues that are detectable down to the level of electron microscopy (see example in *development, Figure 25, p. 81).

Priming

1. **The non*conscious modulation of the processing, *retrieval or production of a mental item by prior exposure to specific information on that item or on items associated with it.**

2. **The presentation of a *stimulus or the induction of a change that prepares the *system for functioning.**

'Priming' in the current memory literature almost always refers to a specific protocol or type of memory (definition 1) rather than to the more general concept (definition 2). This contemporary use was introduced by Cofer (1960), on the basis of earlier observations

(Storms 1958; see also Wohlgemuth 1913; Williams 1953). An experiment by Storms (1958) illustrates what was meant. Storms asked a group of students to study a list of words, *A*, which elicit high-frequency associations, such as 'eagle' (which typically elicits 'bird') or 'hill' ('mountain').[1] He then presented the students with another list of words, *B*, which included the words that are high-frequency responses to the words in *A*, but themselves do not ordinarily elicit words in *A*. For example, although 'eagle' elicits the response 'bird', the converse is not usually the case. Storms found that the production of words in *A* as responses to words in *B* was significantly higher when list *A* was encountered just previously. Cofer (1960) termed this use-dependent augmentation of associative strength as 'priming of associations'.

Over the years the use of the term 'priming' has been extended to include additional protocols and meanings. The current major *taxonomies of priming are based on two types of interrelated distinctions: 'direct' vs. 'indirect', and 'perceptual' vs. 'conceptual' (Richardson-Klavehn and Bjork 1988; Roediger and McDermott 1993). In direct priming, also termed '*repetition priming*', the item presented in the training ('study') *phase is identical to, or is composed of fragments of, the item to be produced in the test phase. In indirect priming, also termed '*associative priming*', the item presented in the study phase is associated with the item to be produced in the test but not identical with it. Direct priming is mostly 'perceptual'; it is modality specific and relatively independent of the meaning (semantics) of the item. It may last for many weeks. Indirect priming, which persists for much shorter periods, is mostly 'conceptual' or 'semantic'; it is dependent on the meaning of the item, and relatively independent of the sensory modality.

Repetition priming is where the frequency, speed, or accuracy of response is facilitated as a consequence of prior exposure to a particular stimulus (Tulving and Schacter 1990; Ochsner *et al.* 1994; Wiggs and Martin 1998). The most commonly used repetition priming *assays include 'perceptual identification', 'word completion', and 'lexical decision' tasks (Schacter 1987; Roediger and McDermott 1993). On a typical *perceptual identification* task (Jacoby and Dallas 1981), the subject is exposed on the study phase to series of words. Each word is flashed on the screen for a fraction of a second only. In the test phase, series or lists of words, including both the previously presented and 'new' words, are presented and the subject is requested to identify them. Priming is reflected in the increase in the accuracy or in the speed of identification of the previously presented words compared to the 'new' words. On the *word completion* task (Roediger *et al.* 1992), the subject is presented in the test with either word stems (e.g. AIR …), or word fragments (e.g. _ R_ _ I _ G), and instructed to complete them with the first word that comes to mind; priming is manifested as the preference for words that have been presented on the study phase (e.g. 'AIRCRAFT', 'PRIMING'). On the *lexical decision* task (Meyer and Schvaneveldt 1971), the subject is required to state whether or not a particular letter string is a legal word, for example, ARDUBOK, BELABOR, GARGOZOM (the middle one is a word, the two others are pseudowords, unless psychologists or molecular biologists have invented something since this has been written). Priming in this case is reflected in the decreased latency to make the decision on the second presentation of the letter string relative to the first. The examples above refer to visual presentation of verbal material; similar tasks could be performed with other sensory modalities and nonverbal material.

Commonly used *associative priming* assays include word associations, category production, and general knowledge priming tasks. On the *word association* task (Storms 1958; Shimamura and Squire 1984), a word presented in the study session results in preference for an associated word, e.g. stem–flower; the study by Storm (1958), mentioned above, is but an example. On the *category production* task (Srinivas and Roediger 1990; Gabrieli *et al.* 1995), the subject is presented with items from a certain category (e.g. animals), and later asked to produce as many as possible category exemplars (e.g. 'lion', 'elephant'); priming is manifested by a *bias toward production of the previously studied category exemplars. On the *general knowledge* task (Blaxton 1989; Vaidya *et al.* 1996), presentation of a word will enhance the production of an answer to trivia questions related to that word; for example, presentation of the word 'Jerusalem' in the study phase, will facilitate the production of the correct answer to the question 'What is the capital of Israel'.

Priming is a hot topic in research on human memory. There are four main reasons for this popularity. First, priming using verbal material is useful in the analysis of the perception, processing, and production of language. Second, priming, similarly to *transfer, provides a window to the processes and mechanisms of retrieval and to their dependence on the conditions and processes of encoding in *acquisition. Third, priming, a non*declarative memory, illuminates distinctions among memory systems (*taxonomy; Squire *et al.* 1993). And fourth, priming protocols are used to tap residual memory in *amnestic patients. It was noted

almost a century ago that past information in 'global' amnesic could sometimes be recovered if the patient is provided with clues to that information (see in Williams 1953). It is now evident that perceptual priming, and possibly some capabilities of conceptual priming, are preserved in amnesics (Warrington and Weiskrantz 1968; Backer Cave and Squire 1992; Schacter and Buckner 1998; for conceptual priming that is impaired in amnesics, see Vaidya *et al.* 1996). As 'global' amnesia is known to occur as a consequence of damage to structures in the medial temporal lobe and the diencephalon, it follows that perceptual priming is not critically dependent upon the integrity of these areas. The introduction of noninvasive *functional neuroimaging has expended tremendously the ability to identify brain regions that subserve priming (Schacter and Buckner 1998; Henson *et al.* 2000; Yasuno *et al.* 2000). In a nutshell, perceptual priming is correlated with reduced neuronal activation in modality specific neo*cortex, especially in higher-level processing areas. Conceptual priming is correlated with a similar change in multiple neocortical areas, including the prefrontal cortex. At the cellular level, repetition priming is thought to be correlated with a *decrease* in neuronal response in cortex with repeated stimulus presentation ('repetition suppression', Desimone 1996).[2] However, the possibility that in some circuits repetition priming involves experience-dependent synaptic *facilitation*, e.g. *long-term potentiation, should not be neglected (Milner 1997; for a candidate mechanism, see Frey and Morris 1997).

It is important to re-emphasize that 'priming' covers heterogeneous processes, which are expected to be subserved by multiple circuits and mechanisms in the brain.[3] The common denominator to all these processes is the nonconscious use-dependent facilitation of the processing and retrieval of an item.[4] *Sensitization also facilitates future processing, retrieval, and *performance, but is nonspecific, whereas priming depends on the specificity of the item(s) presented in the study phase. In some of its properties, such as the independence of *conscious awareness, priming resembles *habit and *skill. In others, it resembles declarative memory: it provides the brain with specific, discriminative, and precise information about events in the world. Tulving (1983) speculated that in performing priming experiments, we tap into memory capabilities that had emerged in phylogenesis after procedural memory systems but before declarative memory, and have played an important part in the life of early hominids (*Homo*). Were those ancestors of ours knowledgeable about the world but not consciously aware of it the way we are? Were they a bit like global amnesics? Even if the role of priming early in the evolution of our species remains a mystery, analysis of the distinction between brain systems that subserve priming and those that subserve declarative knowledge might provide us with clues to the identity of brain circuits that subserve consciousness.

Selected associations: Acquisition, Retrieval, Skill, Taxonomy, Transfer

---

[1]For another *classic example of the use of word associations in unveiling intriguing properties of memory, see *false memory.

[2]This finding is also discussed in the context of *habituation.

[3]This raises the question whether priming is a memory system, or a property that cuts across different memory systems. The *zeitgeist is to classify it as a memory system (*taxonomy), but it is unlikely that repetition and conceptual priming are subserved by the same system. This classification problem is not unique to priming; take, for example, *classical conditioning. It is considered a system of procedural memory, but trace conditioning is declarative, whereas delay conditioning is not. The take-home message is that taxonomies should be taken seriously only as much as they promote new concepts and research.

[4]Those cases in which the prior exposure results in inhibition of processing, are termed 'negative priming'.

Prospective memory

The memory of intentions and things to do.

The term 'prospective memory' was introduced by Meacham (Meacham and Singer 1977). It contrasts with 'retrospective memory', which is the memory for past events and experiences. A scientific *culture trivia will illustrate the distinction. I just got a request from a neuroscience journal to review a manuscript. I glanced through it and decided to read it again thoroughly over the weekend, conclude then whether to recommend acceptance—or rejection, because it may not be sufficiently novel (*scoopophobia), and send my recommendation to the editor via email, with the completed evaluation form in snailmail as a backup. The fact that I got the paper for review, my knowledge of the specific scientific discipline, and the realization that similar results have been reported earlier by another group, all are retrospective memory. But the intention to read the manuscript over the weekend and send my evaluation immediately afterwards is prospective memory. It is on my mind, but it has not yet been done; those are future actions, which I have to remember and remember to

remember till they are either completed or intentionally aborted.[1]

Although the memory for intentions and future actions was occasionally tapped already in the early days of experimental human psychology (Colegrove 1898), its systematic analysis has gained momentum only in the past two decades (Brandimonte *et al.* 1996; Dalla Barba 2000; for a provocative critique, see Crowder 1996). There were several reasons for this delay. First, science is often notorious for neglecting important issues, the science of memory being no exception (Neisser 1978). Second, we may be intuitively *biased by the *paradigm that memory is about the past, not the future. Third, prospective memory might be more difficult to control and interpret than retrospective memory in experimental settings; more than in many retrospective tasks, performance on prospective memory tasks involves non*mnemonic functions that confound the analysis of the mnemonic components of the task (e.g. Dobbs and Reeves 1996).

Consider, for example, the aforementioned manuscript-review assignment, which is now done. At first I had to encode the intention to perform the prospective task, as well as its specific content. (Interestingly, if I were *a priori inclined not to perform the review but rather rethink it only, the memory of the prospective task might have been weaker, see Koriat *et al.* 1990; also 'levels of processing' and 'transfer appropriate processing' in *acquisition, *retrieval.) Following the acquisition *phase, I had to monitor over time the time-to-performance, occasionally rehearsing and refreshing the intention and possibly the content of the intended action. At the appropriate time and *context, I had to retrieve the *internal representations of the intention and the content; perform the task while monitoring the output and matching it with the representation of the goal; and, finally, remove the completed assignment from my cognitive to-do list. All this involved idiosyncratic strategies of allotting and monitoring cognitive resources, executive functions (*working memory), *attention, motivation, tenacity, and more. Furthermore, the job has been accomplished in a multiple tasking situation, i.e. while performing many other behaviours that are not related to the review of the paper.

Whereas the evaluation of a scientific manuscript could be delayed for days, even weeks, prospective memory tests that are used in the laboratory cover only minutes or hours. Two simple tasks could serve as examples (Cockburn 1995). The first is a 'time-based' task. The *subject sits in front of a table with a clock on it and a booklet of sentences. He or she are asked to work through the booklet, putting a tick by those sentences that are true (e.g. 'apples are edibles') and a cross by those that are false (e.g. 'vans read books'). The instructions are to write the start time, answer as many questions as possible in 10 min, stop even if the booklet is not completed, and write the time. The second prospective task is 'event based'. The subject is instructed to work through a booklet containing rows of two- or three-digit numbers per page, cross out the smallest number in each row, and sign the name at the end of the last page after completing the task. Both protocols involve a prospective task (stopping and writing the time after 10 min in the first task, signing the name after completing the job in the second), superimposed on other cognitive tasks. Note that short-lived prospective tasks that are not superimposed on other ongoing tasks, are probably subserved by on-line retention of the internal representation of the intended action over the *delay; this is a typical working memory situation. In *bona fide* prospective memory, the internal representation of the intention is held off-line over the delay, to be retrieved only intermittently and ultimately during the execution of the task. Occasionally, human neuropsychologists who extend the notion of 'working memory' to ongoing tasks that last many days, consider even long-delayed prospective memory as a type of working memory.

Semantics notwithstanding, clearly, remembering to do things plays an important part in our daily life. We use this type of memory extensively at home, at work, in social contexts, and, equally important, while shopping (e.g. Shapiro and Krishnan 1999). Forgetting what we wanted to do may lead to anything from a slight embarrassment to deep distress (*dementia). Interestingly, although many aged individuals would swear that they have prospective memory problems (*metamemory), in controlled laboratory experiments, age-dependent prospective memory impairments are rather elusive (Maylor 1996). This could be due to the presence of useful *habits, and to accumulated experience, that guides the subject to take advantage of optimal strategies to obtain the goal. By the way, slight prospective memory deficits are not so difficult to overcome; no drugs are required (*nootropics), only user-friendly personal digital assistants (PDAs).

The neuropsychology of prospective memory is not as yet developed as that of retrospective memory. All prospective tasks involve retrospective memory. As *amnesics and *demented patients are highly impaired in retrospective memory, identification of brain areas that are specifically involved in the prospective but not the retrospective memory in such patients is difficult. The search is still on for that unfortunate brain damage that erases prospective but not retrospective memory

(e.g. Cockburn 1995). Instead of studying the effect of lesions, one could use the correlative *method, and map brain activity in normal individuals performing prospective memory tasks (*functional neuroimaging). So far, one brain area, itself heterogeneous, is suspected to play an important, although not exclusive, part in prospective memory. This is the frontal *cerebral cortex (Okuda *et al.* 1998; Fuster 2000*b*; but see Brunfaut *et al.* 2000). This will not surprise those readers that have already read about *planning or *working memory.

Do animals have prospective memory? The frontal cortex of other mammals is less developed than ours. Still, if we consider frontal cortex to subserve prospective memory, then these species do have a primitive version of the necessary neuronal gear. Of course, dog owners do not need all this boring scientific argumentation to know for sure that their dog wakes up in the morning having a very clear idea of what should be done throughout the day. Sometimes this dogish memory of things to do seems even stronger than that of the human master. It would be nice, though, to design a smart experiment to verify (*assay) that prospective memory is involved. How boring would the world become if such experiment ends up in *reducing the dog's behaviour into only consecutive, on-line stimulus–response chains (*behaviourism, *instrumental conditioning). Let's hope that this is not the case.

Selected associations: Declarative memory, Metamemory, Planning, Working memory

---

[1]These future actions may involve *planning, but planning and prospective memory are not identical. Planning involves organized scheme(s) of operation for attaining a goal, whereas prospective memory refers also to unstructured intentions and to isolated to-do items.

Protein kinase

A ubiquitous type of enzyme that modifies proteins and regulates their function by catalyzing the addition of a phosphate group.

In biochemical language, protein kinases (PKs) transfer the terminal phosphoryl group of the compound adenosine triphosphate (ATP) to an amino acid in the target protein. It is estimated that as much as 3% of all the genes code for PKs (Hunter 1994; Venter *et al.* 2001).

Protein kinase

After proteins are produced on the ribosomal machinery in the cell by translation from their corresponding messenger RNA (mRNA, *protein synthesis), they are still subjected to a variety of post-translational modifications, which regulate their function. These posttranslational modifications can switch cellular activity from one state to another. PKs are the most ubiquitous agents of post-translational modification in all tissues. The superfamily of PKs is classified into a number of families (Hanks and Hunter 1995). A major meta*criterion in this classification is the target amino acid: serine/threonine, or tyrosine. Most phosphorylation sites on proteins involve serine and threonine residues, and only about 0.1% involve tyrosine ('dual specificity' kinases phosphorylate both serine/threonine and tyrosine). PKs phosphorylate other proteins, but in many cases can also undergo autophosphorylation and regulate their own activity. The multiple families of serine/threonine kinases include PKs regulated by cyclic nucleotides, e.g. cyclic adenosine monophosphate (cAMP)-dependent PK (PKA); diacylglycerolactivated/phospholipid-dependent PKs (PKC), e.g. *calcium-dependent PKCs; calcium/calmodulin dependent PKs, e.g. multifunctional calcium/calmodulin dependent PK (CaMK); and mitogen-activated PKs (MAPKs). Other subfamilies of serine/threonine kinases are also known. Protein tyrosine kinases are conventionally classified into *receptor tyrosine kinases, which are associated with the cell membrane, and nonreceptor tyrosine kinases. Each of these protein tyrosine kinase families is further classified into subfamilies.

The biochemistry and molecular biology of PKs is complex. In the context of memory mechanisms, some generalizations and examples can however be made. PKs respond, either directly or indirectly, to extracellular *stimuli. This means that they fit to serve as components of the molecular *acquisition or *retrieval machinery in neurons (see also *ion channel, *reduction). PKs can switch the cell from one functional state to another, and some types regulate differentiation and growth. This implies that they fit to serve as triggers for *consolidation, memory *phase shifts and long-term memory. Some types of PKs can be converted into a *persistently active form that is autonomous of the activating signal. This implies that these PKs can serve as molecular information storage devices in neurons, and retain activity dependent information over time. A few examples will illustrate the aforementioned generalizations.

1. *PKA*. Here the most detailed data so far are from *Aplysia*, although data from other invertebrates

(e.g. Müller 2000) and from mammals (e.g. Abel *et al.* 1997) are also abundant. In the circuits that encode defensive reflexes in the sea hare, facilitatory interneurons that mediate the sensitizing stimulus release serotonin and other neuromodulators that bind to *receptors on the sensory neurons. These receptors activate the enzyme adenylyl cyclase, generating the second messenger cAMP (*intracellular signal transduction cascade). PKA is composed of two types of subunits, catalytic (C) and regulatory (R) (Figure 57). In the holoenzyme (i.e. C+R), R masks the enzymatic active site on C. When cAMP binds to R, it dissociates it from C and activates the latter. C phosphorylates substrate proteins in the *synapse, culminating in changes in ionic conductances, *neurotransmitter release, and an overall enhanced efficacy of the sensory-to-motor synapse. This results is synaptic facilitation, which is taken to be the cellular correlate of behavioural *sensitization in *simple systems. In the above process, PKA, as part of the cAMP signal transduction cascade, fulfils multiple roles. It is part of an acquisition machinery that creates the short-term trace (probably by phosphorylation of selected types of *ionic channels); it is also a component of the consolidation machinery that

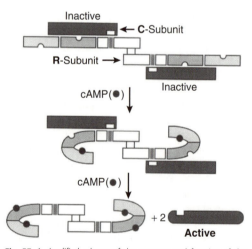

Fig. 57 A simplified scheme of the structure and function of the cAMP-dependent PK (PKA). The enzymatic complex is composed of two types of proteinic subunits, catalytic (C) and regulatory (R). R masks the enzymatic active site on C (upper configuration in the scheme). Binding of the intracellular messenger cAMP to R, dissociates R from C (middle configuration), and renders the latter free to phosphorylate its substrate proteins in the cell (bottom configuration). Cellular processes that degrade R or lower it affinity to C could hence lead to the accumulation of an autonomous, persistently active C. This could sustain use-dependent changes in the synapse for many hours (Buxbaum and Dudai 1989; Chain *et al.* 1999).

stabilizes the long-term trace (see also *CREB). PKA has also been suggested as a candidate information-storage device in the neuron. One of the *immediate early genes induced in consolidation codes for the enzyme ubiquitin hydrolase, which enhances specific proteolysis (breakdown of proteins). A major target of ubiquitin hydrolase is the R subunit of PKA. In the absence of R, C becomes persistently active and autonomous. This mechanism can sustain experience-dependent changes in the synapse for at least 24 h (Chain et al. 1999; for other mechanisms whereby the alteration in the R/C ratio can lead to persistent activation of PKA, see Buxbaum and Dudai 1989).

Studies of *classical conditioning in the *honeybee provide another illustration of the postulated role of PKA in triggering the consolidation of neuronal information in the context of learning. Conditioning of the bee to extend its tongue (proboscis) in response to an odour that is associated with sucrose solution, is correlated with activation of PKA in the antennal lobes, the functional analogues of the mammalian olfactory bulbs (Müller 2000). Only multiple-trial conditioning, which induces long-term memory, but not single-trial conditioning, which induces only short-term memory, leads to prolonged activation of the kinase. Inhibition of the PKA during training blocks long-term memory. Mimicry of the prolonged PKA activation, by a biochemical trick that increases the level of cAMP in the antennal lobes, when combined with a single conditioning trial, is sufficient to induce long-term memory. Hence in this study the *methods of observation, intervention, and mimicry combine to provide evidence that the activity of PKA is correlated in vivo with the induction of long-term memory, is necessary for long-term memory, and is sufficient to trigger the long-term registration of the sensory information in memory.

2. CaMKII. This kinase, highly concentrated in synapses, is implicated in multiple facets of neuronal *plasticity and growth (Braun and Schulman 1995). CaMKII is capable of autophosphorylation, which reduces its dependency on calcium, and produces an autonomous kinase. The enzyme can thus be considered as a molecular switch that becomes persistently activated following a transient calcium burst, i.e. a cellular information storage device (Saitoh and Schwartz 1985). In *long-term potentiation (LTP), CaMKII phosphorylates and enhances the responsiveness and the trafficking into the synapse of AMPA *glutamatergic receptors (Barria et al. 1997; Hayashi et al. 2000), and regulates AMPA receptor synthesis (Nayak et al. 1998). Shifts in the availability of the autonomous enzyme alter the responsiveness of synapses. An increased level of autonomous CaMKII was found to favour long-term depression over LTP, providing an appealing mechanism for regulating *metaplasticity (Chapman et al. 1995; Mayford et al. 1995). And mice expressing a mutant, autonomous CaMKII were found to be defective in certain types of LTP, and incapable of forming stable place *maps in the *hippocampus (Rotenberg et al. 1996).

3. MAPKs. The function of the MAPKs involves sequential activation of several cytoplasmic kinases, resulting in transmission of regulatory signals from the cell surface to the nucleus (Seger and Krebs 1995). MAPKs are involved in response to growth factors, and have been shown to be required for the formation of long-term memory (Martin et al. 1997b; Berman et al. 1998). In this process MAPK functions in concert with PKA (Kornhauser and Greenberg 1997; Martin et al. 1997b).

4. Tyrosine kinases. These are involved in many facets of regulation of differentiation and growth (Schlessinger and Ullrich 1992). Ample evidence attests to their role in synaptic plasticity and learning. For example, mutation in a nonreceptor tyrosine kinase, fyn, impaired LTP, *maze learning, yet also hippocampal development (Grant et al. 1992). In the behaving rat, tyrosine phosphorylation of the glutamatergic NMDA receptor was shown to correlate with LTP (Rosenblum et al. 1996) as well as with taste learning (Rosenblum et al. 1997).

By no means are the above examples exhaustive. Many other PKs are implicated in plasticity, learning, and memory, for example, members of the PKC family (e.g. Thomas et al. 1994). Judging by their multiple, ubiquitous roles in cellular function, and by the extensive cross-talk of networks of PKs in the cell (*coincidence detector), the involvement of PKs in multiple phases of learning and memory is expected to be the rule rather than the exception. Protein phosphatases should also not be forgotten (Mulkey et al. 1993; Winder et al. 1998). Whatever goes up also comes down, and phosphatases are enzymes that undo what the kinases do. Protein phosphatases may inhibit memory formation in the first seconds or minutes in the life of an *engram, and, furthermore, erase cellular traces of immediate- and short-term memories. They should definitely provide interesting targets for modern analogues of the legendary *lotus.

Selected associations: CREB, Consolidation, Intracellular signal transduction cascades, Plasticity, Reduction

Protein synthesis

The process by which cells manufacture protein molecules from amino acids on the basis of the genetic information that is encoded in the DNA.

The genetic code is decoded in all living cells in two major *phases. First it is transcribed from the DNA into a specific messenger RNA (mRNA) molecule. This process is termed 'transcription'. The code is then read from the mRNA molecule to produce the copy of the corresponding protein. This process, which takes place in a complex cellular factory called ribosome, is termed 'translation'. In practice, a group of ribosomes ('polyribosome') performs the task on each mRNA. There are many complex steps in protein synthesis (Alberts *et al.* 1994), but most of the details need not concern us here. Rather, we will concentrate on those aspects of protein synthesis that have become a major focus of research in the biology of learning and memory.

It has all started with the notion that the brain develops with experience, and that, similarly to all *developmental processes, this involves growth. This is an old idea, which has become a tenet of modern neurobiology (Hebb 1949; *zeitgeist). Growth means, among others, synthesis of proteins, which are the major constituents of all living cells. It became evident that experience is indeed accompanied by alteration in protein synthesis in the nervous system (Hamberger and Hyden 1945). Eventually, the proposal was explicitly made that the formation of new memory traces depend on new protein synthesis (Monne 1949; Katz and Halstead 1950). The experimental proof followed (RNA synthesis—Dingman and Sporn 1961; protein synthesis—Flexner *et al.* 1963; Agranoff and Klinger 1964).

Over the years, two types of *methods have been used to demonstrate the role of protein synthesis in memory. The first method involved intervention with the metabolism of the brain, by the use of antibiotics that inhibit RNA or protein synthesis (inference of function from the dysfunction, *method). After the initial successes (Flexner *et al.* 1963; Agranoff and Klinger 1964), scores of laboratories became enthusiastically immersed in the new paradigm, injecting protein synthesis inhibitors into the brain of behaving animals ranging from goldfish to rodents. In spite of occasional worries about the exact target of the antibiotics (e.g. Kyriakis *et al.* 1994), the overwhelming conclusion was that protein synthesis during or up to a few hours after training, but not afterwards, is required for the *consolidation of long-term memory, but not for its *acquisition, short-term retention, or *retrieval once the long-term memory had been formed (Davis and Squire 1984; Dudai 1989; Rose 1995*b*).

In the early days of the protein-synthesis-inhibition-of-memory experiments, the inhibitors were injected into wide areas of the brain, the whole brain, or even the whole body. This created a problem, because the experimenters could not prove that the effect is on neurons, and that the targets have anything to do with the specific memorized task. This difficulty was resolved only in the mid-80s. During that period, new preparations were developed, in which identified memory-subserving neurons are studied in isolation (*Aplysia), and cellular analogues of learning are analysed in brain tissue (*long-term potentiation). Another wave of protein-synthesis-inhibition-of-memory studies soon followed. These experiments finally proved that the initial conclusions about the role of RNA and protein synthesis in consolidation were basically correct (e.g. Montarolo *et al.* 1986, Linden 1996). The new preparations also permitted the effective use of a complementary approach, based on correlation rather than perturbation: identification of neuronal gene products that are induced by experience (*immediate early genes, *late response genes).

The combination of the two aforesaid approaches has led to the following textbook cellular *model of long-term memory: *stimuli that exceed a certain threshold or *coincide in appropriate combinations, operate on the relevant *receptors in the target synapses, and activate *intracellular signal transduction cascades. The latter activate constitutive transcription factors (TFs), and induce the transcription of additional TFs as well as other types of immediate early genes.[1] The TFs trigger phases of gene expression, culminating in the induction of expression of late response genes. The products of the induced genes ultimately induce and embody persistent alterations in the synapses and neurons that encode the memory. Further, whereas neuronal alterations that are based on post-translational modifications are constrained by the limited life span of the modified protein molecule (which is commonly anywhere between a few minutes to a few weeks), the modulation of gene expression could render the alterations immune to the molecular turnover of individual protein molecules. The mechanisms of transcriptional regulation by extracellular signals in neurons are basically similar to those that operate in non-neuronal cells (Hill and Treisman 1995). This suggests, by the way, that the specificity of the *engram should be searched for at higher *levels of organization of the brain (*reduction).

The textbook model is, as usual, too simplistic. The complications are of two types. One type relates to the role of the newly synthesized proteins in the context of memory: Is it permissive, or causal? Do these proteins play a direct role in modifying the use-dependent *internal representation? This issue surfaces in several discussions in this book (e.g. *CREB, *homeostasis, *late response genes); it will not be further elaborated here. The other type of issue refers to the specificity of the process and to cellular economy. Isn't the modulation of cell-wide gene expression by only one or a few synapses remarkably nonparsimonious? And how would synaptic specificity be preserved, if at all?

The solution may lie in the intricacies of a multiphasic mechanism, which is both synapse-specific and cell-wide (Figure 58) (Dudai and Morris 2000). It appears that the activated synapse is somehow 'tagged', possibly by post-translational modification of synaptic protein(s), or by reorganization of such proteins (Katz and Halstead 1950; Dudai 1989; Frey and Morris 1997; Martin *et al.* 1997*a*). This results in a new local synaptic configuration. It could also attract proteins from other parts of the cell. In addition, the stimulus activates constitutive transcription factors, such as CREB, and induces immediate early gene expression, some of which encode inducible transcription factors, others different types of proteins, including enzymes, cytoskeletal elements, and growth factors. The synapse itself contains the full translation apparatus and is capable of synthesizing proteins on location, from mRNA which is delivered from the nucleus (Steward and Levy 1982; Rao and Steward 1991; Weller and Greenough 1993; Martin *et al.* 1997*a*; Steward *et al.* 1998; Huber *et al.* 2000). These locally synthesized proteins strengthen the tagging of the synapse, and/or serve as retrograde messages, which travel to the cell body and inform the nucleus about the change (Casadio *et al.* 1999). This results in modulation of gene expression in the nucleus, and in the production of new mRNAs and proteins, that are funnelled to the tagged synapse. All in all, the process is hence assumed to involve intimate co-ordination between the synapse and the nucleus, which probably optimizes the exploitation of the metabolic resources of the neuron and the specificity of the long-term synaptic change (Dudai and Morris 2000).

We still have a long way to go before we fully understand the mechanisms and roles of synaptic tagging and step-wise synaptic consolidation. We are bound for surprises on the way. For example, it has been reported that the wave of protein synthesis that is triggered by a salient event in one synapse, is capable of affecting the registration of activity in adjacent synapses as well. This

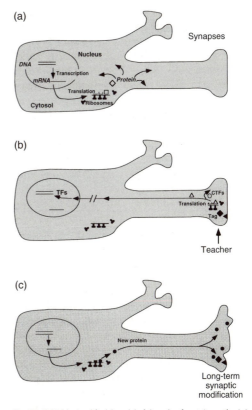

Fig. 58 A highly simplified *model of the role of protein synthesis in the production of long-term synaptic modifications that are assumed to subserve the *acquisition and *consolidation and contribute to the *persistence of long-term memory. (a) Protein synthesis involves transcription in the nucleus and translation on ribosomes in the cytosol (the inner cellular space outside the nucleus). (b) A teaching stimulus ('teacher'), which is sufficiently salient to induce long-term memory, activates membrane receptors and their downstream *intracellular signal transduction cascades. This results in the activation of constitutive transcription factors (CTFs), such as *CREB, and in the induction of the expression of *immediate early genes, which encode inducible transcription factors as well as a variety of other proteins. Immediately after the stimulation, the activated *synapse is tagged in a way that differentiates it from the nonstimulated synapses. The teaching stimulus also induces local protein synthesis in the synapse (the ribosomes in the synapse are not shown in (a) for simplicity). The proteins that are synthesized on location might contribute to the tagging of the activated synapse. They might also comprise or generate a retrograde signal, which travels to the nucleus. The expression of certain genes in the informed nucleus is now modulated by sets of TFs. (c) The newly synthesized proteins travel from the cell body to the activated, tagged synapse, and contribute to its lasting modification. Protein synthesis hence fulfils multiple roles at multiple sites and times after the training, and is controlled by both the activated synapse and the cell body and nucleus.

means that synapses are tuned to the history of each other (Frey and Morris 1997). This could subserve the cellular encoding of *context, *generalization, even *priming. Whether the synaptic phenomenology indeed contributes to the behavioural phenomena of context encoding, generalization or priming, is currently an intriguing yet unresolved issue.

Selected associations: Consolidation, CREB, Development, Immediate early genes, Late response genes

---

[1]On what transcription factors are, and on the distinction between constitutive and inducible TFs, see in *immediate early genes.

Rat

A small mammal of the genus *Rattus*, family *Muridea*, order *Rodentia* (rodents).

The contribution of the rat to the behavioural and brain sciences is second only to that of humans, the main difference being that the contribution of the latter is frequently more voluntary. It has all started with the invasion of Europe by the brown rat (*Rattus norvegicus*). The brown rat arrived from Asia at the beginning of the eighteenth century, almost 400 years after its cousin, *Rattus rattus* (the black or grey rat), spread the devastating Black Death throughout the Continent. The brown rat was very successful in the new niche. The human response was to engage in extensive rat trapping, and to establish rat baiting as a popular sport. The twist in the story came when albino mutants of the brown rat were noted, isolated, and kept for entertainment. The albino rat proved to be much more tameable than the wild type. The relative docility of this mutant provided it with the opportunity for eternal fame; by 1850s, it has already been used in metabolic and genetic experiments in France. England and Germany followed right thereafter. As a matter of fact, this was the first species to be domesticated for scientific purposes (Lockard 1968; Lindsey 1979). In the 1890s, a Swiss scientist who emigrated to the USA imported the albino rat to the University of Chicago.[1] At about the same time, a short-lived attempt was made to use the grey rat at Clark University (Munn 1950), but the white soon replaced the grey in Clark as well. The standardized stocks and inbred strains of laboratory rats used today were developed from the albino as well as from crosses between the albino and wild type (Lindsey 1979).

The championship of the psychology lab did not come easy to the rat. Chicks, cats, and dogs were all at one time or another effective rivals for the attention of researchers (Boakes 1984; *classical conditioning, *imprinting, *instrumental conditioning). The laboratory rat was small, cheap, easily bred and cared for, and, most importantly, smart. At Clark University, it became the subject of the first *maze experiments (Small 1901; Miles 1930). The combination of mazes and rats emerged as a real winner, shaping experimental psychology for generations to come. Rat learning *paradigms became so dominant that at a certain stage, toward the mid-twentieth century, experimental psychologists, especially in North America, became convinced that rat behaviour can faithfully *model human behaviour. Furthermore, they entertained the idea that the rat mind holds many of the clues to human psyche. '… Most of the formal underlying laws of intelligence motivation and instability can still be studied in rats … more easily than in men … (rats) do not go on binges the night before one has planned the experiment; they do not kill each other off in wars; they do not invent engines of destruction, and, if they did, they would not be so dumb about controlling such engines; they do not go in for either class conflicts or race conflicts; they avoid politics, economics and papers on psychology' (Tolman 1945). Whereas avoidance of politics and of papers on psychology does have some merit, the enthusiasm appears today a bit exaggerated.

The advantages of the rat for the science of memory are numerous. Some of these advantages pertain directly to the rat's ability to learn quickly in tasks which are convenient for use in the laboratory. It is especially shrewd in spatial, olfactory, and taste learning (Tolman 1948; Slotnick 1994; Biegler and Morris 1996; Schul *et al.* 1996). Other advantages of the rat relate to its size (not too big, not too small). But probably must important at this stage is the immense body of knowledge that has accumulated over the years on the rat's neuroanatomy, neuropharmacology, neurophysiology, and behaviour. This combination turns the rat into a prime choice for the cross-*level study of certain types of mammalian learning.

The rat, however, has at least two types of disadvantage. First, clearly, in some cognitive tasks, such as *delay tasks, which are of great importance to the understanding of primate *recognition and *recall, the rat is no rival to more advanced species such as the *monkey (Hunter 1913; Keller and Hill 1936; Steckler *et al.* 1998a,b). It is also debated whether it can form genuine *learning sets, a popular *criterion for rudimentary concept formation (Reid and Morris 1992; Slotnick 1994). Second, the molecular genetics of the rat is undeveloped. Transgenics were reported (e.g. Waller *et al.* 1996), but no knockout technology is yet available at the time of writing. This deprives the rat of one of the most powerful tools of molecular neurobiology (*neurogenetics). So far, in this arena, the *mouse outperforms the rat, and if the latter doesn't catch up, which is rather unlikely, it will lose its hegemony in the world of mazes and puzzle boxes.

Selected associations: Maze, Model, Subject, Zeitgeist

---

[1]Whether all the albino rats later used in research in the USA indeed originated from this import is uncertain (Lindsey 1979).

Real-life memory

Memory acquired, used, and investigated in natural settings.

It may come as a surprise to postdocs running mice in water *mazes, poking molluscan neurons in a dish, or flashing computerized test icons in front of bored students—but memory does have a life outside the laboratory. It is this potential detachment from reality, particularly in dealing with human memory, that has prompted Neisser (1978) to deliver in the first International Conference on Practical Aspects of Memory a signal presentation, entitled 'Memory: what are the important questions?'. Neisser claimed, more or less, that the bulk of experimental research on human memory, since its first days some one hundred years earlier (Ebbinghaus 1885), meant very little as much as memory in real life is concerned. He further went on to argue that 'if X is an interesting or socially significant aspect of memory, then psychologists have hardly ever studied X' (*ibid.*). Neisser's scholarly provocation stirred emotional polemics (e.g. Banaji and Crowder 1989; Conway 1991; Loftus 1991), itself a potentially interesting topic for research on everyday memory (Roediger 1991). It also epitomized, and contributed to, a deflection in the direction of human memory research.

It is difficult to underestimate the importance of the first controlled paradigms for quantifying human memory (Ebbinghaus 1885). Without them, memory research would have not been promoted to the rank of a respectable, quantitative, and reproducible science. In parallel, the mainstream research on animal learning, while looking for reproducible methods and quantifiable variables, has also become increasingly dependent on artificial laboratory *paradigms (*classical and

*instrumental conditioning). Many of these paradigms expose the experimental animal to settings and demands far remote from the ecological niches and from the problems that these niches pose (Boakes 1984). The effectiveness and popularity of these animal learning paradigms have tempted prominent investigators to adapt them to human use (e.g. Woodworth and Scholsberg 1954), and even to go as far as to declare that most, if not all, the riddles of human memory will ultimately be solved by understanding the behaviour of the *rat (Munn 1950). There were, of course, early attempts to investigate human memory in its natural settings (e.g. Galton 1879; Colegrove 1898; Thorndike and Woodworth 1901*a,b*; *capacity, *transfer). Furthermore, over the years the mainstream 'laboratory approach' to memory research was not without its ardent opponents, who claimed that most of the studies miss the social and ecological context, function, and complexity of memory in real life (Bartlett 1932). However, the challenge did not gain much momentum until the 1970s.

Real-life memory research was at first formulated as an opposition, devoid of a formal consensus on its precise definition (Klatzky 1991). It is known by multiple names, which refer to the same or similar notions: 'everyday memory' ('an awkward phrase', Neisser 1991); 'ecological memory' (Bruce 1985); and 'real-world memory' (Cohen 1996). In essence, the majority of the traditional research on memory throughout the first half of the twentieth century has focused on the structure and the 'syntax' of memory, i.e. how the system operates and what are the formal relations between *stimuli and actions (*algorithm, *model). Furthermore, this research was dominated by the role of the investigator, who in many respects shaped the behaviour of the *subject in artificial settings by choosing the problems, the constraints, and the *reinforced response. In contrast, real-life memory research concentrates on the subject in its natural environment, on phenomena relevant to daily life, and on familiar types of stimuli and responses. It emphasizes better the 'semantics' of the learned behaviour, i.e. its content, function, context, and meaning. Here is a selection of 'real life' questions: How accurate are our autobiographical reminiscences? Should we trust eyewitnesses? What shall we do to remember better which name belongs to which face? How do we keep a mental record of what we *plan to do later in the day (*prospective memory)? How do experts differ from novices in their everyday *skill? Or, closer to academic life, how much do we remember after attending a classroom lecture (not too much, and unfortunately or not, jokes rather than facts are remembered best; Kintch and Bates 1977).

Criticism of research on real-life memory focuses on what is considered by the critics as lack of *controllability, rigorousness, and reproducibility of the *methods and the generalizability of the conclusions (Banaji and Crowder 1989). But the reduced control of extraneous variables is the price many investigators are ready to pay in exchange for the ability to tackle naturalistic, complex behaviours, and unveil new memory phenomena (Baddley 1981; Klatzky 1991). Explicitly or implicitly, the modern real-life memory movement did exert a significant impact on human memory research.[1] The development of novel techniques that permit on-line analysis of the conscious brain in normal subjects has in parallel extended and enriched the repertoire of methodologies available in the investigation of human memory (e.g. virtual reality, *functional neuroimaging). As a consequence, many *bona fide* real-life phenomena are currently being dealt with at the forefront of human memory research, both inside and outside the laboratory (Cohen 1996; Goel *et al.* 1997; Maguire *et al.* 1997).

Selected associations: Context, False memory, Flashbulb memory, Observational learning, Prospective memory

---

[1]The parallel in the field of animal learning is the ethological approach (Tinbergen 1969; Lorenz 1981). For a review, see Camhi (1984); for more recent variants, see Eichenbaum (1996) and Chiel and Beer (1997); also *birdsong, *imprinting.

Recall

1. **The reactivation or reconstruction of the *internal representation of a target item in the absence of this item.**
2. **The brain process(es) by which this occurs.**
3. ***Recall test:* A test situation by which this is measured.**

Recall is a type of memory (definition 1), brain process (definition 2), and test situation (definition 3). It is important to distinguish between the three. Recall as a memory faculty is the phenomenon that most people have in mind when they refer to 'remembrance' or 'recollection'. It is 'memory par excellence' (Bergson 1908). Some authors, especially in the older literature, equate recall with *retrieval. This should be avoided,

because retrieval is a universal process, which must occur to actualize any type of learned information, even the simplest ones such as *habituation and *sensitization, whereas recall corresponds to retrieval only under the conditions specified in definition 1. Recall as a process is inferred to underlie the recall faculty. Recall as a test involves the generation by the *subject of the internal representation of a fact or event according to instructions, in the absence of the corresponding on-line sensory information, for example, reproduce in mind a remote autobiographical episode while sitting in the laboratory. But recall could also be involved in tasks that are not intentionally meant to tap into it. For example, in a *recognition test, a subject instructed to identify an on-line sensory *stimulus probably uses recall of off-line information to evaluate the meaning of this target.

A few additional words on variants of recall. When recall is tested in the absence of intentional *cues, it is called 'free recall'. When cues are provided, it is called 'cued recall' or 'prompted recall'. Each of these terms can be used, as far as it is remembered that there is probably no recall without cues—only that in prompted recall these cues are provided by the experimenter, whereas in free recall they are generated by the subject. When recall is initiated by instructions or by focused intention, it is focused or intentional recall, whereas if it is the spin-off of a stream of *associations, it is incidental recall. When the recall yields what is judged to be the complete target, it is complete or total recall. But in many cases recall is only partial. Two examples of partial recall are provided by the 'feeling of knowing' (FOK) and the 'tip of the tongue' (TOT) phenomena. In FOK the subject judges that the target is in memory despite a failure to retrieve it at present time (Hart 1965); in TOT, the subject judges as if verbal information resides on the tip of the tongue (*metaphor) despite the failure to express it (Brown and McNeill 1966; *metamemory).[1] An attempt to recall an item in memory may at first prove futile but later succeed without further learning. This is called 'reminiscence', i.e. the recall of previously unrecalled items (Ballard 1913; Payne 1987). Under certain conditions, the overall recall performance of the subject on a certain type of test and material may improve with repeated recall trials; this is termed 'hyperamnesia' (Erdelyi and Becker 1974; Payne 1987).

Starting from the early days of experimental psychology (e.g. MacDougall 1904; Hollingworth 1913), many attempts have been made to explain how recall works, and what distinguishes it from recognition. It should be said at the outset that this focus on the distinction of recall from recognition may be a bit misleading, because it suggests that the two phenomena or processes are decisively different, which may not be true. In a nutshell, there are two main types of recall 'theories', or *models. One type refers to recall and recognition as lying on a continuum of retrieval (Tulving 1976). The main difference between recall and recognition, according to this view, is the nature and availability of *retrieval cues*: supplied in recognition, self-generated in recall (see above). The other type of models distinguishes basic differences between recognition and recall. These models propose that recall operates in *two *phases*, or stages (Bahrick 1970; Kintsch 1970). The first phase is the search, *generation*, or retrieval phase. The second phase is the identification, or decision, or *recognition* phase, once the target has been retrieved.[2]

Two points about the two-stage models of recall are noteworthy. One, recognition also involves retrieval. Therefore, distinguishing one phase of recall as the retrieval phase, as opposed to recognition, disregards the universality of retrieval as the process necessary to actualize stored information. Second, it is tempting to assume that if recognition is a subprocess in recall, recognition will be easier than recall. Intuitively it makes sense: how easy it is to recognize a face, how difficult is it to recall the name that belongs to that face (McWeeny *et al.* 1987). Yet it can be shown that under certain conditions items are recalled but not recognized (Bahrick and Bahrick 1964; Tulving and Thomson 1973). For example, consider the following experiment (Tulving and Thomson 1973): subjects were presented with an input list of pairs of words, one a target word, such as *baby*, the other a weak semantic associate that was intended to be used as a *cue for the target word, e.g. *grasp*. Afterwards, the subjects were presented with strong semantic associates of the target words, e.g. *infant*, and asked to generate a list of associated words. The subjects were then asked to mark all the words in the generated list that they recognized as having occurred in the input list. Finally, the subjects were presented with the original input list cues and asked to recall the target words. Under these conditions, the prompted recall was superior to the recognition of words from the input list. This seems incompatible with recall being a generation-plus-recognition process. The recognition failure was explained by the authors by invoking the 'encoding-specificity principle'. This principle (*acquisition, *retrieval) states that memory performance is best when the cues present at retrieval match those present in acquisition. The encoding of the target words in the input list was in the presence of the input list cues, and influenced by the subjects' expectation that they will be tested with these cues. In the later part of the experiment, which involved the recognition task, the retrieval attempt was made using different cues and in a different *context. The encoding specificity principle predicts that this will hamper the retrieval, hence recognition, of the target words. Another interpretation of the data is that the recognition failure resulted from the formation of two different traces in the different parts of the experiment, rather than from differences in the retrieval efficacy of the same trace (Baddeley 1982). The two different traces could have resulted from the interaction of each target word with two different semantic contexts, shaped by the weak and the strong semantic associates, respectively. If correct, this means that the 'item to be recognized' was not actually identical to the 'item to be recalled', rendering the comparison of the efficacy of recognition and recall in this experiment questionable.

Can animals recall? We find it easy to understand recall because we frequently recall and because we can ask other individuals to declare their own recall experience. But how do we know whether a dog is musing spontaneously, or at least is cued to muse, about things past? In referring to recall, there is an implicit assumption that it does not refer to very short-lived memory, say of a few seconds only. If this assumption is abandoned, than trace conditioning (*classical conditioning) and *working memory involve cued recall functions, and clearly, they can be performed by nonhuman species. Furthermore, animals do seem capable of high-order stimulus–stimulus associations (Dickinson 1980; Mackintosh 1983), so why not consider these as resulting in stimulus-independent retrieval, hence recall? Nonhuman species might also be capable of *conscious awareness of the recall act (Clark and Squire 1998, *declarative memory). A reasonable conclusion is that recall is a spectrum of functions, differing in their dependence on available cues, and their explicitness, and other species are capable of rudimentary forms of recall (see also discussion in *episodic memory).

Which brain circuits subserve recall? The analysis of defective recall in *amnesics indicates that, similarly to recognition, recall depends during the acquisition and *consolidation phases of the memory on the integrity of the *hippocampal formation and other mediotemporal structures (Haist *et al.* 1992). *Functional neuroimaging of normal subjects confirms that the hippocampus is indeed involved in explicit recall (e.g. Maguire *et al.* 1997). With time, however, the memory to be recalled becomes practically independent of the hippocampal formation, and remains in the *cerebral cortex (e.g. Teng and Squire 1999). There is evidence that recalling a target in its absence activates areas in the sensory cortex that were originally involved in *perception of the target (e.g. Kosslyn *et al.* 1995; Zatorre *et al.* 1996; Wheeler *et al.* 2000). And finally, to recall a target, monitor the operation and verify it, the prefrontal cortex is needed (Jetter *et al.* 1986; Buckner and Koustaal 1998; Fletcher *et al.* 1998; Tomita *et al.* 1999; Maril *et al.* 2001). This brings us back to the issue as to whether nonhuman species can recall: those species that have a reasonably developed prefrontal cortex, such as other primates, can probably recall, but less efficiently than *Homo sapiens*, who happens to have a more sophisticated prefrontal cortex.

Selected associations: Amnesia, Confabulation, Recognition, Retrieval, State-dependent learning

---

[1]FOK and TOT apply to *recognition as well.

[2]The notion of recall involves search and identification can be traced to much earlier literature: it is hinted already in Augustine (400; *classic).

Receptor

1. **A molecule or molecular complex that binds other types of molecules in a specific, saturable manner.**
2. **A protein that responds to the binding of specific types of molecules by triggering a distinct type of change in cellular activity.**
3. **A specialized cell or organ at the front end of a sensory channel, capable of responding to specific types of sensory *stimuli by modulating its output to the nervous system.**

'Receptor' is from *recipio*, 'to receive' in Latin. The families of receptors that concern us here are molecular (definition 1), specifically, proteins that respond to molecular stimuli by triggering cellular response (definition 2). Many types of these receptors reside on the surface membrane of the cell. Other types of molecular receptors are on the membrane of intracellular organelles or in the cytoplasm. We will focus on the cell-surface types. Receptor molecules also exist on and in sensory receptors cells (definition 3), where they respond to either chemical or physical stimuli, depending on the sensory modality that the organ or the cell transduces (Hudspeth 1989; Lagnado and Baylor 1992; GarciaAnoveros and Corey 1997; Herness

and Gibertson 1999; Mombartes 1999). The receptive apparatus in sensory receptor cells is not prime candidate for fulfilling memory functions. This is because, being at the front end of the sensory channel, its alteration affects the input globally, whereas most learning is expected to involve a discriminative alteration in response to the input. We shall therefore concentrate on receptor proteins in the brain, particularly on those receptors that reside on *synaptic membranes and bind *neurotransmitters, neuromodulators, and growth factors. Such receptors subserve intercellular communication and could mediate or encode lasting modifications in circuit properties.

The term 'receptor' is used in pharmacology in a broader sense than in cellular neurobiology, and refers to any type of drug–target in living tissue (Ariens and Beld 1977; definition 1). The notion that drugs and poisons mimic or block physiological function by interacting with specific sites in the organism is at least over a century old. Langley (1905), studying the effects of the cholinergic (*acetylcholine) toxins nicotine and curare, was the first to term these sites 'receptive substances'. The decisive proof that receptors are specialized proteins was provided by studies of the nicotinic acetylcholine receptor from the electric organ of electric fish. This receptor was isolated, reconstituted, and its gene was ultimately cloned (Numa *et al.* 1983; Changeux *et al.* 1984; for a personal view on the early history of the field, see Nachmansohn 1959). In its time, the cloning of the nicotinic receptor was a remarkable feat. Less then 20 years later, cloning receptor genes is a routine.

Before proceeding, a few semantic points should be clarified. Receptor proteins contain multiple functional components, which could reside in dissociatable subunits. One type of component is the 'binding site', which recognizes and binds specific molecules ('ligands', from 'bound' in Latin). Most receptors have multiple binding sites, commonly for different types of ligands. Another component is the 'effector', that part that performs the response function. This could be, for example, an *ion channel pore, or an active site of an enzyme (and see below). Some authors refer only to the binding site as a *bona fide* 'receptor' (Cooper *et al.* 1996). Receptors without an effector are sometimes called 'acceptors', and could, for example, play a part in regulating the level of specific ligands in the cell. Specific ligands could either activate the receptor, in which case they are termed 'agonists', or block it, in which case they are 'antagonists'. Ligands could also modulate the binding and action of other agonists. Finally, typically, a receptor protein is named after what is considered to be its major endogenous agonist, e.g. *glutamatergic, *dopaminergic. Similarly, the name of a receptor subtype refers to an endogenous ligand or to a drug or poison that displays selectivity for that subtype (e.g. a cholinergic *muscarinic* receptor). Sometimes, another structural or functional attribute is used for naming, e.g. a '*metabotropic*' family of glutamate receptors (from 'metabolism'). In yet other cases, for the lack of a better alternative, arbitrary notations are employed, such as 1–*n*, α–ν, etc. (e.g. Milligan *et al.* 1994). As the number of identified receptor types and variants keeps growing, notations tend to become cumbersome. The completion of the Human Genome project is expected to lead to a revision that will make the naming of receptor families more rational and convenient.

Cell-surface receptor proteins could be classified by their effector type. The three major effector types are ion channels, G proteins, and enzymes. Ion channel receptors are ligand-gated ion channels, for example, the nicotinic acetylcholine receptor is a Na^+ channel, and the *N*-methyl-D-aspartate (NMDA) receptor primarily a *calcium channel.[1] G-protein-coupled receptors belong to a superfamily of membrane proteins that contain seven hydrophobic transmembrane domains, and function by activating members of a family of regulatory protein called GTP-binding protein (abbreviated G protein; Gutkind 1998; *intracellular signal transduction). The G protein, depending on its specific type, activates or inhibits the activity of other target proteins, such as enzymes, ion channels—or yet other receptors. Examples for G-protein-coupled receptors are muscarinic (*acetylcholine), dopaminergic, and metabotropic glutamatergic receptors. Finally, enzyme-linked receptors function as enzymes or are intimately associated with an enzyme. Examples are receptor *protein kinases (Numa *et al.* 1983; Marshall 1995). *In situ*, receptor proteins do not live in isolation; they interact dynamically with other membrane, cytoskeletal and cytoplasmatic elements to form macromolecular complexes, which together control specific facets of cellular state (Kim and Huganir 1999).

Generally speaking, synaptic receptors fit to fulfil the role of elementary hardware components in biological 'learning machines' (Dudai 1994*a*). They could serve as:

1. **Acquisition devices.* Synaptic messages encoding stimulus information trigger a change in the target nerve cell by first activating receptor proteins. These receptors could therefore be regarded as 'cellular acquisition devices', implementing decoding and registration functions. Examples are various types of glutamatergic receptors that mediate excitatory transmission in the mammalian brain.

2. *Transducers of* **context.* In the acquisition *phase the receptor could mediate information about the conditioned stimulus, about the *reinforcer (e.g. Shimizu *et al.* 2000), or about other, contextual *dimensions of the input.[2] For example, receptors for acetylcholine in the mammalian brain transduce information on the novelty or saliency of stimuli (e.g. Naor and Dudai 1996). *Noradrenergic and dopaminergic receptors probably fulfil similar types of roles. An illustration of the role of receptors in encoding context at the cellular *level is provided by their ability to modulate stimulus-induced long-term alterations in synaptic efficacy (e.g. Kirkwood *et al.* 1999, also *long-term potentiation).

3. **Coincidence detectors.* Receptor proteins could associate incoming stimuli. A popular example is the glutamatergic NMDA receptor, a molecular AND gate that integrates information encoded by glutamate and by membrane depolarization. Another example is provided by the role of serotonergic or peptidergic receptors[3] in the conditioning of defensive reflexes in **Aplysia.* In this case, the transmitter, which carries information about the unconditioned stimulus, activates a receptor-coupled enzyme, adenylyl cyclase. For optimal activation, however, the enzyme also requires calcium, which carries information about the conditioned stimulus. This dually activated receptor was reported to display the order and temporal-specificity constraints that are characteristic of *classical conditioning (Yovell and Abrams 1992).

4. *Information storage devices.* Use-dependent alterations in the sensitivity or availability of receptor molecules could encode long-lasting modifications in synaptic activity, and hence subserve the *persistence of the *engram over time (Changeux *et al.* 1984; Lynch and Baudry 1984). The idea is that even in the absence of other experience-dependent lasting synaptic modifications, increased availability or facilitated kinetics of a receptor is read-out by the retrieval input as a facilitated synaptic state. The proposed role of the AMPA-type glutamate receptor in long-term potentiation is a prominent example (Nayak *et al.* 1998; Shi *et al.* 1999).

In fulfilling the above roles, the specificity and effectiveness of the receptor-mediated information could be contributed by the sender (the ligand), the receiver (the receptor), or, most probably, by both. Candidate dimensions of specificity include the spatial (point of origin), temporal (rate and frequency), and intensity of the incoming stimulus, the location and concentration of the receptor on the cell surface, and the combinatorial activation of the receptor and its downstream intra-cellular signal transduction cascade(s) together with other types of receptors and cascades (e.g. Gutkind 1998; Madhani and Fink 1998).

The multiple roles of synaptic receptors in learning, memory, and retrieval marks them as promising targets for new memory-enhancing drugs (*dementia, *nootropics). For example, agonists of AMPA-type glutamate receptors have already been tested on humans and reported to improve memory (Ingvar et al. 1997).

Selected associations: Acquisition, Coincidence detector, Ion channel, Neurotransmitter, Stimulus

---

[1]Ligand-gated is contrasted with 'voltage-gated' channels (see *ion channel). Ligand-gated receptor channels are sometimes referred to also as 'chemically gated'. It makes sense to reserve the term 'ligand gated' to channels that are regulated by an extracellular ligand such as a neurotransmitter, and use the term 'chemically gated' to refer to channels that are regulated by either extracellular or intracellular compounds.

[2]The types of roles fulfilled by receptors in acquisition, including encoding of context, could also be fulfilled in *retrieval.

[3]'Serotonergic' is a receptor for the neurotransmitter serotonin, and 'peptidergic' is a receptor for peptides that function as neurotransmitters, neuromodulators and hormones.

Recognition

1. **The judgement of previous occurrence.**

2. **The brain process(es) by which this is achieved.**

3. *Recognition test:* **A test situation in which the *subject judges the familiarity or recency of a *stimulus.**

Similarly to *recall, recognition (*re-cognoscĕre*, Latin for to get to know again) refers to a type of memory (definition 1, Mandler 1980), a brain process (definition 2), and a memory test (definition 3). To judge that something has occurred previously may mean different things, ranging from the detection of familiarity or recency to the identification of the specific attributes of the target in its proper *context. Imagine entering a classroom and detecting a new student in the front row. Her face looks familiar, but you have no idea who she is. In this case recognition means detection of familiarity only. But now suppose you enter the classroom and realize that the person in the front row is Ann, whom you first met last month at the Faculty club. This is also recognition, but this time, it involves much more knowledge. Many recognition tests in the laboratory

measure only familiarity, or recency among equally familiar targets.

The aforementioned types of knowledge are reflected in an influential *model of recognition, called the *dual-process* model (Juola et al. 1971; Mandler 1980; Jacoby 1991; Yonelinas 1999). As the name implies, this model depicts recognition as being subserved by two qualitatively different processes. One process is the judgement of *familiarity*; it is generally considered to be automatic and fast.[1] The other process is termed *recollection*, or search, or retrieval.[2] It is considered to be intentional and slower, and refers to the retrieval of information about the target and its context. This complements the familiarity decision, and identifies specific attributes of the target and the context. The familiarity process is also labelled K (for '*know*') and the recollection process R (for '*remember*'). The terms 'recollection', 'remember', and 'know' connote *conscious awareness, and indeed, the use of these terms in the context of recognition stems from human memory research, where remembering and knowing is *declarative (e.g. Tulving 1985b). One can, however, adapt the dual process model to animal studies where conscious awareness is not assumed. An interesting spin-off of the dual-process model is the blurring of distinction between recall and recognition. Prominent models of recall propose two stages, the second of which is recognition (see there). A combination of the two-stage model of recall and the dual-process model of recognition, depicts recall as involving a search phase in which the target is generated, followed by familiarity judgement and recollection. But recollection itself could involve activation or reconstruction of *internal representations in the absence of the target, which is *bona fide* recall. This situation reinforces the notion that both recall and recognition are processes along the continuum of *retrieval (Tulving 1983). These situations differ in the information sought in each case (about the context in recognition, about the target in recall; Hollingworth 1913), and in the retrieval cues (provided by the experimenter or the environment in recognition, self-generated in recall). The clearest distinction between recognition and recall is therefore in the test situation, not necessarily in the type of processes employed by the subject to perform the task.[3]

Whereas whether animals are capable of genuine recall is open to debate, ample evidence proves that they can surely recognize (e.g. *classical conditioning, *instrumental conditioning, *delay task). Two points are noteworthy. First, is the recognition of only detection of familiarity, or also identification of the specific attributes and context of the target, as we humans recognize? The answer is likely to depend on the species and the task, but in any case requires the proper attention in construing the data. Second, in those tests in which recognition is judged by a decreased response to a familiar stimulus, the possibility that the *performance represents *habituation should not be ignored.[4] These caveats notwithstanding, there are clearly tasks in which animals can recognize better than humans, due to superior sensory sensitivity, discriminability, and possibly categorization in the domain of the relevant sensory modality. A beautiful *classic example is provided by Argos, Odyssey's dog: the old dog is the first to recognize Odyssey upon his much belated return to Ithaca, probably by his scent, whereas the nurse Eurykleia needs much more time and the scar on her master's leg as a retrieval cue (Homer, *Odyssey*, *Books XVII, XIX*). There are, of course, tasks in which the recognition capacity of the human brain is impressive (Dudai 1997*a*). For example, in one study subjects learned to recognize no less than 10 000 pictures and the author concluded that even a million are possible (Standing 1973).

What are the brain substrates of recognition? This question can be broken into the following subquestions: (a) What is the flowchart diagram of the circuits that subserve recognition? (b) What is the role of each of the stations in theses circuits in the different postulated subprocesses of recognition? and (c) What are the cellular and molecular mechanisms that subserve these roles in each of the stations? The experimental *systems used in this type of research range from recognition tasks, mostly visual, in humans and in the *monkey, to recognition tasks involving the chemical and other senses in rodents (e.g. Mishkin and Murray 1994; Nakamura and Kubota 1996; Schacter *et al.* 1996c; Reed and Squire 1997; Tanaka 1997; Tulving and Markowitsch 1997; Aguirre and Farah 1998; Berman *et al.* 1998, 2000; Brown and Xiang 1998; Murray and Mishkin 1998; Parker and Gaffan 1998; Steckler *et al.* 1998*a,b*; Suzuki and Eichenbaum 2000; von Zerssen *et al.* 2001). The *methods involved are selective lesions in experimental animals and analysis of brain damage in *amnesics, cellular physiology and molecular biology in laboratory animals, and in recent years, *functional neuroimaging of human subjects. To this one should add psychophysics and modelling, that contribute to the understanding of the *algorithms involved (e.g. Wallis and Bulthoff 1999). But before saying a few words on some general conclusions of this research, it helps to ask what is it that we expect the system to contain. Well, it must contain, as any other memory system, circuits that store the information and are able to retrieve it. But there is an additional component that is a must for recognition: a comparator, that matches the target with stored internal

representation, and detects familiarity/novelty. A brainstem–thalamocortical loop was suggested to subserve this function in taste recognition (Berman *et al.* 2000); other circuits, including corticocortical ones, could fit as well in other systems.

The storage and retrieval circuits that subserve recognition are in general similar to those that subserve recall (Haist *et al.* 1992; Zola-Morgan and Squire 1993), and include the *limbic archicortex, paleocortex, neocortex, and neuromodulatory systems that regulate *acquisition, *consolidation, and retrieval, including monitoring (*cerebral cortex, *hippocampus, *metamemory, *retrieval). The identity of the areas and their subdivisions and their relative contribution depend on the task type and particulars, e.g. sensory modality involved, or whether the task is spatial or not. Within these systems, there are species-adapted specializations that allow recognition of specific features in the world, such as letters and digits in humans (Polk and Farah 1998), faces in mammals (Gross *et al.* 1972; Kendrick and Baldwin 1987; Desimone 1991; Golby *et al.* 2001), or species-specific melodies in birds (*birdsong). Furthermore, different components have been proposed to subserve differentially the two postulated subprocesses of recognition. Hence it was proposed that a neuronal system centred on the perirhinal cortex contributes preferentially to the familiarity judgement, whereas the system centred on the hippocampal formation contributes preferentially to recollection (Brown and Xiang 1998; see also Eldridge *et al.* 2000). Similarly, there is evidence that in word recognition, the left prefrontal, left parietal, and posterior cingulate regions contribute to recollection more than to familiarity judgement (Henson *et al.* 1999). Within cortical circuits that subserve recognition, discrete types of cellular responses are discerned, including a characteristic suppression of the neuronal response to a stimulus once it becomes familiar (Desimone 1996; Brown and Xiang 1998; *priming[5]). Recognition learning may also take advantage of the presence in the cortex of specific molecular 'novelty switches', which are activated only by unfamiliar but not by familiar stimuli, and whose activation triggers *intracellular signal transduction cascades, culminating in use-dependent long-term *plastic changes in the circuit that ultimately encodes the familiarity (Berman *et al.* 1998, 2000).

Selected associations: Delay task, Habituation, Imprinting, Recall, Surprise

---

[1]The detection of familiarity could be examined in the context of system detection theory (e.g. Yonelinas 1999). This theory (Wickens 1984) is applicable to situations in which there are two or more states

of the world that cannot be easily discriminated, and whose discrimination involves two response categories, yes or no, e.g. familiar or unfamiliar. This discrimination is not absolute, but rather based on a number of factors, including the discriminability of input signals and the *criteria used by the *system, themselves shaped by the price paid for false decisions. These factors depend on experience and *context. The signal detection theory was originally developed to deal with the detection of sonar and radar signals in the Second World War. It is a prominent example of the application of engineering and information processing theories to human psychology; a related example is the application of such theories to *attention.

[2]It is important to note that the use of the term retrieval in the dual-process theory of recognition refers to a limited aspect of retrieval (see also *recall). Retrieval in general is a universal *phase of memory, without which no stored information can be actualized. Detection of familiarity, by definition, involves retrieval as well, in this case of the old *internal representations that are compared with the new ones. It is, however, the convention in the discussion of the dual-process models of recognition to use the term 'retrieval' (or 'recollection', or 'search') to refer specifically to the retrieval of information about the identity of the recognized item.

[3]Again, the distinction between recognition and recall becomes even fuzzier when recognition pertains to the judgement of previous occurrence of mental images, propositions, and concepts in the train of thought, rather than of sensory *stimuli only. Hence when one recognizes a thought as contemplated previously, it involves recall and recognition intimately combined.

[4]The relationship of habituation to recognition is not trivial. A *reductionist view considers habituation as rudimentary recognition, because the nervous system functions differently if the stimulus has occurred previously. However, the simplest reflex habituation does not involve matching of stored representations with the percept of the on-line stimulus (e.g. *Aplysia). Complex habituation, such as that of the mammalian orienting reflex (*sensitization), may already involve such matching to detect novelty (Sokolov 1963b).

[5]Although in the cortex cellular response in recognition may resemble that seen in repetition *priming, priming is not the source of familiarity in recognition (Stark and Squire 2000).

Red herring

Something that diverts attention from the real issue or purpose.

A bundle of smelly smoked (red) herrings drawn across a fox's trail confuses the hounds (Cowie et al. 1985). Discovering that a *metaphorical red herring had been hiding in one's path is a scientist's nightmare, although not discovering it if it is there is even worse. It possibly tends to materialize more frequently on the fringe of hectic, fast-advancing disciplines that attract risk-takers

(*scoopophobia). The diversionary data or concepts could pose a real treat to academic careers. Indeed one may toy with the arithmetic of the red herring phenomenon: the magnitude of damage is likely to be proportional to the significance of the research topic, the time elapsed since the diversion, the ego-driven stubbornness of the investigator, and the number of scientists that managed to become enticed by the misleading clue.

Red herrings come in multiple sizes. Tiny herrings are daily encounters in research laboratories, and are frequently identified rapidly as *artefacts and 'disturbances' (e.g. Lynch 1985). They are disguised as imaginary bands on electrophoretic gels, speckles on blots, blips on oscilloscopes, distortions in histological preparations, or erratic software. Experienced investigators are quick to sort out the herrings from the real big fish, and alert the scientific community to the potential problem (e.g. Moser et al. 1994). Furthermore, talented scientists somehow find their way between the exceptional and the expected; in encountering surprising findings, such individuals may insist that what others see as a red herring, is actually not, and ultimately they win.

Medium-size herrings are those that affect a person's career over extended periods but do not necessarily divert the activities of the research community at large. This may happen, for example, in eccentric projects, which are not quick to attract many followers. Imagine a hypothetical scientist sitting in a hypothetical laboratory, aiming to elucidate the function of a hypothetical metabolic pathway. That person erroneously becomes convinced (because of a sampling error, dim light, or too much beer) that a hypothetical rare fly carries a new variant of an enzyme that catalyses a redundant metabolic pathway, and for which 72 variants had already been discovered in other species. As after, that same person devotes a frustrated career to the search for the nonexistent isozyme. Sad, indeed, but the impact on the scientific community is bound to be small, if at all.

Some research programmes that now look rather eccentric were not regarded as such at their time; see, for example, the case of *Clever Hans. In some respects, the horse Hans was a red herring on the path of experimental psychology. In that specific case, the exposure of the interpretational and conceptual mistake had a beneficial effect on subsequent research (Sebeok and Rosenthal 1981), because it led to the identification of sources of errors, for example, of the demand characteristics type (Orne 1962, *bias). Giant herrings, of the order of magnitude of the Clever Hans phenomenon, may stir stormy waves in the scientific community. A more recent example is that of memory transfer. In the early sixties, several laboratories devoted substantial resources in an attempt to replicate the results of the so-called memory transfer experiments. The original reports have claimed that specific memories can be transferred from one individual to another, either via cannibalism (in the flatworm *Planaria*) or in brain extracts (in rats). For a while the possibility existed that many research groups, excited by the striking breakthrough, would embark upon a lengthy journey into a blind ally. As the idea of specific memory transfer is so catchy, the methods and data were soon scrutinized and ultimately the approach was abandoned (Hartry *et al.* 1964; Byrne *et al.* 1966).

The 64 000 herrings question is whether right now we coexist with hidden fat red herrings, that lure scores of labs off-track. One can never be sure. Is there a red herring element in the link of massive modulation of neuronal *protein synthesis and gene expression with memory? (*consolidation, *immediate early genes, *late response genes.) And is *long-term potentiation, a fascinating cellular phenomenon *per se*, actually diverting us away from the ultimate goal of memory research, namely the mechanisms of experience-dependent alterations in *internal representation? Thus are heretic notions, no doubt, but orthodox believers may not be especially good in detecting conceptual mines. We should accept that red herrings are cohabitants of the scientific *culture, and that the success in detecting them is based on a the combination of luck, open-mindedness, intuition, humbleness, and most of all, experience. At least the latter competence can be acquired. A good lab should therefore alert its graduates to the smell of red herrings. Familiarity with the history of the discipline, and with the failures as well as the success stories, is useful in achieving that goal.

Selected associations: Clever Hans, Culture, Phrenology

Reduction

1. **The description or explanation of higher-*level phenomena in terms of lower-level phenomena.**
2. **The formulation of a theory in terms of a more inclusive or basic theory.**

'Reductionism' is a tenet of modern neuroscience. Only its version and explicitness vary among subdisciplines and their practitioners. Neuroscientists attempt to explain mental faculties by brain faculties, hence mental phenomena by biology. In that they are different, for example, from orthodox *behaviourists. Clearly, biology at large has accomplished some of its most impressive triumphs so far by adhering to the radical reductionist approach, epitomized in state-of-the-art molecular and cellular biology, genetic engineering (*neurogenetics), and the Genome project. Whether ardent reductionism also fits all the needs of memory research is, however, still a debatable question.

In science and the philosophy of science, 'reduction' (*reducere*, Latin for 'to bring back') is employed in different connotations (Nagel 1979; Mayr 1982; Dudai 1989). In its most common use, it refers to the mere process of analysing a complex phenomenon by dissecting it into elementary components. This is '*constitutive reductionism*' (definition 1, 'description'). In the context of our discussion, it means that one attempts to identify brain, neuronal, or molecular correlates (*criterion) of learning and memory. This type of reductionist approach is accepted by all neurobiologists and practised by the majority of them; ethologists and behavioural psychologists can still excuse themselves from preaching the reductionistic *zeitgeist. In the course of practising constitutive reductionism, neurobiologists take 'reductive steps'. These are shifts in the level of analysis from the level of a *system as a whole to the level of its components. For example, a shift in the analysis from that of molar electrical activity in *cortex to that of individual cortical neurons, or from single neurons to individual molecules in the *synaptic membrane, is a reductive step. In addition, constitutive reductionism almost always involves 'simplifying steps'. These are procedures taken to facilitate experimental analysis, without altering intentionally the level of analysis. For example, proceeding in the analysis of single neuron activity from *in situ* to a brain slice (e.g. *hippocampus), or removing part of the tissue and hence decreasing the number of cells in a ganglion (e.g. *Aplysia*), while still maintaining the cellular level of analysis, is a 'simplifying step'. This *methodology is best epitomized by Johnson (1751), who noticed that 'Divide and conquer is a principle equally just in science as in policy'. A 'simplifying step' may also mean switching to a simpler organism or circuit that display the phenomenon, process, or mechanism in question (*model, *simple system).

More rigorous than constitutive reductionism is '*explanatory reductionism*' (definition 1, 'explanation'). It assumes that, ultimately, the knowledge of the components will explain properties of the system as a whole. This means, in our case, that having once understood the properties of neurons and molecules, one should be able to show how these properties are necessary and sufficient to explain learning and memory. Most neurobiologists practise constitutive reductionism in the hope of achieving explanatory reductionism. Others doubt whether in the neurosciences, satisfactory explanatory reductionism is always feasible.

Most demanding is '*theory reductionism*', i.e. reducing a theory, including all its concepts and laws, into another, more inclusive or basic theory (definition 2; e.g. Nagel 1979). This would mean that, having a biological theory (such as a future theory of brain function), one would be able to reduce it without residue into a physical theory. Profound doubts are often expressed whether this is appropriate and feasible (for a modern *classic, see Fodor 1974). 'Theory reductionism' requires that 'bridge laws', or 'correspondence rules', be established to enable shifts from the terminology of one theory to the other. A limited concept of 'correspondence rules' is also useful in the less stringent, descriptive, or explanatory reductionist approaches, because it focuses attention on the need to formulate systematic relationships between findings at one level to those at another. For a selection of the literature on explanatory and theory reduction in the neuroscience, see Putnam (1973), Searle (1990), Schaffner (1993), Churchland and Churchland (1998), Crick and Koch (1998), and Fodor (1998). For issues related to other facets of reductionism in biology, which reflect on neurobiology and especially on *development and neurogenetics, see Hull (1981), Sober (1994), and Kirschner et al. (2000). And for a bit more on the philosophy involved, see Brentano (1874) and Kim and Sosa (1999).

Within the context of the present discussion, two issues deserve special attention. The first is what do we expect the relationships to be between properties, processes, and events at a lower level to those at a higher level, and vice versa. It is safe to assume that even conservative psychologists will agree that mental events somehow relate to physical events. But what does the relationship mean? For example, the two may correspond to each other property by property, and ultimately unique mental states would correspond one by one to unique brain states. If this is true, then having identified a certain physicochemical brain state in sufficient detail, we will be in a position to deduce from a set of physiological data what the *subject *recalls. This argument applies to multiple levels of brain function: knowing the molecular details will be expected to tell us precisely what a cell encodes, monitoring the electrical activity of a *cell assembly will be expected to tell us exactly what the assembly represents, etc.[1] An alternative possibility is that a given mental/behavioural state is encoded by different molecular and physiological states. This would mean that indeed, a particular mental/behavioural state corresponds to some physical events in the brain, but the former does not necessarily correspond to a unique configuration of the latter. This view might induce chagrin in many practising neurobiologists who attempt to read into defined codes, representations, and computations. The problem is not merely philosophical. When we devote our career to determining with great pains the activity of *signal-transduction cascades within neurons, or of circuits within brain regions, do we expect to be able, at the end of the day, to conclude from the lower-level data what the overall higher-level meaning is, and at what level of accuracy? Do we have an 'uncertainty principle' operating at the level of neuronal representations? Also, is knowing more lower-level details always means knowing more about the higher-level functional state of the system (Alberts and Miake-Lye 1992; Barkai and Leibler 1997; Sanes and Lichtman 1999; Kirschner et al. 2000)?

The second issue, related to the first one, is how far should one attempt to reduce a system without losing the characteristic properties that had provided the incentive for the research programme in the first place. In other words, how much of the system properties are 'emergent', i.e. appear only at a higher level of organization or function, because of some interactive or integrative properties (Pepper 1926; Meehl and Sellars 1956)? Why not aim at reducing the description of brains to the language of the elementary particles of matter? Most reasonable people will ridicule such a proposal, yet there is nothing in it that contradicts ardent reductionism. If not elementary particles, why not atoms? Or molecular motifs? When do reductionistic aspirations cease to amuse and become a serious scientific goal?[2] It seems that in the case of memory research, the clue lies in the definition of *memory. Once we agree that memory is retention over time of *internal representations, we should look for the level at which behaviourally meaningful representations are encoded. Lower levels (lower than cellular) will provide us with valuable information on mechanisms that subserve memory, but are unlikely *per se* to identify what a specific memory is. Memory research, as in any other branch of biological research, thus requires pragmatic, 'focused reductionism' (Dudai 1992). Otherwise, we may find ourselves in a situation so enchantingly illustrated by Geertz (1983): "There is an Indian story … about an Englishman who, having been told that the world rested on a platform which rested on the back of an elephant which rested in turn on the back of a turtle, asked… what did the turtle rest on? 'Another turtle'. And that turtle? 'Ah, Sahib, after that it's turtles all the way down.'

Selected associations: Criterion, Level, Method, Paradigm, Zeitgeist

---

[1]This argumentation is intentionally restricted to the pragmatic point of view of the experimenter. What is argued here is only whether there is one-to-one, or one-to-many, or many-to-many correspondence between the particular neuronal state and the particular behavioural or mental state. Nothing is claimed about the quality or type identity of the corresponding states, e.g. whether some events are of a 'physical type' and others of a different, 'mental type' (e.g. Block and Fodor 1972). Further, the correspondence may reflect correlation, supervenience, or causality (*criterion).

[2]This is actually still another manifestation of the classic 'Sorites paradox', which is presented in *insight.

Reinforcer

A *stimulus that alters the probability or intensity of response.

'Reinforcer' (*fortis*, 'strong' in Latin), which is an *agent* or *event*, and 'reinforcement', which is the *process* that this agent is assumed to trigger and sustain, are among the most loaded terms in the behavioural literature. This is not because the concepts involved are necessarily more complex than certain other behavioural concepts, but because frequently their discussion connotes particular theoretical constructs, some of which have gravitated toward the status of a religious sect with all the convictions and emotions involved (*paradigm, *zeitgeist). The reinforcer, via the postulated reinforcement, can *shape* behaviour, and also *maintain* the response level once achieved; if the reinforcer is removed, the behaviour risks *extinction. The reinforcer itself is traditionally not considered to *produce* learning, only to augment response, which promotes *associations. Examples for reinforced learning are provided in many contexts in this book (e.g. Figures pp. 70, 76, 129, 131; *instrumental conditioning). Whether this dissociation between the reinforcing and 'teaching' actions of stimuli, respectively, holds water at *reduced *levels of description, is debatable (e.g. Shimizu *et al.* 2000; Berman and Dudai 2001).[1] 'Stimulus' in the above definition refers to stimuli presented intentionally to the *subject, or to incidental stimuli, or to stimuli that result from the exogenous and endogenous effects of the *subject's action; in the nervous system all events, including actions, translate into stimuli. Hence stimuli in general could have both eliciting and reinforcing functions, and the experienced experimenter makes good use of both.

On the history of the concept: two main approaches are distinguished in the *pre-scientific* thinking. One is the totalitarian, 'exogenous' approach, characteristic of certain religions and regimes. It states that conforming to the rules is bound to bring reward by deity or king, whereas opposing the rules will result in inevitable punishment. The other, 'endogenous' attitude attempts to identify drives that shape human behaviour independently of external authority. The most popular example is 'hedonism', the philosophical doctrine holding that only what is pleasant is intrinsically good; it is epitomized in the words of Diogenes Laertius (3C AD): 'All living creatures from the moment of birth take delight in pleasure and resist pain from natural causes independent of reason' (Long 1986).

The *scientific* treatment of reinforcers and reinforcements drew in its early days from two conceptual sources. One, philosophical contemplation of the attributes that foster the association of mental events, such as similarity, contrast, and contiguity. This philosophy can be traced back to Aristotle, but the main influence in the early days of experimental psychology was that of British Associationism (*associative learning). The other influential conceptual source was Darwinian evolutionism (Wilcoxon 1969; Boakes 1984). Evolution, so goes the Darwinian view, is moulded by natural selection of adaptive traits among the pool of genetically generated variations. Spencer, Bain, and Baldwin were the first to adapt this selectionist view to the theory of learning (*ibid.*; Cason 1932).[2] In a nutshell, the idea was that the adaptive processes of the ontogenesis of the individual's behaviour parallel the processes of phylogenesis, in that pleasurable states are selected among other states of the organism, whereas noxious states are selected against. This view has culminated in Thorndike's 'law of effect', a *generalization concerning causality and feedback, which posits that behavioural responses that lead to gratification are reinforced by their effect and repeated whereas those that result in discomfort recur less and less (Thorndike 1911; *instrumental conditioning).

The law of effect was remarkably influential in the theory of reinforcement, although within different conceptual frameworks. A prominent development was the consideration of reinforcement in stimulus terms in the elaborate Skinnerian system of operant conditioning (Skinner 1938; Ferster and Skinner 1957).

Skinner's approach supported the 'empirical law of effect', which is similar to the original law but devoid of the theoretical assumptions about internal states, which orthodox *behaviourists shy away from. Another influential theory considered reinforcement in terms of drive reduction. Drives are hypothetical endogenous processes that impel an individual to act on the world or react to it. The drive reductionists proposed that reinforcements satisfy because they reduce drives. In other words, reinforcers promote *homeostasis. The 'law of primary reinforcement', coined by Hull (1943), epitomizes the idea: 'Whenever a reaction takes place in temporal contiguity with an afferent receptor impulse resulting from the impact upon a receptor of a stimulus energy, and this conjunction is followed closely by the diminution in a need (and the associated diminution in the drive and in the drive receptor discharge), there will result an increment in the tendency for that stimulus on subsequent occasions to evoke that reaction' (*ibid.*; Hull's symbolic notations were omitted from the quote for simplicity) (see also: Miller and Dollard 1941; Birney and Teevan 1961; Wilcoxon 1969).

The reader should not be mislead, however, to think that all the theories of reinforcement were related to the concept of effect. Many prominent thinkers considered the strengthening of response in the absence of the action–effect assumptions. The best example is Pavlov (1927). He used 'reinforcement' to account for the action of the unconditioned stimulus in *classical conditioning, which has nothing to do with the idea of action–effect.[3]

Over the years, additional theoretical approaches to the problem of reinforcement have emerged. A notable example is the proposal that reinforcement is primarily a function of the value of the response, not of the stimulus, and this response value is greater if the opportunity to perform the behaviour is smaller (Premack 1965). For example, water is an effective reinforcer for a thirsty rat because it reinforces a highly valued behaviour, drinking. Responses more valued by the organism reinforce those that are less valued. This also implies that the reinforcement value is relative. The thirsty rat will increase activity in a running wheel if this is followed by delivery of water; but a water-satiated, running-deprived rat will increase its drinking if this gets it access to running (Premack 1962). Some modern approaches to reinforcement abandon the simple cause-and-effect feedback loop of the effect theories, and take into account complex system properties of brains and organisms, drawing from system theory, cognition, and ecology (Timberlake 1993).

A major chapter in the analysis of reinforcers and reinforcement began with the first systematic attempt to identify brain circuits of reward and punishment. In a *classic series of experiments it was shown that rats could become engaged in intensive self-stimulation via chronically implanted brain electrodes, provided these electrodes are inserted into specific sites in the brain, such as the septal area and the medial forebrain bundle (Olds and Milner 1954; Olds 1969; *dopamine).[4] This gave a boost not only to science fiction, but also to the cartography of the brain in terms of circuits that encode the *internal representation of reinforcers and compute reinforcements (Livingston 1967; Robbins and Everitt 1996; *limbic system).

Applied reinforcers and postulated reinforcements vary greatly by the type of experimental *system, *assay and protocol. It is, however, methodologically useful to consider some *generalizations. The *dimensions listed below refer to selected attributes of the reinforcing event, or of inferred reinforcement processes, or of experimental manipulations used to apply the reinforcer in order to exercise the reinforcement. All these factors are often mixed practically in the design and execution of the experiment.

1. *Valence.* A reinforcer, the addition of which strengthens the response, is termed a 'positive reinforcer'. A reinforcer, the removal of which strengthens the response, is termed a 'negative reinforcer'. A candidate reinforcer that leaves the response unaltered is a 'neutral reinforcer'. Many authors use the term positive reinforcer synonymously with 'reward'. This is basically OK, although reward may be delivered without affecting behaviour, as any parent knows, whereas a positive reinforcer by definition affects behaviour. It is not OK, however, to exchange negative reinforcer with 'punishment'. Indeed, both refer to aversive stimuli. But whether an aversive stimulus is a negative reinforcer or punishment depends on the stimulus–response contingencies. Hence an electric shock is a negative reinforcer if its removal is contingent on the response, a removal that is certainly not punishment, but is a punishment if its application is contingent on the response. This is the appropriate point to add that the valence of reinforcers is not always apparent at the time of the experiment. There are situations in which the subject appears to be reinforced in spite of the absence of an apparent reinforcer (e.g. latent *learning, *observational learning). In these cases it makes sense to talk about a 'latent reinforcer'. In the theory of learning there are views that learning is impossible if there is no reinforcer whatsoever; therefore, if there is no apparent reinforcer, there must be a latent one.

2. *Magnitude.* This refers to quality, or quantity, or both. Reinforcers differ in their quality; some types of stimuli are more effective in a given situation than others, e.g. food vs. toys to a hungry subject (Jarvik 1953; Garcia *et al.* 1968). Reinforcers could also differ in quantity, in terms of intensity or schedule of delivery.

3. *Hierarchy.* A reinforcer that has *a priori reinforcing properties to an individual of the species, is a 'primary reinforcer'. A reinforcer whose reinforcing properties are due to association with a primary reinforcer is a 'secondary reinforcer', or, depending on the order of association, 'higher-order reinforcer' (compare with higher-order conditioning in *classical conditioning).

4. *Schedule.* The schedule in which reinforcer/reinforcement is delivered is crucial to the behavioural outcome. Generally speaking, reinforcement could be delivered continuously, so that every response is reinforced, or intermittently, so that some responses are reinforced and some are not. Contrary to the intuition of newcomers to the discipline, intermittent reinforcement is often more effective than continuous reinforcement; we have already encountered this in *experimental extinction (the so-called 'PREE effect', see there). Four main types of schedules are common in intermittent reinforcement: (a) *fixed ratio*, in which a response is reinforced upon completion of a fixed number of responses; (b) *variable ratio*, in which the reinforcement is scheduled according to a random series of response/reinforcement ratios; (c) *fixed interval*, in which the first response occurring after a given interval of time measured from the preceding reinforcement is reinforced; and (d) *variable interval*, in which reinforcements are scheduled according to a random series of intervals (Ferster and Skinner 1957; on the special case of delayed reinforcement and its behavioural consequences, see also Renner 1964).

5. *Level.* At the behavioural level, reinforcers are sensory input. At the circuit level, they are input from other circuits in the brain, or chemical messages such as hormones from other parts of the body. At the cellular and *synaptic level, reinforcers are encoded in *neurotransmitters, neuromodulators, ion currents, and other chemical or electrical messages.

It is currently possible to consider the neural encoding of reinforcers, and the computation of reinforcement, in terms of identified circuits, synapses, and molecules (e.g. Robbins and Everitt 1996; Schultz *et al.* 1997; Picciotto *et al.* 1998; Menzel *et al.* 1999; Corbit and Balleine 2000; Shimizu *et al.* 2000). Key brain structures involve *limbic–corticostriatal–pallidal circuitry (Robbins and Everitt 1996) and diffused neuromodulatory systems (Schultz *et al.* 1997). This accumulated knowledge

contributes to the theory of brain and behaviour, and to the understanding and treatment of pathological conditions in which abused reinforcements result in bad *habits (Picciotto *et al.* 1998; Robbins and Everitt 1999). We should also become tuned to the possibility that soon there will be a need to apply this knowledge to the effective and safe training of smart robots (Saksida *et al.* 1997).

Selected associations: Algorithm, Instrumental conditioning, Model, Neurotransmitter, Stimulus

---

[1] 'Teaching' as used here can refer to instructive, adjustive, or selective actions, as explained under *stimulus.

[2] As in other entries in this book, unless otherwise indicated, theory does not mean a formal physical theory, but rather a conceptual framework for further hypotheses and experiments (see in *algorithm).

[3] Note that in this case the reinforcer does enter into the association. The use of the reinforcer/reinforcement terminology in the context of classical conditioning is considered by some authorities as obsolete.

[4] The original observation was fortuitous: James Olds noted that a rat keeps returning to the place on the table top where it had been when an electrical stimulus was applied to its brain via a chronically implanted electrode. This has led to experiments in which rats were trained to press a lever to self-deliver the stimulus. For more on the history of this important chapter in the neurobiology of reinforcement, drive, motivation, and learning, as well as on the *real-life events beyond the *culture of science, see Milner (1989).

Retrieval

1. **The actualization of learned information.**

2. **The access, selection, reactivation, or reconstruction of stored *internal representations.**

3. **The brain state required to attempt or attain 1 and 2 above.**

Until fairly recently, retrieval was an uncharted terrain in the neurobiology of memory. This was particularly striking when compared with the rich contribution of experimental psychology and modelling to the phenomenology and theory of retrieval (Semon 1904; Shiffrin and Artkinson 1969; Anderson 1983; Tulving 1983). This situation was also in sharp contrast to the signal role of retrieval in behavioural *assays of memory, for, at the end of the test, even if the intention is to study *acquisition, *consolidation, or retention of memory, it is retrieval that is tested. Hence many brain scientists study retrieval without even being aware of it. In a way, they are in the same position as Mr Jourdain, Moliere's bourgeois gentleman (Molière 1670), who suddenly realized (*insight) that he was speaking prose for 40 years without ever knowing it.

Definition 1 is molar, and pertains to both the phenomenon and the process of retrieval. Definitions 2 and 3 refer to the subprocesses and the brain state, respectively, that underlie 'retrieval' as defined in 1. Definition 3 includes also those situations in which the attempt to retrieve a particular item fails, or is only partially successful (e.g. Hart 1965; Brown and McNeill 1966).

The following points highlight selected attributes of retrieval:

1. At the behavioural *level, *a memory unretrieved is undetected.*[1] It is actually possible to go a step further and claim that there is no such thing as a behaviourally-meaningful *engram in a nonre-trieved state (Tulving 1991; *persistence).[2]

2. Similarly to other memory *phases, retrieval refers to *a heterogeneous group of processes* that share a function. The computational theories, *algorithms and circuits that subserve retrieval of simple *reflex-ive memories are clearly different from those that subserve the actualization of abstract thoughts. Some operational principles and elementary build-ing blocks of the molecular and cellular hardware may, however, be universal.

3. Success in retrieval depends on the *availability of appropriate *cues.* These cues are either external or self-generated. Cues are instrumental in retrieval even if unidentified by the *subject or the experi-menter. Cues that are part of the response (e.g. a digit in a multidigit number) prompt gradual reconstruction of the memory; the product is termed 'redintegrative memory' (from 'reintegra-tive'; Horowitz and Prysulak 1969).

4. Retrieval is more effective when attempted in the presence of cues that were present in acquisition (*context, *state-dependent memory). This idea is reflected in the 'encoding specificity principle', which refers to the overall *relations between acquisi-tion and retrieval*: retrieval occurs if and only if properties of the trace are sufficiently similar to the properties of the information available in retrieval (Tulving 1983). In other words, for the *system to retrieve, it must resonate with the input. A related idea is that retrieval is more effective when the subject processes the information in retrieval in the same way that it was processed in acquisition; this is termed 'transfer appropriate processing' (Morris *et al.* 1977). For example, in verbal tests,

semantic processing of verbal material in learn-ing favours success in retrieval using semantic but not phonological processing, and vice versa. Whereas 'encoding specificity' emphasizes the information encoded, 'transfer appropriate process-ing' emphasizes the processing of that information by the subject.

5. Retrieval is not merely a passive readout of infor-mation, it is also an experience; therefore, once retrieved, *the engram is unlikely to remain exactly the same.* This is evident from studies at the behavioural, brain system, cellular, and molecular levels (Bartlett 1932; Schacter *et al.* 1998; Sara 2000; *false memory; see also below).

How does retrieval work in the nervous system? A sim-ple case is illustrated by *classical conditioning of the withdrawal reflex in *Aplysia*. A simplified *model of learning in this system involves use-dependent facilita-tion of sensory-to-motor *synapses. This is expressed as the enhanced release of *neurotransmitter in response to the sensory stimulus. The facilitation is embodied in chemical changes in the presynaptic terminal. Retrieval is the readout of the new state of the synapse by the action potentials that encode the conditioned stimulus (CS) in the sensory neurons. The cue for retrieval is the CS. The neurons that retrieve are those that learn and retain at least part of the trace.[3] The conditions at acquisition influence retrieval, because whether the animal was already *habituated or naive determines the nature and extent of the subsequent cellular modifica-tions in the sensory synapse, hence the synaptic state encountered by the action potentials that encode the CS in retrieval (Byrne and Kandel 1996). And, finally, retrieval, being an experience in the same neuron that retains the memory, might disrupt *homeostasis and induce new *plastic changes.

Most of what we now know about neuronal mecha-nisms of retrieval, however, owes to systems that are far more complex than *Aplysia*. *Functional neuroimag-ing, combined with smart design of behavioural tests, has made it possible to identify neuronal players in the retrieval of explicit (*declarative) memory in humans. Before the introduction of functional neuro-imaging, data on the involvement of specific brain structures in retrieval in humans were based predominantly on clini-cal cases (Shallice 1988; Schacter *et al.* 1996*b*). As brain lesions, once formed, are permanent, and could affect the formation or 'storage' of the memory trace, whereas retrieval is restricted to a brief time window of memory expression, conclusions about retrieval that are based solely on the effect of static pathology are problematic to start with. In contrast, functional neuroimaging could dissociate the neuronal events of retrieval from those of earlier memory phases (e.g. Buckner *et al.* 1995; Nyberg *et al.* 1996; Buckner and Koustaal 1998; Fletcher *et al.* 1998; Wagner *et al.* 1998*a,b*; Schacter and Wagner 1999; Lepage *et al.* 2000; Rugg and Wilding 2000). This is currently one of the most dynamic fields in memory research, and the picture keeps changing. A tentative model of explicit retrieval in the mammalian brain can nevertheless be portrayed.

It is methodologically convenient, and probably correct, to describe the brain system that subserves retrieval as composed of two main types of components: item-specific and item-invariant. The item-specific component subserves the actual recovery of the particular memory item. This process is referred to as 'ecphory' (Greek for 'to be made known'). The term was coined by Semon (1904), the same person who brought us 'engram', and later retrieved by Tulving (1983). Ecphory involves circuits that 'store' (*metaphor) memories (Markowitsch 1995, Schacter *et al.* 1996*a*; Schacter and Wagner 1999; Eldridge *et al.* 2000; Nyberg *et al.* 2000; Wheeler *et al.* 2000). In the case of declarative memory, these circuits are distributed over areas in the *cerebral neocortex, and connect with paleocortical and subcortical structures (*amnesia, *hippocampus, *limbic system).[4] In addition, there is an item-invariant system, which searches for items in memory, allocates the mental resources, controls the process, and verifies the outcome. This system is said to put the brain into a retrieval 'state', 'mode', or 'set'.[5]

Where is this retrieval-mode system located? It has been demonstrated by a number of groups that prefrontal cortex is differentially activated in retrieval (Buckner *et al.* 1995; Schacter *et al,* 1996*a*; Rugg *et al.* 1996; Buckner and Koustaal 1998; Fletcher *et al.* 1998; Wagner *et al.* 1998; Lepage *et al.* 2000). The prefrontal cortex subserves multiple executive functions in the brain (*planning, *working memory), and is therefore a likely candidate for setting the stage for ecphory. There is hemispheric asymmetry in the retrieval-related activity of prefrontal cortex. This finding has led to a model, the hemispheric encoding/retrieval asymmetry (HERA), which proposes that the left prefrontal cortex is differentially involved in retrieval of semantic information and in encoding novel aspects of the retrieved information into *episodic memory, whereas the right prefrontal cortex is involved in retrieval of episodic memory (Nyberg *et al.* 1996). The possibility was further raised that the hemispheric asymmetry observed in retrieval in the prefrontal cortex is contributed by the memory retrieval mode, but not by the ecphory (Lepage *et al.* 2000). Prefrontal areas probably contribute differentially to retrieval mode functions, as well as to the *metamemory processes that monitor and verify retrieval; but again, the picture is incomplete (Schacter and Wagner 1999; Rugg and Wilding 2000).

The main picture of the layout and function of retrieval system(s) in the human brain, including the executive role played by the prefrontal cortex, are supported by lesion studies and cellular physiology in the *monkey (Hasegawa *et al.* 1998; Tomita *et al.* 1999). The investigation of the mechanisms of retrieval at more reduced levels of analysis depends much on the use of additional species. These include rodents (Moser and Moser 1998a; Riedel *et al.* 1999; Maren and Holt 2000; Nader *et al.* 2000; Sara 2000; Berman and Dudai 2001), *Drosophila* (Dubnau *et al.* 2001), and *Aplysia* (see above).

An intriguing proposal, hinted already above, is that retrieval, being an experience, is followed by a new *phase of *consolidation (Spear and Mueller 1984; Sara 2000). Even more provocative is the suggestion that in some systems and conditions the original trace, or at least a part of it, could become markedly labile for a while, after its retrieval (Nader *et al.* 2000). The 'reconsolidation' hypothesis, if validated, could guide the development of new drugs and behavioural methods to alter specific items in memory. This might be used to erase unwanted memories (Dudai 2000), or enhance desired ones. Until such treatments are identified, down-to-earth tricks could be tried to improve retrieval. Well, on the one hand, retrieval appears to be enhanced by glucose (Manning *et al.* 1998; *nutrients); on the other, stress and corticosteroids impair retrieval (De Quervain *et al.* 1998; *lotus). A good dessert in relaxed company might hence provide a reasonable alternative to medical intervention.

Selected associations: Performance, Persistence, Phase, Recall, Recognition

---

[1]Lewis (1979) proposed to call unretrieved memories 'inactive', and retrieved as well as short-term memories 'active' (*taxonomy). This terminology, however, did not catch on.

[2]Retrieval is not obligatory evidence for memory at *reduced levels of analysis. Hence one could identify *persistent memory-related *plastic changes at the molecular, cellular, or circuit level in the absence of actualization of the internal representation. Still, for the engram to acquire its representational meaning, it must be retrieved.

[3]It is possible, though, that other parts of the nervous system of *Aplysia*, which are not involved in acquisition or consolidation of the information, evoke or control retrieval.

[4]The role of the hippocampus in retrieval of declarative memories is limited in time (Teng and Squire 1999; Haist *et al.* 2001; *consolidation).

[5]For more on the general notion of 'set', see *learning set.

Scoopophobia

The *fear of being scooped.

Scoopophobia (sometimes manifested as prioritymania) is a common occupational hazard in contemporary science. The term stems from 'scoop', which literally means to gather or collect swiftly, and *metaphorically, to top or outmanoeuvre a competitor in acquiring and publishing an important news story (it all originated in *schope*, Old Dutch for 'bucket'). Scoopophobia is a very focused phobia: the victim does not fear scoops in general, only those of the competitors. The first signs could become apparent already in Graduate School ('early onset'), but more commonly in postdoctoral training or immediately afterwards ('late onset', but not senile). It is a chronic malady, with a pre-tenure acute phase and subsequent recurrent exacerbations, that could linger well into postretirement. Among the presenting symptoms: manic preoccupation with one's own findings, delusions that include an amazing belief that these findings are indeed the most important in the world ever, and frequent, mostly out-of-place statements about having achieved monthly (and in severe cases weekly) outstanding breakthroughs in research. Treatments based on attempts to augment one's modesty almost always fail. The prognosis is gloomy. Unfortunately, truly afflicted individuals (not the hypochondriacs or those who play the scoopophobe to impress their peers) seldom calm down. Even rarer are the cases in which the patient freezes and stops working (bipolar scoopophobia). Most scoopophobics enter intermittent frenetic states, in which they increase their publication output to a level that precludes even them themselves from reading all the papers that they publish. Their main achievement in such states is occasional induction of an attack of scoopophobia in a true or imaginary competitor. The disease is potentially contagious, as some students tend to contract it from their mentors. It may hence become an endemic epidemic.

Serious and distressing as it is (to victims, family, and friends), scoopophobia is actually only a symptom of the mechanisms and pressures of the scientific *culture. The aetiology of the syndrome is composite. A primary precipitating factor is the sheer competitive drive universally favoured by academic promotion committees. But this does not account for the whole story. The explosion of information in modern science can occasionally turn even a calm person into a paranoiac. It sometimes seems as though so many people are hectically plotting to do exactly the same experiment that you yourself are planning to do at this very moment. The kinetics and volume of the scientific literature only augments this perceived threat. A simple number game illustrates the case: a search for the terms 'learning OR memory' in the citation indexes (Web-of-Science[SM] 2000), yields 3172 publications of a total of 847 708 papers for the year 1989, and 17 199 of 1 176 391 papers in 1999. This means 62 papers per week in 1989, 340 per week in 1999, i.e. a more than fivefold increase in the absolute number and an almost fourfold increase in the proportion of total scientific papers within a decade. Indeed, some of these papers could be easily neglected, but others, and in addition some that do not spell out 'learning' or 'memory' in their title, keywords, or abstract, are important. The conclusions: first, it is impossible to keep abreast of *all* the developments in one's discipline; second, the number of research groups that conduct research in learning and memory is amazingly large, and is on the rise.

An issue that comes immediately to mind is redundancy and its role in research. The mere use of the term 'redundancy' does some injustice to the phenomenon in the *context of science. Literally, 'redundancy' means unnecessary repetition. But usually redundancy in research is not genuine superfluity; different scientific programmes may be similar, but are seldom exactly the same in all their details and conclusions. Though for the individual researcher this similarity is sufficient to cause ego damage, for the scientific discipline it is an essential part of the game, because by virtue of the open, distributed nature of the scientific work, concepts, theories, and data are subjected to the scrutiny of repetitions and modifications. They are then either refuted, or corroborated, or modified, or simply neglected, navigating the discipline into new cycles of research (*culture; *paradigm). Hence the rules of the profession require the individual researcher to accept a certain degree of altruism: although not rewarding for the individual, redundancy is critical for the scientific community at large.

Redundancy can be either simultaneous, i.e. two or more groups start to do the same thing independently at the same time, or consequential, i.e. some groups follow the pioneering work of other groups. Most cases are of the second type. There is undoubtedly an intimate interaction between surges in consequential redundancy and the *zeitgeist. Examples in memory research include sudden interest in topics as diverse as the role of protein synthesis in *consolidation, protein phosphorylation (*protein kinase) in *synaptic plasticity, *long-term potentiation, *neurogenetics, the use of the water *maze as a memory *assay, or the search and analysis of *false memory. (Statistics illustrating the kinetics of publication on topics that had became trendy are provided in *long-term potentiation, *zeitgeist.) Not all important experimental systems in memory research had triggered major waves of publications on the same topic by other labs. For example, although the discovery of memory mutants in *Drosophila arose much interest, not many labs followed. Similarly, although *Aplysia has no doubt contributed tremendously to our understanding of the cellular bases of *plasticity, the level of redundancy generated in other labs was relatively modest. Any attempt to analyse the reason for this in terms of scientific *culture, far exceeds the scope of our current discussion. So is also the question what causes some important findings to emerge truly in parallel in independent labs (Ogburn and Thomas 1922; Merton 1961, 1963).

Can one become immune to scoopophobia? An amateurish little survey suggests to me that some of those who have initiated new fields of inquiry in the neurosciences are more resistant to scoopophobia. Hence genuine self-confidence can obviously help, almost by-definition. (For a historical sampler of prioritymania among scientific giants, see Merton 1957.) Disregard for scoopophobia does not ensure that the fearless individual will be well remembered and cited. Actually, E.O. Wilson (cited in Weiner 1999) remarked that 'Progress in a scientific discipline can be measured by how quickly its founders are forgotten'. Another defence mechanism is the ostrich solution, namely, not to read the literature. Some of my best friends follow this practice. It might provide temporary, illusory relief, but also waste time and money and bounce back as a boomerang of unpleasant *surprise. Not reading the literature might have been a privilege of the old days in neuroscience; for example, Loewi (1936), who did the first experiment to prove that the *neurotransmitter *acetylcholine is secreted in vivo, was unaware of the earlier suggestion published by Elliott (1904) that chemicals mediate messages between neurons. Would familiarity with Elliott's paper have altered the course of Loewi's experiments? Was it better for Loewi not to know? It is difficult to see how all this could have happened nowadays, with the publications/meetings/web explosion.

In some cases, unfortunately too few, the identification of simultaneous discoveries culminates in an agreement between the competing laboratories to publish back to back (e.g. Rosenblum et al. 1996; Rostas et al. 1996). In others it results in endless fights on priority. Advice to newcomers to a scientific discipline are rarely effective. But one might at least

try (Cajal 1916; Cornford 1922). A somewhat useful (yet admittedly naïve) way to cope with scoopophobia, live in peace with inevitable competition, appreciate how science advances, and keep a modest level of modesty, is to *recall the saying of the Jewish sage, Rabbi Tarfon: 'Not yours is the work to complete, neither is yours the freedom to idle' (Mishnah, Avot B15). It surely epitomizes the blessed infiniteness of research, on which scoops are only ephemeral minute vibrations.

Selected associations: Culture, Homo sapiens, Paradigm, Surprise

Sensitization

Augmentation of the responsiveness to *stimuli following the presentation of a salient stimulus.

Sensitization is a type of non*associative learning. The sensitizing stimulus is usually strong or noxious. Sensitization contrasts with another type of nonassociative learning, *habituation, in which there is a *generalized diminution of response following the presentation of a weak or monotonous stimulus. If the response is already habituated, the effect of the sensitizing experience is termed 'dishabituation'. Thus, whether the *subject is said to undergo sensitization or dishabituation, depends on what we know about its history.

Sensitization is a lingering manifestation of arousal. Another manifestation of arousal is the 'investigatory' or 'orienting reflex', which is an immediate, complex somatic and sensory response to an unexpected stimulus (Pavlov 1927; Sokolov 1963b; *attention). Sensitization complements the behavioural adaptation to the *surprising situation by transiently decreasing the threshold to further stimuli. The phylogenetic value of sensitization is rather straightforward: 'An earthworm that has just avoided being eaten by a blackbird that has taken a peck at it, is indeed well advised to respond with a considerably lowered threshold to similar stimuli, because it is almost certain that the bird will still be nearby for the next few seconds' (Lorenz 1981).

The ability of a salient stimulus to alter the subsequent response to other stimuli was systematically investigated already by Pavlov. He reported that after *experimental extinction of a *classically conditioned response, a strong or novel stimulus temporarily restored the original response (Pavlov 1927). Later,

Sensitization

Grether (1938) reported that unpaired presentation of unconditioned and conditioned stimuli could result in conditioned response. This was termed 'pseudoconditioning'. Whereas pseudoconditioning can be described as nonassociative classical conditioning, sensitization can be described as nonassociative α conditioning.[1]

The widespread occurrence and the many expressions of sensitization throughout the phylogenetic spectrum makes it unlikely that a single mechanism will explain it all. Indeed, the investigation of a variety of vertebrates and invertebrates preparations unveils diverse circuit and cellular mechanisms (e.g. Egger 1978; Russo and Ison 1979; Davis *et al.* 1982; Hawkins *et al.* 1998). Dishabituation and sensitization, which at a certain stage were suspected to be two manifestations of the same phenomenon, were later found not to be so on the bases of differences in the behavioural parameters, in the *development of the response with age, and in the neuronal mechanisms (Rankin and Carew 1988; Byrne and Kandel 1996; Hawkins *et al.* 1998).

Among the preparations used to study elementary types of sensitization, a prominent place is reserved to a *simple system, the sea hare, *Aplysia*. In *Aplysia*, sensitization of the defensive withdrawal reflexes, achieved

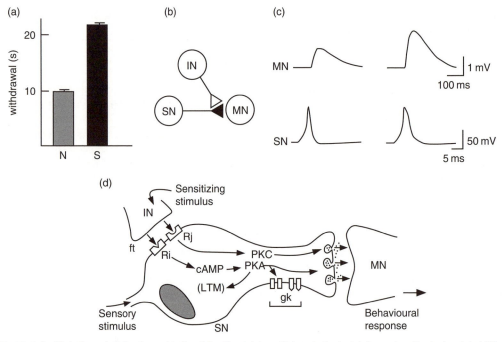

Fig. 59 A simplified scheme depicting the sensitization of the gill and siphon withdrawal reflex in *Aplysia* at various *levels of analysis. (a) The behavioural response (see also page 16). N, 'naive' *Aplysia*, withdrawing the gill and siphon in response to a mild touch to the skin; S, the augmented response of subjects sensitized by a shock to the tail. (b) The elementary module of the central circuit that subserves the behaviour. IN, interneuron; MN, motor neuron; SN, sensory neuron. (c) Synaptic facilitation, the correlate and cellular analogue of behavioural sensitization in this system. The lower curve in each case is the action potential (spike) in SN, and the upper curve is the excitatory postsynaptic potential (EPSP) in the follower MN (left-hand curves, pre-training, right-hand curves, post-training). The broadened spike in SN after sensitization training ultimately results in an enhanced response to subsequent action potentials, and therefore in enhanced transmitter released on to the MN. This contributes to the augmentation over time of the behavioural response. (d) Elements of the molecular machinery that underlies short-term synaptic facilitation. The sensitizing stimulus releases facilitatory transmitter(s) (ft) from the IN on to the SN. These modulatory substances, e.g. serotonin, activate several types of receptors (Ri, Rj) on the SN membrane. The receptors in turn activate *intracellular signal transduction cascades. One type of receptor activates the *protein kinase C cascade, which results in enhancement of transmitter release. Another type of receptor activates the cyclic adenosine monophosphate (cAMP) cascade, leading to phosphorylation of potassium channels (gk), which results in spike broadening and enhanced excitability in response to subsequent stimuli to the SN. The cAMP cascade could also trigger memory *consolidation that involves modulation of gene expression and culminates in the long-term memory of sensitization (LTM; see *CREB). In reality, the relative contributions of multiple signal transduction cascades, enhanced excitability and enhanced transmitter release, depend on the history of the SN as well as on the time after the sensitizing experience. Use-dependent alterations in other components of the circuit are not shown for simplicity. (Modified from Abrams, 1985, and Byrne and Kandel, 1996.)

by applying a noxious stimulus to the skin, is based on multiple time- and *context-dependent alterations in the circuits that subserve the behaviour (Trudeau and Castellucci 1993; Byrne and Kandel 1996; T.E. Cohen *et al.* 1997; Cleary *et al.* 1998). A significant portion of the sensitization of the behavioural response is explained by presynaptic facilitation in a single type of *synapse. This is the synapse between the sensory neuron, which carries information from the skin, and the motor neuron, which commands the withdrawal response (Figure 5, p. 16, and Figure 59.). Synaptic facilitation is a form of use-dependent synaptic *plasticity that is expressed as an enhancement in the strength of the synaptic connection; as synaptic facilitation was found in *Aplysia* to correlate with major aspects of behav-ioural sensitization, it was accepted in this *system as a convenient cellular analogue of sensitization.

In the aforementioned sensory-to-motor synapse in *Aplysia*, a considerable part of the facilitation is induced by a modulatory neuron, which is activated by information about the sensitizing stimulus. This neuron releases modulatory substances, which activate a number of *receptors and their downstream *intracellular signal transduction cascades in the sensory neuron terminal. This culminates in multiple plastic changes, among them enhanced *neurotransmitter release by the sensory neuron on to the motor neuron that controls the withdrawal response. Both short-term sensitization, lasting up to a few hours, and long-term sensitization, lasting more than a day, could be *modelled by short- and long-term synaptic facilitation. Whereas short-term facilitation involves post-translational modifications, long-term facilitation requires modulation of gene expression, *protein synthesis, and morphological changes in the synapse, which are assumed to maintain the facilitation over time in spite of the ongoing molecular turnover (*consolidation). Studies of *classical conditioning in the same preparation have unveiled that facilitation is also a component of this elementary type of associative learning, only that in classical conditioning, the use-dependent enhancement in the synapse is specifically augmented by the *coincidence of the conditioned and the unconditioned stimuli (Abrams 1985). That classical conditioning in this system is an elaboration of sensitization is actually not at all surprising, considering that conditioning is of the α type, involving a pre-existing rather than a new response.

The analysis of sensitization in *Aplysia* is hence a *classical example of a reductive research programme in the field of memory research. It has focused on identified cellular processes in an identified locus in the neuronal circuit that subserves the behaviour, and has succeeded in partially translating the behavioural phenomenon into cellular phenomena that are accessible to mechanistic analysis (*reduction). This programme has identified molecular devices that could perform functions of *acquisition of cellular information (e.g. serotonin receptors), storage (e.g. protein kinases), and readout, or *retrieval, of such information (e.g. potassium channels, components of the transmitter release machinery). A sizeable part of what is so far known about the molecular and cellular mechanisms of short- and long-term memory, is derived from the cellular analysis of short- and long-term facilitation in *Aplysia*. Hence, whoever wishes to understand the *zeitgeist in molecular neurobiology cannot afford to disregard sensitization in *Aplysia*.

Sensitization, although only a primitive form of learning, is of great importance in human behaviour. It can be demonstrated already in the neonate (Lipsitt 1990). Later throughout life, sensitization comes to contribute to a plethora of normal as well as pathological responses. Long-term sensitization was proposed as a model for phobia and generalized anxiety disorder (Marks 1987). Furthermore, 'stress sensitization', which is the augmentation by stress experience of the stress response upon re-éxposure to a stressor (e.g. Nissenbaum *et al.* 1991), was invoked to explain why phobias and neurotic rituals relapse after trauma (Marks 1987; Marks and Tobena 1990).

Selected associations: Context, Generalization, Habituation, Surprise, Taxonomy

---

[1]In α conditioning the conditioned response is intensification of pre-existing response to the conditioned stimulus; see *classical conditioning.

Simple system

A *system, such as an organism or a preparation containing neural tissue, that is less complex than other systems in the same category, and is used to model the category and to facilitate research that involves this category.

Interest in the intelligence of simple organisms, and their use to investigate problems of learning and memory, draws mainly from two conceptual frameworks: Darwinism (Boakes 1984), and *reductionism. The notion that evolution applies to the mind as well, undoubtedly combined with a keen interest in zoology and behaviour, has directed some investigators already a century ago to study the mental powers of organisms such as protozoa and insects (Peckham and Peckham 1887; Jennings 1906; Day and Bentley 1911). Starting at the 1950s and 60s, the use of simple organisms in neurobiology (Benzer 1967), as well as that of simplified preparations from such organisms (Kandel and Spencer 1968), has been further reinforced by the remarkable success of utilizing simple organisms to decode the genetic code and to unravel metabolic pathways.

The selection of a 'simple' organism for the investigation of learning and memory depends on the objective and on the context of the research programme. If the objective is to study the neurobiology of a particular species *per se*, the selection is self-explanatory. If the objective is primarily to advance understanding of a general problem in the neurobiology of learning and memory, the selection is based on properties that offer particular experimental advantages. These could be, for example, simple reflex circuits, large accessible neurons (Kandel and Spencer 1968; T.E. Cohen *et al.* 1997), or amenability to genetic analysis (Benzer 1967; Dudai *et al.* 1976; Tully 1996). Furthermore, whether an organism is regarded 'simple' depends on what is it compared with. In the context of the analysis of human *amnesia, studying a *rat is switching to a simple system, although the rat, of course, is far from being simple.

Intact simple organisms could be employed to analyse distinct phenomena of learning and memory, such as non*associative learning, rudimentary associative learning, *cue revaluation, or elements of memory *consolidation. But the use of such organisms in the dissection of the physiological and molecular mechanisms that subserve the aforementioned phenomena requires a combination of *reductive and simplifying steps.[1] This results in preparations in which fragments of the nervous system, or even individual neurons only, are analysed (Rayport and Schacher 1986; Krasne and Teshiba 1995; T.E. Cohen *et al.* 1997; Frysztak and Crow 1997). In the simplified preparations, certain molecular and cellular phenomena could be used to *model a molar behaviour, for example, *synaptic depression and facilitation to model *habituation and *sensitization, respectively (T.E. Cohen *et al.* 1997), or activity dependent synaptic facilitation to model associative conditioning (Byrne and Kandel 1996).

The analysis of simple organisms and simplified neural preparations from such organisms has generated highly valuable insight into basic phenomena, processes, and mechanisms of learning and memory. Subsequent analysis in more complex systems has established that some basic findings *generalize from the simple systems to the more complex ones (Bailey *et al.* 1996; e.g. *CREB, *consolidation, *immediate early genes, *intracellular signal transduction cascades, *protein synthesis). The caveats should not, however, be overlooked. First, 'primitive' organisms are often not so primitive (e.g. Srinivasan and Chang 1998), and miniature brains do not necessarily imply simplicity (*subject). The so-called 'simple organisms' surely did not evolve to supply neuroscientists with convenient tools to approach complex problems; these organisms were shaped in evolution to survive in a circumscribed ecological niche, and are therefore endowed with certain specialized (and intriguing) properties, but not with others. This means that whatever is the physiology and behaviour of these species, it has been adapted to fulfil needs that might be different from those of other species. But it also means that individuals belonging to primitive species clearly cannot perform some feats that are within the repertoire of more advanced species: likening contemplation in a worm to the retrieval of explicit knowledge in humans, is carrying the analogy a bit too far indeed. Second, within their phylogenetic limitations, some of the specialized tasks carried out by so-called simple organisms are themselves rather elaborate (e.g. Zeil *et al.* 1996). Third, even if the task is simple, the neuronal *algorithms that subserve it may prove complex when the surface is scratched (e.g. Wolpaw 1997).

In recent years, some of the enthusiasm for using simple organisms to analyse the neurobiological bases of behaviour has dwindled, because state-of-the-art molecular biology could now be used to approach problems in higher organisms that previously were approachable only in lower ones. Powerful *neurogenetics, for example, can already be practised in *mice, depriving *Drosophila* of its monopoly in the neurogenetic analysis of memory. It would be, however, a pity if simple organisms were to be abandoned. These species, in addition to being so interesting as such, do offer substantial advantages, for example, in deciphering the *representational code that are used in identified neural circuits that subserve discrete behaviours. In parallel with the aforementioned trend, the use of brain slices (e.g. Barkai and Hasselmo 1997) and of neuronal cell cultures (e.g. Tong *et al.* 1996) from complex nervous systems has gained much popularity, because such simplified preparations permit full exploitation of highly advanced cellular, molecular, and computational techniques (e.g. in the investigation of *long-term potentiation). It is likely that in the future, simple systems may come to include also bionic hybrids of neural tissue and printed circuits (Kuwana *et al.* 1995; Maher *et al.* 1999).

Selected associations: Aplysia, Drosophila, Honeybee, Model, Reduction

---

[1]For the definition of these two types of steps and the distinction between them, see *reduction.

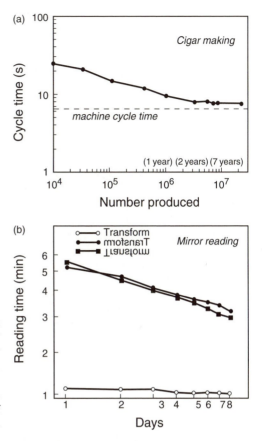

(a) Cigar making

machine cycle time

(1 year) (2 years) (7 years)

Skill

1. **Proficiency in the *performance on a perceptual, motor, or cognitive task, *acquired through cumulative experience.**

2. **The type of knowledge that subserves this proficiency.**

The first systematic investigation of skill learning involved a skill that is now obsolete. This was the study of the acquisition of the American Morse code by employees of railway and telegraph companies (Bryan and Harter 1897, 1899). On the basis of these studies, Bryan and Harter proposed that the formation of skill is a multi*phase process, which involves the mastery of specific elementary *habits that become associated in a hierarchy. The expert is then able to perform the hierarchy of habits automatically, at a speed that in certain individuals approaches the physical limit of the task (Figure 60). The command of automaticity should therefore be given full respect in education: 'It is quite useless to raise the question whether or not children should acquire specific automatic habits. There is no escape from such habits ... The wolf does not escape. Neither Shakespeare nor Caliban escape ... Automatism is not genius, but it is the hands and feet of genius' (Bryan and Harter 1899).

1. *The spectrum of skills.* Sending Morse messages involves a motor, or perceptual-motor skill. Decoding such messages involves primarily a perceptual skill. Other types of skill are cognitive, for example, problem solving. 'Skill' is also used, mainly in colloquial language, to refer to proficiency in other behavioural domains, such as emotional or social, without necessarily distinguishing between an innate (*a priori) predisposition and an acquired ability. Emotional and social skill could be regarded as subtypes of cognitive skill. Cognitive skill is occasionally dubbed 'intellectual skill', but this applies only to humans and may connote

Fig. 60 The acquisition of skill. (a) The average speed of production of cigars by a group of girls operating cigar-making machines. The curve for the first 2 years fits a power function (see text). After producing about 3 million cigars, the performance of the workers approached the machine cycle time. (Adapted from Crossman 1959.) (b) The average reading time of a group of undergraduates for mirror-reading English text. Again, the curves fit a power function. (Adapted from Kolers 1968.)

pretentious capabilities. The term 'mental skill' should be avoided as all skills are mental. Skills could be performed in the absence of *conscious awareness, hence, are classified as non*declarative memory (Squire and Zola 1996). Their acquisition, however, may either involve conscious awareness, i.e. be declarative or explicit, or be independent of conscious awareness, i.e. nondeclarative or implicit.

2. *The acquisition of skills.* The analysis of all types of skill shows that their acquisition involves multiple phases.[1] The nature of these phases is the subject matter of theories of skill acquisition (e.g. Snoddy 1926; Crossman 1959; Fitts 1964; Anderson 1982; Logan

1988). These theories differ in the nature and number of phases, but basically share the view that the first phase involves selection of the proper *algorithm, and the later phase(s) involve(s) perfection and automatization of the suitable solution. Hence the first phase is called either 'adaptation' (Snoddy 1926), 'algorithmic' (Logan 1988), 'understanding' or formation of 'cognitive set' (Fitts 1964),[2] or 'declarative' (Anderson 1982); the later phase is 'facilitation' (Snoddy 1926), or 'automatization' (Logan 1988), or 'procedural' (Anderson 1982). The existence of phases in skill acquisition is supported by behavioural data, and more recently, by *functional neuroimaging data that show the recruitment of different brain circuits with practice (see below).

A common observation is that the improvement of performance with practice follows a power law: $\log C = \log B + n\log X$, where C = a measure of performance, X = number of trials or time on task, B, n = constants (Snoddy 1926; DeJong 1957; Crossman 1959; Newell and Rosenbloom 1981) (Figure 60). This is called the 'power law of performance', or 'of practice', or 'of learning'. Power functions are commonly associated in the literature with perceptual-motor skill, and sometimes are even taken as evidence that the type of learning is indeed such skill. In fact they are common to all learning that involves repetitive training (Newell and Rosenbloom 1981), including learning to *forget (Rubin and Wenzel 1996).

3. The *persistence of skills. Skills could be retained over years in the absence of further practice (Fleishman and Parker 1962), and sometimes even in the absence of recollection of having previously performed the task (Cohen 1984). What loss occurs is quickly regained by re-practicing (Fleishman and Parker 1962; see 'saving' in *experimental extinction).

4. The relationship between skill and other types of procedural memory. Automaticity is an attribute shared by other forms of procedural memory (Squire and Zola 1996; *taxonomy). The question arises what is the relationship between skill and these other forms of memory. Of special interest is the relevance of skill to repetition *priming. Whereas skill learning refers to a *generalized improvement on a task, priming refers to the improvement on a given item within the task.[3] Is the latter a special case of the former? The views differ; priming and skill learning are considered manifestation of the same type of incremental learning process or mechanism by some authors (Logan 1990; Poldrack et al. 1999), but not by others (Schwartz and Hashtroudi 1991; Kirsner and Speelman 1996). A data-based argument brought up by the opponents of the single-process view is that priming is independent of accumulative practice. A conceptual argument in favour of a unified-process approach is that even skill learning is limited to the specific task-related procedures, and therefore is not qualitatively so different from priming. It could be proposed, so goes this argument, that skill and repetition priming represent each a change along a continuum of generalization; the degree of generalization reflects the *level of the processing stream in which the modification occurs. Depending on the item variability in training and the amount of practice, the use-dependent alteration may result in learned information that does not *transfer to other items (repetition priming), or, alternatively, generalizes over a class of items (skill; Ofen-Noy et al. 2002). This view echoes the proposal that different types of learning, including declarative ones, involve a procedural component, yet differ, among others, in the resulting specificity of transfer (Kolers and Roediger 1984).

5. Which brain areas encode and retain skills? The approach to this question relies on two main types of *methodologies. One is the analysis of the performance of patients with 'global' *amnesia, Parkinson's disease, and Huntington's disease; the other, functional neuroimaging of brain activity during the learning and performance of skill in healthy human *subjects. The analysis of performance of amnesics, Parkinsonian and Huntingtonian patients provides information about brain areas that are obligatory for skill (*criterion). This type of studies is complemented by the investigation of the effect of circumscribed brain lesions on tasks that are considered to *model human skill in laboratory animals, e.g. the *monkey. The neuroimaging studies provide information about brain areas whose activity is correlated with skill learning and performance. This type of studies is complemented by cellular physiology methods in laboratory animals (e.g. Recanzone et al. 1993).

Despite their dense declarative amnesia, human patients with extensive damage to the mediotemporal lobe perform remarkably well on perceptual-motor, perceptual, and cognitive skill tasks (Milner et al. 1968; Brooks and Baddeley 1976; Cohen and Squire 1980; Cohen 1984). For example, with experience, they improve normally on motor tracking in a tactual maze (perceptual-motor skill), on mirror-reading (perceptual skill, Figure 60), and on solving the Tower of Hanoi puzzle (cognitive skill, Figure 61). All this, without recollection of having previously performed the task. These findings show that skill is not subserved by the same brain circuits that subserve declarative memory. In contrast to the success of amnesics on skill tasks, Huntington's and Parkinson's patients are impaired on

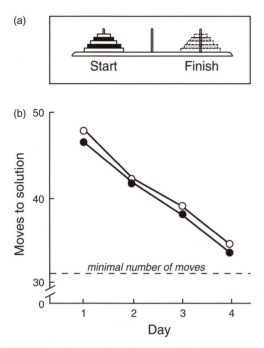

Fig. 61 The performance of amnesics on a cognitive skill. The Tower of Hanoi puzzle consists of five wooden blocks and three pegs (a). At the outset, all five blocks are arranged on the leftmost peg in size order, the smallest block on top. The subject is then asked to move the blocks from the leftmost peg to the rightmost peg, while moving only one block at a time, and without ever placing a larger block on top of a smaller one. The optimal solution, which involves shuttling the blocks back and forth on all three pegs, requires 31 moves. (Compare with the Tower of London, *planning.) In this experiment, training consisted of solving the puzzle four times per session on each of four consecutive days. The performance of amnesics patients on this task is indistinguishable from that of normal controls (b). A follow-up study showed that patient H.M. (*amnesia, *classic) retained the skill after 1 year. (Adapted from Cohen 1984.)

learning of perceptual-motor skill (Heindel *et al.* 1988), perceptual skill (Martone *et al.* 1984), and cognitive skill (Saint-Cyr *et al.* 1988). Huntington's disease and Parkinson's disease both involve striatal pathology, and therefore, the striatum has been proposed to subserve skill learning, similarly to its role in habit formation.

Functional neuroimaging can be used to identify areas that are activated during the acquisition and performance of skill in the normal brain (e.g. Seitz *et al.* 1990; Grafton *et al.* 1995; Karni *et al.* 1998; Petersen *et al.* 1998; Hund-Georgiadis and von Carmon 1999; Nadler *et al.* 2000; Poldrack and Gabrieli 2001).[4] A few tentative generalizations could be extracted from these studies: (a) skill-related changes in brain activity are distributed over multiple brain areas, some of which are task-specific and some task-independent; (b) the task-specific areas include modality specific cortical areas, whereas the corticostriatal system, and possibly the *cerebellum, are involved in skills that span sensory modalities and tasks; and (c) often it is found that the involvement of brain areas in skill learning and performance changes over time in the course of practice. The picture that emerges, although yet preliminary, is that the acquisition of skill involves changes in two types of *internal representations, those of the specific behavioural acts of the particular skill, and those of the 'syntactic' hierarchical routines by which the particular acts are perfected, bound, and executed. Further, above a certain degree of practice, the relevant internal representations may shift to brain circuits other than those employed in the early phases of training. This can be shown when comparing the activation of brain areas over training in an individual, or the activation in the brain of novices vs. experts (e.g. Hund-Georgiadis and von Carmon 1999). Exceptional skill benefits from particular behavioural routines (Ericsson and Lehmann 1996), and the talented brain may process the talent-related material in a unique way (Schlaug *et al.* 1995; Pesenti *et al.* 2001). An interesting question is whether this results merely from the perfection of normal brain resources, or from an innate predisposition in the structure of the brain, or, most likely, from both.

Selected associations: Birdsong, Habit, Instrumental conditioning, Priming, Transfer

---

[1]'Phase' here means stages in the development of skill that are superimposed on the basic universal phases of memory, such as short-term memory, *consolidation, or *retrieval.

[2]On 'set' see *learning set. The terms 'understanding', 'cognitive set', and 'declarative' fit the discussion of human skill but not necessarily that of skill in other species.

[3]That is, whereas skill refers to types of stimuli, priming refers to tokens; on types and tokens see *system.

[4]It is noteworthy that a limited degree of gross localization of function can be obtained in certain skill paradigms by the use of behavioural methods in the absence of neuroimaging. Hence if a visual perceptual skill improves only in one eye without affecting the other, it could be inferred that the process occurs at low-level of the visual processing stream in the brain, before the site of binocular integration (Sagi and Tanne 1994).

Spaced training

Training with intercalated rest intervals.

In many situations, multiple training sessions with intercalated rest intervals (also termed 'distributed training') result in a more robust and long-lasting memory than the same amount of training with no rest intervals ('massed training'). This phenomenon was noted already in the early days of experimental psychology (Jost 1897). It has been observed in species far apart on the phylogenetic scale, from the most primitive to the most advanced (Melton 1970; Carew *et al.* 1972; Cornell 1980; Perruchet 1989; Payne and Wenger 1992; Yin *et al.* 1995; Kogan *et al.* 1996; Pereyra *et al.* 2000). In human *subjects it is unveiled in a variety of verbal, perceptual, and motor tasks, in both *declarative and nondeclarative memory *systems, in the laboratory and in *real-life situation, in adults as well as in infants.

The phylogenetic and ontogenetic conservation of the spaced training effect suggests that it relates to elementary processes and mechanisms of learning. Two main types of explanations have been proposed at the system *level. One is that as the spacing between repetition increases, the familiarity of the repeated items decreases, resulting in enhanced *attention and more thorough processing of the information. As a consequence, overall, the information is learned better under spaced conditions. Explanations of this type are termed 'deficient processing theories' (Greene 1989). The other type of explanations is that spacing allows richer variability and exploitation of the *context, which increases the number of possible *retrieval *cues for the repeated item. This, in turn, is expected to facilitate retrieval. Explanations of this type are termed 'contextual variability theories' (*ibid.*). Contextual variability theories can also be extended to imply that, whereas the experimenter deems the *stimulus equal when presented either in a spaced or in a massed training protocol, the subject may actually *perceive two different stimuli (e.g. Pereyra *et al.* 2000). It is noteworthy that spaced training can be demonstrated in even very simple conditioning *paradigms in which the context is kept highly constant; but one cannot exclude the possibility that brains of other species may discover with time magnificent changes and new worlds in what appears to us an extremely boring environment.

The recent introduction of molecular biology techniques to the analysis of learning and memory in *simple organisms has led to the emergence of a molecular and cellular *model that attempts to explain the increased efficacy of spaced training. This model is embedded in the gene expression hypothesis of long-term memory. The hypothesis states that *consolidation of memory into a long-term form involves modulation of transcription factors and gene expression (*immediate early gene, *late response gene). Specifically, the model proposes that training induces both activator and repressor isoforms of *CREB, which is a type of molecular switch that controls the formation of long-term memory. The downstream processes subserving the formation of long-term memory are activated only when the amount of functional activator within the relevant nerve cells transcends a certain threshold. The key assumption is that immediately after training, enough CREB repressor exists to block the activator. With rest, however, the repressor inactivates faster than the activator. Therefore the activator accumulates with spaced but not with massed training (Yin *et al.* 1995). This highly simplified model thus provides an interesting attempt to link events at the molecular level to those at the system and behavioural level (*reduction; for a related model, see *flashbulb memory.)

Why had the superiority of spaced training evolved in evolution? One possibility is that it confers to species ranging from slugs to humans some extra advantage that we do not yet understand. It cannot be merely the opportunity to take a break and rest in the middle of a study session. Another possibility is that the superiority of spaced, as opposed to massed training, is a spin-off of the way synapses and neuronal circuits are built.[1] And, of course, it is also possible that both assumptions are correct, and that evolution had capitalized on the biological constraints.

The advantage of spaced training is not limited to its potential ability to illuminate elementary mechanisms of learning and memory. It can also be recruited to improve everyday memory (Landauer and Ross 1977; Payne and Wenger 1992). In fact it is one of the very few training and rehearsing procedures that has been repeatedly proven to be of some value in memory improvement (*mnemonics). Yet despite the simplicity of the procedure and the evidence for its effectiveness, for most people it is counterintuitive: when asked to provide a subjective rating, subjects tend to rate massed training as more likely to ensure proper recall than spaced training (Zechmeister and Shaughnessy 1980). The literature on spaced training is thus worth rehearsing, although preferably not in a massed fashion.

Selected associations: Consolidation, CREB, Mnemonics, Real-life memory

State-dependent learning

The phenomenon in which information learned in one state of the organism is *retrieved best if a similar state is reinstated at the time of testing.

The 'state' in state-dependent learning is taken to imply the internal, physiological, and mental milieu, but its reinstatement often requires elements of the original external milieu (*context). The phenomenon is also termed 'dissociated learning'. The more general term 'state-dependent learning' is, however, to be preferred, as 'dissociation' connotes clinical meanings that are not intended.[1] The terms 'state-dependent retrieval', 'state-dependent recall', and 'state-dependent memory' are also used, sometimes with an underlying assumption that the key to the understanding of the state dependency lies in a particular memory *phase but not in another. In practice, state dependency is frequently induced by drugs or intoxication: this special case of state-dependent learning is known as 'drug-dependent' or 'drug-dissociated' learning.

Over the years, the fascination with state-dependent learning has been shared by scientists and non-scientists alike. The latter, though, became intrigued much before the former. It was noted long ago that somnambulists (sleepwalkers, such as Lady Macbeth, Shakespeare 1606), could in their trance do things that are forgotten in their waking state but pursued or recalled in a subsequent episode of sleepwalking (Ellenberger 1970). The same phenomenon was later demonstrated with 'artificial somnambulism', i.e. hypnosis ('animal magnetism', *ibid.*), to which spontaneous somnambulists were found to be especially susceptible. This phenomenon of hypnosis-dependent learning was exploited not only by shamans, performing magicians, and occasionally crooks, but also by authors and screenwriters. In *Dr Caligari*, one of the greatest *classics of the German Expressionist cinema (Wiene *et al.* 1919), the notorious Caligari hypnotizes the somnambulist Cesare to commit murders while in a somnambulistic trance. Perhaps the most popular state-dependencies were, however, attributed to alcohol and narcotics. In describing a *system of *phrenology,

Combe (1830, cited in Siegel 1982) recounts the story of an Irish porter who used to forget, when sober, what he had done while drunk, and yet could recapture the memory once he again became indulged in drinking. This story was later echoed in the writings of several eminent physicians, including Winslow ('On obscure diseases of the brain', 1860, cited in Eich and Birbaum 1982) and Ribot (1882, *amnesia). Additional cases of alcohol-dependent recall also found their way into fictional literature (Dickens, cited in Siegel 1982) and the cinema (Chaplin, cited in Bower 1981).

In Victorian England opium was occasionally used as freely as alcohol (Berridge 1977), and hence opiate-dependent recall became known as well. Opiate-dependent recall was the clue to a contemporary best-seller, *The moonstone* (Collins 1868). In this detective story, a young gentleman, Blake, worried about the safety of his fiancé who possesses a valuable diamond, hides the diamond while he is under the effect of an opium tincture (laudanum). He has no memory of the event, till a physician's assistant advises him to recreate the drugged state. The author, Wilkie Collins, wrote from first-hand knowledge: he was himself an avid opium user, and the rumour went that he was unable to remember where in the novel he concluded the previous writing session unless he became drugged again (Siegel 1982).

Controlled scientific experimentation on state dependency has started with Girden and Culler (1937). They paralysed a dog with curare,[2] and then trained it in a *classical conditioning protocol to associate the sound of a bell with a shock-induced leg flexion. After training, the conditioned response was displayed in the presence of curare, vanished on return to the normal nonparalysed state and reappeared with re-administration of the poison. Conversely, conditioning in the absence of curare was undetected in the presence of the poison. Drug-dissociation learning was subsequently demonstrated by many groups of investigators using a variety of drugs and species (e.g. Overton 1964; Bruins Slot and Colpaert 1999; smoking can do the trick as well, Peters and McGee 1982). In many studies of drug-dissociated learning, rather large doses of drugs are needed, that also affect acquisition. Even the anecdotal alcohol-dependent memory in *Homo sapiens* was respectively verified in the laboratory using a group of joyous volunteers (Goodwin *et al.* 1969). Recall of single experiences displayed a greater sensitivity to drug dependency than *recognition. This latter observation was later found to *generalize to other situations of state-dependent learning.

Many drugs that can produce drug-dissociated learning affect the mood. It is therefore only natural to ask whether affective states *per se* could induce state-dependent learning. The answer is probably yes (Blaney 1986). It was reported that depressed patients, or normal subjects hypnotized to sadness for the sake of science, display a 'mnemonic *bias' toward the recall of unpleasant information (Lloyd and Lishman 1975; Bower 1981; Clark and Teasdale 1982). Similar results have been reported for other emotional disorders (e.g. panic disorder favours panic-related words; Becker *et al.* 1994). The question is whether this is state dependency *bona fide*, i.e. whether the altered mood induces mood dependency in the retrievability of items in memory irrespective of the affective valence of these items. An alternative possibility is that an altered mood at the time of training or testing promotes the learning or recall, respectively, of events or facts that agree with that particular mood. In such a case concordance between mood at learning and mood at retrieval is not obligatory, i.e. it is not true state-dependent learning. The phenomenon in which material is more likely to be attended, learnt, or recalled if it is consistent with the subject's prevailing mood, is termed 'mood congruency' or 'mood congruity' (Bower 1981; Blaney 1986). Overall, the jury is yet out on whether the available data on mood-associated recall favour state dependency, mood congruency, or both (Blaney 1986; Pearce *et al.* 1990; Power and Dalgleish 1997). Regardless of the exact mechanisms, if depressed patients display a bias for depressing memories, they could be expected to become immersed in depressing thoughts and expectations, which in turn will augment and perpetuate the depression. This is a vicious cycle that could contribute to chronic depression (Clark and Teasdale 1982; Ingram 1984; for a critical review of similar ideas and 'cognitive theories' of depression in general, see Haaga *et al.* 1991).

Recently, neuronal, *reduced analogues of state-dependent *plasticity and learning have been reported (Wörgötter *et al.* 1998; Shulz *et al.* 2000). This, together with the analysis of *neurotransmitter and *receptor mechanisms in state dependency (Bruins Slot and Colpaert 1999), paves the way to further understanding of the molecular, cellular, and circuit mechanisms that implement state dependency at the behavioural *level. In the meantime, a practical caveat: the potential contribution of state-dependent learning to the outcome of behavioural experiments should not be ignored. A *control for state-dependent learning is highly advisable in every study in which drugs or conditional gene knockouts (*neurogenetics) are used to manipulate

only the acquisition or retrieval *phase but not both. Furthermore, state dependency must be kept in mind whenever *developmental, hormonal, circadian rhythm, or *nutritional states are not kept under control throughout the experiment. All this, because memory traces may trick us and disappear, only to resurface later, when the original state experienced by the subject in acquisition is reinstated.

Selected associations: Context, Percept, Retrieval, Transfer

---

[1]In psychiatry, 'dissociation implies disruption of integrated functions of personality (DSM-IV 1994).

[2]A blocker of the *acetylcholine *receptor that Native American warriors used to smear on their arrowheads.

Stimulus

1. An event or aspect of the environment that triggers a response in a *system.

2. A signal for action.

Originally, 'to stimulate' meant literally to prick or stub (*stimulus*, Latin for a goad or spur). Over the years, various concepts and usages of 'stimulus' have played a central part in the behavioural and neural sciences. Unless otherwise indicated, definition 1 is the one discussed here. Stimuli could be or could include *cues; further, definition 2 overlaps with definitions 3 and 4 of 'cue'.

The *classic usage of 'stimulus' in memory research refers to an event that triggers a response in the behaving organism. The concept, however, spans *levels, from the behavioural to the molecular. At all levels, stimulus is a packet of information that triggers specific, or less specific, processes in the receiving system.

1. *On stimuli and information.* There are two basic approaches to information. One, 'syntactic', considers the quantity without considering the content. The other, 'semantic', considers the meaning and significance. The 'syntactic' approach is used in information theory, where 'information' is a mathematical abstraction that refers to the uncertainty in coding and transmitting data, irrespective of the semantics (*system). This efficacy of transfer is measured in 'bits'. One bit is the choice between two equally likely possibilities; the number of bits required to select among n alternatives is $\log_2 n$. It is currently difficult, if not impossible, to translate the data in sensory stimuli into bits

(*capacity). Even when the number of bits will be known, still, itself it will tells us nothing about what these bits signify to the receiver. To understand this, we must either observe the behavioural or physiological effect of the stimulus under *controlled conditions, or decipher the neuronal codes used by the sender and the receiver (*internal representation). The semantics of the stimulus depends on at least some of the stimulus *dimensions.

2. *On the dimensions of stimuli.* Autonomous dimensions, which are independent of the *context and of the state of the receiver, involve modality (e.g. wavelength, chemical composition), intensity, duration, rate, frequency, and location in time and space. Contextual dimensions, e.g. saliency, refer to the relation of the stimulus to other stimuli. Subjective dimensions depend on the interaction of the stimulus with the receiver and include functional threshold (*sensitization), familiarity, hedonic valence, saliency, and efficacy.

3. *On the source of stimuli.* From the point of view of source–receiver interaction, stimuli differ in their purposiveness. Purposive stimuli[1] differ in the specificity of their target. Non-purposive stimuli are released inadvertently by animate or inanimate systems. Consider a rabbit hopping in an open field. The moving object is a stimulus that triggers attack by the fox. This stimulus is not released purposively by the source. When the rabbit discovers the attack, it may freeze (*fear conditioning), which is already a purposive stimulus to abort the attack; this purpose was selected by evolution and shaped the innate, *a priori behavioural repertoire of the species. As the meaning of purposive stimuli is context and receiver dependent, it is not necessarily what the sender meant to deliver. Nowhere is it better epitomized than in 'pragmatics', the discipline that studies the meaning of sentences in language (i.e. verbal stimuli, definitions 1 and 2) in the particular contexts in which they are uttered. The same is true for body language. Travel guides to certain countries carry special warnings about this problem.

4. *On the effect of stimuli.* Stimuli could do one of the following: (a) induce new pattern(s) of activity in the receiver, in which case the stimulus is said to be *instructive*; (b) augment or inhibit non-discriminatorily endogenous patterns of activity in the receiver, in which case the stimulus is *adjustive.* (c) augment or inhibit differentially endogenous patterns of activity in the receiver, in which case the stimulus is *selective*; or (d) leave the system as it is, in which case the stimulus is *ineffective.* In each of a–c above, the effect of the stimulus could be either immediate or latent, and may or may not *persist after the stimulus is gone (*memory, *plasticity).

*A *reductive *taxonomy of stimuli encountered in learning and memory research:*

a. *The types of stimuli that affect the behaviour of organisms.* The behaviour of organisms is affected by sensory stimuli from the outside world, and by endogenous stimuli, which are either sensory stimuli from within the organism, or global mental states (e.g. hunger, anxiety), or specific mental operations (e.g. one thought as a stimulus for another, *associative memory). In most learning *paradigms, emphasis is placed on exogenous sensory stimuli. It is the experimenter who selects these stimuli, but the experimental *subject may not honour the selection (e.g. *classical conditioning, *context).

b. *Sensory stimuli* are delivered from the external world to the front end of a specialized sensory channel in the organism, causing sensation, i.e. a functional change in a sensory *receptor. Sensory physiology textbooks distinguish four types of dimensions in sensory stimuli, which can be quantitatively correlated with sensation. These are sensory modality, intensity, duration, and location in sensory space (Martin 1991). 'Proximal stimuli' affect the sensory receptor directly, for example, chemicals that interact with taste receptors, or pressure applied to somatosensory receptors on the skin. 'Distal stimuli' interact with the receptor via proximal stimuli; hence a visual scene is a distal stimulus that interacts with the visual receptor via photons, which are proximal stimuli.

This is a proper point to digress briefly into a conceptual issue. Dominant schools in philosophy trust that sensory stimuli are not autonomous entities but rather 'sense data', i.e. entities that exist as such only because they are sensed (Price 1950; *percept). This view is in accord with the stand taken in this book, that the world drives behaviour only via internal representations, which are inherently *biased *models of the world. In important chapters in the history of psychology, however, 'stimuli' did not connote mental processing. For example, Skinner (1938; *behaviourism) regarded 'stimulus' as part of the environment that affects behaviour, and 'response' as part of behaviour that is affected by the stimulus. The basic idea was that behaviour and environment can be broken into parts, which interact but retain their identity throughout an experiment. That brain processes are involved was not deemed relevant. This type of attitude was accompanied by highly sophisticated stimulus–response ('operant') *methodology and terminology (Guthrie 1935; Skinner 1938; Hull 1943; Bower and Hilgard 1981; *instrumental conditioning).[2] Another discipline in which the focus is on the phenotype of stimuli is ethology. A central notion is that of a 'sign stimulus', or 'releaser', which elicits a particular pattern of innately predisposed behaviour. A popular example is the spring fighting of the male stickleback, which is released by the sight of a conspecific male, or by elongated fish-like dummies with a red belly (Tinbergen 1969; for releasers consider also *birdsong, *imprinting).

c. *Perceptual stimuli* are extracted by the brain from sensory stimuli, creating a *percept, which could become a memory. At this stage, the stimulus is already converted into an internal representation, encoded in the spatiotemporal activity of neuronal circuits, or populations. Further processing could be subserved by stimuli arriving from other neuronal populations (*cell assembly), i.e. 'interpopulation stimuli'.

d. *Interpopulation stimuli* are delivered from one neuronal population to another. They are either the outcome of a percept, or of a global brain state (e.g. *attention), or of endogenous activity of the source circuit. The notion that there are 'stimulus-independent' states in the brain (e.g. McGuire *et al.* 1996) should therefore be regarded only as a pragmatic heuristic of a test protocol, not a *real-life state.

e. *Synaptic stimuli* are either chemical ligands (*neurotransmitter) or ion currents. They engage receptors, *ion channels, and other membrane proteins, and subserve interpopulation stimuli (*d* above). Included here are also diffused ('volume') transmission and circulating hormones. So are glia-neuron messages (Araque *et al.* 1999).

f. *Intracellular stimuli* are delivered from a molecular sender to a molecular receiver within a neuron. For example, a G-protein shuttling between a surface receptor and an enzyme, or a transcription factor shuttling between the *protein kinase and a regulatory site of a gene (e.g. *CREB, *immediate early gene, *intracellular signal transduction cascade). Intracellular stimuli hence operate downstream of intercellular stimuli (*e* above) and ultimately actualize the information in the latter. Ion currents could also serve as intracellular stimuli.

The breakdown of stimulus types by level reminds one of the idea that the world rests on turtles, that rest on turtles, that rest on turtles, 'all the way down' (Geertz 1973; *reduction). For if we proceed in it we could end up with elementary particles as stimuli. This is a dilemma of reductionism, which must be solved by reconciling the multilevel nature of memory with the need to focus on those levels of organization and function in which the most important attributes of memory emerge (Dudai 1992). In the future science of memory, 'correspondence rules' of reductive theories will permit investigators to translate events from the language of one level to that of another. In the meantime, suffice it to remember that *e* and *f* above relate to cellular plasticity and cellular storage, whereas points *c* and *d* relate to representational change, hence *bona fide* memory; and that from a phylogenetic point of view, the survival value of all the stimuli is judged at the behavioural level, *a*.

Finally, in considering memory, it is important to reiterate that not all effective stimuli are successful teachers, and that in many cases the system quickly relaxes into the pre-stimulus state (*homeostasis). Therefore, not every poststimulus change in the brain is a manifestation of learning and memory, even if the report ends up as a catchy title in a respected journal. It is also noteworthy that our interaction with stimuli is use dependent. Sensory systems change their sensitivity to change (e.g. Torre *et al.* 1995; *metaplasticity); the brain learns to extract stimulus attributes by perceptual learning (Goldstone 1998); and we construe stimuli in the context of *culture (e.g. Clark and Clark 1980). We also learn to anticipate some stimuli but not others. If there is a discrepancy between the expectation and the actual stimulus, we experience *surprise, which itself is an effective incentive to form a memory of that stimulus, or, more accurately, of its percept.

Selected associations: Attention, Cue, Dimension, Generalization, Percept

---

[1]Purposiveness does not imply *declarativeness. The emission of the stimulus by the source may subserve a discrete purpose, e.g. warning, without the source being consciously aware of it. Purposiveness should also not be confounded with intentionality, which is the dimension of 'aboutness', considered to distinguish the mental from the physical (see *system).

[2]To do justice to subschools of behaviourism: not all those who considered overt behaviour as the only legitimate type of datum in psychology, discarded the role of internal processes; all, however, regarded stimuli as critical circumscribed variables of the behavioural experimentation and theory (Tolman 1952).

Subject

1. **The object of treatment or experiment.**
2. **An organism or thing under the authority, control, or influence of another organism or thing.**
3. **That which perceives, feels, thinks, or intends.**

Discussion of the multiple meanings of 'subject' could occupy a lengthy monograph, covering subjects from philosophy and linguistics, via the exact and the natural sciences, to politics and law. The few selected definitions provided above are the most relevant to memory research. We could benefit substantially from paying *attention to those implications of 'subject' that tend to be overlooked in the design and analysis of experiments. 'Subject' originates from Latin, where it had originally meant 'to throw or place beneath'. Accordingly, experimenters frequently think that having thrown the subject into the experimental situation (definition 1) ensures control over that subject (definition 2). The truth is that to some degree or another, every subject, especially if unanaesthetized, is an entity that perceives, feels, thinks, etc. (definition 3). An experimenter must be tuned to these attributes, otherwise real embarrassments may ensue.

Although the subject is at the focus of the experiment, frequently the attention devoted to it by the experimenter is surprisingly minimal, even less than that allotted to the computer on which the paper reporting the experiment is later being written. It is not an outraging exaggeration to claim that in some subdisciplines in experimental neuroscience, except possibly those that deal with human subjects (*Homo sapiens), many investigators are unaware of the spectrum of attributes of their subject. This is a mistake that may result in *artefacts. So here are some elementary truths about the subjects of memory experiments, which some investigators tend to ignore, yet you couldn't afford doing so.

1. The subject has a history. It is never the featureless, utterly inexperienced mind that you might wished it were (definitely not a *tabula rasa*, Locke 1690). The appreciation that the subject's life did not start with your experiment (though, unfortunately, it may end with it), is a must for the proper design, *performance, analysis and interpretation of behavioural and physiological experiments (e.g. *priming, *state-dependent learning, *transfer).
2. Individual subjects of the same species differ from each other. (That individuals from different species

are different should be obvious, although sometimes people tend to confuse species traits, expecting a *mouse to behave like a *rat, for example, in a problem box). This also applies to some degree to subjects that share the same genes (*neurogenetics), and moreover, even to subjects raised in the same environment—although, of course, the variability is smaller then in a genetically heterogeneous population in an heterogeneous environment (animals kept in different cages, humans raised in different cultures).

3. Miniature brains do not necessarily have miniature minds. A *honeybee can outperform the smartest of the elephants in some species-specific tasks. And miniature subjects are not homogeneous 'atoms of behaviour'. Surely, complex species are expected to display more behavioural variability than *simple ones, and we should in no way jump to *anthropomorphism. A powerful tool for smoothening behavioural and physiological 'noise' is statistics (Fisher 1966; Martin and Bateson 1993; Kerlinger and Lee 2000). Yet smoothening the noise must be distinguished from neglecting important differences among individuals. Such differences are important, because they may provide clues to potential breakthroughs (Benzer 1967). Statistics is important, attentive observation is even more so. It is useful to keep in mind the following citation from Martin and Bateson's (1993): 'Our general advice is not to become obsessed by statistical techniques, nor too cavalier in their use. Statistical analysis is merely a tool to help answer questions, and should be the servant rather than the master of science.'

4. *Reduced, *simplified preparations (such as isolated *Aplysia ganglia, *hippocampal slices, cell cultures, identified *synapses), the subjects of *reductive research programmes and experiments, do have a history as well. This history modifies the state and the response of the preparation (e.g. Frey and Morris 1997; Dudai and Morris 2000).

5. The subject's behaviour is always more complex than reflected in the data that you collect. This may be due to the fact that you have *a priori decided to choose only a selected parameter to study. Even Pavlov did it, and it was a key to his success: his dogs did a lot more than merely salivate in response to the metronome; Pavlov nevertheless decided to concentrate only on an easily quantifiable part of the conditioned reflex (Pavlov 1927). Another possibility is that you are not aware of the full spectrum of your subject's behaviour, because of lack of familiarity with the *system.

6. The subject has its own idiosyncratic understanding and appreciation of the experimental situation. Furthermore, questions that appear simple and intriguing to you may be of no interest whatsoever to the subject (e.g. *Drosophila* pay attention to odours, students to music; most species will pay much attention to their own visceral sensations following the ingestion of food, surely more than following visual or auditory experience; *conditioned taste aversion). You must hence know which questions to ask and how to pose them, in order to satisfy the curiosity and boost the motivation of the subject to take part in the game (e.g. Pavlov 1927; Benzer 1967; Garcia *et al.* 1968).

7. The subject may trick you by doing what you wish it to do, by noticing your behaviour ('demand characteristics'; Orne 1962, see *bias; *Clever Hans). The subject may also be influenced by the behaviour of other subjects without you ever being aware of it (*observational learning).

8. Know thy subject. Pay special attention to it if you switch a species, a preparation or an *assay. Different species have different perceptions of the world and behave accordingly. An innate response pattern (*a priori) may be mistakenly taken by you as evidence for learning (e.g. Moore and Stuttard 1979; Wolfer *et al.* 1998; *artefact).

9. And last, but not least: beware of falling in love with your experimental subject, especially if it is only a fly (Dethier 1962). It will surely bias you, and may even become painful.

Selected associations: Anthropomorphism, Drosophila, Homo sapiens, Model

---

Surprise

1. A sudden and unexpected encounter.

2. Unanticipated contradiction between *percepts or thoughts and the predictions of organized knowledge.

The trouble with political jokes is that they often get elected. For most if not all the readers, encountering this statement here is a real surprise. This is precisely why it stands a good chance to be remembered. Surprise ('*sur*'- +'*prendre*', Old French, *prehendere*, 'to seize' in Latin) is a perceptual *dimension well known to affect the *acquisition of memory in *real-life; it may lead, for

example, to an enduring *'flashbulb memory'. Descartes regarded 'wonder', or 'sudden surprise', as one of only six primitive 'passions of the soul', and appreciated its role as a trigger of *attention and learning: 'It has two causes: first, an impression in the brain, which represents the object as something unusual and consequently worthy of special consideration; and secondly, a movement of the spirits, which the impression disposes both to flow with greater force to the place in the brain where it is located so as to strengthen and preserve it there...' (Descartes 1649). Note, by the way, how well this paragraph fits five centuries later into discussions of *functional neuroimaging; all you have to do is to replace 'spirits' with 'blood', but this deserves a separate discussion on the history of ideas. A more recent forefather of our scientific *zeitgeist, Darwin (1872), also appreciated the importance of surprise as a primitive, universal emotion, characterized by specific gestures and physiological response. He focused on unpleasant surprises, startles, and fears, whereas we all know that benevolent surprises do exist, albeit they do not show up too often. In contemporary neuroscience, 'surprise' and its roles in learning and memory can be discussed at multiple *levels, from the behavioural to the molecular and vice versa. Let's therefore look at some of its manifestations in the brain, neuronal circuits and individual neurons.

'Surprise' is basically a sudden, significant mismatch between the actual and the expected. In brains, this is between on-line inputs (be them sensory *percepts or endogenous *internal representations) and off-line internal representations, i.e. memories. Definition 2 above emphasizes two additional properties: (a) that the knowledge is organized, and not merely a collection of data, and (b) that such organized knowledge makes predictions about reality (*a priori, *planning). These properties are explicit in the terminology of cognitive psychology. In cognitive terminology, 'surprise' is a sudden discrepancy between input and a 'cognitive schema'. 'Schemata' are structured clusters of generic knowledge, that represent situations, events, actions, or complex objects, enable the comprehension of input, and predict future outcome of action (Eysenck and Keane 1995; those schemata that contain organized sequences of stereotypical actions are 'scripts'). When external or internal data suddenly contradict the prediction of a schema, surprise follows. This may then motivate and enable the analysis of the discrepancy and the adjustment to it (Schutzwohl 1998). Thus, in a way, surprise is a sudden perturbation of cognitive *homeostasis.

Although the aforementioned framework connotes human or at least primate cognition, there is no reason why the basic elements should not be adapted to *reductive treatment of much simpler brains. Conditioning paradigms were particularly instrumental in casting light on the postulated role of surprise in learning in a variety of species. Consider, for example, the phenomenon called 'blocking', which is the inhibition of the conditioning to a stimulus, CS_1, in a compound $CS_1 + CS_2$ stimulus, by previous pairing of CS_2 with the UCS (*classical conditioning). A prevalent interpretation of the effect is that in order for an association between a CS and a UCS to be formed, the UCS must surprise the animal, but in blocking this is not the case, as CS_2 already predicts the UCS (Kamin 1969; for alternative interpretations see Mackintosh 1983). The analysis of conditioning has provided incentives as well as constraints for a number of formal *models of learning. Among them is the noted Rescorla–Wagner *algorithm (Rescorla and Wagner 1972), which, in a nutshell, concludes that the amount of learning is proportional to the amount of surprise. In other words, learning theories, not only layperson intuition, also mark surprise as a driving force in learning.

Recording the electrical activity of the human brain in action by electroencephalography (EEG, *functional neuroimaging), has identified brain waves that appear only under 'surprising' situations. The EEG of individuals that respond to a rare stimulus occurring randomly in a sequence of frequent stimuli, or to an omission of an expected stimulus, shows a characteristic wave about 300 ms after the surprising event ('P300 wave'; Sutton et al. 1965). Similarly, a characteristic evoked-response brain wave about 400 ms after the stimulus is detected in individuals that encounter an out-of-context word in a sentence reading task ('N400 wave'; Kutas and Hillyard 1980). These are striking physiological correlates that differentiate fast cognitive responses by time and type.

What are the brain circuits involved? In theory, one expects circuits that compare on-line with off-line representations, identify the mismatches, induce other circuits to generate the proper behavioural response, and trigger the proper long-lasting representational change. To be useful ecologically, these circuits must operate in the subsecond range, even if they process input modalities that are considered relatively slow, such as taste (Halpern and Tapper 1971). Plausible candidates are systems that involve *cortex (both frontal and modality specific), thalamocortical, or thalamocortical–brainstem circuits. Consider, for example, the following candidate scheme: on-line information is encoded in the brainstem or cortex or both, off-line

information in the cortex, and the thalamus does the comparisons (Ahissar et al. 1997). Furthermore, there are good reasons to assume that the match/mismatch output signal modulates diffused neuromodulatory systems, such as the cholinergic (*acetylcholine; e.g. Mishkin and Murray 1994; Naor and Dudai 1996), *dopaminergic (e.g. Schultz et al. 1997; Redgrave et al. 1999), or *noradrenergic (e.g. Kitchinga et al. 1997). These neuromodulators are then expected to regulate *intracellular signal transduction cascades in the target neurons, culminating in *synaptic remodelling and ultimately in long-term memory (Berman et al. 1998). Thus at the cellular level, the mechanisms that encode surprise merge with those that encode attention and subserve acquisition of memory. If we delve into the nuts and bolts of these signal transduction cascades, we could even end up with molecular models that account for the ability of surprising information to encode a robust *engram after only a single brief experience, by shifting instantly the balance of the signal transduction cascades and the transcription factors in favour of that configuration that activates the appropriate 'long-term *plasticity genes' (Bartsch et al. 1995; *CREB, *immediate early genes, *fear conditioning, *flashbulb memory).

It is noteworthy that some of the aforementioned studies, especially those involving cellular and molecular analysis, do not target 'surprise' specifically, but rather the reaction to unfamiliar events in general. This should not be taken to imply that unfamiliarity and surprise are utterly identical. Unfamiliarity can be detected by any sensory system with an access to memory; surprise as defined here requires in addition the ability to generate expectations on the basis of organized knowledge. In addition, novelty is a continuous dimension (many inputs are only slightly novel), whereas bona fide surprise is probably more of an abrupt event, conforming to a step function. Still, it is likely that brain mechanisms that subserve detection of surprise overlap with those that subserve the response to unfamiliarity in general. In all theses cases, the brain compares the present to the past. In the case of surprise, an additional faculty is engaged, that of computing expectations and evaluating the significance of their sudden clash with reality, in real-time. We do not know whether even the simplest nervous systems that can detect novelty generate such rudimentary expectations and are engaged in comparison of pre-representations with on-line input (*a priori). In mammals, this ability is contributed, among others, by the frontal cortex (Fuster 1995a; Watanabe 1996; Daffner et al. 2000; *attention, *working memory).

Surprises are effective incentives for behavioural modifications that contribute to survival. This is probably why the ability to detect them had been embedded effectively in our brain. Seen this way, the most important ones are the bad surprises, because they may kill; hence, Darwin was not off-track when he emphasized startling, nasty surprises (Darwin 1872; also 'startle reflex' under *attention, *sensitization). With the emergence of human *culture, our capacity to note mismatches with predictions of organized knowledge has gained additional functions, some of which are geared to create pleasure, not pain. Hence, it is said that surprise and 'defamiliarization' are at the basis of our appreciation of art (Shklovsky 1917). On the more practical side of life, surprises, although still mostly bad ones, contribute to our attitudes as consumers of goods (Maute and Dube 1999). And in the small world of universities, professors can exploit pedagogical surprises to enhance the success of their classes (Kintch and Bates 1977; Thorne 1999).

Selected associations: A Priori, Algorithm, Attention, Dimension, Sensitization

---

Synapse

A specialized junction between neurons, or between neurons and other types of excitable cells, capable of transmitting, processing, and retaining neural information.

The term 'synapse' (Greek for *syn-haptein*, 'to make contact') is commonly attributed to Sherrington (Foster and Sherrington 1897). It was actually proposed by Verrall, an expert on *classical drama, to replace *syndesm* (Greek for 'chained together'), which was Sherrington's first choice (Shepherd and Erulkar 1997). 'Synapse' was preferred because it was judged to yield a better adjectival form. It is left for the reader to judge whether 'synaptic *plasticity' indeed rhymes better than 'syndesic plasticity', but, in any case, it is too late for a change. In the background of the introduction of 'synapse' was one of the most important and heated debates in the history of the neurosciences (e.g. Brazier 1988; Finger 1994). Two 'theories' (*model) concerning the cellular organization of the nervous system coexisted toward the end of the nineteenth century. One, 'the reticular theory of nervous organization', promoted among others by Golgi, held that nerve cells are physically interconnected to form an uninterrupted web

(reticulum). This theory held the contacts between the extensions that branch of neuronal cell bodies are only specializations in a fused continuum of tissue. The opposing theory, dubbed 'the neuron theory' or 'the neuron doctrine', promoted among others by Cajal, held that nerve cells are discrete entities.[1] According to this doctrine, the junctions between neurons are specialized miniature devices that engage the juxtaposed individual units in the net. The neuron doctrine triumphed, although not without some skirmishes waged by the retreating 'reticularists' well into the twentieth century (Szentagothai 1975). Sherrington was a neurophysiologist who trusted that nerves terminate in free endings and that the transfer of information from these endings to their targets differs markedly from the propagation of information along neuronal branches. When requested to revise his contribution to an authoritative textbook of physiology (Foster and Sherrington 1897), he reasoned that as research on the functional junction between nerve cells had already matured to become an important topic in physiology, this type of junction deserved a special term. Hence the 'synapse' was born.

Synapses come in many flavours. They can be classified by their morphology, location, function (e.g. inhibitory vs. facilitatory), types of *neurotransmitters and their *receptors, etc. A major *taxonomy distinguishes 'chemical' from 'electrical' synapses. In chemical synapses, information is transmitted from one cell to another by chemical messages (neurotransmitters) over an intercellular gap. In electrical synapses, there is direct electrical communication between the juxtaposed cells by way of a specialized contact, called 'gap junction', which contains *channel complexes called 'connexons' (Goodenough *et al.* 1996). Two connexons, each contributed by one of the juxtaposed cells, interact, and align to form an intercellular channel, which subserves electrical coupling and exchange of small molecules. Cell–cell 'on-line interneting' via connexons occurs in many types of tissues. Electrical synapses are hence specializations in the nervous system of a ubiquitous type of cellular device that allows direct communication and synchronization of activity between adjacent cells. Communication via electrical synapses is fast but the direct coupling imposes some constraints, such as the inability to reverse the sign of the signal or amplify it on location. Electrical synapses do, however, display use-dependent plasticity, which may involve *intracellular signalling cascades triggered by chemical transmitters (Goodenough *et al.* 1996; Pereda and Faber 1996). Synaptic complexes that share elements of both electrical and chemical transmission are termed 'mixed synapses'. An example for the use of electrical synapses in the mammalian brain is provided by widespread networks of inhibitory neurons in the *cerebral cortex (Gibson *et al.* 1999). So far, electrical synapses have received less attention than chemical synapses, but recent years have witnessed a growing interest in their function in the brain.

As noted above, in chemical synapses, in contrast to electrical synapses, the two opposing neurons are separated by an intercellular gap, called the 'synaptic cleft'. The use of 'gap' or 'cleft' does not imply void; there is a rich microcosm in between the pre- and the postsynaptic membranes, and some of the molecules physically bridge the two sides. It is also noteworthy that, although we now take it for granted that chemical synapses exchange chemical messages, the nature of the information transmitted over the synaptic cleft in such synapses had been debated over many years. Two types of possibilities were considered. One, that the information is mediated by electric currents. The other, that it is transmitted by chemical substances. The existence of chemical transmission in the neuromuscular junction was proposed by Du Bois-Reymond in 1877 (cited in Dale 1938). A series of investigations conducted independently by Lewandowsky, Langley, Elliot and later Dale, Loewi, and others have provided convincing evidence

for chemical ('neurohumoral') transmission (Elliot 1904; Dale 1938, 1954; also *acetylcholine, *noradrenaline). The evidence had been provided first for synapses in the peripheral nervous system and only later for the central nervous system. Actually, for a while, some leading investigators considered chemical messages too sluggish to be useful for fast communication in the central nervous system. Notable among them was Eccles (1982). But even the lingering opposition finally succumbed to the data: 'Eccles and his team concluded that … (transmission) could only be due to the release of a chemical agent from the endings of the afferent fibre … A remarkable conversion indeed! One is reminded, almost inevitably, of Saul on his way to Damascus, when the sudden light shone and the scales fell from his eyes' (Dale 1954).

Since their discovery, it has been realized that synapses are faced with an inherently tough job. Basically, they have to transmit information (*stimulus) with acceptable fidelity. But they had also been evolved into miniature transducers that filter, encode, process, modulate, associate and register chunks of that information for their own use and for the sake of the circuit. Accordingly, in the discipline of memory research, synaptic components have been assigned roles of elements in

(a) (b)

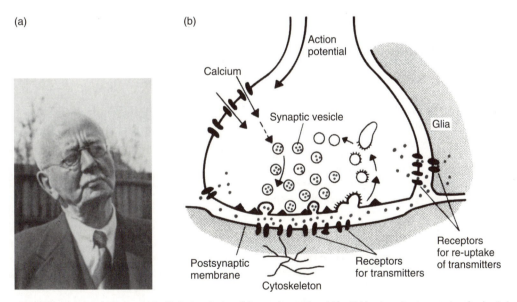

Fig. 62 (a) Sherrington, who is accredited with the introduction of the term 'synapse', and (b) a highly schematic representation of a chemical synapse. Only a few elements of the synapse are shown. The postsynaptic terminal and an adjacent glia cell are depicted in grey. Glia cells (from the Greek 'glue') are traditionally considered to provide neurons with physical and metabolic support; although it is now clear that they do much more (Araque *et al.* 1999; Ullian *et al.* 2001), their exact role in synaptic communication and in synaptic plasticity is still mostly an *enigma. For more on synaptic components and their function, see *calcium, *ion channel, *neurotransmitter, *receptor.

miniature learning machines, such as *acquisition devices, *coincidence detectors and associators, storage devices, etc. (Dudai 1993; *Aplysia, *Drosophila, *long-term potentiation).[2] The synaptic job is carried out by webs of macromolecules in the presynaptic and the postsynaptic terminals. Parts of this web extend into the synaptic cleft as well. The macromolecular web includes *ion channels, *receptors, cytoskeleton, adhesion molecules, and more (Kuno 1995; Hagler and Goda 1998; Kim and Huganir 1999). The presynaptic terminal contains a highly specialized apparatus for transmitter release (Kuno 1995; Schiavo et al. 1995; Geppert and Sudhof 1998), regulated, inter alia, by presynaptic receptors for the same or other transmitters (Langer 1997; Miller 1998). The structure and function of the synaptic machinery is a dynamic function of the stage in *development, the individual experience of the synapse, and the ambient extracellular and intracellular input (e.g. *calcium; *glutamate; Okabe et al. 1999; Thomson 2000). Plastic changes could manifest themselves in anything from gradual alterations in synaptic efficacy, subserved by pre-, post-, or pre + postsynaptic mechanisms (Jessel and Kandel 1993; Markram et al. 1998; Thomson 2000), to a transformation from a silent synapse to one that starts talking (Atwood and Wojtowicz 1999). Some manifestations of synaptic *plasticity last for a fraction of a second to a few seconds only, but other forms of synaptic plasticity could last much longer (*long-term potentiation). To reshape itself in the long term, the synapse apparently takes advantage of local as well as cell-wide *protein synthesis facilities (Steward 1997; Casadio et al. 1999; Gardiol et al. 1999).

The notion that synaptic plasticity subserves developmental and behavioural plasticity is a tenet of neuroscience. In the neurobiology of memory as well as in *modelling, the twentieth century was in many respects the century of the synapse. It has become the major and sometimes the sole focus of attention at the molecular, cellular, and circuit *levels of analysis. The synapse was also identified as the prime target for multiple types of neuroactive drugs, including some that affect memory (*lotus, *nootropics). The popularity of the synapse stems from a smart choice of a domineering *reductive research programme, and from the availability of certain advanced research *methodologies. It is tempting to predict that in the twenty-first century, analysis of the synapse will become even further integrated into the analysis of *internal representations and their experience-dependent modification at the circuit and system level. The data so far do tell us that synapses are critical in making memories. But synapses may not be

sufficient and even more so exclusive agents in establishing a memory (*criteria). Because they are so interesting and captivating, and because we find them more or less amenable to analysis, becoming immersed in the fascinating world of the synapse could easily make one forget what the ultimate goal of memory research is. As far as memory is concerned, what counts for the behaving brain is not the individual synapse but rather the integrated contribution of many synapses to the coherent activity of the networks in which they operate.

Selected associations: Algorithm, Ion channel, Long-term potentiation, Plasticity, Reduction

---

[1]When the term 'synapse' was introduced, the term 'neuron' had itself been a newcomer to the scientific jargon. It was coined by Waldeyer (1891), an ardent supporter of Cajal's neuron doctrine, only a few years earlier.

[2]Beware, however, of the '*homunculus fallacy', which equates the behaviour of the synapse with the behaviour of the brain or even the organism.

System

1. A set of units and their interrelationships.
2. A group of related elements organized for a purpose.
3. A portion of the universe selected for study.

'System' (from sunistanai, 'to combine' in Greek) is abundant in colloquial 'scientinglish'. 'Let me tell you about my system' or 'did you try it in your system' are only selected examples of ritualistic utterances of scientific *culture. An experimental system well-matched to the research goal is a key to successful research programmes. Prolific systems facilitate the road to academic tenure and fame, and trendy systems increase the probability of acceptance of manuscripts into respectable scientific journals. The popularity of 'system', therefore, deserves an attempt to put some order to the system.

What are systems? In the most general sense all systems are sets of interconnected units (definition 1). These units may be either concrete (e.g. parts of a machine) or abstract (e.g. concepts in a theory). In some cases the system is delineated on the basis of its assumed purpose (definition 2), but the teleological raison d'être may exist only in the eyes of the beholder. Even more anthropocentric is the view that a system is defined by its being selected for analysis (definition 3). None of these definitions assumes anything about the composition, size, semantics, and goal of the system. Systems hence vary tremendously in their scale and complexity, dependence on other systems, interdependence of subsystems, function, and dynamics (e.g. Simon and Ando 1961; Mesarovic *et al.* 1970; Houk 1980*b*; Bhalla and Iyengar 1999).

The existence of systems. Systems may be either natural kinds or *artefacts. In many cases they are both. Consider memory research. 'Non*declarative memory' is a heuristic term referring to an artefactual system; it is highly unlikely that all memory faculties included under the umbrella of this term indeed comprise a natural system. The hippocampal system (see *hippocampus) is a reasonable candidate for a natural system but its boundaries are not known for sure. The status of the *amygdala as a natural system is unclear. And is the cyclic adenosine monophosphate cascade (*intracellular signal transduction cascades) a natural kind or an artefact of erroneous *taxonomy?

The boundaries of systems. Systems impermeable to the rest of the universe are termed 'closed'. Those with permeable boundaries are 'open'. In open systems, the variables determined by causes extrinsic to the system are 'input', whereas those dependent upon the action of the system are 'output'. In reality absolute impermeability is nonexistent, but the level of input and output may be extremely low. Open systems differ in their openness. Living systems are open but semipermeable, i.e. they allow some inputs but not others. For example, a neuron is encircled by a semipermeable membrane that allows only selective flux of materials (*ion channel, *receptor).

The relation of systems to other systems. From the aforementioned description it becomes evident that considering any system as truly independent of other systems is an illusion. Systems always harbour other systems and are themselves parts of still others. A paranoiac conclusion is that systems are everywhere, and that everything is a system (for additional notes on the intractability of systems, see Gall 1986). The question arises, therefore, can we deal satisfactorily with variables in a system irrespective of variables in other related systems (*control)? Luckily, the prerogative of a scientist is to decide what 'satisfactorily' is in any given system, so that practically we may decide that interactions below a certain level are ignored. The assumption that variables outside the system are held for all practical means constant (and hence are irrelevant) is referred to as the *ceteris paribus* assumption (Latin for

'other things being equal'). The usefulness of certain *simple systems derives from a focus on one or a few variables combined with adaptation of the *ceteris paribus* assumption.

The generality of systems. Systems chosen for analysis differ in their claim for generality. Some are 'types', others 'tokens'. Type is a class, or a *taxonomic entity, possibly an abstraction only, characterized by sameness in certain *dimensions. Tokens are the particulars that instantiate the type. For example, in the previous sentence as well as in this present one, the word 'the' appears twice, but it is only one word. Hence, those were more than once, tokens of the type 'the'.[1] The distinction between types and tokens depends on the *level of analysis and discourse. *Glutamatergic receptors are tokens of the type '*receptor', but *N*-methyl-D-aspartate (NMDA) receptors (NMDAR) are tokens of the type 'glutamatergic receptors', and copies of the NMDAR are tokens of the type NMDAR. Usually the selection of a system for investigation (or of *models) is driven by a wish to understand the type by studying the token. For example, selection of *Aplysia* as a model system for the analysis of learning and memory, was not guided by an irresistible urge to comprehend the mental life of a slug, but rather by the realization that it provides convenient advantages that might allow understanding of types of simple learning. In general, defining the understanding of a type as the immediate objective of the research programme is mostly impractical, for the research itself always boils down to the analysis of tokens. But if we were to conclude that no tokens could illuminate anything about the (hypothetical) corresponding types, many investigators would have lost interest in their systems.

Information and systems. Systems encode information, although in our current understanding of brain systems we rarely understand for sure what the specific information is. It is pertinent to note that 'information' has different meanings in different treatments. In everyday language, 'information' refers to knowledge, i.e. the meaning and significance ('semantics') of input and output. In contrast, in information theory, 'information' is a mathematical abstraction that refers to the uncertainty in coding and transmitting data, irrespective of the semantics (Shannon and Weaver 1949; Wiener 1961; Pierce 1961; *stimulus). This efficacy of transfer is measured in 'bits'. One bit (*binary digit*) is the choice between two equal likely possibilities. Selection of one of four alternatives requires two bits, and so on; the more alternatives, the more bits are needed to select among them. The number of bits required to select among n alternatives is log$_2$ n. Even if the number of bits is known, it tells us nothing about what these bits signify to neither the sender nor the receiver. A major goal of the neurosciences is to decipher not only the 'information' processed by a nervous system, but also to unveil its meaning (*capacity, *internal representation).

Mental and physical systems. Memory, at least in its more complex manifestations, connotes mental activity. In discussing memory systems it is therefore pertinent to ask what distinguishes mental from physical systems. By posing this question one does not, of course, claim that mental systems are not physical; the issue is merely what turns 'mental' mental. A traditional criterion is that mental systems display 'intentionality', whereas physical systems do not (Brentano 1874). In philosophy, 'intentionality' is 'aboutness'; mental systems exist in states ('intentional states') which are about something, for example, belief, hope, etc. In fact, in most of the systems studied in the biology of memory, the distinction between the mental and the physical is not an acute issue, especially if the system in question is simple and the experimental approach highly *reductive. However, when one approaches issues such as complex *declarative representations, *planning, and possibly even highly developed capabilities of *observational learning, the issue becomes relevant, although not necessarily solvable.

Selection of a system. So how should one select a system for the investigation of memory? Idiosyncratic *bias and training background notwithstanding, several considerations are still noteworthy. First, it is useful to choose a system that provides optimal access to the *methods and level of analysis that one wishes to pursue. In other words, as in many other facets of life, the trick is to match aspiration, capability, and availability all together. Second, although one may wish to illuminate a type, in practice a useful token must be selected, which allows fragmenting the problem into approachable segments. Further, the *ceteris paribus* prerogative should be exploited liberally, yet without being too serious about its validity. And third, never lure yourself to think that you know everything about your system. At the end of the day, sometimes even in its beginning, it will tear off its disguise and present itself as a metasystem or a subsystem of yet another unfamiliar system.

Selected associations: Anthropomorphism, Bias, Generalization, Model, Subject

---

[1]The distinction between 'type' and 'token' goes back to the physicist and philosopher Peirce in the nineteenth century, but itself is a token

manifestation of a much older type distinction between 'universals' and 'particulars'; see Armstrong 1989; also on 'realists' vs. 'nominalists' in *Ockham's razor.

Taxonomy

The systematic grouping of entities into categories according to some *method of arrangement or distribution; classification.

The tendency to categorize the world into 'similar' and 'different' is fundamental to human cognition. It underlies folk knowledge systems in orally-reliant societies as well as sophisticated taxonomies in science (Durkheim 1912; Levi-Strauss 1962; Smith and Medin 1981; Sokal 1985; Berlin 1992). It is shared to some degree even by species far remote from us on the phylogenetic scale (Giurfa *et al.* 1996). The term 'taxonomy' itself is, however, a newcomer to language: *taxinomie*, or *taxonomie*, was introduced in 1813 into French to denote classification of entities, and the discipline that deals with such classifications (from *taxis+ nomie*, meaning *arrangement+ method* in Greek; Le Maxidico 1996). It then found its way into English. In biology, 'taxonomy' came to be associated predominantly with the discipline that classifies biological species (Mayr 1981). But the term is also widely used in other domains of knowledge to denote classifications of a variety of natural kinds, concepts, and artefacts.

A major issue concerning taxonomies of natural entities is whether they represent 'natural' types or only creations of the human mind. Some claim that 'natural' reflects the state of affairs in nature; others that it only reflects the capacities of the human mind; and still others that both the above coincide, as the human mind is expected to have evolved to equate 'natural' in nature with 'natural' in mind (Sokal 1985). A potential clash of 'natural in mind' and 'natural in nature' is illustrated in the taxonomy of biological species: early schools of taxonomy relied on the phenotypic similarity of organisms and therefore shared much with primitive taxonomies; later taxonomies already rely on the more refined scientific understanding of phylogenesis (Mayr 1981; Sokal 1985). Certain classifications do appear intuitively 'unnatural'. Consider, for example, the fictitious taxonomy attributed by Borges (1952) to a Chinese encyclopaedia, *Celestial emporium of benevolent knowledge.* According to this, animals are divided into: '(a) those that belong to the Emperor,

(b) embalmed ones, (c) those that are trained, (d) suckling pigs, (e) mermaids, (f) fabulous ones, (g) stray dogs, (h) those that are included in this classification, (i) those that tremble as if they were mad, (j) innumerable ones, (k) those drawn with a very fine camel's hair brush, (l) others, (m) those that have just broken a flower vase, (n) those that resemble flies from a distance'. The beauty of this taxonomy is in its poetic oddity (*surprise). However, as classifications are intended to facilitate handling and analysis of information, even the aforementioned emporium could have made some sense from the point of view of a ruling Emperor. Further, we should not forget that to the modern mind, 'primitive' classifications of natural phenomena may appear rather confused, even though they were considered perfectly logical to the contemporary mind (Hallpike 1979). For example, the Greek world was depicted as composed of four basic elements, water, air, fire and earth (Plato, *Timaeus* 32b–c); hence taxonomies are *culture dependent and what is regarded as 'natural' in 2001 may not be so in 2100.

Taxonomies prevail at every branch of knowledge and *level of analysis. Examples in the neurosciences are types of neurons, glia, *ion channels, *receptors, *neurotransmitters, *intracellular signal transduction cascades, neuronal firing patterns, brain regions and pathways, etc. These 'types' contain multiple 'tokens', i.e. specimens or instances of the type (Dudai 1993; *system). The taxonomy most characteristic of memory research is no doubt that of memory itself. 'Memory system' could be described as an organized structure of interconnected neural substrates, encoding experience-dependent *representations that subserve some characteristic type(s) of behavioural and cognitive function(s) (Tulving 1985; but see below). Each system could hence be specified by phenotypic, functional, structural, and possibly phylogenetic *criteria (e.g. Tolman 1949; Sherry and Schacter 1987; Shettleworth 1993; Schacter and Tulving 1994).

The mere notion that memory is not monolithic pre-dates science. Over the years, multiple axes or *dimensions have been used to classify memory. For example, sensory *modality*: 'In memory, all things are kept distinct and according to kind. Each is brought in through its own proper entrance: the light and all the colors ... all these enter in, each by its own gateway, and are laid away within it ...' (Augustine 400). Or *duration*, i.e. whether short or long lived (James 1890; Hebb 1949; *phase). Or *actualization*, i.e. whether active or inactive at a given point in time (Lewis 1979; *retrieval). Or the *processes* that drive the system, either top-down, concept-driven, or bottom-up, data-driven

(Roediger 1990).[1] Additional candidate dimensions are illustrated in *collective memory, *dimension, *learning, *prospective memory. Most taxonomies of memory are not mutually exclusive; one could consider a short-term, visual memory, or an inactive, long-term memory.

A cardinal *criterion in the prevailing taxonomy of long-term memory is that of *conscious awareness, i.e. whether the information is accessible to conscious recollection or not. This type of dichotomy was imported into modern neuroscience from philosophy. Kant (1781) distinguished representations with or without consciousness; de Biran (1804) spoke of 'mechanical memory', in which recall is a 'simple repetition of movements', and 'representative memory', in which recall involves 'the clear appearance of ...(an) idea'; Bergson (1908) differentiated between habit, the 'memory that repeats', and 'memory per excellence', or 'the memory that imagines'; and Ryle (1949) distinguished 'knowing how' from 'knowing that'. 'Knowing how' is also known as 'practical knowledge', and 'knowing that' as 'propositional' or 'factual knowledge' (Bernecker and Dretske 2000).

The 'that' vs. 'how' dichotomy is supported by analysis of memory deficits in human *amnesics and to a certain degree by animal *models of amnesia (Mishkin *et al.* 1984; Squire and Zola 1996; Eichenbaum 1997a). Accordingly, the current *zeitgeist taxonomy of memory systems in the brain sciences depicts two metasystems of long-term memory, *declarative (the 'that' system, alias 'explicit') and nondeclarative (the 'how' system, alias 'implicit') (Schacter 1987; Squire and Zola 1996; Figure 63). Declarative memory is further divided into memory for facts ('semantic') and for events ('episodic', 'autobiographical', Tulving 1983). Some authors draw a distinction between 'episodic' and 'declarative' (Tulving and Markowitsch 1998). Similarly, in epistemology, 'knowledge by acquaintance', i.e. of people, places, and things, is distinguished from propositional or factual knowledge (Bernecker and Dretske 2000).

Declarative memory is subserved by diencephalic and mediotemporal structures (*cerebral cortex, *hippocampus, *limbic system). Some authors propose that brain systems that subserve *episodic and semantic memory are partially dissociable, with only episodic memory being fully dependent on the hippocampus (Vargha-Khadem *et al.* 1997; see Tulving and Markowitsch 1998 for support of this view, and Squire and Zola 1998 for a different position). Nondeclarative memory is commonly further subdivided into the following systems (Figure 63): (a) non*associative

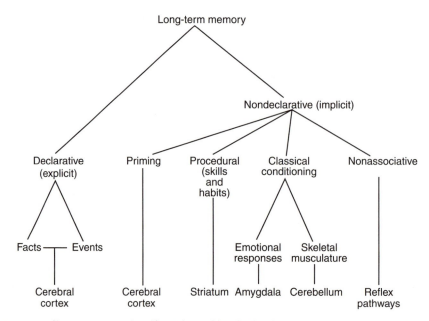

Fig. 63 A taxonomy of long-term memory, adapted from Milner et al. (1998). Selected brain areas that subserve each type of memory system are indicated at the bottom of the diagram.

memory, i.e. *habituation, and *sensitization, sub-served by specific reflex pathways; (b) *classical condi-tioning, which is further classified into conditioning of musculoskeletal reflexes, subserved among others by the *cerebellum, and conditioning of emotional responses, subserved among others by the *amygdala (*fear conditioning); (c) procedural memory, i.e. mem-ory for *habits and *skills, subserved by a corticostriatal system; and (d) *priming, which, in its multiple variants, is believed to be subserved by cortex. It can be readily seen that, whereas the classification of declarative memory is based on a unified concept and seems 'natural', non-declarative memory is defined by exclusion, and its subtaxa are rather hetero-geneous.

The zeitgeist taxonomy of long-term memory systems evokes several types of interrelated problems:

1. *Criteria.* The notorious 'problem of the criterion' pops up again. In order to classify correctly we must know a lot about the system, but in order to know a lot about the system we must be able to classify it correctly. What shall we use as the decisive criterion for the delineation of a memory system? Common behavioural (phenomenological) properties? The faculties affected by circumscribed brain lesions? The evolutionary history of parts of the brain? As mentioned above, Tulving (1985a) proposes to

consider both functional neuroanatomy and behav-iour, but the same brain structure could contribute to different tasks, and a seemingly similar behav-ioural output could reflect different computational goals and *algorithms. For example, perceptual and conceptual priming both involve nonconscious modulation of the processing, retrieval, or produc-tion of a mental item by prior exposure to specific information on that item or on items associated with it. But one could come up with very different systems that share this property. So is there a natural 'priming system' in the brain?[2]

2. Which leads to the issues of *system vs. process* and *system vs. attribute.* Is priming a memory system, or is it a cross-the-board process, or a manifestation of automaticity of different processes, shared by *skill systems (e.g. Logan 1990)?

3. Which leads to the issue of *superfluity.* This taps into the tension between the mind's tendency to classify and the continuity of nature (Aristotle, *Parts of Animals* 642b5–644a12; for selected examples see *amygdala and *limbic system). For it is rather easy and even appealing to come up with new types of memory systems, and the minute they are pro-posed, to come up with neurobiological and behav-ioural justification, turning the tentative proposal into a premature *fait accompli.*

4. Which leads to the other facet of the coin, *generalization*. We could err in grouping into a unified memory system the capabilities of species far remote on the phylogenetic scale. For example, to regard some memory performances in rodents as declarative as opposed to nondeclarative may overgeneralize and disregard the accomplishments of the evolution of the primates. 'Implicit' vs. 'explicit' may better fit the tests used, but again, the issue of whether even these terms apply to lower invertebrates, which are on a different branch of evolution, is questionable. Disregarding this difficulty could culminate in the pursuit of *red herrings. Hence taxonomy should be better used a heuristic aid to research rather than a guiding criterion.

Selected associations: Criterion, Dimension, Model, Memory, System

---

[1]On additional aspects of top-down vs. bottom-up processing, see *attention, *binding, and *insight.

[2]This question makes sense only if we consider definitions 1 and 2 of *system. Definition 3 of *system leaves us with the convenient freedom to declare anything a 'system'.

Transfer

The contribution of experience on one task to *performance on a subsequently different task.

Teachers have appreciated transfer much before neurobiologists did. The teachings of the *classics, when practised, were not necessarily for school children to become experts in Homer or Virgil. The idea was that such studies have a general disciplinary value that will be transferred to the intellect at large. This is why educational psychologists were driven to investigate transfer. They had to prove that some educational *methods do have merit. In doing so they have also developed basic research methodologies of tremendous value. Consider, for example, the use of *control groups: it was introduced in research on transfer in schooling (Thorndike and Woodworth 1901*a,b*; Coover and Angell 1907). A brief example should suffice to illustrate this type of early studies: a group of schoolgirls in London were instructed to memorize a history text and subsequently tested for their *recall. The girls were then divided into two groups. Group A practised poetry over 2 weeks, whereas group B was engaged in working

sums. Both groups were later subjected again to a history test. Although both groups got the same score on the first history test, group A fared much better on the final history test. The conclusion was that improvement gained by practise in memorizing one subject of instruction (poetry) was transferred to memory work in other subjects (history): '…the results do appear… to strengthen the case of those who wish children to learn much poetry; it is not an obstacle, but an aid, to the acquisition of other knowledge' (Winch 1908).

Transfer is said to be 'positive' if the experience on the first task results in improvement on the subsequent task, and 'negative' if that experience on the first task impairs the performance on the subsequent task (e.g. Woltz *et al.* 2000). Of course, experience on task *i* could result in positive transfer on task *j* but negative transfer on task *k*. As transfer is such a comprehensive term, qualifiers are used to specify the type of transfer under consideration. Only the two major uses of the term will be outlined here:

1. *Transfer of training* refers to the contribution of training on one *skill to the performance on a different skill. Some authors use the terms 'transfer of training' and 'transfer' interchangeably. However, in the behavioural literature 'transfer of training' conventionally implies intentional training on a particular overt behaviour, whereas 'transfer' extends also to higher cognitive processes such as the formation of concepts and hypotheses (see below). This distinction notwithstanding, the demonstration of transfer of training in even 'simple' *classical or *instrumental conditioning may also involve the formation of hypotheses and concepts (e.g. Schusterman 1962; *learning set). The study of Winch (1908), mentioned above, epitomizes a simple transfer of training experiment. Multiple protocols of transfer of training have been developed, and with them measures of the efficacy of transfer (Gagne *et al.* 1948; Murdock 1957; Hammerton 1967; Kolers and Roediger 1984). These measures commonly reflect better performance on the initial encounter with the new task, or 'saving' of training time or trials (on 'saving', see also *experimental extinction). Clearly, efficient transfer of training procedures is of great practical importance, as it could save time and money on training for specific jobs, either in the real situation or in simulators (Hammerton 1967; Hammerton and Tickner 1967).

In our discussion so far we have considered transfer of training as an intertask phenomenon. A somewhat different point of view propounds that even in what is formally considered by the experimenter as a single task, *recall is actually a 'retrieval task' that replays the '*acquisition task'. As a consequence, performance on retrieval could benefit from transfer of experience on acquisition. This is further discussed as 'transfer appropriate processing' (Morris *et al.* 1977) under *retrieval.

2. *Analogical transfer* refers to the use of a familiar problem to solve a novel problem of a similar type (Gick and Holyoak 1983; Reeves and Weisberg 1994). The familiar problem is dubbed the 'source problem', 'base analogue', or 'base domain', and the new problem the 'target problem' or 'target domain'. For example, the popular depiction of the Rutherford model of the atom uses an analogy to the solar system (the base domain) to understand atomic structure (the target domain); the nucleus is depicted as the sun and the electrons as the stars (Gentner 1983). Much of our thinking is subserved by noticing similarities and analogies and generating *metaphors (Tversky 1977; Gibbs 1994). It is doubtful whether we could construe the world otherwise, although probably only a minority of scientists would agree with Nietzche that 'truth is a moving army of metaphors' (Nietzche 1873). By the way, 'metaphor' in Greek means 'transfer', in the colloquial meaning of 'transfer'.

Over the years, a number of 'theories', or *models, of analogical transfer have been advanced (Reeves and Weisberg 1994). They propose multiple stages in analogical transfer. First, there is the *acquisition of information about the base and target domains. This could occur long before the attempt is being made to solve the problem. Next there is the noticing of the base domain and its relevance. This critical stage echoes *insight. Next comes the application of the analogy to the target domain. If hints are provided, the situation is termed 'informed transfer'; otherwise, it is 'spontaneous transfer'. What type of information is used by the brain in doing all this? It helps to realize that problems can be defined at multiple *levels of information. The visible details of the particular problem are elements of the 'surface structure' of the problem, whereas the underlying abstract rules and principles comprise the 'deep structure'. Problems with different surface structures could share a deep structure. One aspect in which models of analogical transfer differ is their view of the relative contribution of 'surface' and 'deep' structures, or of data and *stimuli vs. rules, to the successful analogy (Reeves and Weisberg 1994; for a window to related debates in the cognitive sciences, see Gentner and Medina 1998).

A widely cited example will serve to illustrate the surface and deep structure. In this example, a problem entitled 'the radiation problem' is the target problem, and another, 'the general problem', the base problem (Gick and Holyoak 1983). The radiation problem is about a physician, who is faced with a patient with a malignant, life-threatening stomach tumour. It is impossible to operate on the patient. Radiation can destroy the tumour, but at the desired intensity the ray will destroy the healthy tissue on the way to the tumour. Lower density radiation is harmless to the healthy tissue but will not affect the tumour either. What shall the physician do? Now, here is the general problem: a country is ruled from a strong fortress by a dictator. A rebel army general leads his army to capture the fortress. Many roads lead to the fortress from different directions. All of them are mined. The mines are set to be detonated by the passage of large army units but not by small units. An attack by the entire army at once, which otherwise would capture the fortress, will detonate the mines. The solution: dispatch the soldiers in small units via many roads so that the entire army arrives together at the fortress at the same time. Subjects given the general problem were more likely to solve the radiation problem. Its solution: reduce the intensity of the rays but irradiate from several directions simultaneously (this is actually the correct clinical procedure). The two problems differ in their surface elements (physician, patient, hospital, vs. general, fortress, army, etc.), but share a deep structure (disjoining followed by *coincident convergence).

Transfer protocols are incorporated into a variety of studies on *engrams (e.g. Karni and Bertini 1997; Buckley and Gaffan 1998). They are used among others to measure the *generalization and extent of learning as a function of the activity (or damage) in a particular brain area. The identity of the brain areas involved depends on the paradigm used; for example, somatosensory *cortex in motor skill. It is not yet established which brain areas are specifically critical for analogical transfer, although the frontal cortex is a safe bet.

A timely issue concerning transfer relates to the interplay between the extent of generalization of knowledge that is required to support transfer on the one hand, and the extensive specialization demanded from modern technological society on the other. To be effective, transfer must involve some degree of similarity, in data, procedures, rules, or cognitive *maps, between the source and the target tasks. Modern technology encourages more and more differentiation and specialization in order to master skills at an expert level. This may reduce substantially the overlap between old and new skills. How will it affect our ability to transfer knowledge from previous to future jobs? The problem surely calls for rethinking and identification of those cognitive skills that could promote efficient transfer of knowledge from what we know today to what we will have to know tomorrow. The impact on our educational and training systems might be profound.

Selected associations: Acquisition, Generalization, Learning set, Priming

Working memory

1. **A memory *system that holds information in temporary storage during the *planning and execution of a task.**
2. **The process in which newly *perceived information is combined with *retrieved information during the planning and execution of a task, to form and maintain short-lived *internal representations that guide the behavioural response.**

'Working memory' is one of the most important and exciting concepts in modern neuroscience, and rightly so. It refers to a cognitive faculty that is essential for mentation and complex behaviour. This faculty subserves much of our ability to interact with the world in a flexible and intelligent manner, and is essential for thought, planning, and language. For example, reading these lines and combining them into a meaningful message, requires working memory. It is doubtful whether without working memory there would have been a Homer, a Shakespeare, a Mozart, or a Newton, and an audience to appreciate them. A mind without working memory is thus expected to be a rather dull place.

The idea that there should be a cognitive faculty that 'holds things in mind' temporarily, probably occurred long ago to thoughtful individuals while practising their own working memory. The term 'working memory' itself was introduced by Miller *et al.* (1960) in referring to a postulated quick-access brain space where plans can be retained temporarily while they are being formed, manipulated, and executed. Working memory is hence some type of 'short-term memory' (Baddeley 1986; *phase). However, despite the overlap, 'short-term' and 'working' memory are not the same. Generally speaking, 'short-term memory' is a more comprehensive term, which refers to all internal representations that last for only a short while. It is a universal faculty of nervous systems that can learn. In contrast, 'working memory' combines *attention,

short- and long-term memory, retrieval, computations over representations, and planning and decision making, to yield goal-directed short-lived internal representations. It is engaged in on-line processing of data from sensory channels (*percepts) as well as from long-term stores, and maintains the selected representations in a limited *capacity store only until the task is completed. The faculty of working memory is considered to have reached its pinnacle in primates and especially in humans, where it takes years to mature (Luciana and Nelson 1998). Species other than primates display rudimentary capabilities of working memory, e.g. rats while navigating in a *maze or solving olfactory riddles (Olton 1979; Staubli *et al.* 1995; Mumby 1995).

An influential cognitive *model of working memory considers three types of components: a 'central executive', 'phonological loop', and 'visuospatial sketchpad' (Baddeley and Hitch 1974; Baddeley 1986). The 'central executive' is an attentional control system, the 'phonological loop' deals with speech-based information, and the 'visuospatial sketchpad' with visual and spatial information.[1] In recent years, many efforts have been devoted in an attempt to map in the brain the postulated central executive and its subordinate functions. In the process, much has been learned about candidate brain substrates of working memory in primates. In the *monkey, the data are based on circumscribed brain lesions, cellular recordings, and their correlation with performance on *delay tasks that are considered to tax working memory (e.g. Goldman-Rakic 1992). In humans, the data are based on the study of the behaviour of selected brain-damaged patients, as well as on the *functional neuroimaging of patients or healthy volunteers, using tests that tax visuospatial or verbal working memory (e.g. Paulesu *et al.* 1993; Bechara *et al.* 1998; E.E. Smith *et al.* 1998; Ungerleider *et al.* 1998; Prabhakaran *et al.* 2000).

In a nutshell, the findings indicate that working memory is subserved by multiple distributed systems, which vary in their identity from one type of working memory task to another. In all cases, however, the frontal lobe plays a central part (Miller *et al.* 1960; Fuster 2000*b*). Within the frontal lobe, there is division of labour, which appears more intricate as one increases the resolution of the experimental techniques and the sophistication of their use. The dorsolateral and ventrolateral prefrontal cortex differ in their contribution to various types of working memory tasks, but the functional determinants of the specialization and subspecialization are not yet clear. These determinants may relate to the type of information processed (e.g. visual vs. verbal); to the role in maintaining internal representation over the task as opposed to selecting information from other brain areas; and to other attributes of the computations performed over multiple types of information (Petrides 1995; Goldman-Rakic 1996; Ó Scalaidhe *et al.* 1997; Owen 1997; Rushworth *et al.* 1997; Rowe *et al.* 2000). Some of the neurobiological findings so far can be construed within the framework of the aforementioned Baddeley–Hitch model (Baddeley 1998). In addition to the dorsoventral prefrontal dissociations, at least in humans, laterality also counts: the left hemisphere plays a more prominent part in the proposed 'phonological loop', whereas the proposed 'visuospatial sketchpad' is subserved primarily by the right hemisphere (Baddeley 1998; E.E. Smith *et al.* 1998). The location of the hypothetical 'central executive' (Goldman-Rakic 1996; Roberts *et al.* 1996; Baddeley 1998; Carpenter *et al.* 2000) is also not yet established. It is probably embodied in the operation of parallel, distributed polymodal circuits (*homunculus).

To the student of memory, the cellular basis of working memory offers a conceptual challenge (Goldman-Rakic 1995, 1996; *dopamine). Working memory is designed specifically to hold information only transiently. In other memory systems, often the trick is to retain information over an extended period of time, whereas here, it is to prevent the information from lingering too long and interfering with subsequent thought and action. Are the cellular mechanisms

of working memory different from those in other memory circuits? For example, do incoming signals in working memory circuits activate *immediate early and *late response genes, culminating in cellular remodelling? If so, what is the role of these changes, provided that working memory is not stored in the long term? Or is some type of memory stored even here in the long term? Are fast molecular 'memory erasures' involved (e.g. see protein phosphatases in *protein kinase)? Or is the gimmick in the unique mode of operation of the circuit? Studies of working memory may eventually affect current conceptual *paradigms concerning the role of cellular change in the retention of internal representations.

Finally, a note on terminology. In discussions of human memory, the concept of working memory is occasionally extended to include those situations in which information is being held temporarily for periods much longer than just the few seconds it takes to execute an ongoing cognitive task. For example, suppose I travel to a scientific meeting out of town; I remember the number of my hotel room as long as I am there, say a day or two, and then get rid of this information as it becomes useless. Is this 'working memory'? By some accounts it is, because it is a piece of temporary information that is usable only for the purpose of a transient task, in this case, getting back to my room. But on a second thought, it is not. Essential to the original concept of working memory is the active use of the memory (*taxonomy) under *attentional control* throughout the execution of the task.[2] Clearly, my central executive, wherever it is, is not busy with my hotel room number throughout the meeting. Therefore, remembering the number of a hotel room number, or the position of a car in a parking lot, is a type of temporary memory, which deserves special attention from dedicated investigators, but is definitely of a different kind than the *bona fide* working memory.

Selected associations: Attention, Internal representation, Performance, Prospective memory, Retrieval

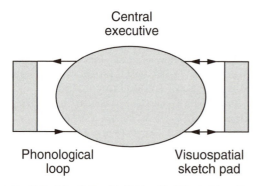

Central executive

Phonological loop

Visuospatial sketch pad

Fig. 64 The influential *model of Hitch and Baddeley depicts working memory in the human brain as two 'slave' systems controlled by a limited *capacity central executive. One system, the phonological loop, is specialized for processing language material, whereas the other, the visuospatial sketch pad, is concerned with visuospatial memory. A new version of the model adds a capacity to *bind temporary episodic representations in an 'episodic buffer' (Baddeley 2000; not shown). Attempts to map working memory into the brain, which are facilitated in recent years by the introduction of *functional neuroimaging, implicate the prefrontal cortex and its interconnections with other cortices in multiple working memory functions. (After Baddeley 1986.)

[1]A revised version of the model proposes a fourth distinct component, or alternatively a subdivision of the central executive, termed the 'episodic buffer', which *binds on-line and off-line information into transient episodes, i.e. events integrated across space and time (Baddeley 2000).

[2]Which should remind us that in animal studies as well, 'working memory' should be reserved to those situations in which the subject can be convincingly assumed to *attend the task information over the trial, or over a closely packed series of brief trials. This is unlikely to apply to protocols that last several hours.

Zeitgeist

1. The spirit of the time.
2. A collection of *paradigms, beliefs, and opinions that dominates a *culture or discipline at a given period, and moulds the intellectual climate against which new findings, interpretations, ideas, and *models are judged.

'Zeitgeist' (German for 'spirit of the time') was introduced into intellectual dialectics by the Romanticism, the anti*classical cultural movement originating in late eighteenth century Europe that displayed heightened interest in nature, emotional expression, and imagination. In the beginning, the meaning of 'zeitgeist' ranged from a semi-mystical force that shapes human history (Hegel 1820) to an opinionated cultural world view (Goethe 1827). Its current meaning is conveyed by definition 2 above. Occasionally the use of the term in the exact and natural sciences is considered purple prose. But what should concern us here is not whether the term itself is trendy or not, but rather what the concept tells us about the way science is practised.

It is not difficult to identify distinct zeitgeists in the history of memory research. A few examples should suffice. Introspection was the zeitgeist in the early days of psychology in Europe (Boring 1950a). *Behaviourism, the doctrine that only publicly observed behaviour is psychological datum, was the zeitgeist in North America for a substantial part of the twentieth century. The sweeping attitude that analysis of the *rat can illuminate universal properties of brain and mind was another long-lasting zeitgeist (e.g. Munn 1950). And the focus on memory in laboratory settings, remote from *real-life situations, is yet another example.

The zeitgeist in the neurosciences and behavioural sciences is not a coherent systematic theory or unified conceptual framework, but rather a collection of paradigms, assumptions, beliefs, and attitudes. Some are more central to the world view of the practitioners of the discipline, some less, all dominate the field, and all, or almost all, have opponents that actively oppose the mainstream or just sit there quietly harbouring the hope that the stream will divert its course. The following list is a limited selection of elements of the contemporary zeitgeist in the science of memory (for a representative manifesto see Milner et al. 1998). Note that not always are the elements as stated here a faithful formulation of the views of those individuals who promote the zeitgeist; rarely do they speak exactly the same language. Some of the statements are a bit exaggerated, but still, they do reflect the spirit:

1. Learning and memory are implemented in *synaptic change. Even when the proposed change involves the neuronal cell body and nucleus (Dudai and Morris 2000), the ultimate focus is still on the synapse.
2. *Long-term potentiation (LTP) = memory (e.g. Stevens 1998). There are, though, recurrent cracks in this zeitgeist (e.g. see discussion in Shors and Matzel 1997).
3. Long-term memory = synaptic remodelling and growth (*development).
4. *Classical conditioning is the tip of the iceberg of intricate information processing in even simple brains.
5. The major natural *taxonomy of mammalian memory distinguishes explicit (*declarative) from implicit (non-declarative) memory. A bold version of this zeitgeist claims that the classification is honoured even in primitive species without a real brain.
6. *Functional neuroimaging of the brain is bound to present us with the *engram.

There were elements of the zeitgeist that persisted till recently but not any more. For example, that it is not productive to approach the mechanistic bases of emotional memory (for the antithesis see LeDoux 1996); or that the study of consciousness 'does not fit' serious active neuroscientists (it does, though admittedly, the growing number of publications on the subject sometimes raises the question whether this zeitgeist was not abandoned prematurely).

What establishes a zeitgeist? The question merits detailed analysis of specific zeitgeist test cases, a worthy task for historians and sociologists of science (ample raw data are available, e.g. Worden et al. 1975). It is tempting, though, to suggest some possibilities. Frequently, one identifies one or a few single discoveries whose outcome can be generalized to a large number of problems and systems. Take LTP as an example. It suggests a cellular *model of *plasticity and learning; it can be searched for in many types of pathways and synapses in a variety of preparations and conditions; drugs that block it may be tested on multiple types of learning; many types of pharmacological congeners may be tested on LTP once the role of a certain *receptor (*glutamate) has been identified; many mutations (*neurogenetics) can be analysed for their effect on LTP, etc. etc. This creates lots of work for lots of people. The use of LTP can hence spread rather efficiently over the entire field of research on neuronal plasticity, infect multiple types of professionals, and recruit them all into the field of learning research. It is plausible to assume that some of these investigators would have not been attracted to memory research had it not been for the availability of the new cellular *assay. Success is clearly contagious, but is not enough: the recipe for a zeitgeist requires additional ingredients. It does not hurt to have dominant investigators that keep blowing the horn. And even this may not suffice. Some earlier zeitgeist may lay the ground for the development of later ones. Consider the zeitgeist notion that gene knockouts are a key to the molecular analysis of memory machinery. This idea was successfully developed in the fruit fly, *Drosophila*, but the number of research groups working on memory mutants in *Drosophila* was never larger than five at a time. The *geist* reached the right *zeit* only when the *mouse entered the scene, because the mouse is a mammal, lots of information is available on its brain and behaviour, but, even more importantly, its brain is more relevant to ours. So here is a manifestation of another timeless zeitgeist, which clearly transcends neuroscience, namely, that we think that we are at the centre of the universe.

Whereas it might be difficult to pin-point in each case why a certain zeitgeist has prevailed, the fact that it did is easily noticed. It is reflected in the preferential acceptance of papers to trendy journals, in the selection of speakers in international conferences, and ultimately in chapters in textbooks that set the tone for the next generation. In rare cases, the zeitgeist may even prevent solid science from being published for years; the inability to publish on the properties of *conditioned taste aversion because it contradicted the zeitgeist concerning how *associative learning should behave, is an example (Garcia 1981). Furthermore, nowadays, one should watch for commercial interests in promoting the zeitgeist. Having said all that, it might seem that stating that a zeitgeist could sometimes slow down the pace of discovery may look like beating a dead horse, and that the discussion of zeitgeist is superfluous. But it is definitely not. The reason is twofold. First, dead horses often prove to be phoenixes; it wouldn't do harm to repeat the warning against conservative paradigms, dominant opinions, and overenthusiastic *esprit de corps*. But, second, zeitgeists carry marked benefits as well, and should not be demoted merely because they are zeitgeists. Most importantly, we shouldn't forget, they might be simply true! In addition, they attract funds. They bring in new investigators, sometimes with types of training new to the discipline (e.g. modellists into LTP, experimental psychologists into neurogenetics). They add to the cohesion of scientific communities and foster collaborations. They also promote reproduction of experiments and ultimately multiple discoveries (Ogburn and Thomas 1922; Merton 1961), all of which are critical for good science. And, almost paradoxically, they target paradigms for future revolt, which may in due time modify the zeitgeist (e.g. Boring 1950b; Chomsky 1959; Hebb 1960; Breland and Breland 1961; Neisser 1978).

The Janus face of zeitgeists hence complicates life. The personal sentiment is, as in many other cases, a function of training and personality. Some prefer the security of the zeitgeist, some the thrill of the rebellion. May be the attitude should be influenced by noting what the outcome of either conformism or revolt might be. The first risks stagnation, the latter provokes doubts and stimulates new intellectual expeditions, even if some of these end up only in *red herrings. Therefore, at least from the point of view of the scientific culture, it would be nice to keep in mind the following rule, although practise it in moderation, especially before reaching academic tenure: whatever discipline, whatever problem you are engaged in, *a priori, question thy zeitgeist.

Selected associations: Culture, Paradigm, Scoopophobia

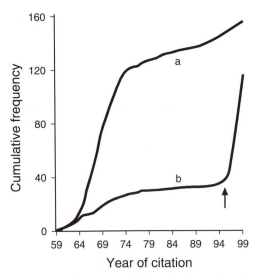

Fig. 65 Zeitgeists in transition. In 1959, the American psychologist James Deese published two papers on human memory in two respectable professional journals. One (a; Deese 1959a) dealt with veridical memory, the other (b; Deese 1959b) with *false memory. The graph depicts the frequency of citations of these papers from their publication to the end of 1999. Until the 1990s, veridical memory was congruent with the zeitgeist of memory research; but then the zeitgeist changed, questioning the fidelity of memories became fashionable, and Deese's paper on false memory gained popularity (arrow). The data till 1997 are adapted from Bruce and Winograd (1998), and those for 1998–99 are compiled from the Science Citation Index Expanded, Web of Science V. 4.1, ©ISI, Institute for Scientific Information. For another example of a bibliometric measure of zeitgeist, see *LTP.

References

Aamodt, S.M., Nordeen, E.J., and Nordeen, K.W. (1996). Blockade of NMDA receptors during song model exposure impairs song development in juvenile zebra finches. *Neurobiology of Learning and Memory*, **65**, 91–98.

Abel, T. and Kandel, E. (1998). Positive and negative regulatory mechanisms that mediate long-term memory storage. *Brain Research Reviews*, **26**, 360–378.

Abel, T., Nguyen, P.V., Barad, M., Deuel, T.A.S., and Kandel, E.R. (1997). Genetic demonstration of a role for PKA in the late phase of LTP and in hippocampus-based long-term memory. *Cell*, **88**, 615–626.

Abeles, M. (1982). *Local cortical circuits*. Springer-Verlag, Berlin.

Abeles, M. (1991). *Corticonics. Neural circuits of the cerebral cortex*. Cambridge University Press, Cambridge, MA.

Abeliovich, A., Chen, C., Goda, Y., Silva, A.J., Stevens, C.F., and Tonegawa, S. (1993). Modified hippocampal long-term potentiation in PKCgamma-mutant mice. *Cell*, **75**, 1253–1262.

Abraham, W.C. and Bear, M.F. (1996). Metaplasticity: the plasticity of synaptic plasticity. *Trends in Neurosciences*, **19**, 126–130.

Abraham, W.C. and Tate, W.P. (1997). Metaplasticity: A new vista across the field of synaptic plasticity. *Progress in Neurobiology*, **52**, 303–323.

Abrams, M.H. (1953). *The mirror and the lamp. Romantic theory and the critical tradition*. Oxford University Press, Oxford.

Abrams, T.W. (1985). Activity-dependent presynaptic facilitation: an associative mechanism in *Aplysia*. *Cellular and Molecular Neurobiology*, **5**, 123–145.

Abrams, T.W. and Kandel, E.R. (1988). Is contiguity detection in classical conditioning a system or a cellular property? Learning in *Aplysia* suggests a possible molecular site. *Trends in Neurosciences*, **11**, 128–135.

Aceves-Pina, E.O., Booker, R., Duerr, J.S., Livingstone, M.S., Quinn, W.G., Smith, R.F., Sziber, P.P., Tempel, B.L., and Tully, T.P. (1983). Learning and memory in *Drosophila*, studied with mutants. *Cold Spring Harbor Symposia on Quantitative Biology*, **48**, 831–840.

Acosta-Urquidi, J., Alkon, D.L., and Neary, J.T. (1984). Ca^{2+}-dependent protein kinase injection in a photoreceptor mimics biophysical effects of associative learning. *Science*, **224**, 1254–1257.

Adams McCord, M. (1987). *William Ockham*, Vol. I. University of Notre Dame Press, Notre Dame, IN.

Adams, M.D., Celniker, S.E., Holt, R.A., Evans, C.A., Gocayne, J.D., Amanatides, P.G., *et al.* (2000). The genome sequence of *Drosophila melanogaster*. *Science*, **287**, 2185–2195.

Adolph, E.F. (1961). Early concepts of physiological regulations. *Physiological Reviews*, **41**, 737–770.

Adolphs, R., Tranel, D., Damasio, H., and Damasio, A.R. (1995). Fear and the human amygdala. *Journal of Neuroscience*, **15**, 5879–5891.

Adolphs, R., Tranel, D., and Damasio, A.R. (1998). The human amygdala in social judgment. *Science*, **393**, 470–474.

Adrian, E.D. and Matthews, B.H.C. (1934). The Berger rhythm: Potential changes from the occipital lobes in man. *Brain*, **57**, 355–385.

Aggleton, J. (ed.) (2000). *The amygdala*. Oxford University Press, Oxford.

Aggleton, J.P. and Brown, M.W. (1999). Episodic memory, amnesia, and the hippocampal-anterior thalamic axis. *Behavioral and Brain Sciences*, **222**, 425–489.

Aggleton, J.P. and Shaw, C. (1996). Amnesia and recognition memory: A re-analysis of psychometric data. *Neuropsychologia*, **34**, 51–62.

Agmon-Snir, H., Carr, C.E., and Rinzel, J. (1998). The role of dendrites in auditory coincidence detection. *Nature*, **393**, 268–272.

Agranoff, B.W. and Klinger, P.D. (1964). Puromycin effect on memory fixation in the goldfish. *Science*, **146**, 952–953.

Agranoff, B.W., Davis, R.E., and Brink, J.J. (1966). Chemical studies on memory fixation in goldfish. *Brain Research*, **1**, 303–309.

Aguirre, G.K. and Farah, M.J. (1998). Human visual object recognition: what have we learned from neuroimaging? *Psychobiology*, **26**, 322–332.

Ahisaar, E., Vaadia, E., Ahissar, M., Bergman, H., Arieli, A., and Abeles, M. (1992). Dependence of cortical plasticity on correlated activity of single neurons and on behavioral context. *Science*, **257**, 1412–1415.

Ahissar, E., Haidarliu, S., and Zacksenhouse, M. (1997). Decoding temporally encoded sensory input by cortical oscillations and thalamic phase comparators. *Proceedings of the National Academy of Sciences USA*, **94**, 11633–11638.

Ahissar, M. and Hochstein, S. (1997). Task difficulty and the specificity of perceptual learning. *Nature*, **387**, 401–406.

Ahmed, B., Anderson, J.C., Douglas, R.J., Martin, K.A.C., and Nelson, J.C. (1994). Polyneuronal innervation of spiny stellate neurons in cat visual cortex. *Journal of Comparative Neurology*, **341**, 39–49.

References

Aidley, D.J. (1998). *The physiology of excitable cells*, 4th edn. Cambridge University Press, Cambridge.

Alberts, B. (1998). The cell as a collection of protein machines: Preparing the next generation of molecular biologists. *Cell*, **92**, 291–294.

Alberts, B. and Miake-Lye, R. (1992). Unscrambling the puzzle of biological machines: The importance of the details. *Cell*, **68**, 415–420.

Alberts, B., Bray, D., Lewis, J., Raff, M., Roberts, K., and Watson, J.D. (1994). *Molecular biology of the cell*, 3rd edn. Gerland, New York.

Albus, J.S. (1971). A theory of cerebellar function. *Mathematical Biosciences*, **10**, 25–61.

Alexander, M.P. and Freedman, M. (1984). Amnesia after anterior communicating artery aneurysm rupture. *Neurology*, **34**, 752–757.

Alvarez-Buylla, A. and Kirn, J.R. (1997). Birth, migration, incorporation, and death of vocal control neurons in adult songbirds. *Journal of Neurobiology*, **33**, 585–601.

Alzheimer, A. (1907/2000). Ueber eine eigenartige Erkrankung der Hirnrinde (About a peculiar disease of the cerebral cortex). Centralblatt fur Nervenheiklunde und Psychiatrie, March 1st. A fascimile of the original plus an English translation, *NeuroScience News*, **3**, 4–7.

Amara, S.G. (ed.) (1998). Neurotransmitter transporters. *Methods in Enzymology*, Vol. 296. Academic Press, San Diego.

Amaral, D.G., Price, J.L., Pitkanen, A., and Carmichael, S.T. (1992). Anatomical organization of the primate amygdaloid complex. In *The amygdala* (ed. J.P. Aggleton), pp. 1–66. Wiley-Liss, New York.

Ambalavanar, R., McCabe, B.J., Potter, K.N., and Horn, G. (1999). Learning-induced Fos-like immunoreactivity in the chick brain: time course and co-localization with GABA and parvalbumin. *Neuroscience*, **93**, 1515–1524.

Amico, R.P. (1993). *The problem of the criterion*. Rouman & Littlefield, Lanham, MD.

Amit, D.J. (1989). *Modeling brain function. The world of attractor neural networks*. Cambridge University Press, New York.

Amit, D.J. and Fusi, S. (1994). Learning in neural networks with material synapses. *Neural Computation*, **6**, 957–973.

Amorapanth, P., LeDoux, J.E., and Nader, K. (2000). Different lateral amygdala outputs mediate reactions and actions elicited by a fear-arousing stimulus. *Nature Neuroscience*, **3**, 74–79.

Amsel, A. (1958). The role of frustrative nonreward in noncontinuous reward situation. *Psychological Bulletin*, **55**, 102–119.

Anazi, Y. and Simon, H.A. (1979). The theory of learning by doing. *Psychological Review*, **86**, 124–140.

Andersen, P. and Lomo, T. (1967). Control of hippocampal output by afferent volley frequency. *Progress in Brain Research*, **27**, 400–412.

Andersen, P. and Moser, E.I. (1995). Brain temperature and hippocampal function. *Hippocampus*, **5**, 491–498.

Andersen, P. and Soleng, A.F. (1998). Long-term potentiation and spatial learning are both associated with the generation of new excitatory synapses. *Brain Research Reviews*, **26**, 353–359.

Andersen, P., Bliss, T.V.P., and Skrede, K. (1971). Lamellar organization of hippocampal excitatory pathways. *Experimental Brain Research*, **13**, 222–238.

Andersen, P., Sundberg, S.H., Sveen, O., and Wigstrom, H. (1977). Specific long-lasting potentiation of synaptic transmission in hippocampal slices. *Nature*, **266**, 736–737.

Andersen, R.A., Snyder, L.H., Bradley, D.C., and Xing, J. (1997). Multimodal representation of space in the posterior parietal cortex and its use in planning movements. *Annual Review of Neuroscience*, **20**, 303–330.

Anderson, J.R. (1982). Acquisition of cognitive skill. *Psychological Review*, **89**, 369–406.

Anderson, J.R. (1983). Retrieval of information from long-term memory. *Science*, **220**, 25–30.

Anderson, J.R. (1990). Use of objects as hammers to open nuts by Capuchin monkeys (*Cebus apella*). *Folia Primatologica (Basel)*, **54**, 138–145.

Anderson, M.C. and Green, C. (2001). Suppressing unwanted memories by executive control. *Nature*, **410**, 366–369.

Andreasen, N.C., Arndt, S., Swayze, V.II, Cizadlo, T., Flaum, M., O'Leary, D., Ehrhardt, J.C., and Yuh, W.T.C. (1994). Thalamic abnormalities in schizophrenia visualized through magnetic resonance image averaging. *Science*, **266**, 294–298.

Anglin, D., Spears, K.L., and Huston, H.R. (1997). Flunitrazepam and its involvement in date or acquaintance rape. *Academic Emergency Medicine*, **4**, 323–326.

Annas, J.E. (1992). *Hellenistic philosophy of mind*. University of California Press, Berkeley, CA.

Anokhin, P.K. (1974). *Biology and neurophysiology of the conditioned reflex and its role in adaptive behavior*. Pergamon Press, Oxford.

Anselm (~1100/1995). *Monologion and Proslogion, with the replies of Gaunilo and Anselm* (trans. T. Williams). Hackett, Indianapolis, IN.

Anson, L.C., Chen, P.E., Wyllie, D.J.A., Colquhoun, D., and Schoepfer, R. (1998). Identification of amino acid residues of the NR2A subunit that control glutamate potency in recombinant NR1/NR2A NMDA receptors. *Journal of Neuroscience*, **18**, 581–589.

Appleby, J., Covington, E., Hoyt, D., Latham, M., and Sneider, A. (ed.) (1996). *Knowledge and postmodernism in historical perspective*. Routledge, New York.

Araque, A., Parpura, V., Sanzgiri, R.P., and Haydon, P.G. (1999). Tripartite synapses: glia, the unacknowledged partner. *Trends in Neurosciences*, **22**, 208–215.

Arbuckle, T.Y. and Cuddy, L.L. (1969). Discrimination of item strength at time of presentation. *Journal of Experimental Psychology*, **81**, 126–131.

Arieli, A., Shoham, D., Hildesheim, R., and Grinvald, A. (1995). Coherent spatiotemporal patterns of ongoing activity revealed by real-time optical imaging coupled with single-unit recording in the cat visual cortex. *Journal of Neurophysiology*, **73**, 2072–2093.

Arieli, A., Sterkin, A., Grinvald, A., and Aertsen, A. (1996). Dynamics of ongoing activity: Explanation of the large variability in evoked cortical responses. *Science*, *273*, 1868–1871.

Ariens, E.J. and Beld, A.J. (1977). The receptor concept in evolution. *Biochemical Pharmacology*, **26**, 913–918.

Aristotle. *The complete works*. The revised Oxford translation (ed. J. Barnes) (1984). Princeton University Press, Princeton, NJ.

Armstrong, C.M. and Hille, B. (1998). Voltage-gated ion channels and electrical excitability. *Neuron*, **20**, 371–380.

Armstrong, D.M. (1989). *Universals. An opinionated introduction*. Westview Press, Boulder, CO.

Arnauld, A. (1662/1964). *The art of thinking. Port-Royal logic* (trans. J. Dickoff and C.W. James), Bobb-Merrill, Indianapolis, IN.

Arnsten, A.F.T. (1998). Catecholamine modulation of prefrontal cortical cognitive function. *Trends in Cognitive Sciences*, **2**, 436–447.

Arnsten, A.F.T. and Goldman-Rakic, P.S. (1998). Noise stress impairs prefrontal cortical cognitive function in monkeys. *Archives of General Psychiatry*, **55**, 362–368.

Aronson, E. (ed.) (1995). *Readings about the social animal*, (7th edn). Freeman, New York.

Arvanitaki, A. and Chalazonitis, N. (1958). Configurations modales de l'activite, propres a differents neurons d'un meme centre. *Journal de Physiologie (Paris)*, **50**, 122–125.

Ashburner, M. (1989). *Drosophila. A laboratory handbook*. Cold Spring Harbor Laboratory Press, Cold Spring Harbor, New York.

Asher, R. (1951). Munchausen's syndrome. *Lancet*, **i**, 339–341.

Aston-Jones, G., Rajkowski, J., Kubiak, P., and Alexinsky, T. (1994). Locus ceruleus neurons in monkey are selectively activated by attended cues in vigilance task. *Journal of Neuroscience*, **14**, 4467–4480.

Atkins, C.M., Selcher, J.C., Petraitis, J.J., Trzaskos, J.M., and Sweatt, J.D. (1998). The MAPK cascade is required for mammalian associative learning. *Nature Neuroscience*, **1**, 602–609.

Atwood, H.L. and Wojtowicz, J.M. (1999). Silent synapses in neural plasticity: Current evidence. *Learning & Memory*, **6**, 542–571.

Auerbach, J.M. and Segal, M. (1996). Muscarinic receptors mediating depression and long-term potentiation in rat hippocampus. *Journal of Physiology (London)*, **492**, 479–493.

Auger, C. and Attwell, D. (2000). Fast removal of synaptic glutamate by postsynaptic transporters. *Neuron*, **28**, 547–558.

Augustine, St (400/1969). *The confessions*. Image, Doubleday, New York.

Azari, N.P., Nickel, J., Wunderlich, G., Niedeggen, M., Hafter, H., Tellmann, L., Herzog, H., Stoeig, P., Birnbacher, D., and Seitz, R.J. (2001). Neural correlates of religious experience. *European Journal of Neuroscience*, **13**, 1649–1652.

Baars, B.J. (1998). Metaphors of consciousness and attention in the brain. *Trends in Neurosciences*, **21**, 58–62.

Babich, F.R., Jacobson, A.L., Bubash, S., and Jacobson, A. (1965). Transfer of a response to naive rats by injection of ribonucleic acid extracts from trained rats. *Science*, **149**, 656–657.

Bach, M.E., Hawkins, R.D., Osman, M., Kandel, E.R., and Mayford, M. (1995). Impairment of spatial but not contextual memory in CaMKII mutant mice with a selective loss of hippocampal LTP in the range of the θ frequency. *Cell*, **81**, 905–915.

Backer Cave, C. and Squire, L.R. (1992). Intact and long-lasting repetition priming in amnesia. *Journal of Experimental Psychology: Learning, Memory, and Cognition*, **18**, 509–520.

Bacon, F. (1620/1994). *Novum organum. With other parts of the great instauration*. (trans. and ed. P. Urbach and J. Gibson). Open Court, Chicago, IL.

Baddeley, A. (1981). The cognitive psychology of everyday life. *British Journal of Psychology*, **72**, 257–269.

Baddeley, A.D. (1982). Domains of recollection. *Psychological Review*, **89**, 709–729.

Baddeley, A. (1986). *Working memory*. Clarendon Press, Oxford.

Baddeley, A. (1993). Working memory or working attention? In *Attention: selection, awareness, and control*, (ed. A. Baddeley and L. Weiskrantz, L.), pp. 152–170. Clarendon Press, Oxford.

Baddeley, A. (1994). The magical number seven: Still magic after all these years? *Psychological Review*, **101**, 353–3556.

Baddeley, A. (1997). *Human memory. Theory and practice*, (revised edn). Psychology Press, Hove.

Baddeley, A. (1998). Recent developments in working memory. *Current Opinion in Neurobiology*, **8**, 234–238.

Baddeley, A. (2000). The episodic buffer: a new component of working memory? *Trends in Cognitive Sciences*, **4**, 417–423.

Baddeley, A.D. and Hitch, G. (1974). Working memory. In *The psychology of learning and motivation*, (ed. G.A. Bower), pp. 47–89. Academic Press, New York.

Bahrick, H.P. (1970). Two-phase model for prompted recall. *Psychological Review*, **77**, 215–222.

Bahrick, H.P. (1984). Semantic memory content in permastore: Fifty years of memory for Spanish learned in schools. *Journal of Experimental Psychology. General*, **113**, 1–29.

References

Bahrick, H.P. and Bahrick, P.O. (1964). A re-examination of the interrelations among measures of retention. *Quarterly Journal of Experimental Psychology,* **16**, 318–324.

Bailey, C.H. and Chen, M. (1983). Morphological basis of long-term habituation and sensitization in *Aplysia. Science,* **220**, 91–93.

Bailey, C.H. and Kandel, E.R. (1993). Structural changes accompanying memory storage. *Annual Review of Physiology,* **55**, 397–426.

Bailey, C.H., Bartsch, D., and Kandel, E.R. (1996). Toward a molecular definition of long-term memory storage. *Proceedings of the National Academy of Sciences USA,* **93**, 13445–13452.

Bain, A. (1859). *The emotions and the will.* J. Parker & Son, London.

Baker, A.G. (1976). Learned irrelevance and learned helplessness: Rats learn that stimuli, reinforcers and responses are uncorrelated. *Journal of Experimental Psychology, Animal Behavior Processes,* **2**, 130–141.

Baker, M.C. and Cunningham, M.A. (1985). The biology of bird-song dialects. *Behavioral and Brain Sciences,* **8**, 85–133.

Ballard, P.B. (1913). Oblivescence and reminiscence. *British Journal of Psychology Monograph Supplements,* **1**, 1–82.

Balleine, B.W. and Dickinson, A. (2000). The effect of lesions of the insular cortex on instrumental conditioning: evidence for a role in incentive memory. *Journal of Neuroscience,* **20**, 8954–8964.

Banaji, M.R. and Crowder, R.G. (1989). The bankruptcy of everyday memory. *American Psychologist,* **44**, 1185–1193.

Bandura, A. (1962). Social learning through imitation. In *Nebraska symposium on motivation,* (ed. M.R. Jones), pp. 211–269. University of Nebraska Press, Lincoln, NB.

Bandura, A. (1986). *Social foundations of thought and action: a social cognitive theory.* Prentice-Hall, Englewood Cliffs, NJ.

Bandura, A. and Walters, R.H. (1963). *Social learning and personality development.* Holt, Rinehart and Winston, New York.

Bandura, A., Ross, D., and Ross, S. (1963). Imitation of film-mediated aggressive models. *Journal of Abnormal and Social Psychology,* **66**, 3–11.

Bannerman, D.M., Good, M.A., Butcher, S.P., Ramsay, M., and Morris, R.G.M. (1995). Distinct components of spatial learning revealed by prior training and NMDA receptor blockade. *Nature,* **378**, 182–186.

Bao, J.X., Kandel, E.R., and Hawkins, R.D. (1998). Involvement of presynaptic and postsynaptic mechanisms in a cellular analog of classical conditioning at *Aplysia* sensory-motor neuron synapses in isolated cell culture. *Journal of Neuroscience,* **18**, 458–466.

Barkai, E. and Hasselmo, M.H. (1997). Acetylcholine and associative memory in the piriform cortex. *Molecular Neurobiology,* **15**, 17–29.

Barkai, N. and Leibler, S. (1997). Robustness in simple biochemical networks. *Nature,* **387**, 913–917.

Barlow, H.B. (1972). Single units and sensation: A neuron doctrine for perceptual psychology? *Perception,* **1**, 371–394.

Barondes, S.H. and Cohen, H.D. (1966). Puromycin effect on successive phases of memory storage. *Science,* **151**, 594–595.

Barresi, J. and Moore, C. (1996). Intentional relations and social understanding. *Behavioral and Brain Sciences,* **19**, 107–154.

Barrett, A.A. (1990). *Caligula. The corruption of power.* Yale University Press, New Haven, CT.

Barria, A., Muller, D., Derkach, V., Griffith, L.C., and Soderling, T.R. (1997). Regulatory phosphorylation of AMPA-type glutamate receptors by CaMKII during long-term potentiation. *Science,* **276**, 2042–2045.

Bartels, A. and Zeki, S. (1998). The theory of multistage integration in the visual brain. *Proceedings of the Royal Society of London [Biology],* **265**, 2327–2332.

Bartlett, F.C. (1932). *Remembering. A study in experimental and social psychology.* Cambridge University Press, London.

Bartsch, D., Ghirardi, M., Skehel, P.A., Karl, K.A., Herder, S.P., Chen, M., Bailey, C.H., and Kandel, E.R. (1995). *Aplysia* CREB2 represses long-term facilitation: Relief of repression converts transient facilitation into long-term functional and structural change. *Cell,* **83**, 979–992.

Bartus, R.T., Dean, R.L., Beer, B., and Lippa, A.S. (1982). The cholinergic hypothesis of geriatric memory dysfunction. *Science,* **217**, 408–417.

Bateson, P.P.G. (1966). The characteristics and context of imprinting. *Biological Reviews of the Cambridge Philosophical Society,* **41**, 177–220.

Bateson, P.P.G. and Wainwright, A.P. (1972). The effects of prior exposure to light on the imprinting process in domestic chicks. *Behaviour,* **42**, 279–290.

Baum, E.B., Moddy, J., and Wilczek, F. (1988). Internal representations for associative memory. *Biological Cybernetics,* **59**, 217–228.

Baumeister, R.F and Hastings, S. (1997). Distortions of collective memory: How groups flatter and deceive themselves. In *Collective memory of political events. Social psychological perspectives,* (ed. J.W. Pennebaker, D. Paez, and B. Rima), pp. 277–293. Lawrence Erlbaum Associates, Mahwah, NJ.

Baxter, M.G., Bucci, D.J., Gorman, L.K., Wiley, R.G., and Gallagher, M. (1995). Selective immunotoxic lesions of basal forebrain cholinergic cells: effects on learning and memory in rats. *Behavioral Neuroscience,* **109**, 714–722.

Baxter, M.G., Parker, A., Lindenr, C.C.C., Izquierdo, A.D., and Murray, E.A. (2000). Control of response selection by reinforcer value requires interaction of amygdala and orbital prefrontal cortex. *Journal of Neuroscience,* **20**, 4311–4319.

Bayenes, F., Vansteenwegen, D., de Houwer, J., and Crombez, G. (1996). Observational conditioning of food valence in humans. *Appetite,* **27**, 235–250.

Baynes, K., Eliassen, J.C., Lutsep, H.L., and Gazzaniga, M.S. (1998). Modular organization of cognitive systems masked by interhemispheric integration. *Science*, **280**, 902–905.

Bealer, G. (1999). The a priori. In *The Blackwell guide to epistemology* (ed. J. Greco and E. Sosa), pp. 243–270. Blackwell, Malden, MA.

Bear, M.F. (1995). Mechanisms for a sliding synaptic modification threshold. *Neuron*, **15**, 1–4.

Bear, M.F. and Malenka, R.C. (1994). Synaptic plasticity: LTP and LTD. *Current Opinion in Neurobiology*, **4**, 389–399.

Bechara, A., Damasio, H., Tranel, D., and Damasio, A.R. (1997). Deciding advantageously before knowing the advantageous strategy. *Science*, **275**, 1293–1295.

Bechara, A., Damasio, H., Tranel, D., and Anderson, S.W. (1998). Dissociation of working memory from decision making within the human prefrontal cortex. *Journal of Neuroscience*, **18**, 428–437.

Bechtel, W. (1982). Two common errors in explaining biological and psychological phenomena. *Philosophy of Science*, **49**, 549–574.

Bechtel, W. (1988). *Philosophy of science. An overview for cognitive science.* Lawrence Erlbaum Associates, Hillsdale, NJ.

Beck, C.D.O. and Rankin, C.H. (1997). Long-term habituation is produced by distributed training at long ISIs and not by massed training or short ISIs in *Caenorhabditis elegans*. *Animal Learning and Behavior*, **25**, 446–457.

Becker, E., Rinck, M., and Margaret, J. (1994). Memory bias in panic disorder. *Journal of Abnormal Psychology*, **103**, 396–399.

Bell, C., Caputi, A., Grant, K., and Serrier, J. (1993). Storage of a sensory pattern by anti-Hebbian synaptic plasticity in an electric fish. *Proceedings of the National Academy of Sciences USA*, **90**, 4650–4654.

Bende, M. and Nordin, S. (1997). Perceptual learning in olfaction: Professional wine tasters versus controls. *Physiology and Behavior*, **62**, 1065–1070.

Benjamin, A.S., Bjork, R.A., and Schwartz, B.L. (1998). The mismeasure of memory: When retrieval fluency is misleading as a metamnemonic index. *Journal of Experimental Psychology: General*, **127**, 55–68.

Benjamin, J., Li, L., Patterson, C., Greenberg, B.D., Murphy, D.L., and Hamer, D.H. (1996). Population and familial association between the D4 dopamine receptor gene and measures of novelty seeking. *Nature Genetics*, **12**, 81–84.

Bennett, A.T.D. (1996). Do animals have cognitive maps? *Journal of Experimental Biology*, **199**, 219–224.

Bennett, B.T., Abee, C.R., and Henrickson, R. (ed.) (1995). *Nonhuman primates in biomedical research. Biology and management.* Academic Press, San Diego.

Benton, D. and Parker, P.Y. (1998). Breakfast, blood glucose, and cognition. *American Journal of Clinical Nutrition*, **67** (Suppl.), 772S–778S.

Benzer, S. (1967). Behavioural mutants of *Drosophila* isolated by countercurrent distribution. *Proceedings of the National Academy of Sciences USA*, **58**, 1112–1119.

Berger, H. (1929). Über das Elektrenkephalogramm des Menschen. *Archiv für Psychiatrie*, **87**, 527–570.

Bergson, H. (1908/1988). *Matter and Memory.* Zone Books, New York.

Berke, J.B. and Hyman, S.E. (2000). Addiction, dopamine, and the molecular mechanisms of memory. *Neuron*, **25**, 515–532.

Berlin, B. (1992). *Ethnobiological classification. Principles of categorization of plants and animals in traditional societies.* Princeton University Press, Princeton, NJ.

Berlyne, N. (1972). Confabulation. *British Journal of Psychiatry*, **120**, 31–39.

Berman, D.E. and Dudai, Y. (2001). Memory extinction, learning anew, and learning the new: dissociations in the molecular machinery of learning in cortex. *Science*, **291**, 2417–2419.

Berman, D.E., Hazvi, S., Rosenblum, K., Seger, R., and Dudai, Y. (1998). Specific and differential activation of mitogen-activated protein kinase cascades by unfamiliar taste in the insular cortex of the behaving rat. *Journal of Neuroscience*, **18**, 10037–10044.

Berman, D.E., Hazvi, S., Neduva, V., and Dudai. Y. (2000). The role of identified neurotransmitter systems in the response of insular cortex to unfamiliar taste: activation of ERK1-2 and formation of a memory trace. *Journal of Neuroscience*, **20**, 7017–7023.

Bernecker, S. and Dretske, F. (ed.) (2000). *Knowledge. Reading in contemporary epistemology.* Oxford University Press, Oxford.

Berridge, M.J. (1993). Inositol triphosphate and calcium signaling. *Nature*, **361**, 315–325.

Berridge, V. (1977). Opium and the historical perspective. *Lancet*, 78–80.

Berry, D.C. and Broadbent, D.E. (1988). Interactive tasks and the implicit-explicit distinction. *British Journal of Psychology*, **79**, 251–272.

Best, P.J. and White, A.M. (1999). Placing hippocampal single-unit studies in a historical context. *Hippocampus*, **9**, 346–351.

Bhalla, U.S. and Iyengar, R. (1999). Emergent properties of networks of biological signalling pathways. *Science*, **283**, 382–387.

Biegler, R. and Morris, R.G.M. (1996). Landmark stability: Studies exploring whether the perceived stability of the environment influences spatial representation. *Journal of Experimental Biology*, **199**, 187–193.

Bienenstock, E.L., Cooper, L.N., and Munro, P.W. (1982). Theory for the development of neuron selectivity: Orientation specificity and binocular interaction in visual cortex. *Journal of Neuroscience*, **2**, 32–48.

de Biran, M. (1804/1929). *The influence of habit on the faculty of thinking* (trans. M. Donaldson Boehm). Williams & Wilkins,

References

Baltimore, MD (Reprinted by University Microfilms International, Ann Arbor, MI, 1982).

Birney, R.C. and Teevan, R.C. (ed.) (1961). *Reinforcement. An enduring problem in psychology.* Van Norstarnd, Princeton, NJ.

Bito, H., Deisseroth, K., and Tsien, R.W. (1996). CREB phosphorylation and dephosphorylation: A Ca^{2+}-and stimulus duration-dependent switch for hippocampal gene expression. *Cell*, **87**, 1203–1214.

Bitterman, M.E., Menzel, R., Fietz, A., and Schafer, S. (1983). Classical conditioning of proboscis extension in the honeybees (*Apis mellifera*). *Journal of Comparative Physiology*, **97**, 107–119.

Bjordahl, T.S., Dimyan, M.A., Weinberger, N.M. (1998). Induction of long-term receptive field plasticity in the auditory cortex of the waking guinea pig by stimulation of the nucleus basalis. *Behavioral Neuroscience,* **112**, 467–479.

Blackwell, K.T. and Alkon, D.L. (1999). Ryanodine receptor modulation of in vitro associative learning in *Hermissenda crassicornis. Brain Research,* **822**, 114–125.

Blake, J.A., Richardson, J.E., Davisson, M.T., Eppig, J.T., and the Mouse Genome Informatics Group (1997). The mouse genome database (MGD). A comprehensive public resource of genetic, phenotypic and genomic data. *Nucleic Acids Research*, **25**, 85–91.

Blakely, R.D. and Bauman, A.L. (2000). Biogenic amine transporters: regulation in flux. *Current Opinion in Neurobiology*, **10**, 328–336.

Blanchard, R.J. and Blanchard, D.C. (1969). Crouching as an index of fear. *Journal of Comparative Physiological Psychology*, **67**, 370–375.

Blaney, P.H. (1986). Affect and memory: a review. *Psychological Bulletin*, **99**, 229–246.

Blaxton, T.A. (1989). Investigating dissociations among memory measures: support for transfer-appropriate processing framework. *Journal of Experimental Psychology: Learning, Memory, and Cognition*, **15**, 657–668.

Blaxton, T.A., Zeffiro, T.A., Gabrieli, J.D.E., Bookheimer, S.Y., Carrillo, M.C., Theodore, W.H., and Disterhoft, J.F. (1996). Functional mapping of human learning: a positron emission tomography activation study of eyeblink conditioning. *Journal of Neuroscience*, **16**, 4032–4040.

Blessing, W.W. (1997). Inadequate frameworks for understanding bodily homeostasis. *Trends in Neurosciences*, **20**, 235–239. (See also correspondence in *Trends in Neurosciences*, **20**, 508–509.)

Bliss, T.V.P. and Collingridge, G.L. (1993). A synaptic model of memory: Long-term potentiation in the hippocampus. *Nature*, **361**, 31–39.

Bliss, T.V.P. and Gardner-Medwin, A.R. (1973). Long-lasting potentiation of synaptic transmission in the dentate area of the unanesthetized rabbit following stimulation of the perforant path. *Journal of Physiology (London)*, **232**, 357–374.

Bliss, T.V.P. and Lomo, T. (1973). Long-lasting potentiation of synaptic transmission in the dentate area of the anaesthetized rabbit following stimulation of the perforant path. *Journal of Physiology (London)*, **232**, 331–356.

Block, N. (1980). What is functionalism? In *Readings in philosophy of psychology*, Vol. 1, (ed. N. Block), pp. 171–184. Harvard University Press, Cambridge, MA.

Block, N. (1995). On a confusion about a function of consciousness. *Behavioral and Brain Sciences*, **18**, 227–287.

Block, N. (1996). How can we find the neural correlate of consciousness? *Trends in Neurosciences*, **19**, 456–459.

Block, N.J. and Fodor, J.A. (1972). What psychological states are not. *Philosophical Review*, **81**, 159–181.

Boakes, R. (1984). *From Darwin to behaviourism. Psychology and the mind of animals.* Cambridge University Press, Cambridge.

Bock, J. and Braun, K. (1999*a*). Filial imprinting in domestic chicks is associated with spine pruning in the associative area, dorsocaudal neostriatum. *European Journal of Neuroscience*, **11**, 2566–2570.

Bock, J. and Braun, K. (1999*b*). Blockade of N-methyl-D-aspartate activation suppresses long-term induced synaptic elimination. *Proceedings of the National Academy of Sciences USA*, **96**, 2485–2490.

Bodis-Wollner, I. (1987). Electroencephalography. In *The Oxford companion to the mind*, (ed. R.L. Gregory and O.L. Zangwill), pp. 214–217. Oxford University Press, Oxford.

Bogen, J.E. (1995). On the neurophysiology of consciousness: I. An overview. *Consciousness and Cognition*, **4**, 52–62.

Bolhuis, J.J. (1999). Early learning and the development of filial preferences in the chick. *Behavioural Brain Research*, **98**, 245–252.

Bonhoeffer, T. and Grinvald, A. (1993). The layout of iso-orientation domains in area-18 of cat visual cortex—optical imaging reveals a pinwheel-like organization. *Journal of Neuroscience*, **13**, 4157–4180.

Bonner, J.T. (1980). *The evolution of culture in animals.* Princeton University Press, Princeton, NJ.

Bontempi, B., Laurent-Demir, C., Destrade, C., and Jaffard, R. (1999). Time-dependent reorganization of brain circuitry underlying long-term memory storage. *Nature*, **400**, 671–675.

Bootman, M.D. and Berridge, M.J. (1995). The elemental principles of calcium signalling. *Cell*, **83**, 675–678.

Bootman, M.D., Berridge, M.J., and Lipp, P. (1997). Cooking with calcium: the recipes for composing global signals from elementary events. *Cell*, **91**, 367–373.

Borges, J.L. (1944/1998). Funes, his memory. In *Collected fictions*. Viking, New York.

Borges, J.L. (1949/1998). The two kings and the two labyrinths. In *Collected fictions*. Viking, New York.

Borges, J.L. (1952/1964). The analytical language of John Wilkins. In *Other inquisitions*. University of Texas Press, Austin, TX.

Borges, J.L. (1964). On rigor in science. In: *Dreamtigers*. University of Texas Press, Austin, TX.

Boring, E.G. (1935). The relation of the attributes of sensation to the dimensions of the stimulus. *Philosophy of Science*, **2**, 236–245.

Boring, E.G. (1950*a*). *A history of experimental psychology*, (2nd edn). Prentice-Hall. Englewood Cliffs, NJ.

Boring, E.G. (1950*b*). Great men and scientific progress. *Proceedings of the American Philosophical Society*, **94**, 339–351.

Boring, E.G. (1954). The nature and history of experimental control. *American Journal of Psychology*, **67**, 573–589.

Bortolotto, Z.A., Clarke, V.R.J., Delany, C.M., Parry, M.C., Smolders, I., Vignes, M., Ho, K.H., Miu, P., Brinton, B.T., Fantaske, R., Ogden, A., Gates, M., Ornstein, P.L., Lodge, D., Bleakman, D., and Collingridge, G.L. (1999). Kainate receptors are involved in synaptic plasticity. *Nature*, **402**, 297–301.

Bothwell, M. and Giniger, E. (2000). Alzheimer's disease: neurodevelopment converges with neurodegeneration. *Cell*, **102**, 271–273.

Bottjer, S.W. and Johnson, F. (1997). Circuits, hormones, and learning: Vocal behavior in songbirds. *Journal of Neurobiology*, **33**, 602–618.

Bourne, G.H. (ed.) (1975). *The rhesus monkey*. Vol. I. *Anatomy and physiology*. Academic Press, New York.

Bourne, H.R. and Nicoll, R. (1993). Molecular machines integrate coincident synaptic signals. *Neuron,* **10** (Suppl.): 65–75.

Bourtchuladze, R., Frenguelli, B., Blendy, J., Cioffi, D., Schutz, G., and Silva, A.J. (1994). Deficient long-term memory in mice with a targeted mutation of the cAMP-responsive element-binding protein. *Cell*, **79**, 59–68.

Bouton, M.E. (1991). Context and retrieval in extinction and in other examples of interference in simple associative learning. In *Current topics in animal learning: brain, emotion, and cognition*, (ed. L. Dachowski and C.F. Flaherty), pp. 25–53. Laurence Erlbaum, Hillsdale, NJ.

Bouton, M.E. (1993). Context, time, and memory retrieval in the interference paradigms of Pavlovian learning. *Psychological Bulletin*, **114**, 80–99.

Bouton, M.E. (1994). Conditioning, remembering, and forgetting. *Journal of Experimental Psychology. Animal Behavior Processes*, **20**, 219–231.

Bouton, M.E. and Swartzentruber, D. (1991). Sources of relapse after extinction in Pavlovian and instrumental conditioning. *Clinical Psychology Review*, **11**, 123–140.

Bower, G.H. (1981). Mood and memory. *American Psychologist*, **36**, 129–148.

Bower, G.H. and Hilgard, E.R. (1981). *Theories of Learning*, (5th edn). Prentice-Hall, Englewood Cliffs, NJ.

Boyer, C.B. (1989). *A history of mathematics*, (2nd edn). Wiley, New York.

Boynton, S. and Tully, T. (1992). *latheo*, a new gene involved in associative learning and memory in *Drosophila melanogaster*, identified from P element mutagenesis. *Genetics*, **131**, 655–672.

Brainard, M.S. and Doupe, A.J. (2000). Interruption of a basal ganglia–forebrain circuit prevents plasticity of learned vocalizations. *Nature*, **404**, 762–766.

Braitenberg, V. (1967). Is the cerebellar cortex a biological clock in the millisecond range? *Progress in Brain Research*, **25**, 334–346.

Braitenberg, V., Heck, D., and Sultan, F. (1997). The detection and generation of sequences as a key to cerebellar function: experiments and theory. *Behavioral and Brain Sciences*, **20**, 229–277.

Brandimonte, M., Einstein, G.O., and McDaniel, M.A. (ed.) (1996). *Prospective memory. Theory and applications*. Lawrence Erlbaum Associates, Mahwah, NJ.

Brandt, J., Bylsma, F.W., Aylward, E.H., Rothlind, J., and Gow, C.A. (1995). Impaired source memory in Huntington's disease and its relation to basal ganglia atrophy. *Journal of Clinical and Experimental Neuropsychology*, **17**, 868–877.

Brannon, E.M. and Terrace, H.S. (1998). Ordering of the numerosities 1 to 9 by monkeys. *Science*, **282**, 746–749.

Braud, W.G. and Broussard, W.J. (1973). Effects of puromycin on memory for shuttle box extinction in goldfish and barpress extinction in rats. *Pharmacology, Biochemistry and Behavior*, **1**, 651–656.

Braun, A.P. and Schulman, H. (1995). The multifunctional calcium/calmodulin dependent protein kinase: from form to function. *Annual Review of Physiology*, **57**, 417–445.

Bray, D. (1995). Protein molecules as computational elements in living cells. *Nature*, **376**, 307–312.

Brazier, M.A.B. (1984). *A history of neurophysiology in the 17th and 18th centuries. from concept to experiment*. Raven Press, New York.

Brazier, M.A.B. (1988). *A history of neurophysiology in the 19th century*. Raven Press, New York.

Brecht, B. (1929–33/1987). About the way to construct enduring works. In *Poems 1912–1956*. Routledge, New York.

Breland, K. and Breland, M. (1961). The misbehavior of organisms. *American Psychologist*, **16**, 681–683.

Brenner, S. (1997). *Loose ends*. Current Biology, London.

Brenowitz, E. A., Margoliash, D., and Nordeen, K.W. (1997). An introduction to birdsong and the avian song system. *Journal of Neurobiology*, **33**, 495–500.

Brentano, F. (1874/1960). The distinction between mental and physical phenomena. In *Realism and the background of phenomenology*, (ed. R.M. Chisholm), pp. 39–61. Ridgeview, CA.

Brewer, J.B., Zhao, Z., Desmond, J.E., Glover, G.H., and Gabrieli, J.D.E. (1998). Making memories: Brain activity that predicts how well visual experience will be remembered. *Science*, **281**, 1185–1187.

References

Brindle, P.K. and Montminy, M.R. (1992). The CREB family of transcription activators. *Current Opinion in Genetics and Development,* **2,** 199–204.

Britten, K.H., Newsome, W.T., Shadlen, M.N., Celebrini, S., and Movshon, J.A. (1996). A relationship between behavioral choice and the visual responses of neurons in macaque MT. *Visual Neuroscience,* **13,** 87–100.

Broadbent, D.E. (1958). *Perception and communication.* Pergamon Press, Oxford.

Broadbent, D.E. (1975). The magic number seven after fifteen years. In *Studies in long-term memory,* (ed. A. Kennedy and A. Wilkes), pp. 3–18. Wiley, London.

Broca, P. (1878). Anatomie compare des circonvolutions cerebrales. Le grand lobe limbique et la scissure limbique dans la serie des mammifieres. *Revue Anthropologique,* **1,** 385–498.

Brodal, A. (1981). *Neurological anatomy in relation to clinical medicine,* (3rd edn). Oxford University Press, New York.

Brodal, P. (1998). *The central nervous system. Structure and function,* (2nd edn). Oxford University Press, New York.

Brogden, W.J. (1939). Sensory pre-conditioning. *Journal of Experimental Psychology,* **25,** 323–332.

Brooks, N.D. and Baddeley, A.D. (1976). What can amnesic patients learn? *Neuropsychologia,* **14,** 111–122.

Brown, E. and Deffenbacher, K. (1995). Forgotten mnemonists. *Journal of the History of the Behavioral Sciences,* **11,** 342–349.

Brown, M.F., Mckeon, D., Curley, T., Weston, B., Lambert, C., and Lebowitz, B. (1998). Working memory for color in honeybees. *Animal Learning and Behavior,* **26,** 264–271.

Brown, M.W. and Xiang, J.Z. (1998). Recognition memory: Neuronal substrates of the judgment of prior occurrence. *Progress in Neurobiology,* **55,** 149–189.

Brown, R. and Kulik, J. (1977). Flashbulb memories. *Cognition,* **5,** 73–99.

Brown, R. and McNeill, D. (1966). The 'Tip of the Tongue' phenomenon. *Journal of Verbal Learning and Verbal Behavior,* **5,** 325–337.

Brown, S. and Schafer, E.A. (1888). XI. an investigation into the functions of the occipital and temporal lobes of the Monkey's brain. *Philosophical Transactions of the Royal Society of London, B,* **179,** 303–327.

Brown, T.H., Kairiss, E.W., and Keenan, C.L. (1990). Hebbian synapses: Biophysical mechanisms and algorithms. *Annual Review of Neuroscience,* **13,** 475–511.

Brownlee, D.J.A. and Fairweather, I. (1999). Exploring the neurotransmitter labyrinth in nematodes. *Trends in Neurosciences,* **22,** 16–24.

Bruce, D. (1985). The how and why of ecological memory. *Journal of Experimental Psychology: General,* **114,** 78–90.

Bruce, D. and Winograd, E. (1998). Remembering Deese's 1959 articles: the Zeitgeist, the sociology of science, and false memories. *Psychonomic Bulletin & Review,* **5,** 615–624.

Bruins Slot, L.A. and Colpaert, F.C. (1999). Opiate states of memory: Receptor mechanisms. *Journal of Neuroscience,* **19,** 10520–10529.

Brunfaut, E., Vanoverberghe, V., and d'Ydewalle, G. (2000). Prospective remembering of Korsakoff's and alcoholics as a function of the prospective-memory and on-going tasks. *Neuropsychologia,* **38,** 975–984.

Bryan, W.L. and Harter, N. (1897). Studies in the physiology and psychology of the telegraphic language. *Psychological Review,* **4,** 27–53.

Bryan, W.L. and Harter, N. (1899). Studies on the telegraphic language. the acquisition of a hierarchy of habits. *Psychological Review,* **6,** 354–375.

Buchel, C., Morris, J., Dolan, R.J., and Friston, K.J. (1998). Brain systems mediating aversive conditioning: an event-related fMRI study. *Neuron,* **20,** 947–957.

Buckley, M.J. and Gaffan, D. (1998). Learning and transfer of object-reward associations and the role of perirhinal cortex. *Behavioral Neuroscience,* **112,** 15–23.

Buckner, R.L. (2000). Neural origins of 'I remember'. *Nature Neuroscience,* **3,** 1068–1069.

Buckner, R.L. and Koustaal, W. (1998). Functional neuroimaging studies of encoding, priming, and explicit memory retrieval. *Proceedings of the National Academy of Sciences USA,* **95,** 891–898.

Buckner, R.L. and Tulving, E. (1995). Neuroimaging studies of memory: Theory and recent PET results. In *Handbook of Neuropsychology,* Vol. 10 (ed. F. Boller and J. Grafman), pp. 439–466. Elsevier, Amsterdam.

Buckner, R.L., Petersen, S.E., Ojemann, J.G., Miezon, F.M., Squire, L.R., and Raichle, M.E. (1995). Functional anatomical studies of explicit and implicit memory retrieval tasks. *Journal of Neuroscience,* **15,** 12–29.

Buckner, R.L., Bandettini, P.A., O'Craven, K.M., Savoy, R.L., Petersen, S.E., Raichle, M.E., and Rosen, B.R. (1996). Detection of cortical activation during averaged single trials of a cognitive task using functional magnetic resonance imaging. *Proceedings of the National Academy of Sciences USA,* **93,** 14878–14883.

Bunge, M. (1960). Levels: a semantical preliminary. *Review of Metaphysics,* **13,** 396–406.

Bunsey, M. and Eichenbaum, H. (1996). Conservation of hippocampal memory function in rats and humans. *Nature,* **379,** 255–257.

Buonomano, D.V. and Merzenich, M.M. (1998). Cortical plasticity: from synapses to maps. *Annual Review of Neuroscience,* **21,** 149–186.

Burchfield, R.W. (1996). *Fowler's modern English usage,* (3rd edn). Clarendon Press, Oxford.

Bures, J., Buresova, O., and Krivanek, J. (1988). *Brain and behavior: paradigms for research in neural mechanisms.* Wiley, New York.

Bures, J., Bermudez-Rattoni, F., and Yamamoto, T. (1998). *Conditioned taste aversion. Memory of a special kind.* Oxford University Press, New York.

Burgess, N. and O'Keefe, J. (1996). Neuronal computations underlying the firing of place cells and their role in navigation. *Hippocampus,* **6,** 749–762.

Burgess, P.W. and McNeil, J.E. (1999). Content-specific confabulation. *Cortex,* **35,** 163–182.

Burke, E. (1757/1990). Introduction on taste. In *A philosophical enquiry into the origin of our ideas of the sublime and the beautiful.* Oxford University Press, Oxford.

Burkert, W. (1985). *Greek religion.* Harvard University Press, Cambridge, MA.

Burnham, W.H. (1889). Memory, historically and experimentally considered. *American Journal of Psychology,* **2,** 39–90.

Burnyeat, M. (1990). T*he Theaetetus of Plato,* (trans. M.J. Levett). Hackett, Indianapolis.

Bush, R.R. and Mosteller, F. (1951). A mathematical model for simple learning. *Psychological Review,* **58,** 313–323.

Butters, N. (1985). Alcoholic Korsakoff's syndrome: Some unresolved issues concerning etiology, neuropathology, and cognitive deficits. *Journal of Clinical and Experimental Neuropsychology,* **7,** 181–210.

Buxbaum, J. and Dudai, Y. (1989). A quantitative model for the kinetics of cAMP-dependent protein kinase (type II) activity: Long-term activation of the kinase and its possible relevance to learning and memory. *Journal of Biological Chemistry,* **264,** 9344–9351.

Byers, D., Davis, R.L., and Kiger, J.A. Jr. (1981). Defect in cyclic AMP phosphodiesterase due to the *dunce* mutation of learning in *Drosophila melanogaster. Nature,* **289,** 79–81.

Byrne, J.H. (1985). Neural and molecular mechanisms underlying information storage in *Aplysia*: implications for learning and memory. *Trends in Neurosciences,* **8,** 478–482.

Byrne, J.H. and Kandel, E.R. (1996). Presynaptic facilitation revisited: State and time dependence. *Journal of Neuroscience,* **16,** 425–435.

Byrne, W.L., Samuel, D., Bennett, E.L., Rosenzweig, M.R., Wasserman, E., Wagner, A.R., *et al.* (1966). Memory transfer. *Science,* **153,** 658–659.

Cabeza, R., Rao, S.M., Wagner, A.D., Mayer, A.R., and Schacter, D.L. (2001). Can medial temporal lobe regions distinguish true from false? An event-related functional MRI study of veridical and illusory recognition memory. *Proceedings of the National Academy of Sciences USA,* **98,** 4805–4810.

Cahill, L. and McGaugh, J.L. (1998). Mechanisms of emotional arousal and lasting declarative memory. *Trends in Neurosciences,* **21,** 294–299.

Cahill, L., Haier, R.J., White, N.S., Fallon, J., Kilpatrick, L., Lawrence, C., Potkin, S.G., and Akire, M.T. (2001). Sex related differences in amygdala activity during emotionally influenced memory storage. *Neurobiology of Learning and Memory,* **75,** 1–9.

Cajal, S.R.y. (1916/2000). *Advice for a young investigator.* MIT Press, Cambridge, MA.

Calkins, M.W. (1921). The truly psychological behaviorism. *Psychological Review,* **28,** 1–18.

Camhi, J.M. (1984). *Neuroethology.* Sinauer, Sunderland, MA.

Cannon, W.B. (1929). Organization for physiological homeostasis. *Physiological Reviews,* **9,** 399–431.

Cannon, W.B. (1932). *The wisdom of the body.* Norton, New York.

Cannon, W.B. (1934). The story of the development of our ideas of chemical mediation of nerve impulses. *American Journal of the Medical Sciences,* **188,** 145–159.

Cantley, L.C., Auger, K.R., Carpenter, C., Duckworth, B., Graziani, A., Kapeller, R., and Soltoff, S. (1991). Oncogenes and signal transduction. *Cell,* **64,** 281–302.

Capaldi, E.J. (1966). Partial reinforcement: an hypothesis of sequential effects. *Psychological Review,* **73,** 459–477.

Capaldi, E.J. and Neath, I. (1995). Remembering and forgetting as context discrimination. *Learning & Memory,* **2,** 107–132.

Capsoni, S., Ugolini, G., Comparini, A., Ruberti, F., Berardi, N., and Cattaneo, A. (2000). Alzheimer-like neurodegeneration in aged antinerve growth factor transgenic mice. *Proceedings of the National Academy of Sciences USA,* **97,** 6826–6831.

Carew, T.J. (1996). Molecular enhancement of memory formation. *Neuron,* **16,** 5–8.

Carew, T.J., Castellucci, V., and Kandel, E.R. (1971). An analysis of dishabituation and sensitization of the gill-withdrawal reflex in Aplysia. *International Journal of Neuroscience,* **2,** 79–98.

Carew, T.J., Pinsker, H.M., and Kandel, E.R. (1972). Long-term habituation of a defensive withdrawal reflex in *Aplysia. Science,* **175,** 451–454.

Carmichael, L., Hogan, H.P., and Walter, A.A. (1932). An experimental study of the effect of language on the reproduction of visually perceived form. *Journal of Experimental Psychology,* **15,** 73–86.

Carnap, R. (1933/1959). Psychology in physical language. In *Logical positivism,* (ed. A.J. Ayer), pp. 165–198. The Free Press, Glencoe, IL.

Carpenter, P.A., Just, M.A., and Reichle, E.D. (2000). Working memory and executive function: evidence from neuroimaging. *Current Opinion in Neurobiology,* **10,** 195–199.

Carroll, L. (1865/1998). *Alice's adventures in wonderland.* Penguin Books, London.

Carroll, L. (1872/1998). *Through the looking glass, and what Alice found there.* Penguin, London. (*Note*: the last line of Carroll's version differs from the popular version cited here, which fits better the 'binding problem'; see *ibid.,* Notes, p. 344.)

References

Carroll, R.C., Morielli, A.D., and Peralta, E.C. (1995). Coincidence detection at the level of phospholipase C activation mediated by the m4 muscarinic acetylcholine receptor. *Current Biology*, **5**, 536–544.

Carruthers, M. (1990). *The book of memory*. Cambridge University Press, Cambridge.

Carter, C.S., Braver, T.S., Barch, D.M., Botvinick, M.M., Noll, D., and Cohen, J.D. (1998). Anterior cingulate cortex, error detection, and the online monitoring of performance. *Science*, **280**, 747–749.

Carvell, G.E. and Simons, D.J. (1996). Abnormal tactile experience early in life disrupts active touch. *Journal of Neuroscience*, **16**, 2750–2757.

Casadio, A., Martin, K.C., Giustetto, M., Zhu, H.X., Chen, M., Bartsch, D., Bailey, C.H., and Kandel, E.R. (1999). A transient, neuron-wide form of CREB-mediated long-term facilitation can be stabilized at specific synapses by local protein synthesis. *Cell*, **99**, 221–237.

Cason, H. (1925). The physical basis of the conditioned response. *American Journal of Psychology*, **36**, 371–393.

Cason, H. (1932). The pleasure-pain theory of learning. *Psychological Review*, **39**, 440–466.

Cassell's Concise Latin Dictionary, (3rd edn). (compiler Simpson, D.P.) (1966). Cassell, London.

Castellucci, V.F. and Kandel, E.R. (1976). Presynaptic facilitation as a mechanism for behavioural sensitization in *Aplysia*. *Science*, **194**, 1176–1178.

del Castillo, J. and Katz, B. (1954). Statistical factors involved in neurotransmitter facilitation and depression. *Journal of Physiology (London)*, **124**, 574–585.

Catalano, S.M., Chang, C.K., and Shatz, C.J. (1997). Activity-dependent regulation of NMDAR1 immunoreactivity in the developing visual cortex. *Journal of Neuroscience*, **17**, 8376–8390.

Caton, R. (1875). The electric current of the brain. *British Medical Journal*, **2**, 278.

Cavallaro, S., Meiri, N., Yi, C.-L., Musso, S., Ma, W., Goldberg, J., and Alkon, D.L. (1997). Late memory-related genes in the hippocampus revealed by RNA fingerprinting. *Proceedings of the National Academy of Sciences USA*, **94**, 9669–9673.

Cavanaugh, J.C. and Perlmutter, M. (1982). Metamemory: a critical examination. *Child Development*, **53**, 11–28.

Caygill, H. (1995). *A Kant dictionary*. Blackwell, Oxford.

Cedar, H., Kandel, E.R., and Schwartz, J.H. (1972). Cyclic adenosine monophosphate in the nervous system of *Aplysia californica*. I. Increased synthesis in response to synaptic stimulation. *Journal of General Physiology*, **60**, 558–569.

Chain, D.G., Casadio, A., Schacher, S., Hegde, A.N., Valbrun, M., Yamamoto, N., Goldberg, A.L., Bartsch, D., Kandel, E.R., and Schwartz, J.H. (1999). Mechanisms for generating the autonomous cAMP-dependent protein kinase required for long-term facilitation in *Aplysia*. *Neuron*, **22**, 147–156.

Chance, P. (1999). Thorndike's puzzle boxes and the origins of the experimental analysis of behavior. *Journal of the Experimental Analysis of Behavior*, **72**, 433–440.

Changeux, J.P. (1985). *Neuronal man*. Pantheon, New York.

Changeux, J.-P. and Danchin, A. (1976). Selective stabilisation of developing synapses as a mechanism for the specification of neuronal networks. *Nature*, **264**, 705–712.

Changeux, J.P., Devillers-Thiery, P., and Chemouilli, P. (1984). Acetylcholine receptor: an allosteric protein. *Science*, **225**, 1335–1345.

Changeux, J.-P., Bertrand, D., Corringer, P.-J., Dehaene, S., Edelstein, S., Lena, C., Le Novere, N., Marubio, L., Picciotto, M., and Zoli, M. (1998). Brain nicotinic receptors: Structure and regulation, role in learning and reinforcement. *Brain Research Reviews*, **26**, 198–216.

Chapman, P.F., Frenguelli, B.G., Smith, A., Chen, C.-M., and Silva, A.J. (1995). The α-Ca^{2+}/calmodulin kinase II: a bidirectional modulator of presynaptic plasticity. *Neuron*, **14**, 591–597.

Charney, D.S., Grillon, C., and Bremner, J.D. (1998). The neurobiological basis of anxiety and fear: Circuits, mechanisms, and neurochemical interactions (Part I). *Neuroscientist*, **4**, 35–44.

Chase, W.G. and Ericsson, K.A. (1982). Skill and working memory. In *The psychology of learning and motivation. Advances in research and theory*, Vol. 16, (ed. G.H. Bower), pp. 1–58. Academic Press, New York.

Chase, W.G. and Simon, H.A. (1973). The mind's eye in chess. In *Visual information processing* (ed. W.G. Chase), pp. 215–279. Academic Press, New York.

Chawla, D., Rees, G., and Friston, K.J. (1999). The physiological basis of attentional modulation in extrastriate visual areas. *Nature Neuroscience*, **2**, 671–676.

Chen, X.Y. and Wolpaw, J.R. (1995). Operant conditioning of H-reflex in freely moving rats. *Journal of Neurophysiology*, **73**, 411–415.

Cheney, D.L. and Seyfarth, R.M. (1990). *How monkeys see the world*. University of Chicago Press, Chicago.

Cherry, S.R. and Phelps, M.E. (1996). Imaging brain function with positron emission tomography. In *Brain mapping. The methods* (ed. A.W. Toga and J.C. Mazziotta), pp. 191–221. Academic Press, San Diego.

Chiel, H.J. and Beer, R.D. (1997). The brain has a body: Adaptive behavior emerges from interactions of nervous system, body and environment. *Trends in Neurosciences*, **20**, 553–557.

Chisholm, R.M. (1982). *The foundations of knowing*. University of Minnesota Press, Minneapolis, MN.

Cho, Y.H., Beracochea, D., and Jaffard, R. (1993). Extended temporal gradient for the retrograde and anterograde amnesia produced by ibotanate enthorhinal cortex lesions in mice. *Journal of Neuroscience*, **13**, 1759–1766.

Chomsky, N. (1959). Verbal behavior. Review of verbal behavior by B.F. Skinner. *Language*, **35**, 26–58.

Chomsky, N. (1966). *Cartesian linguistics. A chapter in the history of rationalist thought.* Harper & Row, New York.

Chow, K.L. (1954). Effects of temporal neocortical ablation on visual discrimination learning sets in monkeys. *Journal of Comparative and Physiological Psychology*, **47**, 194–198.

Christensen, T.A., Pawlowski, V.M., Lei, H., and Hildebrand, J.G. (2000). Multi-unit recordings reveal context-dependent modulation of synchrony in odor-specific neural ensembles. *Nature Neuroscience*, **3**, 927–931.

Christianson, S.-A. (1992). Do flashbulb memories differ from other types of emotional memories? In *Affect and accuracy in recall. Studies of 'flashbulb' memories*, (ed. E. Winograd and U. Neisser), pp. 191–211. Cambridge University Press, New York.

Christie, B.R. and Abraham, W.C. (1992). Priming of associative long-term depression by theta frequency synaptic activity. *Neuron*, **8**, 79–84.

Christoffersen, G.R.J. (1997). Habituation: events in the history of its characterization and linkage to synaptic depression, a new proposed kinetic criterion for its identification. *Progress in Neurobiology*, **53**, 45–66.

Chun, M.M. and Phelps, E.A. (1999). Memory deficits for implicit contextual information in amnesic subjects with hippocampal damage. *Nature Neuroscience*, **2**, 845–847.

Churchland, P.M. and Churchland, P.S. (1998). *On the contrary. Critical essays, 1987–1997.* MIT Press, Cambridge, MA.

Churchland, P.S. and Sejnowski, T.J. (1992). *The computational brain.* MIT Press, Cambridge, MA.

Clanchy, M.T. (1993). *from memory to written record. England 1066–1307.* Blackwell, Oxford.

Claparede, E. (1911). Recognition and 'Me-Ness'. *Archives de Psychologie*, **11**, 79–90. Translated in D. Rapaport (trans. and comment) (1951). *Organization and pathology of thought, selected sources*, pp. 58–75. Columbia University Press, New York.

Clark, D.M. and Teasdale, J.D. (1982). Diurnal variation in clinical depression and accessibility of memories of positive and negative experiences. *Journal of Abnormal Psychology*, **91**, 87–95.

Clark, R.B. (1960). Habituation of the polychaete *Nereis* to sudden stimuli. I. General properties of the habituation process. *Animal Behaviour*, **8**, 82–91.

Clark, R.E. and Squire, L.R. (1998). Classical conditioning and brain systems: the role of awareness. *Science*, **280**, 77–81.

Clark, W.C. and Clark, S.B. (1980). Pain responses in Nepalese porters. *Science*, **209**, 410–412.

Clause, B.T. (1993). The Wistar rat as a right choice: establishing mammalian standards and the ideal of a standarized mammal. *Journal of the History of Biology*, **26**, 329–349.

Clayton, D.A. (1978). Socially facilitated behavior. *Quarterly Review of Biology*, **53**, 373–392.

Clayton, N.S. and Dickinson, A. (1998). Episodic-like memory during cache recovery by scrub jays. *Nature*, **395**, 272–274.

Clayton, N.S., Griffiths, D.P., Emery, N.J., and Dickinson, A. (2001). Elements of episodic-like memory in animals. *Philosophical Transactions of the Royal Society London. Series B.*, **356**, 1483–1491.

Cleary, L.J., Lee, W.L., and Byrne, J.H. (1998). Cellular correlates of long-term sensitization in *Aplysia*. *Journal of Neuroscience*, **18**, 5988–5998.

Cockburn, J. (1995). Task interruption in prospective memory: a frontal lobe function? *Cortex*, **31**, 87–97.

Code, C., Wallesch, C.-W., Joanette, Y., and Roch Lecours, A. (1996). *Classic cases in neuropsychology.* Psychology Press, Hove, East Sussex.

Cofer, C.N. (1960). Experimental studies of the role of verbal processes in concept formation and problem solving. *Annals of the New York Academy of Sciences*, **91**, 94–107.

Cohen, G. (1996). *Memory in the real world*, (2nd edn). Psychology Press, Erlbaum (UK) Taylor & Francis, Hove, UK.

Cohen, L.B., Salzberg, B.M., Davila, H.V., Ross, W.N., Landowne, D., and Waggoner, A.S. (1974). Changes in axon fluorescence during activity: Molecular probes of membrane potential. *Journal of Membrane Biology*, **19**, 1–36.

Cohen, N.J. (1984). Preserved learning capacity in amnesia: evidence for multiple memory systems. In *Neuropsychology of memory* (ed. L.R. Squire and N. Butters), pp. 83–103. The Guilford Press, New York.

Cohen, N.J. and Squire, L.R. (1980). Preserved learning and retention of pattern-analyzing skill in amnesia: dissociation of knowing how from knowing that. *Science*, **210**, 207–210.

Cohen, N.J., Poldrack, R.A., and Eichenbaum, H. (1997). Memory for items and memory for relations in the procedural/declarative memory framework. *Memory*, **5**, 131–178.

Cohen, T.E., Kaplan, S.W., Kandel, E.R., and Hawkins, R.D. (1997). A simplified preparation for relating cellular events to behavior: Mechanisms contributing to habituation, dishabituation, and sensitization of the *Aplysia* gill-withdrawal reflex. *Journal of Neuroscience*, **17**, 2886–2899.

Cole, K.C., VanTilburg, D., Burch-Vernon, A., and Riccio, D.C. (1996). The importance of context in the US preexposure effect in CTA: Novel versus latent inhibited contextual stimuli. *Learning and Motivation*, **27**, 362–374.

Colegrove, F.W. (1898). Individual memories. *American Journal of Psychology*, **10**, 228–255.

Colish, M.L. (1997). *Medieval foundations of the Western intellectual tradition 400–1400.* Yale University Press, London.

References

Collins, A. (1987). *The nature of mental things*. University of Notre Dame Press, Notre Dame, IN.

Collins, A.M. and Quillian, M.R. (1969). Retrieval time from semantic memory. *Journal of Verbal Learning and Verbal Behavior*, **8**, 240–247.

Collins, W. (1868/1992). *The moonstone*. David Campbell Publishers, London.

Colquhoun, D. and Sakmann, B. (1998). From muscle endplate to brain synapses: a short history of synapses and agonist-activated ion channels. *Neuron*, **20**, 381–387.

Colwill, R.M. and Rescorla, R.A. (1985). Post-conditioning devaluation of a reinforcer affects instrumental responding. *Journal of Experimental Psychology: Animal Behavior Processes*, **11**, 120–132.

Colwill, R.M. and Rescorla, R.A. (1986). Associative structures in instrumental conditioning. In *The psychology of learning and motivation*, Vol. 20, (ed. G.H. Bower), pp. 55–104. Academic Press, New York.

Conn, P.M. (ed.) (1998). Ion channels. Part B. *Methods in enzymology*, Vol. 293. Academic Press, San Diego.

Constantine-Paton, M. and Cline, H.T. (1998). LTP and activity-dependent synaptogenesis: the more alike they are, the more different they become. *Current Opinion in Neurobiology*, **8**, 139–148.

Conway, M.A. (1991). In defense of everyday memory. *American Psychologist*, **46**, 19–26.

Conway, M.A. (1995). *Flashbulb memories*. LEA, Hove, UK.

Conway, M.A. (1996). Shifting sands. *Nature*, **380**, 214.

Conway, M.A. (2001). Sensory-perceptual episodic memory and its context: autobiographical memory. *Philosophical Transactions of the Royal Society, London, Series B*, **356**, 1375–1384.

Conway, M.A. and Pleydell-Pearce, C.W. (2000). The construction of autobiographical memories in the self-memory system. *Psychological Review*, **107**, 261–288.

Cook, D.A. (1981). *A history of narrative film*. Norton, New York.

Cook, D.G. and Carew, T.J. (1989). Operant conditioning of head-waving in *Aplysia*. III. Cellular analysis of possible reinforcement pathways. *Journal of Neuroscience*, **9**, 3115–3122.

Coombs, C.H. (1938). Adaptation of the galvanic response to auditory stimuli. *Journal of Experimental Psychology*, **22**, 244–268.

Cooper, D.E. (1972). Innateness: Old and new. *Philosophical Review*, **October**, 465–483.

Cooper, J.R., Bloom, F.E., and Roth, R.H. (1996). *The biochemical basis of neuropharmacology*, (7th edn). Oxford University Press, New York.

Cooper, L.N. (1973). A possible organization of animal memory and learning. In *Proceedings of the Nobel symposium on collective properties of physical systems*, (ed. B. Lundquist and S. Landquist), pp. 252–264, Academic Press, New York.

Coover, J.E. and Angell, F. (1907). General practice effect of special exercise. *American Journal of Psychology*, **17**, 328–340.

Corbit, L.H. and Balleine, B.W. (2000). The role of the hippocampus in instrumental conditioning. *Journal of Neuroscience*, **20**, 4233–4239.

Corbit, L.H., Muir, J.L., and Balleine, B.W. (2001). The role of the nucleus accumbens in instrumental conditioning: evidence of a functional dissociation between accumbens core and shell. *Journal of Neuroscience*, **21**, 3251–3260.

Corfas, G. and Dudai, Y. (1989). Habituation and dishabituation of a cleaning reflex in normal and mutant *Drosophila*. *Journal of Neuroscience*, **9**, 56–62.

Corfas, G. and Dudai, Y. (1990). Adaptation and fatigue of a mechanosensory neuron in wild-type *Drosophila* and in memory mutants. *Journal of Neuroscience*, **10**, 491–499.

Corfas, G. and Dudai, Y. (1991). Memory mutations and age affect the fine structure of an identified sensory neuron in *Drosophila*. *Proceedings of the National Academy of Sciences USA*, **88**, 7252–7256.

Corkin, S. (1968). Acquisition of motor skill after bilateral medial temporal-lobe excision. *Neuropsychologia*, **6**, 255–265.

Corkin, S., Amaral, D.G., Gonzalez, R.G., Johnson, K.A., and Hyman, B.T. (1997). H.M.'s medial temporal lobe lesion: Findings from magnetic resonance imaging. *Journal of Neuroscience*, **17**, 3964–3979.

Cornell, E.H. (1980). Distributed study facilitates infants' delayed recognition memory. *Memory and Cognition*, **8**, 539–542.

Cornford, F.M. (1922). *Microcosmographia academica. Being a guide for the young academic politician*, (2nd edn). Ares, Chicago, IL.

Coull, J.T. and Nobre, A.C. (1998). Where and when to pay attention: the neural systems for directing attention to spatial locations and to time intervals revealed by both PET and fMRI. *Journal of Neuroscience*, **18**, 7426–7435.

Cowan, N. (1988). Evolving conceptions of memory storage, selective attention, and their mutual constraints within the human information-processing system. *Psychological Bulletin*, **104**, 163–191.

Cowan, W.M. (1998). The emergence of modern neuroanatomy and developmental neurobiology. *Neuron*, **20**, 413–426.

Cowie, A.P., Mackin, R., and McCaig, I.R. (1985). *Oxford dictionary of current idiomatic English*. Vol. 2: *Phrase, clause & sentence idioms*. Oxford University Press, Oxford.

Cox, P.A. (2000). Will tribal knowledge survive the millennium? *Science*, **287**, 44–45.

Crabtree, G.R. (1999). Generic signals and specific outcomes: signaling through Ca^{2+}, calcineurin, and NF-AT. Cell, **96**, 611–614.

Craik, F.I.M. and Lockhart, R.S. (1972). Levels of processing: a framework for memory research. *Journal of Verbal Learning and Verbal Behavior*, **11**, 671–684.

Craik, F.I.M. and Tulving, E. (1975). Depth of processing and the retention of words in episodic memory. *Journal of Experimental Psychology: General*, **104**, 268–294.

Crair, M.C., Gillespie, D.C., and Stryker, M.P. (1998). The use of visual experience in the development of columns in cat visual cortex. *Science*, **279**, 566–570.

Crawley, J.N. and Paylor, R. (1997). A proposed test battery and constellations of specific behavioral paradigms to investigate the behavioral phenotypes of transgenic and knockout mice. *Hormones and Behavior*, **31**, 197–211.

Crick, F. (1984*a*). Function of the thalamic reticular complex: the searchlight hypothesis. *Proceedings of the National Academy of Sciences*, **81**, 4586–4590.

Crick, F. (1984*b*). Memory and molecular turnover. *Nature*, **312**, 101.

Crick, F. (1994). *The astonishing hypothesis. the scientific search for the soul*. Simon and Schuster, London.

Crick, F. and Koch, C. (1990). Towards a neurobiological theory of consciousness. *Seminars in Neuroscience*, **2**, 263–275.

Crick, F. and Koch, C. (1992). The problem of consciousness. *Scientific American*, (September), 153–159.

Crick, F. and Koch, C. (1995). Are we aware of neural activity in primary visual cortex? *Nature*, **375**, 121–123.

Crick, F. and Koch, C. (1998). Consciousness and neuroscience. *Cerebral Cortex*, **8**, 97–107.

Crick, F. and Mitchison, G. (1983). The function of dream sleep. *Nature*, **304**, 111–114.

Crimson, M.L. (1994). Tacrine: the first drug approved for Alzheimer's disease. *Annals of Pharmacotherapy*, **28**, 744–751.

Cross, H.A., Halcomb, C.G., and Matter, W.W. (1967). Imprinting or exposure learning in rats given early auditory stimulation. *Psychonomic Science*, **7**, 233–234.

Crossman, E.R.F.W. (1959). A theory of the acquisition of speed-skill. *Ergonomics*, **2**, 153–166.

Crowder, R.G. (1996). The trouble with prospective memory: a provocation. In *Prospective memory. Theory and applications* (ed. M. Brandimonte, G.O. Einstein, and M.A. McDaniel), pp. 143–147. Lawrence Erlbaum Associates, Mahwah, NJ.

Cruikshank, S.J. and Weinberger, N.M. (1996). Evidence for the Hebbian hypothesis in experience-dependent physiological plasticity of neocortex: a critical review. *Brain Research Reviews*, **22**, 191–228.

Cuddon, J.A. (1979). *A dictionary of literary terms*. Penguin Books, London.

Cummins, R. (1975). Functional analysis. *Journal of Philosophy*, **72**, 741–745.

Curran, T. and Morgan, J.I. (1994). Fos: an immediate-early transcription factor in neurons. *Journal of Neurobiology*, **26**, 403–412.

Daffner, K.R., Mesulam, M.M., Scinto, L.F.M., Acar, D., Calvo, V., Faust, R., Chabrerie, A., Kennedy, B., and Holcomb, P. (2000). The central role of the prefrontal cortex in directing attention to novel events. *Brain*, **123**, 927–939.

Dagher, A., Owen, A.M., Boecker, H., and Brooks, D.J. (1999). Mapping the network for planning: a correlational PET activation study with the tower of London task. *Brain*, **122**, 1973–1987.

Dale, H.H. (1914). The action of certain esters and ethers of choline, and their relation to muscarine. *Journal of Pharmacology and Experimental Therapeutics*, **6**, 147–190.

Dale, H.H. (1938/1953). The William Henry Welch Lectures, 1937. Acetylcholine as a chemical transmitter of the effects of nerve impulses. In *Adventures in physiology, with excursions into autopharmacology*, pp. 611–637. Pergamon Press, London. (A selection from the scientific publications of Sir Henry Hallett Dale, with an introduction and recent comments by the author.)

Dale, H. (1948). Accident and opportunism in medical research. *British Medical Journal,* **2**, 451–455.

Dale, H.H. (1954). The beginnings and the prospects of neurohumoral transmission. *Pharmacological Reviews*, **6**, 7–13.

Dalla Barba, G. (2000). Prospective memory: a 'new' memory system? In *Handbook of neuropsychology*, Vol. 8 (ed. H. Spinnler and F. Boller), pp. 239–251. Elsevier, Amsterdam.

Damasio, A.R. (1989). Time-locked multiregional retroactivation: A systems-level proposal for the neural substrates of recall and recognition. *Cognition*, **33**, 25–62.

Damasio, A.R. (1990). Category-related recognition defects as a clue to neural substrates of knowledge. *Trends in Neurosciences*, **13**, 95–98.

Damasio, A. (1999). *The feeling of what happens: body and emotion in the making of consciousness*. Harvest, New York.

Dan, Y., Alonso, J.-M., Usrey, W.M., and Reid, R.C. (1998). Coding of visual information by precisely correlated spikes in the lateral geniculate nucleus. *Nature Neuroscience*, **1**, 501–507.

d'Andrade, R. (1995). *The development of cognitive anthropology*. Cambridge University Press, New York.

Daniel, W.F. and Crovitz, H.F. (1983). Acute memory impairment following electroconvulsive therapy: A review of the literature. 1. The effects of electrical stimulus waveform and number of treatments. *Acta Psychiatrica Scandinavica*, **67**, 1–7.

Danion, J.M., Weingartner, H., File, S.E., Jaffard, R., Sunderland, T., Tulving, E., and Warburton, D.M. (1993). Pharmacology of human memory and cognition: Illustrations from the effects of benzodiazepines and cholinergic drugs. *Journal of Psychopharmacology*, **7**, 371–377.

References

Dante, A. (1314/1996). *The divine comedy: inferno*. Canto 4, line 45, and p. 552. Oxford University Press, New York.

Darwin, C. (1838/1987*a*). Notebook M. In *Charles Darwin's notebooks, 1836–1844. Geology, transmutation of species, metaphysical enquiries* (ed. P.H. Barrett, P.J. Gautrey, S. Herbert, D. Kohn, and S. Smith), p. 128. British Museum (Natural History) and Cornell University Press, Ithaca, NY.

Darwin, C. (1838/1987*b*). Notebook B, p. 169. In *Charles Darwin's notebooks, 1836–1844. Geology, transmutation of species, metaphysical enquiries* (ed. Barrett, P.H., Gautrey, P.J., Herbert, S., Kohn, D., and Smith, S.), British Museum (Natural History) and Cornell University Press, Ithaca, NY.

Darwin, C. (1871/1981). *The descent of Man, and selection in relation to sex*. Princeton University Press, Princeton, NJ.

Darwin, C. (1872/1998). *The expression of the emotions in man and animals* (ed. P. Ekman), Harper Collins, London.

Dash, P.K., Hochner, B., and Kandel, E.R. (1990). Injection of the cAMP-response element into the nucleus of *Aplysia* sensory neurons blocks long-term facilitation. *Nature, 345*, 718–721.

Dave, A.S. and Margoliash, D. (2000). Song replay during sleep and computational rules for sensorimotor vocal learning. *Science, 290*, 812–816.

Davidson, D. (1979). What metaphors mean. In *On metaphor* (ed. S. Sacks), pp. 29–45. University of Chicago Press, Chicago.

Davidson, D. (1980). *Essays on actions and events*. Oxford University Press, Oxford.

Davidson, R.J. and Irwin, W. (1999). The functional neuroanatomy of emotion and affective style. *Trends in Cognitive Sciences, 3*, 11–21.

Davies, J.D. (1971). *Phrenology fad or science. A 19th-century American crusade*. Archon Books, Shoe String, Hamden, CT.

Davis, G.W. and Goodman, C.S. (1998). Genetic analysis of synaptic development and plasticity: Homeostatic regulation of synaptic efficacy. *Current Opinion in Neurobiology, 8*, 149–156.

Davis, G.W., Schuster, C.M., and Goodman, C.S. (1996). Genetic dissection of structural and functional components of synaptic plasticity. III. CREB is necessary for presynaptic functional plasticity. *Neuron, 17*, 669–679.

Davis, H. and Perusse, R. (1988). Numerical competence in animals: Definitional issues, current evidence, and a new research agenda. *Behavioral and Brain Sciences, 11*, 561–615.

Davis, H.P. and Squire, L.R. (1984). Protein synthesis and memory: A review. *Psychological Bulletin, 96*, 518–559.

Davis, M. (1970). Effects of interstimulus interval length and variability on startle response habituation in the rat. *Journal of Comparative and Physiological Psychology, 72*, 177–192.

Davis, M. (1992). The role of the amygdala in fear and anxiety. *Annual Review of Neuroscience, 15*, 353–375.

Davis, M., Parisi, T., Gendelman, D.S., Tischler, M., and Kehne, J.H. (1982). Habituation and sensitization of startle reflexes elicited electrically from the brainstem. *Science, 218*, 688–690.

Davis, R.L. (1993). Mushroom bodies and *Drosophila* learning. *Neuron, 11*, 1–14.

Dawson, R.G. and McGaugh, J.L. (1969). Electroconvulsive shock effect on a reactivated memory: further examination. *Science, 166*, 525–527.

Dawson, R.M.C., Elliott, D.C., Elliott, W.H., and Jones, M.J. (1986). *Data for biochemical research*, (3rd edn). Clarendon Press, Oxford.

Day, L.B., Weisend, M., Sutherland, R.J., and Schallert, T. (1999). The hippocampus is not necessary for a place response but may be necessary for pliancy. *Behavioral Neuroscience, 113*, 914–924.

Day, L.M. and Bentley, M. (1911). A note on learning in Paramecium. *Journal of Animal Behavior, 1*, 67–73.

d'Azevedo, W.L. (1962). Uses of the past in Gola discourse. *Journal of African History, 3*, 11–34.

De Koninck, P. and Schulman, H. (1998). Sensitivity of CaM kinase II to the frequency of Ca^{2+} oscillations. *Science, 279*, 227–230.

De Olmos, J.S. and Heimer, L. (1999). The concepts of the ventral striatopallidal system and extended amygdala. *Annals of the New York Academy of Sciences, 877*, 1–32.

De Quervain, D,J.F., Roosendaal, B., and McGaugh, J.L. (1998). Stress and glucocorticoids impair retrieval of long-term spatial memory. *Nature, 394*, 787–790.

De Quincey, T. (1866). *Suspiria de Profundis, being a sequel to the confessions of an English opium eater*. Ticknor and Fields, Boston.

Deahl, J.N. (1900). *Imitation in education. Its nature, scope and significance*. Macmillan, New York.

Deberdt, W. (1994). Interaction between psychological and pharmacological treatment in cognitive impairment. *Life Sciences, 55*, 2057–2066.

Decety, J., Grezes, J., Costes, N., Perani, D., Jeannerod, M., Procyk, E., Grassi, F., and Fazio, F. (1997). Brain activity during observation of actions. Influence of action content and subject's strategy. *Brain, 120*, 1763–1777.

Decker, M.W. and McGaugh, J.L. (1991). The role of interactions between the cholinergic system and other neuromodulatory systems in learning and memory. *Synapse, 7*, 151–168.

Deese, J. (1951). The extinction of a discrimination without performance of the choice response. *Journal of Comparative and Physiological Psychology, 44*, 362–366.

Deese, J. (1959*a*). Influence of interitem associative strength upon immediate free recall. *Psychological Reports, 5*, 305–312.

Deese, J. (1959*b*). On the prediction of occurrence of particular verbal intrusions in immediate recall. *Journal of Experimental Psychology, 58*, 17–22.

DeFelipe, J. and Jones, E.G. (1988). *Cajal on the cerebral cortex*. Oxford University Press, New York.

Dehaene, S. and Changeux, J.-P. (1997). A hierarchical neuronal network for planning behavior. *Proceedings of the National Academy of Sciences USA*, **94**, 13293–13298.

Dehaene, S., Spelke, E., Pinel, P., Stanescu, R., and Tsivkin, S. (1999). Sources of mathematical thinking: behavioral and brain-imaging evidence. *Science*, **284**, 970–974.

Dehue, T. (1997). Deception, efficiency, and random groups. Psychology and the gradual origination of the random group design. *Isis*, **88**, 653–673.

Deisseroth, K., Bito, H., Schulman, H., and Tsien, R.W. (1995). A molecular mechanism for metaplasticity. *Current Biology*, **5**, 1334–1338.

Deisseroth, K., Bito, H., and Tsien, R.W. (1996). Signaling from synapse to nucleus: Postsynaptic CREB phosphorylation during multiple forms of hippocampal synaptic plasticity. *Neuron*, **16**, 89–101.

DeJong, R.J. (1957). The effects of increasing skill on cycle-time and its consequences for time-standards. *Ergonomics*, **1**, 51–60.

DeLuca, J. and Cicerone, K.D. (1991). Confabulation following aneurysm of the anterior communicating artery. *Cortex*, **27**, 417–423.

Dennett, D.C. (1978). *Brainstorms: philosophical essays on mind and psychology*. MIT Press, Cambridge, MA.

Dennett, D.C. (1983). Intentional systems in cognitive ethology: the 'Panglossian paradigm' defended. *Behavioral and Brain Sciences*, **6**, 343–390.

Dennett, D.C. (1987). *The intentional stance*. MIT Press, Cambridge, MA.

Dennett, D.C. (1991). *Consciousness explained*. Little, Brown and Co., Boston, MA.

Descartes, R. (1633/1985). Treatise on man. In *The philosophical writings of Descartes*, Vol. I (trans. J. Cottingham, R. Stoothoff, and D. Murdoch). Cambridge University Press, Cambridge.

Descartes, R. (1649/1985). The passions of the soul. In *The philosophical writings of Descartes*, Vol. I (trans. J. Cottingham, R. Stoothoff, and D. Murdoch). Cambridge University Press, Cambridge.

Desimone, R. (1991). Face-selective cells in the temporal cortex of monkeys. *Journal of Cognitive Neuroscience*, **3**, 1–7.

Desimone, R. (1996). Neural mechanisms for visual memory and their role in attention. *Proceedings of the National Academy of Sciences USA*, **93**, 13494–13499.

Desimone, R. and Duncan, J. (1995). Neural mechanisms of selective visual attention. *Annual Review of Neuroscience*, **18**, 193–222.

Desmedt, A., Garcia, R., and Jaffard, R. (1998). Differential modulation of changes in hippocampal-septal synaptic excitability by the amygdala as a function of either elemental or contextual fear conditioning in mice. *Journal of Neuroscience*, **18**, 480–487.

Desmond, J.E. and Fiez, J.A. (1998). Neuroimaging studies of the cerebellum: language, learning and memory. *Trends in Cognitive Sciences*, **2**, 355–362.

Dethier, V.G. (1962). *To know a fly*. Holden-Day, San Francisco, CA.

Deutsch, J.A. (1993). Spatial learning in mutant mice. *Science*, **262**, 760–761.

DeYoe, E.A., Felleman, D.J., Van Essen, D.C., and McClendon, E. (1994). Multiple processing streams in occipitotemporal visual cortex. *Nature*, **371**, 151–154.

DeZazzo, J. and Tully, T. (1995). Dissection of memory formation: From behavioral pharmacology to molecular genetics. *Trends in Neurosciences*, **18**, 212–218.

DeZazzo, J., Sandstrom, D., De Belle, S., Velinzon, K., Smith, P., Grady, L., DelVecchio, M., Ramaswami, M., and Tully, T. (2000). *nalyot*, a mutation of the *Drosophila* Myb-related *Adf1* transcription factor, disrupts synapse formation and olfactory memory. *Neuron*, **27**, 145–158.

Di Carlo, A., Baldereschi, M., Amaducci, L., Maggi, S., Grigoletto, F., Scarlatom G., and Inzitari, D. (2000). Cognitive impairment without dementia in older people: prevalence, vascular risk factors, impact on disability. The Italian longitudinal study on aging. *Journal of the American Geriatrics Society*, **48**, 775–782.

Dickinson, A. (1980). *Contemporary animal learning theory*. Cambridge University Press, Cambridge.

Dickinson, A. and Balleine, B. (1994). Motivational control of goal-directed action. *Animal Learning & Behavior*, **22**, 1–18.

Dickinson, E. (1896/1988). The brain is wider than the sky. In *The Norton anthology of modern poetry*, (2nd edn), (ed. R. Ellmann and R. O'Clair), p. 51. Norton, New York.

Dingman, W. and Sporn, M.B. (1961). The incorporation of 8-azaguanine into rat brain RNA and its effect on maze-learning by the rat: An inquiry into the biochemical basis of memory. *Journal of Psychiatric Research*, **1**, 1–11.

Dittamn, A.H. and Quinn, T.P. (1996). Homing in Pacific salmon: mechanisms and ecological basis. *Journal of Experimental Biology*, **199**, 83–91.

D'Mello, G.D. and Steckler, T. (1996). Animal models in cognitive behavioural pharmacology: An overview. *Cognitive Brain Research*, **3**, 345–352.

Dobbs, A.R. and Reeves, M.B. (1996). Prospective memory: More than memory. In *Prospective memory. Theory and applications*, (ed. M. Brandimonte, G.O. Einstein, and M.A. McDaniel), pp. 199–225. Lawrence Erlbaum Associates, Mahwah, NJ.

Dodge, R. (1923). Habituation to rotation. *Journal of Experimental Psychology*, **6**, 1–35.

References

Dolan, R.J. and Fletcher, P.F. (1999). Encoding and retrieval in human medial temporal lobes: Am empirical investigation using functional magnetic resonance imaging (fMRI). *Hippocampus*, **9**, 25–34.

Dolmetsch, R.E., Xu, K.L., and Lewis, R.S. (1998). Calcium oscillations increase the efficiency and specificity of gene expression. *Nature*, **392**, 933–936.

Donoghue, M.J. (1992). Homology. In *Keywords in evolutionary biology*, (ed. E.F. Keller and E.A. Lloyd), pp. 170–179. Harvard University Press, Cambridge, MA.

Dosher, B.A. and Sperling, G. (1998). A century of human information-processing theory. Vision, attention, and memory. In *Perception and cognition at century's end*, (ed. J. Hochberg), pp. 199–252. Academic Press, San Diego.

Doty, B.A., Jones, C.N., and Doty, L.A. (1967). Learning-set formation by mink, ferrets, skunks, and cats. *Science*, **155**, 1579–1580.

Doty, R.W. (1998). The five mysteries of the mind, and their consequences. *Neuropsychologia*, **36**, 1069–1076.

Douglas, R.J., Koch, K., Mahowald, M., Martin, K.A.C., and Suarez, H.H. (1995). Recurrent excitation in neocortical circuits. *Science*, **269**, 981–985.

DSM-IV (1994). *Diagnostic and statistical manual of mental disorders*, (4th edn), (ed. A. Frances, H.A. Pincus, M.B. First, and Task force on DSM-IV). American Psychiatric Association, Washington, DC.

Dubnau, J. and Tully, T. (1998). Gene discovery in *Drosophila*: New insights for learning and memory. *Annual Review of Neuroscience*, **21**, 407–444.

Dubnau, J., Grady, L., Ktamoto, T., and Tully, T. (2001). Disruption of neurotransmission in *Drosophila* mushroom body blocks retrieval but not acquisition of memory. *Nature*, **411**, 476–480.

Dudai, Y. (1985). Some properties of adenylate cyclase which might be important for memory formation. *Federation of European Biological Societies Letters*, **191**, 165–170.

Dudai, Y. (1988). Genetic dissection of learning and short-term memory in *Drosophila*. *Annual Review of Neuroscience*, **11**, 537–563.

Dudai, Y. (1989). *The neurobiology of memory. Concepts, findings, trends*. Oxford University Press, Oxford.

Dudai, Y. (1992). Why should 'learning' and 'memory' be redefined, (or, an agenda for focused reductionism). *Concepts in Neuroscience*, **3**, 99–121.

Dudai, Y. (1993). Molecular devices of learning: types and tokens. In *Memory concepts, basic and clinical aspects*. Novo Nordisk Foundation Symposium 7 (ed. P. Andersen, O. Hvalby, O. Paulsen, and B. Hokfelt), pp. 65–76. Elsevier, Amsterdam.

Dudai, Y. (1994a). Molecular devices in neuronal learning machines (or, the syntactic approach to biological learning). In *The memory system of the brain* (ed. J. Delacour), pp. 319–336. World Scientific, Singapore.

Dudai, Y. (1994b). On the relevance of *in vivo* neurobiological observations to learning and memory. In *Cellular and molecular mechanisms underlying higher neural functions* (ed. A.I. Selverston and P. Ascher), pp. 71–79. Wiley, Chichester.

Dudai, Y. (1995). On the relevance of LTP to learning and memory. In *Brain and memory* (ed. J.L. McGaugh, N.M. Weinberger, and G. Lynch), pp. 319–327. Oxford University Press, New York.

Dudai, Y. (1996). Consolidation: fragility on the road to the engram. *Neuron*, **17**, 367–370.

Dudai, Y. (1997a). How big is human memory, or on being just useful enough. *Learning & Memory*, **3**, 341–365.

Dudai, Y. (1997b). Time to remember. *Neuron*, **18**, 179–182.

Dudai, Y. (1999). The smell of representations. *Neuron*, **23**, 633–635.

Dudai, Y. (2000). The shaky trace. *Nature*, **406**, 686–687.

Dudai, Y. and Morris, R.G.M. (2000). To consolidate or not to consolidate: What are the questions? In *Brain, perception, memory. Advances in cognitive sciences* (ed. J.J. Bolhuis). Oxford University Press, Oxford.

Dudai, Y., Jan, Y.N., Byers, D., Quinn, W.G., and Benzer, S. (1976). *dunce*, a mutant of *Drosophila* deficient in learning. *Proceedings of the National Academy of Sciences USA*, **73**, 1684–1688.

Dudai, Y., Uzzan, A., and Zvi, S. (1983). Abnormal activity of adenylate cyclase in the *Drosophila* memory mutant *rutabaga*. *Neuroscience Letters*, **42**, 207–212.

Dudai, Y. (Rapporteur), Amari, S.I., Bienestock, E., Dehaene, S., Fuster, J., Goddard, G.V., Konishi, M., Menzel, R., Mishkin, M., Muller, C.M., Rolls, E.T., Schwegler, H.H., and von der Malsburg, C. (1987). On neuronal assemblies and memories. In *The neural and molecular bases of learning*, (ed. J.P. Changeux and M. Konishi), pp. 399–410. Wiley, Chichester.

Dudycha, G.J. and Dudycha, M.M. (1941). Childhood memories: A review of the literature. *Psychological Bulletin*, **38**, 668–682.

Duhem, P. (1914/1954). *The aim and structure of physical theory*. Princeton University Press, NJ.

Duncan, C.P. (1948). The retroactive effect of electroshock on learning. *Journal of Comparative Psychology*, **42**, 32–44.

Duncan, R. and Weston-Smith, M. (ed.) (1977). *The encyclopedia of ignorance. Everything you ever wanted to know about the unknown*. Pocket Books, New York.

Dura, J.M., Taillebourg, E., and Preat, T. (1995). The *Drosophila* learning and memory gene *linotte* encodes a putative receptor tyrosine kinase homologous to the human ryk gene product. *FEBS Letters*, **370**, 250–254.

Durkheim, E. (1895/1964). *The rules of sociological method*. Free Press, Glencoe, IL.

Durkheim, E. (1912/1961). *The elementary forms of the religious life*. George, Allen & Unwin, London.

Duzel, E., Yonelinas, A.P., Managun, G.R., Heinze, H.-J., and Tulving, E. (1997). Event-related brain potential correlates of two states of conscious awareness in memory. *Proceedings of the National Academy of Sciences USA*, **94**, 5973–5978.

Eacott, M.J. and Crawley, R.A. (1998). The offset of childhood amnesia: Memory for events that occurred before age 3. *Journal of Experimental Psychology: General*, **127**, 27–33.

Ebbinghaus, H. (1885/1964). *Memory: A contribution to experimental psychology.* Teachers College, Columbia University, New York/Dover New York.

Ebstein, R.P., Novick, O., Umansky, R., Priel, B., Osher, Y., Blaine, D., Bennett, E.R., Nemanov, L., Katz, M., and Belmaker, R.H. (1996). Dopamine D4 (D4DR) exon III polymorphism associated with the human personality trait of novelty seeking. *Nature Genetics*, **12**, 78–80.

EBT (1923). Relearning after forty six years. *American Journal of Psychology*, **34**, 468–469.

Eccles, J.C. (1973). The cerebellum as a computer: patterns in space and time. *Journal of Physiology (London)*, **229**, 1–32.

Eccles, J.C. (1982). The synapse: from electrical to chemical transmission. *Annual Review of Neuroscience*, **5**, 325–339.

Eckhorn, R., Bauer, R., Jordan, W., Brosch, M., Kruse, W., Munk, M., and Reilboeck, H.J. (1988). Coherent oscillations: A mechanism of feature linking in the visual cortex. *Biological Cybernetics*, **60**, 121–130.

Edelberg, H.K. and Wei, J.Y. (1996). The biology of Alzheimer's disease. *Mechanisms of Ageing and Development*, **91**, 95–114.

Edelman, G.M. (1987). *Neural Darwinism. The theory of neuronal group selection.* Basic Books, New York.

Edelman, G.M. (1990). *The remembered present: a biological theory of consciousness.* Basic Books, New York.

Edelman, G.M. (1993). Neural Darwinism: Selection and reentrant signaling in higher brain function. *Neuron*, **10**, 115–125.

Edelman, G.M. (1995). Memory and the individual soul: against silly reductionism. In *Nature's imagination. The frontiers of scientific vision* (ed. J. Cornwell), pp. 200–206. Oxford University Press, Oxford.

Eder, K. (1996). *The social construction of nature.* SAGE, London.

Edwards, A.J. (1993). *Dementia.* Plenum Press, New York.

Edwards, D.H., Yeh, S.-R., and Krasne, F.B. (1998). Neuronal coincidence detection by voltage-sensitive electrical synapses. *Proceedings of the National Academy of Sciences USA*, **95**, 7145–7150.

Edwards, D.H., Heitler, W.J., and Krasne, F.B. (1999). Fifty years of a command neuron: The neurobiology of escape behavior in the crayfish. *Trends in Neurosciences*, **22**, 153–161.

Efron, R. (1970). The relationships between the duration of a stimulus and the duration of a perception. *Neuropsychologia*, **8**, 37–55.

Egeth, H.E. and Yantis, S. (1997). Visual attention: Control, representation, and time course. *Annual Review of Psychology*, **48**, 269–297.

Egger, M.D. (1978). Sensitization and habituation of dorsal horn cells in cats. *Journal of Physiology*, **279**, 153–166.

Eich, E. and Birbaum, I.M. (1982). Repetition, cueing, and state-dependent memory. *Memory and Cognition*, **10**, 103–114.

Eichenbaum, H. (1996). The real-life/laboratory controversy as viewed from the cognitive neurobiology of animal learning and memory. *Behavioral and Brain Sciences*, **19**, 196–197.

Eichenbaum, H. (1997*a*). Declarative memory: Insights from cognitive neurobiology. *Annual Review of Psychology*, **48**, 547–572.

Eichenbaum, H. (1997*b*). To cortex: thanks for the memories. *Neuron*, **19**, 481–484.

Eichenbaum, H. (1999). Conscious awareness, memory and the hippocampus. *Nature Neuroscience*, **2**, 775–776.

Eichenbaum, H., Fagan, A., and Cohen, N.J. (1986). Normal olfactory discrimination learning set and facilitation of reversal learning after medial-temporal damage in rats: implications for an account of preserved learning abilities in dementia. *Journal of Neuroscience*, **6**, 1876–1884.

Eichenbaum, H., Otto, T., and Cohen, N. (1994). Two functional components of the hippocampal memory system. *Behavioral and Brain Sciences*, **17**, 449–518.

Eichenbaum, H., Schoenbaum, G., Young, B., and Bunsey, M. (1996). Functional organization of the hippocampal memory system. *Proceedings of the National Academy of Sciences USA*, **93**, 13500–13506.

Eid, C.N. and Rose, G.M. (1999). Cognition enhancement strategies by ion channel modulation of neurotransmission. *Current Pharmaceutical Design*, **5**, 345–361.

Eisenstein, E.M. (1997). Selecting a model system for neurobiological studies of learning and memory. *Behavioural Brain Research*, **82**, 121–132.

Eldridge, L.L., Knowlton, B.J., Furmanski, C.S., Bookheimer, S.Y., and Engel, S.A. (2000). Remembering episodes: a selective role for the hippocampus during retrieval. *Nature Neuroscience*, **3**, 1149–1152.

Eliot, T.S. (1939/1982). The naming of cats, In *Old Possum's book of practical cats.* Harcourt Brace Jovanovich, New York.

Eliot, T.S. (1963). Burnt Norton. In *Collected poems 1909–1962.* Faber and Faber, London.

Ellenberger, H.F. (1970). *The discovery of the unconscious. The history and evolution of dynamic psychiatry.* Basic Books, New York.

Elliott, T.R. (1904). On the action of adrenalin. *Proceedings of the Physiological Society, London*, **31**, XX–XXI.

Emery, C.F., Huppert, F.A., and Schein, R.L. (1997). Do pulmonary function and smoking behavior predict cognitive function? Findings from a British sample. *Psychology & Health*, **12**, 265–275.

References

Emptage, N.J. and Carew, T.J. (1993). Long-term synaptic facilitation in the absence of short-term facilitation in *Aplysia* neurons. *Science*, **262**, 253–256.

Engel, A.K., Roelfsema, P.R., Fries, P., Brecht, M., and Singer, W. (1997). Role of the temporal domain for response selection and perceptual binding. *Cerebral Cortex*, **7**, 571–582.

Engert, F. and Bonhoeffer, T. (1997). Synapse specificity of long-term potentiation breaks down at short distances. *Nature*, **388**, 279–284.

Epstein, R., Kirshnit, C.E., Lanza, R.P., and Rubin, L.C. (1984). 'Insight' in the pigeon: Antecedents and determinants of an intelligent performance. *Nature*, **308**, 61–62.

Epstein, R., Harris, A., Stanley, D., and Kanwisher, N. (1999). The parahippocampal place area: Recognition, navigation, or encoding? *Neuron*, **23**, 115–125.

Erber, J., Kierzek, S., Sander, E., and Grandy, K. (1998). Tactile learning in the honeybee. *Journal of Comparative Physiology [A]*, **183**, 737–744.

Erdelyi, M.H. and Becker, J. (1974). Hyperamnesia for pictures: Incremental memory for pictures but not for words in multiple recall trials. *Cognitive Psychology*, **6**, 159–171.

Erickson, C.A. and Desimone, R. (1999). Responses of macaque perirhinal neurons during and after visual stimulus association learning. *Journal of Neuroscience*, **19**, 10404–10416.

Ericsson, K.A. and Lehmann, A.C. (1996). Expert and exceptional performance: evidence of maximal adaptation to task constraints. *Annual Review of Psychology*, **47**, 273–305.

Eriksen, C.W. (1960). Discrimination and learning without awareness: A methodological survey and evaluation. *Psychological Review*, **67**, 279–300.

Eriksson, P.S., Perfilieva, E., Bjork-Eriksson, T., Alborn, A.-M., Nordenborg, C., Peterson, D.A., and Gage, F.H. (1998). Neurogenesis in the adult human hippocampus. *Nature Medicine*, **4**, 1313–1317.

Esch, H.E., Zhang, S., Srinivasan, M.V., and Tautz, J. (2001). Honeybee dances communicate distances measured by optic flow. *Nature*, **411**, 581–583.

Evans, E.P. (1906/1987). *The criminal prosecution and capital punishment of animals.* Faber and Faber, London.

Everitt, B.J. and Robbins, T.W. (1997). Central cholinergic systems and cognition. *Annual Review of Psychology*, **48**, 649–684.

Eysenck, M.W. and Keane, M.T. (1995). *Cognitive psychology. A student's handbook*, (3rd edn). Psychology Press, Hove, UK.

Faber, T., Joerges, J., and Menzel, R. (1999). Associative learning modifies neural representations of odors in the insect brain. *Nature Neuroscience*, **2**, 74–78.

Falconer, D.S. (1960). *Introduction to quantitative genetics.* Oliver and Boyd, Edinburgh.

Falls, W.A., Miserendino, J.D., and Davis, M. (1992). Extinction of fear-potentiated startle: Blockade by infusion of an NMDA antagonist into the amygdala. *Journal of Neuroscience*, **12**, 854–863.

Fanselow, M.S. (1998). Pavlovian conditioning, negative feedback, and blocking: Mechanisms that regulate association formation. *Neuron*, **20**, 625–627.

Farley, J.M., Richards, W.G., Ling, L.J., Liman, E., and Alkon, D.L. (1983). Membrane changes in a single photoreceptor cause associative learning in *Hermissenda*. *Science*, **221**, 1201–1203.

Fausett, L. (1994). *Fundamentals of neural networks. Architectures, algorithms, and applications.* Prentice Hall, Englewood Cliffs, NJ.

Feldman, D.E. and Knudsen, E.I. (1997). An anatomical basis for visual calibration of the auditory space map in the Barn Owl's midbrain. *Journal of Neuroscience*, **17**, 6820–6837.

Feldman, M.D. (2000). Munchausen by Internet: detecting factitious illness and crisis on the Internet. *Southern Medical Journal*, **93**, 669–672.

Fellous, J.-M. (1999). Neuromodulatory basis of emotion. *Neuroscientist*, **5**, 283–294.

Fernández, G., Weyerts, H., Schrader-Bölsche, M., Tendolkar, I., Smid, H.G.O.M., Tempelmann, C., Hinrichs, H., Scheich, H., Elger, C.E., Mangun, G.R., and Heinze, H.J. (1998). Successful verbal encoding into episodic memory engages the posterior hippocampus: A parametrically analyzed functional magnetic resonance imaging study. *Journal of Neuroscience*, **18**, 1841–1847.

Fernández, G., Effern, A., Grunwald, T., Pezer, N., Lehnertz, K., Dumpelmann, M., Van Roost, D., and Elger, C.E. (1999). Real-time tracking of memory formation in the human rhinal cortex and hippocampus. *Science*, **285**, 1582–1585.

Ferry, B., Roozendaal, B., and McGaugh, J.L. (1999). Basolateral amygdala noradrenergic influences on memory storage are mediated by an interaction between β- and α_1-adrenoceptors. *Journal of Neuroscience*, **19**, 5119–5123.

Ferster, C.B. and Skinner, B.F. (1957). *Schedules of reinforcement.* Apple-Century-Crofts, New York.

Finger, S. (1994). *Origins of neuroscience. A history of explorations into brain functions.* Oxford University Press, New York.

Finger, S. (2000). *Minds behind the brain. A history of the pioneers and their discoveries.* Oxford University Press, New York.

Finkbeiner, S. (2000). CREB couples neurotrophin signals to survival messages. *Neuron*, **25**, 11–14.

Fiorito, G. and Scotto, P. (1992). Observational learning in *Octopus vulgaris*. *Science*, **256**, 545–547.

Fischer, T.M., Blazis, D.E.J., Priver, N.A., and Carew, T.J. (1997). Metaplasticity at identified inhibitory synapses in *Aplysia*. *Nature*, **389**, 860–865.

Fisher, F.M. and Ando, A. (1963). Two theorems of *ceteris paribus* in the analysis of dynamic systems. In *Essays on the structure of social science models* (ed. A. Ando, F.M. Fisher, and H.A. Simon), pp. 107–112. MIT Press, Cambridge, MA.

Fisher, R.A. (1966). *The design of experiments*, (8th edn). Hafner, New York.

Fitts, P.M. (1964). Perceptual-motor skill learning. In *Categories of human learning* (ed. A.W. Melton), pp. 243–285. Academic Press, New York.

Fivush, R. (ed.) (1994). *Long-term retention of infant memories.* Lawrence Erlbaum Associates, Hove.

Flaherty, C.F. (1985). *Animal learning and cognition.* Knopf, New York.

Flanagan, J.R. and Wing, A.M. (1997). The role of internal models in motion planning and control: Evidence from grip force adjustments during movements of hand-hand loads. *Journal of Neuroscience*, **17**, 1519–1528.

Flavell, J.H. (1971). What is memory development the development of? *Human Development*, **14**, 272–278.

Flavell, J.H. and Wellman, H.M. (1977). Metamemory. In *Perspective in the development of memory and cognition* (ed. R.V. Krail and J.W. Hagen), pp. 3–33. Laurence Erlbaum Associates, Hillsdale, NJ.

Fleishman, E.A. and Parker, J.F. Jr. (1962). Factors in the retention and relearning of perceptual motor skills. *Journal of Experimental Psychology*, **64**, 215–226.

Fletcher, P.C., Frith, C.D., and Rugg, M.D. (1997). The functional neuroanatomy of episodic memory. *Trends in Neurosciences*, **20**, 213–218.

Fletcher, P.C., Shallice, T., Frith, C.D., Frackowiak, R.S.J., and Dolan, R.J. (1998). The functional roles of prefrontal cortex in episodic memory—II. Retrieval. *Brain*, **121**, 1249–1256.

Flexner, J.B., Flexner, L.B., and Stellar, E. (1963). Memory in mice as affected by intracerebral puromycin. *Science*, **141**, 57–59.

Flint, J. (1999). The genetic basis of cognition. *Brain*, **122**, 2015–2031.

Fodor, J.A. (1974). Special sciences. *Synthese*, **28**, 77–115.

Fodor, J.A. (1983). *The modularity of mind.* MIT Press, Cambridge, MA.

Fodor, J.A. (1998). *In critical condition. Polemical essays on cognitive science and the philosophy of mind.* MIT Press, Cambridge, MA.

Fodor, J.A. and Pylyshyn, Z.W. (1988). Connectionism and cognitive architecture: A critical analysis. *Cognition*, **28**, 3–71.

Folkers, E., Drain, P., and Quinn, W.G. (1993). *radish,* A *Drosophila* mutant deficient in consolidated memory. *Proceedings of the National Academy of Sciences USA*, **90**, 8123–8127.

Fontenrose, J. (1978). *The Delphic oracle. Its responses and operations with a catalogue of responses.* University of California Press, Berkeley.

Fortin, N.J., Agster, K.L., and Eichenbaum, H.B. (2002). Critical role of the hippocampus in memory for sequences of events. *Nature neuroscience*, **5**, 458–462.

Foster, M. and Sherrington, C.S. (1897). *A text book of physiology*, (7th edn), Part III. *The central nervous system.* Macmillan, London.

Fowler, H.W. and Burchfield, R.W. (1996). *Fowler's modern English usage*, (3rd edn). Clarendon Press, Oxford.

Fox, P.T., Raichle, M.E., Mintun, M.A., and Dence, C. (1988). Nonoxidative glucose consumption during focal physiologic neural activity. *Science*, **241**, 462–464.

Frankland, P.W., Cestari, V., Filipkowski, R.K., McDonald, R.J., and Silva, A.J. (1998). The dorsal hippocampus is essential for context discrimination but not for contextual conditioning. *Behavioral Neuroscience*, **112**, 863–874.

Fraser, M. (1987). *Dementia: Its nature and management.* Wiley, Chichester.

Fraser, S.E. and Harland, R.M. (2000). The molecular metamorphosis of experimental embryology. *Cell*, **100**, 41–55.

Freedman, D., Pisani, R., and Purves, R. (1998). *Statistics*, (3rd edn). Norton, New York.

Freeman, F.M., Rose, S.P.R., and Scholey, A.B. (1995). Two time windows of anisomycin-induced amnesia for passive avoidance training in the day-old chick. *Neurobiology of Learning and Memory*, **63**, 291–295.

Fregnac, Y. and Schulz, D. (1994). Models of synaptic plasticity and cellular analogs of learning in the developing and adult vertebrate visual cortex. In *Advances in neural and behavioral development*, Vol. 4 (ed. V.A. Casagrande and P.G. Shinkamn), pp. 149–235. Ablex, Norwood, NJ.

Freud, S. (1899/1950). *Screen memories.* In Collected papers, Vol. V (ed. J. Strachey), pp. 47–69. Hogarth Press, London.

Freud, S. (1900/1976). *The interpretation of dreams* (trans. J. Strachey), Penguin Books, London.

Freud, S. (1901/1991). *The psychopathology of everyday life* (ed. J. Strachey, A. Richards, and A. Tyson), Penguin Books, London.

Freud, S. (1908–1933/1985). *Civilization, society and religion,* The Penguin Freud Library (trans. J. Strachey; ed. A. Richards and A. Dickson), Vol. 12. Penguin Books, London.

Freud, S. (1915/1953–1973). *Repression.* In Collected papers, Vol. XIV (ed. J. Strachey), pp. 156–158. Hogarth Press, London.

Freud, S. (1925/1950). *A note upon the 'mystic writing-pad'.* In Collected Papers, Vol. V (ed. J. Strachey), pp. 175–180. Hogarth Press, London.

Frey, J.U., Mantamadiotis, T., Gass, P., Balschun, D., and Schutz, G. (2000). Normal neuronal plasticity in CREB-deficient mouse strains. *European Journal of Neuroscience*, **12** (Suppl.), 30.

References

Frey, U. and Morris, R.G.M. (1997). Synaptic tagging and long-term potentiation. *Nature*, **385**, 533–536.

Frey, U., Krug, M., Reymann, K.G., and Matthies, H. (1988). Anisomycin, an inhibitor of protein synthesis, blocks the late phases of LTP phenomena in the hippocampal CA1 region *in vitro*. *Brain Research*, **452**, 57–65.

Friedman, D., Ritter, W., and Snodgrass, J.G. (1996). ERPs during study as a function of subsequent direct and indirect memory testing in young and old adults. *Cognitive Brain Research*, **4**, 1–13.

Friedman, H.R. and Goldman-Rakic, P.S. (1994). Coactivation of prefrontal cortex and inferior parietal cortex in working memory tasks revealed by 2DG functional mapping in the rhesus monkey. *Journal of Neuroscience*, **14**, 2775–2788.

Frith, C.D. and Frith, U. (1999). Interacting minds—a biological basis. *Science*, **286**, 1692–1695.

Frost, L., Kaplan, S.W., Cohen, T.E., Henzi, V., Kandel, E.R., and Hawkins, R.D. (1997). A simplified preparation for relating cellular events to behavior: Contribution of LE and unidentified siphon sensory neurons to mediation and habituation of the *Aplysia* gill- and siphon-withdrawal reflex. *Journal of Neuroscience*, **17**, 2900–2913.

Frysztak, R.J. and Crow, T. (1997). Synaptic enhancement and enhanced excitability in presynaptic and postsynaptic neurons in the conditioned stimulus pathway of *Hermissenda*. *Journal of Neuroscience*, **17**, 4426–4433.

Funahashi, S., Bruce, C.J., and Goldman-Rakic, P.S. (1989). Mnemonic coding of visual space in the monkey's dorsolateral prefrontal cortex. *Journal of Neurophysiology*, **61**, 331–349.

Fuster, J.M. (1973). Unit activity in prefrontal cortex during delayed-response performance: neuronal correlates of transient memory. *Journal of Neurophysiology*, **36**, 61–78.

Fuster, J.M. (1992). Prefrontal cortex and memory in primates. In *Encyclopedia of learning and memory* (ed. Squire, L.R.), Macmillan, New York, pp. 532–536.

Fuster, J.M. (1995*a*). Memory and planning: Two temporal perspectives of frontal lobe function. *Advances in Neurology*, **66**, 9–20.

Fuster, J.M. (1995*b*). *Memory in the cerebral cortex. An empirical approach to neural networks in the human and nonhuman primate.* MIT Press, Cambridge, MA.

Fuster, J.M. (2000*a*). The module: crisis of a paradigm. *Neuron*, **26**, 51–53.

Fuster, J.M. (2000*b*). The prefrontal cortex of the primate: a synopsis. *Psychobiology*, **28**, 125–131.

Fuster, J.M. and Jervey, J.P. (1982). Neuronal firing in the inferotemporal cortex of the monkey in a visual memory task. *Journal of Neuroscience*, **2**, 361–375.

Gabrieli, J.D.E., Fleischman, D.A., Keane, M.M., Reminger, S.L., and Morrell, F. (1995). Double dissociation between memory systems underlying explicit and implicit memory in the human brain. *Psychological Science*, **6**, 76–82.

Gaffan, D. (1974). Recognition impaired and association intact in the memory of monkeys after transection of the fornix. *Journal of Comparative and Physiological Psychology*, **86**, 1100–1109.

Gaffan, D. (1994). Dissociated effects of perirhinal cortex ablation, fornix transection and amygdalectomy: Evidence for multiple memory systems in the primate temporal lobe. *Experimental Brain Research*, **99**, 411–422.

Gaffan, D. (1998). Idiothetic input into object-place configuration as the contribution to memory of the monkey and human hippocampus: A review. *Experimental Brain Research*, **123**, 201–209.

Gagne, R.M., Foster, H., and Crowley, M.E. (1948). The measurement of transfer of training. *Psychological Bulletin*, **45**, 97–130.

Galef, B.G., Kennett, D.J., and Wigmore, S.W. (1984). Transfer of information concerning distant foods in rats: A robust phenomenon. *Animal Learning and Behavior*, **12**, 292–296.

Gall, J. (1986). *Systemantics. The underground text of systems lore. How systems work and how they fail*, (2nd edn). The General Systemantics Press, Ann Arbor, MI.

Gallagher, M. and Holland, P.C. (1994). The amygdala complex: Multiple roles in associative learning and attention. *Proceedings of the National Academy of Sciences USA*, **91**, 11771–11776.

Gallagher, M. and Rapp, P.R. (1997). The use of animal models to study the effects of aging on cognition. *Annual Review of Psychology*, **48**, 339–370.

Gallese, V. and Goldman, A. (1998). Mirror neurons and the simulation theory of mind reading. *Trends in Cognitive Sciences*, **2**, 493–501.

Gallistel, C.R. (1989). Animal cognition: The representation of space, time, and number. *Annual Review of Psychology*, **40**, 155–189.

Galton, F. (1869). *Hereditary genius: An inquiry into its laws and consequences*. Macmillan, London.

Galton, F. (1872). Statistical inquiries into the efficacy of prayer. *Forthnightly Review*, **12**, 125–135.

Galton, F. (1879). Psychometric experiments. *Brain*, **2**, 149–162.

Ganong, W.F. (1993). *Review of medical physiology*. 16th ed. Appleton & Lange, Norwalk, CT.

Ganz, L. (1975). Temporal factors in visual perception. In *Handbook of perception*, Vol. V, (ed. E.C. Carterette and M.P. Friedman), pp. 169–231. Academic Press, New York.

Garcia, J. (1981). Tilting at the paper mills of academe. *American Psychologist*, **36**, 149–158.

Garcia, J., Kimmeldorf, D.J., and Koelling, R.A. (1955). Conditioned aversion to saccharin resulting from exposure to gamma radiation. *Science*, **122**, 157–158.

Garcia, J., Ervin, F.R., and Koeling, R.A. (1966). Learning with prolonged delay of reinforcement. *Psychonomic Science*, **5**, 121–122.

Garcia, J., McGowan, B.K., Ervin, F.R., and Koelling, R.A. (1968). Cues: Their relative effectiveness as a function of the reinforcer. *Science*, **160**, 794–795.

Garcia, M.L. and Cleveland, D.V. (2001). Going new places using an old MAP: tau, micortubules and human neurodegenerative disease. *Current Opinion in Cell Biology*, **13**, 41–48.

GarciaAnoveros, J. and Corey, D.P. (1997). The molecules of mechanotransduction. *Annual Review of Neuroscience*, **20**, 507–594.

Gardiol, A., Racca, C., and Triller, A. (1999). Dendritic and postsynaptic protein synthetic machinery. *Journal of Neuroscience*, **19**, 168–179.

Gardner, H. (1993). *Multiple intelligeneces. The theory in practice.* Basic Books, New York.

Gawne, T.J. and Richmond, B.J. (1993). How independent are the messages carried by adjacent inferior temporal cortical neurons? *Journal of Neuroscience*, **13**, 2758–2771.

Geertz, C. (1983). *The interpretation of culture. Selected essays.* Basic Books, NY.

Gelernter, J., Kranzler, H., Coccaro, E., Siever, L., New, A., and Mulgrew, C.L. (1997). D4 dopamine-receptor (DRD4) alleles and novelty seeking in substance-dependent, personality-disorder, and control subjects. *American Journal of Human Genetics*, **61**, 1144–1152.

Genette, G. (1997). *Palimpsests. Literature in the second degree.* University of Nebraska Press.

Gentner, D. (1983). Structure-mapping: a theoretical framework for analogy. *Cognitive Science*, **7**, 155–170.

Gentner, D. and Medina, J. (1998). Similarity and the development of rules. *Cognition*, **65**, 263–297.

Georgopoulos, A.P. (1994). New concepts in generation of movement. *Neuron*, **13**, 257–268.

Georgopoulos, A.P. (1996). Arm movements in monkeys: Behavior and neurophysiology. *Journal of Comparative Physiology [A]*, **179**, 603–612.

Georgopoulos, A.P., Crutcher, M.D., and Schwartz, A.B. (1989). Cognitive spatial-motor processes. 3. Motor cortical prediction of movement direction during an instructed delay period. *Experimental Brain Research*, **75**, 183–194.

Geppert, M. and Sudhof, T.C. (1998). RAB3 and synaptotagmin: The yin and yang of synaptic membrane fusion. *Annual Review of Neuroscience*, **21**, 75–95.

Gereau, R.W. IV and Conn, P.J. (1994). A cyclic AMP-dependent form of associative synaptic plasticity induced by coactivation of β-adrenergic receptors and metabotropic glutamate receptors in rat hippocampus. *Journal of Neuroscience*, **14**, 3310–3318.

Gerstein, L.G., Bedenbaugh, P., and Aertsen, A. (1989). Neuronal assemblies. *IEEE Transactions on Biomedical Engineering*, **36**, 4–14.

Gescheider, G.A. (1997). *Psychophysics: the fundamentals*, (3rd edn). LEA, Mahwah, NJ.

Getz, W.M. and Page, R.E.J. (1991). Chemosensory kin-communication systems and kin recognition in honey bees. *Ethology*, **87**, 298–315.

Gevins, A., Smith, M.E., McEvoy, L.K., Leong, H., and Le, J. (1999). Electroencephalographic imaging of higher brain function. *Philosophical Transactions of the Royal Society of London, Series B: Biological Sciences*, **354**, 1125–1134.

Gewirtz, J.C., McNish, K.A., and Davis, M. (2000). Is the hippocampus necessary for contextual fear conditioning? *Behavioural Brain Research*, **110**, 83–95.

Ghez, C. (1991). The cerebellum. In *Principles of neural science*, (3rd edn)., (ed. E.R. Kandel, J.H. Schwartz, and T.M. Jessel), pp. 626–646. Elsevier, New York.

Ghirardi, M., Montarolo, P.G., and Kandel, E.R. (1995). A novel intermediate stage in the transition between short- and long-term facilitation in the sensory to motor neuron synapse of *Aplysia*. *Neuron*, **14**, 413–420.

Gholson, B. and Barker, P. (1985). Kuhn, Lakatos, Laudan. Applications in the history of physics and psychology. *American Psychologist*, **40**, 755–769.

Ghoneim, M.M. and Mewaldt, S.P. (1990). Benzodiazepines and human memory: A review. *Anesthesiology*, **72**, 926–938.

Ghosh, A. and Greenberg, M.E. (1995). Calcium signalling in neurons: Molecular mechanisms and cellular consequences. *Science*, **268**, 239–247.

Giacobini, E. and McGeer, P.L. (2000). Approaches to the treatment of Alzheimer's disease. *NeuroScience News*, **3**, 62–70.

Gibbons, M. (1999). Science's new social contract with society. *Nature*, **402** (Suppl.), C81–C84.

Gibbs, R.W. Jr. (1994). *The poetics of mind. Figurative thought, language, and understanding.* Cambridge University Press, New York.

Gibson, J.J. (1941). A critical review of the concept of set in contemporary experimental psychology. *Psychological Bulletin*, **38**, 781–817.

Gibson, J.J. (1979). *The ecological approach to visual perception.* Houghton Mifflin, Boston, MA.

Gibson, J.R., Beierlein, M., and Connors, B.W. (1999). Two networks of electrically coupled inhibitory neurons in neocortex. *Nature*, **402**, 75–79.

Gick, M.L. and Holyoak, K.J. (1983). Schema induction and analogical transfer. *Cognitive Psychology*, **15**, 1–38.

Gingrich, J.A. and Hen, R. (2000). The broken mouse: The role of development, plasticity and environment in the interpretation of phenotypic changes in knockout mice. *Current Opinion in Neurobiology*, **10**, 146–152.

Girden, E. and Culler, E.A. (1937). Conditioned responses in curarized striate muscle in dogs. *Journal of Comparative Psychology*, **23**, 261–274.

References

Giurfa, M. and Menzel, R. (1997). Insect visual perception: Complex abilities of simple nervous systems. *Current Opinion in Neurobiology*, **7**, 505–513.

Giurfa, M., Eichmann, B., and Menzel, R. (1996). Symmetry perception in an insect. *Nature*, **382**, 458–461.

Giurgea, C. (1973). The 'nootropic' approach to the pharmacology of the integrative activity of the brain. *Conditional Reflex*, **8**, 108–115.

Glanzman, D.L. (1995). The cellular basis of classical conditioning in *Aplysia californica*—it's less simple than you think. *Trends in Neurosciences*, **18**, 30–36.

Glaser, E.M. (1966). *The physiological basis of habituation*. Oxford University Press, London.

Glaser, O.C. (1910). The formation of habits at high speed. *Journal of Comparative Neurology and Psychology*, **20**, 165–184.

Glass, A.L. and Holyoak, K.J. (1986). *Cognition*, (2nd edn). Random House, New York.

Glassman, R.B. (1978). The logic of the lesion experiment and its role in the neural science. In *Recovery from brain damage*, (ed. S. Finger), pp. 3–31. Plenum Press, New York.

Glock, H.-J. (1996). *A Wittgenstein dictionary*. Blackwell, Oxford.

Goate, A., Chartier-Harlin, M.-C., Mullan, M., Brown, J., Crawford, F., Fidani, L., Giuffra, L., Haynes, A., Irving, N., James, L., Mant, R., Newton, P., Rooke, K., Roques, P., Talbot, C., Pericak-Vance, M., Roses, A., Williamson, R., Rossor, M., Owen, M., and Hardy, J. (1991). Segregation of a missense mutation in the amyloid precursor protein gene with familial Alzheimer's disease. *Nature*, **349**, 704–706.

Gochin, P.M., Colombo, M., Dorfman, G.A., Gerstein, G.L., and Gross, C.G. (1994). Neural ensemble coding in inferior temporal cortex. *Journal of Neurophysiology*, **71**, 2325–2337.

Goda, Y. and Sudhof, T.C. (1997). Calcium regulation of neurotransmitter release: Reliably unreliable? *Current Opinion in Cell Biology*, **9**, 513–518.

Godden, D.R. and Baddeley, A.D. (1975). Context-dependent memory in two natural environments: on land and underwater. *British Journal of Psychology*, **66**, 325–331.

Goel, V., Grafman, J., Tajik, J., Gana, S., and Danto, D. (1997). A study of the performance of patients with frontal lobe lesions in a financial planning task. *Brain*, **120**, 1805–1822.

Goelet, P., Castellucci, V.F., Schacher, S., and Kandel, E.R. (1986). The long and the short of long-term memory—a molecular framework. *Nature*, **322**, 419–422.

Goethe, J.G. (1827/1891). *Homer noch einmal*. Vol. 38, Schriften zür Literatur, Driter Teil. J.G. Gottesche Buchhandlung Nachfolger, Stuttgart and Berlin.

Golby, A.J., Gabrieli, J.D.E., Chiao, J.Y., and Eberhardt, J.L. (2001). Differential responses in the fusiform region to same-race and other-race faces. *Nature Neuroscience*, **4**, 845–850.

Goldman, S.A. and Nottebohm, F. (1983). Neuronal production, migration, and differentiation in a vocal control nucleus of the adult female canary brain. *Proceedings of the National Academy of Sciences USA*, **80**, 2390–2394.

Goldman-Rakic, P.S. (1992). Working memory and the mind. *Scientific American*, **267** (Sept.), 111–117.

Goldman-Rakic, P.S. (1995). Cellular basis of working memory. *Neuron*, **14**, 477–485.

Goldman-Rakic, P.S. (1996). Regional and cellular fractionation of working memory. *Proceedings of the National Academy of Sciences USA*, **93**, 13473–13480.

Goldstone, R.L. (1998). Perceptual learning. *Annual Review of Psychology*, **49**, 585–612.

Gomulicki, B.R. (1953). The development and present status of the trace theory of memory. *British Journal of Psychology Monographs Suppl.*, **XXIX**.

Goodenough, D.A., Goliger, J.A., and Paul, D.L. (1996). Connexins, connexons, and intercellular communication. *Annual Review of Biochemistry*, **65**, 475–502.

Goodman, C.S. and Shatz, C.J. (1993). Developmental mechanisms that generate patterns of neuronal connectivity. *Cell*, 72, **10** (Suppl.), 77–98.

Goodwin, D.W., Powell, B., Bremer, D., Hoine, H., and Stern, J. (1969). Alcohol and recall: state-dependent effects in man. *Science*, **163**, 1358–1360.

Goodwin, S.F., Del Vecchio, M., Velinzon, K., Hogel, C., Russell, S.R.H., Tully, T., and Kaiser, K. (1997). Defective learning in mutants of the *Drosophila* gene for a regulatory subunit of cAMP-dependent protein kinase. *Journal of Neuroscience*, **17**, 8817–8827.

Gorenstein, C., Bernik, M.A., Pompeia, S., and Marcourakis, T. (1995). Impairment of performance associated with long-term use of benzodiazepines. *Journal of Psychopharmacology*, **9**, 313–318.

Gorfein, D.S. and Hoffman, R.R. (ed.) (1987). *Memory and learning. The Ebbinghaus centennial conference*. Lawrence Earlbaum Associates, Hillsdale, NJ.

Gottfried, K. and Wilson, K.G. (1997). Science as a social construct. *Nature*, **386**, 545–547.

Gould, E., Beylin, A., Tanapat, P., Reeves, A., and Shors, T.J. (1999a). Learning enhances adult neurogenesis in the hippocampal formation. *Nature Neuroscience*, **2**, 260–265.

Gould, E., Reeves, A.J., Graziano, M.S.A., and Gross, C.G. (1999b). Neurogenesis in the neocortex of adult primates. *Science*, **286**, 548–552.

Gould, J.L. (1984). The natural history of honey bee learning. In *The biology of learning*, (ed. P. Marler and H. Terrace), pp. 149–180. Springer-Verlag, Berlin.

Gould, S.J. (1981). *The mismeasure of man*. Norton, New York.

Gould, S.J. and Lewontin, R.C. (1979). The spandrels of San Marco and the Panglossian paradigm: a critique of the adaptationist programme. *Proceedings of the Royal Society of London B*, **205**, 581–598.

Gouliaev, A.H. and Senning, A. (1994). Piracetam and other structurally related nootropics. *Brain Research Reviews*, **19**, 180–222.

Graf, P. and Schacter, D.L. (1985). Implicit and explicit memory for new associations in normal and amnesic subjects. *Journal of Experimental Psychology. Learning, Memory, and Cognition*, **1**, 501–518.

Grafman, J. and Wassermann, E. (1999). Transcranial magnetic stimulation can measure and modulate learning and memory. *Neuropsychologia*, **37**, 159–167.

Grafton, S.T., Hazeltine, E., and Ivry, R. (1995). Functional mapping of sequence learning in normal humans. *Journal of Cognitive Neuroscience*, **7**, 497–510.

Graham, K.S. (1999). Semantic dementia: a challenge to the multiple-trace theory? *Trends in Cognitive Sciences*, **3**, 85–87.

Grahame, N.J., Barnet, R.C., Gunther, L.M., and Miller, R.R. (1994). Latent inhibition as a performance deficit resulting from CS-context associations. *Animal Learning and Behavior*, **22**, 395–408.

Granholm, E. and Butters, N. (1988). Associative encoding and retrieval in Alzheimer's and Huntington's disease. *Brain and Cognition*, **7**, 335–347.

Grant, S.G.N., O'Dell, T.J., Karl, K.A., Stein, P.L., Soriano, P., and Kandel, E.R. (1992). Impaired long-term potentiation, spatial learning, and hippocampal development in *fyn* mutant mice. *Science*, **258**, 1903–1910.

Gratzer, W. (1996). *A bedside Nature. Genius and eccentricity in science 1869–1953*, p. 3. Macmillan Magazines, London.

Gray, R., Rajan, A.S., Radcliffe, K.A., Yakehiro, M., and Dani, J.A. (1996). Hippocampal synaptic transmission enhanced by low concentrations of nicotine. *Nature*, **383**, 713–716.

Graybiel, A.M. (1998). The basal ganglia and chunking of action repertoires. *Neurobiology of Learning and Memory*, **70**, 119–136.

Grayling, A.C. (1997). *An introduction to philosophical logic*, (3rd edn). Blackwell, Oxford.

Grecksch, G. and Matthies, H. (1980). Two sensitive periods for the amnesic effect of anisomycin. *Pharmacology, Biochemistry and Behavior*, **12**, 663–665.

Green, D.M. and Swets, J.A. (1988). *Signal detection theory and psycophysics*. Peninsula Publishing, Los Altos, CA.

Green, E.J., McNaughton, B.L., and Barnes, C.A. (1990). Exploration-dependent modulation of evoked responses in fascias dentata: Dissociation of motor, EEG, and sensory factors and evidence for a synaptic efficacy change. *Journal of Neuroscience*, **10**, 1455–1471.

Green, E.L. (ed.) and the staff of the Jackson laboratory (1966). *Biology of the laboratory mouse*. Dover, New York.

Green, M. (1991). Visual search, visual streams, and visual architectures. *Perception and Psychophysics*, **50**, 388–403.

Green, M.H. (1991). *Classic experiments in modern biology*. Freeman, New York.

Greenblatt, S.H. (1995). Phrenology in the science and culture of the 19th century. *Neurosurgery*, **37**, 790–804.

Greene, B. (1999). *The elegant universe*. Vintage Books, New York.

Greene, R.L. (1989). Spacing effects in memory: Evidence for a two-process account. *Journal of Experimental Psychology: Learning, Memory, and Cognition*, **15**, 371–377.

Greenfield, P.M. and Savage-Rumbaugh, E.S. (1993). Comparing communicative competence in child and chimp: The pragmatics of repetition. *Journal of Child Language*, **20**, 1–26.

Gregory, R.L. (1966). *Eye and brain. The psychology of seeing*, (2nd edn). McGraw-Hill, New York.

Grether, W.F. (1938). Pseudo-conditioning without paired stimulation encountered in attempted backward conditioning. *Journal of Comparative Psychology*, **25**, 91–96.

Griffin, D.R. (1984). *Animal thinking*. Harvard University Press, Cambridge, MA.

Griffin, D.R. (1985). Animal consciousness. *Neuroscience & Biobehavioral Reviews*, **9**, 615–622.

Grinvald, A., Ross, W.N., and Farber, I. (1981). Simultaneous optical measurements of electrical activity from multiple sites on processes of cultured neurons. *Proceedings of the National Academy of Sciences USA*, **78**, 3245–3249.

Grinvald, A., Lieke, E., Frosting, R.D., Gilbert, C.D., and Wiesel, T.N. (1986). Functional architecture of cortex revealed by optical imaging of intrinsic signals. *Nature*, **324**, 361–364.

Grofein, D.S. and Hoffman, R.R. (ed.) (1987). *Memory and learning. The Ebbinghaus centennial conference*. Lawrence Erlbaum Associates, Hillsdale, NJ.

Groh, J.M., Born, R.T., and Newsome, W.T. (1997). How is a sensory map read out? Effects of microstimulation in visual area MT on saccades and smooth pursuit eye movements. *Journal of Neuroscience*, **17**, 4312–4330.

Gross, C.G., Rocha-Miranda, C.E., and Bender, D.B. (1972). Visual properties of neurons in inferotemporal cortex of the macaque. *Journal of Neurophysiology*, **35**, 96–111.

Grossberg, S., Mingolla, E., and Ross, W.D. (1997). Visual brain and visual perception: How does the cortex do perceptual grouping? *Trends in Neurosciences*, **20**, 106–111.

Groves, P.M. and Thompson, R.F. (1970). Habituation: A dual-process theory. *Psychological Review*, **77**, 419–450.

Gruber, H.E. (1995). Insight and affect in the history of science. In *The nature of insight*, (ed. R.J. Sternberg and J.E. Davidson), pp. 397–431. MIT Press, Cambridge, MA.

Guo, A., Xia, S.Z., Feng, C.H., Wolf, R., and Heisenberg, M. (1996). Conditioned visual flight orientation in *Drosophila*: dependence on age, practice, and diet. *Learning & Memory*, **3**, 49–59.

Gustafsson, B. and Wigstrom, H. (1986). Hippocampal long–lasting potentiation produced by pairing single volleys and brief conditioning tetani evoked in separate afferents. *Journal of Neuroscience*, **6**, 1575–1582.

References

Guthrie, E.R. (1935/1952). *The psychology of learning*. Harper & Row, New York.

Guthrie, W.K. (1962). *A history of Greek philosophy. I. The earlier Presocratics and the Pythagoeans*. Cambridge University Press, Cambridge.

Guthrie, W.K.C. (1975). *A history of Greek philosophy. IV. Plato: the man and his dialogues. Earlier Period*, p. 118 (also V. *The Later Plato and the Academy*, pp. 173–175). Cambridge University Press, Cambridge.

Guthrie, W.K.C. (1981). *A history of Greek philosophy. IV. Arsitotle, an encounter*. Cambridge University Press, Cambridge.

Gutierrez, H., Hernandez-Echeagaray, E., Ramirez-Amaya, U., and Bermudez-Rattoni, F. (1999). Blockade of N-methyl-D-aspartate receptors in the insular cortex disrupts taste aversion and spatial memory formation. *Neuroscience*, **89**, 751–758.

Gutkind, J.S. (1998). The pathways connecting G protein-coupled receptors to the nucleus through divergent mitogen-activated protein kinase cascades. *Journal of Biological Chemistry*, **273**, 1839–1842.

Guttman, N. and Kalish, H.I. (1956). Discriminability and stimulus generalization. *Journal of Experimental Psychology*, **51**, 79–88.

Guyton, A.C. (1991). *Textbook of medical physiology*, (8th edn). WB Saunders, Philadelphia, PA.

Guzowski, J.F. and McGaugh, J.L. (1997). Antisense oligodeoxynucleotide-mediated disruption of hippocampal CREB protein levels impairs memory of a spatial task. *Proceedings of the National Academy of Sciences USA*, **94**, 2693–2698.

Guzowski, J.F., McNaughton, B.L., Barnes, C.A., and Worley, P.F. (1999). Environment-specific expression of the immediate-early gene *Arc* in hippocampal neuronal ensembles. *Nature Neuroscience*, **2**, 1120–1124.

Haaga, D.A.F., Dyck, M.J., and Ernst, D. (1991). Empirical status of cognitive theory of depression. *Psychological Bulletin*, **110**, 215–236.

Haber, R.N. (1966). Nature of the effects of set on perception. *Psychological Review*, **73**, 335–351.

Hacking, I. (ed.) (1981). *Scientific revolutions*. Oxford University Press, Oxford.

Hagler, D.J. and Goda, Y. (1998). Synaptic adhesion: the building blocks of memory? *Neuron*, **20**, 1059–1062.

Haist, F., Bowden Gore, J., and Mao, H. (2001). Consolidation of human memory over decades revealed by functional magnetic resonance imaging. *Nature neuroscience*, **4**, 1139–1145.

Haist, F., Shimamura, A.P., and Squire, L.R. (1992). On the relationship between recall and recognition memory. *Journal of Experimental Psychology: Learning, Memory, and Cognition*, **18**, 691–702.

Halbwachs, M. (1925/1992). The social frameworks of memory. In *On collective memory*, (ed. and trans. L.A. Cosar), pp. 37–189. The University of Chicago Press, Chicago, IL.

Haldane, J.B.S. (1923). *Dedalus, or science and the future*. Kegan Paul, London.

Hall, G. and Honey, R.C. (1989). Contextual effects in conditioning, latent inhibition, and habituation: Associative and retrieval functions of contextual cues. *Journal of Experimental Psychology: Animal Behavior Process*, **15**, 232–241.

Hall, J., Thomas, K.L., and Everitt, B.J. (2000). Rapid and selective induction of BDNF expression in the hippocampus during contextual learning. *Nature Neuroscience*, **3**, 533–535.

Hall, J.C. (1986). Learning and rhythms in courting, mutant *Drosophila. Trends in Neurosciences*, **9**, 414–418.

Hall, R. (1964). The term 'sense-datum'. *Mind*, 130–131.

Halligan, P.W. and Marshall, J.C. (1996). Visuospatial disorders. In *The Blackwell dictionary of neuropsychology*, (ed. J.G. Beaumont, P.M. Kenealy, and M.J. Rogers), pp. 763–767. Blackwell, Oxford.

Hallpike, C.R. (1979). *The foundations of primitive thought*. Clarendon Press, Oxford.

Halpern, B.P. and Tapper, D.N. (1971). Taste stimuli: Quality coding time. *Science*, **171**, 156–1258.

Hamberger, C.A. and Hyden, H. (1945). Cytochemical changes in the cochlear ganglion caused by acoustic stimulation and trauma. *Acta Oto-Laryngologica*, **61** (Suppl.), 5–89.

Hammer, M. (1993). An identified neuron mediates the unconditioned stimulus in associative olfactory learning in honeybees. *Nature*, **366**, 59–63.

Hammer, M. and Menzel, R. (1995). Learning and memory in the honeybee. *Journal of Neuroscience*, **15**, 1617–1630.

Hammer, M. and Menzel, R. (1998). Multiple sites of associative odor learning as revealed by local brain microinjections of octopamine in honeybees. *Learning & Memory*, **5**, 146–156.

Hammerton, M. (1967). Measures for the efficiency of simulators as training devices. *Ergonomics*, **10**, 63–65.

Hammerton, M. and Tickner, A.H. (1967). Visual factors affecting transfer of training from a simulated to a real control situation. *Journal of Applied Psychology*, **51**, 46–49.

Hammond, N.G.L. and Scullard, H.H. (1970). *The Oxford classical dictionary*, (2nd edn). Oxford University Press.

Hampton, R.R. (2001). Rhesus monkeys know when they remember. *Proceedings of the National Academy of Science USA*, **98**, 5359–5362.

Hanks, S.K. and Hunter, T. (1995). The eukaryotic protein kinase superfamily: Kinase (catalytic) domain structure and classification. *FASEB Journal*, **9**, 576–596.

Hardcastle, V.G. (1994). Psychology's binding problem and possible neurobiological solution. *Journal of Consciousness Studies*, **1**, 66–90.

Hardy, J., Duff, K., Hardy, K.G., Perez-Tur, J., and Hutton, M. (1998). Genetic dissection of Alzheimer's disease and related dementias: Amyloid and its relationship to tau. *Nature Neuroscience*, **1**, 355–358.

Hare, R.M. (1984). Supervenience. *The Aristotelean Society Supplementary Volume*, **58**, 1–16.

Harel, D. (1987). *Algorithmics. The spirit of computing*. Addison-Wesley, Wokingham.

Harlow, H.F. (1949). The formation of learning sets. *Psychological Review*, **56**, 51–65.

Harlow, H.F. (1959). Learning set and error factor theory. In *Psychology: a study of a science*, Vol. 2, (ed. Koch, S.), pp. 492–537. McGraw-Hill, New York.

Harlow, H.F. and Bromer, J.A. (1938). A test-apparatus for monkeys. *Psychological Record*, **2**, 434–436.

Harmon, W. (ed.) (1998). *The classic hundred poems. All time favorites*, (2nd edn). Columbia University Press, New York.

Harris, B. (1979). Whatever happened to Little Albert? *American Psychologist*, **34**, 151–160.

Harrison, M. (1998). *The language of theatre*. Routledge, New York.

Harrison, P.J. (1999). The neuropathology of schizophrenia—a critical review of the data and their interpretation. *Brain*, **122**, 593–624.

Harris-Warrick, R.M. and Marder, E. (1991). Modulation of neural networks for behavior. *Annual Review of Neuroscience*, **14**, 39–57.

Hart, J.T. (1965). Memory and the feeling-of-knowing experience. *Journal of Educational Psychology*, **56**, 208–216.

Hartry, A.L., Keith-Lee, P., and Morton, W.D. (1964). Planaria: Memory transfer through cannibalism reexamined. *Science*, **146**, 274–275.

Hartshorn, K., Rovee-Collier, C., Gerhardstein, P., Bhatt, R.S., Wondoloski, T.L., Klein, P., Gilch, J., Wurtzel, N., and Campos-de-Carvalho, M. (1998). The ontogeny of long-term memory over the first year-and-a-half of life. *Developmental Psychobiology*, **32**, 69–89.

Harvey, P. (1937/1984). *The Oxford companion to classical literature*. Oxford University Press, Oxford.

Harvey, P. (1990). *An introduction to Buddhism. Teachings, history and practices*. Cambridge University Press, Cambridge.

Hasegawa, I., Fukushima, T., Ihara, T., and Miyashita, Y. (1998). Callosal window between prefrontal cortices: cognitive interaction to retrieve long-term memory. *Science*, **281**, 814–818.

Hasselmo, M.E. (1995). Neuromodulation and cortical function: modeling the physiological basis of behavior. *Behavioural Brain Research*, **67**, 1–27.

Hatten, M.E. (1999). Central nervous system neuronal migration. *Annual Review of Neuroscience*, **22**, 511–539.

Hawkins, R.D., Cohen, T.E., Greene, W., and Kandel, E.R. (1998). relationships between dishabituation, sensitization, and inhibition of the gill- and siphon-withdrawal reflex in *Aplysia californica*: effects of response measure, test time, and training stimulus. *Behavioral Neuroscience*, **112**, 24–38.

Hayashi, Y., Shi, S.-H., Esteban, J.A., Piccini, A., Poncer, J.C., and Malinow, R. (2000). Driving AMPA receptors into synapses by LTP and CaMKII: Requirement for GluR1 and PDZ domain interaction. *Science*, **287**, 2262–2267.

Hayes, D.P. (1992). The growing inaccessibility of science. *Nature*, **356**, 739–740.

Hayes, K.J., Thompson, R., and Hayes, C. (1953). Discrimination learning set in chimpanzees. *Journal of Comparative Physiological Psychology*, **46**, 99–104.

Haynes, R.D. (1994). *From Faust to Strangelove. Representation of the scientist in Western literature*. The Johns Hopkins University Press, Baltimore, MD.

Hebb, D.O. (1949). *The organization of behavior: A neuropsychological theory*. Wiley, New York.

Hebb, D.O. (1959). Karl Spencer Lashley: 1890–1958. *American Journal of Psychology*, **72**, 142–150.

Hebb, D.O. (1960). The American revolution. *American Psychologist*, **15**, 735–745.

Hebb, D.O. and Williams, K. (1946). A method of rating animal intelligence. *Journal of General Psychology*, **34**, 59–65.

Hediger, H.K.P. (1981). The Clever Hans phenomenon from an animal psychologist's point of view. *Annals of the New York Academy of Sciences*, **364**, 1–17.

Hegel, G.W.F. (1820s/1998). *Introduction to the philosophy of history*. In The Hegel Reader, (ed. S. Houlgate). Blackwell, Oxford.

Heidmann, A., Heidmann, T.M., and Changeux, J.-P. (1984). Stabilisation selective de représentations neuronals per résonance entre 'préreprésentations' spontanées du réseau cérébral et 'percepts' évoqués par interactions avec le monde extérieur. *Comptes Rendus de l'Academie des Sciences Paris Serie III*, **299**, 839–843.

Heilig, G.K. (1997). *Demographics '96. A population education tool from the United Nations Population Fund (UNFPA)*. CD, UNFPA, New York.

Heindel, W.C., Butters, N., and Salmon, D.P. (1988). Impaired learning of a motor skill in patients with Huntington's disease. *Behavioral Neuroscience*, **102**, 141–147.

Heird, J.C., Lennon, A.M., and Bell, R.W. (1981). Effects of early experience on the learning ability of yearling horses. *Journal of Animal Science*, **53**, 1204–1209.

Helenius, P., Salmelin, R., Service, E., and Connolly, J.F. (1998). Distinct time courses of word and context comprehension in the left temporal cortex. *Brain*, **121**, 1133–1142.

Henson, R.N.A., Rugg, M.D., Shallice, T., Josephs, O., and Dolan, R.J. (1999). Recollection and familiarity in recognition memory: An event-related functional magnetic resonance imaging study. *Journal of Neuroscience*, **19**, 3962–3972.

Henson, R., Shallice, T., and Dolan, R. (2000). Neuroimaging evidence for dissociable forms of repetition priming. *Science*, **287**, 1269–1272.

References

Hepper, P.G. (1996). Fetal memory: does it exist? What does it do? *Acta Paediatrica Supplementum*, **416**, 16–20.

Herdegen, T. and Leah, J.D. (1998). Inducible and constitutive transcription factors in the mammalian nervous system: control of gene expression by Jun, Fox and Krox, and CREB/ATF proteins. *Brain Research Reviews*, **28**, 370–490.

Herness, M.S. and Gibertson, T.A. (1999). Cellular mechanisms of taste transduction. *Annual Review of Physiology*, **61**, 873–900.

Herrenstein, R.J. and Boring, E.G. (ed.) (1965). Cerebral localization. In *A source book in the history of psychology*, Ch. VII. Harvard University Press, Cambridge, MA.

Herrmann, D.J. (1982). Know thy memory: The use of questionnaires to assess and study memory. *Psychological Bulletin*, **92**, 434–452.

Hertzog, C. (1992). Improving memory: The possible roles of metamemory. In *Memory improvement. Implications for memory theory*, (ed. D.J. Herrmann, H. Weingartner, A. Searleman, and C. McEvoy), pp. 61–78. Springer-Verlag, New York.

Hesiod (8th Century BC/1988). *Theogony* (trans. M.L. West). Oxford University Press, Oxford.

Hess, E.H. (1959). Imprinting. *Science*, **130**, 133–141.

Hesse, M.B. (1963). *Models and analogies in science*. Sheed and Ward, London.

Heyes, C. and Huber, L. (ed.) (2000). *The evolution of cognition*. MIT Press, Cambridge, MA.

Heyes, C.M., Jaldow, E., Nokes, T., and Dawson, G.R. (1994). Imitation in rats (*Rattus norvegicus*): the role of demonstrator action. *Behavioural Processes*, **32**, 173–182.

Hilgard, E.R. and Marquis, D.G. (1940). *Conditioning and learning*. Appleton-Century, New York.

Hill, C.S. and Treisman, R. (1995). Transcriptional regulation by extracellular signals: Mechanisms and specificity. *Cell*, **80**, 199–211.

Hill, D.K. and Keynes, R.D. (1949). Opacity changes in stimulated nerve. *Journal of Physiology (London)*, **108**, 278–281.

Hille, B. (1992). *Ionic channels of excitable membranes*, (2nd edn). Sinauer, Sunderland, MA.

Hinton, G.E.(1989). Connectionist learning procedures. *Artificial Intelligence*, **40**, 185–234.

Hirsch, J. (1959). Studies in experimental behavior genetics: II. Individual differences in geotaxis as a function of chromosome variations in synthesized *Drosophila* populations. *Journal of Comparative and Physiological Psychology*, **52**, 304–308.

Hirsch, J. (1963). Behavior genetics and individuality understood. *Science*, **142**, 1436–1442.

Hirsh, R. (1974). The hippocampus and contextual retrieval of information from memory: a theory. *Behavioral Biology*, **12**, 421–444.

Hirsh, R. (1980). The hippocampus, conditional operations, and cognition. *Physiological Psychology*, **8**, 175–182.

Hirst, W. (1988). Improving memory. In *Perspectives in memory research*, (ed. M.S. Gazzaniga), pp. 219–244. MIT Press, Cambridge, MA.

Hitchcock, A. (1935). *The 39 steps*. Gaumont British Film Corporation of America.

Hobbes, T. (1651/1997). *Leviathan*. Norton, New York.

Hochberg, J. (ed.) (1998). *Perception and cognition at century's end. Handbook of perception and cognition*, (2nd edn). Academic Press, San Diego.

Hochberg, J. (1998). Gestalt theory and its legacy. Organization in eye and brain, in attention and mental representation. In *Perception and cognition at century's end*, (ed. J. Hochberg), pp. 253–306. Academic Press, San Diego.

Hock, B.J. and Bunsey, M.D. (1998). Differential effects of dorsal and ventral hippocampal lesions. *Journal of Neuroscience*, **18**, 7027–7032.

Hock, F.J. (1995). Therapeutic approaches for memory impairments. *Behavioural Brain Research*, **66**, 143–150.

Hodges, J.R., Patterson, K., Ward, R., Gerrard, P., Bak, T., Perry, R., and Gregory, C. (1999). The differentiation of semantic dementia and frontal lobe dementia (temporal and frontal variants of fronto-temporal dementia) from early Alzheimer's disease: a comparative neuropsychological study. *Neuropsychology*, **13**, 31–40.

Hodgkin, A.L. and Huxley, A.F. (1952). A quantitative description of membrane current and its application to conduction and excitation in nerve. *Journal of Physiology (London)*, **117**, 500–544.

Hodgkin, A.L., Huxley, A.F., Feldberg, W., Rushton, W.A.H., Gregory, R.A., McCance RA (1977). *The pursuit of nature. Informal essays on the history of physiology*. Cambridge University Press, Cambridge.

Hodos, W. (1970). Evolutionary interpretation of neural and behavioral studies of living vertebrates. In *The neuroscience, 2nd study program*, (ed. F.O. Schmidt), pp. 26–39.

Hogan, B., Beddington, R., Costantini, F., and Lacy, E. (1994). *Manipulating the mouse embryo. A laboratory manual*. Cold Spring Harbor Laboratory Press, Cold Spring Harbor, NY.

Holland, P.C. (1988). Excitation and inhibition in unblocking. *Journal of Experimental Psychology, Animal Behavior Processes*, **14**, 261–279.

Holland, P.C. (1992). Occasion setting in Pavlovian conditioning. *Psychology of Learning and Motivation*, **28**, 69–125.

Holland, P.C. (1993). Cognitive aspects of classical conditioning. *Current Opinion in Neurobiology*, **3**, 230–236.

Holland, P.C. and Bouton, M.E. (1999). Hippocampus and context in classical conditioning. *Current Opinion in Neurobiology*, **9**, 195–202.

Holland, P.C. and Straub, J.J. (1979). Differential effects of two ways of devaluating the unconditioned stimulus after

Pavlovian appetitive conditioning. *Journal of Experimental Psychology*, **5**, 65–78.

Hollingworth, H.L. (1913). Characteristic differences between recall and recognition. *American Journal of Psychology*, **24**, 532–544.

Hollmann, M. and Heinemann, S. (1994). Cloned glutamate receptors. *Annual Review of Neuroscience*, **17**, 31–108.

Holmes, G. (1930). The cerebellum of man. *Brain*, **62**, 1–30.

Holt, E.B. (1931). *Animal drive and the learning process.* Holt, New York.

Homer (~ 9C BC/1975). *The Odyssey* (trans. R. Lattimore). Harper, New York.

Hommel, B. (1998). Event files: evidence for automatic integration of stimulus-response episodes. *Visual Cognition*, **5**, 183–216.

Honess, R.W. and Roizman, B. (1974). Regulation of herpesvirus macromolecular synthesis: I. Cascade regulation of the synthesis of three groups of viral proteins. *Journal of Virology*, **14**, 8–19.

Hopfield, J.J. (1982). Neural networks and physical systems with emergent collective computational abilities. *Proceedings of the National Academy of Sciences USA*, **79**, 2554–2558.

Hopfield, J.J. (1995). Pattern recognition computation using action potential timing for stimulus representation. *Nature*, 376: 33–36.

Hopfield, J.J., Feinstein, D.I., and Palmar, R.G. (1983). 'Unlearning' has a stabilizing effect on collective memories. *Nature*, **304**, 158–159.

Horn, G. (1985). *Memory, imprinting, and the brain.* Oxford University Press, Oxford.

Horn, G. and McCabe, B.J. (1990). Learning by seeing: N-methyl-D-aspartate receptors and recognition memory. *Advances in Experimental Medicine and Biology*, **268**, 187–196.

Horowitz, L.M. and Prysulak, L.S. (1969). Redintegrative memory. *Psychological Review*, **76**, 519–531.

Horowitz, T.S. and Wolfe, J.M. (1998). Visual search has no memory. *Nature*, **394**, 575–577.

Houk, J.C. (1980a). Systems and models. In *Medical physiology*, (14th edn), (ed. V.B. Mountcastle), Vol. 1, Part III, Ch. 7, pp. 227–245. C.V. Mosby Co., St Louis.

Houk, J.C. (1980b). Homeostasis and control principles. In *Medical physiology*, (14th edn), (ed. V.B. Mountcastle), Vol. 1, Part III, Ch. 8, pp. 246–267. C.V. Mosby Co., St Louis, MO.

Houpt, K.A., Zahorik, D.M., and Swartzman-Andert, J.A. (1990). Taste aversion learning in horses. *Journal of Animal Science*, **68**, 2340–2344.

Howe, M.L. and Courage, M.L. (1997). The emergence and early development of autobiographical memory. *Psychological Review*, **104**, 499–523.

Huang, Y.-Y., Colino, A., Selig, D.K., and Malenka, R.C. (1992). The influence of prior synaptic activity on the induction of long-term potentiation. *Science*, **255**, 730–733.

Hubel, D.H. and Wiesel, T.N. (1977). Ferrier lecture: Functional architecture of macaque monkey visual cortex. *Proceedings of the Royal Society London, Biological Sciences*, **198**, 1–59.

Huber, K.M., Kayser, M.S., and Bear, M.F. (2000). Role for rapid dendritic protein synthesis in hippocampal mGluR-dependent long-term depression. *Science*, **288**, 1254–1256.

Hudson, R. (1993). Olfactory imprinting. *Current Opinion in Neurobiology*, **3**, 548–552.

Hudspeth, A.J. (1989). How the ear's works work. *Nature*, **341**, 397–404.

Huh, K.-H. and Wenthold, R.J. (1999). Turnover analysis of glutamate receptors identifies a rapidly degraded pool of the N-methyl-D-aspartate receptor subunit, NR1, in cultured cerebellar granule cells. *Journal of Biological Chemistry*, **274**, 151–157.

Hull, C.L. (1943). *Principles of behavior. An introduction to behavior theory.* Appleton-Century-Crofts, New York.

Hull, D.L. (1981). Reduction and genetics. *Journal of Medicine and Philosophy*, **6**, 125–143.

Hume, D. (1739/1958). *Treatise on human nature.* Oxford University Press, New York.

Humphreys, L.G. (1939). The effect of random alternation of reinforcement on the acquisition and extinction of conditioned eyelid reactions. *Journal of Experimental Psychology*, **25**, 141–158.

Hund-Georgiadis, M. and von Carmon, D.Y. (1999). Motor-learning-related changes in piano players and non-musicians revealed by functional magnetic-resonance signals. *Experimental Brain Research*, **125**, 417–425.

Hunter, I.M.L. (1977). An exceptional memory. *British Journal of Psychology*, **68**, 155–164.

Hunter, I.M.L. (1978). The role of memory in expert mental calculations. In *Practical aspects of memory*, (ed. M.M. Greenberg, P.E. Morris, and R.N. Sykes), pp. 339–345. Academic Press, London.

Hunter, T. (1994). 1001 protein kinases redux—towards 2000. *Seminars in Cell Biology*, **5**, 367–376.

Hunter, T. (1995). Protein kinases and phosphatases: The Yin and Yang of protein phosphorylation and signaling. *Cell*, **80**, 225–236.

Hunter, T. and Karin, M. (1992). The regulation of transcription by phosphorylation. *Cell*, **70**, 375–387.

Hunter, W.S. (1913). The delayed reaction in animals and children. *Behavior Monographs*, **2**, 1–86.

Hunter, W.S. (1930). A consideration of Lashley's theory of the equipotentiality of cerebral action. *Journal of General Psychology*, **3**, 455–468.

References

Hurlbert, A.C. and Derrington, A.M. (1993). How many neurons it takes to see? *Current Biology*, **3**, 510–512.

Hyde, T.S. and Jenkins, J.J. (1973). Recall of words as a function of semantic, graphic, and syntactic orienting tasks. *Journal of Verbal Learning and Verbal Behavior*, **12**, 471–480.

Iacoboni, M., Woods, R.P., Brass, M., Bekkering, H., Mazziotta, J.C., and Rizzolatti, G. (1999). Cortical mechanisms of human imitation. *Science*, **286**, 2526–2528.

Immelmann, K. (1972). Sexual and other long-term aspects of imprinting in birds and other species. *Advances in the Study of Behavior*, **4**, 147–174.

Impey, S., Mark, M., Villacres, E.C., Poser, S., Chavkin, C., and Storm, D.R. (1996). Induction of CRE-mediated gene expression by stimuli that generate long-lasting LTP in area CA1 of the hippocampus. *Neuron*, **16**, 973–982.

Impey, S., Wayman, G., Wu, Z., and Storm, D.R. (1994). Type I adenylyl cyclase functions as a coincidence detector for control of cyclic AMP response element-mediated transcription: Synergistic regulation of transcription by Ca^{2+} and isoproterenol. *Molecular Cell Biology*, **14**, 8272–8281.

Impey, S., Smith, D.M., Obritean, R., Wade, C., and Storm, D. (1998). Stimulation of cAMP response element (CRE)-mediated transcription during contextual learning. *Nature Neuroscience*, **1**, 595–601.

Ingram, D.K., Shimada, A., Spangler, E.L., Ikari, H., Hengemihle, J., Kuo, H., and Greig, N. (1996). Cognitive enhancement. New strategies for stimulating cholinergic, glutamatergic, and nitric oxide systems. *Annals of the New York Academy of Sciences*, **786**, 348–361.

Ingram, R.E. (1984). Toward and information-processing analysis of depression. *Cognitive Therapy and Research*, **8**, 443–478.

Ingvar, M., Ambros-Ingerson, J., Davis, M., Granger, R., Kessler, M., Rogers, G.A., Schehr, R.S., and Lynch, G. (1997). Enhancement by an ampakine of memory encoding in humans. *Experimental Neurology*, **146**, 553–559.

Inman, A. and Shettleworth, S.J. (1999). Detecting metamemory in nonverbal subjects: A test with pigeons. *Journal of Experimental Psychology: Animal Behavior Processes*, **25**, 389–395.

International Human Genome Sequencing Consortium (2001). Initial sequencing and analysis of the human genome. *Nature*, **409**, 860–921.

Irion, A.L. (1959). Rote learning. In *Psychology: a study of a science. Study I. Conceptual and systematic. Vol. 2. General systematic formulations, learning, and special processes*, (ed. S. Koch). McGraw-Hill, New York.

Irwin, T.H. (1991). Aristotle's philosophy of mind. In *Psychology. Companions to ancient thought*. 2, (ed. S. Everson), pp. 56–83. Cambridge University Press, Cambridge.

Irzik, G. (1996). Can causes be reduced to correlations? *British Journal for the Philosophy of Science*, **47**, 249–270.

Isaacson, R.L. (1992). A fuzzy limbic system. *Behavioural Brain Research*, **52**, 129–131.

Isenberg, N., Silbersweig, D., Engelien, A., Emmerich, S., Malavade, K., Beattie, B., Leon, A.C., and Stern, E. (1999). Linguistic threat activates the human amygdala. *Proceedings of the National Academy of Sciences USA*, **96**, 10456–10459.

Ito, M. (1972). Neural design of the cerebellar motor control system. *Brain Research*, **40**, 81–84.

Ito, M. (1984). *The cerebellum and neural control*. Raven Press, New York.

Ito, M. (1998). Cerebellar learning in the vestibulo-ocular reflex. *Trends in Cognitive Sciences*, **2**, 313–321.

Ito, M. (2001). Cerebellar long-term depression: characterization, signal transduction, and functional roles. *Physiological Reviews*, **81**, 1143–1195.

Izquierdo, I. and Medina, J.H. (1991). $GABA_A$ receptor modulation of memory: The role of endogenous benzodiazepines. *Trends in Pharmacological Sciences*, **12**, 260–625.

Jacobs, J. (1887). Experiments on 'prehension'. *Mind*, **12**, 75–79.

Jacobsen, C.F. and Nissen, H.W. (1937). Studies of cerebral function in primates. IV. The effects of frontal lobe lesions in the delayed alternations habit in monkeys. *Journal of Comparative Psychology*, **23**, 101–112.

Jacobson, M. (1991). *Developmental neurobiology*, (3rd edn). Plenum Press, New York.

Jacoby, L.L. (1991). A process dissociation framework: separating automatic from intentional uses of memory. *Journal of Memory and Language*, **30**, 513–541.

Jacoby, L.L. and Dallas, M. (1981). On the relationship between autobiographical memory and perceptual learning. *Journal of Experimental Psychology: General*, **110**, 306–340.

Jaenisch, R. (1988). Transgenic animals. *Science*, **240**, 1468–1474.

James, W. (1890/1950). *The principles of psychology*. Dover, New York.

Jan, L.Y. and Jan, Y.N. (1992). Tracing the roots of ion channels. *Cell*, **69**, 715–718.

Janknecht, R., Cahill, M.A., and Nordheim, A. (1995). Signal integration at the *c-fos* promoter. *Carcinogenesis*, **16**, 443–450.

Janus, C., D'Amelio, S., Amitay, O., Chishti, M.A., Strome, R., Fraser, P., Carlson, G.A., Roder, J.C., St. George-Hyslop, P., and Westaway, D. (2000). Spatial learning in transgenic mice expressing human presenilin 1 (PS1) transgenics. *Neurobiology of Aging*, **21**, 541–549.

Jarvik, M.E. (1953). Discrimination of colored food and food signs by primates. *Journal of Comparative and Physiological Psychology*, **46**, 390–392.

Jarvis, E.D., Riberio, S., da Silva, M.L., Ventura, D., Vielliard, J., and Mello, C.V. (2000). Behaviourally driven gene expression reveals song nuclei in hummingbird brain. *Nature*, **406**, 628–632.

Jeannerod, M. (1994). The representing brain: Neural correlates of motor intention and imagery. *Behavioral and Brain Sciences*, **17**, 187–245.

Jeannerod, M. and Decety, J. (1995). Mental motor imagery: A window into the representational stages of action. *Current Opinion in Neurobiology*, **5**, 727–732.

Jenkins, C.D., Hurst, M.W., and Rose, R.M. (1979). Life changes. Do people really remember? *Archives of General Psychiatry*, **36**, 379–384.

Jenkins, H.M. and Moore, B.R. (1973). The form of the auto-shaped response with food or water reinforcers. *Journal of the Experimental Analysis of Behavior*, **20**, 163–181.

Jenkins, W.M. and Merzenich, M.M. (1987). Reorganization of neocortical representations after brain injury: a neurophysiological model of the bases of recovery from stroke. *Progress in Brain Research*, **71**, 249–266.

Jennings, H.S. (1899). The psychology of a protozoan. *American Journal of Psychology*, **X**, 503–515.

Jennings, H.S. (1906). *The behaviour of the lower organisms*. Columbia University Press, New York.

Jessell, T.M. and Kandel, E.R. (1993). Synaptic transmission: A bidirectional and self-modifiable form of cell–cell communication. *Cell*, **72** (Suppl.), 1–30.

Jetter, W., Poser, U., Freeman, R.B.Jr., and Markowitsch, J.H. (1986). A verbal long term memory deficit in frontal lobe-damaged patients. *Cortex*, **22**, 229–242.

Jiang, M., Griff, E.R., Ennis, M., Zimmer, L.A., and Shipley, M.T. (1996). Activation of locus coeruleus enhances the responses of olfactory bulb mitral cells to weak olfactory nerve input. *Journal of Neuroscience*, **16**, 6319–6329.

Joerges, J., Kuttner, A., Galizia, C.G., and Menzel, R. (1997). Representations of odours and odor mixtures visualized in the honeybee brain. *Nature*, **387**, 285–288.

Jog, M.S., Kubota, Y., Connolly, C.I., Hillegaart, V., and Graybiel, A.M. (1999). Building neural representations of habits. *Science*, **286**, 1745–1749.

John, E.R. (1967). *Mechanisms of memory*. Academic Press, New York.

John, E.R., Chesler, P., Bartlett, F., and Victor, I. (1968). Observation learning in cats. *Science*, **159**, 1489–1491.

Johnson, M.H. and Horn, G. (1987). The role of a restricted region of the chick forebrain in the recognition of individual conspecifics. *Behavioural Brain Research*, **23**, 269–275.

Johnson, M.K. and Hasher, L. (1987). Human learning and memory. *Annual Review of Psychology*, **38**, 631–668.

Johnson, R. Jr. (1995). Event-related potential insights into the neurobiology of memory systems. In *Handbook of Neuropsychology*, Vol. 10, (ed. F. Boller and J. Grafman). Elsevier, Amsterdam, pp. 135–163.

Johnson, S. (1751/2000). *The need for general knowledge*. In *Samuel Johnson. The major works*, (ed. D. Greene). Oxford University Press, Oxford.

Johnson, S. (1755/2000). *A dictionary of the English language. Preface*. In *Samuel Johnson. The Major Works*, (ed. D. Greene). Oxford University Press, Oxford.

Johnston, D. and Wu, S.M.-S. (1995). *Foundations of cellular neurophysiology*. MIT Press, Cambridge, MA.

Johnston, M.V., McKinney, M., and Coyle, J.T. (1981). Neo-cortical cholinergic innervation: a description of extrinsic and intrinsic components in the rat. *Experimental Brain Research*, **43**, 159–172.

Jones, E.G. and Peters, A. (ed.) (1984–1994). *Cerebral cortex*, Vols. 1–10. Plenum, New York.

Jones, E.R. (1972). Switchboard versus statistical theories of learning and memory. *Science*, **177**, 850–864.

Jones, H.E. (1930). The retention of conditioned emotional reactions in infancy. *Journal of Genetic Psychology*, **37**, 485–498.

Jones, M.J., Sinha, P., Vetter, T., and Poggio, T. (1997). Top-down learning of low-level vision tasks. *Current Biology*, **7**, 991–994.

Jones, R.W. (1973). *Principles of biological regulation. An introduction to feedback systems*. Academic Press, New York.

Jordan, W.P. and Leaton, R.N. (1983). Habituation of the acoustic startle response in rats after lesions in the mesencephalic reticular formation or the inferior colliculus. *Behavioral Neuroscience*, **97**, 710–724.

Jorm, A.F., Korten, A.E., and Henderson, A.S. (1987). The prevalence of dementia: A quantitative integration of the literature. *Acta Psychiatrica Scandinavica*, **76**, 465–479.

Joseph, J.S., Chun, M.M., and Nakayama, K. (1997). Attentional requirements in a 'preattentive' feature search task. *Nature*, **387**, 805–807.

Jost, A. (1897). Die assoziationstestigkeit in iherer abhängigkeit der verteilung der wiederholungen. *Zeitschrift für Psychologie*, **14**, 436–472.

Joyce, E., Blumenthal, S., and Wessely, S. (1996). Memory, attention, and executive function in chronic fatigue syndrome. *Journal of Neurology, Neurosurgery and Psychiatry*, **60**, 495–503.

Joyner, A.L. (1993). *Gene targeting. A practical approach*. Oxford University Press, Oxford.

Julesz, B. (1981). Textons, the elements of texture perception, and their interactions. *Nature*, **290**, 91–97.

Jung, C.G. (1969). The archetype and the collective unconscious. *The collective works*, Vol. 9, Part I. Princeton University Press, Princeton.

Juola, J.F., Fischler, I., Wood, C.T., and Atkinson, R.C. (1971). Recognition time for information stored in long-term memory. *Perception & Psychophysics*, **10**, 8–14.

Jusczyk, P.W. and Aohne, E.A. (1997). Infants' memory for spoken words. *Science*, **277**, 1984–1986.

Kaas, J.H. (1997). Topographic maps are fundamental to sensory processing. *Brain Research Bulletin*, **44**, 107–112.

References

Kaba, H., Hayashi, Y., Higushi, T., and Nakanishi, S. (1994). Induction of an olfactory memory by the activation of a metabotropic glutamate receptors. *Science*, **265**, 262–264.

Kaczmarek, L.K. and Levitan, I.B. (1987). *Neuromodulation. The biochemical control of neuronal excitability*. Oxford University Press, New York.

Kahneman, D. and Tversky, A. (1982). The psychology of preferences. *Scientific American*, **246**, 136–142.

Kamil, A.C. and Mauldin, J.E. (1975). Intraproblem retention during learning-set acquisition in blue jays (*Cyanocitta cristata*). *Animal Learning and Behavior*, **3**, 125–130.

Kamin, L.J. (1968). 'Attention-like' processes in classical conditioning. In *Miami symposium on the prediction of behavior, 1967: Aversive stimulation*, (ed. M.R. Jones), pp. 9–31. University of Miami Press, Coral Gables, FL.

Kamin, L.J. (1969). Predictability, surprise, attention and conditioning. In *Punishment and aversive behavior*, (ed. B.A. Campbell and R.M. Church), pp. 279–296. Appleton-Century-Crofts, New York.

Kandel, E.R. (1976). *Cellular basis of behavior. An introduction to behavioral neurobiology*. Freeman, San Francisco.

Kandel, E.R. (1979). *Behavioral biology of Aplysia. A contribution to the comparative study of opistobranch molluscs*. Freeman, San Francisco.

Kandel, E.R. and Schwartz, J.H. (1982). Molecular biology of learning: Modulation of transmitter release. *Science*, **218**, 433–443.

Kandel, E.R. and Spencer, W.A. (1968). Cellular neurophysiological approaches in the study of Learning. *Psychological Review*, **48**, 65–134.

Kandel, E.R. and Tauc, L. (1965). Heterosynaptic facilitation in neurones of the abdominal ganglion of *Aplysia depilans. Journal of Physiology (London)*, **181**, 1–27.

Kandel, E.R., Schwartz, J.H., and Jessel, T.M. (2000). *Principles of neural science*, (4th edn). McGraw-Hill, New York.

Kaneko, S., Maeda, T., and Satoh, M. (1997). Cognitive enhancers and hippocampal long-term potentiation in vitro. *Behavioural Brain Research*, **83**, 45–49.

Kant, I. (1781/1998). *Critique of pure reason*. Cambridge University Press, Cambridge.

Kant, I. (1800/1988). *Logic*. Dover, New York.

Kanwisher, N. and Wojciulik, E. (2000). Visual attention: insights from brain imaging. *Nature Reviews Neuroscience*, **1**, 91–100.

Kaplan, C.A. and Simon, H.A. (1990). In search of insight. *Cognitive Psychology*, **22**, 374–419.

Kappers, C.U.A. (1917). Further contribution on neurobiotaxis. IX. An attempt to compare the phenomenon of neurobiotaxis with other phenomena of taxis and tropism. The dynamic polarization of the neurone. *Journal of Comparative Neurology*, **27**, 261–298.

Kapur, S., Craik, F.I.M., Tulving, E., Wilson, A.A., Houle, S., and Brown, G.M. (1994). Neuroanatomical correlates of encoding in episodic memory: Levels of processing effect. *Proceedings of the National Academy of Sciences USA*, **91**, 2008–2011.

Karlin, A. and Akabas, M. (1996). Toward a structural basis for the function of the nicotinic acetylcholine receptors and their cousins. *Neuron*, **15**, 1231–1244.

Karmiloff-Smith, A. (1994). Precis of *Beyond modularity: a developmental perspective on cognitive science. Behavioral and Brain Science*, **17**, 693–745.

Karni, A. and Bertini, G. (1997). Learning perceptual skills: behavioral probes into adult cortical plasticity. *Current Opinion in Neurobiology*, **7**, 530–535.

Karni, A., Meyer, G., Rey-Hipolito, C., Jezzard, P., Adams, M.M., Turner, R., and Ungerleider, L.G. (1998). The acquisition of skilled motor performance: fast and slow experience-driven changes in primary motor cortex. *Proceedings of the National Academy of Sciences USA*, **95**, 861–868.

Kartsounis, L.D., Rudge, P., and Stevens, J.M. (1995). Bilateral lesions of CA1 and CA2 fields of the hippocampus are sufficient to cause a severe amnesic syndrome in humans. *Journal of Neurology, Neurosurgery and Psychiatry*, **59**, 95–98.

Kastner, S., De Weerd, P., Desimone, R., and Ungerleider, L.G. (1998). Mechanisms of directed attention in the human extrastriate cortex as revealed by functional MRI. *Science*, **282**, 108–111.

Kaszniak, A.W. and Zak, M.G. (1996). On the neuropsychology of metamemory: Contributions from the study of amnesia and dementia. *Learning and Individual Differences*, **8**, 355–381.

Katz, J.J. and Halstead, W.C. (1950). Protein organization and mental function. *Comparative Psychology Monographs*, **20**, 1–38.

Katz, L.C. (1999). What's critical for the critical period in visual cortex? *Cell*, **99**, 673–676.

Katz, L.C., Weliky, M., and Dalva, M. (1998). Relationship between local synaptic connections and orientation domains in primary visual cortex. *Neuron*, **20**(4).

Katz, P.S. and Frost, W.N. (1996). Intrinsic neuromodulation: altering neuronal activity from within. *Trends in Neurosciences*, **19**, 54–61.

Kawai, N. and Matsuzawa, T. (2000). Numerical memory span in a chimpanzee. *Nature*, **403**, 39–40.

Kawasaki, H., Springett, G.M., Mochizuki, N., Toki, S., Nakaya, M., Matsuda, M., Housman, D.E., and Graybiel, A.M. (1998). A family of cAMP-binding proteins that directly activate Rap1. *Science*, **282**, 2275–2279.

Kawashima, R., O'Sullivan, B.T., and Roland, P. (1995). Positron-emission tomography studies of cross-modality inhibition in selective attentional tasks: Closing the 'mind's eye'. *Proceedings of the National Academy of Sciences USA*, **92**, 5969–5972.

Kawato, M. (1999). Internal models for motor control and trajectory planning. *Current Opinion in Neurobiology*, **9**, 718–727.

Kelemen, W.L. and Weaver, C.A.III (1997). Enhanced metamemory at delays: Why do judgments of learning improve over time? *Journal of Experimental Psychology: Learning, Memory and Cognition*, **23**, 1394–1409.

Keller, F.S. and Hill, L.M. (1936). Another 'insight' experiment. *Journal of Genetic Psychology*, **48**, 484–489.

Keller, F.S. and Schoenfeld, W.N. (1950). *Principles of psychology. A systematic text in the science of behavior*. Appleton-Century-Crofts, New York.

Kelley, W.M., Miezin, F.M., McDermott, K.B., Buckner, R.L., Racihle, M.E., Cohen, N.J., Ollinger, J.M., Akbudak, E., Conturo, T.E., Snyder, A.Z., and Petersen, S.E. (1998). Hemispheric specialization in human dorsal frontal cortex and medial temporal lobe for verbal and nonverbal memory encoding. *Neuron*, **20**, 927–936.

Kendrick, K.M. and Baldwin, B.A. (1987). Cells in temporal cortex of conscious sheep can respond preferentially to the sight of faces. *Science*, **236**, 448–450.

Kennedy, C. and Sokoloff, L. (1957). An adaptation of the nitrous oxide method to the study of the cerebral circulation in children: Normal values for cerebral blood flow and cerebral metabolic rate in childhood. *Journal of Clinical Investigation*, **36**, 1130–1137.

Kennedy, J.S. (1992). *The new anthropomorphism*. Cambridge University Press, Cambridge.

Kennedy, T.E., Kuhl, D., Barzilai, A., Sweatt, J.D., and Kandel, E.R. (1992). Long-term sensitization training in *Aplysia* leads to an increase in calreticulin, a major presynaptic calcium-binding protein. *Neuron*, **9**, 1013–1024.

Kennell, J.H., Voos, D.K., and Klaus, M.H. (1979). Parent-infant bonding. In *Handbook of infant development*, (ed. J.D. Osofsky), pp. 786–798. Wiley, New York.

Kenny, A.J.P. (1971). *The homunculus fallacy*. In *Interpretations of life and mind. Essays around the problem of reduction*, (ed. M. Grene), pp. 65–83. Routledge & Kegan Paul, London.

Kentros, C., Hargreaves, E., Hawkins, R.D., Kandel, E.R., Shapiro, M., and Muller, R.V. (1998). Abolition of long-term stability of new hippocampal place cell maps by NMDA receptor blockade. *Science*, **280**, 2121–2126.

Keown, D. (2000). Buddhism. A very short introduction. Oxford University Press, Oxford.

Kerlinger, F.N. and Lee, H.B. (2000). *Foundations of behavioural research*. Harcourt College Publishers, Ft Worth, TX.

Kety, S.S. (1970). The biogenic amines in the central nervous system: their possible roles in arousal, emotion and learning. In *The neurosciences, second study program*, (ed. F.O. Schmitt), pp. 324–336. Rockefeller University Press, New York.

Keverne, E.B. (1997). An evaluation of what the mouse knock-out experiments are telling us about mammalian behaviour. *BioEssays*, **19**, 1091–1098.

Kilgard, M.P. and Merzenich, M.M. (1998). Cortical map reorganization enabled by nucleus basalis activity. *Science*, **279**, 1714–1718.

Killcross, S., Robbins, T.W., and Everitt, B.J. (1997). Different types of fear-conditioned behaviour mediated by separate nuclei within amygdala. *Nature*, **388**, 377–380.

Kim, D.S., Duong, T.Q., and Kim, S.G. (2000). High resolution mapping of iso-orientation columns by fMRI. *Nature Neuroscience*, **3**, 164–169.

Kim, J. (1978). IX. Supervenience and nomological incommensurables. *American Philosophical Quarterly*, **15**, 149–156.

Kim, J. and Sosa, E. (ed.) (1999). *Metaphysics. An anthology*, pp. 483–556. Blackwell, Oxford.

Kim, J.H. and Huganir, R.L. (1999). Organization and regulation of proteins in synapses. *Current Opinion in Cell Biology*, **11**, 248–254.

Kim, J.J. and Fanselow, M.S. (1992). Modality-specific retrograde amnesia of fear. *Science*, **256**, 675–677.

Kim, J.J. and Thompson, R.F. (1997). Cerebellar circuits and synaptic mechanisms involved in classical eyeblink conditioning. *Trends in Neurosciences*, **20**, 177–181.

Kim, J.J., Krupka, D.J., and Thompson, R.F. (1998). Inhibitory cerebello-olivary projections and blocking effect in classical conditioning. *Science*, **279**, 570–573.

Kim, S.-S., Duong, T.Q., and Kim, S.-G. (2000). High-resolution mapping of iso-orientation columns by fMRI. *Nature Neuroscience*, **3**, 164–169.

Kimmel, H.D. (1977). Notes from 'Pavlov's Wednesdays': sensory preconditioning. *American Journal of Psychology*, **90**, 319–321.

Kintch, W. and Bates, E. (1977). Recognition memory for statements from a classroom lecture. *Journal of Experimental Psychology, Human Learning and Memory*, **3**, 150–159.

Kintsch, W. (1970). Models for free recall and recognition. In *Models of human memory*, (ed. D.A. Norman). Academic Press, New York.

Kirchhoff, B.A., Wagner, A.D., Maril, A., and Stern, C.E. (2000). Preforntal-temporal circuitry for episodic encoding and subsequent memory. *Journal of Neuroscience*, **20**, 6173–6180.

Kirkpatrick, B. (1996). There's no such thing as the amygdala. *Biological Psychiatry*, **39**, 309–310.

Kirkwood, A., Rioult, M.G., and Bear, M.F. (1996). Experience-dependent modification of synaptic plasticity in visual cortex. *Nature*, **381**, 526–528.

Kirkwood, A., Rozas, C., Kirkwood, J., Perez, F., and Bear, M.F. (1999). Modulation of long-term synaptic depression in visual cortex by acetylcholine and norepinephrine. *Journal of Neuroscience*, **19**, 1599–1609.

References

Kirn, J., O'Loughlin, B., Kasparian, S., and Nottebohm, F. (1994). Cell death and neuronal recruitment in the high vocal center of adult male canaries are temporally related to changes in song. *Proceedings of the National Academy of Sciences USA*, **91**, 7844–7848.

Kirschner, M., Gerhart, J., and Mitchison, T. (2000). Molecular 'vitalism'. *Cell*, **100**, 79–88.

Kirsner, K. and Speelman, C. (1996). Skill acquisition and repetition priming: one principle, many processes? *Journal of Experimental Psychology: Learning, Memory, and Cognition*, **22**, 563–575.

Kitamoto, T. (2001). Conditional modification of behaviour in *Drosophila* by targeted expression of a temperature-sensitive *Shibire* allele in defined neurons. *Journal of Neurobiology*, **47**, 81–92.

Kitamoto, T., Ikeda, K., and Salvaterra, P.M. (1992). Analysis of cis-regulatory elements in the 5′ flanking region of the *Drosophila melanogaster* choline acetyltransferase gene. *Journal of Neuroscience*, **12**, 1628–1639.

Kitazawa, S., Kimura, T., and Yin, P.-B. (1998). Cerebellar complex spikes encode both destinations and errors in arm movements. *Nature*, **392**, 494–497.

Kitchinga, V., Vankov, A., Harley, C., and Sara, S. (1997). Novelty-elicited, noradrenaline-dependent enhancement of excitability in the dentate gyrus. *European Journal of Neuroscience*, **9**, 41–47.

Klatzky, R.L. (1991). Let's be friends. *American Psychologist*, **46**, 43–45.

Kleim, J.A., Vij, K., Ballar, D.H., and Greenough, W.T. (1997). Learning-dependent synaptic modifications in the cerebellar cortex of the adult rat persist for at least four weeks. *Journal of Neuroscience*, **17**, 717–721.

Klin, C.M., Guzman, A.E., and Levine, W.H. (1997). Knowing that you don't know: Metamemory and discourse processing. *Journal of Experimental Psychology: Learning, Memory and Cognition*, **23**, 1378–1393.

Kluver, H. and Bucy, P.C. (1938). An analysis of certain effects of bilateral temporal lobectomy in the rhesus monkey, with special reference to 'psychic blindness'. *Journal of Psychology*, **5**, 33–54.

Knall, C. and Johnson, G.L. (1998). G-protein regulatory pathways: Rocketing into the twenty-first century. *Journal of Cellular Biochemistry*, **30–31** (Suppl.), 137–146.

Knierim, J.J. and Van Essen, D.C. (1992). Visual cortex: Cartography, connectivity, and concurrent processing. *Current Opinion in Neurobiology*, **2**, 150–155.

Knierim, J.J., McNaughton, B.L., and Poe, G.R. (2000). Three-dimensional spatial selectivity of hippocampal neurons during space flight. *Nature Neuroscience*, **3**, 211–212.

Knopman, D. (1993). The non-Alzheimer degenerative dementias. In *Handbook of neuropsychology*. Vol. 8, (ed. F. Boller and J. Grafman), pp. 295–313. Elsevier, Amsterdam.

Knowlton, B.J. and Fanselow, M.S. (1998). The hippocampus, consolidation and on-line memory. *Current Opinion in Neurobiology*, **8**, 293–296.

Knowlton, B.J., Mangels, J.A., and Squire, L.R. (1996). A neostrital habit learning system in humans. *Science*, **273**, 1399–1402.

Knudsen, E.I. (1998). Capacity for plasticity in the adult owl auditory system expanded by juvenile experience. *Science*, **279**, 1531–1533.

Knudsen, E.I., du Lac, S., and Esterly, S.D. (1987). Computational maps in the brain. *Annual Review of Neuroscience*, **10**, 41–65.

Koch, C. (1997). Computation and the single neuron. *Nature*, **385**, 207–210.

Koch, C.A., Anderson, D., Moran, M.F., Ellis, C., and Pawson, T. (1991). SH2 and SH3 domains: Elements that control interactions of cytoplasmic signaling proteins. *Science*, **252**, 668–674.

Koehler, O. (1951). Der Vogelsang als Vorstufe von Musik und Sprache. *Journal fuer Ornithologie*, **93**, 3–20.

Koepp, M.J., Gunn, R.N., Lawrence, A.D., Cunningham, V.J., Dagher, A., Jones, T., Brooks, D.J., Bench, C.J., and Grasby, P.M. (1998). Evidence for striatal dopamine release during a video game. *Nature*, **393**, 266–268.

Koester, H.J. and Sakmann, B. (1998). Calcium dynamics in single spines during coincident pre- and postsynaptic activity depend on relative timing of back-propagating action potentials and subthreshold excitatory postsynaptic potentials. *Proceedings of the National Academy of Sciences USA*, **95**, 9596–9601.

Koffka, K. (1935/1963). *Principles of Gestalt psychology*. Harcourt, Brace & World, New York.

Kogan, J.H., Frankland, P.W., Blendy, J.A., Coblentz, J., Marowitz, Z., Schutz, G., and Silva, A.J. (1996). Spaced training induces normal long-term memory in CREB mutant mice. *Current Biology*, **7**, 1–11.

Kohler, R.E. (1994). *Lords of the fly. Drosophila genetics and the experimental life*. The University of Chicago Press, Chicago, IL.

Kohler, W. (1917/1965). On the insight of apes. In *A source book in the history of psychology*, (ed. R.J. Herrenstein and E.G. Boring, E.G.), pp. 569–578. Harvard University Press, Cambridge, MA.

Kohler, W. (1925). *The mentality of apes*. Routledge & Kegan Paul, London.

Kolers, P.A. (1968). The recognition of geometrically transformed text. *Perception & Psychophysics*, **3**, 57–64.

Kolers, P.A. and Roediger, H.L.III (1984). Procedures of mind. *Journal of Verbal learning and Verbal Behavior*, **23**, 425–449.

Konig, P., Engel, A.K., and Singer, W. (1996). Integrator or coincidence detector? The role of the cortical neuron revisited. *Trends in Neurosciences*, **19**, 130–137.

Konishi, M. (1965). The role of auditory feedback in the control of vocalization in the white-crowned sparrow. *Zeitschrift fuer Tierpsychologie*, **22**, 770–783.

Konishi, M. (1985). Birdsong: From behavior to neuron. *Annual Review of Neuroscience*, **8**, 125–170.

Konishi, M. (1986). Centrally synthesized maps of sensory space. *Trends in Neurosciences*, **9**, 163–168.

Konorski, J. (1948). *Conditioned reflexes and neuron organization*. Cambridge University Press, Cambridge.

Konorski, J. (1967). *Integrative activity of the brain. An interdisciplinary approach*. University of Chicago Press, Chicago, IL.

Kopelman, M.D. (1987). Two types of confabulation. *Journal of Neurology, Neurosurgery, and Psychiatry*, **50**, 1482–1487.

Kopelman, M.D. (1999). Varieties of false memory. *Cognitive Neuropsychology*, **16**, 197–214.

Koriat, A. (1993). How do we know that we know? The accessibility model of the feeling of knowing. *Psychological Review*, **100**, 609–639.

Koriat, A., Ben-Zur, H., and Nussbaun, A. (1990). Encoding information for future action: memory for to-be-performed tasks versus memory for to-be-recalled tasks. *Memory & Cognition*, **18**, 568–578.

Koriat, A. and Goldsmith, M. (1996). Memory metaphors and the real-life/laboratory controversy: Correspondence versus storehouse conceptions of memory. *Behavioral and Brain Sciences*, **19**, 167–228.

Koriat, A., Goldsmith, M., and Pansky, A. (2000). Toward a psychology of memory accuracy. *Annual Review of Psychology*, **51**, 481–537.

Kornhauser, J.M. and Greenberg, M.E. (1997). A kinase to remember: Dual roles for MAP kinase in long-term memory. *Neuron*, **18**, 839–842.

Korsakoff, S.S. (1887). Disturbance of psychic function in alcoholic paralysis and its relation to the disturbance of the psychic sphere in multiple neuritis of non-alcoholic origin. *Vestnick Klincheskoi Psychiatrii i Neurologii*, **4** (2).

Kosik, K.S. (1994). The Alzheimer's disease sphinx: A riddle with plaques and tangles. *Journal of Cell Biology*, **127**, 1501–1504.

Kosslyn, S.M. (1999). If neuroimaging is the answer, what is the question? *Philosophical Transactions of the Royal Society of London, Series B: Biological Sciences*, **354**, 1283–1294.

Kosslyn, S.M., Thompson, W.L., Kim, I.J., and Alpert, N.M. (1995). Topographical representations of mental images in primary visual cortex. *Nature*, **378**, 496–498.

Kotter, R. and Meyer, N. (1992). The limbic system: A review of its empirical foundation. *Behavioural Brain Research*, **52**, 105–127.

Krasne, F.B. and Teshiba, T.M. (1995). Habituation of an invertebrate escape reflex due to modulation by higher centers rather than local events. *Proceedings of the National Academy of Sciences USA*, **92**, 3362–3366.

Krech, D., Rosenzweig, M.R., and Bennett, E.L. (1960). Effects of environmental complexity and training on brain chemistry. *Journal of Comparative and Physiological Psychology*, **53**, 509–519.

Kremer, E.F. (1971). Truly random and traditional control procedures in CER conditioning in the rat. *Journal of Comparative and Physiological Psychology*, **76**, 441–448.

Kroeber, A.L. and Kluckhohn, C. (1963). *Culture: a critical review of concepts and definitions*. Knopf, New York.

Krupnick, J.G. and Benovic, J.L. (1998). The role of receptor kinases and arrestins in G protein-coupled receptor regulation. *Annual Review of Pharmacology and Toxicology*, **38**, 289–319.

Kuan, C.-Y., Roth, K.A., Flavell, R.A., and Rakic, P. (2000). Mechanisms of programmed cell death in the developing brain. *Trends in Neurosciences*, **23**, 291–297.

Kuhl, D., Kennedy, T.E., Barzilai, A., and Kandel, E.R. (1992). Long-term sensitization training in *Aplysia* leads to an increase in the expression of BiP, the major protein chaperon of the ER. *Journal of Cell Biology*, **119**, 1069–1076.

Kuhn, T.S. (1962). *The structure of scientific revolutions*. University of Chicago Press, Chicago, IL.

Kuno, M. (1995). *The synapse: function, plasticity, and neurotrophism*. Oxford University Press, Oxford.

Kupfermann, I. and Weiss, K.R. (1978). The command neuron concept. *Behavioral and Brain Sciences*, **1**, 3–39.

Kurosawa, A. (1950/1992). *Rashomon*. Janus Films, RKO Radio Pictures, USA.

Kutas, M. (1988). Review of event-related potential studies of memory. In *Perspectives in memory research*, (ed. M.S. Gazzaniga), pp. 181–217. MIT Press, Cambridge, MA.

Kutas, M. and Hillyard, S.A. (1980). Reading senseless sentences: Brain potentials reflect semantic incongruity. *Science*, **207**, 203–205.

Kuwana, Y., Shimoyama, I., and Miura, H. (1995). Hybrid insect robot. Steering control of a mobile robot using insect antennae. *Proceedings of the 6th International Symposium of Molecular Electronics and Biocomputing, Okinawa, Japan*, pp. 302–305.

Kvavilashvili, L. and Ellis, J.A. (1999). The effects of positive and negative placebos on human memory performances. *Memory*, **7**, 421–437.

Kwon, S.E., Nadeau, S.E., and Heilman, K.M. (1990). Retrosplenial cortex: Possible role in habituation of the orienting response. *Journal of Neuroscience*, **10**, 3559–3563.

Kyriakis, J.M., Banerjee, P., Nikolakai, E., Dai, T., Rubie, E.A., Ahmad, M.F., Avruch, J., and Woodgett, J.R. (1994). The stress-activated protein kinase subfamily of c-Jun kinases. *Nature*, **369**, 156–160.

La Mettrie, J.O. (1748/1912). *Man a machine*. Open Court, La Salle, IL.

References

LaBar, K.S., Gatenby, J.C., Gore, J.C., LeDoux, J.E., and Phelps, E.A. (1998). Human amygdala activation during conditioned fear acquisition and extinction: a mixed-trial fMRI study. *Neuron*, **20**, 937–945.

du Lac, S., Raymond, J.L., Sejnowski, T.J., and Lisberger, S.G. (1995). Learning and memory in the vestibulo-ocular reflex. *Annual Review of Neuroscience*, **18**, 409–441.

Lacey, A.R. (1996). *A dictionary of philosophy*, (3rd edn). Routledge & Kegan Paul, London.

Lagnado, L. and Baylor, D. (1992). Signal flow in visual transduction. *Neuron*, **8**, 995–1002.

Lakatos, I. (1978). *The methodology of scientific research programmes*, (ed. J. Worrall and G. Currie). Cambridge University Press, Cambridge.

Lakoff, G. and Johnson, M. (1980). *Metaphors we live by*. University of Chicago Press, Chicago, IL.

Laland, K.N. and Williams, K. (1997). Shoaling generates social learning of foraging information in guppies. *Animal Behaviour*, **53**, 1161–1169.

Lamprecht, R. and Dudai, Y. (1995). Differential modulation of brain immediate early genes by intraperitoneal LiCl. *NeuroReport*, **7**, 289–293.

Lamprecht, R. and Dudai, Y. (2000). The amygdala in conditioned taste aversion: it's there, but where. In *The amygdala*, (2nd edn), (ed. J.P. Aggleton), pp. 331–351. Oxford University Press, Oxford.

Lamprecht, R., Hazvi, S., and Dudai, Y. (1997). cAMP response element-binding protein in the amygdala is required for long- but not short-term conditioned taste aversion memory. *Journal of Neuroscience*, **17**, 8443–8450.

Lanahan, A., Williams, J.B., Sanders, L.K., and Nathans, D. (1992). Growth factor-induced delayed response genes. *Molecular and Cellular Biology*, **12**, 3919–3929.

Landauer, T.K. (1988). Optimum rehearsal patterns and name learning. In *Practical aspects of memory*, (ed. M.M. Gruneberg, P.E. Morris, and R.N. Sykes), pp. 625–632. Wiley, Chichester, NY.

Landauer, T.K. and Ross, B.H. (1977). Can simple instructions to use spaced practice improve ability to remember a fact?: an experimental test using telephone numbers. *Bulletin of the Psychonomic Society*, **10**, 215–218.

Langer, S.Z. (1997). 25 years since the discovery of pre-synaptic receptors: present knowledge and future perspectives. *Trends in Pharmacological Sciences*, **18**, 95–99.

Langley, J.N. (1878). On the physiology of the salivary secretion. *Journal of Physiology (London)*, **1**, 339–369.

Langley, J.N. (1905). On the reaction of cells and of nerve-endings to certain poisons, chiefly as regards the reaction of striated muscle to nicotine and curari. *Journal of Physiology (London)*, **33**, 374–413.

Laplanche, J. and Pontalis, J.-B. (1973). *The language of psychoanalysis*. Norton, New York.

Larrabee, M.G. and Bronk, D.W. (1947). Prolonged facilitation of synaptic excitation in sympathetic ganglia. *Journal of Neurophysiology (London)*, **10**, 139–154.

Larson, E.B. and Imai, Y. (1996). An overview of dementia and ethnicity with special emphasis on the epidemiology of dementia. In *The dementias*, (ed. G. Yeo and D. Galagher-Thompson), pp. 9–20. Taylor & Francis, Washington DC.

Lashley, K.S. (1916). The human salivary reflex and its use in psychology. *Psychological Review*, **23**, 446–464.

Lashley, K.S. (1917). The effects of strychnine and caffeine upon the rate of learning. *Psychobiology*, **1**, 141–170.

Lashley, K.S. (1929). *Brain mechanisms and intelligence*. The University of Chicago Press, Chicago, IL.

Lashley, K.S. (1933). Integrative functions of the cerebral cortex. *Physiological Reviews*, **13**, 1–42.

Lashley, K.S. (1950). In search of the engram. *Symposia of the Society for Experimental Biology*, **4**, 454–482.

Lashley, K.S. and Wade, M. (1946). The Pavlovian theory of generalization. *Psychological Review*, **53**, 72–87.

Lashley, K.S., Choa, K.L., and Semms, J. (1951). An examination of the electric field theory of cerebral integration. *Psychological Review*, **58**, 123–136.

Laszlo, E., Artigiani, R., Combs, A., and Csanyi, V. (1996). *Changing visions. Human cognitive maps: past, present, and future*. Praeger, Westport, CT.

Laudan, L. (1977). *Progress and its problems*. University of California Press, Berkeley.

Laurent, G. (1997). Olfactory processing: maps, time and codes. *Current Opinion in Neurobiology*, **7**, 547–553.

Laurent, G. and Davidowitz, H. (1994). Encoding of olfactory information with oscillating neural assemblies. *Science*, **265**, 1872–1875.

Le Maxidico, Dicitionaire encyclopédique de la langue Française (1996). Editions de la Connaissance, France.

Leakey, M.G., Spoor, F., Brown, F.H., Gathogo, P.N., Klarie, C., Leakey, L.N., and McDougall, I. (2001). New hominin genus from eastern Africa shows diverse middle Pliocene lineages. *Nature*, **410**, 433–440.

Leboyer, M., Bellivier, F., Nosten–Bertrand, M., Jouvent, R., Pauls, D., and Mallet, J. (1998). Psychiatric genetics: search for phenotypes. *Trends in Neurosciences*, **21**, 102–105.

Lechner, H.A. and Byrne, J.H. (1998). New perspectives on classical conditioning: A synthesis of Hebbian and non-Hebbian mechanisms. *Neuron*, **20**, 355–358.

Lechner, H.A., Baxter, D.A., and Byrne, J.H. (2000). Classical conditioning of feeding in *Aplysia*: I. Neurophysiological correlates. *Journal of Neuroscience*, **20**, 3377–3386.

Leckman, J.F. and Riddle, M.A. (2000). Tourette's syndrome: when habit-forming systems form habits of their own? *Neuron*, **28**, 349–354.

LeDoux, J.E. (1991). Emotion and the limbic system concept. *Concepts in Neuroscience*, **2**, 169–199.

LeDoux, J.E. (1996). *The emotional brain. The mysterious underpinings of emotional life*. Simon & Schuster, New York.

Lee, C., Rohrer, W.H., and Sparks, D.L. (1988). Population coding of saccadic eye movements by neurons in the superior colliculus. *Nature*, **332**, 357–360.

Lehrer, M. (1993). Why do bees turn back and look? *Journal of Comparative Physiology [A]*, **172**, 549–563.

Leibniz, G.W. (1704/1981). *New essays on human understanding*, (ed. & trans. P. Remnant and J. Bennett). Cambridge University Press, Cambridge.

Leiner, H.C., leiner, A.L., and Dow, R.S. (1993). Cognitive and language functions of the human cerebellum. *Trends in Neurosciences*, **16**, 444–447.

Leon, M. (1992). The neurobiology of filial learning. *Annual Review of Psychology*, **43**, 377–398.

Leonard, B.W., Amaral, D.G., Squire, L.R., and Zola-Morgan, S. (1995). Transient memory impairment in monkeys with bilateral lesions of the entorhinal cortex. *Journal of Neuroscience*, **15**, 5637–5659.

Leonardo, A. and Konishi, M. (1999). Decrystallization of adult birdsong by perturbation of auditory feedback. *Nature*, **399**, 466–470.

Lepage, M., Habib, R., and Tulving, E. (1998). Hippocampal PET activations of memory encoding and retrieval: The HIPPER model. *Hippocampus*, **8**, 313–322.

Lepage, M., Ghaffar, O., Nyberg, L., and Tulving, E. (2000). Prefrontal cortex and episodic memory retrieval mode. *Proceedings of the National Academy of Sciences USA*, **97**, 506–511.

Lettvin, J.Y., Maturana, H.R., McCulloch, W.S., and Pitts, W.H. (1959). What the frog's eye tells the frog's brain. *Proceedings of the Institute of Electrical and Electronic Engineers*, **47**, 1940–1951.

Levine, M. (1959). A model of hypothesis behavior in discrimination learning set. *Psychological Review*, **66**, 353–366.

Levi-Strauss, C. (1966). *The savage mind*. University of Chicago Press, Chicago, IL.

Levy, W.B. and Steward, O. (1979). Synapses as associative memory elements in the hippocampal formation. *Brain Research*, **175**, 233–245.

Levy-Lahad, E. and Bird, T.D. (1996). Genetic factors in Alzheimer's disease: A review of recent advances. *Annals of Neurology*, **40**, 829–840.

Lewin, B. (1994). *Genes V*. Oxford University Press, Oxford.

Lewis, A.S. and Gibson, M.D. (1900). *Palestinian Syriac texts from palimpsest fragments in the Taylor-Schechter collection*. Republished by Raritas, Jerusalem (1971).

Lewis, D.J. (1979). Psychobiology of active and inactive memory. *Psychological Bulletin*, **86**, 1054–1083.

Lewis, F.T. (1923). The significance of the term *hippocampus*. *Journal of Comparative Neurology*, **35**, 213–230.

Liberman, A.M., Cooper, F.S., Shankweiler, D.P., and Studder-Kennedy, M. (1967). Perception of the speech code. *Psychological Review*, **74**, 431–461.

Lidow, M.S., Williams, G.V., and Goldman-Rakic, P.S. (1998). The cerebral cortex: A case for a common site of action of antipsychotics. *Trends in Pharmacological Sciences*, **19**, 136–140.

Lightman, A. and Gingerich, O. (1991). When do anomalies begin? *Science*, **255**, 690–695.

Lindauer, M. (1967). Recent advances in bee communication and orientation. *Annual Review of Entomology*, **12**, 439–470.

Linden, D.J. (1996). A protein synthesis-dependent late phase of cerebellar long-term depression. *Neuron*, **17**, 483–490.

Lindsey, J.R. (1979). Historical foundations. In *The laboratory rat*. Vol. I. *Biology and disease*, (ed. H.J. Baker, J.R. Lindsey, and S.H. Weisbroth). Academic Press, New York.

Linton, M. (1978). Real world memory after six years: an *in vivo* study of very long term memory. In *Practical aspects of memory*, (ed. M.M. Gruneberg, P.E. Morris, and R.N. Sykes), pp. 69–76. Academic Press, Orlando, FL.

Lipsitt, L.P. (1990). Learning processes in the human newborn. *Annals of the New York Academy of Sciences,* **608**, 113–127.

Lisberger, S.G. (1998). Cerebellar LTD: A molecular mechanism of behavioral learning? *Cell*, **92**, 701–704.

Lishman, W.A. (1998). *Organic psychiatry. The psychological consequences of cerebral disorder*, (3rd edn). Blackwell, Oxford.

Lisman, J.E. (1985). A mechanism for memory storage insensitive to molecular turnover: A bistable autophosphorylating kinase. *Proceedings of the National Academy of Sciences USA*, **82**, 3055–3057.

Lisman, J. (1989). A mechanism for the Hebb and the anti-Hebb processes underlying learning and memory. *Proceedings of the National Academy of Sciences USA*, **86**, 9574–9578.

Lisman, J.E. and Fallon, J.R. (1999). What maintains memories. *Science*, **283**, 339–340.

Liu, F.-C. and Graybiel, A.M. (1996). Spatiotemporal dynamics of CREB phosphorylation: Transient versus sustained phosphorylation in the developing striatum. *Neuron*, **17**, 1133–1144.

Liu, L., Wolf, R., Ernst, R., and Heisenberg, M. (1999). Context generalization in *Drosophila* visual learning requires the mushroom bodies. *Nature*, **400**, 753–756.

Livingston, K.F. and Escobar, A. (1971). Anatomical bias of the limbic system concept. *Archives of Neurology*, **24**, 17–21.

Livingston, R.B. (1967). Reinforcement. In *The neurosciences: A study program*, (ed. G.C. Quarton, T. Melnechuck, and F.O. Schmitt), pp. 568–576. The Rockefeller University Press, New York.

Livingstone, M.S., Sziber, P.P., and Quinn, W.G. (1984). Loss of calcium/calmodulin responsiveness in adenylate cyclase

References

of *rutabaga*, a *Drosophila* learning mutant. *Cell*, **137**, 205–215.

Lloyd, D.P. (1949). Post-tetanic potentiation of response in monosynaptic reflex pathways of the spinal cord. *Journal of General Physiology*, **33**, 147–170.

Lloyd, G.G. and Lishman, W.A. (1975). The effect of depression on the speed of recall of pleasant and unpleasant experiences. *Psychological Medicine*, **5**, 173–180.

Lo, Y.-J. and Poo, M. (1991). Activity-dependent synaptic competition in vitro: Heterosynaptic suppression of developing synapses. *Science*, **254**, 1019–1022.

Lockard, R.B. (1968). The albino rat. *American Psychologist*, **23**, 734–742.

Locke, J. (1690/1975). *An essay concerning human understanding.* Clarendon Press, Oxford.

Loewi, O. (1921). Uber humorale Ubertragbarkeit der Herznervenwirkung. *Pflüger's Archive für die gesamte Physiologie*, **189**, 239–242.

Loewi, O. (1936/1965). The chemical transmission of nerve action. In *Nobel lectures including presentation speeches and laureates' biographies. Physiology or medicine, 1922–1941*, pp. 416–432. Elsevier, Amsterdam.

Loftus, E.F. (1991). The glitter of everyday memory…, and the gold. *American Psychologist*, **46**, 16–18.

Loftus, E.F. (1996). Memory distortion and false memory creation. *Bulletin of the American Academy of Psychiatry and the Law*, **24**, 281–295.

Loftus, E.F. and Kaufman, L. (1992). Why do traumatic experiences sometimes produce good memory (flashbulbs) and sometimes no memory (repression)? In *Affect and accuracy in recall. Studies of 'flashbulb' memories*, (ed. E. Winograd and U. Neisser), pp. 212–223. Cambridge University Press, New York.

Loftus, E.F. and Loftus, G.R. (1980). On the permanence of stored information in the human brain. *American Psychologist*, **35**, 409–420.

Loftus, E.F., Feldman, J., and Dashiell, R. (1995), The reality of illusory memories. In *Memory distortions*, (ed. D.L. Schacter), pp. 47–68. Harvard University Press, Cambridge, MA.

Logan, G.D. (1988). Toward an instance theory of automatization. *Psychological Review*, **95**, 492–527.

Logan, G.D. (1990). Repetition priming and automaticity: common underlying mechanisms? *Cognitive Psychology*, **22**, 1–35.

Logothetis, N. (2000). Can current fMRI techniques reveal the microarchitecture of cortex? *Nature Neuroscience*, **3**, 413.

Logothetis, N.K., Guggenberger, H., Peled, S., and Pauls, J. (1999). Functional imaging of the monkey brain. *Nature Neuroscience*, **2**, 555–562.

Logothetis, N.K., Pauls, J., Augath, M., Trinath, T., and Beltermann, A. (2001). Neurophysiological investigation of the basis of the fMRI signal. *Nature*, **412**, 150–157.

Loisette, A. (1899). *Assimilative memory, or how to attend and never forget.* Funk & Wagnalls, New York.

Lomo, T. (1966). Frequency potentiation of excitatory synaptic activity in the dentate area of the hippocampal formation. *Acta Physiologica Scandinavica*, **68** (Suppl. 277), 128.

Long, A.A. (1986). *Hellenistic philosophy. stoics, epicureans, sceptics*, (2nd edn). University of California Press, Berkeley, CA.

Long, A.A. (1991). Representation and the self in Stoicism. In *Psychology. Companions to ancient thought 2*, (ed. S. Everson), pp. 102–120. Cambridge University Press, Cambridge.

Long, E.S. and Miltenberger, R.G. (1998). A review of behavioral and pharmacological treatments for habit disorders in individuals with mental retardation. *Journal of Behavior Therapy and Experimental Psychiatry*, **29**, 143–156.

Lopes da Silva, F. (1991). Neural mechanisms underlying brain waves: From neural membranes to networks. *Electroencephalography and Clinical Neurophysiology*, **79**, 81–93.

Lopez, H.S. and Brown, A.M. (1992). Neuromodulation. *Current Opinion in Neurobiology*, **2**, 317–322.

Lorenz, K.Z. (1937). The companion in the bird's world. *Auk*, **54**, 245–273.

Lorenz, K.Z. (1981). *The foundations of ethology.* Springer-Verlag, New York.

Loucas, R.B. (1936). The experimental delimitation of neural structures essential for learning: the attempt to condition striped muscle responses with Faradization of the sigmoid gyri. *Journal of Psychology*, **1**, 5–44.

Lu, X.-C.M. and Slotnick, B.M. (1990). Acquisition of an olfactory learning-set in rats with lesions of the mediodorsal thalamic nucleus. *Chemical Senses*, **15**, 713–724.

Lubow, R.E. (1989). *Latent inhibition and conditioned attention theory.* Cambridge University Press, Cambridge.

Lubow, R.E. and Gewirtz, J.C. (1995). Latent inhibition in humans: Data, theory, and implications for schizophrenia. *Psychological Bulletin*, **117**, 87–103.

Lubow, R.E. and Moore, A.U. (1959). Latent inhibition: The effect of nonreinforced pre-exposure to the conditional stimulus. *Journal of Comparative and Physiological Psychology*, **52**, 415–419.

Luciana, M. and Nelson, C.A. (1998). The functional emergence of prefrontally-guided working memory systems in four- to eight-year-old children. *Neuropsychologia*, **36**, 273–293.

Luria, A.R. (1966). *Higher cortical function in man* (2nd edn.). Basic Books, New York.

Luria, A.R. (1969). *The mind of a mnemonist.* Jonathan Cape, London.

Lynch, A. (1996). *Thought contagion. How belief spreads through society.* Basic Books, New York.

Lynch, G. and Baudry, M. (1984). The biochemistry of learning: A new specific hypothesis. *Science*, **224**, 1057–1063.

Lynch, G.S., Dunwiddie, T., and Gribkoff, V. (1977). Heterosynaptic depression: a postsynaptic correlate of long-term potentiation. *Nature*, **266**, 737–739.

Lynch, M. (1985). *Art and artifact in laboratory science. A study of shop work and shop talk in a research laboratory.* Routledge & Kegan Paul, London.

Lynch, M.E. (1988). Sacrifice and the transformation of the animal body into a scientific object: Laboratory culture and ritual practice in the neurosciences. *Social Studies of Science,* **18**, 265–289.

Lyons, J. (1977). *Semantics,* Vol. I. Cambridge University Press, Cambridge.

MacDermott, A.B., Role, L.W., and Siegelbaum, S.A. (1999). Presynaptic ionotropic receptors and the control of transmitter release. *Annual Review of Neuroscience,* **22**, 443–485.

MacDougall, R. (1904). Recognition and recall. *Journal of Philosophy, Psychology and Scientific Methods,* **1**, 229–233.

Mackintosh, N.J. (1973). Stimulus selection: Learning to ignore stimuli that predict no change in reinforcement. In *Constraints on learning. Limitations and predispositions,* (ed. R.A. Hinde and J. Stevenson-Hinde), pp. 75–96. Academic Press, London.

Mackintosh, N.J. (1983). *Conditioning and associative learning.* Oxford University Press, Oxford.

MacLean, P.D. (1952). Some psychiatric implications of physiological studies of frontotemporal portion of limbic system (visceral brain). *Electroencephalography and Clinical Neurophysiology,* **4**, 407–418.

MacLean, P.D. (1970). The triune brain, emotion, and scientific bias. In *The neurosciences. Second study program,* (ed. F.O. Schmitt), pp. 336–349. The Rockefeller University Press, New York.

Macphail, E.M. (1996). Cognitive function in mammals: the evolutionary perspective. *Cognitive Brain Research,* **3**, 279–290.

Madhani, H.D. and Fink, G.R. (1998). The riddle of MAP kinase signaling specificity. *Trends in Genetics,* **14**, 151–155.

Magee, J., Hoffman, D., Colbert, C., and Johnston, D. (1998). Electrical and calcium signalling in dendrites of hippocampal pyramidal neurons. *Annual Review of Physiology,* **60**, 327–346.

Magoun, H.W. (1952). An ascending reticular activating system in the brain stem. *Archives of Neurology and Psychiatry,* **67**, 145–154.

Maguire, E.A., Frackowiak, R.S.J., and Frith, C.D. (1997). Recalling routes around London: activation of the right hippocampus in taxi drivers. *Journal of Neuroscience,* **17**, 7103–7110.

Maguire, E.A., Burgess. N., Donnett, J.G., Frackowiak, R.S.J., Frith, C.D., and O'Keefe, J. (1998). Knowing where and getting there: A human navigation network. *Nature,* **280**, 921–924.

Maguire, E.A., Gadian, D.G., Johnsrude, I.S., Good, C.D., Ashburner, J., Frackowiak, R.S.J., and Frith, C.D. (2000). Navigation-related structural change in the hippocampi of taxi drivers. *Proceedings of the National Academy of Sciences USA,* **97**, 4398–4403.

Maher, M.P., Pine, J., Wright, J., and Tai, Y.-C. (1999). The neurochip: A new multielectrode device for stimulating and recording from cultured neurons. *Journal of Neuroscience Methods,* **87**, 45–56.

Maier, N.R.F. (1931). Reasoning in humans II: The solution of a problem and its appearance in consciousness. *Journal of Comparative Psychology,* **12**, 181–194.

Maier, V. and Scheich, H. (1983). Acoustic imprinting leads to differential 2-deoxy-D-glucose uptake in the chick forebrain. *Proceedings of the National Academy of Sciences USA,* **80**, 3860–3864.

Maimonides (Moshe Ben Maimon) (1180/1984). Hilchot Daat (The instructions of knowledge), Chapter 1. In *The Mishneh Torah* (The repetition of the law). Codex Maimuni. Mosses Maimonides code of law. The illuminated pages of the Kaufmann Mishneh Torah. Corviton/Hlikon/Straussburger, Hungary.

Mainzer, K. (1994). *Thinking in complexity. The complex dynamics of matter, mind, and mankind.* Springer-Verlag, Heidelberg.

Malonek, D. and Grinvald, A. (1996). Interactions between electrical activity and cortical microcirculation revealed by imaging spectroscopy: Implications for functional brain mapping. *Science,* **272**, 551–554.

Malonek, D., Dirnagl, U., Lindauer, U., Yamada, K., Kanno, I., and Grinvald, A. (1997). Vascular imprints of neuronal activity: Relationships between the dynamics of cortical blood flow, oxygenation, and volume changes following sensory stimulation. *Proceedings of the National Academy of Sciences USA,* **94**, 14826–14831.

von der Malsburg, C. (1987). Synaptic plasticity as basis of brain organization. In *The neural and molecular bases of learning,* (ed. J.P. Changeux and M. Konishi), pp. 411–432. Wiley, Chichester.

von der Malsburg, C. (1995). Binding in models of perception and brain function. *Current Opinion in Neurobiology,* **5**, 520–526.

Mandelbrot, B.B. (1977). *The fractal geometry of nature.* Freeman, New York.

Mandler, G. (1980). Recognizing: the judgment of previous occurrence. *Psychological Review,* **87**, 252–271.

Manning, A. and Dawkins, M.S. (1998). *An introduction to animal behaviour,* (5th edn). Cambridge University Press, Cambridge.

Manning, C.A., Stone, W.S., Korol, D.L., and Gold, P.E. (1998). Glucose enhancement of 24-h memory retrieval in healthy elderly humans. *Behavioural Brain Research,* **93**, 71–76.

Manns, J.R., Clark, R.E., and Squire, L.R. (2000). Awareness predicts the magnitude of single-cue trace eyeblink conditioning. *Hippocampus,* **10**, 181–186.

References

Mansvelder, H.D. and McGehee, D.S. (2000). Long-term potentiation of excitatory inputs to brain reward areas by nicotine. *Neuron*, **27**, 349–357.

Marcus, E.A., Nolen, T.G., Rankin, C.H., and Carew, T.J. (1988). Behavioral dissociation of dishabituation, sensitization, and inhibition in *Aplysia*. *Science*, **241**, 210–213.

Maren, S. and Fanslow, M.S. (1996). The amygdala and fear conditioning: Has the nut been cracked? *Neuron*, **16**, 237–240.

Maren, S. and Holt, W. (2000). The hippocampus and contextual memory retrieval in Pavlovian conditioning. *Behavioural Brain Research*, **110**, 97–108.

Maren, S., Aharonov, G., Stote, D.L., and Fanselow, M.S. (1996). *N*-methyl-D-aspartate receptors in the basolateral amygdala are required for both acquisition and expression of conditional fear in rats. *Behavioral Neuroscience*, **110**, 1365–1374.

Maren, S., Anagnostaras, S.G., and Fanselow, M.S. (1998). The startled seahorse: Is the hippocampus necessary for contextual fear conditioning? *Trends in Cognitive Sciences*, **2**, 39–43.

Margoliash, D. (1997). Functional organization of forebrain pathways for song production and perception. *Journal of Neurobiology*, **33**, 671–693.

Maril, A., Wagner, A.D., and Schacter, D.L. (2001). On the tip of the tongue: an event-related fMRI study of semantic retrieval failure and cognitive conflict. *Neuron*, **31**, 653–660.

Markman, A.B. and Dietrich, E. (2000). In defense of representation. *Cognitive Psychology*, **40**, 138–171.

Markowitsch, H.J. (1995). Which brain regions are critically involved in the retrieval of old episodic memory? *Brain Research Reviews*, **21**, 117–127.

Markram, H. and Segal, M. (1990). Long-lasting facilitation of excitatory postsynaptic potentials in the rat hippocampus by acetylcholine. *Journal of Physiology*, **427**, 381–393.

Markram, H. and Tsodyks, M. (1996). Redistribution of synaptic efficacy between neocortical pyramidal neurons. *Nature*, **382**, 807–810.

Markram, H., Helm, P.J., and Sakmann, B. (1995). Dendritic calcium transients evoked by single back-propagating action potentials in rat neocortical pyramidal neurons. *Journal of Physiology (London)*, **485**, 1–20.

Markram, H., Lubke, J., Frotscher, M., and Sakmann, B. (1997). regulation of synaptic efficacy by coincidence of postsynaptic action potentials and EPSPs. *Science*, **275**, 213–215.

Markram, H., Gupta, A., Uziel, A., Wang, Y., and Tsodyks, M. (1998*a*). Information processing with frequency–dependent synaptic connections. *Neurobiology of Learning and Memory*, **70**, 101–112.

Markram, H., Roth, A., and Helmchen, F. (1998*b*). Competitive calcium binding: implications for dendritic calcium signaling. *Journal of Computational Neuroscience*, **5**, 331–348.

Marks, I. and Tobena, A. (1990). Learning and unlearning fear: A clinical and evolutionary perspective. *Neuroscience and Biobehavioral Reviews*, **14**, 365–384.

Marks, I.M. (1987). *Fears, fobias, and rituals*. Oxford University Press, New York.

Markson, L. and Bloom, P. (1997). Evidence against a dedicated system for word learning in children. *Nature*, **385**, 813–815.

Markus, E.J., Qin, Y.L., Leonard, B., Skaggs, W.E., McNaughton, B.L., and Barnes, C.A. (1995). Interactions between location and task affect the spatial and directional firing of hippocampal neurons. *Journal of Neuroscience*, **15**, 7079–7094.

Marler, P. (1984). Song learning: Innate species differences in the learning process. In *The biology of learning*, (ed. P. Marler and H.S. Terrace), pp. 289–309. Springer-Verlag, Berlin.

Marler, P. (1997). Three models of song learning: Evidence from behavior. *Journal of Neurobiology*, **33**, 501–516.

Marler, P. and Tamura, M. (1964). Culturally transmitted patterns of vocal behavior in sparrows. *Science*, **146**, 1483–1486.

Marlin, N.A. and Miller, R.R. (1981). Association to contextual stimuli as a determinant of long-term habituation. *Journal of Experimental Psychology: Animal Behavior Processes*, **7**, 313–333.

Marr, D. (1969). A theory of cerebellar cortex. *Journal of Physiology (London)*, **202**, 437–470.

Marr, D. (1982). *Vision*. Freeman, San Francisco.

Marshall, C.J. (1995). Specificity of receptor tyrosine kinase signaling: Transient versus sustained extracellular signal-regulated kinase activation. *Cell*, **80**, 179–185.

Marshall, J. (1980). The new organology. *Behavioral and Brain Sciences*, **3**, 23–25.

Marshall, W.H., Woolsey, C.N., and Bard, P. (1941). Observations on cortical somatic sensory mechanisms of cat and monkey. *Journal of Neurophysiology*, **4**, 1–24.

Martin, J.H. (1991). Coding and processing of Sensory Information. In *Principles of neural science*, (3rd edn), (ed. E.R. Kandel, J.H. Schwartz, and T.M. Jessel), pp. 329–340. Elsevier, New York.

Martin, K.C. and Kandel, E.R. (1996). Cell adhesion molecules, CREB, and the formation of new synaptic connections. *Neuron*, **17**, 567–570.

Martin, K.C., Casadio, A., Zhu, H., Yaping, E., Rose, J.C., Chen, M., Bailey, C.H., and Kandel, E.R. (1997*a*). Synapse-specific, long-term facilitation of *Aplysia* sensory to motor synapses: A function for local protein synthesis in memory storage. *Cell*, **91**, 927–938.

Martin, K.C., Michael, D., Rose, J.C., Barad, M., Casadio, A., Zhu, H.X., and Kandel, E.R. (1997*b*). MAP kinase translocates into the nucleus of the presynaptic cell and is required for long-term facilitation in *Aplysia*. *Neuron*, **18**, 899–912.

Martin, L.J., Spicer, D.M., Lewis, M.H., Gluck, J.P., and Cork, L.C. (1991). Social deprivation of infant rhesus monkeys alters the chemoarchitecture of the brain: I. Subcortical regions. *Journal of Neuroscience*, **11**, 3344–3358.

Martin, P. and Bateson, P. (1993). *Measuring behaviour. An introductory guide*, (2nd edn). Cambridge University Press, Cambridge.

Martin, R. (ed.) (1997). *Neuroscience methods. A guide for advanced students*. Academic Publishers, Amsterdam.

Martin, S.J., Grimwood, P.D., and Morris, R.G.M. (2000). Synaptic plasticity and memory: an evaluation of the hypothesis. *Annual Review of Neuroscience*, **23**, 649–711.

Martone, M., Butters, N., Payne, M., Becker, J.T., and Sax, D.S. (1984). Dissociations between skill learning and verbal recognition in amnesia and dementia. *Archives of Neurology*, **41**, 965–970.

Mason, S.T. (1984). *Catecholamines and behaviour*. Cambridge University Press, Cambridge.

Matthews, G. (1996). Neurotransmitter release. *Annual Review of Neuroscience*, **19**, 219–233.

Mattson, M.P. (1998). Modification of ion homeostasis by lipid peroxidation: Roles in neuronal degeneration and adaptive plasticity. *Trends in Neurosciences*, **21**, 53–57.

Maute, M.F. and Dube, L. (1999). Patterns of emotional responses and behavioural consequences of dissatisfaction. *Applied Psychology, An International Review*, **48**, 349–366.

Mayes, A.R. (1988). *Human organic memory disorders*. Cambridge University Press, Cambridge.

Mayes, A.R. (1995). Memory and amnesia. *Behavioural Brain Research*, **66**, 29–36.

Mayford, M., Wang, J., Kandel, E.R., and O'Dell, T.J. (1995). CaMKII regulates the frequency-response function of hippocampal synapses for the production of both LTD and LTP. *Cell*, **81**, 891–904.

Mayford, M., Bach, M.E., Huang, Y.-Y, Wang, L., Hawkins, R.D., and Kandel, E.R. (1996). Control of memory formation through regulated expression of a CaMKII transgene. *Science*, **274**, 1678–1683.

Maylor, E.A. (1996). Does prospective memory decline with age? In *Prospective memory. Theory and applications*, (ed. M. Brandimonte, G.O. Einstein, and M.A. McDaniel), pp. 173–197. Lawrence Erlbaum Associates, Mahwah, NJ.

Mayr, E. (1981). Biological classification: toward a synthesis of opposing methodologies. *Science*, **214**, 510–516.

Mayr, E. (1982). *The growth of biological thought*. Harvard University Press, Cambridge, MA.

McAllister, A.K., Katz, L.C., and Lo, D.C. (1999). Neurotrophins and synaptic plasticity. *Annual Review of Neuroscience*, **22**, 295–318.

McCarthy, R.A. and Warrington, E.K. (1990). Auditory-verbal span of apprehension: a phenomenon in search of a function? In *Neuropsychological impairments of short-term memory*, (ed. G. Vallar and T. Shallice), pp. 167–186. Cambridge University Press, Cambridge.

McClearn, G.E., Johansson, B., Berg, S., Pedersen, N.L., Ahern, F., Petrill, S.A., and Plomin, R. (1997). Substantial genetic influence on cognitive abilities in twins 80 or more years old. *Science*, **276**, 1560–1563.

McClelland, J.L. and Goddard, N.H. (1996). Considerations arising from a complementary learning systems perspective on hippocampus and neocortex. *Hippocampus*, **6**, 654–665.

McClelland, J.L., McNaughton, B.L., and O'Reilly, R.C. (1995). Why are there complementary learning systems in the hippocampus and neocortex: Insights from the successes and failures of connectionist models of learning and memory. *Psychological Review*, **102**, 419–457.

McCloskey, M., Wible, C.G., and Cohen, N.J. (1988). Is there a special flashbulb memory mechanism? *Journal of Experimental Psychology: General*, **117**, 171–181.

McCormick, D.A. (1989). Cholinergic and noradrenergic modulation of thalamocortical processing. *Trends in Neurosciences*, **12**, 215–221.

McCulloch, W.S. and Pitts, W. (1943). A logical calculus of the ideas immanent in nervous activity. *Bulletin of Mathematical Biophysics*, **5**, 115–133.

McDonald, R.J. and White, N.M. (1993). A triple dissociation of memory systems: Hippocampus, amygdala, and dorsal striatum. *Behavioral Neuroscience*, **107**, 3–22.

McDougall, W. (1923/1949). *An outline of psychology*. Methuen, London.

McEwen, B.S. (1997). Hormones as regulators of brain development: Life-long effects related to health and disease. *Acta Pediatrica* (Suppl.) **422**, 41–44.

McFadden, P.N. and Koshland, D.E. Jr. (1990). Parallel pathways for habituation in repetitively stimulated PC12 cells. *Neuron*, **4**, 615–621.

McGaugh, J.L. (1966). Time-dependent processes in memory storage. *Science*, **153**, 1351–1358.

McGaugh, J.L. (2000). A century of consolidation. *Science*, **287**, 248–251.

McGaugh, J.L. and Cahill, L. (1997). Interaction of neuromodulatory systems in modulating memory storage. *Behavioural Brain Research*, **83**, 31–38.

McGaugh, J.L., Introini-Collison, I.B., Cahill, L.F., Castellano, C., Dalmaz, C., Parent, M.B., and Williams, C.L. (1993). Neuromodulatory systems and memory storage: Role of amygdala. *Behavioural Brain Research*, **58**, 81–90.

McGeer, P.L., McGeer, E.G., Suzuki, J., Dolman, C.E., and Nagai, T. (1984). Aging, Alzheimer's disease, and the cholinergic system of the basal forebrain. *Neurology*, **34**, 741–745.

McGeoch, J.A. (1932). Forgetting and the law of disuse. *Psychological Review*, **39**, 352–370.

McGinn, M. (1997). *Witgenstein and the philosophical investigations*. Routledge, London.

References

McGuire, P.K., Paulesu, E., Frackowiak, R.S.J., and Frith, C.D. (1996). Brain activity during stimulus independent thought. *NeuroReport*, **7**, 2095–2099.

McGuire, W.J. (1961). A multiprocess model for paired-associate learning. *Journal of Experimental Psychology*, **62**, 335–347.

McIntosh, A.R., Rajah, M.N., and Lobaugh, N.J. (1999). Interactions of prefrontal cortex in relation to awareness in sensory learning. *Science*, **284**, 1531–1533.

McKhann, G., Drachman, D., Folstein, M., Katzman, R., Price, D., and Stadlan, E.M. (1984). Clinical diagnosis of Alzheimer's disease: Report of the NINCDS-ADRDA work group under the auspices of the Department of Health and Human Services task force on Alzheimer's disease. *Neurology*, **34**, 939–941.

McNaughton, B.L., Douglas, R.M., and Goddard, G.W. (1978). Synaptic enhancement in facia dentata: cooperativity among coactive afferents. *Brain Research*, **157**, 277–293.

McNish, K.A., Gewirtz, J.C., and Davis, M. (1997). Evidence of contextual fear after lesions of the hippocampus: A disruption of freezing but not fear potentiated startle. *Journal of Neuroscience*, **17**, 9353–9360.

McWeeny, K.H., Young, A.W., Hay, D.C., and Ellis, A.W. (1987). Putting names to faces. *British Journal of Psychology*, **78**, 143–149.

Meacham, J.A. and Singer, J. (1977). Incentive effects in prospective remembering. *Journal of Psychology*, **97**, 191–197.

Meadow, R. (1977). Munchausen syndrome by proxy: the hinterland of child abuse. *Lancet*, **ii**, 343–345.

Medina, J.H. and Izquierdo, I. (1995). Retrograde messengers, long-term potentiation and memory. *Brain Research Reviews*, **21**, 185–194.

Meehl, P.E. and Sellars, W. (1956). The concept of emergence. In *Minnesota studies in the philosophy of science*, Vol. I, (ed. H. Feigl and M. Scriven), pp. 239–252. University of Minnesota Press, Minnesota, MN.

Mehrota, K., Mohan, C.K., and Ranka, S. (1997). *Elements of artificial neural networks*. MIT Press, Cambridge, MA.

Mehta, M.R., Barnes, C.A., and McNaughton, B.L. (1997). Experience-dependent, asymmetric expansion of hippocampal place fields. *Proceedings of the National Academy of Sciences USA*, **94**, 8918–8921.

Mehta, M.R., Quirk, M.C., and Wilson, M.A. (2000). Experience-dependent asymmetric shape of hippocampal receptive field. *Neuron*, **25**, 707–715.

Meldrum, B. and Garthwaite, J. (1990). Excitatory amino acid neurotoxicity and neurodegenerative disease. *Trends in Pharmacological Sciences*, **11**, 379–387.

Melton, A.W. (1970). The situation with respect to the spacing of repetitions and memory. *Journal of Verbal Learning and Verbal Behavior*, **9**, 596–606.

Meltzoff, A.N. and Moore, M.K. (1977). Imitation of facial and manual gestures by human neonates. *Science*, **198**, 75–78.

Menzel, E.W. and Juno, C. (1982). Marmosets (*Saguinus fuscicollis*): are learning sets learned? *Science*, **217**, 750–752.

Menzel, R. and Mercer, A. (ed.) (1987). *Neurobiology and behavior of honeybees*. Springer-Verlag, Berlin.

Menzel, R. and Müller, U. (1996). Learning and memory in the honeybees: from behavior to neural substrates. *Annual Review of Neuroscience*, **19**, 379–404.

Menzel, R., Geiger, K., Chittka, L., Joerges, J., Kunze, J., and Müller, U. (1996). The knowledge base of bee navigation. *Journal of Experimental Biology*, **199**, 141–146.

Menzel, R., Heyne, A., Kinzel, C., Gerber, B., and Fiala, A. (1999). Pharmacological dissociation between the reinforcing, sensitizing, and response-releasing functions of reward in honeybee classical conditioning. *Behavioral Neuroscience*, **113**, 744–754.

Mertfessel, M. (1935). Roller canary song produced without learning from external sources. *Science*, **81**, 470.

Merton, R.K. (1957). Priorities in scientific discovery: a chapter in the sociology of science. *American Sociological Review*, **22**, 635–659.

Merton, R.K. (1961). Singletons and multiples in scientific discovery: a chapter in the sociology of science. *Proceedings of the American Philosophical Society*, **105**, 470–486.

Merton, R.K. (1963). Resistance to the systematic study of multiple discoveries in science. *Archives Europeenes Sociologie*, **4**, 237–262.

Merton, R.K. (1993). *On the shoulders of giants*. The University of Chicago Press, Chicago, IL.

Mesarovic, M.D., Macko, D., and Takahara, Y. (1970). *Theory of hierarchical, multilevel, systems*. Academic Press, New York.

Mesulam, M.M. (1999). Neuroplasticity failure in Alzheimer's disease. Bridging the gap between plaques and tangles. *Neuron*, **24**, 521–529.

Mesulam, M.M., Mufson, E.J., Levey, A.I., and Wainer, B.H. (1983). Cholinergic innervation of cortex by the basal forebrain: cytochemistry and cortical connections of the septal area, diagonal band nuclei, nucleus basalis (substantia innominata), and hypothalamus in the rhesus monkey. *Journal of Comparative Neurology*, **214**, 170–197.

Meumann, E. (1913). *The psychology of learning. An experimental investigation of the economy and technique of memory*. Appleton, New York.

Meunier, M., Bachevalier, J., Mishkin, M., and Murray, E.A. (1993). Effects on visual recognition of combined and separate ablations of the entorhinal and perirhinal cortex in rhesus monkeys. *Journal of Neuroscience*, **13**, 5418–5432.

Meyer, A. (1971). *Historical aspects of cerebral anatomy*. Oxford University Press, London.

Meyer, D.E. and Schvaneveldt, R.W. (1971). Facilitation in recognizing pairs of words: Evidence of a dependence between retrieval operations. *Journal of Experimental Psychology*, **90**, 227–234.

Meyer, J.J., Allen, D.D., and Yokel, R.A. (1996). Hippocampal acetylcholine increases during eyeblink conditioning in the rabbit. *Physiology and Behavior*, **60**, 1199–1203.

Michaelis, E.K. (1998). Molecular biology of glutamate receptors in the central nervous system and their role in excitotoxicity, oxidative stress and aging. *Progress in Neurobiology*, **54**, 369–415.

Michaels, C.E. and Carello, C. (1981). *Direct perception*. Prentice-Hall, Englewood Cliffs, NJ.

Midgley, M. (1992). *Science as salvation. A modern myth and its meaning*. Routledge, London.

Miles, W.R. (1930). On the history of research with rats and mazes: a collection of notes. *Journal of General Psychology*, **3**, 324–337.

Mill, J.S. (1884). *System of logic ratiocinative and inductive. Being a connected view of the principles of evidence and the methods of scientific investigation*. People's edition. Longman, Green, and Co., London.

Miller, E.K. and Desimone, R. (1994). Parallel neuronal mechanisms for short-term memory. *Science*, **263**, 520–522.

Miller, G.A. (1956). The magical number seven, plus or minus two: Some limits on our capacity for processing information. *Psychological Review*, **63**, 81–97.

Miller, G.A., Galanter, E.G., and Pribram, K.H. (1960). *Plans and the structure of behavior*. Holt, Rinehart and Winston.

Miller, J.S., Jagielo, J.A., and Spear, N.E. (1993). The influence of retention interval on the US preexposure effect: changes in the contextual blocking over time. *Learning and Motivation*, **24**, 376–394.

Miller, M.B. and Gazzaniga, M.S. (1998). Creating false memories for visual scenes. *Neuropsychologia*, **36**, 513–520.

Miller, N.E. and Dollard, J. (1941). *Social learning and imitation*. Yale University Press, New Haven, CT.

Miller, R.J. (1998). Presynaptic receptors. *Annual Review of Pharmacology and Toxicology*, **38**, 201–227.

Miller, R.R. and Matute, H. (1996). Biological significance in forward and backward blocking: Resolution of a discrepancy between animal conditioning and human causal judgment. *Journal of Experimental Psychology, General*, **125**, 370–386.

Miller, S. and Konorski, J. (1928). Sur une forme particulière des réflexes conditionnels. *Comptes Rendus des Seances de la Societe de Biologie and de ses Filiales, Paris*, **99**, 1155–1157.

Miller, S.G. and Kennedy, M.B. (1986). Regulation of brain type II Ca²⁺/calmodulin-dependent protein kinase by autophosphorylation: A Ca²⁺-triggered molecular switch. *Cell*, **44**, 861–870.

Milligan, G., Svoboda, P., and Brown, C.M. (1994). Why are there so many adrenoreceptor subtypes? *Biochemical Pharmacology*, **48**, 1059–1071.

Milner, B., Corkin, S., and Teiber, H.L. (1968). Further analysis of the hippocampal amnesic syndrome: 14-year follow-up study of H.M. *Neuropsychologia*, **6**, 215–234.

Milner, B., Squire, L.R., and Kandel, E.R. (1998). Cognitive neuroscience and the study of memory. *Neuron*, **20**, 445–468.

Milner, P.M. (1986). Donald Olding Hebb (1904–1985). *Trends in Neurosciences*, **9**, 347–351.

Milner, P.M. (1989). The discovery of self-stimulation and other stories. *Neuroscience & Biobehavioral Reviiews*, **13**, 61–67.

Milner, P.M. (1997). Repetition priming: Memory or attention? *Behavioral and Brain Sciences*, **20**, 623.

Miltner, W.H.R., Braun, C., Arnold, M., Witte, H., and Taub, E. (1999). Coherence of gamma-band EEG activity as a basis for associative learning. *Nature*, **397**, 434–436.

Minsky, M. (1985). *The society of mind*. Simon & Schuster, New York.

Misanin, J.R., Miller, R.R., and Lewis, D.J. (1968). Retrograde amnesia produced by electroconvulsive shock after reactivation of a consolidated memory trace. *Science*, **159**, 554–555.

Mishkin, M. (1957). Effects of small frontal lesions on delayed alternation in monkeys. *Journal of Neurophysiology*, **20**, 615–622.

Mishkin, M. (1982). A memory system in the monkey. *Philosophical Transactions of the Royal Society of London, B*, **298**, 85–95.

Mishkin, M. and Appenzeller, T. (1987). The anatomy of memory. *Scientific American*, **256**(6), 62–71.

Mishkin, M. and Delacour, J. (1975). An analysis of short-term visual memory in the monkey. *Journal of Experimental Psychology: Animal Behaviour Processes*, **1**, 326–334.

Mishkin, M. and Murray, E.A. (1994). Stimulus recognition. *Current Opinion in Neurobiology*, **4**, 200–206.

Mishkin, M., Malamut, B., and Bachevalier, J. (1984). Memories and habits: Two neural systems. In *Neurobiology of learning and memory*, (ed. G. Lynch, J.L. McGaugh, and N.M. Weinberger), pp. 65–77. Guilford Press, New York.

Mishkin, M., Suzuki, W.A., Gadian, D.G., and Vargha-Khadem, F. (1997). Hierarchical organization of cognitive memory. *Philosophical Transactions of the Royal Society of London, B*, **352**, 1461–1467.

Mishkin, M., Vargha-Kadem, F., and Gadian, D.G. (1998). Amnesia and the organization of the hippocampal system. *Hippocampus*, **8**, 212–216.

Missale, C., Nash, S.R., Robinson, S.W., Jaber, M., and Caron, M.G. (1998). Dopamine receptors: From structure to function. *Physiological Reviews*, **78**, 189–225.

Miyashita, Y. and Hayashi, T. (2000). Neural representation of visual objects: encoding and top-down activation. *Current Opinion in Neurobiology*, **10**, 187–194.

Molière, J.B. (1670/2000). *The bourgeois gentleman*. Ivan R. Dee, Chicago, IL.

References

Mombartes, P. (1999). Molecular biology of odorant receptors in vertebrates. *Annual Review of Neuroscience*, **22**, 487–509.

Mondadori, C. (1993). The pharmacology of the nootropics; new insights and new questions. *Behavioural Brain Research*, **59**, 1–9.

Mondadori, C., Ducret, T., and Borowski, J. (1991). How long does 'memory consolidation' take? New compounds can improve retention performance, even if administered up to 24 hours after the learning experience. *Brain Research*, **555**, 107–111.

Monne, L. (1949). Structure and function of neurones in relation to mental activity. *Biological Reviews of the Cambridge Philosophical Society*, **24**, 297–315.

Montarolo, P.G., Goelet, P., Castellucci, V.F., Morgan, J., Kandel, E.R., and Schacher, S. (1986). A critical period for macromolecular synthesis in long-term heterosynaptic facilitation in *Aplysia*. *Science*, **234**, 1249–1254.

Moore, B.R. and Stuttard, S. (1979). Dr. Guthrie and *Felix domesticus* or: Tripping over the cat. *Science*, **205**, 1031–1033.

Moran, J. and Desimone, R. (1985). Selective attention gates visual processing in the extrastiatal cortex. *Science*, **229**, 782–784.

Moravec, H. (1988). *Mind children. The future of robot and human intelligence*. Harvard University Press, Cambridge, MA.

Morgan, C.L. (1894). *An introduction to comparative psychology*. Walter Scott, London.

Morgan, C.L. (1896/1973). *Habit and instinct*. Arno Press, New York.

Morris, C.D., Bransford, J.D., and Franks, J.J. (1977). Levels of processing versus transfer appropriate processing. *Journal of Verbal Learning and Verbal Behavior*, **16**, 519–533.

Morris, J.S., Öhman, A., and Dolan, R.J. (1998). Conscious and unconscious emotional learning in the human amygdala. *Nature*, **393**, 467–470.

Morris, J.S., Ohman, A., and Dolan, R.J. (1999). A subcortical pathway to the right amygdala mediating 'unseen' fear. *Proceedings of the National Academy of Sciences USA*, **96**, 1680–1685.

Morris, R. and Morris, D. (1966). *Men and apes*. Hutchinson, London.

Morris, R.G.M. (1981). Spatial localization does not require the presence of local cues. *Learning and Motivation*, **12**, 239–260.

Morris, R.G.M., Anderson, E., Lynch, G., and Baudry, M. (1986). Selective impairment of learning and blockade of long-term potentiation by an *N*-methyl-D-aspartate receptor antagonist, AP5. *Nature*, **319**, 774–776.

Morton, J. (1967). A singular lack of incidental learning. *Nature*, **215**, 203–204.

Moscovitch, M. (1989). Confabulation and the frontal systems: strategic versus associative retrieval in neuropsychological theories of memory. In *Varieties of memory and consciousness: essays in honour of Endel Tulving*, (ed. H.L. Roediger III and F.I.M. Craik), pp. 133–160. Laurence Erlbaum Associates, Hillsdale, NJ.

Moscovitch, M. (1996). Recovered consciousness: A proposal for making consciousness integral to neuropsychological theories of memory in humans and nonhumans. *Behavioral and Brain Sciences*, **19**, 768–770.

Moscovitch, M. and Nadel, L. (1998). Consolidation and the hippocampal complex revisited: In defense of the multiple-trace model. *Current Opinion in Neurobiology*, **8**, 297–300.

Moser, E.I., Moser, M.-B., and Andersen, P. (1994). Potentiation of dentate synapses initiated by exploratory learning in rats: Dissociation from brain temperature, motor activity, and arousal. *Learning & Memory*, **1**, 55–73.

Moser, E.I., Krobert, K.A., Moser, M.-B., and Morris, R.G.M. (1998). Impaired spatial learning after saturation of long-term potentiation. *Science*, **281**, 2038–2042.

Moser, M.B. and Moser, E.I. (1998a). Distributed encoding and retrieval of spatial memory in the hippocampus. *Journal of Neuroscience*, **18**, 7535–7542.

Moser, M.B. and Moser, E.I. (1998b). Functional differentiation in the hippocampus. *Hippocampus*, **8**, 608–619.

Moser, M.-B., Trommald, M., Egeland, T., and Andersen, P. (1997). Spatial training in a complex environment and isolation alter the spine distribution differently in rat CA1 pyramidal cells. *Journal of Comparative Neurology*, **380**, 373–381.

Moser, P.K. (ed.) (1987). *A Priori knowledge*. Oxford University Press, Oxford.

Moulin, C.J.A., Perfect, T.J., and Jones, R.W. (2000). Evidence for intact memory monitoring in Alzheimer's disease: metamemory sensitivity at encoding. *Neuropsychologia*, **38**, 1242–1250.

Mountcastle, V.B. (1997). The columnar organization of the neocortex. *Brain*, **120**, 701–722.

Mouse Genome Informatics and Mouse Genome Database (Ongoing), World Wide Web, URL: *http://www.informatics.jax.org*

Mowrer, O.H. (1939). A stimulus-response analysis of anxiety and its role as a reinforcing agent. *Psychological Review*, **46**, 553–565.

Moyer, J.R., Deyo, R.A., and Disterhoft, J.F. (1990). Hippocapectomy disrupts trace eye-blink conditioning in rabbits. *Behavioral Neuroscience*, **104**, 243–252.

Mulkey, R.M., Herron, C.E., and Malenka, R.C. (1993). An essential role for protein phosphatases in hippocampal long-term depression. *Science*, **261**, 1051–1055.

Muller, G.E. and Pilzecker, A. (1900). Experimentelle Beitrage zur Lehre von Gedachtnis. *Zeitschrift fuer Psychologie*, **1**, 1–300.

Müller, U. (2000). Prolonged activation of cAMP-dependent protein kinase during conditioning induces long-term memory in honeybees. *Neuron, 27,* 159–168.

Mumby, D.G. (1995). Assessing working memory for objects in rats: No one said it was easy. *NeuroReport, 6,* 1960–1962.

Munn, N.L. (1950). *Handbook of psychological research on the rat.* Houghton Mifflin, Boston, MA.

Murdock, B.B. (1957). Transfer designs and formulas. *Psychological Bulletin, 54,* 313–326.

Murray, E.A. and Mishkin, M. (1998). Object recognition and location memory in monkeys with excitotoxic lesions of the amygdala and hippocampus. *Journal of Neuroscience, 18,* 6568–6582.

Murray, E.A., Davidson, M., Gaffan, D., Olton, D.S., and Souomi, S. (1988). Effect of fornix transection and cingulate cortex ablation on spatial memory in rhesus monkeys. *Experimental Brain Research, 74,* 173–186.

Murray, E.A., Gaffan, D., and Mishkin, M. (1993). Neural substrates of visual stimulus-stimulus association in Rhesus monkeys. *Journal of Neuroscience, 13,* 4549–4561.

Nachmansohn, D. (1959). *Chemical and molecular basis of nerve activity.* Academic Press, New York.

Nadal, J.P., Toulouse, G., Changeux, J.P., and Dehaene, S. (1986). Networks of formal neurons and memory palimpsests. *Europhysics Letters, 1,* 535–542.

Nadel, L. and Moscovitch, M. (1997). Memory consolidation, retrograde amnesia and the hippocampal complex. *Current Opinion in Neurobiology, 7,* 217–227.

Nadel, L. and Zola-Morgan, S. (1984). Infantile amnesia: A neurobiological perspective. In *Infant memory: its relation to normal and pathological memory in humans and other animals,* (ed. M. Moscovitch), pp. 145–166. Plenum, New York.

Nader, K. and LeDoux, J.E. (1997). Is it time to invoke multiple fear learning systems in the amygdala? *Trends in Cognitive Sciences, 1,* 241–243.

Nader, K., Bechara, A., and van der Kooy, D. (1997). Neurobiological constraints on behavioral models of motivation. *Annual Review of Psychology, 48,* 85–114.

Nader, K., Schafe, G.E., and LeDoux, J.E. (2000). Fear memories require protein synthesis in the amygdala for reconsolidation after retrieval. *Nature, 406,* 722–726.

Nadler, M.A., Harrison, L.M., and Stephens, J.A. (2000). Acquisition of a new motor skill is accompanied by changes in cutaneomuscular responses recorded from finger muscles in man. *Experimental Brain Research, 134,* 246–254.

Nagel, E. (1979). *The structure of science. Problems in the logic of scientific explanation.* 2nd. ed. Hackett, Indianapolis, IN.

Nagel, T. (1974). What is it like to be a bat? *Philosophical Review, 83,* 435–450.

Nagel, T. (Chair) (1993). *Experimental and theoretical studies of consciousness.* Ciba Foundation Symposium 174. Wiley, Chichester.

Nagy, A. (1996). Engineering the mouse genome. In *Mammalian development,* (ed. P. Lonai), pp. 339–382. Harwood Academic Publishers, Amsterdam.

Nagy, W.E. and Anderson, R.C. (1984). How many words are there in printed school English? *Reading Research Quarterly, 19,* 304–330.

Nail-Boucherie, K., Dourmap, N., Jaffard, R., and Costentin, J. (2000). Contextual fear conditioning is associated with an increase of acetylcholine release in the hippocampus of rat. *Cognitive Brain Research, 9,* 193–197.

Nakamura, K. and Kubota, K. (1996). The primate temporal pole: Its putative role in object recognition and memory. *Behavioural Brain Research, 77,* 53–77.

Nakayama, K. (1998). Vision fin de siècle. A reductionistic explanation of perception for the 21st century? In *Perception and cognition at century's end,* (ed. J. Hochberg), pp. 307–331. Academic Press, San Diego.

Naor, C. and Dudai, Y. (1996). Transient impairment of cholinergic function in the rat insular cortex disrupts the encoding of taste in conditioned taste aversion. *Behavioral Brain Research, 79,* 61–67.

Nargeot, R., Baxter, D.A., and Byrne, J.H. (1997). Contingent-dependent enhancement of rhythmic motor patterns: An *in vitro* analog of operant conditioning. *Journal of Neuroscience, 17,* 8093–8105.

Nargeot, R., Baxter, D.A., and Byrne, J.H. (1999). In vitro analog of operant conditioning in Aplysia. I. Contingent reinforcement modifies the functional dynamics of an identified neuron. *Journal of Neuroscience, 19,* 2247–2260.

Nathans, D., Lau, L.F., Chrsity, B., Hartzell, S., Nakabeppu, Y., and Ryder, K. (1988). Genomic response to growth factors. *Cold Spring Harbor Symposia on Quantitative Biology, 53,* 893–900.

Nayak, A., Zastrow, D.J., Lickteig, R., Zahniser, N.R., and Browning, M.D. (1998). Maintenance of late-phase LTP is accompanied by PKA-dependent increase in AMPA receptor synthesis. *Nature, 394,* 680–683.

Neisser, U. (1967). *Cognitive psychology.* Appleton-Century-Crofts, New York.

Neisser, U. (1978). What are the important questions? In *Practical aspects of memory,* (ed. M.M. Gruneberg, P.E. Morris, and R.N. Sykes), pp. 3–24. Academic Press, London.

Neisser, U. (1991). A case of misplaced nostalgia. *American Psychologist, 46,* 34–36.

Neisser, U. and Harsch, N. (1992). Phantom flashbulbs: False recollections of hearing the news about Challenger. In *Affect and accuracy in recall. Studies of 'flashbulb' memories,* (ed. E. Winograd and U. Neisser), pp. 9–31. Cambridge University Press, New York.

Nelson, C.A. (1998). The nature of early memory. *Preventive Medicine, 27,* 172–179.

References

Nelson, D.A. and Marler, P. (1994). Selection-based learning in bird song development. *Proceedings of the National Academy of Sciences USA*, **91**, 10498–10501.

Nelson, K. (1992). Emergence of autobiographical memory at age 4. *Human Development*, **35**, 172–177.

Nelson, K. (1993). The psychological and social origins of autobiographical memory. *Psychological Science*, **4**, 7–14.

Nelson, R. (Director), Keyes, D. (Author), Silliphant, S. (Screenplay) (1968). *Charley*. ABC/CBS Fox Video.

Nelson, R.J. and Young, K.A. (1998). Behavior in mice with targeted disruption of single genes. *Neuroscience and Biobehavioral Reviews*, **22**, 453–462.

Nestler, E.J. and Aghajanian, G.K. (1997). Molecular and cellular basis of addiction. *Science*, **278**, 58–63.

Newell, A. and Rosenbloom, P.S. (1981). Mechanisms of skill acquisition and the law of practice. In *Cognitive skills and their acquisition*, pp. 1–55. Lawrence Erlbaum Associates, Hillsdale, NJ.

Newell, A. and Simon, H.A. (1972). *Human problem solving*. Prentice-Hall, Englewood Cliffs, NJ.

Nguyen, P.V., Abel, T., and Kandel, E.R. (1994). Requirement of a critical period of transcription for induction of late phase of LTP. *Science*, **265**, 1104–1107.

Nicholls, J.G., Baylor, D.A., Wickelgren, W.O., Rosenthal, J., Martin, A.R., Betz, W., Chandler, W.K., Fein, H., Stuart, A.E., Finn, A.L., Odurjh, M., Ridge, R.A. (1967). Persistence transfer. *Science*, **158**, 1524–1525.

Nichols, R. (1994). *The diaries of Robert Hooke, the Leonardo of London, 1635-1703*. The Book Guild, Lewes, Sussex.

Nicolelis, M.A.L., Fanselow, E.E., and Ghazanfar, A.A. (1997). Hebb's dream: The resurgence of cell assemblies. *Neuron*, **19**, 219–221.

Nicolis, G. and Prigogine, I. (1989). *Exploring complexity. An introduction*. Freeman, New York.

Nicoll, R.A. and Malenka, R.C. (1995). Contrasting properties of two forms of long-term potentiation in the hippocampus. *Nature*, **377**, 115–118.

Nieder, A. and Wagner, H. (1999). Perception and neuronal coding of subjective contours in the owl. *Nature Neuroscience*, **2**, 660–663.

Niethammer, M., Kim, E., and Sheng, M. (1996). Interaction between the C terminus of NMDA receptor subunits and multiple members of the PSD-95 family of membrane-associated guanylate kinases. *Journal of Neuroscience*, **16**, 2157–2163.

Nietzche, F. (1873/1990). Ueber Wahrheit und Luge im aussermoralischen Sinne. (Hebrew trans. J. Golomb). In *Essays on aesthetics*. HaKibutz HaMehuhad, Tel-Aviv.

Nieuwenhuys, T., Voogd, J., and van Huijzen, C. (1988). *The human central nervous system. A synopsis and atlas*, (3rd edn). Springer-Verlag, Berlin.

Nilsson, L.-G., Backman, L., Erugrund, K., and Nyberg, L. (1997). The Betula prospective cohort study: memory, health, and aging. *Aging and Cognition*, **1**, 1–36.

Nissenbaum, L.K., Zigmund, M.J., Sved, A.F., and Abercrombie, E. (1991). Prior exposure to chronic stress results in enhanced synthesis and release of hippocampal norepinephrine in response to a novel stressor. *Journal of Neuroscience*, **11**, 1478–1484.

de No, R.L. (1934). Studies on the structure of the cerebral cortex. II. Continuation of the study of the Ammonic system. *Journal für Psychologie und Neurologie*, **46**, 113–177.

de No, R.L. (1938). Analysis of the activity of the chains of internuncial neurons. *Journal of Neurophysiology*, **1**, 207–244.

Noble, E.P., Ozkaragoz, T.Z., Ritchie, T.L., Zhang, X.X., Belin, T.R., and Sparkes, R.S. (1998). D_2 and D_4 dopamine receptor polymorphisms and personality. *American Journal of Medical Genetics*, **81**, 257–267.

Norcross, J.C. and Tomcho, T.J. (1994). Great books in psychology: Three studies in search of a consensus. *Teaching of Psychology*, **21**, 86–90.

Norman, D.A. and Bobrow, D.G. (1975). On data-limited and resource-limited processes. *Cognitive Psychology*, **7**, 44–64.

Normile, D. (1999). Building working cells 'in Silico'. *Science*, **284**, 80–81.

Nottebohm, F. (1970). Ontogeny of bird song. *Science*, **167**, 950–956.

Nottebohm, F., Stokes, T.M., and Leonard, C.M. (1976). Central control of song in the canary, *Serinus canaris*. *Journal of Comparative Neurology*, **165**, 457–486.

Nudo, R.J., Milliken, G.W., Jenkins, W.M., and Merzenich, M.M. (1996). Use-dependent alterations of movement representations in primary motor cortex of adult squirrel monkeys. *Journal of Neuroscience*, **16**, 785–807.

Numa, S., Noda, M., Takahashi, H., Tanabe, T., Toyosato, M., Furutani, Y., and Kikyotani, S. (1983). Molecular structure of the nicotinic acetylcholine receptor. *Cold Spring Harbor Symposia on Quantitative Biology*, **48**, 57–69.

Nyberg, L., Cabeza, R., and Tulving, E. (1996). PET studies of encoding and retrieval: The HERA model. *Psychonomic Bulletin & Review*, **3**, 135–148.

Nyberg, L., Habib, R., McIntosh, A.R., and Tulving, E. (2000). Recativation of encoding-related brain activity during memory retrieval. *Proceedings of the National Academy of Sciences USA*, **97**, 11120–11124.

Ó Scalaidhe, S.P., Wilson, F.A.W., and Goldman-Rakic, P.S. (1997). Areal segregation of face-processing neurons in prefrontal cortex. *Science*, **278**, 1135–1138.

Ochsner, K.N., Chiu, C.-Y.P., and Schacter, D.L. (1994). Varieties of priming. *Current Biology*, **4**, 189–194.

Ofen-Noy, N., Dudai, Y., and Karni, A. (2002). Levels of specificity in the acquisition of mirror reading skill (in preparation).

Ogawa, S., Lee, T.M., Kay, A.R., and Tank, D.W. (1990). Brain magnetic resonance imaging with contrast dependent on blood oxygenation. *Proceedings of the National Academy of Sciences USA*, **87**, 9868–9872.

Ogawa, S., Menon, R.S., Kim, S.G., and Ugurbil, K. (1998). On the characteristics of functional magnetic resonance imaging of the brain. *Annual Review of Biophysics and Biomolecular Structure*, **27**, 447–474.

Ogburn, W.F. and Thomas, D. (1922). Are inventions inevitable? A note on social evolution. *Political Science Quarterly*, **37**, 83–98.

Ohlsson, S. (1984*a*). Restructuring revisited. I. Summary and critique of the Gestalt theory of problem solving. *Scandinavian Journal of Psychology*, **25**, 65–78.

Ohlsson, S. (1984*b*). Restructuring revisited. II. An information processing theory of restructuring and insight. *Scandinavian Journal of Psychology*, **25**, 117–129.

Okabe, S., Kim, H.-D., Miwa, A., Kuriu, T., and Okado, H. (1999). Continual remodeling of postsynaptic density and its regulation by synaptic activity. *Nature Neuroscience*, **2**, 804–811.

O'Keefe, J. (1996). The spatial prepositions in English, vector grammar and the cognitive map theory. In *Language and space*, (ed. P. Bloom, M.A. Peterson, L. Nadel, and M.F. Garrett), pp. 277–316. MIT Press, Cambridge, MA.

O'Keefe, J. (1999). Do hippocampal pyramidal cells signal non-spatial as well as spatial information? *Hippocampus*, **9**, 352–364.

O'Keefe, J. and Conway, D.H. (1978). Hippocampal place units in the freely moving rat: Why they fire where they fire. *Experimental Brain Research*, **31**, 573–590.

O'Keefe, J. and Dostrovsky, J. (1971). The hippocampus as a spatial map. Preliminary evidence from unit activity in the freely-moving rat. *Brain Research*, **34**, 171–175.

O'Keefe, J. and Nadel, L. (1978). *The hippocampus as a cognitive map*. Oxford University Press, Oxford.

O'Keefe, J. and Speakman, A. (1987). Single unit activity in the rat hippocampus during a spatial memory task. *Experimental Brain Research*, **68**, 1–27.

Okubo, Y., Suhara, T., Suzuki, K., Kobayashi, K., Inoue, O., Terasaki, O., Someya, Y., Sassa, T., Suso, Y., Matsushima, E., Iyo, M., Tateno, Y., and Toru, M. (1997). Decreased prefrontal dopamine D1 receptors in schizophrenia revealed by PET. *Nature*, **385**, 634–636.

Okuda, J., Fujii, T., Yamadori, A., Kawashima, R., Tsukiura, T., Fukatsu, R., Suzuki, K., Ito, M., and Fukuda, H. (1998). Participation of the prefrontal cortices in prospective memory: Evidence from a PET study in humans. *Neuroscience Letters*, **253**, 127–130.

Olby, R.C., Cantor, G.N., Christie, J.R.R., and Hodge, M.J.S. (ed.) (1990). *Companion to the history of modern science*. Routledge, London.

Olds, J. (1969). The central nervous system and the reinforcement of behavior. *American Psychologist*, **24**, 114–132.

Olds, J. and Milner, P. (1954). Positive reinforcement produced by electrical stimulation of septal area and other regions of rat brain. *Journal of Comparative and Physiological Psychology*, **47**, 419–427.

Oliet, S.H.R., Piet, R., and Poulain, D.A. (2001). Control of glutamate clearance and synaptic efficacy by glial coverage of neurons. *Science*, **292**, 923–926.

Oliver, G. and Schafer, E.O. (1894). On the physiological action of extract of the suprarenal capsule. *Journal of Physiology (London)*, **16**, 1–4.

Olmsted, J.M.D. (1938). *Claude Bernard. Physiologist*. Harper, New York.

Olpe, H.-R. and Lynch, G.S. (1982). The action of piracetam on the electrical activity of the hippocampal slice preparation: a field potential analysis. *European Journal of Pharmacology*, **80**, 415–419.

Olshansky, S.J., Carnes, B.A., and Cassel, C.K. (1993). The aging of the human species. *Scientific American*, **268** (April), 18–24.

Olton, D.S. (1979). Mazes, maps, and memory. *American Psychologist*, **34**, 583–596.

Olton, D.S. and Feustle, W.A. (1981). Hippocampal function required for nonspatial working memory. *Experimental Brain Research*, **41**, 380–389.

Olton, D.S. and Samuelson, R.J. (1976). Remembrance of places passed: spatial memory in rats. *Journal of Experimental Psychology: Animal Behavior Processes*, **2**, 97–116.

Olton, D.S. and Schlosberg, P. (1978). Food-searching strategies in young rats: win-shift predominates over win-stay. *Journal of Comparative and Physiological Psychology*, **92**, 609–618.

Ong, W.J. (1982). *Orality & literacy. The technology of the word*. Routledge, London.

Orne, M.T. (1962). On the social psychology of the psychological experiment: With particular reference to demand characteristics and their implications. *American Psychologist*, **17**, 776–783.

O'Shea, M.F., Saling, M.M., and Bladin, P.F. (1994). Can metamemory be localized? *Journal of Clinical and Experimental Neuropsychology*, **16**, 640–646.

Ottersen, O.P. and Landsend, A.S. (1997). Organization of glutamate receptors at the synapse. *European Journal of Neuroscience*, **9**, 2219–2224.

Overton, D.A. (1964). State-dependent or 'dissociated' learning produced with pentobarbital. *Journal of Comparative and Physiological Psychology*, **57**, 3–12.

Owen, A.M. (1997). The functional organization of working memory processes within human lateral frontal cortex: The contribution of functional neuroimaging. *European Journal of Neuroscience*, **9**, 1329–1339.

References

Owen, A.Q.M. (1997). Cognitive planning in humans: Neuropsychological, neuroanatomical and neuropharmacolgical perspectives. *Progress in Neurobiology*, **53**, 431–450.

Packard, M.G., Hirsh, R., and White, N. (1989). Differential effects of fornix and caudate nucleus lesions on two radial maze tasks: evidence for multiple memory systems. *Journal of Neuroscience*, **9**, 1465–1472.

Paller, K.A., Kutas, M., and McIsaac, H.K. (1995). Monitoring conscious recollection via the electrical-activity of the brain. *Psychological Science*, **6**, 107–111.

Palm, G. (1982). *Neuronal assemblies. An alternative approach to artificial intelligence.* Springer-Verlag, Berlin.

Pantelis, C., Barnes, T.R.E., Nelson, H.E., Tanner, S., Weatherley, L., Owen, A.M., and Robbins, T.W. (1997). Frontal-striatal cognitive deficits in patients with chronic schizophrenia. *Brain*, **120**, 1823–1843.

Papez, J.W. (1937). A proposed mechanism of emotion. *Archives of Neurology and Psychiatry*, **38**, 725–743.

Papini, M.R. and Bitterman, M.E. (1990). The role of contingency in classical conditioning. *Psychological Review*, **97**, 396–403.

Parker, A. and Gaffan, D. (1998). Interaction of frontal and perirhinal cortices in visual recognition memory in monkeys. *European Journal of Neuroscience*, **10**, 3044–3057.

Parker, A.J. and Newsome, W.T. (1998). Sense and the single neuron: Probing the physiology of perception. *Annual Review of Neuroscience*, **21**, 227–277.

Parkin, A.J. (1987). *Memory and amnesia.* Basil Blackwell, Oxford.

Parkinson, J.A., Robbins, T.W., and Everitt, B.J. (2000). Dissociable roles of the central and basolateral amygdala in appetitive emotional learning. *European Journal of Neuroscience*, **12**, 405–413.

Paterson, S.J., Brown, J.H., Gsodl, M.K., Johnson, M.H., and Karmiloff-Smith, A. (1999). Cognitive modularity and genetic disorders. *Science*, **286**, 2355–2358.

Paulesu, E., Frith, C.D., and Frackowiak, R.S.J. (1993). The neural correlates of the verbal component of working memory. *Nature*, **362**, 342–345.

Pauling, L. and Coryell, C.D. (1936). The magnetic properties and structure of hemoglobin, oxyhemoglobin and carbon-monoxyhemoglobin. *Proceedings of the National Academy of Sciences USA*, **22**, 210–216.

Pavlov, I.P. (1906). The scientific investigation of the physical faculties or processes in the higher animals. *Science*, **24**, 613–619.

Pavlov, I.P. (1927). *Conditioned reflexes. An investigation of the physiological activity of the cerebral cortex.* Oxford University Press, London.

Pavlov, I.P.P. (1928). *Lectures in conditioned reflexes. Twenty-five years of objective study of the higher nervous activity (behavior) of animals.* International Publishers, New York.

Payne, D.G. (1987). Hyperamnesia and reminiscence in recall: A historical and empirical review. *Psychological Bulletin*, **101**, 5–27.

Payne, D.G. and Wenger, M.J. (1992). Improving memory through practice. In *Memory improvement*, (ed. D.J. Hermann, H. Weingartner, A. Searlman, and C. McEvoy), pp. 187–209. Springer-Verlag, New York.

Peach, R.K. (ed.) (1986). *Readings in agnosia.* Longman, New York.

Pearce, J.M. and Bouton, M.E. (2001). Theories of associative learning in animals. *Annual Review of Psychology*, **52**, 111–139.

Pearce, J.M. and Hall, G. (1978). Overshadowing the instrumental conditioning of a lever-press response by a more valid predictor of the reinforcer. *Journal of Experimental Psychology, Animal Behavior Processes*, **4**, 356–367.

Pearce, S.A., Isherwood, S., Hrouda, D., Richardson, P.H., Erskine, A., and Skinner, J. (1990). Memory and pain: Tests of mood congruity and state dependent learning in experimentally induced and clinical pain. *Pain*, **43**, 187–193.

Peckham, G.W. and Peckham, E.G. (1887). Some observations on the mental powers of spiders. *Journal of Morphology*, **1**, 383–419.

Pellegrini-Giampietro, D.E., Gorter, J.A., Bennett, M.V.L., and Zukin, R.S. (1997). The GluR2 (GluR-B) hypothesis: Ca^{2+}-permeable AMPA receptors in neurological disorders. *Trends in Neurosciences*, **20**, 464–470.

di Pellegrino, G., Fadiga, L., Fogassi, L., Gallese, V., and Rizzolatti, G. (1992). Understanding motor events: a neurophysiological study. *Experimental Brain Research*, **91**, 176–180.

Penfield, W. and Rasmussen, T. (1950/1968). *The cerebral cortex of man. A clinical study of localization of function.* Hafner, New York.

Penfold, P.S. (1996). The repressed memory controversy: Is there a middle ground? *Canadian Medical Association Journal*, **155**, 647–653.

Penick, S. and Solomon, P.R. (1991). Hippocampus, context, and conditioning. *Behavioral Neuroscience*, **105**, 611–617.

Pennebaker, J.W. and Banasik, B.L. (1997). On the creation and maintenance of collective memories: History as social psychology. In *Collective memory of political events. Social psychological perspectives*, (ed. J.W. Pennebaker, D. Paez, and B. Rima), pp. 3–19. Lawrence Erlbaum Associates, Mahwah, NJ.

Pepper, S.C. (1926). Emergence. *Journal of Philosophy*, **23**, 241–245.

Pereda, A.E. and Faber, D.S. (1996). Activity-dependent short-term enhancement of intercellular coupling. *Journal of Neuroscience*, **16**, 983–992.

Pereyra, P., Portino, R.E.G., and Maldonado, H. (2000). Long-lasting and context-specific freezing preference is acquired after spaced repeated presentations of a danger stimulus in the crab Chasmagnathus. *Neurobiology of Learning and Memory*, **74**, 119–134.

Perkinton, M.S., Sihra, T.S., and Williams, R.J. (1999). Ca²⁺-permeable AMPA receptors induce phosphorylation of cAMP response element-binding protein through a phosphatidylinositol 3-kinase-dependent stimulation of the mitogen-activated protein kinase signaling cascade in neurons. *Journal of Neuroscience*, **19**, 5861–5874.

Perruchet, P. (1989). The effect of spaced practice on explicit and implicit memory. *British Journal of Psychology*, **80**, 113–130.

Pesenti, M., Zago, L., Crivello, F., Mellet, E., Samson, D., Duroux, B., *et al.* (2001). Mental calulation in a prodigy is sustained by right prefrontal and medial temporal areas. *Nature Neuroscience*, **4**, 103–107.

Pessoa, F. (1914?/1998). In *Fernando Pessoa & Co. Selected poems*. (trans. and ed. R. Zenith). Grove Press, New York.

Peters, A. (1985). The visual cortex of the rat. In *Cerebral cortex*, Vol. 3, (ed. A. Peters and E.G. Jones), pp. 19–80. Plenum Press, New York.

Peters, J.A. (1959). *Classic papers in genetics*. Prentice-Hall. Englewood Cliffs, NJ.

Peters, R. and McGee, R. (1982). Cigarette smoking and state-dependent memory. *Psychopharmacology*, **76**, 232–235.

Petersen, O.H., Petersen, C.C.H., and Kasai, H. (1994). Calcium and hormone action. *Annual Review of Physiology*, 56, 297–319.

Petersen, S.E., Mier, H.v., Fiez, J.A., and Reichle, M.E. (1998). The effects of practice on the functional anatomy of task performance. *Proceedings of the National Academy of Sciences USA*, **95**, 853–860.

Peterson, L.R. and Peterson, M.J. (1959). Short-term retention of individual verbal items. *Journal of Experimental Psychology*, **58**, 193–198.

Peterson, M.R. and Jusczyk, P.W. (1984). On perceptual predispositions for human speech and monkey vocalizations. In *The biology of learning*, (ed. P. Marler and H.S. Terraced), pp. 585–616, Springer-Verlag, Berlin.

Petrides, M. (1995). Functional organization of the human frontal cortex for mnemonic processing. *Annals of the New York Academy of Sciences*, **769**, 85–96.

Pfaffenberger, C.J. and Scott, J.P. (1959). The relationship between delayed socialization and trainability in guide dogs. *Journal of Genetic Psychology*, **95**, 145–155.

Pfungst, O. (1911). *Clever Hans. The horse of Mr. von Osten*. Holt, Rinehart and Winston, New York. (Reissued, R. Rosenthal (ed.), Holt, Rinehart and Winston, New York, 1965.)

Pham, T.A., Impey, S., Storm, D.R., and Stryker, M.P. (1999). CRE-mediated gene transcription in neocortical neuronal plasticity during the developmental critical period. *Neuron*, **22**, 63–72.

Phillips, R.G. and LeDoux, J.E. (1992). Differential contribution of amygdala and hippocampus to cued and contextual fear conditioning. *Behavioral Neuroscience*, **106**, 274–286.

Piaget, J. (1962). *Play, dreams and imitation in childhood*. Norton, New York.

Piaget, J. (1969). *The child's conception of time*. Routledge and Kegan Paul, London.

Picciotto, M.R., Zoli, M., Rimondini, R., Léna, C., Marubio, L.M., Pich, E.M., *et al.* (1998). Acetylcholine receptors containing the β2 subunit are involved in the reinforcing properties of nicotine. *Nature*, **391**, 173–177.

Pickering, A. (ed.) (1992). *Science as practice and culture*. University of Chicago Press, Chicago.

Picton, T.W., Lins, O. G., and Scherg, M. (1995). The recording and analysis of event-related potentials. In *Handbook of neuropsychology*, Vol. 10, (ed. F. Boller and J. Grafman), pp. 3–73. Elsevier, Amsterdam.

Pierce, A.H. (1908). The subconscious again. *Journal of Philosophy, Psychology and Scientific Methods*, **5**, 264–271.

Pierce, J.R. (1961). *Symbols, signals and noise: The nature and process of communication*. Harper, New York.

Pinker, S. (1994). *The language instinct. How the mind creates language*. William Morrow and Co., New York.

Pinto, S., Quintana, D.G., Smith, P., Mihalek, R.M., Hou, Z.H., Boynton, S., Jones, C.J., Hendricks, M., Velinzon, K., Wohlschlegel, J.A., Austin, R.J., Lane, W.S., Tully, T., and Dutta, A. (1999). *latheo* encodes a subunit of the origin recognition complex and disrupts neuronal proliferation and adult olfactory memory when mutant. *Neuron*, **23**, 45–54.

Pitkanen, A., Savander, V., and LeDoux, J.E. (1997). Organization of intra-amygaloid circuitries in the rat: An emerging framework for understanding functions of the amygdala. *Trends in Neurosciences*, **20**, 517–523.

Plato. *The collected dialogues*, (ed. E. Hamilton and H. Cairns) (1961). Princeton University Press, Princeton, NJ.

Plomin, R. (1999). Genetics and general cognitive ability. *Nature*, **402** (Suppl.), C25–C29.

Plutarch (1–2C AD/1914*a*). *Table-talk Book One, Moralia VIII*. Loeb Classical Library, Harvard University Press, Cambridge, MA.

Plutarch (1–2C AD/1914*b*). *Lives. Theseus XXIII*. Loeb Classical Library. Harvard University Press, Cambridge, MA.

Poe, E.A. (1846/1970). *The philosophy of composition*. Graham's Lady's and Gentelman's Magazine XX, May 1846, reprinted in: Great short works of Edgar Allan Poe, (ed. G.R. Thompson). Harper & Row, New York.

Pointer, S.C. and Bond, N.W. (1998). Context-dependent memory: Colour versus odour. *Chemical Senses*, **23**, 359–362.

Poldrack, R.A. and Gabrieli, J.D.E. (2001). Characterizing the neural mechanisms of skill learning and repetition priming. Evidence from mirror reading. *Brain*, **124**, 67–82.

References

Poldrack, R.A., Desmond, J.E., Glover, G.H., and Gabrieli, J.D.E. (1998). The neural basis of visual skill learning: An fMRI study of mirror reading. *Cerebral Cortex*, **8**, 1–10.

Poldrack, R.A., Selco, S.L., Field, J.E., and Cohen, N.J. (1999). The relationship between skill learning and repetition priming: experimental and computational analyses. *Journal of Experimental Psychology: Learning, Memory, and Cognition*, **25**, 208–235.

Polk, T.A. and Farah, M.J. (1998). The neural development and organization of letter recongition: evidence from functional neuroimaging, computational modeling, and behavioral studies. *Proceedings of National Academy of Science USA*, **95**, 847–852.

Pontecorvo, M.J., Clissold, D.B., and Conti, L.H. (1988). Age-related cognitive impairments as assessed with an automated repeated measures memory task: Implications for the possible role of acetylcholine and norepinephrine in memory dysfunction. *Neurobiology of Aging*, **9**, 617–625.

Pontieri, F.E., Tanda, G., Orzi, F., and Di Chiara, G. (1996). Effects of nicotine on the nucleus accumbens and similarity to those of addictive drugs. *Nature*, **382**, 255–257.

Pope, K.S. (1996). Memory, abuse, and science. *American Psychologist*, **51**, 957–974.

Posner, M.I. and Petersen, S.E. (1990). The attention system of the human brain. *Annual Review of Neuroscience*, **13**, 25–42.

Potts, R., Runyan, D., Zerger, A., and Narchetti, K. (1996). A content analysis of safety behaviors of television characters: implications for children's safety and injury. *Journal of Pediatric Psychology*, **21**, 517–528.

Power, A.E., Thai, L.J., and McGaugh, J.L. (2002). Lesions of the nucleus basalis magnocellularis induced by 192 IgG-saporin block memory enhancement with posttraining norepinephrine in the basolateral amygdala. *Proceedings of the National Academy of Science USA*, **99**, 2315–2319.

Power, M. and Dalgleish, T. (1997). *Cognition and emotion. From order to disorder*. Psychology Press, Hove.

Powis, D.A. and Bunn, S.J. (1995). *Neurotransmitter release and its modulation. Biochemical mechanisms, physiological function and clinical relevance*. Cambridge University Press, Cambridge.

Prabhakaran, V., Narayanan, K., Zhao, Z., and Gabrieli, J.D.E. (2000). Integration of diverse information in working memory within the frontal lobe. *Nature Neuroscience*, **3**, 85–90.

Préat, T. (1998). Decreased odor avoidance after electric shock in *Drosophila* mutants biases learning and memory tests. *Journal of Neuroscience*, **18**, 8534–8538.

Premack, D. (1962). Reversibility of the reinforcement relation. *Science*, **136**, 255–257.

Premack, D. (1965). Reinforcement theory. In *Nebraska symposium on motivation*, (ed. D. Levine), Vol. 13, pp. 123–180. University of Nebraska Press, Lincoln, NB.

Premack, D. and Woodruff, G. (1978). Does the chimpanzee have a theory of mind? *Behavioral and Brain Sciences*, **1**, 515–526.

Pribram, K.H., Mishkin, M., Rosvold, H.E., and Kaplan, S.J. (1952). Effects on delayed-response performance of lesions of dorsolateral and ventromedial frontal cortex of baboons. *Journal of Comparative and Physiological Psychology*, **45**, 565–575.

Price, D.L. and Sisodia, S.S. (1998). Mutant genes in familial Alzheimer's disease and transgenic models. *Annual Review of Neuroscience*, **21**, 479–505.

Price, D.L., Sisodia, S.S., Wong, P.C., and Borchelt, D.R. (2000). Alzheimer's disease: the value of transgenic and gene targeted models. *NeuroScience News*, **3**, 71–81.

Price, H.H. (1950). *Perception*, (2nd edn). Methuen, London.

Pringle, J.W.S. (1951). On the parallel between learning and evolution. *Behaviour*, **3**, 174–215.

Proust, M. (1913/1997). *Swann's way*. Penguin, New York.

Przybyslawski, J. and Sara, S.J. (1997). Reconsolidation of memory after its reactivation. *Behavioural Brain Research*, **84**, 241–246.

Purves, D., Hadley, R.D., and Voyvodic, J.T. (1986). Dynamic changes in the dendritic geometry of individual neurons visualized over periods of up to three months in the superior cervical ganglion of living mice. *Journal of Neuroscience*, **6**, 1051–1060.

Putnam, H. (1973). Reductionism and the nature of psychology. *Cognition*, **2**, 131–146.

Qian, Z., Gilbert, M.E., Colicos, M.A., Kandel, E.R., and Kuhl, D. (1993). Tissue-plasminogen activator is induced as an immediate-early gene during seizure, kindling and long-term potentiation. *Nature*, **361**, 453–457.

Quartz, S.R. and Sejnowski, T.J. (1997). The neural basis of cognitive development: A constructivist manifesto. *Behavioral and Brain Sciences*, **20**, 537–596.

Quinn, W.G., Harris, W.A., and Benzer, S. (1974). Conditioned behavior in *Drosophila melanogaster*. *Proceedings of the National Academy of Sciences USA*, **71**, 708–712.

Quintana-Murci, L., Semino, O., Bandelt, H.-J., Passarino, G., McElreavey, K., and Santachiara-Benerecetti, S.S. (1999). Genetic evidence of an early exit of *Homo sapiens sapiens* from Africa through eastern Africa. *Nature Genetics*, **23**, 437–441.

Quintillian (1C AD/1985). *Institutio oratoria*, Book XI. In *Memory in historical perspective: the literature before Ebbinghaus*, (ed. D.J. Hermann, and R. Chaffin). Springer-Verlag.

Quirk, G.J., Armony, J.L., and LeDoux, J.E. (1997). Fear conditioning enhances different temporal components of tone-evoked spike trains in auditory cortex and lateral amygdala. *Neuron*, **19**, 613–624.

Raaijmakers, J.G.W. and Shiffrin, R.M. (1992). Models for recall and recognition. *Annual Review of Psychology*, **43**, 205–234.

Rachman, S. (1998). *Anxiety*. Psychology Press, Hove, UK.

Radstock, P. (1886). *Habit and its importance in education. An essay in pedagogical psychology*. Heath & Co., Boston, MA.

Raffalli-Sebille, M.-J., Chaputhier, G., Venault, P., and Dodd, R.H. (1990). Methyl β-carboline-3-carboxylate enhances performance in a multiple-trial learning task in mice. *Pharmacology, Biochemistry and Behavior*, **35**, 281–284.

Raichle, M.E. (1983). Positron emission tomography. *Annual Review of Neuroscience*, **6**, 249–268.

Raichle, M.E. (1994). Visualizing the mind. *Scientific American*, **270**(4), 36–42.

Rakic, P. (2002). Adult neurogenesis: an identity crisis. *Journal of Neuroscience*, **22**, 614–618.

Raman, I.M., Tong, G., and Jahr, C.E. (1996). β-Adrenergic regulation of synaptic NMDA receptors by cAMP-dependent protein kinase. *Neuron*, **16**, 415–421.

Ramus, F., Hauser, M.D., Miller, C., Morris, D., and Mehler, J. (2000). Language discrimination by human newborns and by cotton-top Tamarin monkeys. *Science*, **288**, 349–351.

Ranck, J.B. (1973). Studies on single neurons in dorsal hippocampal formation and septum in unrestrained rats. Part I. Behavioral correlates and firing repertoires. *Experimental Neurology*, **41**, 461–531.

Randich, A. and LoLordo, V.M. (1979). Associative and non-associative theories of the UCS preexposure phenomenon: Implications for Pavlovian conditioning. *Psychological Bulletin*, **86**, 523–548.

Rankin, C.H. (2000). Context conditioning in habituation in the nematode *Caenorhabditis elegans*. *Behavioral Neuroscience*, **114**, 496–505.

Rankin, C.H. and Carew, T.J. (1988). Dishabituation and sensitization emerge as separate processes during development in *Aplysia*. *Journal of Neuroscience*, **8**, 197–211.

Rao, A. and Steward, O. (1991). Evidence that protein constituents of postsynaptic membrane specializations are locally synthesized: analysis of proteins synthesized within synaptosomes. *Journal of Neuroscience*, **11**, 2881–2895.

Rasmusson, D.D. (2000). The role of acetylcholine in cortical synaptic plasticity. *Behavioural Brain Research*, **115**, 205–218.

Raspe, R.E. (1785/1944). *The surprising adventures of Baron Munchausen*. Peter Pauper Press, Mount Vernon, New York.

Rawles, R.E. (1978). The past and present of mnemotechny. In *Practical aspects of memory*, (ed. M.M. Gruneberg, P.E. Morris, and R.N. Sykes), pp. 164–171. Academic Press, London.

Raymond, J.L., Lisberger, S.G., and Mauk, M.D. (1996). The cerebellum: a neuronal learning machine? *Science*, **272**, 1126–1131.

Rayport, S.G. and Schacher, S. (1986). Synaptic plasticity *in vitro*: Cell culture of identified *Aplysia* neurons mediating short-term habituation and sensitization. *Journal of Neuroscience*, **6**, 759–763.

Razran, G. (1958). Pavlov and Lamarck. *Science*, **128**, 758–760.

Reber, A.S. (1967). Implicit learning of artificial grammars. *Journal of Verbal Learning and Verbal Behavior*, **6**, 855–863.

Recanzone, G.H., Schreiner, C.E., and Merzenich, M.M. (1993). Plasticity in the frequency representation of primary auditory-cortex following discrimination-training in adult owl monkeys. *Journal of Neuroscience*, **13**, 87–103.

Reder, L.M. and Ritter, F.E. (1992). What determines initial feeling of knowing? Familiarity with questions terms, not the answer. *Journal of Experimental Psychology: Learning, Memory and Cognition*, **18**, 435–451.

Redgrave, P., Prescott, T.J., and Gurney, K. (1999). Is the short-latency dopamine response too short to signal reward error? *Trends in Neurosciences*, **22**, 146–151.

Reed, J.M. and Squire, L.R. (1997). Impaired recognition memory in patients with lesions limited to the hippocampal formation. *Behavioral Neuroscience*, **111**, 667–675.

Reed, J.M. and Squire, L.R. (1998). Retrograde amnesia for facts and events: Findings from four new cases. *Journal of Neuroscience*, **18**, 3943–3954.

Rees, C.T. and Spatz, H.-C. (1989). Habituation of the landing response of *Drosophila* wild-type and mutants defective in olfactory learning. *Journal of Neurogenetics*, **5**, 105–118.

Reeves, L.M. and Weisberg, R.W. (1994). The role of content and abstract information in analogical transfer. *Psychological Bulletin*, **115**, 381–400.

Reid, I.C. and Morris, R.G.M. (1992). Smells are no surer: rapid improvement in olfactory discrimination is not due to the acquisition of a learning set. *Proceedings of the Royal Society London Series B*, **247**, 137–143.

Reid, I.C. and Morris, R.G.M. (1993). The enigma of olfactory learning. *Trends in Neurosciences*, **16**, 17–20.

Reith, M.E.A. (ed.) (1997). *Neurotransmitter transporters. Structure, function, and regulation*. Humana Press, Totowa, NJ.

Renner, K.E. (1964). Delay of reinforcement. A historical review. *Psychological Bulletin*, **61**, 341–361.

Rescorla, R.A. (1967). Pavlovian conditioning and its proper control procedures. *Psychological Review*, **74**, 71–80.

Rescorla, R.A. (1968). Probability of shock in the presence and absence of CS in fear conditioning. *Journal of Comparative and Physiological Psychology*, **66**, 1–5.

Rescorla, R.A. (1973). Effect of US habituation following conditioning. *Journal of Comparative and Physiological Psychology*, **82**, 137–143.

Rescorla, R.A. (1980). *Pavlovian second-order conditioning: studies in associative learning*. Lawrence Erlbaum Associates, Hillsdale, NJ.

References

Rescorla, R.A. (1988). Behavioral studies of Pavlovian conditioning. *Annual Review of Neuroscience*, **11**, 329–352.

Rescorla, R.A. (1996). Preservation of Pavlovian associations through extinction. *Quarterly Journal of Experimental Psychology*, **49B**, 245–258.

Rescorla, R.A. (1999). Within-subject partial reinforcement extinction effect in autoshaping. *Quarterly Journal of Experimental Psychology*, **52B**, 75–87.

Rescorla, R.A. and Heth, C.D. (1975). Reinstatement of fear to an extinguished conditioned stimulus. *Journal of Experimental Psychology. Animal Behavior Processes*, **1**, 88–96.

Rescorla, R.A. and Solomon, R.L. (1967). Two-process learning theory: Relationships between Pavlovian conditioning and instrumental learning. *Psychological Review*, **74**, 151–182.

Rescorla, R.A. and Wagner, A.R. (1972). A theory of Pavlovian conditioning: Variations in the effectiveness of reinforcement and nonreinforcement. In *Classical conditioning II: Current research and theory*, (ed. A.H. Black and W.F. Prokasy), pp. 64–99. Appleton-Century-Crofts, New York.

Restle, F. (1958). Toward a quantitative description of learning set data. *Psychological Review*, **65**, 77–91.

Revusky, S.H. and Bedarf, E.W. (1967). Association of illness with prior ingestion of novel foods. *Science*, **155**, 219–220.

Reynolds, J.H., Chelazzi, L., and Desimone, R. (1999). Competitive mechanisms subserve attention in macaque areas V2 and V4. *Journal of Neuroscience*, **19**, 1736–1753.

Ribot, T.A. (1882/1977). *Diseases of memory.* University Publications of America, Washington DC.

Richards, I.A. (1936). *The philosophy of rhetoric.* Oxford University Press, London.

Richardson-Klavehn, A. and Bjork, R.A. (1988). Measures of memory. *Annual Review of Psychology*, **39**, 475–543.

Ridley, R.M. and Baker, H.F. (1991). A critical evaluation of monkey models of amnesia and dementia. *Brain Research Reviews*, **16**, 15–37.

Riedel, G. (1996). Function of metabotropic glutamate receptors in learning and memory. *Trends in Neurosciences*, **19**, 219–224.

Riedel, G., Micheau, J., Lam, A.G.M., Roloff, E.V., Martin, S.J., Bridge, H., De Hoz, L., Poeschel, B., McCulloch, J., and Morris, R.G.M. (1999). Reversible neural inactivation reveals hippocampal participation in several memory processes. *Nature Neuroscience*, **2**, 898–905.

Riopelle, A.J., Alper, R.G., Strong, P.N., and Ades, H.W. (1953). Multiple discrimination and patterned string performance of normal and temporal-lobectomized monkeys. *Journal of Comparative Physiological Psychology*, **46**, 145–149.

Rioult-Pedotti, M.-S., Friedman, D., and Donoghue, J.P. (2000). Learning-induced LTP in neocortex. *Science*, **290**, 533–536.

Risold, P.Y., Thompson, R.H., and Swanson, L.W. (1997). The structural organization of connections between hypothalamus and cerebral cortex. *Brain Research Reviews*, **24**, 197–254.

Ristau, C.A. (ed.) (1991). *Cognitive ethology. The mind of other animals.* Lawrence Erlbaum Associates, Hillsdale, NJ.

Rizzolatti, G., Fadiga, L., Gallese, V., and Fogassi, L. (1996). Premotor cortex and the recognition of motor actions. *Cognitive Brain Research*, **3**, 131–141.

Robbins, T.W. (1998). Homology in behavioural pharmacology: An approach to animal models of human cognition. *Behavioural Pharmacology*, **9**, 509–519.

Robbins, T.W. and Everitt, B.J. (1996). Neurobehavioural mechanisms of reward and motivation. *Current Opinion in Neurobiology*, **6**, 228–236.

Robbins, T.W. and Everitt, B.J. (1999). Drug addiction: bad habits add up. *Nature*, **398**, 567–570.

Roberts, A.C., Robbins, T.W., and Weiskrantz, L. (ed.) (1996). Executive and cognitive functions of the prefrontal cortex. *Philosophical Transactions of the Royal Society, London B*, **351**, 1387–1527.

Robinson, R. (1954). *Definition.* Oxford University Press, London.

Rochester, N., Holland, J.H., Haibt, L.H., and Duda, W.L. (1956). Tests on a cell assembly theory of the action of the brain, using a large digital computer. *IRE Transactions on Information Theory*, **IT-2**, 80–93.

Rock, I. (1957). The role of repetition in associative learning. *American Journal of Psychology*, **70**, 186–193.

Roediger, H.L. III (1980). Memory metaphors in cognitive psychology. *Memory & Cognition*, **8**, 231–246.

Roediger, H.L. (1990). Implicit memory: retention without remembering. *American Psychologist*, **45**, 1043–1056.

Roediger, H.L. III (1991). They read an article? A commentary on the everyday memory controversy. *American Psychologist*, **46**, 37–40.

Roediger, H.L. III (1996). Memory illusions. *Journal of Memory and Language*, **35**, 76–100.

Roediger, H.L. III and McDermott, K.B. (1993). Implicit memory in normal human subjects. In *Handbook of neuropsychology*, Vol. 8, (ed. H. Spinnler and F. Boller), pp. 63–131. Elsevier, Amsterdam.

Roediger, H.L. III and McDermott, K.B. (1995). Creating false memories: remembering words not presented in lists. *Journal of Experimental Psychology: Learning, Memory, and Cognition*, **21**, 893–814.

Roediger, H.L., Weldon, M.S., Stadler, M.A., and Riegler, G.H. (1992). Direct comparison of word stems and word fragments in implicit and explicit retention tests. *Journal of Experimental Psychology: Learning, Memory, and Cognition*, **18**, 1251–1269.

Rogan, M.T. and LeDoux, J.E. (1996). Emotion: Systems, cells, synaptic plasticity. *Cell*, **85**, 469–475.

Rogan, T.R., Staubli, U.V., and LeDoux, J.E. (1997). Fear conditioning induces associative long-term potentiation in the amygdala. *Nature*, **390**, 604–610.

Rogers, J., Yang, L.-B., Lue, L.F., Strhmeyer, R., Liang, Z., Konishi, Y., Li, R., Walker, D., and Shen, Y. (2000). Inflammatory mediators in the Alzheimer's disease brain. *Neuroscience News*, **3**, 38–45.

Rogers, L.J. (1994). The molecular neurobiology of early learning, development, and sensitive periods, with emphasis on the avian brain. *Molecular Neurobiology*, **7**, 161–187.

Rollins, M. (1998). Philosophy, perception, and cognitive science. In *Perception and cognition at century's end* (ed. J. Hochberg), pp. 23–44. Academic Press, San Diego.

Rolls, E.T. and Tovee, M.J. (1994). Processing speed in the cerebral cortex and the neurophysiology of visual masking. *Proceedings of the Royal Society of London [Biology]*, **257**, 9–15.

Rolls, E.T., Rolls, B.J., Kelly, P.H., Shaw, S.G., Wood, R.J., and Dale, R. (1974). The relative attenuation of self-stimulation, eating and drinking produced by dopamine-receptor blockade. *Psychopharmacologia*, **38**, 219–230.

Rolls, E.T., Treves, A., and Tovee, M.J. (1997). The representational capacity of the distributed encoding of information provided by populations of neurons in primate temporal visual cortex. *Experimental Brain Research*, **114**, 149–162.

Romanes, G.J. (1882). *Animal intelligence*. Kegan Paul, Trench, & Co., London.

Romo, R., Hernandez, A., Zainos, A., Brody, C.D., and Lemus, L. (2000). Sensing without touching: psychophysical performance based on cortical microstimulation. *Neuron*, **26**, 273–278.

Root, A.I. (1972). *The ABC and XYZ of bee culture. An encyclopedia pertaining to scientific and practical culture of bees*, (34th edn). AI Root, Medina, OH.

Rosch, E., Mervis, C.B., Gray, W.D., Johnson, D., and Boyes-Braem, P. (1976). Basic objects in natural categories. *Cognitive Psychology*, **8**, 382–439.

Rose, S.P.R. (1981). What should a biochemistry of learning and memory be about? *Neuroscience*, **6**, 811–821.

Rose, S. (1995a). The rise of neurogenetic determinism. *Nature*, **373**, 380–382.

Rose, S.P.R. (1995b). Glycoproteins and memory function. *Behavioural Brain Research*, **66**, 73–78.

Rosen, B., Belliveau, J., and Chien, D. (1989). Perfusion imaging by nuclear magnetic resonance. *Magnetic Resonance Quarterly*, **5**, 263–281.

Rosenblum, K., Meiri, N., and Dudai, Y. (1993): Taste memory: the role of protein synthesis in gustatory cortex. *Behavioral and Neural Biology*, **59**, 49–56.

Rosenblum, K., Dudai, Y., and Richter-Levin, G. (1996). Long-term potentiation increases tyrosine phosphorylation of the N-methyl-D-aspartate receptor subunit 2B in rat dentate gyrus *in vivo*. *Proceedings of the National Academy of Sciences USA*, **93**, 10457–10460.

Rosenblum, K., Berman, D.E., Hazvi, S., Lamprecht, R., and Dudai, Y. (1997). NMDA receptor and the tyrosine phosphorylation of its 2B subunit in taste learning in the rat insular cortex. *Journal of Neuroscience*, **17**, 5129–5135.

Rosenmund, C., Stern-Bach, Y., and Stevens, C.F. (1998). The tetrameric structure of glutamate receptor channel. *Science*, **280**, 1596–1599.

Rosenthal, R. (1965). *Clever Hans: A case study of scientific method*. Introduction to Pfungst (1911).

Rosenthal, R. and Rubin, D.B. (1978). Interpersonal expectancy effects: The first 345 studies. *Behavioral and Brain Sciences*, **1**, 377–415.

Rosenzweig, M.R. and Bennett, E.L. (1996). Psychobiology of plasticity: Effects of training and experience on brain and behavior. *Behavioral Brain Research*, **78**, 57–65.

Rosenzweig, M.R., Bennett, E.L., Colombo, P.J., Lee, D.W., and Serrano, P.A. (1993). Short-term, intermediate-term, and long-term memories. *Behavioural Brain Research*, **57**, 193–198.

Rossi, S., Cappa, S.F., Babiloni, C., Pasqualetti, P., Miniussi, C., Carducci, F., Babiloni, F., and Rossini, P.M. (2001). Prefrontal cortex in long-term memory: an "interference" approach using magnetic stimulation. *Nature neuroscience*, **4**, 948–952.

Rostas, J.A.P., Brent, V.A., Voss, K., Errington, M.L., Bliss, T.V.P., and Gurd, J.W. (1996). Enhanced tyrosine phosphorylation of the 2B subunit of the N-methyl-D-aspartate receptor in long-term potentiation. *Proceedings of the National Academy of Sciences USA*, **93**, 10452–10456.

Rosvold, H.E. and Mirsky, A.F. (1954). The closed-field intelligence test for rats adapted for water-escape motivation. *Canadian Journal of Psychology*, **8**, 10–16.

Rotenberg, A., Mayford, M., Hawkins, R.D., Kandel, E.R., and Muller, R.U. (1996). Mice expressing activated CaMKII lack low frequency LTP and do not form stable place cells in the CA1 region of the hippocampus. *Cell*, **87**, 1351–1361.

Roth, M.S. (1989). Remembering forgetting: maladies de la memoire in nineteenth-century France. *Representations*, **26** (Spring), 49–68.

Roullet, P. and Sara, S. (1998). Consolidation of memory after its reactivation: involvement of beta noradrenergic receptors in the late phase. *Neural Plasticity*, **6**, 63–68.

Rousseau, J.-J. (1762/1993). *Emile*. Everyman, J.M. Dent, London.

Rousseau, J.-J. (1798/2000). *Confessions*. Oxford University Press, Oxford.

Rovee-Collier, C. (1997). Dissociations in infant memory; Rethinking the development of implicit and explicit memory. *Psychological Review*, **104**, 467–498.

Rowe, J.B., Toni, I., Josephs, O., Frackowiak, R.J.S., and Passingham, R.E. (2000). The prefrontal cortex: response selection or maintenance within working memory? *Science*, **288**, 1656–1660.

Rowe, S.H. (1909). *Habit-formation and the science of teaching*. Longmans, Green and Co., New York.

Roy, C.S. and Sherrington, C.S. (1890). On the regulation of the blood supply to the brain. *Journal of Physiology (London)*, **11**, 85–108.

Royer, S., Coulson, R.L., and Klein, M. (2000). Switching off and on of synaptic sites at *Aplysia* sensorimotor synapses. *Journal of Neuroscience*, **20**, 626–638.

Rozin, P. (1976). The evolution of intelligence and access to the cognitive unconscious. In *Progress in Psychobiology and Physiological Psychology*, (ed. J.M. Sprague and A.N. Epstein), Vol. 6, pp. 245–280. Academic Press, New York.

Rubin, B.D. and Katz, L.C. (1999). Optical imaging of odorant representation in the mammalian olfactory bulb. *Neuron*, **23**, 499–511.

Rubin, D.C. (1995). *Memory in oral traditions*. Oxford University Press, New York.

Rubin, D.C. and Greenberg, D.L. (1998). Visual memory-deficit amnesia: A distinct presentation and etiology. *Proceedings of the National Academy of Sciences USA*, **95**, 5413–5416.

Rubin, D.C. and Wenzel, A.E. (1996). One hundred years of forgetting: a quantitative description of the literature. *Psychological Review*, **103**, 734–760.

Rubin, N., Nakayama, K., and Shapley, R. (1997). Abrupt learning and retinal size specificity in illusory-contour perception. *Current Biology*, **7**, 461–467.

Rudy, B. and Iverson, L.E. (ed.) (1992). Ion channels. In *Methods in Enzymology*, Vol. 207. Academic Press, San Diego.

Rugg, M.D. and Wilding, E.L. (2000). Retrieval processing and episodic memory. *Trends in Cognitive Sciences*, **4**, 108–115.

Rugg, M.D., Fletcher, P.C., Frith, C.D., Frackowiak, R.S.J., and Dolan, R.J. (1996). Differential activation of the prefrontal cortex in successful and unsuccessful memory retrieval. *Brain*, **119**, 2073–2083.

Rugg, M.D., Fletcher, P.C., Frith, C.D., Frakowiak, R.S.J., and Dolan, R.J. (1997). Brain regions supporting intentional and incidental memory: A PET study. *NeuroReport*, **8**, 1283–1287.

Rumelhart, D.E., Hinton, G.E., and Williams, R.J. (1986*a*). Learning representations by back-propagating errors. *Nature*, **323**, 533–536.

Rumelhart, D.E., Hinton, G.E., and Williams, R.J. (1986*b*). Learning internal representations by error propagation. In *Parallel distributed processing: explorations in the microstructures of cognition*, Vol. 1, (ed. D.E. Rumelhart and J.L. McClelland), pp. 318–362. MIT Press, Cambridge, MA.

Rumelhart, D.E., McClelland, J.L., and the PDP Research Group (1986*c*). *Parallel distributed processing*, Vol. I. MIT Press, Cambridge, MA.

Rushworth, M.F.S., Nixon, P.D., Eacott, M.J., and Passingham, R.E. (1997). Ventral prefrontal cortex is not essential for working memory. *Journal of Neuroscience*, **17**, 4829–4838.

Rusiniak, K.W., Hankins, W.G., Garcia, J., and Brett, L.P. (1979). Flavor-illness aversions: Potentiation of odor by taste in rats. *Behavioral and Neural Biology*, **25**, 1–17.

Russell, B. (1945). *A history of Western philosophy*. Simon & Schuster, New York.

Russo, J.M. and Ison, J.R. (1979). Sensitization of the rat's acoustic startle response by repetition of a photic stimulus. *Physiological Psychology*, **7**, 102–106.

Rutner, F. (1988). *Biogeography and taxonomy of honeybees*. Springer-Verlag, Berlin.

Ryle, G. (1949). *The concept of mind*. Hutchinson, London.

Rzoska, J. (1953). Bait shyness, a study in rat behavior. *British Journal of Animal Behaviour*, **1**, 128–135.

Sacktor, M.C. and Mayeux, R. (1995). Delirium and dementia. In *Merritt's textbook of neurology*, (9th edn), (ed. L.P. Rowland), pp. 1–8. William & Wilkins, Baltimore.

Sadato, N., Pascual-Leone, A., Grafman, J., Ibañez, V., Deiber, M.P., Dold, G., and Hallett, M. (1996). Activation of the primary visual cortex by Braille reading in blind subjects. *Nature*, **380**, 526–528.

Saffran, J.R., Aslin, R.N., and Newport, E.L. (1996). Statistical learning by 8-month-old infants. *Science*, **274**, 1926–1928.

Safire, W. (1999). Ockham's razor's close shave. *New York Times Magazine*, January 31, 14.

Sagi, D. and Tanne, D. (1994). Perceptual learning: learning to see. *Current Opinion in Neurobiology*, **4**, 195–199.

Saint-Beuve, C.-A. (1850/1951). What is a classic? In *The great critics. An anthology of literary criticism*, (3rd edn), (ed. J.H. Smith and E.W. Parks), pp. 596–607. Norton, New York.

Saint-Cyr, J.A., Taylor, A.E., and Lang, A.E. (1988). Procedural learning and neostriatal dysfunction in man. *Brain*, **111**, 941–959.

Saitoh, T. and Schwartz, J.H. (1985). Phosphorylation-dependent subcellular translocation of a Ca^{2+}/calmodulin-dependent protein kinase produces an autonomous enzyme in *Aplysia*. *Journal of Cell Biology*, **100**, 835–842.

Sakai, K. and Miyashita, Y. (1991). Neural organization for the long-term memory of paired associates. *Nature*, **354**, 152–155.

Saksida, L.M., Raymond, S.M., and Touretzky, D.S. (1997). Shaping robot behavior using principles from instrumental conditioning. *Robotics and Autonomous Systems*, **22**, 231–249.

Sakurai, Y. (1998). The search for cell assemblies in the working brain. *Behavioural Brain Research*, **91**, 1–13.

Salmon, D.P. and Butters, N. (1995). Neurobiology of skill and habit learning. *Current Opinion in Neurobiology*, **5**, 184–190.

Sanes, J.R. and Lichtman, J.W. (1999). Can molecules explain long-term potentiation? *Nature Neuroscience*, **2**, 597–604.

Sara, S. (2000). Retrieval and reconsolidation: toward a neurobiology of remembering. *Learning & Memory*, **7**, 73–84.

Sassone-Corsi, P. (1995). Transcription factors responsive to cAMP. *Annual Review of Cell and Developmental Biology*, **11**, 355–377.

Saunders, R.C. and Weiskrantz, L. (1989). The effects of fornix transaction and combined fornix transaction, mammilary body lesions and hippocampal ablations on object-pair association memory in the rhesus monkey. *Behavioural Brain Research*, **35**, 85–94.

Schactel, E.G. (1947). On memory and childhood amnesia. *Psychiatry*, **10**, 1–26.

Schacter, D.L. (1982). *Stranger behind the engram. Theories of memory and the psychology of science.* Lawrence Erlbaum Associates, Hillsdale, NJ.

Schacter, D.L. (1987). Implicit memory: History and current status. *Journal of Experimental Psychology. Learning, Memory and Cognition*, **13**, 501–518.

Schacter, D.L. (1996). Illusory memory: a cognitive neuroscience analysis. *Proceedings of the National Academy of Sciences USA*, **93**, 13527–13533.

Schacter, D.L. and Buckner, R.L. (1998). Priming and the brain. *Neuron*, **20**, 185–195.

Schacter, D.L. and Tulving, E. (1994). What are the memory systems of 1994? In *Memory systems 1994*, (ed. D.L. Schacter and E. Tulving), pp. 1–38. MIT Press, Cambridge, MA.

Schacter, D.L. and Wagner, A.DE. (1999). Medial temporal lobe activation in fMRI and PET studies of episodic encoding and retrieval. *Hippocampus*, **9**, 7–24.

Schacter, D.L., Harbluk, J.L., and McLachlan, D.R. (1984). Retrieval without recollection: An experimental analysis of source amnesia. *Journal of Verbal Learning and Verbal Behavior*, **23**, 593–611.

Schacter, D.L., Alpert, N.M., Savage, C.R., Rauch, S.L., and Albert, M.S. (1996*a*). Conscious recollection and the human hippocampal formation: Evidence from positron emission tomography. *Proceedings of the National Academy of Sciences USA*, **93**, 321–325.

Schacter, D.L., Curran, T., Galluccio, L., Milberg, W.P., and Bates, J.F. (1996*b*). False recognition and the right frontal lobe: A case study. *Neuropsychologia*, **34**, 793–808.

Schacter, D.L., Reiman, E., Curran, T., Yun, L.S., Bandy, D., McDermott, K.B., and Roediger, H.L. III (1996*c*). Neuroanatomical correlates of veridical and illusory recognition memory: evidence from positron emission tomography. *Neuron*, **17**, 267–274.

Schacter, D.L., Norman, K.A., and Koustaal, W. (1998). The cognitive neuroscience of constructive memory. *Annual Review of Psychology*, **49**, 289–318.

Schafe, G.E. and Bernstein, I.L. (1998). Forebrain contribution to the induction of a brainstem correlate of conditioned taste aversion—II. Insular (gustatory) cortex. *Brain Research*, **800**, 40–47.

Schafe, G.E., Sollars, S.I., and Bernstein, I.L. (1995). The CS–US interval and taste aversion learning: A brief look. *Behavioral Neuroscience*, **109**, 799–802.

Schaffner, K.F. (1993). Theory structure, reduction, and disciplinary integration in biology. *Biology and Philosophy*, **8**, 319–347.

Scharenberg, A.M., Olds, J.L., Schreurs, B.G., Craig, A.M., and Alkon, D.L. (1991). Protein kinase C redistribution within CA3 stratum oriens during acquisition of nictitating membrane conditioning in the rabbit. *Proceedings of the National Academy of Sciences USA*, **88**, 6637–6641.

Schiavo, G., Gmachl, M.J.S., Stenbeck, G., Söllner, T.H., and Rothman, J.E. (1995). A possible docking and fusion particle for synaptic transmission. *Nature*, **378**, 733–736.

Schiller, F. (1992). *Paul Broca: Founder of French anthropology, explorer of the brain.* Oxford University Press, New York.

Schlaug, G., Jäncke, L., Huang, Y., and Steinmetz, H. (1995). *In vivo* evidence of structural brain asymmetry in musicians. *Science*, **267**, 699–701.

Schleidt, M. and Genzel, C. (1990). The significance of mother's perfume for infants in the first weeks of their life. *Ethology and Sociobiology*, **11**, 145–154.

Schlessinger, J. and Ullrich, A. (1992). Growth factor signaling by receptor tyrosine kinases. *Neuron*, **9**, 383–391.

Schmidt, S.R. (1994). Effects of humor on sentence memory. *Journal of Experimental Psychology: Learning, Memory and Cognition*, **20**, 953–967.

Schmidtke, K. and Vollmer, H. (1997). Retrograde amnesia: a study of its relation to anterograde amnesia and semantic memory deficits. *Neuropsychologia*, **35**, 505–518.

Schneider, W. (1999). The development of metamemory in children. *Attention and Performance*, **17**, 487–514.

Schnider, A. and Ptak, R. (1999). Spontaneous confabulations fail to suppress currently irrelevant memory traces. *Nature Neuroscience*, **2**, 677–681.

Schnider, A., von Daniken, C., and Gutbrod, K. (1996*a*). The mechanisms of spontaneous and provoked confabulations. *Brain*, **119**, 1365–1375.

Schnider, A., Gutbrod, K., Hess, C.W., and Schroth, G. (1996*b*). Memory without context: amnesia with confabulations after infraction of the right capsular genu. *Journal of Neurology, Neurosurgery, and Psychiatry*, **61**, 186–193.

Schoenbaum, G. and Eichenbaum, H. (1995). Information coding in the rodent prefrontal cortex. 1. Single-neuron activity in orbitofrontal cortex compared with that in pyriform cortex. *Journal of Neurophysiology*, **74**, 733–750.

References

Schreiner, C.E. (1995). Order and disorder in auditory cortical maps. *Current Opinion in Neurobiology*, **5**, 489–496.

Schrier, A.M. and Thompson, C.R. (1984). Are learning set learned? A reply. *Animal Learning and Behavior*, **12**, 109–112.

Schudson, M. (1995). Dynamics of distortion in collective memory. In *Memory distortion. How minds, brains, and societies reconstruct the past*, (ed. D.L. Schachter), pp. 346–364. Harvard University Press, Cambridge, MA.

Schul, R., Slotnick, B.M., and Dudai, Y. (1996). Flavor and the frontal cortex. *Behavioral Neuroscience*, **110**, 760–765.

Schultz, W. (1998). Predictive reward signal of dopamine neurons. *Journal of Neurophysiology*, **80**, 1–27.

Schultz, W., Dayan, P., and Montague, P.R. (1997). A neural substrate of prediction and reward. *Science*, **275**, 1593–1599.

Schuman, H. and Scott, J. (1989). Generations and collective memories. *American Sociological Review*, **54**, 359–381.

Schuster, C.M., Davis, G.W., Fetter, R.D., and Goodman, C.S. (1996). Genetic dissection of structural and functional components of synaptic plasticity. II. Fasciclin II controls presynaptic structural plasticity. *Neuron*, **17**, 655–667.

Schusterman, R.J. (1962). Transfer effects of successive discrimination-reversal training in chimpanzees. *Science*, **137**, 422–423.

Schutzwohl, A. (1998). Surprise and schema strength. *Journal of Experimental Psychology, Learning, Memory and Cognition*, **24**, 1182–1199.

Schwartz, B., Zerubavel, Y., and Barnett, B. (1986). The recovery of Masada: A study in collective memory. *Sociological Quarterly*, **27**, 147–164.

Schwartz, B.L. and Hashtroudi, S. (1991). Priming is independent of skill learning. *Journal of Experimental Psychology: Learning, Memory, and Cognition*, **17**, 1177–1187.

Science Citation Index (2001). *Web of Science V. 4.1*, ©ISI, Institute for Scientific Information. http://wos.isiglobalnet.com.

Scott, M.P. (2000). Development: the natural history of genes. *Cell*, **100**, 27–40.

Scott, S.K., Young, A.W., Calder, A.J., Hellawell, D.J., Aggleton, J.P., and Johnson, M. (1997). Impaired auditory recognition of fear and anger following bilateral amygdala lesions. *Nature*, **385**, 254–257.

Scoville, W.B. and Milner, B. (1957). Loss of recent memory after bilateral hippocampal lesions. *Journal of Neurology, Neurosurgery and Psychiatry*, **20**, 11–21.

Scrimshaw, N.S. (1998). Malnutrition, brain development, learning, and behavior. *Nutrition Research*, **18**, 351–379.

Searle, J.R. (1990). Is the brain's mind a computer program? *Scientific American*, **262**, 26–31.

Searle, J.R. (1992). *The rediscovery of mind*. MIT Press, Cambridge, MA.

Seashore, R.H. and Eckerson, L.D. (1940). The measurement of individual differences in general English vocabularies. *Journal of Educational Psychology*, **31**, 14–38.

Sebeok, T.A. and Rosenthal, R. (ed.) (1981). The Clever Hans phenomenon: Communication with horses, whales, apes and people. *Annals of the New York Academy of Sciences*, **364**.

Sechenov, I. (1862/1965). *Reflexes of the brain*. MIT Press, Cambridge, MA.

Seeburg, P.H. (1993). The molecular biology of mammalian glutamate receptor channels. *Trends in Pharmacological Sciences*, **14**, 297–303.

Seeburg, P.H., Burnashev, N., Kohr, G., Kuner, T., Sprengel, R., and Monyer, H. (1995). The NMDA receptor channel: Molecular design of a coincidence detector. *Recent Progress in Hormone Research*, **50**, 19–34.

Seeley, T.D. (1995). *The wisdom of the hive*. Harvard University Press, Cambridge, MA.

Segal, M. and Bloom, F.E. (1976). The action of norepinephrine in the rat hippocampus. IV. The effect of locus coeruleus stimulation on evoked hippocampal unit activity. *Brain Research*, **107**, 513–525.

Segal, M., Korkotian, E., and Murphy, D.D. (2000). Dendritic spine formation and pruning: common cellular mechanisms? *Trends in Neurosciences*, **23**, 53–57.

Seger, C.A. (1994). Implicit learning. *Psychological Bulletin*, **115**, 163–196.

Seger, R. and Krebs, E.G. (1995). The MAPK signaling cascade. *FASEB Journal*, **9**, 726–735.

Segev, I. (1992). Single neurone models: Oversimple, complex and reduced. *Trends in Neurosciences*, **15**, 414–421.

Seitz, R.J., Roland, P.E., Bohm, C., Greitz, T., and Stone-Elander, S. (1990). Motor learning in man: a PET study. *NeuroReport*, **1**, 57–60.

Sejnowski, T.J. (1995). Sleep and memory. *Current Biology*, **5**, 832–834.

Seligman, M.E.P. (1970). On the generality of the laws of learning. *Psychological Review*, **77**, 406–418.

Semon, R. (1904/1921). *The mneme*. George Allen & Unwin, London.

Seneca (63–65/1917). *Ad Lucilium Epistulae Morales, XLVII* (trans. Gummere, R.M.), Harvard University Press, London.

Service, R.F. (1999). Scanners get a fix on lab animals. *Science*, **286**, 2261–2262.

Shadlen, M.N. and Movshon, J.A. (1999). Synchrony unbound: a critical evaluation of the temporal binding hypothesis. *Neuron*, **24**, 67–77.

Shadlen, M.N. and Newsome, W.T. (1994). Noise, neural codes and cortical organization. *Current Opinion in Neurobiology*, **4**, 569–579.

Shadlen, M.N. and Newsome, W.T. (1998). The variable discharge of cortical neurons: Implications for connectivity, computation, and information coding. *Journal of Neuroscience*, **18**, 3870–3896.

Shadlen, M.N., Britten, K.H., Newsome, W.T., and Movshon, J.A. (1996). A computational analysis of the relationship between neuronal and behavioral responses to visual motion. *Journal of Neuroscience*, **16**, 1486–1510.

Shadmehr, R. and Brashers-Krug, T. (1997*a*). Functional stages in the formation of human long-term motor memory. *Journal of Neuroscience*, **17**, 409–419.

Shadmehr, R. and Holcomb, H.H. (1997*b*). Neural correlates of motor memory consolidation. *Science*, **277**, 821–825.

Shailor, B.A. (1988). *The medieval book.* Yale University Library, New Haven.

Shakespeare, W. (1600/1974). *The life of king Henry the fifth.* In The Complete Work, (ed. Craig, W.J.), Oxford University Press, London.

Shakespeare, W. (1606/1974). *Macbeth.* In *The Complete Works*, (ed. Craig, W.J.), Oxford University Press, London.

Shallice, T. (1982). Specific impairments of learning. *Philosophical Transactions of the Royal Society of London [B]*, **298**, 199–209.

Shallice, T. (1988). *From neuropsychology to mental structure.* Cambridge University Press, Cambridge.

Shallice, T. and Warrington, E.K. (1970). Independent functioning of verbal memory stores: A neuropsychological study. *Quarterly Journal of Experimental Psychology*, **22**, 261–273.

Shallice, T., Fletcher, P., Frith, C.D., Grasby, P., Frakowiak, R.S.J., and Dolan, R.J. (1994). Brain regions associated with acquisition and retrieval of verbal episodic memory. *Nature*, **368**, 633–635.

Shanks, D.R. and Darby, R.J. (1998). Feature- and rule-based generalization in human associative learning. *Journal of Experimental Psychology. Animal Behavior Processes*, **24**, 405–415.

Shannon, C.E. and Weaver, W. (1949). *The mathematical theory of communication.* Urbana.

Shapiro, S. and Krishnan, H.S. (1999). Consumer memory for intentions: A prospective memory perspective. *Journal of Experimental Psychology: Applied*, **5**, 169–189.

Sharpless, S. and Jasper, H. (1956). Habituation of the arousal reaction. *Brain*, **79**, 655–682.

Shaw, G.L., McGaugh, J.L., and Rose, S.P.R. (1990). *Neurobiology of learning and memory. Reprint volume*, World Scientific, Singapore.

Shaywitz, B.A., Fletcher, J.M., and Shaywitz, S.E. (1997). Attention-deficit/hyperactivity disorder. *Advances in Pediatrics*, **44**, 331–367.

Sheng, M. and Greenberg, M.E. (1990). The regulation and function of *c-fos* and other immediate early genes in the nervous system. *Neuron*, **4**, 477–485.

Sheng, M., Thompson, M.A., and Greenberg, M.E. (1991). CREB: A Ca^{2+}-regulated transcription factor phosphorylated by calmodulin-dependent kinases. *Science*, **252**, 1427–1430.

Shepherd, G.M. (1988). A basic circuit of cortical organization. In *Perspectives in memory research*, (ed. M.S. Gazzaniga), pp. 93–134. MIT Press, Cambridge, MA.

Shepherd, G.M. and Erulkar, S.D. (1997). Centenary of the synapse: from Sherrington to the molecular biology of the synapse and beyond. *Trends in Neurosciences*, **20**, 385–392.

Sherrington, C. (1941). *Man on his nature.* Cambridge University Press, Cambridge.

Sherry, D.F. and Schacter, D.L. (1987). The evolution of multiple memory systems. *Psychological Review*, **94**, 439–454.

Shettleworth, S.J. (1993). Varieties of learning and memory in animals. *Journal of Experimental Psychology. Animal Behavior Processes*, **19**, 5–14.

Sheu, F.-S., McCabe, B.J., Horn, G., and Routtenberg, A. (1993). Learning selectively increases protein kinase C substrate phosphorylation in specific regions of the chick brain. *Proceedings of the National Academy of Sciences USA*, **90**, 2705–2709.

Shi, G., Nakahira, K., Hammond, S., Rhodes, K.J., Schechter, L.E., and Trimmer, J.S. (1996). β Subunits promote K+ channel surface expression through effects early in biosynthesis. *Neuron*, **16**, 843–852.

Shi, S.-H., Hayashi, Y., Petralia, R.S., Zaman, S.H., Wenthold, R.J., Svoboda, K., and Malinow, R. (1999). Rapid spine delivery and redistribution of AMPA receptors after synaptic NMDA receptor activation. *Science*, **284**, 1811–1816.

Shiffrin, R.M. and Atkinson, R.C. (1969). Storage and retrieval processes in long-term memory. *Psychological Review*, **76**, 179–193.

Shiffrin, R.M. and Nosofsky, R.M. (1994). Seven plus or minus two: A commentary on capacity limitations. *Psychological Review*, **101**, 357–361.

Shimamura, A.P. (1995). Memory and the prefrontal cortex. *Annals of the New York Academy of Sciences*, **769**, 151–159.

Shimamura, A.P. and Squire, L.R. (1984). Paired-associate learning and priming effects in amnesia: a neuropsychological analysis. *Journal of Experimental Psychology: General*, **113**, 556–570.

Shimamura, A.P. and Squire, L.R. (1986). Memory and metamemory: A study of the feeling-of-knowing phenomenon in amnesic patients. *Journal of Experimental Psychology: Learning, Memory and Cognition*, **12**, 452–460.

Shimamura, A.P. and Squire, L.R. (1987). A neuropsychological study of fact memory and source amnesia. *Journal of Experimental Psychology. Learning, Memory and Cognition*, **13**, 464–473.

Shimamura, A.P., Jernigan, T.L., and Squire, L.R. (1988). Korsakoff's syndrome: Radiological (CT) findings and neuropsychological correlates. *Journal of Neuroscience*, **8**, 4400–4410.

Shimizu, E., Tang, Y.-P., Rampon, C., and Tsien, J.Z. (2000). NMDA receptor-dependent synaptic reinforcement as a crucial process for memory consolidation. *Science*, **290**, 1170–1174.

Shipley, T. and Sanders, M.S. (1982). Special senses are really special: Evidence for a reciprocal, bilateral pathway between insular cortex and nucleus parabrachialis. *Brain Research Bulletin*, **8**, 493–501.

Shklovsky, V. (1917/1965). Art as technique. In *Russian formalist criticism. Four essays* (trans. T.L. Lemon and M.J. Reis), pp. 3–24. University of Nebraska Press, Lincoln, NB.

Shoham, D., Glaser, D.E., Arieli, A., Kenet, T., Wijnbergen, C., Toledo, Y., Hildsheim, R., and Grinvald, A. (1999). Imaging cortical dynamics at high spatial and temporal resolution with novel voltage-sensitive dyes. *Neuron*, **24**, 791–802.

Shoop, R.D., Yamada, N., and Berg, D.K. (2000). Cytoskeletal links of neuronal acetylcholine receptors containing α7 subunits. *Journal of Neuroscience*, **20**, 4021–4029.

Shors, T.J. and Matzel, L.D. (1997). Long-term potentiation: What's learning got to do with it? *Behavioral and Brain Sciences*, **20**, 597–655.

Shors, T.J., Miesegaes, G., Beylin, A., Zhao, M., Rydel, T., and Gould, E. (2001). Neurogenesis in the adult is involved in the formation of trace memories. *Nature*, **410**, 372–376.

Shulz, D.E., Sosnik, R., Ego, V., Haidraliu, S., and Ahissar, E. (2000). A neuronal analogue of state-dependent learning. *Nature*, **403**, 549–553.

Shuster, M.J., Camardo, J.S., Siegelbaum, S.A., and Kandel, E.R. (1985). Cyclic AMP-dependent protein kinase closes the serotonin-sensitive K⁺ channel of *Aplysia* sensory neurones in cell free membrane patches. *Nature*, **313**, 392–395.

Siegel, S. (1982). Drug dissociations in the nineteenth century. In *Drug discrimination: application in CNS pharmacology*, (ed. F.C. Colpaert and J.L. Slangen), pp. 257–261. Elsevier, Amsterdam.

Siesjo, B.K. (1978). *Brain energy metabolism*. Wiley, Chichester.

Sigg, D., Thompson, C.M., and Mercer, A.R. (1997). Activity-dependent changes to the brain and behavior of the honey bee, *Apis mellifera* (L.). *Journal of Neuroscience*, **17**, 7148–7156.

Silva, A.J., Paylor, R., Wehner, J.M., and Tonegawa, S. (1992). Impaired spatial learning in α-calcium-calmodulin kinase II mutant mice. *Science*, **257**, 206–211.

Silva, A.J., Smith, A.M., and Giese, K.P. (1997*a*). Gene targeting and the biology of learning and memory. *Annual Review of Genetics*, **31**, 527–546.

Silva, A.J., and the participants at the Banbury Conference on Genetic Background in Mice (1997*b*). Mutant mice and neuroscience: recommendations concerning genetic background. *Neuron*, **19**, 755–759.

Silva, A.J., Kogan, J.H., Frankland, P.W., and Kida, S. (1998). CREB and memory. *Annual Review of Neuroscience*, **21**, 127–148.

Simon, H. (1962). The architecture of complexity. *Proceedings of the American Philosophical Society*, **106**, 467–482.

Simon, H.A. (1974). How big is a chunk? *Science*, **183**, 482–488.

Simon, H.A. and Ando, A. (1961). Aggregation of variables in dynamic systems. *Econometrica*, **29**, 111–137.

Singer, W. and Gray, C.M. (1995). Visual feature integration and the temporal correlation hypothesis. *Annual Review of Neuroscience*, **18**, 555–586.

Singer, W., Gray, C., Engel, A., Konig, P., Artola, A., and Brocher, S. (1990). Formation of cortical cell assemblies. *Cold Spring Harbor Symposium of Quantitative Biology*, **55**, 939–952.

Sirinivasan, M.V., Zhang, S., Altwein, M., and Tautz, J. (2000). Honeybee navigation: nature and calibration of the 'odometer'. *Science*, **287**, 851–853.

Skelton, R.W., Miller. J.J., and Philips, A.G. (1985). Long-term potentiation facilitates behavioral responding to single-pulse potentiation of the perforant path. *Behavioral Neuroscience*, **99**, 603–620.

Skinner, B.F. (1938). *The behavior of organisms: an experimental analysis*. Appleton-Century-Crofts, New York.

Skinner, B.F. (1957). *Verbal behavior*. Appleton-Century-Crofts, New York.

Skinner, B.F. (1960). Pigeons in a pelican. *American Psychologist*, **15**, 28–37.

Skinner, B.F. (1961). *Walden two*. New York.

Skinner, B.F. (1971). *Beyond freedom and dignity*. Knopf, New York.

Skinner, B.F. (1984). Canonical papers. *Behavioral and Brain Sciences*, **7**, 473–724.

Skinner, B.F. (1988/1995). The behavior of organisms at fifty. In *Modern perspectives on B.F. Skinner and contemporary behaviorism*, (ed. J.T. Todd and E.K. Morris), pp. 149–161. Greenwood Press, Westport, CT.

Slotnick, B.M. (1994). The enigma of olfactory learning revisited. *Neuroscience*, **58**, 1–12.

Slotnick, B.M. and Katz, H.M. (1974). Olfactory learning-set formation in rats. *Science*, **185**, 796–798.

Slotnick, B.M., Westbrook, F., and Darling, F.M.C. (1997). What the rat's nose tells the rat's mouth: Long delay aversion conditioning with aqueous odors and potentiation of taste by odors. *Animal Learning and Behavior*, **25**, 357–369.

Smalheiser, N.R., Manev, H., and Costa, E. (2001). RNAi and brain function: was McConnell on the right track? *Trends in Neurosciences*, **24**, 216–218.

Small, W.S. (1901). Experimental study of the mental processes of the rat. II. *American Journal of Psychology*, **12**, 206–239.

Smith, A. and Nutt, D. (1996). Noradrenaline and attention lapses. *Nature*, **380**, 291.

Smith, A.F. (1991). Cognitive processes in long-term dietary recall. *Vital and health statistics*, Series 6, No. 4, *Cognition and survey measurement*. US Department of Health and

Human Services, Publication no. (PHS) 92-1079, NCHS. Hyatsville, MD.

Smith, E.E. and Jonides, J. (1977). Working memory: A view from neuroimaging. *Cognitive Psychology*, **33**, 5–42.

Smith, E.E. and Medin, D.L. (1981). *Categories and concepts*. Harvard University Press, Cambridge, MA.

Smith, E.E., Jonides, J., Marshuetz, C., and Koeppe, R.A. (1998). Components of verbal working memory: evidence from neuroimaging. *Proceedings of the National Academy of Sciences USA*, **95**, 876–882.

Smith, F.V. and Bird, M.W. (1963). The relative attraction for the domestic chick of combinations of stimuli in different sensory modalities. *Animal Behaviour*, **11**, 300–305.

Smith, J.D., Shields, W.E., Allendoerfer, K.R., and Washburn, D.A. (1998). Memory monitoring by animals and humans. *Journal of Experimental Psychology: General*, **127**, 227–250.

Snoddy, G.S. (1926). Learning and stability: a psychophysiological analysis of a case of motor learning with clinical applications. *Journal of Applied Psychology*, **10**, 1–36.

Snow, C.P. (1963). *The two cultures: and a second look*. The New American Library, New York.

Sober, E. (ed.) (1994). *Conceptual issues in evolutionary biology*, (2nd edn). MIT Press, Cambridge. MA.

Sokal, A. and Bricmont, J. (1999). *Fashionable nonsense*. Picador, New York.

Sokal, R.R. (1985). The continuing search for order. *American Naturalist*, **126**, 729–749.

Sokoloff, L. (1989). Circulation and energy metabolism of the brain. In *Basic neurochemistry. Molecular, cellular, and medical aspects*, (ed. G.J. Siegel, B.W. Agranoff, R.W. Albers, and P.B. Molinoff), pp. 565–590. Raven Press, New York.

Sokoloff, L., Reivich, M., Kennedy, C., Des Rosiers, M.H., Patlak, C.S., Pettigrew, K.D., Sakurada, O., and Shinohara, M. (1977). The [^{14}C]deoxyglucose method for the measurement of local cerebral glucose utilization: Theory, procedure, and normal values in the conscious and anesthetized albino rat. *Journal of Neurochemistry*, **28**, 897–916.

Sokolov, E.N. (1963*a*). *Perception and the conditioned reflex*. Pergamon Press, Oxford.

Sokolov, E.N. (1963*b*). Higher nervous functions: The orienting reflex. *Annual Review of Physiology*, **25**, 545–580.

Solomon, R.L. (1949). An extension of control group design. *Psychological Bulletin*, **46**, 137–150.

Solomon, R.L. and Turner, L.H. (1962). Discriminative classical conditioning in dogs paralyzed by curare can later control discriminative avoidance responses in the normal state. *Psychological Review,* **69**, 202–219.

Solomonia, R.O., McCabe, B.J., and Horn, G. (1998). Neural cell adhesion molecules, learning and memory in the domestic chick. *Behavioral Neuroscience*, **112**, 646–655.

Sorabji, R. (1972). *Aristotle on memory*. Duckworth, London.

Sorensen, R.A. (1992). *Thought experiments*. Oxford University Press, New York.

Spalding, D.A. (1873). Instinct, with original observations on young animals. *Macmillans Magazine*, **27**, 282–293. (Reprinted in *British Journal of Animal Behaviour* (1954), **2**, 2–11.)

Spanagel, R. and Weiss, F. (1999). The dopamine hypothesis of reward: past and current status. *Trends in Neurosciences*, **22**, 521–527.

Spear, N.E. and Mueller, C.W. (1984). Consolidation as a function of retrieval. In *Memory consolidation. Psychobiology of cognition*, (ed. H. Weingartner and E.S. Parker), pp. 111–147. Laurence Erlbaum Associates, Hillsdale, NJ.

Spearman, C. (1904). General intelligence, objectively determined and measured. *American Journal of Psychology*, **15**, 201–293.

Spelke, E. (1994). Initial knowledge—6 suggestions. *Cognition*, **50**, 431–445.

Spence, K.W., Bergamnn, G., and Lippitt, R.R. (1950). A study of simple learning under irrelevant motivational-reward conditions. *Journal of Experimental Psychology*, **40**, 539–542.

Spencer, W.A., Thompson, R.F., and Neilson, D.R. (1966). Alterations in responsiveness of ascending and reflex pathways activated by iterated cutaneous afferent volleys. *Journal of Neurophysiology*, **29**, 240–252.

Sperling, G. (1960). The information available in brief visual presentations. *Psychological Monographs: General and Applied*, **74**, 1–29.

Sperling, G. and Weichslgartner, E. (1987). Dynamics of automatic and controlled visual attention. *Science*, **238**, 778–780.

Squire, L.R. (1987). *Memory and brain*. Oxford University Press, New York.

Squire, L.R. and Zola, S.M. (1996). Structure and function of declarative and nondeclarative memory systems. *Proceedings of the National Academy of Sciences USA*, **93**, 13515–13522.

Squire, L.R. and Zola, S.M. (1997). Amnesia, memory and brain systems. *Philosophical Transactions of the Royal Society of London, B*, **352**, 1663–1673.

Squire, L.R. and Zola, S.M. (1998). Episodic memory, semantic memory, and amnesia. *Hippocampus*, **8**, 205–211.

Squire, L.R. and Zola-Morgan, S. (1991). The medial temporal lobe memory system. *Science*, **253**, 1380–1386.

Squire, L.R., Slater, P.C., and Chace, P.M. (1975). Retrograde amnesia: Temporal gradient in very-long-term memory following electroconvulsive therapy. *Science*, **187**, 77–79.

Squire, L.R., Cohen, N.J., and Nadel, L. (1984). The medial temporal region and memory consolidation: A new hypothesis. In *Memory consolidation. Psychobiology of cognition*, pp. 185–210. Laurence Erlbaum Associates, Hillsdale, NJ.

Squire, L.R., Knowlton, B., and Musen, G. (1993). The structure and organization of memory. *Annual Review of Psychology*, **44**, 453–495.

References

Srinivas, K. and Roediger, H.L. (1990). Classifying implicit memory tests: category association and anagram solution. *Journal of Memory and Language, 29,* 389–412.

Srinivasan, M. and Zhang, S.W. (1998). Probing perception in a miniature brain: Pattern recognition and maze navigation in honeybees. *Zoology—Analysis of Complex Systems,* **101,** 246–259.

Staddon, J.E.R. and Higa, J.J. (1996). Multiple time scales in simple habituation. *Psychological Review,* **103,** 720–733.

Stahl, S.M. (1996). *Essential psychopharmacology. Neuroscientific basis and clinical applications.* Cambridge University Press, Cambridge.

Standing, L. (1973). Learning 10,000 pictures. *Quarterly Journal of Experimental Psychology,* **25,** 207–222.

Stanley, G.B., Li, F.F., and Dan, Y. (1999). Reconstruction of natural scenes from ensemble responses in the lateral geniculate nucleus. *Journal of Neuroscience,* **19,** 8036–8042.

Stanton, M.E. (2000). Multiple memory systems, development and conditioning. *Behavioral Brain Research,* **110,** 25–37.

Stark, C.E.L. and Squire, L.R. (2000). Recognition memory and familiarity judgments in severe amnesia: No evidence for a contribution of repetition priming. *Behavioral Neuroscience,* **114,** 459–467.

Staubli, U., Ivy, G., and Lynch, G. (1984). Hippocampal denervation causes rapid forgetting of olfactory information in rats. *Proceedings of the National Academy of Sciences USA,* **81,** 5885–5887.

Staubli, U., Rogers, G., and Lynch, G. (1994). Facilitation of glutamate receptors enhance memory. *Proceedings of the National Academy of Sciences USA,* **91,** 777–781.

Staubli, U., Le, T.-T., and Lynch, G. (1995). Variants of olfactory memory and their dependencies on the hippocampal formation. *Journal of Neuroscience,* **15,** 1162–1171.

Steckler, T., Drinkenburg, W.H.I.M., Sahgal, A., and Aggleton, J.P. (1998*a*). Recognition memory in rats—I. Concepts and classification. *Progress in Neurobiology,* **54,** 289–311.

Steckler, T., Drinkenburg, W.H.I.M., Sahgal, A., and Aggleton, J.P. (1998*b*). Recognition memory in rats—II. Neuroanatomical substrates. *Progress in Neurobiology,* **54,** 313–332.

Steinmetz, J.E. (2000). Brain substrates of classical conditioning: a highly localized but also distributed system. *Behavioural Brain Research,* **110,** 13–24.

Steketee, J.D., Silverman, P.B., and Swann, A.C. (1989). Forebrain norepinephrine involvement in selective attention and neophobia. *Physiology and Behavior,* **46,** 577–583.

Sternberg, R.J. and Davidson, J.E. (ed.) (1995). *The nature of insight.* MIT Press, Cambridge, MA.

Stevens, C.F. (1998). A million dollar question: Does LTP = memory? *Neuron,* **20,** 1–2.

Stevenson, H.W. (1954). Latent learning in children. *Journal of Experimental Psychology,* **47,** 17–21.

Steward, O. (1997). mRNA localization in neurons: A multipurpose mechanism? *Neuron,* **18,** 9–12.

Steward, O. and Levy, W.B. (1982). Preferential localization of polyribosomes under the base of dendritic spines in granule cells of the dentate gyrus. *Journal of Neuroscience,* **2,** 248–291.

Steward, O., Wallace, C.S., Lyford, G.L., and Worley, P.F. (1998). Synaptic activation causes the mRNA for the IEG *Arc* to localize selectively near activated postsynaptic sites on dendrites. *Neuron,* **21,** 741–751.

Stich, S.P. and Warfield, T.A. (ed.) (1994). *Mental representation. A reader.* Blackwell, Oxford.

Stillings, N.A., Feinstein, M.H., Garfield, J.L., Rissland, E.L., Rosenbaum, D.A., Weisler, S.E., and Baker-Ward, L. (1987). *Cognitive science. An introduction.* MIT Press, Cambridge, MA.

Stopfer, M. and Laurent, G. (1999). Short-term memory in olfactory network dynamics. *Nature,* **402,** 664–668.

Storms, L.H. (1958). Apparent backward association: A situational effect. *Journal of Experimental Psychology,* **55,** 390–395.

Stratton, G.M. (1917). The mnemonic feat of the 'Shass Polak'. *Psychological Review,* **24,** 244–247.

Stuss, D.T. and Benson, D.F. (1984). Neuropsychological studies of the frontal lobes. *Psychological Bulletin,* **95,** 3–28.

Sullivan, L.G. (1995). Myth, metaphor and hypothesis: how anthropomorphism defeats science. *Philosophical Transactions of the Royal Society of London. B. Biological Sciences,* **349,** 215–218.

Sullivan, W.E. and Konishi, M. (1986). Neural map of interaural phase difference in the owl's brainstem. *Proceedings of the National Academy of Sciences USA,* **83,** 8400–8404.

Sun, Z.Y. and Schacher, S. (1998). Binding of serotonin to receptors at multiple sites is required for structural plasticity accompanying long-term facilitation of *Aplysia* sensorimotor synapses. *Journal of Neuroscience,* **18,** 3991–4000.

Sunahara, R.K., Dessauer, C.W., and Gilman, A.G. (1996). Complexity and diversity of mammalian adenylyl cyclases. *Annual Review of Pharmacology and Toxicology,* **36,** 461–480.

Sunayashiki-Kusuzaki, K., Lester, D.S., Schreurs, B.G., and Alkon, D.L. (1993). Associative learning potentiates protein kinase C activation in synaptosomes of the rabbit hippocampus. *Proceedings of the National Academy of Sciences USA,* **90,** 4286–4289.

Super, H., Spekreijse, H., and Lamme, V.A.F. (2001). A neural correlate of working memory in the monkey primary visual cortex. *Science,* **293,** 120–124.

Suppes, P., Pavel, M., and Falmagne, J.-Cl. (1994). Representations and models in psychology. *Annual Review of Psycho-logy,* **45,** 517–544.

Sutherland, E.W. and Rall, T.W. (1960). The relation of adenosine-3′,5′-phosphate and phosphorylase to the actions of catecholamines and other hormones. *Pharmacological Reviews*, **12**, 265–299.

Sutherland, E.W., Oye, I., and Butcher, R.W. (1965). The action of epinephrine and the role of the adenyl cyclase system in hormone action. *Recent Progress in Hormone Research*, **21**, 623–642.

Sutton, M.A., Masters, S.E., Bagnall, M.W., and Carew, T.J. (2001). Molecular mechanisms underlying a unique intermediate phase of memory in *Aplysia*. *Neuron*, **31**, 143–154.

Sutton, S., Braren, M., Zubin, J., and John, E. (1965). Evoked potential correlates of stimulus uncertainty. *Science*, **150**, 1187–1188.

Suzuki, W.A. and Eichenbaum, H. (2000). The neurophysiology of memory. *Annals of the New York Academy of Sciences*, **911**, 175–191.

Suzuki, W.A., Zola-Morgan, S., Squire, L.R., and Amaral, D.G. (1993). Lesions of the perirhinal and parahippocampal cortices in the monkey produce long-lasting memory impairment in the visual and tactual modalities. *Journal of Neuroscience*, **13**, 2430–2451.

Swank, M.W. and Bernstein, I.L. (1994). c-Fos induction in response to a conditioned stimulus after single trial taste aversion learning. *Brain Research*, **636**, 202–208.

Swanson, L.W. (1987). Limbic System. In *Encyclopedia of neuroscience*, (ed. G. Adelman), pp. 589–591. Birkhauser, Boston, MA.

Swanson, L.W. and Petrovich, G.D. (1998). What is the amygdala? *Trends in Neurosciences*, **21**, 323–331.

Swartz, K.B. (1997). What is mirror self-recognition in non-human primates, and what is it not? *Annals of the New York Academy of Sciences*, **818**, 65–71.

Swartzman, L.C. and Burkell, J. (1998). Expectations and the placebo effect in clinical drug trials: Why we should not turn a blind eye to unblinding, and other cautionary notes. *Clinical Pharmacology & Therapeutics*, **64**, 1–7.

Sylva, K. (1997). Critical periods in childhood learning. *British Medical Bulletin*, **53**, 185–197.

Szentagothai, J. (1975). From the last skirmishes around the neuron theory to the functional anatomy of neuron networks. In *The neurosciences: Paths of discovery*, (ed. F.G. Worden, J.P. Swazey and G. Adelman), pp. 103–120. MIT Press, Cambridge, MA.

Szymborska, W. (1995). Brueghel's two monkeys. From: *Calling out to Yeti* (1972). In *View with a grain of sand*. Harcourt Brace & Co., San Diego.

Talland, G.A. (1965). *Deranged memory. A psychonomic study of the amnesic syndrome*. Academic Press, New York.

Tanaka, K. (1993). Neuronal mechanisms of object recognition. *Science*, **262**, 685–688.

Tanaka, K. (1997). Mechanisms of visual object recognition: monkey and human studies. *Current Opinion in Neurobiology*, **7**, 523–529.

Tang, Y., Mishkin, M., and Aigner, T.G. (1997). Effects of muscarinic blockade in perirhinal cortex during visual recognition. *Proceedings of the National Academy of Sciences USA*, **94**, 12667–12669.

Tang, Y.-P., Shimizu, E., Dube, G.R., Rampon, C., Kerchner, G.A., Zhuo, M., Liu, G., and Tsien, J.Z. (1999). Genetic enhancement of learning and memory in mice. *Nature*, **401**, 63–69.

Tasaki, I., Watanabe., A., Sandlin, R., and Carnay, L. (1968). Changes in fluorescence turbidity and birefringence associated with nerve excitation. *Proceedings of the National Academy of Sciences USA*, **61**, 883–888.

Taube, J.S., Muller, R.U., and Ranck, J.B. (1990). Head-direction cells recorded from the postsubiculum in freely moving rats. I. Description and quantitative analysis. *Journal of Neuroscience*, **10**, 420–435.

Taubenfeld, S.M., Milekic, M.H., Monti, B., and Alberini, C.M. (2001). The consolidation of new but not reactivated memory requires hippocampal C/EBPβ. *Nature Neuroscience*, **4**, 813–818.

Tauc, L. and Gershenfeld, H.M. (1961). Cholinergic transmission mechanisms for both excitation and inhibition in molluscan central synapses. *Nature*, **192**, 366–367.

Taylor, P. and Radic, Z. (1994). The cholinesterases: from genes to proteins. *Annual Review of Pharmacology and Toxicology*, **34**, 281–320.

Temkin, O. (1947). Gall and the phrenological movement. *Bulletin of the History of Medicine*, **XXI**, 275–321.

Templeton, J.J. (1998). Learning from other's mistake: A paradox revisited. *Animal Behaviour*, **55**, 79–85.

ten Cate, C. and Vos, D.R. (1999). Sexual imprinting and evolutionary processes in birds: a reassessment. *Advances in the Study of Behavior*, 28, 1–31.

Teng, E. and Squire, L.R. (1999). Memory for places learned long ago is intact after hippocampal damage. *Nature*, **400**, 675–677.

Tesmer, J.J.G., Sunahara, R.K., Johnson, R.A., Gosselin, G., Gilman, A.G., and Sprang, S.R. (1999). Two-metal-ion catalysis in adenylyl cyclase. *Science*, **285**, 756–760.

Teuber, H.-L. (1955). Physiological psychology. *Annual Review of Psychology*, **6**, 267–296.

Teyler, T.J. and DiScenna, P. (1986). The hippocampal memory indexing theory. *Behavioral Neuroscience*, **100**, 147–154.

Thach, W.T. (1996). On the specific role of the cerebellum in motor learning and cognition: clues from PET activation and lesion studies in man. *Behavioral and Brain Sciences*, **19**, 411–431.

Thach, W.T. (1998). What is the role of the cerebellum in motor learning and cognition? *Trends in Cognitive Sciences*, **2**, 331–337.

Thomas, K.L., Laroche, S., Errington, M.L., Bliss, T.V.P., and Hunt, S.P. (1994). Spatial and temporal changes in signal transduction pathways during LTP. *Neuron*, **13**, 737–745.

References

Thomas, S.A. and Palmiter, R.D. (1997a). Thermoregulatory and metabolic phenotypes of mice lacking noradrenaline and adrenaline. *Nature*, **387**, 94–97.

Thomas, S.A. and Palmiter, R.D. (1997b). Disruption of the dopamine β-hydroxylase gene in mice suggests roles for norepinephrine in motor function, learning, and memory. *Behavioral Neuroscience*, **111**, 579–589.

Thomas, S.A. and Palmiter, R.D. (1997c). Impaired maternal behavior in mice lacking norepinephrine and epinephrine. *Cell*, **91**, 583–592.

Thomas, S.A., Matsumoto, A.M., and Palmiter, R.D. (1995). Noradrenaline is essential for mouse fetal development. *Nature*, **374**, 643–646.

Thompson, C.P., Cowan, T.M., and Frieman, J. (1993). *Memory search by a mnemonist*. Laurence Erlbaum Associates, Hillsdale, NJ.

Thompson, R.F. and Kim, J.J. (1996). Memory systems in the brain and localization of a memory. *Proceedings of the National Academy of Sciences USA*, **93**, 13438–13444.

Thompson, R.F. and Spencer, W.A. (1966). Habituation: A model phenomenon for the study of neuronal substrates of behavior. *Psychological Review*, **73**, 16–43.

Thompson, R.F., Swain, R., Clark, R., and Shinkman, P. (2000). Intracerebellar conditioning—Brogden and Gantt revisited. *Behavioural Brain Research*, **110**, 3–11.

Thomson, A.M. (2000). Facilitation, augmentation and potentiation at central synapses. *Trends in Neurosciences*, **23**, 305–312.

Thorndike, E.I. (1907/1920). *The elements of psychology*, (2nd edn). Seiler, New York.

Thorndike, E.L. (1911/1965). *Animal intelligence. Experimental studies*. Hafner, New York.

Thorndike, E.L. and Woodworth, R.S. (1901a). The influence of improvement in one mental function upon the efficiency of other functions. (I.). *Psychological Review*, **8**, 247–261.

Thorndike, E.L. and Woodworth, R.S. (1901b). The influence of improvement in one mental function upon the efficiency of other functions. III. Functions involving attention, observation and discrimination. *Psychological Review*, **8**, 553–564.

Thorndike, L. (1923). *A history of magic and experimental science*. Columbia University Press, New York.

Thorne, B.M. (1999). Using irony in teaching the history of psychology. *Teaching of Psychology*, **26**, 222–224.

Thorpe, S., Fize, D., and Marlot, C. (1996). Speed of processing in the human visual system. *Nature*, **381**, 520–522.

Thorpe, W.H. (1954). The process of song-learning in the chaffinch as studied by means of the sound spectrograph. *Nature*, **173**, 465.

Thurstone, L.L. (1947). *Multiple factor analysis*. University of Chicago Press, Chicago, IL.

Timberlake, W. (1993). Behavior systems and reinforcement: an integrative approach. *Journal of the Experimental Analysis of Behavior*, **60**, 105–128.

Tinbergen, N. (1969). *The study of instinct*. Oxford University Press, New York.

Titchner, E.B. (1908/1924). *Lectures on the elementary psychology of feeling and attention*. MacMillan, New York.

Todd, J.T. and Morris, E.K. (ed.) (1995). *Modern perspectives on B.F. Skinner and contemporary behaviorism*. Greenwood Press, Westport, CT.

Todt, D. and Hultsch, H. (1998). How songbirds deal with large amounts of serial information: Retrieval rules suggest a hierarchical song memory. *Biological Cybernetics*, **79**, 487–500.

Tolman, E.C. (1924). The inheritance of maze-learning ability in rats. *Journal of Comparative Psychology*, **4**, 1–18.

Tolman, E.C. (1932/1967). *Purposive behavior in animals and men*. Appleton-Century-Crofts, New York.

Tolman, E.C. (1938). The determiners of behavior at a choice point. *Psychological Review*, **45**, 1–41.

Tolman, E.C. (1945). A stimulus-expectancy need-cathexis psychology. *Science*, **101**, 160–166.

Tolman, E.C. (1948). Cognitive maps in rats and men. *Psychological Review*, **55**, 189–208.

Tolman, E.C. (1949). There is more than one kind of learning. *Psychological Review*, **56**, 144–155.

Tolman, E.C. (1952). Autobiography. In *A history of psychology in autobiography*, pp. 323–329. Clark University Press, Worcester, MA.

Tomasello, M., Kruger, A.C., and Ratner, H.H. (1993). Cultural learning. *Behavioral and Brain Sciences*, **16**, 495–552.

Tomita, H., Ohbayashi, M., Nakahara, K., Hasegawa, I., and Miyashita, Y. (1999). Top-down signal from prefrontal cortex in executive control of memory retrieval. *Nature*, **401**, 699–703.

Tong, G., Malenka, R.C., and Nicoll, R.A. (1996). Long-term potentiation in cultures of single hippocampal granule cells: A presynaptic form of plasticity. *Neuron*, **16**, 1147–1157.

Torre, V., Ashmore, J.F., Lamb, T.D., and Menini, A. (1995). Transduction and adaptation in sensory receptor cells. *Journal of Neuroscience*, **15**, 7757–7768.

Torres, R.M. and Kuhn, R. (1997). *Laboratory protocols for conditional gene targeting*. Oxford University Press, Oxford.

Treffert, D.A. (2000). *Extraordinary people: understanding savant syndrome*. iUniverse.com, Lincoln, NB.

Treisman, A.M. (1985). Preattentive processing in vision. *Computer Vision, Graphics, and Image Processing*, **31**, 156–177.

Treisman, A. (1993). The perception of features and objects. In *Attention: selection, awareness, and control* (ed. A. Baddeley and L. Weiskrantz), pp. 5–35. Clarendon Press, Oxford.

Treisman, A. (1995). Modulatory and attention: Is the binding problem real? *Visual Cognition*, **2**, 303–311.

Treisman, A. (1999). Solutions to the binding problem: progress through controversy and convergence. *Neuron*, **24**, 105–100.

Treisman, A.M. and Gelade, G. (1980). A feature-integration theory of attention. *Cognitive Psychology*, **12**, 87–136.

Tremblay, L., Hollerman, J.R., and Schultz, W. (1998). Modifications of reward expectation-related neuronal activity during learning in primate striatum. *Journal of Neurophysiology*, **80**, 964–977.

Trembley, L. and Schultz, W. (1999). Relative reward preference in primate orbitofrontal cortex. *Nature*, **398**, 704–708.

Treves, A. and Rolls, E.T. (1994). Computational analysis of the role of the hippocampus in memory. *Hippocampus*, **4**, 374–391.

Trudeau, L.-E. and Castellucci, V.F. (1993). Sensitization of the gill and siphon withdrawal reflex of *Aplysia*: Multiple sites of change in the neuronal network. *Journal of Neurophysiology*, **70**, 1210–1220.

Tsien, J.Z., Chen, D.F., Gerber, D., Tom, C., Mercer, E.H., Andersdon, D.J., Mayford, M., Kandel, E.R., and Tonegawa, S. (1996*a*). Subregion- and cell type-restricted gene knock-out in mouse brain. *Cell*, **87**, 1317–1326.

Tsien, J.Z., Huerta, P.T., and Tonegawa, S. (1996*b*). The essential role of hippocampal CA1 NMDA receptor-dependent synaptic plasticity in spatial memory. *Cell*, **87**, 1327–1338.

Tsodyks, M., Kenet, T., Grinvald, A., and Arieli, A. (1999). Linking spontaneous activity of single cortical neurons and the underlying functional architecture. *Science*, **286**, 1943–1946.

Tully, T. (1996). Discovery of genes involved with learning and memory: An experimental synthesis of Hirschian and Benzerian perspectives. *Proceedings of the National Academy of Sciences USA*, **93**, 13460–13467.

Tully, T. and Quinn, W.G. (1985). Classical conditioning and retention in normal and mutant *Drosophila melanogaster*. *Journal of Comparative Physiology A*, **157**, 263–277.

Tully, T., Preat, T., Boynton, S.C., and Del Vecchio, M. (1994). Genetic dissection of consolidated memory in *Drosophila*. *Cell*, **79**, 35–47.

Tulving, E. (1972). Episodic and semantic memory. In: *Organization of memory* (ed. E. Tulving and W. Donaldson), Academic Press, N.Y.

Tulving, E. (1976). Ecphoric processes in recall and recognition. In *Recall and recognition*, (ed. J. Brown). Wiley, London.

Tulving, E. (1983). *Elements of episodic memory*. Oxford University Press, Oxford.

Tulving, E. (1985*a*). How many memory systems are there? *American Psychologist*, **40**, 385–398.

Tulving, E. (1985*b*). Memory and consciousness. *Canadian Psychology*, **26**, 1–12.

Tulving, E. (1991). Interview. *Journal of Cognitive Neuroscience*, **3**, 89–94.

Tulving, E. and Donaldson, W. (ed.)(1972). Organization of memory, Academic Press, N.Y.

Tulving, E. and Madigan, S. (1970). Memory and verbal learning. *Annual Review of Psychology*, **21**, 437–484.

Tulving, E. and Markowitsch, H.J. (1997). Memory beyond the hippocampus. *Current Opinion in Neurobiology*, **7**, 209–216.

Tulving, E. and Markowitsch, H.J. (1998). Episodic and declarative memory: Role of the hippocampus. *Hippocampus*, **8**, 198–204.

Tulving, E. and Schacter, D.L. (1990). Priming and human memory systems. *Science*, **247**, 301–306.

Tulving, E. and Thomson, D.M. (1973). Encoding specificity and retrieval processes in episodic memory. *Psychological Review*, **80**, 352–373.

Tulving, E., Schacter, D.L., McLachlan, D.R., and Moscovitch, M. (1988). Priming of semantic autobiographical knowledge: a case study of retrograde amnesia. *Brain and Cognition*, **8**, 3–20.

Tversky, A. (1977). Features of similarity. *Psychological Review*, **84**, 327–352.

Tversky, B. and Marsh, E.J. (2000). Biased retelling of events yield biased memories. *Cognitive Psychology*, **40**, 1–38.

Ugrubil, K., Hu, X., Zhu, X.-H., Kim, S.-G., and Georgopoulos, A. (1999). Functional mapping in the human brain using high magnetic fields. *Philosophical Transactions of the Royal Society of London, Series B: Biological Sciences*, **354**, 1195–1213.

Ullian, E.M., Sapperstein, S.K., Christopherson, K.S., and Barres, B.A. (2001). Control of synapse number by glia. *Science*, **291**, 657–661.

Ullman, S. (1980). Against direct perception. *Behavioral and Brain Sciences*, **3**, 373–415.

Ullman, S. (1996). *High level vision*. MIT Press, Cambridge, MA.

Underwood, B.J. (1966). Individual and group predictions of item difficulty for free learning. *Journal of Experimental Psychology*, **71**, 673–679.

Underwood, B.J. and Ekstrand, B.R. (1966). An analysis of some shortcomings in the interference theory of forgetting. *Psychological Review*, **73**, 540–549.

Ungar, G. and Oceguera-Navarro, C. (1965). Transfer of habituation by material extracted from brain. *Nature*, **207**, 301–302.

Ungerleider, L.G., Courtney, S.M., and Haxby, J.V. (1998). A neural system for human working memory. *Proceedings of the National Academy of Sciences USA*, **95**, 883–890.

Usherwood, P.N.R. (1994). Insect glutamate receptors. *Advances in Insect Physiology*, **24**, 309–341.

Vaadia, E., Haaiman, I., Abeles, M., Bergman, H., Prut, Y., Slovin, H., and Aertsen, A. (1995). Dynamics of neuronal interactions in monkey cortex in relation to behavioural events. *Nature*, **373**, 515–518.

Vaidya, C.J., Gabrieli, J.D.E., Demb, J.B., Keane, M.M., and Wetzel, L.C. (1996). Impaired priming on the general knowledge task in amnesia. *Neuropsychology*, **10**, 529–537.

References

Vaillant, G.E. (1992). The historical origins and future potential of Sigmund Freud's concept of the mechanisms of defence. *International Review of Psycho-Analysis*, **19**, 35–50.

Valverde, M.A., Diaz, M., Sepulveda, F.V., Gill, D.R., Hyde, S.C., and Higgins, C.F. (1992). Volume-regulated chloride channels associated with the human multidrug-resistance P-glycoprotein. *Nature*, **355**, 830–833.

Van der Heijden, A.H.C. (1995). Modularity and attention. *Visual Cognition*, **2**, 269–302.

Van Essen, D.C. (1997). A tension-based theory of morphogenesis and compact wiring in the central nervous system. *Nature*, **385**, 313–318.

van Praag, H., Christie, B.R., Sejnowski, T.J., and Gage, F.H. (1999). Running enhances neurogenesis, learning, and long-term potentiation in mice. *Proceedings of the National Academy of Sciences USA*, **96**, 13427–13431.

van Turennout, M., Hagoort, P., and Brown, C.M. (1998). Brain activity during speaking: From syntax to phonology in 40 milliseconds. *Science*, **280**, 572–574.

Vanzetta, I. and Grinvald, A. (1999). Increased cortical oxidative metabolism due to sensory stimulation: Implications for functional brain imaging. *Science*, **286**, 1555–1558.

Vargha-Khadem, F., Gadian, D.G., Watkins, K.E., Connelly, A., Van Paesschen, W., and Mishkin, M. (1997). Differential effects of early hippocampal pathology on episodic and semantic memory. *Science*, **277**, 376–380.

Varshavsky, A. (1992). The N-end rule. *Cell*, **69**, 725–735.

Venter, J.C., Adams, M.D., Myers, E.W., Li, P.W., Mural, R.J., Sutton, G.G., *et al.* (2001). The sequence of the human genome. *Science*, **291**, 1304–1351.

Verhage, M., Maia, A.S., Plomp, J.J., Brussard, A.B., Heeroma, J.H., Vermeer, H., Toonen, R.F., Hammer, R.E., van den Berg, T.K., Missler, M., Geuze, H.J., and Sudhof, T.C. (2000). Synaptic assembly of the brain in the absence of neurotransmitter secretion. *Science*, **287**, 864–869.

Vico, G. (1710/1988). *On the most ancient wisdom of the Italians unearthed from the origins of the Latin language.* Cornell University Press, Ithaca, NY.

Vidal, J.-M. (1980). The relations between filial and sexual imprinting in the domestic fowl: Effects of age and social experience. *Animal Behaviour*, **28**, 880–891.

Voltaire (1759/1991). *Candide, or the optimist.* Dover, New York.

von Frisch, K. (1967). *The dance language and orientation of bees.* Harvard University Press, Cambridge, MA.

Voogd, J. and Glickstein, M. (1998). The anatomy of the cerebellum. *Trends in Neurosciences*, **21**, 370–375.

Waddell, S., Armstrong, J.D., Kitamoto, T., Kaiser, K., and Quinn, W.G. (2000). The *amnesiac* gene product is expressed in two neurons in the *Drosophila* brain that are critical for memory. *Cell*, **103**, 805–813.

Wagenaar, W.A. (1986). My memory: a study of autobiographical memory over six years. *Cognitive Psychology*, **18**, 225–252.

Wagner, A.D., Desmond, J.E., Glover, G.H., and Gabrieli, D.E. (1998*a*). Prefrontal cortex and recognition memory. Functional-MRI evidence for context-dependent retrieval processes. *Brain*, **121**, 1985–2002.

Wagner, A.D., Schacter, D.L., Rotte, M., Koutstaal, W., Maril, A., Dale, A.M., Rosen, B.R., and Buckner, R.L. (1998*b*). Building memories: remembering and forgetting of verbal experience as predicted by brain activity. *Science*, **281**, 1188–1191.

Wagner, A.D., Koustaal, W., and Schacter, D.L. (1999). When encoding yields remembering: Insights from event-related neuroimaging. *Philosophical Transactions of the Royal Society of London, Series B: Biological Sciences*, **354**, 1307–1324.

Wagner, A.R. (1979). Habituation and memory. In *Mechanisms of learning and motivation*, (ed. A. Dickinson and R.A. Boakes), pp. 53–82. Laurence Erlbaum Associates, Hillsdale, NJ.

Wagner, A.R., Siegel, S., Thomas, E., and Ellison, G.D. (1964). Reinforcement history and the extinction of a conditioned salivary response. *Journal of Comparative Physiological Psychology*, **58**, 354–358.

Wakayama, T., Perry, A.C.F., Zuccotti, M., Johnson, K.R., and Yanagimachi, R. (1998). Full-term development of mice from enucleated oocytes injected with cumulus cell nuclei. *Nature*, **394**, 369–374.

Waldeyer, W. (1891). V. Uber einige neuere Forschungen im Gebiete der Anatomie des Centralnervensystems. *Deutsche medizinische Wochenschrift*, **17**, 1352–1356.

Walker, D.L. and Davis, M. (1997). Double dissociation between the involvement of the bed nucleus of the stria terminalis and the central nucleus of the amygdala in startle increases produced by conditioned versus unconditioned fear. *Journal of Neuroscience*, **17**, 9375–9383.

Walker, S. (1983). *Animal thought.* Routledge & Kegan Paul, London.

Wallace, A.F.C. (1961). On being just complicated enough. *Proceedings of the National Academy of Sciences USA*, **47**, 458–461.

Wallace, M.T., Wilkinson, L.K., and Stein, B.E. (1996). Representation and integration of multiple sensory inputs in primate superior colliculus. *Journal of Neurosphysiology*, **76**, 1246–1266.

Wallenstein, G.V., Eichenbaum, H., and Hasselmo, M.E. (1998). The hippocampus as an associator of discontiguous events. *Trends in Neurosciences*, **21**, 317–323.

Waller, S., Fairhall, K.M., Xu, J., Robinson, I.C.A.F., and Murphy, D. (1996). Neurohypophyseal and fluid homeostasis in transgenic rats expressing a tagged rat vasopressin prepropeptide in hypothalamic neurons. *Endocrinology*, **137**, 5068–5077.

Wallis, G. and Bulthoff, H. (1999). Learning to recognize objects. *Trends in Cognitive Sciences*, **3**, 22–31.

Walter, W.G., Cooper, R., Aldrige, V.J., McCallum, W.C., and Winter, A.L. (1964). Contingent negative variation: An electric sign of sensorimotor association and expectancy in the human brain. *Nature*, **203**, 380–384.

Walton, M.R. and Dragunow, M. (2000). Is CREB a key to neuronal survival? *Trends in Neurosciences*, **23**, 48–53.

Warren, H.C. (1921). *A history of the association psychology from Hartley to Lewes*. The Johns Hopkins University, Baltimore, MD.

Warren, J.M. (1966). Reversal learning and the formation of learning sets by cats and rhesus monkeys. *Journal of Comparative Physiological Psychology*, **61**, 421–428.

Warrington, E.K. and Weiskrantz, L. (1968). New method of testing long-term retention with special reference to amnesic patients. *Nature*, **217**, 972–974.

Warrington, E.K. and Weiskrantz, L. (1982). Amnesia: A disconnection syndrome? *Neuropsychologia*, **20**, 233–248.

Wasserman, P.M. and DePamphilis, M.L. (ed.) (1993). Guide to techniques in mouse development. *Methods in Enzymology*, **225**.

Wasserman, E.A. and Miller, R.R. (1997). What's elementary about associative learning? *Annual Review of Psychology*, **48**, 573–607.

Watanabe, M. (1996). Reward expectancy in primate prefrontal neurons. *Nature*, **382**, 629–632.

Watkins, M.J. (1990). Mediationism and the obfuscation of memory. *American Psychologist*, **45**, 328–335.

Watson, J.B. (1913). Psychology as the behaviorist views it. *Psychological Review*, **20**, 158–177.

Watson, J.B. (1914). *Behavior. An introduction to comparative psychology*, pp. 299–303. Holt, Rinehart and Winston, New York. (Reissued 1967.)

Watson, J.B. and Rayner, R. (1920). Conditioned emotional reactions. *Journal of Experimental Psychology*, **3**, 1–14.

Watson, J.D. (1968/1980). *The double helix*, (Norton Critical edn) (ed. G.S. Stent). Norton, New York.

Web-of-Science[SM] scientific databases (2000). *http://wos.isiglobalnet.com/* Institute for Scientific Information, Philadelphia.

Wehner, R. and Menzel, R. (1990). Do insects have cognitive maps? *Annual Review of Neuroscience*, **13**, 403–414.

Weiler, I.J., Hawrylak, N., and Greenough, W.T. (1995). Morphogenesis in memory formation: synaptic and cellular mechanisms. *Behavioural Brain Research*, **66**, 1–6.

Weimer, W.B. and Palermo, D.S. (1973). Paradigms and normal science in psychology. *Science Studies*, **3**, 211–244.

Weinberger, N.M. (1995). Dynamic regulation of receptive fields and maps in the adult sensory cortex. *Annual Review of Neuroscience*, **18**, 129–158.

Weiner, J. (1999). *Time, love, and memory: a great biologist and his quest for the origins of behavior*. Faber and Faber, New York.

Weinheimer, S.P. and McKnight, S.L. (1987). Transcriptional and post-transcriptional controls establish the cascade of herpes simplex virus protein synthesis. *Journal of Molecular Biology*, **195**, 819–833.

Weinstock, S. (1954). Resistance to extinction of a running response following partial reinforcement under widely spaced trials. *Journal of Comparative Physiological Psychology*, **47**, 318–322.

Weisberg, R.W. and Alba, J.W. (1981). An examination of the alleged role of 'fixation' in the solution of several 'insight' problems. *Journal of Experimental Psychology. General*, **110**, 169–192.

Weiskrantz, L. (1956). Behavioural changes associated with ablation of the amygdaloid complex in monkeys. *Journal of Comparative and Physiological Psychology*, **49**, 381–391.

Weiskrantz, L. (1995). The problem of animal consciousness in relation to neuropsychology. *Behavioural Brain Research*, **71**, 171–175.

Weiskrantz, L. (1997). Fragments of memory. *Neuropsychologia*, **35**, 1051–1057.

Weiss, B. and Laties, V.G. (1962). Enhancement of human performance by caffeine and amphetamines. *Pharmacological Reviews*, 14, 1–35.

Weller, I.J. and Greenough, W.T. (1993). Metabotropic glutamate receptors trigger postsynaptic protein synthesis. *Proceedings of the National Academy of Sciences USA*, **90**, 7168–7171.

Wells, G.L. and Loftus, E.F. (ed.) (1984). *Eyewitness testimony. Psychological perspectives*. Cambridge University Press, New York.

Welsh, J.P. and Llinas, R. (1997). Some organizing principles for the control of movement based on olivo-cerebellar physiology. *Progress in Brain Research*, **114**, 449–461.

Weng, G., Bhalla, U.S., and Iyengar, R. (1999). Complexity in biological signaling systems. *Science*, **284**, 92–96.

Weng, J., McClelland, J.U., Pentland, A., Sporns, O., Stockman, I., Sur, M., and Thelen, E. (2001). Autonomous mental development by robots and animals. *Science*, **291**, 599–600.

Wenk, G.L. (1997). The nucleus basalis magnocellularis cholinergic system: one hundred years of progress. *Neurobiology of Learning and Memory*, **67**, 85–95.

Werman, R. (1966). Criteria for identification of a central nervous system transmitter. *Comparative Biochemistry and Physiology*, **18**, 745–766.

Wertsch, J.V. (1985). *Vygotsky and the social formation of mind*. Harvard University Press, Cambridge, MA.

Wess, J. (1993). Molecular basis of muscarinic acetylcholine receptor function. *Trends in Pharmacological Sciences*, **14**, 308–313.

Wetzel, C.D., Squire, L.R., and Janowsky, D.S. (1981). Methylphenidate impairs learning and memory in normal adults. *Behavioral and Neural Biology*, **31**, 413–424.

Wetzler, S.E. and Sweeney, J.A. (1986). Childhood amnesia: an empirical demonstration. In *Autobiographical memory*,

References

(ed. D.C. Rubin), pp. 191–201. Cambridge University Press, New York.

Wheeler, M.E., Petersen, S.E., and Bucnker, R.L. (2000). Memory's echo: vivid remembering reactivates sensory-specific cortex. *Proceedings of the National Academy of Sciences USA*, **97**, 11125–11129.

White, E.L. (1989). *Cortical circuits. Synaptic organization of the cerebral cortex. Structure, function, and theory*. Birkhauser, Boston, MA.

Whiten, A., Custance, D.M., Gomez, J.-C., Teixidor, P., and Bard, K.A. (1996). Imitative learning of artificial fruit processing in children (*Homo sapiens*) and chimpanzees (*Pan troglodytes*). *Journal of Comparative Psychology*, **110**, 3–14.

Whiten, A., Goodall, J., McFrew, W.C., Nishida, T., Reynolds, V., Sugiyama, Y., Tutin, C.E.G., Wrangham, R.W., and Boesch, C. (1999). Cultures in chimpanzees. *Nature*, **399**, 682–685.

Whitmarsh, A.J., Cavangh, J., Tournier, C., Yasuda, J., and Davis, R.J. (1998). A mammalian scaffold complex that selectively mediates MAP kinase activation. *Science,* **281**, 1671–1674.

Whittlesea, W.A. and Wright, R.L. (1997). Implicit (and explicit) learning: Acting adaptively without knowing the consequences. *Journal of Experimental Psychology: Learning, Memory and Cognition*, **23**, 181–200.

Whitty, C.W.M. and Zangwill, O.L. (ed.) (1966). *Amnesia*. Butterworths, London.

Whyte, L.L., Wilson, A.G., and Wilson, D. (ed.) (1969). *Hierarchical structures*. American Elsevier, New York.

Wickens, C.D. (1984). *Engineering psychology and human performance*. Charles E. Meririll, Columbus, OH.

Wickens, D.D. (1987). The dual meaning of context: implications for research, theory, and applications. In *Memory and learning. The Ebbinghaus centennial conference*, pp. 135–152. Lawrence Erlbaum Associates, Hillsdale, NJ.

Wiene, R., Meyer, C., and Janowitz, H. (1919/1992). *The cabinet of Dr. Caligari*. Video release, Aikman Archives, Simitar Entertainment. Script (1919/1984) (revised edn. trans. and ed. R.V. Adkinson). Classic Film Scripts, Lorrimer, London.

Wiener, N. (1961). *Cybernetics, or control and communication in the animal and the machine*. MIT Press, Cambridge, MA.

Wiersma, C.A.G. and Ikeda, K. (1964). Interneurons commanding swimmeret movements in the crayfish, *Procambarus clarki* (girard). *Comparative Biochemistry and Physiology*, **12**, 509–525.

Wiesel, T.N. (1982). Postnatal development of the visual cortex and the influence of environment. *Nature*, **299**, 583–591.

Wiggs, C.L. and Martin, A. (1998). Properties and mechanisms of perceptual priming. *Current Opinion in Neurobiology,* **8**, 227–233.

Wiggs, C.L., Weisberg, J., and Martin, A. (1999). Neural correlates of semantic and episodic memory retrieval. *Neuropsychologia*, **37**, 103–118.

Wikswo, J.P., Gevins, A.S., and Williamson, S.J. (1993). The future of EEG and MEG. *Electroencephalography and Clinical Neurophysiology*, **87**, 1–9.

Wilcoxon, H.C. (1969). Historical introduction to the problem of reinforcement. In *Reinforcement and behavior*, (ed. J.T. Tapp), pp. 1–46. Academic Press, New York.

Wilkins, W.K. and Wakefield, J. (1995). Brain evolution and neurolinguistic preconditions. *Behavioral and Brain Sciences*, **18**, 161–226.

Williams, E. and Scott, J.P. (1953). The development of social behavior patterns in the mouse in relation to natural periods. *Behaviour*, **6**, 35–65.

Williams, H. and Nottebohm, F. (1985). Auditory responses in avian vocal motor neurons: A motor theory for song per-ception in birds. *Science*, **229**, 279–282.

Williams, M. (1953). Investigation of amnesic defects by progressive prompting. *Journal of Neurology, Neurosurgery and Psychiatry*, **16**, 14–18.

Williamson, T. (1994). *Vagueness*. Routledge, London.

Willingham, D.B. (1998). What differentiates declarative and procedural memories: reply to Cohen, Poldrack, and Eichenbaum (1997). *Memory*, **6**, 689–699.

Willner, P. (1997). The dopamine hypothesis of schizophrenia: current status, future prospects. *International Clinical Psychopharmacology*, **12**, 297–308.

Wilson, C. (1995). *The invisible world. Early modern philosophy and the invention of the microscope*. Princeton University Press, Princeton, NJ.

Wilson, M.A. and Tonegawa, S. (1997). Synaptic plasticity, place cells and spatial memory: Study with second generation knockouts. *Trends in Neurosciences*, **20**, 102–106.

Winbolt, B. (1996). False memory syndrome—an issue clouded by emotion. *Medicine Science and the Law*, **36**, 100–109.

Winch, W.H. (1908). The transfer of improvement in memory in school-children. *British Journal of Psychology*, **2**, 284–293.

Winder, D.G., Mansuy, I.M., Osman, M., Moallem, T.M., and Kandel, E.R. (1998). Genetic and pharmacological evidence for a novel, intermediate phase of long-term potentiation suppressed by calcineurin. *Cell*, **92**, 25–37.

Winkler, J., Suhr, S.T., Gage, F.H., Thal, L.J., and Fisher, L.J. (1995). Essential role of neocortical acetylcholine in spatial memory. *Nature*, **375**, 484–487.

Winocur, G. (1990). Anterograde and retrograde amnesia in rats with dorsal hippocampal or dorsomedial thalamic lesion. *Behavioral Brain Research*, **38**, 145–154.

Winocur, G. and Weiskrantz, L. (1976). An investigation of paired-associate learning in amnesic patients. *Neuropsychologia*, **14**, 97–110.

Winograd, T. (1972). *Understanding natural language*. Academic Press, New York.

Wise, R.A. and Rompre, P.-P. (1989). Brain dopamine and reward. *Annual Review of Psychology*, **40**, 191–225.

Witter, M.P., Groenewegen, H.J., Lopes ds Silva, F.H., and Lohman, A.H.M. (1989). Functional organization of the extrinsic and intrinsic circuitry of the parahippocampal region. *Progress in Neurobiology*, **33**, 161–254.

Wohlgemuth, A. (1913). On memory and the direction of associations. *British Journal of Psychology*, **5**, 447–465.

Wolfer, D.P., Stagljar-Bozicevic, M., Errington, M.L., and Lipp, H.-P. (1998). Spatial memory and learning in transgenic mice: Fact or artifact? *News in Physiological Sciences*, **13**, 118–123.

Wolpaw, J.R. (1997). The complex structure of a simple memory. *Trends in Neurosciences*, **20**, 588–594.

Wolpe, J. (1963). *The practice of behavior therapy*. Pergamon, New York.

Wolpert, L., Beddington, R., Brockes, J., Jessel, T., Lawrence, P., and Meyerowitz, E. (1998). *Principles of development*. Current Biology, London & Oxford University Press, Oxford.

Woltz, D.J., Gradner, M.K., and Bell, B.G. (2000). Negative transfer errors in sequential cognitive skills: strong-but-wrong sequence application. *Journal of Experimental Psychology. Learning, Memory, and Cognition*, **26**, 601–625.

Wood, B. (1996). Human evolution. *BioEssays*, **18**, 945–954.

Wood, B. and Collard, M. (1999). The human genus. *Science*, **284**, 65–71.

Wood, E.R., Dudchenko, P.A., and Eichenbaum, H. (1999). The global record of memory in hippocampal neuronal activity. *Nature*, **397**, 613–616.

Woods, P.J. (1974). A taxonomy of instrumental conditioning. *American Psychologist*, **29**, 584–597.

Woodworth, R.S. and Schlosberg, H. (1954). *Experimental psychology*. Holt, Rinehart and Winston, New York.

Worden, F.G., Swazey, J.P., and Adelman, G. (eds.)(1975). *The neurosciences: paths of discovery*. MIT Press, Cambridge, MA.

Wörgötter, F., Suder, K., Zhao, Y.Q., Kerscher, N., Eysel, U.T., and Funke, K. (1998). State-dependent receptive-field restructuring in the visual cortex. *Nature*, **396**, 165–168.

Wright, A.A., Cook, R.G., Rivera, J.J., Sands, S.F., and Delius, J.D. (1988). Concept learning by pigeons: Matching-to-sample with trial-unique video picture stimuli. *Animal Learning and Behavior*, **16**, 436–444.

Wu, G.-Y. and Cline, H.T. (1998). Stabilization of dendritic arbor structure in vivo by CaMKII. *Science*, **279**, 222–226.

Wundt, W. (1896/1965). Outlines of psychology. In : *A source book in the history of psychology*, (ed. R.J. Herrenstein and E.G. Boring), pp. 399–406. Harvard University Press, Cambridge, MA.

Wüstenberg, D., Gerber, B.T., and Menzel, R. (1998). Long-but not medium-term retention of olfactory memories in honeybees is impaired by actinomycin D and anisomycin. *European Journal of Neuroscience*, **10**, 2742–2745.

Wyszynski, M., Lin, J., Rao, A., Nigh, E., Beggs, A.H., Craig, A.M., and Sheng, M. (1997). Competitive binding of α-actinin and calmodulin to the NMDA receptor. *Nature*, **385**, 439–442.

Xia, Z., Dudek, H., Miranti, C.K., and Greenberg, M.E. (1996). Calcium influx via the NMDA receptor induces immediate early gene transcription by a MAP kinase/ERK-dependent mechanism. *Journal of Neuroscience*, **16**, 5425–5436.

Xu, R. and Salpeter, M.M. (1999). Rate constants of acetylcholine receptor internalization and degradation in mouse muscles. *Journal of Cellular Physiology*, **181**, 107–112.

Yagil, G. (1999). Complexity and hierarchy: a level rule. *Complexity*, **4**, 22–27.

Yágüez, L., Nagel, D., Hoffman, H., Canavan, A.G.M., Wist, E., and Hömberg, V. (1998). A mental route to motor learning: Improving trajectorial kinematics through imagery training. *Behavioral Brain Research*, **90**, 95–106.

Yakovlev, P.I. (1948). Motility, behavior and brain. *Journal of Nervous and Mental Disease*, **107**, 313–335.

Yamamoto, Y., Shimura, T., Sako, N., Yasoshima, Y., and Sakai, N. (1994). Neural substrates for conditioned taste aversion in the rat. *Behavioural Brain Research*, **65**, 123–137.

Yamei, H., Potts, R., Baoyin, Y., Zhengtang, G., Deino, A., Wei, W., Clark, J., Guangmao, X., and Weiwen, H. (2000). Mid-pleistocene Acheulean-like stone technology of the Bose basin, South China. *Science*, **287**, 1622–1626.

Yasuno, F., Nishikawa, T., Tokunaga, H., Yoshiyama, K., Nakagawa, Y., Ikeijiri, Y., Oku, N., Hashikawa, K., Tanabe, H., Shinozaki, K., Sugita, Y., Nishimura, T., and Takeda, M. (2000). The neural basis of perceptual and conceptual word priming—a PET study. *Cortex*, **36**, 59–69.

Yates, F.A. (1966). *The art of memory*. ARK, London.

Yehuda, S. and Carasso, R.L. (1993). Modulation of learning, pain thresholds, and thermoregulation in the rat by preparations of free α-linoleic and linoleic acids: Determination of the optimal ω3 to ω6 ratio. *Proceedings of the National Academy of Sciences USA*, **90**, 10345–10349.

Yehuda, S., Rabinovtz, S., Carasso, R.L., and Mostofsky, D.I. (1996). Essential fatty acids preparation (SR-3) improves Alzheimer's patients quality of life. *International Journal of Neuroscience*, **87**, 141–149.

Yeo, C.H. and Hesslow, G. (1998). Cerebellum and conditioned reflexes. *Trends in Cognitive Sciences*, **2**, 322–330.

Yerkes, R.M. (1907/1973). *The dancing mouse. A study in animal behavior*. Arno Press, New York.

Yerkes, R.M. and Dodson, J.D. (1908). The relation of strength of stimulus to rapidity of habit-formation. *Journal of Comparative Neurology and Psychology*, **18**, 459–482.

Yerkes, R.M. and Yerkes, D.N. (1928). Concerning memory in the chimpanzee. *Journal of Comparative Psychology*, **8**, 237–271.

References

Yin, J.C.P. and Tully, T. (1996). CREB and the formation of long-term memory. *Current Opinion in Neurobiology*, **6**, 264–268.

Yin, J.C.P., Del Vecchio, M., Zhou, H., and Tully, T. (1995). CREB as a memory modulator: Induced expression of a *dCREB2* activator isoform enhances long-term memory in *Drosophila*. *Cell*, **81**, 107–115.

Yonelinas, A.P. (1999). The contribution of recollection and familiarity to recognition and source-memory judgments: a formal dual-process model and an analysis of receiver operating characteristics. *Journal of Experimental Psychology: Learning, Memory, and Cognition*, **25**, 1415–1434.

Yonelinas, A.P. (2001). Components of episodic memory: the contribution of recollection and familiarity. *Proceedings of the Royal Society, London, Series B.*, **356**, 1363–1374.

Young, J.Z. (1965). *The organization of a memory system*. Proceedings of the Royal Society London B **163**, 285–320.

Young, J.Z. (1979). Learning as a process of selection and amplification. *Journal of the Royal Society of Medicine*, **72**, 801–814.

Young, J.Z. (1987). Memory. In *The Oxford companion of the mind*. Oxford University Press, Oxford.

Young, M.P. and Yamane, S. (1992). Sparse population coding of faces in the inferotemporal cortex. *Science*, **256**, 1327–1331.

Young, T. (1802). The Bakerian Lecture. On the theory of light and colours. *Philosophical Transactions of the Royal Society (London)*, **92**, 12–48.

Yovell, Y. and Abrams, T.W. (1992). Temporal asymmetry in activation of *Aplysia* adenylyl cyclase by calcium and transmitter may explain temporal requirements of conditioning. *Proceedings of the National Academy of Sciences USA*, **89**, 6526–6530.

Yzerbyt, V.Y., Lories, G., and Dardenne, B. (ed.) (1998). *Metacognition. Cognitive and social dimensions*. SAGE Publications, London.

Zaidel, E., Zaidel, D.W., and Bogen, J.E. (1996). Disconnection syndrome. In *The Blackwell dictionary of neuropsychology*, (ed. J.G. Beaumont, P.M. Kenealy, and M.J.C. Rogers), pp. 279–285. Blackwell, Cambridge, MA.

Zamanillo, D., Sprengel, R., Hvalby, O., Jensen, V., Burnashev, N., Rozov, A., Kaiser, K.M.M., Koster, H.J., Borchardt, T., Worley, P., Lubke, J., Frotscher, M., Kelly, P.H., Sommer, B., Andersen, P., Seeburg, P.H., and Sakmann, B. (1999). Importance of AMPA receptors for hippocampal synaptic plasticity but not for spatial learning. *Science*, **284**, 1805–1811.

Zars, T., Fischer, M., Schulz, R., and Heisenberg, M. (2000). Localization of a short-term memory in *Drosophila*. *Science*, **288**, 672–675.

Zatorre, R.J., Halpern, A.R., Perry, D.W., Meyer, E., and Evans, A.C. (1996). Hearing in the mind's ear: a PET investigation of musical imagery and perception. *Journal of Cognitive Neuroscience*, **8**, 29–46.

Zechmeister, E.B. and Shaughnessy, J.J. (1980). When you know that you know and when you think that you know but you don't. *Bulletin of the Psychonomic Society*, **15**, 41–44.

Zeil, J., Kelber, A., and Voss, R. (1996). Structure and function of learning flights in bees and wasps. *Journal of Experimental Biology*, **199**, 245–252.

von Zerssen, G.C., Mecklinger, A., Opitz, B., and von Carmon, D.Y. (2001). Conscious recollection and illusory recognition: an event-related fMRI study. *European Journal of Neuroscience*, **13**, 2148–2156.

Zhang, J. and Snyder, S.H. (1995). Nitric oxide in the nervous system. *Annual Review of Pharmacology and Toxicology*, **35**, 213–233.

Zhang, M.S. and Barash, S. (2000). Neuronal switching of sensory motor transformations for antisaccades. *Nature*, **408**, 971–975.

Zhong, Y., Budnik, V., and Wu, C.-F. (1992). Synaptic plasticity in *Drosophila* memory and hyperexcitable mutants: role of cAMP cascade. *Journal of Neuroscience*, **12**, 644–651.

Zhou, Y.D. and Fuster, J.M. (1996). Mnemonic neuronal activity in somatosensory cortex. *Proceedings of the National Academy of Sciences USA*, **93**, 10533–10537.

Zhou, Y.D. and Fuster, J.M. (1997). Neuronal activity of somatosensory cortex in a cross-modal (visuo-haptic) memory task. *Experimental Brain Research*, **116**, 551–555.

Zhou, Z., Champagnet, J., and Poon, C.-S. (1997). Phasic and long-term depression in brainstem nucleus tractus solitarus neurons: Differing roles of AMPA receptor desensitization. *Journal of Neuroscience*, **17**, 5349–5356.

Zigmond, M.J., Bloom, F.E., Landis, S.C., Roberts, J.L., and Squire, L.R. (ed.) (1999). *Fundamental neuroscience*. Academic Press.

Zimmer-Hart, C.L. and Rescorla, R.A. (1974). Extinction of Pavlovian conditioned inhibition. *Journal of Comparative and Physiological Psychology*, **86**, 837–845.

Zipser, D. and Andersen, R.A. (1988). A back-propagation programmed network that simulates response properties of a subset of posterior parietal neurons. *Nature*, **331**, 679–684.

Zipser, D. and Rumelhart, D.E. (1990). The neurobiological significance of the new learning models. In *Computational neuroscience*, (ed. E.L. Schwartz), pp. 192–200. MIT Press, Cambridge, MA.

Zipser, K., Lamme, V.A.F., and Schiller, P.H. (1996). Contextual modulation in primary visual cortex. *Journal of Neuroscience*, **16**, 7376–7389.

Zola-Morgan, S. and Squire, L.R. (1985). Medial temporal lesions in monkeys impair memory on a variety of tasks sensitive to human amnesia. *Behavioral Neuroscience*, **99**, 22–34.

Zola-Morgan, S. and Squire, L.R. (1993). Neuroanatomy of memory. *Annual Review of Neuroscience*, **16**, 547–563.

Zola-Morgan, S., Cohen, N.J., and Squire, L.R. (1983). Recall of remote episodic memory in amnesia. *Neuropsychologia*, **21**, 487–500.

Zola-Morgan, S., Squire, L.R., and Amaral, D.G. (1986). Human amnesia and the medial temporal region: Enduring memory impairment following a bilateral lesion limited to field CA1 of the hippocampus. *Journal of Neuroscience,* **6**, 2950–2967.

Zola-Morgan, S., Squire, L.R., and Amaral, D.G. (1989*a*). Lesions of the amygdala that spare the adjacent cortical regions do not impair or exacerbate the impairment following lesions of the hippocampal formation. *Journal of Neuroscience,* **9**, 1922–1936.

Zola-Morgan, S., Squire, L.R., Amaral, D.G., and Suzuki, W.A. (1989*b*). Lesions of perirhinal and parahippocampal formation that spare the amygdala and hippocampal formation produce severe memory impairment. *Journal of Neuroscience,* **9**, 4355–4370.

Zola-Morgan, S., Squire, L.R., Clower, R.P., and Rempel, N.L. (1993). Damage to the perirhinal cortex exacerbates memory impairment following lesions to the hippocampal formation. *Journal of Neuroscience,* **13**, 251–265.

Zoli, M., Jansson, A., Sykova, E., Agnati, L.F., and Fuxe, K. (1999). Volume transmission in the CNS and its relevance for neuropsychopharmacology. *Trends in Pharmacological Sciences,* **20**, 142–150.

Zuriff, G.E. (1986). Precis of *Behaviorism: A conceptual reconstruction. Behavioral and Brain Sciences,* **9**, 687–724.

Index

(Bold numbers indicate main entry. Terms used extensively throughout the text are referred to only by their main entry page numbers. Terms are also linked to each other by selective associations at the end of each entry.)

Index

Index

Index

Index

Index